- A new section in Part Three, "The Web and the Library: What They Offer Research Projects," helps students to evaluate when the Web is useful to research. projects and to understand the range of resources, such as searchable online databases and library subscription services, available in the library.

- Expanded coverage of plagiarism in Chapter 13 discusses a recent case in popular fiction to help students understand how to avoid plagiarism in their own writing.

- Updated visual design coverage expands students' knowledge of visual communication through such genres as letters of appeal, graphic novels, photo-essays, pictorial timelines, and travel guides.

- The Online Study Center and Online Teaching Center is accessible at college.hmco.com/pic/trimbur4e. The Online Study Center includes information for students including chapter overviews, interactive writing assignments, student writing samples, Internet resources, and useful links. The Online Teaching Center provides background information on the genre approach, as well as practical teaching approaches to public writing, the ethics of writing, literacy narratives, portfolios, and collaboration. Sample syllabi and teaching tips for each chapter are included as well.

 **Online Study Center**   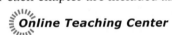 **Online Teaching Center**

A NOTE ABOUT THE ART IN *THE CALL TO WRITE*

The art featured on the cover, part openers, and chapter openers of *The Call to Write* comes from some of the best-known and most exciting contemporary graphic designers and visual artists.

- **Tibor Kalman** designed the cover for the Talking Heads' *Remain in Light*.

- **Jaime** and **Gilbert Hernandez** write and draw the widely praised independent comic *Love and Rockets*.

- **April Greiman** created the 3-D poster "Your Turn, My Turn" for the Pacific Design Center in Los Angeles. (The original came with 3-D glasses.)

- **Art Chantry** designed the poster for the Night Gallery performance art series at the Center on Contemporary Art in Seattle.

- **Paula Scher** created the poster for Jennifer Lewis and Richard Wright's *The Diva Is Dismissed* for the Public Theater in New York.

The Call to Write

brief fourth edition

John Trimbur

WORCESTER POLYTECHNIC INSTITUTE

Online Study Center

Online Teaching Center

college.hmco.com/pic/trimbur4e

Houghton Mifflin Company
Boston   New York

Library of Congress Control Number: 2006940294

Instructor's examination copy
 ISBN-13: 978-0-618-91811-9
For orders, use student text ISBNs
 ISBN-13: 978-0-618-92377-9

3456789-VH-11 10 09 08 07

brief contents

contents

■ **CHAPTER 3**

PERSUASION AND RESPONSIBILITY: ANALYZING ARGUMENTS 56

■ CHAPTER 6

PUBLIC DOCUMENTS: CODIFYING BELIEFS AND PRACTICES   171

■ **CHAPTER 9**

COMMENTARY: IDENTIFYING PATTERNS OF MEANING 288

■ **CHAPTER 11**

REVIEWS: EVALUATING WORKS AND PERFORMANCES 353

PART 3   WRITING AND RESEARCH PROJECTS   387

■ CHAPTER 12

THE RESEARCH PROCESS: CRITICAL ESSAYS AND RESEARCH PROJECTS   390

■ CHAPTER 13

WORKING WITH SOURCES   439

PART 5   PRESENTING YOUR WORK   561

guide to visual design

LOGOS

MURALS AND BANNERS

PAGE DESIGN

PHOTO ESSAY

POSTCARD

POSTERS

POWERPOINT

REVIEWS AND RATING SYSTEMS

TRAVEL GUIDE

WEB PAGES

preface

The Call to Write, Brief Fourth Edition, offers students a broad introduction to writing, so that they can learn to write with flexibility and influence in a variety of settings. Many of the assignments in the following chapters are typical of the writing college students are called on to do. A central aim of this book is to help students become effective writers in their college coursework. At the same time, *The Call to Write* takes as its starting point the view that writing is much more than a school subject. Writing is an activity individuals and groups rely on to communicate with others, organize their social lives, get work done, entertain themselves, and voice their needs and aspirations. Accordingly, this textbook presents a wide range of situations that call on people to write—in everyday life, in school, in the workplace, and in the public sphere.

Just as the situations that give rise to writing differ, so do the tools available to writers. Writing can no longer refer simply to the traditional forms of print literacy. It also involves the visual design of the page and screen and the new digital media that enable the integration of text, graphics, sound, and video. Although *The Call to Write* cannot teach many of the skills needed to operate the new writing technologies, it takes into account how writers use these new means of communication and how many forms of writing combine words and graphics to deliver a message.

One of the main premises of the book is that writing should belong to everyone in the various roles people play. *The Call to Write* offers students an education in writing, with the goal of enabling them to see how writing connects individuals to others and to the cultural practices and social institutions that shape their lives. In this regard, the call to write—the felt sense that something needs to be said—presents writing not just as a skill to master but as a means to participate meaningfully in the common life and to influence its direction.

DISTINCTIVE FEATURES OF *THE CALL TO WRITE*

The goal of *The Call to Write* is to offer teachers and students a range of activities that are grounded in rhetorical traditions and the accumulated experience of successful writing instruction. It has been enormously gratifying that teachers and students who used the first three editions of *The Call to Write* have confirmed the practical value of its approach. The fourth edition builds on—and seeks to refine—the basic features that give *The Call to Write* its distinctive character:

- **An emphasis on the rhetorical situation.** *The Call to Write* begins with the idea that writing doesn't just happen but instead takes place in particular social contexts. Throughout the textbook, students are provided with opportunities to analyze how rhetorical situations give rise to the call to write. A wide array of writing—from speeches, news stories, government reports, and op-ed pieces to posters, graffiti, ads, flyers, and newsletters, as well as academic articles, literary essays, and student work—illustrates the range and richness of situations that call on people to write.

- **Genre-based writing assignments.** To help students understand the choices available to them when they respond to the call to write, the "Writing Projects" in Part Two use the notion of genre as the basis for guided writing assignments. Each chapter includes individual and collaborative writing assignments based on familiar genres; extensive treatment of invention, planning, peer commentary, and revision; samples of student writing; and an opportunity for students to reflect on the process of writing.

- **Integration of reading and writing.** Chapter 2, "Reading for Academic Purposes: Analyzing the Rhetorical Situation," emphasizes the kind of reading students are called on to do in college courses. The opening section focuses on the rhetorical situation of academic writing to help students see that reading in college is not merely a matter of acquiring new information but also involves understanding how academic writing formulates issues to investigate by considering what others have written. This focus on the connections between reading and writing continues in the Working with Sources feature in Part Two, as well as the For Critical Inquiry questions that ask students to read closely and carefully, to understand their response as readers and the decisions writers make when they take up the call to write.

- **A focus on visual design.** *The Call to Write* emphasizes not only how many types of writing integrate text and graphics but that writing itself is a form of visible language. Each chapter in Part Two includes a Visual Design reading that asks students to evaluate critically how a particular example of visual communication works. Chapter 19, "Visual Design," explores how visual design is used for purposes of identification, information, and persuasion; the chapter also provides instruction in effective page design. Chapter 20, "Web Design," considers how Web pages integrate word and image, and Chapter 21, "Oral Presentations," includes some guidelines for PowerPoint™.

- **An emphasis on ethics and the writer's responsibilities.** *The Call to Write* presents boxes on the ethics of writing that raise issues concerning writers' responsibilities toward their readers and their subjects. Chapter 3, "Persuasion and Responsibility: Analyzing Arguments," includes extensive coverage of how writers can deal responsibly with disagreements and negotiate their differences with others.

- **An emphasis on collaborative learning.** *The Call to Write* includes many opportunities for group discussions, as well as a collaborative project and guidelines for peer commentaries in each of the chapters in Part Two. Chapter 16, "The Writing Process: A Case Study of a Writing Assignment," traces how a student used peer response to write an academic paper, and Chapter 18, "Working Together: Collaborative Writing Projects," offers information and advice about group writing projects.

NEW TO THE FOURTH EDITION

The fourth edition includes new and revised features to help students understand and respond to the call to write. These additions come in large part from discussions with writing teachers who used the first three editions of *The Call to Write*. A number of the new features emphasize research and writing from sources, to strengthen the book's focus on academic writing.

- **Completely revised book design** has improved the usability of *The Call to Write*, making features easier to identify and enhancing readability.

- **Annotated readings** appear in each chapter in Part Two to demonstrate features of a particular genre of writing.

- **Writing in a Digital World**, a new feature included in each chapter in Part Two explores electronic literacies such as text-messaging, social networking Web sites, multimedia, informational Web sites, blogs, and online public campaigns.

- **A new section, The Web and the Library: What They Offer Research Projects,** in Chapter 12 "The Research Process" helps students to evaluate when the Web is useful to research projects and to understand the range of resources, such as searchable online databases and library subscription services, that they can find in the library.

- **Expanded coverage of plagiarism** in Chapter 13 "Working with Sources" provides examples from a recent case of plagiarism in publishing to help students understand what plagiarism is. Revised and expanded guidelines help students avoid plagiarism.

- **Updated Visual Design** features in Part Two expand students' knowledge of visual communication by including such genres as the letter of appeal, graphic novels, photo-essays, pictorial timelines, and travel guides.

- **Examples in Chapter 19 "Visual Design" and throughout have been updated** to reflect the best in contemporary work in graphic and information design, including an expanded section in Chapter 21 "Oral Presentations" on PowerPoint.

- **Coverage in Chapter 7 "Profiles" has been expanded** to include profiles of places as well as of people.

USING *THE CALL TO WRITE*

The Call to Write is meant to be used flexibly, to fit the goals and local needs of teachers, courses, and writing programs. While there is no single path to follow in teaching *The Call to Write*, for most teachers the core of the book will be the Writing Projects in Part Two—the guided writing assignments based on common genres. Teachers can choose from among these genres and assign them in the order that best suits their course design.

A rich array of material appears in the other sections of *The Call to Write*, and teachers may draw on the various chapters to introduce key concepts and deepen students' understanding of reading and writing. It can be helpful to think of the organization of the book as a modular one that enables teachers to combine chapters in ways that emphasize their own interests and priorities.

The following overview of the organization of *The Call to Write* describes the five main parts of the book.

- **Part One, "Writing and Reading,"** introduces students to the notion of the call to write, offers strategies for critical reading and rhetorical analysis, and presents methods for identifying disputed issues, planning responsible arguments, and negotiating differences with others. These chapters can serve to introduce central themes at the beginning of a course, or they can be integrated throughout the course.

- **Part Two, "Writing Projects,"** presents familiar genres of writing, with examples, For Critical Inquiry questions, and individual and collaborative writing assignments. Assignments call on students to write for a number of different audiences and in a number of different settings, ranging from everyday life to the academic world to public forums. These chapters form the core of *The Call to Write*.

- **Part Three, "Writing and Research Projects,"** explores the genres of the critical essay, the research paper, and the fieldwork report. It considers what calls on people to do research, how they formulate meaningful questions, and the sources they typically use. Part Three provides an overview of the research process, introduces students to library and online research, and includes information about research projects that use observation, interviews, and questionnaires. This section is particularly appropriate for writing courses that emphasize writing from sources and research-based writing.

- **Part Four, "Writers at Work,"** presents a case study of a student using peer commentary to complete an academic writing assignment, explores the genre of the essay and the meaning and purpose of form in writing, and looks at how writers work together on collaborative writing projects. These chapters can be integrated into a course at a number of points—to initiate discussion of how writers manage individual writing projects, to enhance student understanding of peer commentary, to prepare students for collaborative writing projects, and to deepen students' understanding of form.

- **Part Five, "Presenting Your Work,"** looks at how writers communicate the results of their work to readers. It includes information on visual design, Web design, oral presentations, essay exams, and portfolios. These chapters can be integrated into a course at many points, depending on the teacher's goals.

ADDITIONAL RESOURCES FOR *THE CALL TO WRITE*

The Call to Write, Brief Fourth Edition, is accompanied by many helpful supplements for both teachers and students. Both the Online Study Center and Online Teaching Center can be accessed at **college.hmco.com/pic/trimbur4e.**

FOR STUDENTS

Online Study Center

 *Online Study Center*

A companion Web site includes information for students including chapter overviews, interactive writing assignments, Internet resources and useful links, and samples of student writing. The Online Study Center icon appears in relevant locations within each chapter. Students should be encouraged to make use of the supplementary materials provided at this site.

FOR INSTRUCTORS

Online Teaching Center

Online Teaching Center

The Online Teaching Center provides background information on the genre approach of *The Call to Write,* as well as practical teaching approaches to public writing, the ethics of writing, literacy narratives, portfolios, and collaboration.

The *Instructor's Resource Manual* contains sample syllabi and teaching tips for each chapter in the fourth edition. Instructors should acquaint themselves with all the materials available on the Online Study Center and refer students to the site for extra practice and additional information.

ACKNOWLEDGMENTS

Preparing *The Call to Write* has made me acutely aware of the intellectual, professional, and personal debts I have accumulated over the years teaching writing, training writing teachers and peer tutors, and administering writing programs and writing centers. I want to acknowledge the contributions so many rhetoricians and composition specialists have made to my thinking about the study and teaching of writing, and I hope they will recognize—and perhaps approve of—the way their work has influenced the design of this book.

The unifying theme of the "call to write," as many will note immediately, comes from Lloyd Bitzer's notion of "exigence" and the "rhetorical situation." My treatment of argument and persuasion is informed by Aristotle's appeals (by way of Wayne Booth's sense of "rhetorical stance") and stasis theory (as articulated in Dick Fulkerson's *Teaching Argument in Writing*), and my understanding of reasoning in argument is altogether indebted to Stephen Toulmin (though the terminology I use differs somewhat). The influence of Carolyn Miller's seminal work on genre as "social action" should be apparent at every turn.

I learned to teach writing from two great mentors, Ken Bruffee and Peter Elbow, and their mark is everywhere in the book. My interest in visual design grows in part out of an ongoing collaboration with Diana George. Lester Faigley got me to pay attention to electronic communication and cyberspace. Bob Schwegler listened and offered key advice at many points.

I am happy to feature so much writing from students I have taught at Worcester Polytechnic Institute, where I developed and taught the bulk of the material that now appears in *The Call to Write*. Some of the student writing, I should note, has been edited for this book.

Katharine Glynn was the development editor for *The Call to Write,* Brief Fourth Edition, and Lynn Huddon was the sponsoring editor; I want to acknowledge their hard work, careful attention, good senses of humor, and loyalty to this project.

To the many reviewers who provided valuable feedback at many points, my thanks: Stevens Amidon, Indiana University, Purdue; Debra L. Burgauer, Bradley University; J. C. Clapp, North Seattle Community College; William Lalicker, West Chester University; Sally Levan, Grannon University; Rob Lively, Truckee Meadows Community College; and Carol Westcamp, University of Arkansas–Fort Smith.

Finally I want to acknowledge the contributions to *The Call to Write* made by members of my family—Lundy Braun and Clare, Lucia, and Martha Catherine Trimbur. They not only provided emotional support; they were coworkers, contributing samples of their writing, suggesting readings and assignments, and locating Web sites and online resources. This has been, in many respects, a joint venture, and I am gratified by their presence in the book.

JOHN TRIMBUR

The Call
to Write

writing and reading

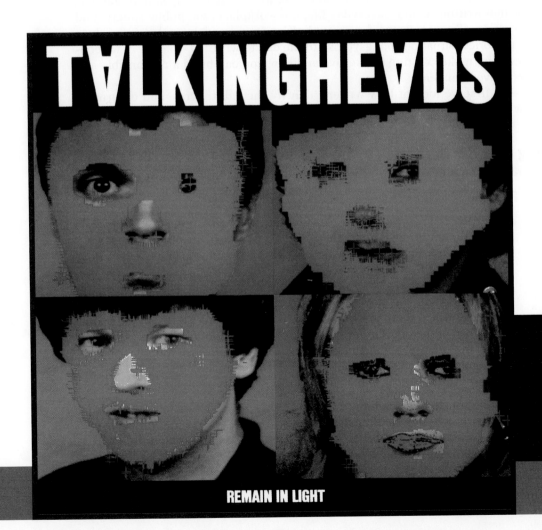

1

INTRODUCTION: THE CALL TO WRITE

The call to write may come from a teacher who assigns a paper, a friend who sends you an email, or a supervisor at work. You may feel called to write a letter to your congressman or senator on an issue you care about. Or you belong to a campus organization or community group and want to publicize its aims and activities. In any case, as you will see throughout this book, people who write typically experience some sense of need that can be met by writing. Accordingly, what a person writes will be shaped by the situation that gave rise to that need.

By thinking about these various occasions for writing, you can deepen your understanding of your own and other people's writing and develop a set of strategies that will help you become a more effective writer. The three chapters in Part One of this textbook offer a way of looking at why and how people respond to the call to write. In Chapter 1, we look more closely at four contexts in which writing occurs—everyday life, the workplace, the public sphere, and school. In Chapter 2, we focus on how writers read in order to analyze the rhetorical situation that gave rise to the call to write. In Chapter 3, we consider what makes writing persuasive and how you can build a responsible and persuasive argument.

But first we look at how writers identify the call to write and determine how to respond to it.

Identifying and Responding to the Call to Write

Here are some of the factors writers typically take into account when they identify a call to write and turn it into a writing task:

- **Purpose:** Writers need to clarify what they are trying to accomplish with their writing. How do they want to influence the situation that gave rise to the call to write? What effect do they intend to have, and how will the writing achieve this effect?

   Let's say there is a proposal to cut financial aid at your college or university. If you decide to respond to this situation, what kind of change will you try to bring about? Is it your purpose to call for a total reversal of the decision or only to propose a reduction of cuts? How will you try to bring about this change? Is it your purpose to rally students to oppose the cuts or to call on the decision makers directly? Depending on your purpose, what genre can best accomplish your goals?

- **Relationship to readers:** How you construct a writing task depends in part on whom you choose as your intended readers and on what you know about them, their familiarity with the situation, and their interests and opinions.

   As you determine who your readers will be, you will also make decisions about your relationship to them. For example, if you are trying to convince students to demonstrate against the financial aid cuts, you can appeal to your relationship as peers and emphasize your common interests. On the other hand, if you are writing to decision makers in positions of authority, you are probably addressing readers who have more power than you do. Do you want to approach these readers as a humble petitioner, as a concerned student, as a morally outraged victim, as a threat, or as something else?

- **Voice:** The tone of voice in a piece of writing will vary depending on the purpose and the kind of relationship you want to establish with your readers. *Voice* is basically the attitude writers want to project to readers. Should your tone be formal or informal, intimate or distanced? Is it appropriate to express concern, sarcasm, or anger? These decisions hinge on what you want to achieve and whom you are addressing.

  In the case of the financial aid cuts, a tone that's appropriate for a piece of writing intended to call on students to take action may not be appropriate when intended to persuade decision makers or to inform the public. An important part of responding to the call to write is knowing how to modulate your voice to take on the right tone for the situation.

- **The social context:** To shape their writing tasks, writers draw on their knowledge of the social context they are operating in—its history and its current issues, the people involved and their relationships to each other, and the kinds of writing typically used.

  At the same time, the act of writing not only draws on what you know about the social context but connects you to it in various ways, depending on your situation and purposes. Writing answers to an exam, for instance, is very different from writing flyers to rally students against cuts in financial aid. And both forms differ from doodling in the margins of your notebook during a dull lecture. The social context in which each piece of writing takes place is the same, namely an American college or university. Nonetheless, each instance of writing puts you in a different relationship to the institutional context—whether as an academic performer trying to get a good grade, as an activist trying to change the direction of the institution, or as a bored student trying to make class time pass more easily.

- **Genre of writing:** Genres are the different types of writing people draw on to respond to the call to write. If you think about the genres listed in the discussion of financial aid cuts—leaflets, letters of protest, letters to the editor, and fact sheets—you can see that each one has characteristics that enable readers to recognize the writer's purpose and to understand the type of relationship the writer wants to establish with them. Accordingly, your choice of genre is always a key factor, because different genres approach readers in different ways and express different strategies to influence the situation at hand.

There are, of course, many genres of writing. In Part Two, we treat some of the most familiar ones—letters, memoirs, public documents, profiles, reports, commentary, proposals, and reviews. Each genre offers a distinct strategy for dealing with typical writing situations.

■ REFLECTING ON YOUR WRITING

The Call to Write

1. Choose a piece of writing you've done at some time in the past. It could be a writing assignment in school, a note to a friend, something you wrote at work, a diary entry, a letter, an article for a student newspaper or community newsletter, a petition, a flyer, or a leaflet for an organization you belong to. Whatever the writing happens to be, write a page or two in which you describe the call that prompted you to write.

   ■ Describe the situation that made you feel a need to respond in writing.

   ■ Why did you decide to respond in writing instead of taking some other action or not responding at all?

   ■ How did you construct your writing task? Describe your purpose, the relationship you wanted to establish with your readers, and the tone of voice you decided to use in your writing. How did you make these decisions? What knowledge of the social context did you draw on to make those decisions? What type or genre of writing did you use to communicate your purpose?

2. With two or three other students, take turns reading aloud what you have written. Compare the situations that gave rise to the call to write and the way each of you responded. What, if anything, is similar about the ways you identified and responded to the call to write? What was different? How would you account for the differences and similarities?

See Chapter 23, "Writing Portfolios," for more on integrating Reflecting on Your Writing exercises into a portfolio.

what is writing? analyzing literacy events

Learning to write involves an understanding of your own experience as a writer—seeing how various situations have called on you to write, how you have shaped your writing tasks accordingly, and how your writing has involved you in relationships with people in various social contexts. In this chapter, we look at how people respond to the call to write in four contexts:

1. Writing in everyday life
2. Writing in the workplace
3. Writing in the public sphere
4. Writing in school

We present a wide range of writing samples to illustrate how writing is an integral part of our lives as private individuals, as workers, as citizens, and as students. The writing samples and assignments in this chapter ask you to come up with your own answer to the question "What is writing?" by looking at how writing works in these contexts and how it can differ in purpose, intended readers, tone, and genre.

The goal of this chapter is to enable you to analyze how writing actually takes place in the world and how you and others make sense of the writing you encounter and produce. The writing assignment at the end of the chapter—"Analyzing a Literacy Event"—calls on you to examine an occasion in which writing played an important role in people's interactions and the social context in which the writing took place.

Analyzing such "literacy events" can help you understand the role writing plays in your life. And it can help you become a more flexible writer who understands the effects writing has in the wider social world. In this way, you can learn to fit what you want to say to the occasions that call on you to write.

WRITING IN EVERYDAY LIFE

The call to write in everyday life emerges from a range of situations. People write lists to remember things and notes for roommates or family members. They write to maintain social relationships—for example, by a letter of condolence, a thank-you card for a birthday present, or a note to a friend in class. Some people keep diaries to record their experiences—and to let off steam, put their feelings in perspective, and cope with the stresses of life. Others write poetry or fiction for similar purposes and for the pleasure of using language to create imaginary worlds.

The purposes of writing in everyday life tend to be personal, and intended readers are generally people we know well or encounter in our immediate surroundings. Not surprisingly, the tone is characteristically informal and familiar. And although these writings are personal, they are, like everyday life itself, tied to the larger social context.

ANALYZING WRITING IN EVERYDAY LIFE: A SHOPPING LIST

Nothing could be more ordinary than a shopping list. Shopping lists reveal one of the most powerful aspects of writing: they free us from having to commit everything to memory. It's easier and more efficient to list items on paper and let the list remind us of what we want.

A typical shopping list might look something like this:

apples	butter	rice
spaghetti	meat for Sunday dinner	hot dog rolls
bananas	milk	cat food
eggs	bread	paper towels
chicken	two cans of tomatoes	salad stuff

Notice that only the writer could actually bring home exactly what he or she wants. Someone else wouldn't know, for example, how many apples or what kind of meat to buy. This type of writing is a kind of private code that works when you want to talk to yourself. How would this list have to be rewritten if someone other than the writer were going to do the shopping?

With some small changes, the shopping list could be written to be an organizing tool as well as a memory aid. You could compose the list so that it corresponds to the aisles in the grocery store:

apples	bananas	salad stuff
Chicken	meat for Sunday dinner	
two cans of tomatoes		
spaghetti	rice	
paper towels		
butter	milk	eggs
bread	hot dog rolls	
cat food		

Even as simple and straightforward a piece of writing as a shopping list shows how writing occurs within—and connects the writer to—the larger social context. Consider, for example, how the act of writing a shopping list reveals the shopper's relationship to the everyday work of preparing meals and managing a household.

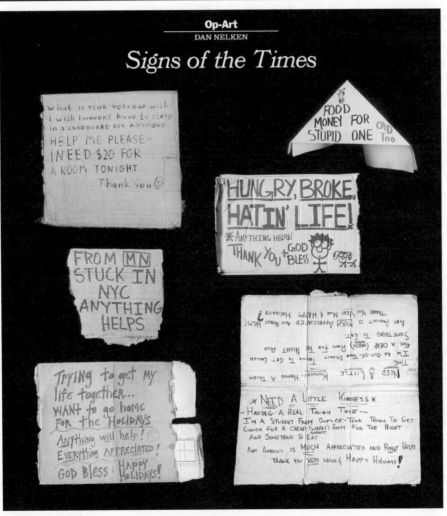

These are placards people in New York City have used to ask for help. On the next page, there is an example of Instant Messenger. Compare the technologies and styles of writing. Consider the purpose each piece of writing serves and what it expresses about the writer's relationship to the social context.

CatTrimbur (7:03:14 PM): hihi
PookyBeaRe (7:03:36 PM): hihi
PookyBeaRe (7:03:53 PM): how are you doing?
CatTrimbur (7:04:50 PM): okie, so tell me abt yr wknd!
PookyBeaRe (7:05:11 PM): it was so gr8
CatTrimbur (7:05:33 PM): hehe, what did u guys do when u got there?
PookyBeaRe (7:06:09 PM): we went rafting and i fell in the water .. and it was so embarrassing bc every1 was rofl at me
CatTrimbur (7:06:37 PM): omg! was the water wicked cold?
PookyBeaRe (7:06:54 PM): WICKED wicked cold!!
CatTrimbur (7:07:09 PM): oh no! and what abt the boys *
PookyBeaRe (7:07:42 PM): they suck :-$
CatTrimbur (7:08:02 PM): yea, im w/ u on that!
CatTrimbur (7:08:22 PM): buts thats ok, now its summer time and we dont have anymore school work to take up all our time!
PookyBeaRe (7:08:33 PM): LOL
CatTrimbur (7:08:47 PM): so when do u start work?
PookyBeaRe (7:09:19 PM): like in june?
PookyBeaRe (7:09:33 PM): btw, did you call that guy?
CatTrimbur (7:09:47 PM): no, i gotto do that, i havent had time!
PookyBeaRe (7:10:39 PM): yeah you do!
CatTrimbur (7:11:07 PM): yea, i know :-(
CatTrimbur (7:11:37 PM): whatever, i dont feel like it now, but i take my practice mcat tomorrow night
PookyBeaRe (7:11:49 PM): loser
CatTrimbur (7:12:09 PM): luza!
PookyBeaRe (7:12:10 PM): we really need to gal this summer
CatTrimbur (7:13:20 PM): no, U need to gal this summer, i like my boring life, doing nothing but watching tv and eating!
PookyBeaRe (7:13:43 PM): omg
PookyBeaRe (7:13:50 PM): u can't mean that!!!!
PookyBeaRe (7:14:17 PM): oh!! btw, b4 2nite i didn't think mark had a gf but i think he does
CatTrimbur (7:14:26 PM): ok, i dont, so we'll go out more this summer, im gonna apply for jobs at rira and usb for waitressing so i can make the big bucks!
CatTrimbur (7:14:40 PM): mark....
PookyBeaRe (7:14:44 PM): brady
PookyBeaRe (7:14:50 PM): can i apply 2?
CatTrimbur (7:14:51 PM): WHAT!!!!!!!!
PookyBeaRe (7:14:56 PM): i'm not sure
CatTrimbur (7:14:57 PM): yuppers!
CatTrimbur (7:15:04 PM): wait, he has a gf?
PookyBeaRe (7:15:05 PM): gr888888888!

WRITING IN THE WORKPLACE

ANALYZING WRITING IN THE WORKPLACE

THE GAP'S SOCIAL RESPONSIBILITY REPORT

Under the names Gap, Banana Republic, and Old Navy, Gap, Inc. runs a $16 billion-a-year enterprise, with retail stores in the United States, Canada, Europe, and Japan that sell clothes made in factories that Gap contracts with all over the world. Through a combination of pressure from antisweatshop groups (citing subpoverty wages, use of child labor, unhealthy working conditions, intimidation of workers and union organizers, and adverse environmental impact) and business leadership on Gap's part, the company has enacted a code of standards for its vendors and issued Social Responsibility Reports in 2003 and 2004.

You can access these reports at the Gap Web site www.gapinc.com/public/ SocialResponsibility/sr_report.shtml. Consider how Gap evaluates its efforts to monitor and improve working conditions. For another evaluation, see Ethical Trading Action Group's "Coming Clean on the Clothes We Wear: Transparency Report Card" at www.maquiladorasolidarity.org/campaigns.reportcard/ index/htm

The call to write emerges repeatedly in the workplace. For financial and legal reasons, companies need to keep careful records of all their transactions, their inventory and sales, the contracts they enter into, and their dealings with unions and federal and state regulatory agencies.

Equally important is written communication among the members of an organization. Such writing serves to establish a sense of shared purpose, a business plan, a clear chain of command, and procedures to evaluate performance. Writing helps manage the flow of work and the progress of individual projects.

Companies, moreover, need to make their goods and services known to potential customers and clients, and advertising and public relations have become major industries in their own right.

Writing in the workplace is often specialized. Many professions have their own genres of writing—for example, legal briefs of lawyers; case histories of doctors, psychologists, and social workers; and the proposals of engineering, marketing research, management consulting, and other professional firms. So crucial has specialized writing become that the ability to master the genre of a profession is crucial to success in the world of work.

Compare the series of emails written by and to Michael Brown, who was director of the Federal Emergency Management Agency when Hurricane Katrina hit on August 26, 2005, to the memo written to coworkers (but addressed to "The thief that has been stealing the pens"). Consider what the call to write seems to have been in each case.

FEMA AND KATRINA

EMAILS FROM AND TO MICHAEL BROWN

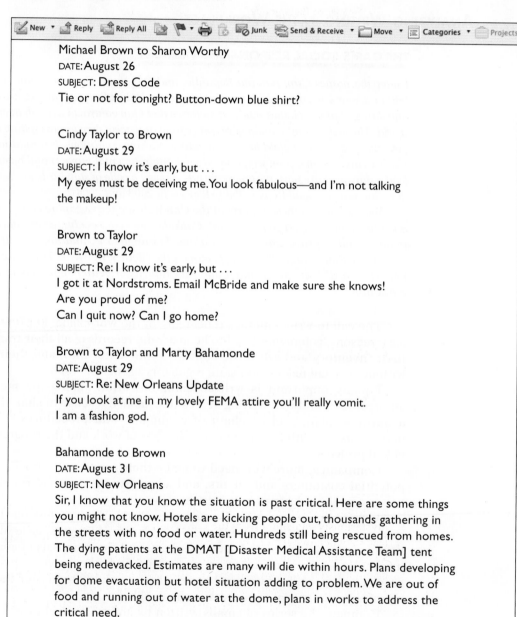

Michael Brown to Sharon Worthy
DATE: August 26
SUBJECT: Dress Code
Tie or not for tonight? Button-down blue shirt?

Cindy Taylor to Brown
DATE: August 29
SUBJECT: I know it's early, but . . .
My eyes must be deceiving me. You look fabulous—and I'm not talking the makeup!

Brown to Taylor
DATE: August 29
SUBJECT: Re: I know it's early, but . . .
I got it at Nordstroms. Email McBride and make sure she knows!
Are you proud of me?
Can I quit now? Can I go home?

Brown to Taylor and Marty Bahamonde
DATE: August 29
SUBJECT: Re: New Orleans Update
If you look at me in my lovely FEMA attire you'll really vomit.
I am a fashion god.

Bahamonde to Brown
DATE: August 31
SUBJECT: New Orleans
Sir, I know that you know the situation is past critical. Here are some things you might not know. Hotels are kicking people out, thousands gathering in the streets with no food or water. Hundreds still being rescued from homes. The dying patients at the DMAT [Disaster Medical Assistance Team] tent being medevacked. Estimates are many will die within hours. Plans developing for dome evacuation but hotel situation adding to problem. We are out of food and running out of water at the dome, plans in works to address the critical need.
     Phone connectivity impossible. More later.

Brown to Bahamonde
DATE: August 31
SUBJECT: Re: New Orleans
Thanks for update. Anything specific I need to do or tweak?

Worthy to Brown
DATE: September 4
SUBJECT: Your shirt
Please roll up the sleeves of your shirt . . . all shirts. Even the President rolled his sleeves to just below the elbow.
   In this crisis and on TV you just need to look more hard-working . . . ROLL UP THE SLEEVES!

MEMO TO A THIEF

memorandum

To: The thief that has been stealing pens from the IBM.

From: A very angry phone receptionist who is constantly putting more pens near the IBM and who is perpetually frustrated with the fact that whenever he/she goes to use them they are missing.

Re: A way to remedy this situation.

Date: The summer

Over the course of the summer it has come to my attention that pens were mysteriously vanishing from the IBM computer. The action causes significant trouble when one tries to take a PHONE MESSAGE or attempts to take a START and commit it to memory. Instead of philosophizing about the possible criminals who insist on making my life harder (I know who who are!),
I simply ask that if you, per chance, notice the absence of a pen or pencil near the IBM that you take it upon yourself to correct this mishap and replace one immediately.

I thank you for your time and efforts in this matter.

WRITING IN THE PUBLIC SPHERE

In the broadest sense, writing in the public sphere refers to all the writing we encounter in public places—official signs (for example, street names, building names and addresses, and parking signs), notices put out by companies and groups (for example, posters announcing meetings and concerts, billboards advertising movies and products, and leaflets seeking support for causes), books, newspapers and magazines, and even the graffiti spray-painted on the sides of buildings and subway cars.

This section focuses on a particular use of writing in the public sphere—namely, writing intended to inform and influence members of the public on matters of concern to all. Here, the public sphere can be understood as the context in which people deliberate on the important issues of the day and seek to shape the direction of society.

ETHICS OF WRITING

Graffiti has become an omnipresent feature of contemporary urban life. Spray-painted or otherwise pasted on walls and subway cars, graffiti can perform a number of functions: marking a gang's turf, putting forth political messages, expressing the individual writer's

©Martha Cooper

ANALYZING WRITING IN THE PUBLIC SPHERE

ACORN KATRINA SURVIVORS ASSOCIATION

Hurricane Katrina made thousands of New Orleans residents into refugees, their homes destroyed. ACORN (Association of Community Organizations for Reform Now) helped set up the Katrina Survivors Association to speak on behalf of the refugees scattered to nearby states and more distant locations. The two-page flyer shown on the following pages presents the platform (or general goals) of the organization to deal with the devastation of Hurricane Katrina and the struggle of local residents to return home on the first page, with Organizing and Direct Action continuing on the second page. For more on the ACORN Katrina Survivors Association, go to http://acorn.org/index .php?id=10284

identity, expressing grief for someone killed or anger at an enemy. Our reactions to graffiti differ dramatically. Some see it simply as a crime—an antisocial act of vandalism—while others see it as a form of artistic expression and political statement by the disenfranchised. What ethical issues are raised for you by such examples of graffiti as the two printed here? Do you consider graffiti a justified form of writing even though it is illegal? Why or why not? ■

ACORN
Katrina Survivors Association

The **ACORN Katrina Survivors Association** is the first nationwide organization of displaced New Orleans residents and other Katrina survivors. The Survivors Association unites members of our displaced communities in order to demand more effective relief efforts and a voice for survivors in the rebuilding process.

The ACORN Katrina Survivors Association uses public pressure, direct action, and dialogue with elected officials and public policy experts to win respect and a voice for survivors, the resources needed for families to survive, and a rebuilding plan that builds stronger communities for all.

The Platform of the ACORN Katrina Survivors Association

Right of return – The people of New Orleans will not be kept out by deliberate attempts to change the make-up of the city, or by neglect, which gives the richer and more powerful first access to choices and resources.

The means to take care of ourselves and our families – Survivors need help with housing, healthcare, income from unemployment, and assistance for those who've helped us.

Rebuilding the right way – Reconstruction should include affordable housing, living wage jobs, and good schools for our children.

Recovering together – The Hurricane should not be used as an excuse to cut health care and food assistance programs that help families across the country.

Accountability and honesty – An independent investigation is necessary so we can understand what went wrong and how to protect ourselves in the future.

ACORN Organizing and Direct Action

The Survivors Association will continue and expand the organizing that local ACORN chapters have accomplished since Katrina first hit, which has already resulted in some notable actions and victories.

- On October 7th, the Houston ACORN Katrina Survivors Association confronted Houston FEMA Director about a lack of response to the needs of the survivors. After negotiations, ACORN members won a shuttle bus to their service center, translated materials, and extended benefits to Rita survivors.

SAVE OUR NEIGHBORHOOD
No Bulldozing!
Contact ACORN
1-800-239-7379

o Louisiana ACORN members staged a caravan into the Lower 9th Ward on October 15th to claim their right to return and to placard hundreds of homes with signs stating "No Bulldozing!"

o A thousand people gathered on the steps of the Louisiana State Capitol for the October 28th Rally to Rebuild Louisiana, to demand job priority, training, and good wages for Louisiana's displaced working families.

ACORN Community Forum on Rebuilding New Orleans

o The Survivors Association sponsored the ACORN Community Forum on Rebuilding New Orleans, which convened in Baton Rouge, Louisiana on November 7th and 8th.

o The conference brought together low-income and minority residents of New Orleans and top urban planning, architecture, and development professionals from around the country.

o Forum participants took a bus tour of affected areas and held discussions on how to rebuild New Orleans to speak to the needs of all New Orleans' residents.

o More than 130 participants at the forum site were joined online by participants from all over the globe, who took part via webcast.

Katrina Survivors Continue to Fight to Return Home

o On November 22nd, 100 ACORN members marched to the Houston FEMA office to deliver a letter demanding that FEMA rescind its recently announced decision to stop paying bills for roughly 150,000 hurricane victims still in motel rooms come December 1st.

o Later that same afternoon, FEMA rescinded the unpopular policy and said that it would extend its hotel-housing program by a month in 10 states.

o Advancement Project obtained a favorable settlement on November 22nd in a lawsuit filed on behalf of ACORN and other groups in response to evictions that had been proceeding without notice to the tenants.

o The agreement requires FEMA to turn over to the courts in Orleans and Jefferson parishes the addresses of tenants facing evictions, and requires that hearings be scheduled no sooner than 45 days after notice is mailed to the evacuees.

The ACORN Katrina Survivors Association members are continuing the fight for the practical resources families need to return home: access to trailers on or near their property; water and electricity back all over New Orleans; federal dollars dedicated to rebuilding individual homes; assistance in Texas to find safe, quality rental housing; and assistance with furniture and transportation.

Here are two samples of writing in the public sphere. The first is a billboard "Do Women Have to Be Naked to Get into The Met. Museum?" designed by the art and media activists Guerrilla Girls. (You can find more of their work at www.guerillagirls.com/index.shtml.) The other is a T-shirt "Hands off Iraq" to protest the U.S.-led invasion of Iraq in 2003. Compare these two forms of public writing—the billboard and the T-shirt. Notice differences in how the two writings are designed. Who are likely to be the intended readers? What sort of relationship do the writers seek to establish with their readers?

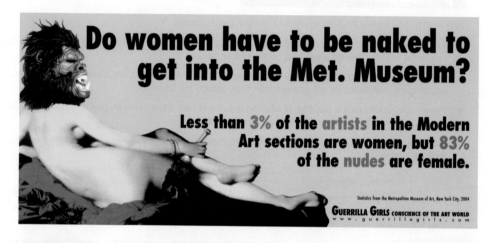

WRITING IN SCHOOL

At first glance it may appear that writing in school is relatively uncomplicated—a call to write, from a teacher who is also the audience, with the purpose of showing how well the student understands the material. From this perspective, school writing fits into the social context of schooling, in which students are in the role of performers, teachers are in the role of evaluators, and writing serves as the basis for ranking students according to the prevailing reward system of grades.

Writing in school, however, is more complex than this description allows us to see. First, students do lots of writing for their own purposes that is not directly evaluated by teachers—taking notes in lectures, for example, or writing summaries of textbook chapters to study for tests. And papers that students turn in to teachers for grades may not include all the writing—for example, research notes, outlines, first drafts, and false starts—a student has done to complete the assignment.

Second, even when students are writing for grades, they are not just displaying knowledge of the material. They must also take into account how the different academic fields call for different genres of writing—a lab report in chemistry, a critical essay on a poem for English, or a case study in psychology. For this reason, learning a subject is in part learning how chemists, literary critics, psychologists, and others use writing to communicate in their respective fields.

ANALYZING WRITING IN SCHOOL: SAMPLES FROM GRADE 3

Before we look at the kind of writing college teachers ask students to write, let's stop for a moment and think about whether writing as a display of learning is the only kind of writing you have been called on to do in school.

Here are two samples of writing drawn from a student in a third-grade class:

Sample 1

I will not forget my name and number.

I will not forget my name and number.

I will not forget my name and number.

I will not forget my name and number.

I will not forget my name and number.

Sample 2

Dear Dad,

    I had to stand in the lunch room today. I am very, very sorry. Mrs. Bailey is horrified. I love you.

Love,
Martha

Consider the purpose of these two writings. What is the relationship in each case between the student and the teacher? In the second sample, how does the student's relationship to her father play a role in the writing?

The same student also wrote the following piece:

Sample 3

My Big and Small Dream

One morning when I woke up I was a monster with pink eyes, purple faded hair, a green body, and a fluorescent yellow face. I went downstairs and ate the stove, the fridg, and all the food. I started shrinking. I was so surprised, then for the next five days I stopped eating. Then to my surprise I was as big and as high as the sky. Since I was big I bumped into a tree that was smaller than me. Also, by mistake, I stepped on a house with people having a party. Then I went to bed and the next morning I woke up and was myself again.

Consider how this sample of writing differs from the first two. What does the student's purpose seem to be? How does this purpose compare to her purposes in the first two samples? What is she learning in the three samples about school and her relationship to teachers?

SAMPLES OF WRITING IN SCHOOL

The following two pieces were both written by the same student. The first is a high school research paper, on a subject chosen by the student. The second was written in college as a response to an assigned reading. As you read, compare the two pieces.

- How does the writer seem to understand the assignments? What does his purpose seem to be in each instance?

- What kind of relationship does he establish with his reader and his subject?

- What features distinguish the college writing from the high school writing? Does the college writing seem to be more "mature" or "advanced" than the high school writing?

SAMPLE 1: HIGH SCHOOL RESEARCH PAPER

Davis 1

Zack Davis

English 3

Mrs. Tanner

1 May 2000

Politics and the Olympic Games

The revival of the modern Olympic Games was influenced by the politics of the late nineteenth century. The Baron de Coubertin had two motives in reviving the Olympic Games. After France lost the Franco-Prussian War, a gloom set over all of France. The Baron wanted to revive the games to inspire the youth of France. In the lycées of France, the intellectual aspects dominated the school. There were no physical education classes and very little, if any, athletic training. The Baron wanted both athletics and education in the schools. When creating these perfect schools of France he used the ephebes of ancient Greece and the public schools of England as examples when education and athletics played a major role in the young boy's lives; there would be a perfect school. The Baron's other purpose in recreating the Olympics was to promote world peace by gathering all the countries together.

Though the Baron's intentions were to produce world amity he did the opposite. Instead of peaceful relations the games created many conflicts. In 1936, for example, there was much conflict at the summer games in Berlin. The problem of the games was racism. Adolf Hitler wrote the following in *Mein Kampf,* while in prison in 1924. "Americans ought to be ashamed of themselves for letting their medals be won by Negroes. I myself would never even shake hands with one of them." Adolf Hitler, the leader of Germany at the time, was clearly very racist. When Jesse Owens, a black American, won the gold medal in the 100 meter dash, Hitler was infuriated. Hitler refused to congratulate him. Political incidents like these increased over the course of the Olympic Games.

In 1968 the politics shifted from racism to protests against racism. Before the games sprinter Tommie Smith and other students suggested to boycott the

Davis 2

Olympics because of the racial conditions in the United States. Although Tommie Smith went to Mexico City, he expressed his feelings on racism there as well. During the ceremony for the two hundred meter dash the "Star Spangled Banner" was played. At that time, both Tommie Smith and John Carlos staged a protest by giving the black power salute. They were suspended by the International Olympic Committee and ordered to leave the country.

Another incident that politics played a major role in was the boycott of the Moscow Olympics in 1980. After Russian troops were sent into Afghanistan in 1979, President Jimmy Carter proposed that the games be rescheduled and moved to another location. The response of the International Olympic Committee was that "politics should be of no influence in the Olympic Games." After failing to reschedule and move the games to another location, the President and sixty-four other countries boycotted. Of the one-hundred and forty-five nations that were invited to take part in the games, only eighty-one entered. Some nations that boycotted the games were West Germany, China, Japan, Canada, Kenya, Australia, New Zealand, Great Britain, France, and Italy. Though many athletes within the United States protested that politics should be of no factor in the games, Carter refused to reconsider. By boycotting the Olympics, Carter did not get the troops out of Afghanistan, but simply increased the tension between the United States and the Soviet Union.

In 1984, in response to the boycott four years earlier, Russia, along with East Germany, Czechoslovakia, Poland, Hungary, Bulgaria, and Cuba, declined the invitation to participate in the summer games in Los Angeles. The Soviets denied the boycott was revenge, but argued that the publicity and ten billion dollar cost of the games were outrageous. They also argued that the security in Los Angeles was not sufficient.

In the most recent games, politics as usual influenced the games. The games were held in South Korea. Though the bid was won fairly by South Korea, North Korea felt they deserved to be the co-hosts. Fearing what North Korea might do out of jealousy, South Korea had 120,000 specially trained antiterrorist fighters,

Davis 3

700,000 men of the Republic of Korea's armed forces, 40,000 permanently stationed United States soldiers and marines, and 100,000 United States sailors aboard aircraft carriers patrolling the Korean shores. In addition, there was 63 armed personnel for each of the 13,000 athletes. Both the United States and South Korea had to take drastic measures to secure the safety of the athletes. If politics played no role in the Olympics none of those measures would be necessary.

When Baron de Coubertin revived the Olympic Games he had nothing but good intentions. His hope was that the Olympics could be a place where people from all over the world could gather together in peace doing what they all had in common. Though his intentions were good, politicians took advantage of the Olympics. They used the games as chances to boycott what they thought was wrong and, in other cases, as revenge. Jesse Owens and all the athletes that were not able to go to the 1980 and 1984 Olympics suffered from politics. The purpose of the Olympics has changed into something that is not right. Let's leave the politics to the politicians and competition to the athletes.

SAMPLE 2: COLLEGE RESPONSE PAPER

Assignment: What is the role of popular religion—as portrayed through the worship of the Madonna—in defining the ethnic identity of the Italian community of East Harlem?

Davis 1

Zack Davis

English 120

Prof. Oboler

1 May 2004

Popular Religion and Ethnic Identity

As I read through The Madonna of 115th Street: Faith and Community in Italian Harlem, 1880–1950, and the important role that popular religion played

Davis 2

in the role of defining ethnic identity in the Italian community of East Harlem, I could not help but think of my hometown, Cranston, and the similarities that popular religion played there as well. As I read about the feasts of the Madonna of 115th Street I was reminded of the Feast of St. Mary in Cranston and the almost identical origins of the feasts. In Cranston, the feast of St. Mary was started to honor La Madonna della Citta or the Madonna of the city, who was from a small village in southern Italy where many of the first Cranstonians originated. It also served as a distinguishing feature from other Catholics in the area and a marker of ethnic identity. Both of the creations of the Madonnas and the feasts in their honor were popular religion. Popular religion was an important role in shaping ethnic identities in Italian communities.

Both of the feasts in Cranston and East Harlem's purpose were to honor the Madonnas, each from a specific place in Italy, where many of the honorees were from. The Madonna served as a shared history in the new world and gave immigrants something to serve as a reference point. Each immigrant could relate to the Madonna and trusted her with their most sacred prayers. The Madonna listened to the needs of the newly arrived immigrants. As quoted from the work, The Madonna of 115th Street, the author says of immigrant Italians, "the Italian feels safer when he plays homage to the patron saint of his hometown or village who in the past was considerate to the people."

The feast of the Madonna of 115th Street began in the summer of 1881 when immigrants from the town of Polla formed a mutual aid society. One of the functions of the mutual aid society was to give unemployment and burial benefits to immigrants. But a larger function of the mutual aid societies and the feasts that it started was to gather immigrants and preserve as well as observe traditional customs in the new world. Because mutual aid societies were unique to Italian Roman Catholics they served as a model for ethnic identity. Furthermore, Catholics of other ethnic backgrounds, such as Irish Catholics, were hostile to feasts of the Madonna of 115th Street. Orsi speaks of an attack published in the Catholic World in 1888. The attack criticized the

Davis 3

shrines, holy cards and pagan superstitions and "devotions" of the Italian Roman Catholic and the ignorance for "great faith of religion." These attacks on Italian Catholics served to further separate Italians from other Catholics and create a stronger ethnic identity.

In addition the building of certain specifically Italian churches (chiesa), which, again, is popular religion, in East Harlem served as another ethnic identity. Italians as a group gathered to build their own churches. The building was a gathering of everyone, of an ethnic group to create something that they could call their own. As the book noted, junkmen and icemen donated their carts and horses to help manage the burden of building materials as people prepared refreshments for the workers. This act was substantial in the creation of ethnic identity.

During the late nineteenth century, popular religion served as an ethnic identity for Italians in East Harlem, Cranston, RI, as well as in other parts of the eastern seaboard. The creation of Madonnas from hometowns as well as feasts for their honor were the most unique feature and distinguishing characteristic. The separation of Italian Catholics from other Catholics such as Irish Catholics provided further ethnic identity in America.

ANALYZING A LITERACY EVENT

The term *literacy event* gives us a way to think about how reading and writing enter our lives and shape our interactions with others. All the samples of writing in this chapter, for example, can be considered literacy events, because they focus our attention on the role that particular moments of reading and writing play in our experience. These literacy events take place in different social contexts, but each of them, in one way or another, reveals an aspect of what writing does in the world.

When analyzing a literacy event, you are asked to examine how people make sense of their encounters with reading and writing—how they understand what writing is and what it does. You will need to focus on a particular moment in which writing takes on a meaningful role in your life or in the lives of others. The three reading selections that follow provide further examples of literacy events. As you will see, each example concentrates on a specific encounter with writing and the social relationships involved.

- The first selection is from *Narrative of the Life of Frederick Douglass,* the account of Douglass's life as a slave and his escape from slavery.

- The second selection appears in Eudora Welty's memoir *One Writer's Beginnings,* about her childhood in Jackson, Mississippi, in the early twentieth century.

- The third selection comes from Margaret J. Finders's *Just Girls: Hidden Literacies and Life in Junior High,* a study of how junior high girls used reading and writing to establish personal identities and social networks.

FROM *NARRATIVE OF THE LIFE OF FREDERICK DOUGLASS*

FREDERICK DOUGLASS

Very soon after I went to live with Mr. and Mrs. Auld, she very kindly commenced to teach me the A, B, C. After I had learned this, she assisted me in learning to spell words of three or four letters. Just at this point of my progress, Mr. Auld found out what was going on, and at once forbade Mrs. Auld to instruct me further, telling her, among other things, that it was unlawful, as well as unsafe, to teach a slave to read. To use his own words, further, he said, "If you give a nigger an inch, he will take an ell. A nigger should know nothing but to obey his master—to do as he is told to do. Learning would spoil the best nigger in the world. Now," said he, "if you teach that nigger (speaking of myself) how to read, there would be no keeping him. It would forever unfit him to be a slave. He would at once become unmanageable, and of no value to his master. As to himself, it could do him no good, but a great deal of harm. It would make him discontented and unhappy." These words sank deep into my heart, stirred up sentiments within that lay slumbering, and called into existence an entirely new train of thought. It was a new and special revelation, explaining dark and mysterious things, with which my youthful understanding had struggled, but struggled in vain. I now understood what had been to me a most perplexing difficulty—to wit, the white man's power to enslave the black man. It was a grand achievement, and I prized it highly. From that moment, I understood the pathway from slavery to freedom. It was just what I wanted, and I got it at a time when I the least expected it. Whilst I was saddened by the thought of losing the aid of my kind mistress, I was gladdened by the invaluable instruction which, by the merest accident, I had gained from my master. Though conscious of the difficulty of learning without a teacher, I set out with high hope, and a fixed purpose, at whatever cost of trouble, to learn how to read. The very decided manner with which he spoke, and strove to impress his wife with the evil consequences of giving me instruction, served to convince me that he was deeply sensible of the truths he was uttering. It gave me the best assurance that I might rely with the utmost confidence on the results which, he said, would flow from teaching me to read. What he most dreaded, that I most desired. What he most loved, that I most hated. That which to him was a great evil, to be carefully shunned, was to me a great good, to be diligently sought; and the argument which he so warmly urged, against my learning to read, only served to inspire me with a desire and determination to learn. In learning to read, I owe almost as much to the bitter opposition of my master, as to the kindly aid of my mistress. I acknowledge the benefit of both.

FROM *ONE WRITER'S BEGINNINGS*
EUDORA WELTY

1   Jackson's Carnegie Library was on the same street where our house was, on the other side of the State Capitol. "Through the Capitol" was the way to go to the Library. You could glide through it on your bicycle or even coast through on roller skates, though without family permission.

2   I never knew anyone who'd grown up in Jackson without being afraid of Mrs. Calloway, our librarian. She ran the Library absolutely by herself, from the desk where she sat with her back to the books and facing the stairs, her dragon eye on the front door, where who knew what kind of person might come in from the public? SILENCE in big black letters was on signs tacked up everywhere. She herself spoke in her normally commanding voice; every word could be heard all over the Library above a steady seething sound coming from her electric fan; it was the only fan in the Library and stood on her desk, turned directly onto her streaming face.

3   As you came in from the bright outside, if you were a girl, she sent her strong eyes down the stairway to test you; if she could see through your skirt she sent you straight back home; you could just put on another petticoat if you wanted a book that badly from the public library. I was willing; I would do anything to read.

4   My mother was not afraid of Mrs. Calloway. She wished me to have my own library card to check out books for myself. She took me in to introduce me and I saw I had met a witch. "Eudora is nine years old and has my permission to read any book she wants from the shelves, children or adult," Mother said. "With the exception of *Elsie Dinsmore*," she added. Later she explained to me that she'd made this rule because Elsie the heroine, being made by her father to practice too long and hard at the piano, fainted and fell off the piano stool. "You're too impressionable, dear," she told me. "You'd read that and the very first thing you'd do, you'd fall off the piano stool." "Impressionable" was a new word. I never hear it yet without the image that comes with it of falling straight off the piano stool.

5   Mrs. Calloway made her own rules about books. You could not take back a book to the Library on the same day you'd taken it out; it made no difference to her that you'd read every word in it and needed another to start. You could take out two books at a time and two only; this applied as long as you were a child and also for the rest of your life, to my mother as severely as to me. So, two by two, I read library books as fast as I could go, rushing them home in the basket of my bicycle. From the minute I reached our house, I started to read. Every book I seized on, from *Bunny Brown and His Sister Sue at Camp Rest-a-While* to *Twenty Thousand Leagues under the Sea,* stood for the devouring wish to read being instantly granted. I knew this was bliss, I knew it at the time. Taste isn't nearly so important; it comes in its own time. I wanted to read *immediately.* The only fear was that of books coming to an end.

FROM *JUST GIRLS: HIDDEN LITERACIES AND LIFE IN JUNIOR HIGH*
MARGARET J. FINDERS

1   As school years draw to a close, students across the nation anticipate the biggest school-sanctioned literacy event of the year: the sale and distribution of the school yearbook. Like students elsewhere, Northern Hills Junior High students anxiously awaited its arrival.

2   Produced by 65 students working together with the help of two staff advisors, the yearbook, a 48-page soft-bound document, captured the year through photographs, student-produced artwork, and captions. Sports held a prominent place in the pages of the yearbook: photos of football, track, basketball, and wrestling events for the boys and

track, tennis, volleyball, and basketball for the girls filled the pages. The book also contained photos of Soda—a drug and alcohol awareness club—and drama club.

3   I believe that most teachers would agree with one of the yearbook's faculty advisors, the media specialist, who described the importance of the yearbook this way:

4   > If you can find your mug in here [yearbook], it gives you a tremendous sense of belonging. We tried to cover all the major events, and it's important to find yourself. We took a lot of pictures. If you and your mom can find yourself in here, then everything is just A-OK.

5   At Northern Hills Junior High, the yearbook had become a central part of the end-of-the-year curriculum. . . . For the most part, teachers described the yearbook as a celebration and well-earned reward for hard work. They allocated class time for signing and sharing yearbooks. Perceived as a way to control the behavior of the 531 seventh and eighth graders who in late May may not be eager to participate in discussions or complete end-of-semester projects, signing time was a tool for negotiating with students, often appearing as a bribe. Teachers told students: "If we get all our work done . . ." "If you are all good . . ." "If you cooperate, and we can hurry through this . . ." The following teacher comment received several nods and "me-toos" from staff in the teacher's lounge: "I give them the last five to ten minutes to write depending on how the class goes. It's a reward. It's a privilege. It's their reward for good behavior."

6   The yearbook played such a large role in the end-of-school activities because the teachers and administrators all believed, as the media specialist articulated, that it gave a tremendous sense of belonging. The discourse of adolescence that privileges peer-group allegiances constructed filters, it seems, that prevented school personnel from seeing the yearbook as exclusionary. Although the yearbook was viewed as a symbol of solidarity for all students, only a particular population of students was made to feel as if they belonged to this club. Other students remained outsiders.

7   Constant comments from Northern Hills staff that "Everybody gets one" and "Everyone loves them" reveal that Cleo and Dottie [social outsiders from poor families who did not buy yearbooks] and many others were invisible to school personnel. Current enrollment was 531; 425 books were ordered. Eight were sold to adults, 10 distributed as complimentary copies, 10 were mailed to students who no longer lived in the district, and 5 remained unsold. 397 copies were sold to students, which left 134 students without yearbooks. That figure represents 25% of the total student population. While students may not have purchased a yearbook for a variety of reasons, the socioeconomic status of families

may have been a critical issue. For whatever reason, when teachers rewarded students with "signing time," one out of four students was not able to participate.

8   Katie: Can I sign your yearbook?

9   Barb: No.

10   A quick glance at the yearbooks shows row after row of white faces ordered by alphabetical arrangement. The seeming homogeneity conceals diversity: invisible barriers such as attitudes, beliefs, economics, and experiences separate these young people into at least two camps. The girls created markers to maintain the borders between them. Allegiances became visible in both the act of writing and in the messages themselves. What is written and to whom is controlled by one's social status. Yearbooks circulated across social boundaries, yet those with the greatest social status stood in judgment of those less powerful. Students carefully monitored who could sign their yearbooks. To allow one of lesser status to mark one's book appeared to lower the status of the book owner. Students often asked for and were denied signing privileges. . . . Some students were in fact told "No," after asking, "Can I sign your yearbook?" In the same way, some students refused to sign yearbooks of those perceived to be outside the circle of significance. Who had the right to write was clearly an issue of entitlement. . . . If one was perceived as an outsider, then one was not entitled to write. Likewise, one might or might not be entitled to even view the message. Students guarded their written texts and controlled who had the right to see them.

11   Students with the greatest status were freed from judgment, and their written comments became models for others to copy. As I watched, one student carefully moved her finger across the page, working cautiously to transfer a phrase exactly from one yearbook to another. Because a particular phrase was perceived as carrying more currency in this arena, this teen appropriated the words of another student as her own in order for her voice to contain that power. Students shared texts and at times took another person's message for her own, copying the same phrase from one yearbook to the next to the next. In such borrowing of texts, one, in a sense, borrowed the social status of another. In taking another's message as her own, each girl had to be careful not to overstep her boundaries and write . . . what she was not entitled to write.

12   In the act of writing, students inadvertently may mark themselves as outsiders by writing a message judged inappropriate by others. If one was not savvy enough to create an appropriate text or powerful enough to forgo judgment, often, out of fear of marking oneself as an outsider, one just scribbled safe messages such as "Have a good summer" or "See ya next year."

13   Some students, in order to preserve their social position, asked a friend, "What should I write? What do you want me to say?" Students took this opportunity to exert their position of authority and made such playful comments as "Say I'm 'just too cool' " or "Say 'she's always got a taco' " (a current description for shorts or jeans that were considered too tight across the seat of the pants) or "Write, 'BFF ASS' " (a code for best friends forever and always stay sweet or sexy). Many comments were so highly coded that only those few insiders could translate them.

14   In order for students to demonstrate that they were with it, comments carrying the current pop jargon taken from movies, television, and local sources become etched into this school-sanctioned document, creating an unusual juxtaposition of sanctioned and out-of-bounds literacies. Dark, graffiti-like messages boldly cut across the white-bordered layout and quite literally "defaced" students and teachers alike. With big pink erasers, students rubbed out the faces of outsiders.

15   In all of this signing, the [social] queens [a group of the most popular girls] demonstrated a tremendous sense of play. Signing yearbooks had the feeling of recess, providing playtime away from the institutional demands of schooling, away from adult supervision. Similar to the playground, who could play was controlled by the peer dynamic. The yearbook was used to stake out territory and control social interactions.

16   Conceived as an opportunity for all to celebrate the completion of another successful academic year, the yearbook provided much more. For Tiffany and all the other social queens it reaffirmed their position in the school arena and in the larger community. They measured their status by the number and size of their pictures and by the number of requests to sign books: "Everybody wants me to sign their book." For Cleo and her friends, it also reaffirmed their position: "None of my friends are in there anyway."

17   The role of the yearbook in the institutional context remains central to the closing of the school year. The yearbook stands as an icon. Unknowingly, some are allowed to speak while others are silenced, some to write while others are written upon.

■ FOR CRITICAL INQUIRY

1. The literacy event Frederick Douglass recounts involved a "new and special revelation, explaining dark and mysterious things." What is the literacy event to which Douglass refers? What exactly is this revelation?

2. What insights does Eudora Welty gain from getting a library card and access to books? What roles do her mother and the librarian, Mrs. Calloway, play in this literacy event? Explain how each makes sense of Welty's encounter with

literacy and how their interactions shape the literacy event. What role, if any, does Welty's gender play?

3. Margaret J. Finders begins by describing the end-of-school ritual of the junior high yearbook from the perspective of teachers and staff. How do school personnel make sense of the yearbook? How do their views differ from those of students? How does Finders analyze and explain the interactions among students that take place around signing yearbooks?

WRITING ASSIGNMENT

Analyzing a Literacy Event

Online Study Center

Now it's your turn to analyze a literacy event. Your task is to identify a particularly meaningful encounter with writing—whether those involved are in the role of a writer, a reader, or both. Then you need to explain how the people involved made sense of the event and the role that writing played in their interactions.

Directions

1. Select a particular encounter with writing in which you were directly involved or that you observed. Look for encounters with writing that reveal powerful feelings or strong responses on the part of the people involved. Look for misunderstandings, conflicts, resolutions, or alliances in which writing plays a key role. Look for instances of writing that had an effect on people's sense of themselves as individuals or as part of a group. If you have time, discuss with a partner three or four literacy events that you are considering for this assignment. See what seems most interesting to another person. Use this information to help you make a decision about the literacy event you want to analyze.

2. Analyze the literacy event. Here are some questions to take into account:

   - Describe what happened. What is the social context of the encounter with writing? Who was involved? What did they do?

   - What type of writing did the encounter center on? What were the specific features of the writing? What was its purpose?

   - How did the participants make sense of the literacy event? Did they share the same perspective or differ? How would you account for these differences or similarities?

   - What were the relationships among the participants? What role did writing play in their interactions? What were the results or consequences of these interactions?

3. Write an analysis of the literacy event. You will need to describe what happened and to explain how the participants made sense of the literacy event and how this particular encounter with writing shaped their interactions. ∎

reading for academic purposes: analyzing the rhetorical situation

Like writing, reading is stitched into the very fabric of our lives as an essential activity in carrying out our personal and social purposes. In this chapter, we focus on reading in college, where reading is central to the intellectual work students are called on to do. The strategies presented are typical of those that readers use in college for such academic purposes as understanding the current state of knowledge in a field of study, explaining the perspectives of experts, analyzing existing debates and controversies, applying concepts, and interpreting important issues.

Whether you are writing a critical review of a scholarly article in a sociology class, working on a term paper in environmental studies, or preparing for an essay exam in business management, you will depend, in important respects, on assembling a useful and usable repertoire of reading strategies. The strategies in this chapter can help you do the kind of reading needed to handle these and many other kinds of writing tasks, inside and outside the academy.

The chapter looks at two ways of reading:

1. **Strategies for close reading.** These strategies give you ways to understand what a text means and how a writer presents ideas and conveys meanings.

2. **Strategies to analyze the rhetorical situation.** These strategies give you ways to understand the larger context of issues and how a writer identifies and responds to the call to write.

The reading strategies you decide to use—and in what combination—will depend on your purpose for reading and the writing task you're working on. If you're reading to understand, say, the effect of acid rain on the environment or how a particular scholar explains Freud's theory of instincts, then the first set of close reading strategies may be sufficient. In other cases,

however, especially when there are a range of views on an issue, you may need not only to understand the information and analysis but also to investigate the rhetorical situation in which the writing occurs.

The *rhetorical situation*, in the broadest sense, refers to the circumstances that a writer takes into account when he or she responds to the call to write. In academic settings, the notion of rhetorical situation is critical to understanding how scholars formulate the issues they write about in relation to what others have already said. By learning to analyze the rhetorical situation, you can take a key step in your college education by going beyond simply acquiring information to see what's at stake in how academics and other writers produce knowledge.

In the writing assignment at the end of this chapter, "Analyzing the Rhetorical Situation," we ask you to use the reading strategies to look closely at a particular piece of writing and to analyze its rhetorical situation.

READING AS RESEARCH: WORKING WITH SOURCES

One of the key premises of *The Call to Write* is that reading is research in the root sense of the word: to seek out or search again. From this perspective, reading as research isn't limited to term papers or other research assignments. Any time you spend reading can amount to research, whether you're preparing for an exam, deciding which new movie to see, or trying to grasp the positions of candidates in an upcoming election. As these examples show, reading is invariably tied to people's purposes and social contexts—to their sense of what they need to know and what sources of information to seek out. By working with print and electronic sources, people put together ways of understanding the world, interacting with others, and clarifying their own ideas and beliefs.

The reading strategies in this chapter—close reading and analysis of the rhetorical situation—can enable you to work actively and critically with print and electronic sources you encounter in the classroom, the workplace, or the public sphere. In the next chapter, "Persuasion and Responsibility," you can add to your reading strategies by learning to analyze arguments. In Part Two, "Writing Projects," many of the assignments emphasize reading as research, and most of the chapters include a "Working with Sources" assignment that calls for close and critical reading.

GETTING STARTED: PREVIEWING

A first step toward knowing what reading strategies to use is to identify your own purpose for reading and the genre of the writing you are about to read. To preview a piece of writing, read the title, headings, and the first sentence of each paragraph. Also examine the captions under any photos or graphic displays of information. Then answer these questions:

1. What is your purpose for reading? What use are you planning to make of your reading? What do you expect to find?

2. What does the writer's purpose seem to be? What does the title convey to you? Is there a statement that explicitly describes the writer's purpose? Or is it implied?

3. What does the genre of writing seem to be? Can you put the reading into a category of writing you are familiar with? What other writings does it remind you of?

4. If the reading seems unfamiliar, how can you get a handle on it? Do editorial comments, prefaces, author notes, or blurbs on book jackets provide background information for your reading? Is there someone you can talk to for more information—for example, another student, your teacher, or a librarian?

5. Who is the intended audience? What are their purposes likely to be in reading the writing?

STRATEGIES FOR CLOSE READING

You have probably used some or all of these strategies while reading textbooks, but they are helpful with other readings as well. To examine strategies for close reading and for analyzing the rhetorical situation, we will use Jonathan Kozol's essay "Distancing the Homeless." The essay offers a typical example of the kind of reading on complex and contested issues that you'll be asked to do in college courses.

ETHICS OF READING

BOREDOM AND PERSISTENCE

Going to college means that you will encounter a wide range of academic and professional writing, some of which may be specialized and technical. You may find at times that the reading you're assigned is intimidating and hard to follow. You may wonder what the writer is trying to prove, or you may think the writer is splitting hairs. The writing may seem abstract, detached from the real world.

These are all symptoms of boredom, and the danger is that you will give up at this point and say you weren't really interested in the first place. What is often the case, though, is not that you aren't interested but rather that you are unfamiliar with the particular type of writing, its forms, specialized vocabularies, and ways of reasoning.

To act responsibly in college, the workplace, and the public domain, you need to read writing that is pertinent and carries weight. An ethics of reading holds that readers need to give difficult material a chance. It's not simply a matter of being fair to the writer. By working on new and difficult material, you also, in effect, refuse to be alienated from it. In this regard, you avoid the threat of boredom leading to the premature closure of communication. ■

UNDERLINING

Underlining the writer's key points helps you identify and keep track of main ideas and important information. It also enables you to return to the marked phrases to reconstruct the writing's meaning quickly. Underlining should be done selectively. If you underline everything, you will not be able to use your underlinings to recall the overall meaning of the writing. Selective underlining enables you to identify where the writer presents important information, claims, evidence, interpretations, and conclusions.

ANNOTATION

Annotations are comments that readers write in the margins of a piece of writing. The purposes of annotation are to help you actively engage in what you are reading and create a record of your experience as you come to grips with its meaning.

There are no rules about annotation, but here are some suggestions:

1. Write brief notes on what you see as major points.
2. Agree or disagree with what the writer is saying.
3. Refer to what the writer is doing at a particular point (for example, making a claim, giving an example, presenting statistical evidence, or refuting an opposing view).
4. Raise questions or voice confusion about something you need to clarify.
5. Draw connections to other things you have read or know about.

FROM "DISTANCING THE HOMELESS"

JONATHAN KOZOL

1   It is commonly believed by many journalists and politicians that the homeless of America are, in large part, former patients of large mental hospitals who were deinstitutionalized in the 1970s—the consequence, it is sometimes said, of misguided liberal opinion that favored the treatment of such persons in community-based centers. It is argued that this policy, and the subsequent failure of society to build such centers or to provide them in sufficient number, is the primary cause of homelessness in the United States.

2   Those who work among the homeless do not find that explanation satisfactory. While conceding that a certain number of the homeless are or have been mentally unwell, they believe that, in the case of most unsheltered people, the primary reason is economic rather than clinical. The cause of homelessness, they say with disarming logic, is the lack of homes and of income with which to rent or acquire them.

3   They point to the loss of traditional jobs in industry (2 million every year since 1980) and to the fact that half of those who are laid off end up in work that pays a poverty-level

wage. They point out that since 1968 the number of children living in poverty has grown by 3 million, while welfare benefits to families with children have declined by 35 percent.

4   And they note, too, that these developments have occurred during a time in which the shortage of low-income housing has intensified as the gentrification of our major cities has accelerated. Half a million units of low-income housing are lost each year to condominium conversion as well as to arson, demolition, or abandonment. Between 1978 and 1980, median rents climbed 30 percent for people in the lowest income sector, driving many of these families into the streets. Since 1980, rents have risen at even faster rates.

5   Hard numbers, in this instance, would appear to be of greater help than psychiatric labels in telling us why so many people become homeless. Eight million American families now use half or more of their income to pay their rent or mortgage. At the same time, federal support for low-income housing dropped from $30 billion (1980) to $7.5 billion (1988). Under Presidents Ford and Carter, 500,000 subsidized private housing units were constructed. By President Reagan's second term, the number had dropped to 25,000.

6   In our rush to explain the homeless as a psychiatric problem, even the words of medical practitioners who care for homeless people have been curiously ignored. A study published by the Massachusetts Medical Society, for instance, has noted that, with the exceptions of alcohol and drug use, the most frequent illnesses among a sample of the homeless population were trauma (31 percent), upper-respiratory disorders (28 percent), limb disorders (19 percent), mental illness (16 percent), skin diseases (15 percent), hypertension (14 percent), and neurological illnesses (12 percent). Why, we may ask, of all these calamities, does mental illness command so much political and press attention? The answer may be that the label of mental illness places the destitute outside the sphere of ordinary life. It personalizes an anguish that is public in its genesis; it individualizes a misery that is both general in cause and general in application.

7   There is another reason to assign labels to the destitute and single out mental illness from among their many afflictions. All these other problems—tuberculosis, asthma, scabies, diarrhea, bleeding gums, impacted teeth, etc.—bear no stigma, and mental illness does. It conveys a stigma in the United States. It conveys a stigma in the Soviet Union as well. In both nations the label is used, whether as a matter of deliberate policy or not, to isolate and treat as special cases those who, by deed or word or by sheer presence, represent a threat to national complacence. The two situations are obviously not identical, but they are enough alike to give Americans reason for concern.

8   The notion that the homeless are largely psychotics who belong in institutions, rather than victims of displacement at the hands of enterprising realtors, spares us from the

need to offer realistic solutions to the deep and widening extremes of wealth and poverty in the United States. It also enables us to tell ourselves that the despair of homeless people bears no intimate connection to the privileged existence we enjoy—when, for example, we rent or purchase one of those restored town houses that once provided shelter for people now huddled in the street.

SUMMARIZING

A summary condenses clearly and accurately what you have read. Like underlining, a good summary identifies the main idea and important supporting material. But it also calls on you to explain the connections between points.

To write an effective summary, follow these steps:

1. Read the text carefully, underlining and annotating it. Identify the writer's purpose and the main point of the reading (this main point might or might not be explicitly stated). Underline and, where relevant, annotate the ideas that support the main point and the key details that support these ideas.

2. Review your underlinings and annotations. Think about what questions you may have. If the writer didn't explicitly state his or her main point, write the main point as you see it. (The main point is often tied to the writer's purpose, so thinking about purpose might help in stating the main point.)

3. Start your summary with a statement in your own words that identifies the writer's purpose and expresses the main point.

4. Consult your underlinings and annotations to identify the most important supporting details. Rewrite these details in your own words, combining ideas when you can.

5. Check your summary to see if it holds together as a coherent piece of writing and is not simply a series of unconnected statements. Add transitions where needed to make connections between parts of the summary.

Sample Summary of "Distancing the Homeless"

In "Distancing the Homeless," Jonathan Kozol calls on readers to reconsider common understandings of the causes of homelessness. According to Kozol, journalists and politicians have identified the release of mental patients as the cause of homelessness. In contrast, he argues that the lack of low-cost housing has caused homelessness. He cites the shortage of jobs and low-income housing, along with increasing rents, to explain why people are homeless. Kozol says that blaming homelessness on the mentally ill both stigmatizes mental illness and distances people from the plight of the homeless.

EXPLORATORY WRITING

Exploratory writing offers you a chance to explore your thoughts and feelings about the ideas in a piece of writing. You can use what you have read as a springboard to see where your thoughts lead you.

The only direction is that you begin with whatever you have just read, and write nonstop for a predetermined amount of time, say five or ten minutes. The idea is to build up momentum, so don't stop to revise, edit, or correct anything you have written. Don't worry about whether your ideas are consistent or contradictory. Just see where your writing takes you.

Sample Exploratory Writing

The way Jonathan Kozol uses data makes it hard to refute his interpretation of homelessness. He makes a very powerful case that the loss of income and the neglect of low-cost housing have caused people to be homeless. Even more interesting to me is his explanation of how people avoid the issue of homelessness by defining the homeless as mentally ill. Labels are definitely a way of distancing ourselves from other people. I have felt this myself when I visited San Francisco and was asked for money by a homeless man. It made me feel extremely uncomfortable, and I didn't know how to react. I felt sorry for the man, but I couldn't help thinking he would use the money for drugs or alcohol. And most of all, the encounter made me want to get away from the man. So I just avoided him as much as I could and started walking faster.

After reading Kozol, I realize that my response comes from a desire to avoid people who have been stigmatized. I felt terribly guilty about the incident, but also I was genuinely frightened of the man. Because of my guilt and fear, I couldn't think of him as a normal human being. I was seeing him through the category of "mentally ill" and potentially dangerous. This is what I'm afraid is now happening on a wider scale, as San Francisco and other cities are enacting laws that limit where the homeless can be. It's an out of sight, out of mind mentality. As downtown areas gentrify, the middle class professionals who live and work there don't want to see or come into contact with the homeless. Gentrification in this way depends on dehumanizing the people it displaces.

OUTLINING

Outlining can help you analyze how writers arrange their material—what the parts are and how they are organized. There are various ways to set up an outline. A standard way, like the outline below, is to divide the writing into three main sections—the introduction, the body, and the conclusion. The outline states the main point at the beginning, uses roman numerals to mark off the main sections, uses capital letters to identify important ideas within each section, and uses arabic numerals to note details that support these ideas.

The benefit of such an outline is that it gives you a clear, concise record of what the piece of writing says. In this way, it is similar to a summary. However, it also goes beyond a summary by helping you visualize the relationships among the parts of the writing so that you can analyze the writer's strategy, as discussed in the next section.

The following outline shows how Kozol has organized his argument.

Sample Outline

Main point: The cause of homelessness is not mental illness but rather the lack of homes and of income with which to rent or acquire them.

I. Introduction: Two views of the cause of homelessness
- a. Common view: Deinstitutionalizing the mentally ill
- b. Kozol's view: The lack of homes and income

II. Body: Supporting evidence for Kozol's view
- a. Lack of income
  1. Loss of traditional jobs in industry
  2. Increase in numbers of people working for poverty-level wages
  3. Increase in children living in poverty
  4. Decrease in welfare benefits
- b. Shortage of low-cost housing
  1. Loss of public housing to condominium conversion and to arson, demolition, and abandonment
  2. Increase in rents
- c. Other revealing statistics
  1. Eight million families using half or more of their incomes for rent or mortgage
  2. Drop in federal support for low-income housing
  3. Decrease in construction of subsidized private housing
- d. Statistics on most frequent illnesses among homeless

III. Conclusion: Reasons for labeling homeless as mentally ill

    a. Treating problem as individual rather than public

    b. Stigma of mental illness isolating homeless as special cases

    c. Way of not dealing with real problems

    d. Distancing ourselves from plight of homeless

DESCRIBING THE WRITER'S STRATEGY

As you have seen, an outline helps you identify how a writer organizes his or her ideas to support a main point. The next step is to analyze the organization by describing the strategy the writer uses to connect these parts.

This reading strategy asks you to identify the main sections in a piece of writing and to explain how each section functions in the piece of writing as a whole. By focusing on what the writer is doing—comparing and contrasting, supporting with evidence, explaining causes and effects—you can see the strategies the writer uses to connect the sections and thereby accomplish his or her overall purpose. (See the Writing Strategies box below for a fuller listing of such strategies.)

To describe a writer's strategy:

1. Write a statement that describes the writer's overall purpose. What is the writer trying to accomplish: provide information, challenge a common view (as Kozol does), or do something else? You can probably think of a number of other purposes writers have: for example, profiling a person or place, rendering personal experience, endorsing a policy, reviewing a book or movie, interpreting an event, or explaining a concept.

2. Divide the writing into what appear to be the main sections, grouping paragraphs that seem to go together. Look for an opening section that introduces the topic or main idea, a middle section or sections that develop the writer's subject, and an ending.

3. Label the function each major section performs. Your label should explain how the section fits into the writing as a whole. Consider how the opening section introduces the topic or main idea, how a middle section or sections develop it, and how the writing ends.

4. Label the parts within each main section according to the function they perform. Explain how each part develops the main idea of the section in which it appears.

To label the parts in steps 3 and 4, you may find it useful to consult the Writing Strategies box. Since the box only gives some of the most common strategies, however, be prepared to invent your own terms.

Notice how the Sample Description of a Writer's Strategy on the next page divides the writing into three main sections by grouping paragraphs together according to the function they perform—introducing the argument, providing supporting evidence, and explaining the consequences of the argument.

Sample Description of a Writer's Strategy

Overall purpose: To challenge a common view about the causes of homelessness

¶1–2: Introduces the main idea.

> Replaces a common belief about the cause of homelessness with an alternative view.

¶3–6: Provides supporting evidence for the main idea.

> Offers the testimony of experts, statistical evidence, and a medical study to refute the common view.

> Raises a question about why the common view commands attention and offers an answer.

¶7–8: Explains the implications of the argument.

> Offers a second reason for the common view.

> Compares how the common view operates in the United States and the Soviet Union.

> Explains important consequences of the common view.

■ WORKING TOGETHER

Analyzing an Argument

Working with two or three other students, pick a short piece of writing that makes an argument. A good source for this assignment is the editorial page of a newspaper—whether it's a student, local, or national newspaper (such as the *New York Times* or

---

WRITING STRATEGIES

What a Writer Does

❑ Narrates, tells a story, relates an anecdote or incident

❑ Describes things, people, places, processes

❑ Illustrates by using examples, details, data

❑ Defines key terms, problems, issues, trends

❑ Compares and/or contrasts things, ideas, persons, places, processes

❑ Classifies things, ideas, people, places, processes into categories

❑ Explains causes and effects

❑ Gives reasons

❑ Offers evidence (statistics, established facts, expert testimony)

❑ Cites other writers

❑ Makes concessions

❑ Refutes opposing views

USA Today). Look for a piece of writing that is five to ten paragraphs long. Then follow these steps:

1. Working individually, underline and annotate. Then write a one-paragraph summary. Finally, write one or two paragraphs of exploratory writing in response to the reading.

2. As a group, compare your underlinings, annotations, summaries, and exploratory writings. What are the main similarities and differences? Don't argue about who is right or wrong. Instead, notice what each person's work on the reading has brought to light.

STRATEGIES FOR ANALYZING THE RHETORICAL SITUATION

Analyzing the rhetorical situation of a piece of writing is a matter of building on the reading strategies already presented to examine how and why a particular piece of writing got written in the first place, who its intended readers are, and what its writer is trying to accomplish. In other words, the goal of analyzing the rhetorical situation is not just to understand the content of a piece of writing or how the writer put it together but to understand its context. Analyzing the rhetorical situation involves asking questions like these: Who is the writer? What called on the writer to put his or her views down on the page? What kind of relationship is the writer trying to establish with readers? How does the writer's work relate to the larger context of discussion about an issue?

This section presents three strategies for analyzing the rhetorical situation—using background information about the context of issues, the writer, and the place of publication; analyzing the writer's purpose and relationship to readers; and analyzing the writer's use of language as clues about the rhetorical situation.

USING BACKGROUND INFORMATION

Background information about the context of issues, the writer, and the publication where the writer's work appears can be useful in understanding the rhetorical situation and how the writer identifies the call to write.

As you will see, the information you turn up about the context, the writer, and the place of publication does not speak for itself. You need to interpret this information in order to determine what it means for your analysis.

The Context of Issues

One of the main themes of this book is that writing doesn't just happen. It is called up when writers are moved by some sense of urgency that makes them want to be heard. This means that there is often a debate, discussion, or controversy already under way that, for one reason or another, the writer feels compelled to enter. This is the case with Jonathan Kozol, who sees the dominant explanations of homelessness as inadequate and misleading.

EVALUATING WEB SITES

Evaluating information on the Web poses special problems for the reader. Unlike printed material such as newspapers, magazines, government documents, academic journals, and books, Web sites do not necessarily go through a process of editing and peer review that filters out unreliable and unsubstantiated information. Instead, what appears on the Web is largely unregulated and sometimes of questionable credibility. After all, anyone can put up a Web site and include in it whatever they wish. That is, of course, part of the Web's attraction, but it is also the primary reason that readers need to approach Web sites with care. Here are some basic suggestions for evaluating the reliability and authority of information found on the Web.

Reading a Web Document

Web documents contain three main elements: header, body, and footer. Knowing where to look in the document should enable you to answer the following questions as a starting point for evaluating the Web site:

1. Who is the author or contact person? This is usually located in the footer.

2. What institution or Internet provider supports the Web site? This is usually located in the header or footer. (*.edu* indicates an educational institution; *.org*, a nonprofit organization; *.gov*, a government institution; and *.com*, a commercial source.)

3. When was the Web site created or updated? This is usually located in the footer.

4. What is the purpose of the information contained in the Web site? This is determined by examining the body.

5. Who is the intended audience? This is determined by examining the body.

Evaluating the Information on a Web Site

You can use the information you have gathered to ask the following questions. Your answers should enable you to evaluate the reliability of the information at the Web site.

1. What do you know about the author? Does he or she list an occupation, institutional affiliation, years of experience, or other information or qualifications? Does the author seem to be qualified to write and present information on the topic at hand?

2. What do you know about the institution or Internet provider that supports the Web site? What influence, if any, is the author's affiliation to this particular organization, institution, or provider likely to have on the information presented at the Web site?

3. What seems to be the purpose of the Web site— to inform, explain, persuade, or some combination? Who is the site's audience likely to be? What uses are visitors likely to make of the site?

4. How much of the information at the Web site has the author created? How much is already existing material that the author has organized? Where does such information come from? Do these sources seem reliable? Is the Web site linked to other sites? Do linked sites seem reliable and authoritative? How can you tell?

Exercise

Use the questions to visit and evaluate the two Web sites shown here—The Insider (http://www.theinsider.org) and

the Southern Folklife Collection (http://www.lib.unc. edu/mss/sfc11/). How do they differ in terms of credibility? What has shaped your judgment?

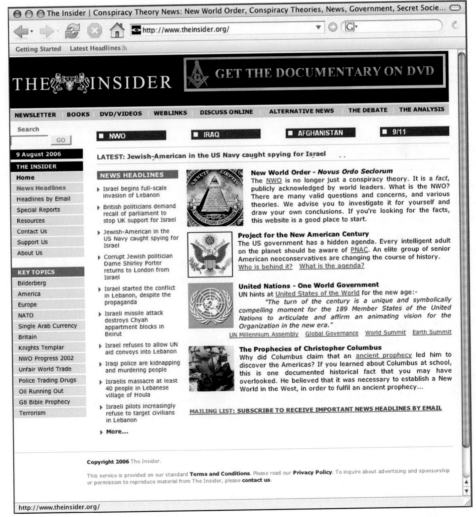

(continues)

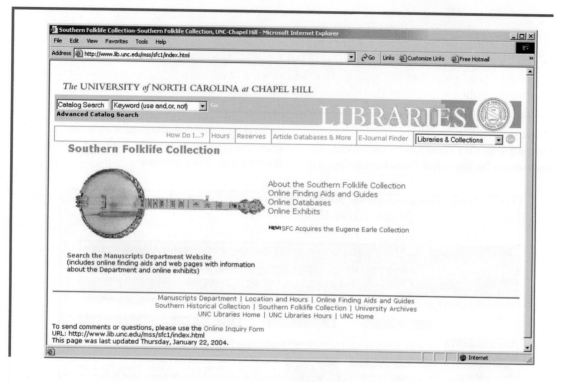

To understand the context of issues for the writing you're analyzing, you'll need to fill in some background information. Here are some questions to help you do so:

1. What do you know about the particular topic the writer is treating? If your knowledge is limited, where can you get reliable background information? You might do some library research—the *Readers' Guide to Periodical Literature* is a good place to start for contemporary issues—or a search on the Web. You can also talk to friends, older students, parents, teachers, librarians, or other adults.

2. What have people been saying about the topic? What do they think the main issues are? What seems to be at stake in these discussions?

3. Do people seem divided over these issues? If so, what positions have various people taken? What proposals or interpretations have they offered?

The Writer

Information about the writer—his or her education, credentials, experience, politics, prior publications, awards, institutional affiliations, reputation—is often summarized briefly in an author note following an article or on a book's dust jacket. You may also find the writer listed in the standard reference source *Contemporary Authors*.

This background information can give you some clues about the writer's authority to speak on the topic and the perspective he or she is likely to bring to it. Such background information can also make you aware of the assumptions readers might make about the writer. For example, knowing that Jonathan Kozol is an award-winning nonfiction writer, radical educator, and social activist whose publications include *Death at an Early Age* (his account of teaching in Boston's inner-city schools in the 1960s) and *Savage Inequalities* (a study of underfunded inner-city schools) can give readers a sense of Kozol's purposes and point of view.

Here are some questions you may find useful:

1. Based on what you know about his or her background, how much authority and credibility can you attribute to the writer? Is there reason to believe that the writer will provide informed accounts and responsible arguments, whether you agree with them or not?

2. Does the information you've found offer suggestions about why the writer was moved to write on the topic? What political, cultural, social, or other commitments is the writer known for? How are these commitments likely to influence the writer's argument?

3. How do these commitments relate to your own views? How is this relationship likely to influence your evaluation of the writer's argument?

The Publication

Type of publication can also provide you with some useful background information. Readers are likely to form very different impressions based on the type of publication in which a writer's work appears. You can find background information on the intended audience and editorial slant of many magazines in the standard reference source *Magazines for Libraries*.

In the case of Jonathan Kozol's "Distancing the Homeless," readers, whether they agree with his analysis or not, will acknowledge that his work appears in reputable publications. "Distancing the Homeless" first appeared in the *Yale Review* (a well-regarded journal that publishes social commentary, literary criticism, fiction, and poetry) and then was incorporated into Kozol's book-length study *Rachel and Her Children: Homeless Families in America*, published by one of the leading publishing houses.

Here are some questions to ask about the type of publication:

1. What do you know about the publication? Who is the publisher? Is it a commercial publication? Does it have an institutional affiliation—to a college or university, an academic field of study, a professional organization, a church? Does it espouse an identifiable political, social, cultural, economic, or religious ideology?

2. If the publication is a periodical, what other writers—and types of writing and topics—appear in the issue?

3. Who would be likely to read the publication?

ANALYZING THE WRITER'S PURPOSE AND RELATIONSHIP TO READERS

The purpose of analyzing the writer's relationship to readers is to understand where the writer is coming from, on whose behalf he or she is speaking, and the common ground the writer is asking readers to share. In some instances, the writer will address one particular audience, while in others the writer will try to appeal to many different audiences. In either case, the writer will have to make some key assumptions about readers' knowledge of the topic and their point of view on the issues it raises.

In the case of "Distancing the Homeless," notice how Kozol quickly locates himself in opposition to the common belief of journalists and politicians that the homeless are mainly former mental patients. Instead, he aligns himself with those "who work among the homeless" and believe that the cause of homelessness is the lack of homes and income. In that sense, he hopes to speak on behalf of the homeless, who, he believes, have been unfairly represented in the media and politics. Kozol is probably anticipating that some of his readers already share or will be predisposed to accept his perspective and social allegiances.

After presenting evidence for his counterinterpretation of the causes of homelessness, Kozol shifts in the sixth paragraph to speak in the collective voice of first-person plural ("we may ask"). At this point, Kozol seems to assume that he has offered enough compelling evidence about the actual causes of homelessness to expect readers who did not originally side with him to join with him on common ground to ask why the mental illness label has been persistently applied to the homeless.

As you can see in the passage from "Distancing the Homeless," writers' relationships to their readers seek points of identification—to establish the common ground that joins individuals together as "we." As the passage illustrates, forming a "we" can often imply the existence of a "they" from whom "we" are somehow distinguished, different, perhaps antagonistic. For these reasons, analyzing the writer's relationship to readers is an especially important reading strategy where the issues under consideration are contested and the writer is attempting to line up readers on one side or another. It can help you figure out where you stand on the issues and where your own allegiances reside.

Here are some questions to help you identify the writer's allegiances and relationship to readers:

1. Based on what you have read and the available background information on the writer, can you identify on whose behalf the writer is speaking? Whose interests does the writer seem to represent? Where do her or his loyalties seem to reside?

2. What assumptions does the writer seem to make about readers? Is the writer trying to establish common ground with a particular audience or with many different audiences? Does the writer seem to assume that

some readers are already predisposed to share her or his perspective and social allegiances?

3. What would it mean to agree (or disagree) with the writer? How would agreement (or disagreement) position readers in relation to what the writer and others have said about the topic? Would agreement (or disagreement) align readers with certain groups, individuals, points of view, institutions, values—and put them into opposition with others? What would readers have to believe to agree (or disagree) with the writer?

ANALYZING THE WRITER'S LANGUAGE

Words and phrases carry powerful associations that can sway readers to share or reject what a writer is saying. It is one thing, after all, to refer to business executives as "corporate leaders" or "entrepreneurial visionaries" and quite another to call them "fat cats" or "robber barons." The choice of terms reveals the writer's attitude and the perspective the writer is inviting readers to share. For this reason, it is useful to look at some of the ways writers use language to influence their readers. Reading closely the actual words that writers use can give you some clues to understanding where they are coming from and what they are trying to accomplish.

Tone

The tone in a writer's voice is one of the first things readers respond to because tone projects the writer's attitude and a sense of the writing's intended effect. In some cases, such as Jonathan Kozol's "Distancing the Homeless," the tone of voice is serious, objective, and authoritative. Readers are likely to feel that they are reading the work of someone who knows what he is talking about and that the purpose of the passage is basically informative. But Kozol's readers will also detect a sense of urgency and engagement. Kozol wants to inform his readers in order for them to do something—to see that "the despair of homeless people" does bear an "intimate connection to the privileged existence we enjoy."

A writer's tone can be serious or lighthearted, formal or informal, stuffy or down-to-earth, distanced or intimate. Sometimes readers can hear sarcasm, anger, self-importance, flippancy, and many other attitudes in a writer's tone. Notice, for example, how the informal, conversational tone of the newspaper columnist Mark Patinkin creates a commonsense, man-on-the-street attitude.

> Yes, I know caning is harsh, but am I the only one who's tired of Michael Fay's whining? Am I the only one who feels President Clinton has better things to do than write letters appealing for leniency?

Denotation/Connotation

Words have precise meanings, which you can find in the dictionary. These are their *denotative* meanings. For example, the denotative meaning of *virus* is "a microscopic organism that can replicate only within the cells of a living host," and *nationalism* means "a feeling of loyalty to a particular country."

Nonetheless, the meaning of these terms is not exhausted by their denotation. They also conjure up connotative meanings, depending on the circumstances in which they are used. *Connotation* is the coloring and emotional force that words take on based on how writers use them. *Nationalism*, for example, might call up images of unity and belongingness, but it can also release fears of war and ethnic antagonisms. *Virus* may lead the reader to think of new and mysterious "killer diseases" invading the country.

Notice, for example, how denotation and connotation work in Kozol's comparison of the United States and the Soviet Union, particularly in regard to the latter. At the level of denotation, the Soviet Union simply refers to the government system that resulted from the Russian Revolution in 1917—and one that collapsed in 1989, just after Kozol published "Distancing the Homeless." At a connotative level, however, the term *Soviet Union* has negative associations for many Americans, conjuring up images of a totalitarian police state. Kozol, of course, is quite aware of these negative connotations, and he uses them to indict the United States by way of comparison.

Figures of Speech

Figures of speech include simile, metaphor, analogy, overstatement, and personification, among others. The most commonly used are simile and metaphor—figures of speech that compare one thing to another. You have probably learned that similes use the words *like* and *as* to make a comparison. ("My love is like a red, red rose." "He is as happy as a clam.") Metaphors make an implicit comparison, as though one thing is actually another. ("She was a thin reed of a girl." "The long arm of the law grabbed him and brought him to trial.") Often these figures of speech are used to describe—to set a scene or create a mood—as in the following instance:

> If buildings could shiver, this Camden, N.J., tenement would have the shakes.
> *Jason DeParle, "Learning Poverty Firsthand"*

Figures of speech, however, are not simply decorative. They also provide ways of thinking, and they may carry judgments on the writer's part. In "Distancing the Homeless," for example, Kozol writes:

> Hard numbers, in this instance, would be of greater help than psychiatric labels in telling us why so many people become homeless.

Numbers, of course, are neither hard nor soft, but their "hardness" here is meant to invest authority in the evidence Kozol presents, in contrast to "psychiatric labels."

When Kozol writes that the homeless are "victims of displacement at the hands of enterprising realtors," he does not mean literally that realtors ejected people in person from their homes. But to say that the homeless were displaced "at the hands of enterprising realtors" accentuates the sense of responsibility Kozol assigns to gentrification in causing homelessness.

Stereotypes

Stereotypes are oversimplified representations that fit people into unvarying categories. These broad generalizations break down under careful scrutiny but appear to carry powerful (and often self-serving) explanations.

"Women are more emotional than men" is a classic stereotypical statement that a writer might use to argue that women won't do well under the stress of positions of authority (and therefore shouldn't be promoted over men). Along the same line, stereotypes of poor and working-class people and racial and ethnic minorities have created popular images (of "white trash," "drunken Indians," "welfare queens") that make subordination of one group to another seem necessary and inevitable. They are used to shame people who fall under the stereotype.

In this sense, stereotyping people, events, and behaviors can, as Kozol says concerning the stereotype of homeless people as mentally ill, stigmatize others and thereby distance us from their fates.

ANALYSIS OF A RHETORICAL SITUATION

The following analysis draws on a number of reading strategies presented in this chapter to examine how the writer Kevin Powell identifies and responds to the call to write in his commentary "My Culture at the Crossroads."

"My Culture at the Crossroads" appeared in the October 9, 2000, issue of *Newsweek*, one of the three leading news magazines in the United States (along with *Time* and *US News & World Report*), as part of its special feature cover story "The Rap on Rap." As you will see, Powell establishes his own credentials for speaking on hip-hop culture in the opening paragraph. *Newsweek* provides further useful background information in the author blurb at the end of Powell's commentary:

> Powell is the editor of *Step Into a World: A Global Anthology of the New Black Literature*, to be published in November [2000] (Wiley), and is guest curator of the Brooklyn Museum of Art's "Hip-Hop Nation: Roots, Rhymes and Rage."

Following Powell's commentary is a sample rhetorical analysis with annotations.

My Culture at the Crossroads

A rap devotee watches corporate control and apolitical times encroach on the music he has loved all his life. BY KEVIN POWELL

I AM A HIP-HOP HEAD FOR LIFE. I HAVE TAGGED MY moniker—"kepo1"—on walls; break-danced on cardboard; bumped elbows with fellow hip-hoppers at legendary clubs like The Rooftop, Union Square and Latin Quarter in New York City, and done everything from organizing rap shows to working as a hip-hop journalist and managing music producers. This culture has not only rescued the lives of countless masses who look like me, but it has empowered more young, working-class black and Latino cats than the civil-rights movement.

Yet something peculiar erupts when you've been around hip-hop for a while. Although you still love it, you look at its culture from a more critical perspective, particularly if you have studied other music genres, traveled widely and reflected intensely. You realize that what began as party music has come to be the soundtrack for post-civil-rights America. You realize that hip-hop is urban folk art, and as much an indication of the conditions in impoverished areas as bluesman Robert Johnson's laments in the 1930s. Naturally, you see a connection between the lives of Johnson and Tupac Shakur, not to mention a not-so-funny link between the mainstream hyping of Elvis and Eminem as innovators of black music forms. And, for sure, you wonder, loudly, if what happened to rock and roll will happen to hip-hop, if it hasn't already.

That is the external battle for hip-hop today: corporate control and cooptation. But there is also a civil war going on within the hip-hop nation. Part of it, unquestionably, has to do with this corporate stranglehold. Part of it has to do with the incredibly apolitical times in which we live: for some white Americans the current economic boom has created the myth that things are swell for all Americans. Not the case; 20 years after the Reagan backlash on civil rights, the influx of crack and guns and the acceleration of a disturbing class divide in black America, hip-hop has come to symbolize a generation fragmented by integration, migration, abandonment, alienation and, yes, self-hatred. Thus, hip-hop, once vibrant, edgy, fresh and def, is now as materialis-

Urban art: '80s graffiti, D.M.C. of Run-D.M.C.'s glasses, Powell

tic, hedonistic, misogynistic, shallow and violent as some of the films and TV shows launched from Hollywood.

It wasn't always that way. But, unfortunately, the golden era of hip-hop—that period in the late '80s and early '90s when such diverse artists as Public Enemy, N.W.A, Queen Latifah, MC Hammer, LL Cool J and De La Soul coexisted and there was no such thing as "positive" or "negative" rap—has long been dead. Gone as well is an embrace of hip-hop's four elements: graffiti writing, the dance element (or what some call break-dancing), DJing and MCing. The MC or "rapper" has been singled out to be his own man in this very male-centered arena, and the formula for a hit record is simple: fancy yourself a thug, pimp or gangster; rhyme about jewelry, clothing and alcohol; denigrate women in every conceivable way, and party and b.s. ad nauseam.

None of this would matter much to me if videos didn't pump visual crack into the minds of young people across the planet. Or if "urban radio" actually played something other than the same 10–12 songs every day. Or if some of our fabulous hip-hop magazines didn't make constant references to marijuana, liquor and "niggas" under the guise of keeping things real. The above notwithstanding, I am not a hater, or someone who disses for the sake of dissing. Nor do I feel hip-hop has created urban misery, racism, sexism, homophobia or classism. That said, what I do believe is that hip-hop is at a crossroads, struggling for control over its creativity, while truly creative artists like Mos Def, Bahamadia and Common wonder when they will get the attention they deserve.

In other words, Jay-Z's "Big Pimpin'" would not bother me so much if Dead Prez's "Mind Sex" received as much notice. Perhaps Chuck D is correct in stating that the Internet is the great equalizer for would-be artists. But what does it matter if homeboys are still screaming "nigga" or "bitch" for global consumption, with no regard for who is inhaling those sentiments?

POWELL is the editor of "Step Into a World: A Global Anthology of the New Black Literature," to be published in November (Wiley), and is guest curator of the Brooklyn Museum of Art's "Hip-Hop Nation: Roots, Rhymes & Rage."

FROM TOP: GIFT OF CAROL AND CONRAD JANIS, NO CREDIT, GUY AROCH

Nadeau 1

Allison Nadeau
English 101
Prof. Malek
15 October 2006

Rhetorical Analysis of "My Culture at the Crossroads"

"My Culture at the Crossroads" by Kevin Powell appeared in the Newsweek issue of October 9, 2000, as part of a special feature in the Arts and Entertainment section on the current crisis in rap music and hip-hop culture. In Powell's view, there is a "civil war going on within the hip-hop nation," caused in part by corporate control of the music and in part by an apolitical climate in post-civil rights America. The result, as Powell sees it, is that hip-hop is now as "materialistic, hedonistic, misogynistic, shallow, and violent" as Hollywood movies and TV shows. Powell points out that hip-hop was not always this way. In the "golden age" of the late 1980s and early 1990s, hip-hop was a vital "urban folk art" that included graffiti writing, breakdancing, DJing, and MCing. Since that time, however, the single focus on the MC or rapper as a thug, pimp, or gangster has brought hip-hop culture to a crossroads. The issue for Powell is whether the most creative artists can gain control of the music and take it in a positive direction.

Powell's commentary is part of a larger debate about the current status of rap. Hip-hop culture has always been controversial, but for many people, black and white, inside and outside the hip-hop nation, rap music now seems to focus exclusively on money, sex, and violence. The murders of Tupac Shakur and Biggie Smalls have heightened concerns about rap's "gangsta" image, and the constant preoccupation with guns, expensive jewelry, fancy cars, drugs, and partying worry many that rap is feeding racist stereotypes and has turned the music away from its original promise to tell the truth about black America. As Michael Eric Dyson is quoted in another article in Newsweek's coverage of rap. "There's a war going on for the soul of hip-hop."

Identifies publication

Summarizes the commentary

Explains the context of issues

Nadeau 2

Identifies the call to write

Describes writer's credentials

Describes purpose

The term "war" that both Dyson and Powell use gives the commentary its sense of urgency and enables readers to see what was calling on Powell to write. He appears to have excellent credentials to speak on the topic. As he notes in the opening paragraph, Powell has a lot of experience in the hip-hop world and, despite recent trends that bother him, he is a "hip-hop head for life." In fact, it is his devotion to hip-hop culture as creative and empowering that defines his purposes in this commentary. He wants first to explain what has gone wrong and then to call for change within the hip-hop nation. It would not make much sense to call for reform unless there was something worth preserving, and Powell describes rap as an "urban folk art" and discusses the "golden age of hip-hop" to establish the positive possibilities.

Analyzes relationship to one intended audience

Powell's relationship to his readers is a complicated one because he has a number of intended audiences. One audience is the broad readership of Newsweek and includes many people who know very little about rap and may have negative feelings about it. For these readers, it might come as a surprise that someone within hip-hop is so critical of it, and Powell seems to use this fact to explain the power of hip-hop for "young, working-class black and Latino cats" and to provide readers with a way of understanding how corporate control and an apolitical times have brought out the worst in hip-hop culture. Powell's criticism of hip-hop may well increase his credibility with these readers and encourage them to see that hip-hop did not create "urban misery, racism, sexism, homophobia, or classism" and that its glorification of money, sex, and violence is no different from what Hollywood and the TV networks put out.

Analyzes relationship to second intended audience

These mainstream readers, however, are not the people who can change the hip-hop nation. If Powell's goal is to educate Newsweek readers about the crisis in rap (and perhaps to neutralize feelings of hostility toward it), he has another goal in addressing intended readers within hip-hop culture, namely to acknowledge the crisis and do something about it. Powell must have been aware (and may be worried) that these readers might be skeptical about his publishing criticisms of hip-hop in a mainstream magazine. This perhaps accounts for the way Powell lists his own roots in hip-hop and proclaims his devotion to it. He also tries to make it clear that he is not "someone who disses for dissing sake." But he must also know that he is unlikely to convince those MCs who are making millions rapping about pimps, "niggas," and "bitches." Instead, his commentary seems to seek out those readers within hip-hop who might join with him to turn things around.

Analyzes language use

Powell's language is one technique he uses to establish his allegiances to hip-hop and a common ground where progressive forces can join together. The commentary has an informal, conversational tone that emphasizes Powell's

Tone

sincerity and makes it seem he is speaking directly to his readers. Powell sprinkles his commentary with rap terms such as "tagged," "def," and "DJing" and the names of rap artists, not so many that mainstream readers will lose the train of thought but enough to ensure Powell's authenticity for his hip-hop

Denotation/ connotation

readers. The use of the term "fresh," for example, will probably just go by many readers as denoting something new, while hip-hop readers will recognize its connotative use as a key term in rap vocabulary. Finally, Powell's most powerful

Figure of speech

figure of speech—the phrase describing videos that "pump visual crack into the minds of young people"—provides all readers with a striking image of what he sees as wrong with the current rap scene.

My analysis suggests that Powell's commentary is rhetorically effective, given the constraints of space and the fact that we cannot assume that Powell's argument will actually rally progressive rappers and produce genuine change. The commentary does, however, make available to many readers what

Evaluates rhetorical effectiveness

may well be a new and more complicated understanding of hip-hop, and it clearly offers points of identification for "positive" rappers. For some readers, Powell's argument that "the current economic boom has created the myth that things are swell for all Americans" may be too brief and lacking in evidence, but this in part is a problem of space. Those predisposed to share Powell's view

Nadeau 4

that there is an accelerating class divide may just be glad to see this idea put forward in a major mainstream publication like Newsweek. In all, Powell has done a skillful job of conveying the sense of urgency that called on him to write this commentary and a skillful balancing act in establishing the authority to address two very different audiences.

WRITING ASSIGNMENT

Analyzing the Rhetorical Situation

 *Online Study Center*

Your task is to select a piece of writing that argues a position and analyze its rhetorical situation. Use the sample rhetorical analysis as a flexible guide—not as a rigid model. How you organize your analysis will depend in part on the writing you choose and in part on the decisions you make about how to arrange the parts of your analysis.

Directions

1. Select a short (five to ten paragraphs) piece of written text that takes a position on an issue. Newspaper editorials and op-ed pieces, featured columnists published in newspapers and magazines, magazine commentary, political ads, and ads from advocacy groups are all good sources for this assignment. It helps if you know something about the topic and the issues involved. Make sure you are interested.

2. To prepare for your analysis, use the reading strategies presented in this chapter to do a careful preliminary reading of the writing you've chosen.

   - Do a first reading that uses strategies such as underlining, annotation, summarizing, and exploratory writing to make sure you understand what the writer is saying. Go back to any sections that need clarification.

   - On a second reading, start to pay attention to what the writer is doing. You may want to outline the writing and describe the writer's strategy. Notice how the writer uses facts to support claims and the types of evidence.

3. Once you've completed these preliminary readings and believe you have a good grasp of the writing, you can now turn to analyzing the rhetorical situation. Here are some questions to guide your analysis:

- What is the context of issues? What do you know about the topic? What issues does the topic raise? Is there a larger debate, discussion, or controversy already going on? What seems to be at stake?

- Who is the writer? What do you know about the writer's background, credibility, knowledge of the topic, beliefs, and social allegiances?

- What is the publication? What do you know about its intended readers, reputability, political slant, and the topics it covers?

- What is the call to write? Why is the writer addressing the issue and taking a position at this particular time? Is there some sense of urgency involved? How does the writer identify the significance of the issues involved?

- What is the writer's purpose? What is he or she trying to accomplish? Is the purpose stated explicitly or implicitly?

- Who is the intended audience? Is the writer addressing one group of readers or more than one? What kind of relationship is the writer trying to establish with readers? What assumptions about readers does the writer seem to make?

- How does the writer use language? What is the writer's tone? What does the writer's word choice show about his or her assumptions about readers? Does the writer use specialized terms or slang? Are there memorable figures of speech? Does the writer stereotype?

- What is your evaluation of the rhetorical effectiveness? Does the writer accomplish his or her purposes? What constraints, if any, qualify the writing's effectiveness?

4. Write an essay that analyzes the writing you've chosen. Begin by summarizing the main line of reasoning. Use your answers to the questions just listed to help you develop your essay, but remember: your essay should be an integrated analysis and not just a list of answers. Conclude with your evaluation of the writing's rhetorical effectiveness. ■

persuasion and responsibility: analyzing arguments

Imagine you are taking a walk and encounter an elderly man whose car has broken down in the middle of the street. His request "Can you give me a hand?" requires no explanation. What makes his request persuasive is the shared belief that people should help each other in times of need. Persuasion seems to occur spontaneously, based largely on a mutual understanding that goes without saying.

You can probably think of other occasions when persuasion takes place as a spontaneous meeting of the minds. A friend suggests that you go to the basketball game together on Friday night, and you agree. Neighbors ask if you can feed their cat when they are away for the weekend. Woven into the fabric of social life, persuasion refers to moments when people reach agreements and join together to accomplish a wide range of purposes and activities.

Moments such as these require no elaborate explanation. You don't need an explicit argument to convince you to go to the basketball game or to feed your neighbors' cat. The reasons are implied in the situation and the shared understandings of the people involved.

In many other instances, however, we do need to make explicit arguments—to give reasons and explanations—to persuade others. Here are some situations that call on people to make explicit arguments:

- A Muslim man and a Christian woman want to get married. Both families are very devout and always imagined that their children would marry someone of their faith in a religious ceremony. Grandchildren, of course, would be raised in the family religion. The couple, however, decide that the best way to handle their different religious backgrounds is to get married in a civil ceremony and let their children make their own decisions about religion. Since the couple are of legal age, they could just go ahead and get married, but they want their parents' blessing. Clearly, they have a problem of persuasion and need to come up with some good arguments.

Online Study Center

- Persuasion poses a problem for a public relations executive assigned to write a news release explaining why her company has decided to lay off a quarter of the workforce. She knows her audience consists of different interests—stockholders concerned with the company's profit margin, company executives responsible for the layoffs, the individuals who have lost their jobs, the public and its low opinion of downsizing and corporate restructuring. What reasons can she give that will present the public image of the company in the best way?

- As part of a campaign to increase childhood immunization, a group of health workers has been commissioned to develop public service announcements for television. They have some decisions to make about the pitch of their publicity. What is the most persuasive approach? Should they emphasize the health risks and what can happen if children are not inoculated? Or should they appeal instead to positive images of good parents taking care of their children? Should they target mothers as the primary audience?

- As a student, you know from experience that essay exams amount to exercises in persuasion. The point is to convince the teacher you have mastered the material and can intelligently answer questions about it. Part of learning in any course involves knowing what counts as a good answer, what kinds of statements teachers find persuasive, and the supporting evidence they expect. How can you use this understanding to prepare for tests and perform well on them?

As you can see, situations that call for explicit arguments to persuade others can be complicated. Part of learning to write is learning how to deal with such situations. That is precisely the purpose of this chapter.

This chapter is arranged to help you:

- Understand the nature of argument

- Analyze issues to write about

- Develop a persuasive position

- Plan convincing arguments

- Negotiate differences with others

■ WORKING TOGETHER

Successful Persuasion

Work with two or three other students. Before you meet, write a short description of three occasions when someone or something persuaded someone else. Then follow these directions:

1. Take turns reading the descriptions aloud. Working together, choose one example from each group member. As much as possible, select examples that differ so

that you wind up with three or four instances that describe different situations, interactions, and types of persuasion.

2. Working together, analyze the examples you have chosen. In each case, what calls on someone to persuade someone else? Who is trying to influence whom? For what purpose? By what means (written, spoken, visual)? Does the persuasion rely on an explicit argument or on something else? What makes the persuasion successful? What common ground, shared values, mutual understandings are involved?

3. Prepare a report, written or oral depending on your teacher's directions, to present to the class. Use the group reports to identify similarities and differences in the acts of persuasion.

UNDERSTANDING ARGUMENT

People often think of arguments as heated moments when tempers flare and discussion degenerates into a shouting match. There is no question such arguments can be seen frequently on television, whether on daytime talk shows like *Jerry Spinger* or on political commentaries like *Capital Gang.*

For our purposes, however, such images of argument are not very useful. We want to think of argument instead as a particular type of persuasion that writers and speakers turn to when people have reasonable differences about the issues that face them. This definition may sound obvious. If people didn't disagree, there would be nothing to argue about. Still, the idea that argument occurs when people have reasonable disagreements is worth examining.

WHAT IS ARGUMENT? DEALING WITH REASONABLE DIFFERENCES

Some disagreements among people are not, properly speaking, reasonable ones. Two people might disagree, for example, about the driving distance between New York City and Buffalo, New York, or about the chemical composition of dioxin. These are not reasonable disagreements because they can be resolved by consulting a road atlas or a chemistry book. There are sources available to settle the matter, so there's really no point in arguing.

On the other hand, people might reasonably disagree about the best route to drive to Buffalo or about the best policy concerning the production and use of dioxin. In disagreements such as these, there are no final, definitive answers available. One person may prefer a certain route to Buffalo because of the scenery, while another wants only the fastest way possible. By the same token, some may argue that policy on dioxin needs above all to take environmental and health risks into account, while for others the effect of policy on the economy and workers' jobs must also be a prime consideration.

Issues of Evaluation

Issues of evaluation are questions about whether something is good or bad, right or wrong, desirable or undesirable, effective or ineffective, valuable or worthless. The second speaker addresses an issue of evaluation when he says that invading Iraq was the right thing to do on the grounds of human rights. In this case, support or refutation of the claim will necessarily rely on a value judgment.

Issues of evaluation appear routinely in all spheres of life:

- Is a Macintosh or a PC computer system best suited to your computing needs?

- Is *American Idol* a cruel display of untalented performers or an old-fashioned talent show that everyone can enjoy?

- Is affirmative action unfair to white males?

- What novels should be included in an American literature course?

Issues of Policy

Issues of policy are questions about what we should do and how we should implement our aims. The third speaker takes on a policy issue when he finds fault with the invasion of Iraq. Support or refutation of policy issues will typically focus on how well the policy solves an existing problem or addresses a demonstrable need.

Issues about policy are pervasive in public discussions. Typically, they use the terms *should, ought,* or *must* to signal the courses of action they recommend:

- Should the federal government ban late-term abortions?

- Must all students be required to take a first-year writing course?

- Should there be a moratorium on capital punishment?

- Should schools provide bilingual education?

Identifying what type of issue is at stake in a speaker's claim offers a way to cut into an ongoing controversy and get oriented. This does not mean, however, that controversies come neatly packaged according to type of issue. The three types of issues are tools of analysis to help you identify how and why people disagree. As you prepare to enter an ongoing controversy, you are likely to find that the three types of issues are connected and lead from one to the next.

Here is an example of how the three types of issues can be used to explore a controversy and invent arguments.

Sample Exploration of a Controversy

Should High Schools Abolish Tracking and Assign Students to Mixed-Ability Classrooms Instead?

1. Issues that can be substantiated: How widespread is the practice of tracking? When did it begin? Why was tracking instituted in the first place? What purposes was it designed for? What are the effects of tracking on students? What experiments have taken place to use mixed-ability groupings instead of tracking? What are the results?

2. Issues of evaluation: What educational values are put into practice in tracking? Are these values worthy? Is tracking fair to all students? Does it benefit some students more than others? What values are embodied in mixed-ability classrooms? How do these compare to the values of tracking?

3. Issues of policy: What should we do? What are the reasons for maintaining tracking? What are the reasons for implementing mixed-ability groupings? Can mixed-ability classrooms succeed? What changes would be required? What would the long-term consequences be?

TAKING A POSITION: FROM ISSUES TO CLAIMS

The point of analyzing the issues in any ongoing controversy is to clarify your own thinking and determine where you stand. Taking a position amounts to entering into the debate to have your own say. Determining your position means you have an arguable claim to make—an informed opinion, belief, recommendation, or call to action you want your readers to consider.

Look at the following two statements:

Tracking was recently dismantled in a local school district.

Tracking has become a very heated issue.

As you can see, these sentences simply describe a situation. They aren't really arguable claims because no one would reasonably disagree with them. They don't tell readers what the writer believes or thinks should be done. Now take a look at these two statements:

For the dismantling of tracking to be successful, our local school district should provide teachers with in-service training in working with mixed-ability groups.

Tracking has become such a heated issue because parents of honors students worry unnecessarily that their children won't get into the best colleges.

Notice that in each statement you can see the writer's stand on the issue right away. The first writer treats an issue of policy, while the second is trying to substantiate the cause of the tracking controversy. What makes each claim arguable is that there can be differing views regarding the issue. Readers could respond that in-service training is a waste of money because teachers already know how to teach different levels of students, or that the real reason tracking is so controversial is because it holds back the brightest students. To make sure a claim is arguable, ask yourself whether someone could reasonably disagree with it—whether there could be at least two differing views on the issue on which you've taken a position.

Both writers have successfully cued readers to their positions, in part by using key words that typically appear in position statements. Notice that in the first sentence, the writer uses *should* (but could have used similar terms such as *must, ought to, needs to,* or *has to*) to signal a proposed solution. In the second, the writer uses a *because* statement to indicate to readers that there is evidence available to back up the claim. Writers also use terms such as *therefore, consequently, thus, it follows that, the point is* to signal their positions.

■ EXERCISE

Steps Toward a Tentative Position

Take a current controversy you know something about, where reasonable differences divide people. It could be the death penalty, drug testing for high school or college athletes, censorship of lyrics, curfews for adolescents under 18. The main consideration is that the controversy interests you and that you believe it is important.

1. State the controversy in its most general terms in the form of a question: "Should colleges routinely conduct drug tests on varsity athletes?" "Do we need a rating system for television shows similar to the one used for movies?"

2. Then use the three types of issues—substantiation, evaluation, and policy—to generate a list of more specific questions: "How do drug tests work?" "Why were drug tests developed in the first place, and what are their consequences?" "Do drug tests violate constitutional freedoms?" "Is drug testing sound policy?"

3. Pick one set of questions from your list of types of issues. For example, you might pick the interrelated questions "Do drug tests actually work?" "Are they reliable?" "Can they be circumvented?" Develop a tentative position that responds to the question or questions. Make sure it presents an arguable claim.

4. Consider whether your tentative position is an informed claim. At this point, you may need more information to analyze the issues responsibly and develop an arguable claim with sufficient evidence.

DEVELOPING A PERSUASIVE POSITION

WHAT ARE THE RHETORICAL APPEALS?

Once you have a tentative position in mind, you can begin to think about how to present it to your readers in the most persuasive way possible. One powerful set of persuasive strategies is known in classical rhetoric as *the appeals*. The three appeals—*ethos*, *pathos*, and *logos*—offer three different but interrelated ways to influence your readers by appealing to their ideas and values, sympathies, and beliefs.

- Ethos: *Ethos* refers to the writer's character as it is projected to readers through the written text. The modern terms *personality* and *attitude* capture some of the meaning of ethos and how readers build an impression of the writer's character—how credible, fair, and authoritative.

- Pathos: *Pathos* refers to the readers' emotions and the responses a piece of writing arouses in them. Pathos should not be associated simply with emotional appeals to readers' fears and prejudices. Instead, it offers a way to analyze their state of mind and the intensity with which they hold various beliefs and values.

- Logos: *Logos* refers to what is said or written. Its original meaning was "voice" or "speech," though the term later took on an association with logic and reasoning. For our purposes, the term offers a way to focus on the writer's message and the line of reasoning the writer develops.

The term *rhetorical stance* refers to the way writers coordinate ethos, pathos, and logos as interrelated components in persuasive writing. To see how this coordination of the three appeals works in practice, let's look at a passage, shown on the next page, from one of Malcolm X's most famous speeches, "The Ballot or the Bullet," delivered to a largely black audience in 1964. At the time Malcolm X gave his speech, the U.S. Senate was debating the Civil Rights Act of 1964, which passed later in the year, following a filibuster by its opponents.

ANALYSIS OF PERSUASIVE APPEALS IN "THE BALLOT OR THE BULLET"

Ethos

Malcolm X identifies himself first by explaining what he is not—a politician, a student of politics, a Democrat, or a Republican. In fact, he does not even consider himself an American. Instead, he identifies himself as "one of the 22 million black people who are victims of Americanism."

Malcolm X presents himself as someone who is willing to look at the racial situation in America without illusions. "I am one," he says, "who doesn't believe in deluding myself." Just being in America, he argues, doesn't make black people Americans. Otherwise, black people would not need Civil Rights legislation to achieve equality.

The tone and attitude Malcolm X projects are militant and unrelenting, chosen in part to distinguish his appeal from the appeals of Civil Rights leaders such as Dr. Martin Luther King Jr., who emphasized racial reconciliation and working through the system. For Malcolm X, there is no point in appealing to American democratic values, as King often did, because the system has always been hypocritical—not a dream but a nightmare.

FROM "THE BALLOT OR THE BULLET"

MALCOLM X

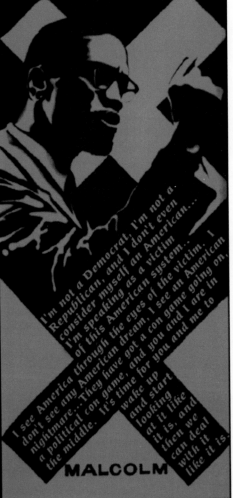

Malcolm X banner by Mike Alewitz

1   I'm not a politician, not even a student of politics; in fact, I'm not a student of much of anything. I'm not a Democrat, I'm not a Republican, and I don't even consider myself an American. If you and I were Americans, there'd be no problem. Those Hunkies that just got off the boat, they're already Americans; Polacks are already Americans; the Italian refugees are already Americans. Everything that came out of Europe, every blue-eyed thing, is already an American. And as long as you and I have been over here, we aren't Americans yet.

2   Well, I am one who doesn't believe in deluding myself. I'm not going to sit at your table and watch you eat, with nothing on my plate, and call myself a diner. Sitting at the table doesn't make you a diner, unless you eat some of what's on that plate. Being here in America doesn't make you an American. Why, if birth made you American, you wouldn't need any legislation, you wouldn't need any amendments to the Constitution, you wouldn't be faced with civil-rights

filibustering in Washington, D.C., right now. They don't have to pass civil-rights legislation to make a Polack an American.

3   No, I'm not an American. I'm one of the 22 million black people who are the victims of Americanism. One of the 22 million black people who are the victims of democracy, nothing but disguised hypocrisy. So, I'm not standing here speaking to you as an American, or a patriot, or a flag-saluter, or a flag-waver—no, not I. I'm speaking as a victim of this American system. And I see America through the eyes of the victim. I don't see any American dream; I see an American nightmare.

Pathos

By locating a stance outside the system, Malcolm X invites his audience to join him in rejecting the moderation of Civil Rights leaders and to share a new, more militant politics.

He seeks, on one hand, to mobilize his black listeners' feelings about what it means to be an American. By offering an explanation of how blacks have been systematically excluded from the American dream, Malcolm X seeks to redirect the intensity of his black listeners' emotions—away from the hope of racial integration and toward a new identity based on the power and self-reliance of black people united in struggle. He is offering them a way to see themselves not as humble petitioners to the white power structure but as a power in their own right.

On the other hand, it may well appear that Malcolm X has written off white listeners. For some, his use of ethnic slurs such as *Hunkies* and *Polacks* are offensive and can hardly have endeared him to his white audience (many whites did indeed reject his message as antiwhite and potentially dangerous). But for others, Malcolm X's unflinching analysis of race relations in America brought with it the shock of recognition that white-skin privilege is a pervasive feature of American life. In fact, Malcolm X did gain a wide audience of whites who came to admire his unyielding insistence on "telling it like it is" and who were thereby led to rethink the consequences of racism in America.

Logos

As you have just seen, Malcolm X established a relationship with his listeners by projecting an attitude and a message that elicited powerful responses. If anything, the way he presents himself (ethos) and his listeners' responses (pathos) are inseparable from the form and content of his message (logos). Still, it is worth noting how cogently reasoned this message is.

Malcolm X's reasoning is simple yet devastating. It all revolves around the issue of how people get to be considered Americans. According to Malcolm X, people who came from Europe are already considered Americans. They don't need Civil Rights legislation. At the same time, the fact of being born in America is not necessarily enough for a person to be considered an American; otherwise black people born in America would not need Civil Rights legislation. Put these two propositions together and you get the unavoidable conclusion: the fact that black people need Civil Rights legislation proves in effect that they are not considered Americans, and the implication is that they are therefore something else—not the inheritors of the American dream but the victims of an American nightmare.

CONSTRUCTING AN APPROPRIATE RHETORICAL STANCE

Experienced writers know that to make persuasive arguments they need to construct an appropriate rhetorical stance. Whether the rhetorical stance you construct is appropriate will, of course, depend on the situation that calls for writing, your purposes, and the beliefs of your readers. Arguments that are appropriate and persuasive in one situation may not necessarily be appropriate and persuasive in another.

The following letters were written by a student applying for a summer internship at a cable television station—Greater Worcester Media Cable Company. As you read, notice that the student is making an arguable claim, namely, "you should hire me as an intern." The question is whether the rhetorical stance he develops is appropriate to the occasion.

Sample Letters of Application

Letter 1

I would like to apply for a summer internship at Greater Worcester Media Cable Company. I've just switched my major from pre-med to mass communication, and I'm really excited about getting out of those boring science classes and into something that interests me. I just finished this great video production class and made a short documentary called "Road Kill," about all the animals that get run over on Highway 61. It was pretty arty and punk, with a sound track dubbed from Sonic Youth.

I want to learn everything I can about television. I'd love to eventually be an anchorman on the national news, like Dan Rather or Peter Jennings or Tom Brokaw. I've always known that television is one of the most influential parts of American life, and I think it would be awesome to be seen nightly by millions of viewers. Think of all the influence—and fun—you could have, with everyone watching you.

Of course, if I do get the internship, I won't be able to go home this summer, and that will be kind of a bummer because my parents and girlfriend are pretty much expecting I'll be around. But still, it would be worth it to get into television because that's where I see myself going long-term.

Letter 2

I would like to apply for a summer internship at Greater Worcester Media Cable Company. As my résumé indicates, I am a Mass Communication major in my sophomore year, with course work in video production, mass communication theory, and the history of television. In addition, I have a strong background in the natural sciences.

I believe that my studies in Mass Communication have given me skills and experience that would be valuable in a summer internship. In my video production class, I filmed and edited a short documentary, and I am eager to gain more experience in production and editing.

A summer internship would be a wonderful opportunity for me to learn how the day-to-day world of cable television works. This kind of practical experience would be an invaluable complement to my coursework in the history and theory of the media.

■ WORKING TOGETHER

Rhetorical Stance

You have probably concluded that the first letter is inappropriate as a letter of application to Greater Worcester Media Cable Company and that the second letter has a greater chance of success. Your task now is to explain why. Work together with two or three other students. Follow these directions:

1. Compare the two letters in terms of the rhetorical stance the writer has constructed in each case. Be specific here and point to words, phrases, and passages that reveal how the writer coordinates ethos, logos, and pathos.

2. Think of a situation in which the first letter would be appropriate to the writer's purposes and the interests of readers. It may be inappropriate when applying for a summer internship, but that doesn't mean it is not as well-written as the second. Notice that in certain respects it has more life, more telling details, and more of a sense of the writer's personality than the second letter.

■ EXERCISE

Crafting an Argument

Assume the role of the student who is applying for a summer internship. Use the information in the two letters to write a third letter addressed to either a parent or a boyfriend or girlfriend. The letter should explain why you want to apply for the summer internship and should persuade your reader that this is a good idea, even though it would mean not being able to come home for the summer. Consider how an appropriate and persuasive rhetorical stance would coordinate the three appeals—ethos, pathos, and logos.

MAKING AN ARGUMENT

Good arguments aren't found ready to use. They have to be made. To make a persuasive argument, you need to develop an effective line of reasoning. To do that, it is helpful to look at the parts that go into making an argument. In this section, we draw on a model of argument developed by the philosopher Stephen Toulmin, although we use somewhat different terms.

WHAT ARE THE PARTS OF AN ARGUMENT?

Here is a quick sketch of the parts of an argument that we'll be considering in more detail in this section:

Claim	Your position, the basic point you want readers to accept
Evidence	The supporting material for the claim
Enabling assumption	The line of reasoning that explains how the evidence supports the claim
Backing	Reasons that show that the enabling assumption is valid
Differing views	Disagreements with all or part of your argument
Qualifiers	Words that modify or limit the claim

CLAIMS, EVIDENCE, AND ENABLING ASSUMPTIONS

As you have seen, you can't have a responsible argument unless you have an arguable claim, and you've looked at some ways to develop claims by analyzing issues and constructing an appropriate rhetorical stance. In this section, we look in detail at the three basic parts of an argument—claims, evidence, and enabling assumptions. Taken together, these terms give us a way to think about the line of reasoning in an argument. Readers justifiably expect writers to provide evidence for the claims they make. Moreover, they expect the evidence a writer offers to have a clear connection to the claim. As you will see, enabling assumptions are explanations of how the evidence supports a writer's claim.

To see how these connections work, take a look at the following two evaluations that students wrote of their composition instructor.

Sample Evaluations

Evaluation 1

Ms. Smith is probably the worst teacher I've had so far in college. I've never been so frustrated. I could never figure out what the teacher wanted us to do. She didn't grade the papers we turned in but instead just wrote comments on them. Then we had to evaluate each other's writings. How are students qualified to judge each other's writing? This is the teacher's job. We had to revise some of our writing to put in a portfolio at the end of the term. How were we supposed to know which papers were any good?

Evaluation 2

Ms. Smith is probably the best teacher I've had so far in college. I really liked how she organized the work. By not grading our papers, she gave us the opportunity to select our best writing and revise it for a portfolio at the end of the term. The comments she offered on drafts and the evaluations we did of each others' papers really helped. I found this freed me to experiment with my writing in new ways and not worry about getting low grades. This system made me realize how important revision is.

In one sense, both evaluations are persuasive. It's hard not to be convinced, at the level of lived experience, that the first student did not like the class, while the second student did. But what are we to make of these differences? What do they tell us about the teacher and her way of teaching writing?

In this case, to understand why the two students differ, it will help to see *how* they differ. Each has made an argument, and we can analyze how the arguments have been made. Each consists of the same basic parts.

Claims

In the two student evaluations, the competing claims are easy to find: Ms. Smith is either the best or the worst teacher in the student's experience. Each claim, moreover, meets the test for writing arguable claims.

- **Reasonable differences:** Both claims are matters of judgment that can't be decided by referring to an established, authoritative source. The question of whether Ms. Smith is a good teacher is worth arguing about.

- **Plausibility:** Both claims could be true. Each has a certain credibility that a claim like "An invasion of flying saucers will take place next week" doesn't have.

- **Sharable claims:** Both claims can be argued on terms that can be shared by others. In contrast, there's no reason to argue that blue is your favorite color or that you love the feel of velvet. Such a claim refers to a personal preference based on subjective experience and can't really be shared by others.

Evidence

Evidence is all the information available in a particular situation. Like detectives in the investigation of a crime, writers begin with the available evidence—data, information, facts, observations, personal testimony, statistics, common knowledge, or any other relevant material.

QUESTIONS TO ASK ABOUT EVIDENCE

To make a persuasive argument, you need evidence for your claim—and you also need some guidelines to evaluate whether the evidence you turn up will work for your argument. Here are some questions to ask yourself:

1. **Is the evidence clearly related to the claim?** As you plan an argument, you are likely to come up with lots of interesting material. Not all of it, however, will necessarily be relevant to the claim you want to support. For example, if you are arguing about how Darwin's theory of evolution influenced fiction writers in the nineteenth century, it doesn't make sense to give a lot of biographical details on Darwin. They may be interesting, but it's unlikely that they will help you explain the influence of his theory.

2. **Do you have enough evidence?** Basing a claim on one or two facts is hardly likely to persuade your readers. They are likely to dismiss your argument as hasty and unjustifiable because of insufficient evidence. The fact that two people in your neighborhood were laid off recently from their construction jobs is not enough evidence for claiming that the construction industry is in crisis. You would need to establish a pattern by showing, say, a decline in housing starts, the postponement of many major building projects, layoffs across the country, or bankruptcies of construction companies.

3. **Is your evidence verifiable?** Readers are likely to be suspicious of your argument unless they can check out the evidence for themselves. For instance, to support an argument for campaign finance reform, you might use examples of how corporate donations influenced politicians' voting, but if you don't tell readers who the politicians and corporations are, they will have no way to verify your evidence.

4. **Is your evidence up-to-date?** Readers expect you to do your homework and provide them with the latest information available. If your evidence is dated, readers may well suspect that newer information has supplanted it, and may therefore find your argument unpersuasive. If you are arguing for gender equity in medical education, citing figures on the enrollment of women in medical schools in the 1960s (around 10 percent) will be quickly dismissed because women currently represent around 50 percent of students entering medical school classes. (You might build a better case for gender equity by looking at possible patterns of discrimination in residency assignments or at the specializations women go into.)

5. **Does your evidence come from reliable sources?** You would probably not make an argument based on the *Weekly World News*'s latest Elvis sighting. As mentioned in Chapter 2, evidence needs to be evaluated and interpreted in light of its sources. Scientific studies, government reports, and research by academics, professional associations, and independent research institutes are likely to carry considerable authority for readers. Partisan sources—magazines such as the conservative *National Review* or the liberal *Nation*—often contain important evidence you can use persuasively, especially if you acknowledge the bias and ask readers to consider the merits of the information in the context of your argument.

Writers use this evidence to construct a sense of what happened and what the unresolved issues are. Notice in the two evaluations of Ms. Smith that the students do not seem to differ about what happened in class. Both describe the same teaching strategies: students wrote papers that were not graded; they received comments from the teacher and from other students; they were required to revise a number of the papers for a final portfolio. The difference is in how each uses this evidence.

Enabling Assumptions

Consider how the two students move from the available evidence—the facts that neither disputes—to their differing claims. This is a crucial move that each argument relies on. For an argument to be persuasive, readers need to know how and why the evidence cited by the writer entitles him or her to make a claim. This link—the connection in an argument between the evidence and the writer's claim—is called the *enabling assumption* because it refers to the line of reasoning that explains how the evidence supports the claim. Such assumptions are often implied rather than stated explicitly.

Notice that the enabling assumptions in the two student evaluations are implied but not directly stated. To find out how the two students connect the evidence to their claims, let's imagine we could interview them, to push them to articulate this missing link in their arguments:

Sample Interviews

Interview with Student 1

Q. How was your writing teacher?

A. She was the worst teacher I've had so far [*claim*].

Q. What makes you say that?

A. The teacher never graded our papers. We had to evaluate each other's papers and then revise a few and put them in a portfolio [*evidence*].

Q. So why was that so bad?

A. Well, because good teachers give you lots of graded evaluations so you know exactly where you stand in a class [*enabling assumption*].

Interview with Student 2

Q. How was your writing teacher?

A. She was great, best I've had so far [*claim*].

Q. What makes you say that?

A. The teacher never graded our papers. We had to evaluate each other's papers and then revise a few and put them in a portfolio [*evidence*].

Q. So why was that so good?

A. Well, because good teachers help you develop your own judgment by experimenting without worrying about grades [*enabling assumption*].

Of course, we could push each writer further to explore the assumptions that underlie the one he or she has articulated. If we push far enough, we are likely to find fundamental beliefs that each holds about the nature of education and learning. For example, in the case of the second student, an exploration of assumptions might look like this:

Assumption 1: Good teaching helps students develop judgment by experimenting and not having to worry about grades.

Assumption 2: Too much emphasis on grades can get in the way of developing judgment through trial and error.

Assumption 3: Education should emphasize the development of individual judgment as much as or more than the learning of subject material.

Assumption 4: Students naturally want to learn, and will do so if given the chance.

This process could continue indefinitely, and exploring the assumptions underlying assumptions can be a useful exercise. The practical question in making an argument is to decide which of these assumptions—or some combination of them—are likely to be shared by your readers and which ones can best clarify differences you have with others.

■ WORKING TOGETHER

Analyzing Claims, Evidence, and Enabling Assumptions

To work with the terms introduced here, analyze the statements that appear below. Identify the claim each statement makes. Identify the evidence that each statement relies on. Finally, explain how an enabling assumption, which may or may not be stated explicitly, connects the evidence to the claim.

1. Ultraviolent video games will inevitably lead to more school shootings.

2. The current increase in cases of tuberculosis can be attributed to new strains of the disease that are resistant to treatment by antibiotics.

3. The fact that both parents have to work just to make ends meet is destroying the American family.

4. It is reasonable that the CEOs of American corporations make over one hundred times in salary and bonuses what the average worker in the company earns.

Backing

Backing refers to evidence and explanations showing that an argument's enabling assumption is valid and reliable. If your readers accept your enabling assumption, whether explicit or implied, there is probably no reason to provide backing for it. But, as in the case of the two student evaluations, where enabling assumptions differ, you need to explain why your enabling assumptions are preferable or more important than competing ones.

As you have seen, the differences that divide the two student evaluations of Ms. Smith hinge on the different enabling assumption each uses to connect the evidence to the claim. Only by identifying these unstated assumptions can we really understand what is at stake. To construct responsible arguments that can clarify their differences, the two writers need to make their enabling assumptions explicit. Here is what the opening of the first student's evaluation might look like if he or she made the enabling assumption explicit:

> One of the marks of good teaching is giving students frequent graded evaluations of their work so that they understand the teacher's expectations and know where they stand in the class. I just had a composition teacher who demonstrates the disaster that can happen when teachers don't take this basic principle of teaching into account.

This is certainly a clearer version of what the writer is trying to argue, but it still leaves open the question of whether giving frequent grades is a "mark of good teaching" and a "basic principle." Is this a safe assumption to make, one that readers will find a reliable measure of good teaching? We may or may not be persuaded, depending on our own assumptions about teaching. In fact, as you can see, the enabling assumption itself is arguable and therefore needs support if the student hopes to persuade readers.

For this reason, the writer could strengthen the argument further by adding backing to the enabling assumption. To bolster the persuasiveness of the enabling assumption, the writer could provide supporting evidence and explanations: research studies about the level of student anxiety in classes where there is little graded work; expert testimony on the subject of what constitutes good teaching; statistics showing how students learn more in classes where the teacher frequently hands out grades; personal accounts from other students about how they slack off when their work isn't graded.

■ WORKING TOGETHER

Backing an Argument

Work together in groups of two or three. What kind of backing can you think of that would support the following enabling assumptions? What sources would you turn to?

1. In the final analysis, the state of the economy determines presidential elections.

2. In time, we will see that most diseases are hereditary.

3. We must strengthen the American family.

4. Big business is greedy.

DIFFERING VIEWS

To argue responsibly, you can't pretend that no one disagrees with you or that there are no alternative perspectives. To note these differences does not, as students sometimes think, undermine your own argument. In fact, it can strengthen it by showing that you are willing to take all sides into account, that you can refute objections to your argument, and, when necessary, that you can concede the validity of differing views.

Summarize Differing Views Fairly and Accurately

Readers often detect when writers handle differing views in a distorted way. In fact, their impressions of a writer's credibility and good character—the writer's ethos—depend in part on how reasonably the writer deals with differences. For that reason, the ability to summarize fairly and accurately is quite important to the success of your argument. By summarizing fairly and accurately, you can show readers that you have anticipated reasonable differences and intend to deal with them responsibly.

This can help avoid having your readers jump into your argument with objections you've overlooked—"Sure, the government creating jobs for people on welfare sounds like a good idea, but what about the cost? And what about personal responsibility? Doesn't this just make people dependent in a different way?"—or rushing to the defense of objections you have characterized unfairly—"Not all conservative Christians believe women should be barefoot and pregnant."

Refuting Differing Views

For views that differ from yours, summarize them briefly, fairly, and accurately. Then explain what's wrong with them. Your best chance of persuading readers that your position is preferable to others is to clarify the differences that divide you and explain what you see as the weaknesses in other lines of reasoning.

To return to the student evaluations, the first student could strengthen his or her argument about what good teaching is by anticipating, summarizing, and refuting elements in the second student's argument. He or she might argue, for example, that while peer response to the written work of others may sound like a good idea, in fact it doesn't really help students improve their writing; he or she would then explain why. It would enhance the persuasiveness of the argument, of course, if the explanation consisted of more than personal anecdotes ("why peer review didn't help me")—for example, references to research studies on the effects of peer review.

Note: The author of this book does not endorse the view that peer review doesn't work, but does recognize it as an arguable claim.

Conceding Differing Views

When differing views have merit, don't avoid them. Remember that your readers will likely think of these objections, so you're better off taking them head on. Summarize the view and explain what you concede. Such concessions are often signaled by words and phrases such as *admittedly, granted, while it may be true, despite the fact*, and *of course she is right to say*.

The purpose of concession is not to give up on your argument but to explain how it relates to differing views. In this sense, it's another means of clarifying differences and explaining your position in the fullest possible way. To concede effectively, follow it up right away with an explanation of how your position relates to the point you have conceded. Otherwise, you may give readers the impression that you endorse the point.

In the case of the student evaluations, the first student could make good use of concession. For example, he or she might concede the second student's point that an important goal of education is developing independent judgment. The student then could go on to show that in practice the teacher's methods don't really lead to independent judgment but instead leave students to flounder on their own. In fact, conceding the point offers the student a line of reasoning he or she could pursue to strengthen the argument by explaining how the development of independent judgment depends on constant interaction with and regular evaluation from a more experienced and knowledgeable person.

Negotiating Differing Views

Negotiating differences means finding points of agreement in differing views. Once again, your purpose is not to abandon your views but to see if you can find any common ground with those who hold differing positions. Negotiating differences may sound like unnecessarily compromising what you believe or giving in just to make other people happy, but it doesn't have to lead to such results. Think of it as combining elements in reasonable differences in order to come up with new solutions and perspectives. Sometimes this is possible, but not always. Still, it's worth trying, because negotiated differences can strengthen your argument by broadening its appeal and demonstrating your desire to take into account as many views as possible.

Back to the student evaluations. The first student might concede that the teacher's portfolio system of evaluation has some merit because it bases grades on student improvement. But from this student's perspective, it still has the problem of not providing enough evaluation and information on the teacher's expectations. To negotiate these differences, the student might propose that the teacher grade but not count the first writing assignment so that students can see the teacher's evaluative standards in practice. The student might also suggest that the teacher give students a midterm progress report on where they stand in the class, and again grade but not count one paper between midterm and the end of class.

Such a solution may not satisfy everyone, but it is likely to enhance the reader's impression of the student as someone who doesn't just criticize but tries to deal with differences constructively.

QUALIFIERS

Qualifiers modify or limit the claim in an argument by making it less sweeping, global, and categorical. For most claims, after all, there are exceptions that don't necessarily disprove the claim but need to be noted. Otherwise, you will needlessly open your claim to attack and disbelief. In many instances, a qualifier is as simple as saying "Many students at Ellroy State drink to excess" instead of "The students at my school get drunk all the time." Qualifiers admit exceptions without undermining your point, and they make statements harder to refute with a counterexample—"I know students who never drink" or "Some students drink only occasionally" or "My friends drink moderately."

You can qualify your claim with words and phrases such as *in many cases, often, frequently, probably, perhaps, may* or *might, maybe, likely,* or *usually.* In some instances, you will want to use a qualifying clause that begins with *unless* to limit the conditions in which the claim will hold true: "Unless the DNA evidence proves negative, everything points to the accused as the murderer."

PUTTING THE PARTS TOGETHER

To see how the various parts of argument we've just discussed can help you make an argument, let's look at the notes a student wrote to plan an argument opposing a recent proposal to the local school committee that would require students to wear uniforms at Middlebrook High School. No one contests that there are real problems at Middlebrook—declining test scores, drug use, racial tensions, lack of school spirit, a growing sense of student alienation. But, as you will see, the student doesn't think school uniforms can really address these problems.

Claim

Middlebrook High School should not require students to wear uniforms.

Evidence

School uniforms don't have the intended effects. I could use examples from schools that require uniforms to show they don't increase discipline, improve self-esteem, or alleviate social tensions.

Teachers oppose requiring uniforms because it would make them into cops. I could get some good quotes from teachers.

Even if they are required to wear uniforms, students will figure out other ways to show what group they are in. Jewelry, hairstyles, shoes, jackets, body piercing, tattoos, and so on will just become all the more important.

Uniforms violate students' right to self-expression. I could call the American Civil Liberties Union to see if they have any information I could use.

Requiring uniforms will make students hate school. I could get more on this by talking to students.

Enabling Assumption

A uniform requirement doesn't really address the problems at Middlebrook. Instead, it would make things worse.

Backing

The uniform proposal is based on a faulty view of what influences student behavior. More rules will just lead to more alienation from school.

To address Middlebrook's problems, students must be given more responsibility, instead of given regulations from above. They need to be brought into the decision-making process so they can develop a stake in what happens at school.

The proposal to require uniforms is based on the desire to return to some mythic age in Middlebrook's past when students were orderly, disciplined, filled with school spirit—namely, all the same kind of white, middle-class students. Middlebrook has changed, and the proposal doesn't deal with these changes.

Differing Views

Some uniform supporters claim that the success of Catholic and private schools is based on the fact students are required to wear uniforms. I need to show the causes of success are not uniforms but other factors.

I'll concede that there are real problems at Middlebrook but maintain my position that uniforms aren't the way to deal with them.

I could also concede that what students wear sometimes gets out of hand but argue that the best way to deal with this is to get students involved, along with teachers and parents, in writing a new dress code. In fact, I could extend this argument to say that the way to deal with some of the problems is for the school to get the different groups—whites, Latinos, blacks, and Cambodians—together to look at the problems and propose some solutions.

Qualifiers

My position is set. I'm against uniforms, period. But maybe I should state my claim in a way that takes uniform supporters' views into account. For example, I could say, "Admittedly there are a number of problems at Middlebrook that need attention, but requiring uniforms will not solve these problems."

As you can see, using the parts of argument has given this student a lot of material to work with and some leads about where to get more. Just as important, using the parts of argument offers a way to see the connections among the available material and how they might fit together in developing the writer's line of reasoning. Not all of this material will necessarily turn up in the final version of the student's argument, of course. This can only be determined through the process of drafting and revising. In fact, she might turn up new material and new arguments as she composes.

■ WORKING TOGETHER

Analyzing the Making of an Argument

Working in small groups, analyze the "Vigilant Neighbors or Big Brother's Informants" ad on the following page. This American Bar Association (ABA) ad appeared in the *New York Times* in September 2002, when the Homeland Security Act was being debated in Congress. One of the act's provisions, Operation TIPS (Terrorism Information and Prevention System), was devised by Attorney General John Ashcroft to create a hotline for mail carriers, truckers, utility workers, and others to report "suspicious" behavior. The ABA ad offers a fair and informative account of the arguments for and against Operation TIPS, which was ultimately removed from the legislation that passed Congress.

■ FOR CRITICAL INQUIRY

1. In the "Vigilant Neighbors or Big Brother's Informants" ad, what evidence do the Pro and Con columns present to support their positions on Operation TIPS? What enabling assumptions connect evidence to their claims?

2. Does the ad present any backing to explain and support the enabling assumptions? What backing can you imagine would be persuasive in supporting the Pro and Con positions?

3. Does the ad use concession and refutation in describing the arguments for and against Operation TIPS?

4. What qualifiers, if any, does the ad use in its description of the two positions?

5. Do you find the Pro or Con position more persuasive? Why?

NEGOTIATING DIFFERENCES

Newspapers, talk shows, and political debates often treat disagreements as arguments that have two sides—pro and con, for and against. You are either pro-choice or antiabortion, for or against the death penalty, a tax-and-spend liberal or a budget-slashing conservative.

Knowing how to argue persuasively and responsibly for your side is an important skill. Without it, people would be powerless in many situations. Unless you can make an effective argument, there may well be occasions when your

Operation TIPS

VIGILANT NEIGHBORS
—— OR ——
BIG BROTHER'S INFORMANTS?

The government has announced the creation of the TIPS program, a national system for concerned Americans to report to law enforcement officials suspicious activity that could be related to terrorism.

PRO

Terrorism threatens our way of life and must be stopped. Operation TIPS provides an essential way for American workers in appropriate industries, such as truckers and others involved in transportation, to assist overburdened law enforcement agencies in detecting, preventing, and disrupting terrorist activity.

This is a voluntary program, involving the reporting of only publicly observable activities that would supplement block/neighborhood watch programs, which have been in place for many years without abuse or opposition.

A national system for receiving tips on possible terrorists would allow law enforcement officials to "connect the dots" and take quick and appropriate action on potentially terrorist-related incidents that are occurring simultaneously.

CON

Operation TIPS would create a community of snoops like those in Iron Curtain countries during the Cold War, with little gain for our safety. Basic civil liberties will be undermined by creating a national database of unreliable reports and allegations accessible by a variety of government agencies.

Since Government officials admit that most tips will wash out, why needlessly invade the privacy of law-abiding citizens and divert attention from potentially more productive investigations?

Officials admit that many terrorist activities are indistinguishable from everyday, lawful activities. Therefore, the TIPS program may simply result in fostering ethnic or religious scapegoating and nothing more.

There are at least two sides to every issue. Our democracy is built on the rule of law. We resolve differences of opinion through dialogue and debate. Disagreement is inevitable. Violence is not.

American Bar Association

Defending Liberty
Pursuing Justice

www.ABA-Dialogue.org

perspective will go unheard and your views unrepresented. Moreover, if you do not argue for what you and others with shared values hold in common, someone else is likely to do your talking for you.

There is little question, then, that arguing for your side is a crucial means of participating in public life and influencing public opinion. Still, as important as argument is, you need to look carefully at how arguments are conducted and what happens to the character and quality of public discussions when issues are polarized into pro-and-con, for-and-against positions.

Consider, for example, the following three ways pro-and-con, for-and-against arguments can limit discussion.

1. **Adversarial stance:** One of the limits of pro-and-con arguments is that they put people in an adversarial stance toward those with whom they disagree. Instead of clarifying the issues and reaching mutual understandings, the goal of the argument may turn into defeating your opponent.

2. **Limited perspectives:** By polarizing issues along adversarial lines, pro-and-con arguments frequently limit the perspectives available in public debate to two—and only two—sides: those for and those against. This may well restrict who is entitled to be heard to the members of rival camps and thereby limit the alternatives considered in making decisions.

3. **Lack of common ground:** The pro-and-con, winner-take-all style of adversarial argument makes it nearly impossible for participants to identify the points of agreement and common ground they might share with others. The search for common ground does not assume that everyone is going to drop their differences and harmonize their interests. Instead, trying to find common ground can establish areas of agreement, large or small, that people can use as a basis to talk about their differences.

■ **EXERCISE**

Looking at Polarized Arguments

Write an account or prepare an oral presentation of an argument you witnessed or took part in that polarized into opposing sides. Describe what happened, and explain why the polarization took place. The point of this exercise is not to condemn the people involved but to understand what happened and why. Remember, polarization is not necessarily a bad thing. It may be unavoidable as people begin to identify their differences or invoke a matter of principle, where a person finds no alternative but to make a counterargument and take a stand. Your task here is to analyze what took place and to consider whether the polarization was inevitable or could have been avoided.

BEYOND PRO AND CON

A number of strategies offer writers approaches to reasonable differences that divide people. In sections that follow, we examine three:

1. Dialogue with others.
2. Recognizing ambiguities and contradictions.
3. Locating common ground.

These strategies enable writers to remain committed to their own goals and values but at the same time avoid some of the limitations of simply arguing for or against, pro and con, in an adversarial relation to others. They will help you to engage people with whom you may differ—to enter into a dialogue that seeks not a victory in debate but a clarification of the issues that may ultimately make it easier for you and others to live together and perhaps to locate common ground.

As you will see, these strategies do not deny differences in the name of having everyone get along for the common good. Nor do they assume that people can easily reconcile their differences or harmonize conflicting interests. Too often, some members of society—women, minorities, working people, seniors, teenagers, and children—have been asked to keep quiet and sacrifice their interests to create what is in fact a false unity. Instead of setting aside differences, these strategies seek to use them constructively in order to take more interests and perspectives into account.

The strategies that follow seek to bring differences out into the open—but not in an adversarial way. Instead of imagining issues in terms of warring camps, you can use these strategies to negotiate—to understand how others feel about the issues, why people might be divided in their views, and what is thereby at stake for all involved. Negotiating differences does not mean abandoning the goal of influencing others, but it does recognize that we need to be open to influence from others—if not to change our minds, at least to deepen our understanding of other views and ways of thinking.

DIALOGUE WITH OTHERS

It is difficult to think of people negotiating their differences unless they recognize one another as reasonable beings in the first place. To recognize another person does not mean to see him or her as an opponent to be defeated in debate or as someone to overwhelm with convincing arguments or manipulate with emotional appeals. It means to start by listening to what that person has to say—to put yourself in his or her shoes and imagine how the world looks from his or her perspective. It is presumptuous, of course, to think that you can be totally successful in understanding those with whom you differ. (Just assuming you can understand them, after all, may well imply a sense of your own superiority.) But it is the engagement with others that counts—the willingness to keep talking and trying to understand.

The reading selection that follows illustrates how recognizing others can lead people into dialogue and open the possibility of mutual understanding. As you read, notice that the strategy of recognizing others differs in important respects from the standard moves of adversarial argument—refuting opposing views or making concessions to them.

AN ELECTRONIC EXCHANGE OF VIEWS

The following correspondence brings together two people who are strangers—a gay teacher and a Vietnam vet—joined in conversation on an electronic bulletin board by the technology of the Internet. While the two correspondents do not know each other personally, they are nonetheless engaged, as you will see, in a deeply personal dialogue.

New ▾   Reply   Reply All   ▾   Junk   Send & Receive ▾   Move ▾   Categories ▾   Projects

1   Do you have any idea what it is like to be gay? To hide the most important thing about yourself, even though you had no choice about it? To live in terror of discovery? To be laughed at, isolated and beaten up? To live around people who hide their children from you? Who wouldn't let you teach them if they knew? Because I am a teacher who dreads every call to the principal's office. I always wonder if it will be my last. How can you love a country that finds you too disgusting to serve? That permits people to attack you and your friends, throw things at them from car windows, deny them the right to be married, have families? Can you conceive of that? Does this get through to you on any level at all?

2   Two years ago, my lover and I walked through the French Quarter of New Orleans. We vacationed there because we knew it to be a tolerant place. We left a restaurant just off Bourbon Street, and three men jumped out of their cars. They knocked my lover and me down. They kicked us in the face, in the kidneys, in the groin. They knocked four of my teeth out, broke my jaw. Then they urinated on us. They laughed and said they were soldiers. That they'd love to have us in the military. I couldn't tell the police what happened. I was afraid the school district might find out back home.

And a reply:

New ▾   Reply   Reply All   ▾   Junk   Send & Receive ▾   Move ▾   Categories ▾   Projects

1   I was very touched by your message, buddy. What happened to you was horrible, unsupportable. That's not what I lost three toes for in Vietnam, for scum to beat up on people like you and your friend. I fought so you could do whatever you wanted so long as you didn't hurt anybody or break the law. You and I have no quarrel. But we do have these problems, and I'll be straight with you about it, just like you were with me. Do you have any idea what it's like to be in a field or jungle or valley with bullets and shells blowing up all around you? With your friends being cut down, ripped apart, bleeding, dying right next to you screaming for their moms or kids or wives? Do you know how much trust and communication it takes to get through that? Do you have any idea what it's like to go through that if there's tension among you?

2

> I'm not saying this can't be worked out. I'm saying, go slow. Don't come in here with executive orders and try to change things in a day that should take longer. Don't make me into a bigot because I know it takes an unbelievable amount of feeling to crawl down there into a valley of death. It takes love of your buddy. And that's something both of us can understand, right? But if you hate him, or fear him or don't understand him—how can you do it?

■ FOR CRITICAL INQUIRY

1. Describe the gay teacher's posting. What does his purpose seem to be? What kind of relationship is he trying to establish with his readers? How can you tell? What cues does he give readers about how he would like them to respond?

2. Consider the Vietnam vet's reply. What does he see as at stake in the gay teacher's posting? To what extent is he able to see things from the teacher's perspective? What is he getting at when he says, "You and I have no quarrel. But we do have these problems"? What, if anything, does the writer offer to work these problems out? To what extent does the Vietnam vet seem committed to a dialogue with the teacher?

3. Imagine that the gay teacher had replied to the Vietnam vet. What kind of response would help keep the dialogue open? What kind of response would tend to close it or turn it into a polarized argument?

4. The teacher and the vet are strangers. They do not know each other personally. What is the effect of such anonymity on this exchange of views?

5. Find someone who holds a position or represents a point of view that you don't share. Arrange an interview with the person. The point of the interview is to engage in a dialogue that can help you understand where the person is coming from and why. You will need to explain your own position or point of view, but your goal is not to argue with the other person. Instead, try to reach some understanding of how and why you differ. If you can, tape and transcribe the interview. Follow a presentation of the interview with your own account of what you learned about the differences that divide you and the other person. Indicate how or whether you changed your mind in any respect.

RECOGNIZING AMBIGUITIES AND CONTRADICTIONS

To negotiate differences is to recognize ambiguities and contradictions. Recognizing ambiguities and contradictions goes beyond acknowledging that there are differing sides, perspectives, and interests that divide people over particular issues. It further suggests that the positions people hold may themselves contain internal differences—that things may not be as simple as they seem at first glance, with views neatly arranged for and against.

Recognizing the ambiguities or contradictions in your position does not mean that you are abandoning what you believe in. It means that you maintain your views but are willing to talk about gray areas, troubling aspects, and conflicting loyalties.

LOCATING COMMON GROUND: CALL FOR A MORATORIUM ON EXECUTIONS

Locating common ground is built on the strategies we have just looked at but seeks to go one step further by identifying how people can join together, in spite of their differences, to address an issue of mutual concern. Locating common ground is a strategy for looking for ways out of the impasse of polarized debate. Instead of focusing on the arguments that divide people, it tries to establish basic points of agreement in order to get people talking to each other about what can be done. In this sense, locating common ground amounts to consensus building—forming alliances and coalitions with others.

As you can see, the "*New York Times* Ad Campaign" letter and the "Call for a Moratorium on Executions" advertisement seek to unite individuals and organizations, whether they support or oppose the death penalty.

No one would doubt that capital punishment has been one of the most divisive and volatile issues in American political life. Recently, however, there has been a growing dialogue among people who are worried that the death penalty is not being applied fairly, whether they support executions on principle or not. The "*New York Times* Ad Campaign" letter seeking support for the "Call for a Moratorium on Executions" ad shows how people who differ in fundamental beliefs about capital punishment can nonetheless find common ground and identify issues of shared concern.

The "*New York Times* Ad Campaign" and "Call for a Moratorium on Executions" are shown on the next two pages.

■ FOR CRITICAL INQUIRY

1. Analyze the argument presented in the "*New York Times* Ad Campaign" letter and the "Call for a Moratorium on Executions" ad. What is the main claim? What evidence is offered to support it? What enabling assumptions link the claim and evidence?

2. Explain what you see as the common ground the letter seeks to establish. What line of reasoning might lead someone who supports the death penalty to support the call for a moratorium on executions?

3. How do you think people who oppose the death penalty would respond to the letter and the ad?

4. Take up an issue that has divided your campus, your community, or the nation. Imagine ways to offer common ground on which people with polarized views might nonetheless join together in a shared undertaking such as the call for a moratorium on executions. What arguments would be needed to establish such a common ground?

New York Times Ad Campaign

Dear Friend,   September 1999

Later this fall, the United Nations General Assembly is expected to vote on a resolution calling for a moratorium on executions worldwide. This vote will prove pivotal to the international community's vision of human rights as we enter the next millennium.

The reasons for a moratorium on executions *here in the US* are particularly compelling:

▶ Legal representation for most capital defendants – the vast majority of whom are indigent – is grossly inadequate. Poor people are most likely to be sentenced to death, and innocent people are inevitably going to be executed.

▶ Race continues to play a primary role in determining who lives and who dies.

▶ Juvenile offenders and the mentally disabled continue to be subject to executions despite international condemnation.

This reality led the American Bar Association, which has never taken a position for or against the death penalty, to call for an immediate halt on executions in 1997. The ABA has concluded that inequities in our system are so pervasive that they undermine confidence in the outcome of capital trials *and* appeals.

In 1998, the United Nations Commission on Human Rights issued a condemnatory report on the US death penalty, urging the US government to halt all executions while it brings the states into compliance with international standards and law.

Yet our nation's use of the death penalty is increasing. Already, 66 people have been executed this year. At this pace, the number of executions in 1999 could top 100, approaching rates last seen during the Great Depression.

The UN vote presents an international moment for citizens of the US to raise our voices for a moratorium.

We urge you to join us in signing an ad urging a moratorium to run in *The New York Times* in the weeks preceding the General Assembly's vote.

The ad statement is on the reverse side. Your name can be added for a gift $35. Organizational signatures are $50. Consider becoming a endorser for $100 or a co-sponsor for $1,000. We will send a copy of the final ad to all signers, and it will be published on our website, www.quixote.org/ej. *The deadline for signatures is November 4.*

Whether you support or oppose the death penalty, please stand with us publicly in this call for simple justice. We need to hear from you soon!

Sincerely,

Bianca Jagger
Human Rights Activist

Bud Welch
father of Oklahoma City
bombing victim, Julie Welch

Noam Chomsky
Professor of Linguistics, M.I.T.

Arthur Schlesinger, Jr.
Historian

Bishop Thomas J. Gumbleton
(Roman Catholic)

Susan Sarandon
Actress

The Very Rev. James Parks Morton
The Interfaith Center of New York

QUIXOTE CENTER
PURSUING JUSTICE, PEACE & EQUALITY
P.O. Box 5206, HYATTSVILLE, MD 20782
301-699-0042 / [FAX] 301-864-2182 / WWW.QUIXOTE.ORG / EJUSA@QUIXOTE.ORG

(Ad Statement)

Call for a Moratorium on Executions

Signature Deadline: November 4

A Story from Death Row

Anthony Porter was to be executed by the State of Illinois on September 23, 1998. Just 48 hours before his scheduled death, the Illinois Supreme Court granted a stay to consider last-minute questions about whether Porter, whose IQ is 51, should be legally barred from execution because he could not understand what was happening to him.

The delay gave four Northwestern University journalism students time to conduct an independent investigation of the case. No physical evidence tied Porter to the 1982 double murder in Chicago. His conviction was based solely on eyewitness testimony. After visiting the crime scene, the students found that this testimony did not add up. With the aid of a private investigator, they began questioning witnesses. Thanks to the students' efforts, another man confessed to the murders for which Porter was almost executed. Porter was freed in February 1999 after 17 years on death row.

We, the undersigned, are US citizens and organizations. Some of us support the death penalty and some oppose it. Yet we *all* join together today to call for an immediate moratorium on executions because of the way capital punishment is applied in our country.

We support a moratorium because of the increasing risk of executing innocent people like Anthony Porter. Nationwide, 82* innocent death row prisoners have been released since 1973 – six in 1999 alone. Some were saved only days before their scheduled execution. The average time these prisoners spent on death row was seven years.[1] Efforts by courts and legislatures to speed up the time between conviction and execution mean that other prisoners likely have been and will be executed before their innocence is discovered. Porter's story is a painful reminder that all too often, a prisoner's innocence is discovered only because of the extraordinary and fortuitous efforts of people *outside* the system.

We support a moratorium because – as the American Bar Association (ABA) has concluded – "fundamental due process is now systematically lacking in capital cases."[2] Porter's case is symptomatic of this crisis in death penalty jurisprudence. Like *90 percent* of those facing capital charges, Porter was too poor to hire his own attorney.

Most indigent defendants suffer from grossly inadequate legal representation.[3] Furthermore, the US General Accounting Office has found "a pattern of evidence indicating racial disparities in charging, sentencing and imposition of the death penalty."[4] Many states continue to execute people who are mentally retarded or who were under age 18 at the time of their crimes or both – even in the face of nearly unanimous international condemnation.

Unfairness and mistakes in the application of the death penalty are undermining public confidence in the criminal justice system and fueling the call for a moratorium. **More than 600* groups and tens of thousands of people across the US are now calling for an immediate halt to executions.** Among them is the ABA, which led the way in early 1997. Opinion polls show that many people in the US embrace alternatives to a death sentence if other means are taken to ensure that the guilty do not further endanger the innocent.[5]

In the coming weeks, the United Nations General Assembly will vote on a resolution urging an international moratorium on executions. We note that many governments of the world are already observing a moratorium, while 105 countries have abandoned capital punishment in law or practice. We urge our government to join in the proposed UN resolution.

We also urge President Clinton, all members of the US Congress, our respective governors and state legislators and members of our state and federal judiciary to enact an immediate moratorium on executions.

*Numbers will be updated at publication of ad as necessary.

[1] *Innocence and the Death Penalty: The Increasing Danger of Executing the Innocent,* Death Penalty Information Center, 1320 18th St. NW, 5th Floor, Washington, DC 20036, 202-293-6970, July 1997. See also www.essential.org/dpic.

[2] Report accompanying ABA Death Penalty Moratorium Resolution (107) adopted by the ABA House of Delegates in February 1997.

[3] Same as note 2. To date, no state has met *all* of the American Bar Association (ABA) policies for administration of the death penalty, including standards for representation for indigent defendants.

[4] *Death Penalty Sentencing: Research Indicates a Pattern of Racial Disparities,* General Accounting Office report, February 1990.

[5] See Death Penalty Information Center website at www.essential.org/dpic/po.html.

RHETORICAL ANALYSIS OF AN ARGUMENT

The annotations on the sample analysis of the argument in "Call for a Moratorium on Executions" point out some of the things you can do in your own analysis of an argument.

SAMPLE ANALYSIS OF THE ARGUMENT IN "CALL FOR A MORATORIUM ON EXECUTIONS"

Shah 1

Vikram Shah
English 17
Prof. Sole
18 March 2003

Identifies the timing and purpose of the call

The "Call for a Moratorium on Executions," along with an accompanying letter, was sent out in September 1999 to solicit signatures and contributions for an ad in the New York Times, just before the United Nations General Assembly voted on a resolution calling for a moratorium on the death penalty. The Call focuses on the issue of capital punishment in the United States. It does not argue against the death penalty in principle. Instead, the Call argues

Summarizes the argument

that "[u]nfairness and mistakes in the application of the death penalty" are "undermining public confidence in the criminal justice system." In particular, the Call notes the lack of due process in capital cases, the inadequate legal representation of poor people charged with capital crimes, the racial disparities in the use of the death penalty, and the fact that juveniles and the mentally retarded are executed in the U.S. Since 1973, 82 innocent death row prisoners were released, due largely to efforts of people outside the criminal justice system, such as the Northwestern University journalism students who succeeded in freeing Anthony Porter in 1999, after another man confessed to the crime for which Porter was to be executed.

Shah 2

The debate over the death penalty, of course, has long divided the American people. As the Call says the number of executions has been increasing in recent years. In general the American public supports capital punishment, although support has dropped from 80% in 1997 to 66% today. The Call, however, includes both supporters and opponents of the death penalty as its intended readers. By focusing on whether the death penalty is being applied fairly, the Call reaches out to both sides in the death penalty debate on the basis of people's shared beliefs in due process and justice.

The Call establishes its rhetorical stance by saying that some of us "support the death penalty and some oppose it." The ethos it projects is that of reasonable, concerned citizens and groups who are troubled by the current flaws in capital punishment. The tone is serious, and the Call seeks to enhance its authority and credibility by drawing on the conclusions of such reputable organizations as the American Bar Association and the General Accounting Office of the federal government. In terms of pathos, the Call appeals to readers who will be worried by unfairness in the current system and do not want to see innocent people executed. The inclusion of the Story from Death Row personalizes the policy issue of capital punishment and gives it a sense of urgency and immediacy for readers. The logos of the Call sends the message that readers do not have to be against the death penalty to recognize that the system is not working the way it is supposed to.

The argument in the Call begins with the claim that executions should be suspended because of the unfairness of the system. The evidence includes the story about Anthony Porter, the number of innocent death row prisoners released since 1973, the American Bar Association's report that poor defendants lack adequate legal representation, and the General Accounting Office's finding of racial disparities in charging and sentencing in capital cases. The enabling assumptions that link this evidence to the Call's claim are beliefs in due process and the right to competent legal counsel. These assumptions are

Describes the context of issues

Analyzes the rhetorical stance

Ethos

Pathos

Logos

Analyzes the parts of the argument

Claim

Evidence

Enabling Assumptions

Shah 3

backed up by the U.S. Constitution and the American legal tradition that everyone (rich or poor, black or white) is equal in the eyes of the law. The Call does not include either differing views or qualifiers in regard to its argument for a moratorium on executions.

Examines strategy for negotiating differences

Identifies type of issue

Evaluation of overall effectiveness

The major purpose of the Call is to provide a common ground on which both opponents and supporters of the death penalty can join together to deal with inequities in the present system. This emphasis on an issue of policy helps both to clarify the current situation of the death penalty and to allow the broadest group of readers to join the call for a moratorium. Some supporters of the death penalty might argue that a moratorium would permit guilty death row prisoners to evade capital punishment. Nonetheless, one of the enabling assumptions in the Call is that the concern for fairness and the public good is worth the risk. It is always difficult to know whether individual readers will be persuaded, but the Call's overall strategy of reaching out on the basis of fairness is certainly a reasonable one in the circumstances.

WRITING ASSIGNMENT

Analyzing an Argument

Online Study Center

Your task is to write an essay that analyzes a short argument. Use the sample rhetorical analysis of an argument as a guideline, but be flexible in the way you approach the argument you're analyzing. What you emphasize will depend in large part on the nature of the argument you're analyzing.

Directions

1. Select a short argument (five to ten paragraphs is a good length). You can use one of the readings in this chapter or elsewhere in this book, a newspaper editorial or op-ed piece, a featured column in a newspaper or magazine, magazine commentary, political ads, or ads for advocacy groups as sources for your analysis.

2. Analyze the argument. Here are some guidelines for your analysis:

- Summarize the argument. What is the main claim?

- Identify the type of issue—substantiation, evaluation, policy.

- Describe the context of issues. Is the argument part of an ongoing debate, discussion, or controversy? What positions have people taken in the past?

- Describe the intended readers and explain how the argument seeks to influence them (to take action, support or oppose a policy, reconsider an established fact or belief, make a value judgment).

- Analyze the rhetorical stance. How does the writer integrate ethos, pathos, and logos?

- Analyze the parts of the argument—claim, evidence, enabling assumptions, backing, differing views, qualifiers—and how the writer puts them together.

- Examine any strategies used to negotiate differences.

- Evaluate the overall effectiveness of the argument. Keep in mind that the goal of argument is to clarify reasonable differences as well as to convince others.

3. Use your analysis to write your essay. Begin by summarizing the argument. Then provide an analysis in the order that best suits your material. End with your evaluation of the argument's effectiveness. ■

part two

writing projects

2

INTRODUCTION: GENRES OF WRITING

The mail has just arrived, and you glance through it, putting letters in one pile, magazines in another, and junk mail in still another. You may do this automatically, but your ability to sort the mail is based on some very real experience with the written materials of print culture. That is why people can distinguish immediately between, say, an L. L. Bean catalog and the recent issue of *Newsweek*. The same is true of the letters they receive—a personal letter from a friend, a fund-raising appeal from Amnesty International, a library overdue notice, and junk mail advertising storm windows or aluminum siding.

Each type of writing is likely to have a different appearance—a four-color catalog, a slick news magazine, handwritten stationery, a form letter with profiles of human rights abuse, a computer printout, and a promotional flyer addressed to "Resident." People use such visual cues to make sense of the written material they receive and what they should do with it.

People are likely to notice how the different types of writing address them in different ways. A personal letter may call for a reply, whether by letter, phone call, or email message. A library notice calls for prompt action if you want to avoid running up a fine. A fund-raising letter may lead to a financial contribution to support a particular cause. A catalog from L. L. Bean may lead to placing an order or just to fantasy reading about the lifestyles of the outdoorsy middle class.

This example of sorting the mail is meant to illustrate how people classify different types of writing into categories in order to get a handle on what they are reading—to know what to expect from it and how to respond. Based on their past experience with written texts, people fit what they read into *patterns*.

Writing and Genre Knowledge

Similarly, writers draw on genre knowledge to make sense of the situations that call on them to write. As writers identify a call to write, they typically review past experience to help them determine the genre best suited to the current occasion. To do this, they look for recurring patterns:

- How is this writing situation similar to ones I've encountered in the past?

- How well do genres of writing I've used in the past match the demands of the present?

- Are there genres I haven't used before that fit this situation?

- What genre best fits my purposes, given the situation and the intended readers?

In the following chapters, you'll see how writers use various genres to respond to recurring writing situations. You'll see how writers' choice of genre takes into account the occasion that calls for writing, the writer's purposes, and the relationship the writer seeks to establish with readers.

While writing teachers do not always agree on how best to classify genres of writing, the eight chapters in Part Two offer practical examples of how writers use some of the most familiar genres. These chapters are by no means a comprehensive account of all genres of writing. Nor are the genres of writing fixed once and for all. New genres are always emerging in response to new conditions, as you can see in the proliferation of email, instant messaging, message boards, blogs, and Web sites. In the following chapters, some of the most common genres illustrate how writers respond to the call to write. You will find these genres helpful when you are called on to write in college, in the workplace, and in public life.

letters: establishing and maintaining relationships

THINKING ABOUT THE GENRE

Letters are easy to recognize. Whether handwritten, typed, word-processed, or composed as email, letters have a predictable format that usually includes the date of writing, a salutation that addresses the reader directly ("Dear Jim"), a message, a closing (such as "Sincerely" or "Yours truly"), and a signature. There are many different occasions for and purposes of letter writing, and the genre of letters can be divided into a number of subgenres, such as personal letters, business letters, letters to the editor, or letters of appeal. Nonetheless, letters are easy to identify because of the way they appear on the page or computer screen.

But it's not only the visual form of the writing that makes letters a distinct genre. Just as important is the way letters address their readers and establish a relationship between the writer and the reader. In part because of two elements of their form—the salutation and the closing and signature—the letter is the genre that comes closest to conversation between people.

The relationship established between writer and reader is one of the main attractions of the genre of letters. It's also one of its most basic functions: letters are important links that help you maintain your networks of personal and social relations. When you read a letter, you can almost hear the voice of the person writing to you.

Letters are also like conversation in that the writer seeks to engage the reader in an ongoing interaction. They often call for a response from their readers—whether it's to RSVP a party invitation, attend a meeting, donate to a worthy cause, pay an overdue bill, or just write back.

One way that letters differ from conversation is that the person you're writing to can't talk back, at least not immediately. As a writer with something to say, you therefore have certain advantages. In a letter, you can talk directly

Online Study Center

to someone without being interrupted. And you know that the reader can return several times to your letter and reflect on its message before responding to you.

Thus, permanence is also a difference between letters and conversation. Once you've sent a letter, you can't take your words back as easily as you can in conversation. By expressing thoughts and feelings in a letter and sending it to someone, the letter writer may be taking a greater risk than by talking face to face or on the phone.

G. K. Chesterton once described the mailbox as "a sanctuary of the human heart" and the letter as "one of the few things left entirely romantic, for to be entirely romantic, a thing must be irrevocable." Many people save the letters they receive from relatives, friends, lovers, and other correspondents as a personal record of what their life was like at a particular time. There is a long tradition of letters in which writers reveal their deepest, most intimate thoughts to readers in a language that would be unimaginable in conversation—love letters, letters of advice, letters of friendship, letters of condolence, letters of despair, and letters written on the eve of death.

Other kinds of letters play just as important a role as personal letters in maintaining the social networks that link people together. Business letters serve a wide range of indispensable functions for businesses and government, going to clients and customers, suppliers and contractors, employees, and the general public in order to advertise products and services, discuss policy changes, request payment, and negotiate agreements.

Letters written for the public realm are equally wide ranging, from the letters individuals and groups write to politicians to influence the direction of public policy to letters to the editor, which give readers a chance to respond to news stories and editorials, as well as to raise neglected issues.

Advocacy groups such as the Sierra Club or the National Rifle Association write fund-raising letters appealing for memberships and donations. Another kind of letter of appeal, often called an open letter because it is circulated widely, is a political tradition in democratic cultures. Sent out through the mail or Internet and sometimes appearing as a paid advertisement in a magazine or newspaper, the letter of appeal calls on its readers to support a cause, protest a policy, or otherwise take action.

■ WRITING FROM EXPERIENCE

List the kinds of letters you write and receive, including email correspondence. Classify the letters according to the relationship they are based on—letters to and from family, letters to and from friends, love letters, letters to you as a consumer or a potential donor, letters from your college, and so on. Are there particular letters you wrote or received that are especially important to you? What makes these letters important? Do you save letters? If so, what kinds of letters, and why? Compare your answers with those of your classmates.

READINGS

OPEN LETTER

METH SCIENCE NOT STIGMA: OPEN LETTER TO THE MEDIA

As the following letter indicates, the media has been filled in recent years with sensationalistic accounts of "meth" or "ice" babies left in the wake of a nationwide methamphetamine epidemic. Circulated widely on the Internet by David C. Lewis and Donald G. Millar of Brown University, this open letter of July 25, 2005, was signed by 92 researchers and clinicians who study the effects of prenatal exposure to drugs.

July 25, 2005

Contact: David C. Lewis, M.D.
Professor of Community Health and Medicine
Donald G. Millar Distinguished Professor of Alcohol & Addiction
Studies
Brown University
Phone: 401-444-1818
E-Mail: David_Lewis@brown.edu

To Whom It May Concern:

1 | *Opening establishes credentials of open letter signers and purpose of letter*

As medical and psychological researchers, with many years of experience studying prenatal exposure to psychoactive substances, and as medical researchers, treatment providers and specialists with many years of experience studying addictions and addiction treatment, we are writing to request that policies addressing prenatal exposure to methamphetamines and media coverage of this issue be based on science, not presumption or prejudice.

2 | *Explains problem of stigmatizing labels.*

Uses comparison as evidence

The use of stigmatizing terms, such as "ice babies" and "meth babies," lacks scientific validity and should not be used. Experience with similar labels applied to children exposed prenatally to cocaine demonstrates that such labels harm the children to which they are applied, lowering expectations for their academic and life achievements, discouraging investigation into other causes for physical and social problems the child might encounter, and leading to policies that ignore factors, including poverty, that may play a much more significant role in their lives. The suggestion that treatment will not work for people dependent upon methamphetamines, particularly mothers, also lacks any scientific basis.

3 |

Despite the lack of a medical or scientific basis for the use of such terms as "ice" and "meth" babies, these pejorative and stigmatizing labels are increasingly being used in the popular media, in a wide variety of contexts across the country. Even when articles themselves acknowledge that the effects of prenatal exposure to methamphetamine are still unknown, headlines across the country are using alarmist and unjustified labels such as "meth babies."

4

Gives examples of stigma-tizing labels

Just a few examples come from both local and national media:

- CBS NATIONAL NEWS, "Generation of Meth Babies" (April 28, 2005) at CBSNews.com
- ARKANSAS NEWS BUREAU, Doug Thompson, "Meth Baby Bill Survives Amendment Vote" (Mar. 5, 2005)
- CHICAGO TRIBUNE, Judith Graham, "Only Future Will Tell Full Damage Speed Wreaks on Kids" ("At birth, meth babies are like 'dishrags'") (Mar. 7, 2004)
- THE LOS ANGELES TIMES, Lance Pugmire, "Meth Baby Murder Trial Winds Up" (Sept. 5, 2003 at B3)
- THE SUNDAY OKLAHOMAN, "Meth Babies" (Oklahoma City, OK; May 23, 2004 at 8A)
- APBNEWS.COM, "Meth Infants Called the New 'Crack Babies' (June 23, 2000).

5

Other examples include an article about methamphetamine use in the MINNEAPOLIS STAR TRIBUNE that lists a litany of medical problems allegedly caused by methamphetamine use during pregnancy, using sensationalized language that appears intended to shock and appall rather than inform, ". . . babies can be born with missing and misplaced body parts. She heard of a meth baby born with an arm growing out of the neck and another who was missing a femur." Sarah McCann, "Meth ravages lives in northern counties" (Nov. 17, 2004, at N1). In May, one Fox News station warned that "meth babies" "could make the crack baby look like a walk in the nursery." Cited in "The Damage Done: Crack Babies Talk Back," Mariah Blake, COLUMBIA JOURNALISM REVIEW Oct/Nov 2004.

6

Conces-sion

Appeal to experience and exper-tise

Although research on the medical and developmental effects of prenatal methamphetamine exposure is still in its early stages, our experience with almost 20 years of research on the chemically related drug, cocaine, has not identified a recognizable condition, syndrome or disorder that should be termed "crack baby" nor found the degree of harm reported in the media and then used to justify numerous punitive legislative proposals.

7

Gives defi-nition of "addic-tion"

The term "meth addicted baby" is no less defensible. Addiction is a technical term that refers to compulsive behavior that continues in spite of adverse consequences. By definition, babies cannot be "addicted" to methamphetamines or anything else. The news media continues to ignore this fact.

- A CNN report was aired repeatedly over the span of a month, showing a picture of a baby who had allegedly been exposed to methamphetamines

Further examples

prenatally and stating: "This is what a meth baby looks like, premature, hooked on meth and suffering the pangs of withdrawal. They don't want to eat or sleep and the simplest things cause great pain." CNN, "The Methamphetamine Epidemic in the United States," Randi Kaye. (Aired Feb. 3, 2005–Mar. 10, 2005).

■ One local National Public Radio station claims that "In one Minnesota County, there is a baby born addicted to meth each week." (Found at news.minnesota.publicradio.org from June 14, 2004).

8

Provides research findings

In utero physiologic dependence on opiates (not addiction), known as Neonatal Narcotic Abstinence Syndrome, is readily diagnosable and treatable, but no such symptoms have been found to occur following prenatal cocaine or methamphetamine exposure.

9

Similarly, claims that methamphetamine users are virtually untreatable with small recovery rates lack foundation in medical research. Analysis of dropout, retention in treatment and re-incarceration rates and other measures of outcome, in several recent studies indicate that methamphetamine users respond in an equivalent manner as individuals admitted for other drug abuse problems. Research also suggests the need to improve and expand treatment offered to methamphetamine users.

10

Questions media sources

Too often, media and policymakers rely on people who lack any scientific experience or expertise for their information about the effects of prenatal exposure to methamphetamine and about the efficacy of treatment. For example, a NEW YORK TIMES story about methamphetamine labs and children relies on a law enforcement official rather than a medical expert to describe the effects of methamphetamine exposure on children. A police captain is quoted stating: "Meth makes crack look like child's play, both in terms of what it does to the body and how hard it is to get off." (Fox Butterfield, Home Drug-Making Laboratories Expose Children to Toxic Fallout, Feb. 23, 2004 A1)

11

Points out policy implications

How to access signers of open letter

We are deeply disappointed that American and international media as well as some policymakers continue to use stigmatizing terms and unfounded assumptions that not only lack any scientific basis but also endanger and disenfranchise the children to whom these labels and claims are applied. Similarly, we are concerned that policies based on false assumptions will result in punitive civil and child welfare interventions that are harmful to women, children and families rather than in the ongoing research and improvement and provision of treatment services that are so clearly needed.

12

Please click here for a pdf version of the open letter with the complete list of signatures.

13 We would be happy to furnish additional information if requested or to
Offers send representatives to meet with policy advisors, staff or editorial boards to
further provide more detailed technical information. Please feel free to contact David
assistance C. Lewis, M.D., 401-444-1818, David_Lewis@brown.edu, Professor of Community Health and Medicine, Brown University, who has agreed to coordinate such
requests on our behalf.

Analysis: Responding to the Call to Write

"Meth Science Not Stigma: Open Letter to the Media" offers a good example of
how open letters respond to a shared sense of urgency on the part of a group
of people, in this case leading medical and psychological researchers. Notice
how the letter first establishes the credentials of the signers and next identifies the occasion for writing, namely the media coverage of "meth" babies. To
establish the reality of the problem, the letter provides examples and then
examines two particular fallacies in the media accounts—the idea that new-
borns can be addicted and the claim that methamphetamine users cannot be
treated. Throughout, the letter uses scientific evidence to correct what the
signers argue is flawed and misleading coverage in the media.

■ FOR CRITICAL INQUIRY

1. Describe the ethos of the letter. How does it establish the signers' credibility?
   What role does it give the authority of science?

2. Examine the argument in the letter. How does it support the claim that media
   coverage of "meth" babies is stigmatizing? How does the letter connect such a
   claim to wider policy consequences in the last paragraph? What assumptions
   enable this connection?

3. Notice the open letter is addressed to "To Whom It May Concern." Why do you
   think the writers used this convention? What does it reveal about who they
   imagine their audience to be?

LETTERS TO THE EDITOR

The newspaper column and letters to the editor presented in this section follow a cycle of writing that is common in newspapers—a pattern of call and
response where the writers respond to the views of those who wrote before
them. First, newspaper columnist Mark Patinkin of the *Providence Journal-
Bulletin* wrote a column on an item in the news: the authorities in Singapore
had sentenced Michael Fay, an American teenager who lived there, to be
caned as a punishment for spray-painting cars. Patinkin's column led to a
round of letters, including those from Kristin Tardiff and John N. Taylor.

THE COLUMN

Commit a crime, suffer the consequences

Mark Patinkin

At their best, columnists are supposed to leave people thinking, "That's just how I feel and didn't know it until reading that." Well, it took reading a column by an 18-year-old student to crystallize my own feelings about an issue I've been perusing day to day.

The Singapore caning case: The American teenager who's about to be flogged because he spray-painted several cars. From the start, I'd viewed it as a barbaric punishment for a poor kid who just did a little mischief. Then I read a column by an 18-year-old telling Michael Fay, the convicted American, to take it like a man, and learn from it.

Something in me instantly said, "She's right."

Yes, I know caning is harsh, but am I the only one who's tired of Michael Fay's whining? Am I the only one who feels President Clinton has better things to do than to write letters appealing for leniency?

Singaporeans get caned all the time for vandalism. Are we Americans supposed to be exempt when we break their laws? What are we — princes?

I'll tell you what else I'm tired of: Michael Fay's father — his biological father here in America — traveling the country insisting his precious boy didn't do it.

It's a setup, the father says. Supposedly, he says, Michael only pleaded guilty as a bargain with the police — after the local cops leaned on him — with the promise of little punishment.

But suddenly the judge sentenced him to six strikes with a cane.

Not once have I read Michael's parents saying their child was out of line. They just make excuses. Gee, I wonder if a life of such excuse-making is part of why he's so troubled.

See, that's the other line here. First, the father says he didn't do it. Then he says, well, Michael also has personal problems, like Attention Deficit Disorder. I happen to think that's a legitimate syndrome, but not for excusing crimes like vandalizing cars.

All this is just part of the new American game of always saying, "It's not my fault." No one, when caught, seems ready to admit having done wrong anymore. They just whine and appeal. As in: "Your honor, the stabbing was not my client's fault. He had a bad childhood. And was caught up in a riot at the time. In fact, he's not a criminal at all, he's one of society's victims."

That's Michael Fay. All those cars he spray-painted? Not his fault. He's had a hard life.

I might have had sympathy for him if he'd only said, "I admit it. I did a dumb thing. I was with the wrong crowd and crossed the line into criminality. I deserve to pay. And I'm truly sorry for the victims."

But we're not hearing that.

There's another thing. Many articles on this — including a paragraph in a column I wrote — have referred to what Michael Fay did as "mischief."

Well, it's not. It's hardcore vandalism. He spray-painted a bunch of cars.

Michael Fay might want to think about what it feels like to the car owners. Anyone whose car has been vandalized knows. Personally, I've had about four car stereos stolen. I still remember the shock — each time — of seeing the broken window and the damage. I remember having to take a good half day out of work to deal with it. And during the times I had little money, I remember how badly it pinched to have to pay the deductible on the insurance.

Finally, I remember how creepy and unnerving it was. It took weeks before I could approach my car again without feeling nervous. It erodes your trust in the world. And it's worse for women, I think, who feel a heightened vulnerability to crime in the first place.

In short, it's beyond mischief, beyond obnoxious — it's vandalism. A violation. And it's downright mean-spirited.

But after he was caught, Michael Fay and his family have been telling the world that he — not the car owners but HE — is the victim.

Sorry, Michael, you're not the victim. You're the criminal. Caning may well be rough.

But if you do the crime, you've got to pay the price.

Mark Patinkin is a Journal-Bulletin columnist. His column appears in Lifebeat each Tuesday and Thursday, and in the Metro section each Sunday.

KRISTIN TARDIFF, LETTER TO THE EDITOR

To the Editor,

1   I wonder why I continue to read Mark Patinkin's columns. At best they bore me, at worst they anger me. I've thought before of responding to his maudlin whining or self-righteous hypocrisy, but this time I really had to put pen to paper.

2   Mr. Patinkin has chosen this time to attack Michael Fay, the 18-year-old boy who has been accused of spray-painting some cars in Singapore. Mark, jury of one, has decided that Fay is unequivocally guilty, and that his sentence of jail term, fine, and caning is fitting punishment. "Stop whining, take it like a man," he says.

3   I find it interesting that Mr. Patinkin has completely ignored the statements of those who may have a little more experience with the Singaporean police than he does. What about the Navy officer who said that our military police were under order to immediately take into custody any American soldier who was going to be arrested by the Singaporean police to protect them? Did he make that up? What about those who have had the experience of being detained in Singapore and tell of torture and forced confessions? Are they just wimpy bleeding hearts in Mark's eyes?

4   Perhaps as a teenager Mr. Patinkin never made a mistake, never did anything considered wrong in the eyes of the law. Hard to believe, but I'll give him the benefit of the doubt. Had he, however, ever been caught and punished for some infraction, that punishment certainly would not have involved being tied up with his pants around his ankles while someone split his cheeks the opposite way with a water-soaked cane. Nor do I think he would have considered that just. The punishment should fit the crime.

5   Michael Fay is willing to serve his time in jail and make restitution. He has already suffered physically and psychologically, and has, I'm sure, seen the error of his ways. Is this not enough punishment? Have we become so warped by the violence of our society that we now see justice as incomplete without the imposition of physical pain? Do we really want to see the young graffiti artist in our neighborhood caned? (I hear some saying yes, but what if it turns out to be your child? Think about it.) Is this really the way we want society to turn? What comes next? Amputation for thieves and maybe prolonged torture and death for drug dealers? Should we just kill all the "bad" people? Why can't we for once work on the causes instead of lashing out blindly at the symptoms?

6   Just one more thing. Regarding Mr. Patinkin's criticism of Fay's parents' pleas for leniency for their son, as a parent he should have more empathy. What else can parents do when they truly feel that their child is being unjustly treated?

7   I hope Mark's children all turn out as perfect as their dad. Maybe he should send to Singapore for a cane. Just in case.

Kristin Tardiff
Providence

JOHN N. TAYLOR, LETTER TO THE EDITOR

To the Editor,

1   The letters . . . denouncing Mark Patinkin's support for caning Michael Fay ("Patinkin should know better than to advocate caning," 5/3) are no different from any of the other whiny, moralizing claptrap we hear from those mawkish people who fear more for Mr. Fay's buttocks than for those who are victimized everyday by the crimes of young punks like Fay. The arguments . . . are laden with the rancid, canting self-righteousness common to all opposing Fay's caning, and evince concern only for the criminal while telling crime victims to go eat cake.

2   From Ms. Tardiff, we get a lot of sarcasm, a lot of questions, and no answers. If she can't propose any semblance of an idea for controlling crime, then neither she (nor anyone else) has the moral authority to condemn a nation which has come up with its own means of dealing with criminals. . . .

3   Singapore has in recent years carried out canings of 14 of its own citizens who were convicted of offenses similar in nature to those of Mr. Fay. Why should Fay be treated any differently from these people? Just because Fay is an affluent white American with many powerful supporters in America (like President Clinton) doesn't mean he should be above the law of the nation where he resides. To let Fay out of the caning simply because he has the support of powerful leaders is an affront to the people of Singapore, who have abided by the law or taken their lumps for violating same. Clemency for Fay would effectively divide Americans and Singaporeans into separate, unequal classes, whereby the former avoid punishment because of America's political and economic clout while the latter, who do not enjoy such powerful connections, suffer the consequences.

4   The caning of Fay is simply an affirmation of the principle that all people, whether they are wealthy white Americans or poor Chinese Singaporeans, are equal in the eyes of the law. . . . It has much to do with upholding Singaporean mores and nothing to do with Fay being American or U.S. political traditions; these sanctions, as applied to crimes like vandalism and other non-political offenses, are designed to discourage repetition of criminal behavior. And they succeed in this goal. How many drive-by shootings go down in Singapore?

5   Like American authorities, the Singaporeans perceive crimes to be the individual act and choice of the perpetrator.

6   There is no doubt Singapore is a non-democratic nation which punishes even peaceable political dissent, and there is no doubt that Singapore's criminal laws are harsh. But Michael Fay knew what the laws were like and freely assumed the risks of getting punished when he engaged in his spree of vandalism. It is the height of arrogance and folly for Americans living or traveling abroad to expect to be protected by the Bill of Rights when they break other nations' laws.

7   Americans have no right demanding a blanket exemption from foreign laws they violate, or that foreign governments give them easier treatment than they would give their own people under similar circumstances.

8   And if caning is immoral, is not the American criminal justice system itself laden with unfairness? Where is the morality in releasing quadruple murderer Craig Price into the community after only four years? Is it right that in the U.S., a murderer draws an average sentence of only about six years? Is it right that dangerous criminals are dumped onto communities simply because the prisons don't meet the standards of some soft-headed judge? We in America sacrifice the lives of innocent people in the name of criminals' civil rights, and then have the gall to denounce Singapore as harsh and oppressive! If anyone's justice is extremist, it is America's.

9   America's approach to crime is to do nothing and let the community be damned, while Singapore has opted to let the offender be damned. What the Michael Fay fan club here in America conveniently forgets while moaning about Singaporean tyranny is the everyday tyranny of violence and fear imposed on millions of Americans by violent criminals in our inner cities and suburbs. These people are oppressed by a dictatorship of criminals and their rights are violated on a massive scale every day. Yet I see more concern for Michael Fay's rear end than I do for people who bear the scars of bullets and knives of criminals.

10   My heart will not bleed if Fay's rear end does. Given the carnage on America's streets, and in Rwanda, Bosnia and Haiti, the supporters of Michael Fay will just have to excuse me if I fail to shed a tear.

John N. Taylor Jr.
North Providence

Analysis: A Public Forum

Like a lot of newspaper columnists, Mark Patinkin uses short paragraphs, an informal, conversational tone, and a commonsense man-in-the-street approach to his readers. Notice that he speaks to his readers as an equal, not as someone who is more knowledgeable or somehow above them. This approach in effect positions the column as something that readers can and should respond to. The controversial nature of the topic—and of some of Patinkin's comments about the topic—make it all the more likely that readers will respond.

In the letters to the editor, the writers argue a position in response to what they've read. The letters to the editor reveal an intensity of feeling, and at times they resort to logical fallacies and other questionable tactics. These tactics include name-calling: Kristin Tardiff refers to Patinkin's "maudlin whining" and "self-righteous hypocrisy." By the same token, John N. Taylor says Tardiff's letter contains the "whiny, moralizing claptrap" of "mawkish people." The writers use exaggeration: "What comes next? Amputation for thieves and maybe prolonged torture and death for drug dealers?" (Tardiff). They are not always completely accurate: "in the U.S., a murderer draws an average sentence of only about six years" (Taylor). At times, they beg the question instead of explaining the point: "What else can parents do?" (Tardiff) and make questionable comparisons: "If caning is immoral, is not the American justice system laden with unfairness?" (Taylor). The letters are definitely opinionated, and finally that is the point: letters to the editor give people the chance to talk back, to take strong positions, to have their say in a public forum.

■ FOR CRITICAL INQUIRY

1. Reread Tardiff's letter to the editor. What is it about Patinkin's column that seems to call on her to respond? How does she define her own position in relation to what Patinkin has written? To what extent does her letter respond directly to Patinkin's column? To what extent does it introduce other issues?

2. Reread the letter from Taylor. How would you describe his response to the call to write? How does he define his own position in relation to Patinkin and Tardiff?

3. What is this exchange of letters really about? Although the letters are ostensibly about Michael Fay, his punishment doesn't exactly seem to be the main issue. Try to distill the main issues that emerge and explain how the letters relate to these issues and to each other. What is at stake for these writers?

OPEN LETTER

MY DUNGEON SHOOK: LETTER TO MY NEPHEW
JAMES BALDWIN

James Baldwin (1924–1987) was a novelist, playwright, and essayist, whose works include the essays Notes of a Native Son *(1955), the novels* Go Tell It on the Mountain *(1953) and* Another County *(1962), and the play* Blues for Mister Charlie *(1964). This letter from Baldwin to his nephew was published in* The Fire Next Time *(1962).*

Dear James:

1   I have begun this letter five times and torn it up five times. I keep seeing your face, which is also the face of your father and my brother. Like him, you are tough, dark, vulnerable, moody—with a very definite tendency to sound

truculent because you want no one to think you are soft. You may be like your grandfather in this, I don't know, but certainly both you and your father resemble him very much physically. Well, he is dead, he never saw you, and he had a terrible life; he was defeated long before he died because, at the bottom of his heart, he really believed what white people said about him. This is one of the reasons that he became so holy. I am sure that your father has told you something about all that. Neither you nor your father exhibit any tendency towards holiness: you really are of another era, part of what happened when the Negro left the land and came into what the late E. Franklin Frazier called "the cities of destruction." You can only be destroyed by believing that you really are what the white world calls a *nigger*. I tell you this because I love you, and please don't you forget it.

2   I have known both of you all your lives, have carried your Daddy in my arms and on my shoulders, kissed and spanked him and watched him learn to walk. I don't know if you've known anybody from that far back; if you've loved anybody that long, first as an infant, then as a child, then as a man, you gain a strange perspective on time and human pain and effort. Other people cannot see what I see whenever I look into your father's face, for behind your father's face as it is today are all those other faces which were his. Let him laugh and I see a cellar your father does not remember and a house he does not remember and I hear in his present laughter his laughter as a child. Let him curse and I remember him falling down the cellar steps, and howling, and I remember, with pain, his tears, which my hand or your grandmother's so easily wiped away. But no one's hand can wipe away those tears he sheds invisibly today, which one hears in his laughter and in his speech and in his songs. I know what the world has done to my brother and how narrowly he has survived it. And I know, which is much worse, and this is the crime of which I accuse my country and my countrymen, and for which neither I nor time nor history will ever forgive them, that they have destroyed and are destroying hundreds of thousands of lives and do not know it and do not want to know it. One can be, indeed one must strive to become, tough and philosophical concerning destruction and death, for this is what most of mankind has been best at since we have heard of man. (But remember: most of mankind is not all of mankind.) But it is not permissible that the authors of devastation should also be innocent. It is the innocence which constitutes the crime.

3   Now, my dear namesake, these innocent and well-meaning people, your countrymen, have caused you to be born under conditions not very far removed from those described for us by Charles Dickens in the London of more than a hundred years ago. (I hear the chorus of the innocents screaming, "No! This is not true! How *bitter* you are!"—but I am writing this letter to *you*, to try

to tell you something about how to handle *them,* for most of them do not really know that you exist. I *know* the conditions under which you were born, for I was there. Your countrymen were *not* there, and haven't made it yet. Your grandmother was also there, and no one has ever accused her of being bitter. I suggest that the innocents check with her. She isn't hard to find. Your country-men don't know that *she* exists, either, though she has been working for them all their lives.)

4   Well, you were born, here you came, something like fourteen years ago; and though your father and mother and grandmother, looking about the streets through which they were carrying you, staring at the walls into which they brought you, had every reason to be heavy-hearted, yet they were not. For here you were, Big James, named for me—you were a big baby. I was not—here you were: to be loved. To be loved, baby, hard, at once, and forever, to strengthen you against the loveless world. Remember that: I know how black it looks today, for you. It looked bad that day, too, yes, we were trembling. We have not stopped trembling yet, but if we had not loved each other none of us would have survived. And now you must survive because we love you, and for the sake of your children and your children's children.

5   This innocent country set you down in a ghetto in which, in fact, it intended that you should perish. Let me spell out precisely what I mean by that, for the heart of the matter is here, and the root of my dispute with my country. You were born where you were born and faced the future that you faced because you were black and *for no other reason.* The limits of your am-bition were, thus, expected to be set forever. You were born into a society which spelled out with brutal clarity, and in as many ways as possible, that you were a worthless human being. You were not expected to aspire to ex-cellence: you were expected to make peace with mediocrity. Wherever you have turned, James, in your short time on this earth, you have been told where you could go and what you could do (and *how* you could do it) and where you could live and whom you could marry. I know your countrymen do not agree with me about this, and I hear them saying, "You exaggerate." They do not know Harlem, and I do. So do you. Take no one's word for any-thing, including mine—but trust your experience. Know whence you came. If you know whence you came, there is really no limit to where you can go. The details and symbols of your life have been deliberately constructed to make you believe what white people say about you. Please try to remember that what they believe, as well as what they do and cause you to endure, does not testify to your inferiority but to their inhumanity and fear. Please try to be clear, dear James, through the storm which rages about your youth-ful head today, about the reality which lies behind the words *acceptance* and

integration. There is no reason for you to try to become like white people and there is no basis whatever for their impertinent assumption that *they* must accept *you*. The really terrible thing, old buddy, is that *you* must accept *them*. And I mean that very seriously. You must accept them and accept them with love. For these innocent people have no other hope. They are, in effect, still trapped in a history which they do not understand; and until they understand it, they cannot be released from it. They have had to believe for many years, and for innumerable reasons, that black men are inferior to white men. Many of them, indeed, know better, but, as you will discover, people find it very difficult to act on what they know. To act is to be committed, and to be committed is to be in danger. In this case, the danger, in the minds of most white Americans, is the loss of their identity. Try to imagine how you would feel if you woke up one morning to find the sun shining and all the stars aflame. You would be frightened because it is out of the order of nature. Any upheaval in the universe is terrifying because it so profoundly attacks one's sense of one's own reality. Well, the black man has functioned in the white man's world as a fixed star, as an immovable pillar: and as he moves out of his place, heaven and earth are shaken to their foundations. You, don't be afraid. I said that it was intended that you should perish in the ghetto, perish by never being allowed to go behind the white man's definitions, by never being allowed to spell your proper name. You have, and many of us have, defeated this intention; and, by a terrible law, a terrible paradox, those innocents who believed that your imprisonment made them safe are losing their grasp of reality. But these men are your brothers—your lost, younger brothers. And if the word *integration* means anything, that is what it means: that we, with love, shall force our brothers to see themselves as they are, to cease fleeing from reality and begin to change it. For this is your home, my friend, do not be driven from it, great men have done great things here, and will again, and we can make America what America must become. It will be hard, James, but you come from sturdy, peasant stock, men who picked cotton and dammed rivers and built railroads, and, in the teeth of the most terrifying odds, achieved an unassailable and monumental dignity. You come from a long line of great poets, some of the greatest poets since Homer. One of them said, *The very time I thought I was lost, My dungeon shook and my chains fell off.*

6   You know, and I know, that the country is celebrating one hundred years of freedom one hundred years too soon. We cannot be free until they are free. God bless you, James, and Godspeed.

Your Uncle,
James

Analysis: Private and Public Audiences

Of all the genres of writing gathered in this book, letter writing may appear to be the most personal and the most intimate. As James Baldwin writes to his nephew, "I keep seeing your face."

But as the opening lines of Baldwin's letter indicate—"I have begun this letter five times and torn it up five times"—writing on such intimate terms can bring with it certain complications, especially in this case, because Baldwin actually has two audiences, his nephew and a public audience of readers.

On the one hand, Baldwin represents himself as a concerned and loving uncle writing a letter of advice to his namesake nephew, thereby invoking the sacred institution of the family as the ground to speak. On the other hand, the advice he offers his nephew—to accept white people without accepting their definitions of him—is meant to be overheard by Baldwin's other audience.

When Baldwin explains to his nephew that white people are trapped in a history of race relations they don't understand and can't escape, he is also explaining to his white readers how their own identities have been based on a belief in the inferiority of African Americans. By using the form of a letter of advice from one family member to another, Baldwin is simultaneously offering his white readers a way to reposition themselves in relation to their own history and identities.

■ FOR CRITICAL INQUIRY

1. Where in the letter does Baldwin first indicate his main point and reason for writing to his nephew? Mark this passage and explain why you think he locates his main point here. How does this passage connect what comes before and what follows?

2. A good deal of the long fifth paragraph involves Baldwin's admonition to his nephew "to be clear . . . about the reality that lies behind the words *acceptance* and *integration.*" What is the reality Baldwin alludes to here? What does he see as the relation between "acceptance" and "integration"? What assumptions have led him to this view?

3. Baldwin wrote a number of essays concerning race relations in the United States. In this instance, however, he has chosen the more personal form of a family letter addressed directly to his nephew but published for all to read. How does this traditional letter of advice from an older family member to a younger one influence the way you read the letter? What advantages do you see in Baldwin's strategy of addressing his nephew instead of the more anonymous audience of people who read *The Fire Next Time,* in which "My Dungeon Shook: Letter to My Nephew" appeared? Are there things Baldwin can say to his nephew that he can't say directly to this audience?

WRITING IN A DIGITAL WORLD

Text Messages

THE PLEASURES OF THE TEXT

CHARLES McGRATH

Charles McGrath is a writer at large for the New York Times, *where this brief article appeared in* "The Way We Live Now" *section of the* New York Times Magazine *January 22, 2006.*

There used to be an ad on subway cars, next to the ones for bail bondsmen and hemorrhoid creams, that said: "if u cn rd ths u cn gt a gd job & mo pa." The ad was promoting a kind of stenography training that is now extinct, presumably. Who uses stenographers anymore? But the notion that there might be value in easily understood shorthand has proved to be prescient. If u cn rd these days, and, just as important, if your thumbs are nimble enough so that u cn als snd, you can conduct your entire emotional life just by transmitting and receiving messages on the screen of your cellphone. You can flirt there, arrange a date, break up and—in Malaysia at least—even get a divorce.

A WORLD OF TEXT

Text messages sent, by country, in the third quarter of 2005.

- China — 76.4 billion
- Philippines — 21.4 billion
- United States* — 19.4 billion
- United Kingdom — 8.1 billion

*The figure for the United States is based on the four major carriers (Cingular, Verizon, Sprint Nextel and T-Mobile).

Source: Informa Telecoms & Media

Shorthand contractions, along with letter-number homophones ("gr8" and "2moro," for example), emoticons (like the tiresome colon-and-parenthesis smiley face) and acronyms (like the ubiquitous "lol," for "laughing out loud"), constitute the language of text-messaging—or txt msg, to use the term that txt msgrs prefer. Text-messaging is a refinement of computer instant-messaging, which came into vogue five or six years ago. But because the typical cellphone screen can accommodate no more than 160 characters, and because the phone touchpad is far less versatile than the computer keyboard, text-messaging puts an even greater premium on concision. Here, for example, is a text-message version of "Paradise Lost" disseminated by some scholars in England: "Devl kikd outa hevn coz jelus of jesus&strts war. pd'off wiv god so corupts man (md by god) wiv apel. devl stays serpnt 4hole life&man ruind. Woe un2mnkind."

As such messages go, that one is fairly straightforward and unadorned. There is also an entire code book of acronyms and abbreviations, ranging from CWOT (complete waste of time) to DLTBBB (don't let the bedbugs bite). And emoticonography has progressed way beyond the smiley-face stage, and now includes hieroglyphics to indicate drooling, for example (:-) . . .), as well as secrecy (:X), Hitler (/.#() and the rose (@};–). Keep these in mind; we'll need them later.

As with any language, efficiency isn't everything. There's also the issue of style. Among inventive users, and younger ones especially, text-messaging has taken on many of the characteristics of hip-hop, with so much of which it conveniently overlaps—in the substitution of "z" for "s," for example,

"a," for "er" and "d" for "th." Like hip-hop, text-messaging is what the scholars call "performative"; it's writing that aspires to the condition of speech. And sometimes when it makes abundant use of emoticons, it strives not for clarity so much as a kind of rebus-like cleverness, in which showing off is part of the point. A text-message version of "Paradise Lost"—or of the prologue, anyway—that tries for a little more shnizzle might go like this: "Sing hvnly mewz dat on d :X mtntp inspyrd dat shephrd hu 1st tot d chozn seed in d begnin hw d hvn n erth @};– outa chaos."

Not that there is much call for Miltonic messaging these days. To use the scholarly jargon again, text-messaging is "lateral" rather than "penetrative," and the medium encourages blandness and even mindlessness. On the Internet there are several Web sites that function as virtual Hallmark stores and offer ready-made text messages of breathtaking banality. There are even ready-made Dear John letters, enabling you to dump someone without actually speaking to him or her. Far from being considered rude, in Britain this has proved to be a particularly popular way of ending a relationship—a little more thoughtful than leaving an e-mail message but not nearly as messy as breaking up in person—and it's also catching on over here.

Compared with the rest of the world, Americans are actually laggards when it comes to text-messaging. This is partly for technical reasons. Because we don't have a single, national phone company, there are several competing and incompatible wireless technologies in use, and at the same time actual voice calls are far cheaper here than in most places, so there is less incentive for texting. But in many developing countries, mobile-phone technology has so far outstripped land-line availability that cellphones are the preferred, and sometimes the only, means of communication, and text messages are cheaper than voice ones. The most avid text-messagers are clustered in Southeast Asia, particularly in Singapore and the Philippines.

There are also cultural reasons for the spread of text-messaging elsewhere. The Chinese language is particularly well-suited to the telephone keypad, because in Mandarin the names of the numbers are also close to the sounds of certain words: to say "I love you," for example, all you have to do is press 520. (For "drop dead," it's 748.) In China, moreover, many people believe that to leave voice mail is rude, and it's a loss of face to make a call to someone important and have it answered by an underling. Text messages preserve everyone's dignity by eliminating the human voice.

This may be the universal attraction of text-messaging, in fact: it's a kind of avoidance mechanism that preserves the feeling of communication—the immediacy—without, for the most part, the burden of actual intimacy or substance. The great majority of text messages are of the "Hey, how are you, whassup?" variety, and they're sent sometimes when the messenger and the recipient are within speaking distance of each other—across classrooms, say, or from one row of a stadium to another. They're little electronic waves and nods that, just like real waves and nods, aren't meant to do much more than establish a connection—or a disconnection, as the case may be—without getting into specifics.

"We're all wired together" is the collective message, and we'll signal again in a couple of minutes, not to say anything, probably, but just to make sure the lines are still working. The most depressing thing about the communications revolution is that when at last we have succeeded in making it possible for anyone to reach anyone else anywhere and at any time, it turns out that we really don't have much we want to say.

Analysis: txt msg

Many commentators have noted that instant messages and text messages are examples of how new communication media have blurred the line between speaking and writing that seemed so set in print culture. Writing takes on some of the aspects of speech. Instant messaging, for example, enables the immediacy of spoken conversation, while text messages are a form of writing that goes through the telephone—and in many parts of the world provides a cheaper alternative to the phone call.

Though these forms of communication resemble speech in some ways, they have also developed new visual codes for writing that are maximally compact, inventive, and playful. What may be most significant about text messages is how they have reconfigured the available modes of communication—speaking, writing, and visual communication.

■ **FOR CRITICAL INQUIRY**

1. Consider the relations among speaking, writing, and visual communication in instant messages and text messages. How are the new forms like or unlike older ways of communicating? How do they resemble letters? How are they different? How do they put the modes of communication together in new ways?

2. If you have access to instant messaging sessions, analyze an exchange or two. What questions would you use to examine the language and the interactions that take place?

3. Charles McGrath ends his article on a rather dismissive note, saying that the attraction of text messaging is that it's an "avoidance mechanism." For him, the "most depressing thing about the communication revolution" is that people have very little to say. What enabling assumptions might lead to such claims? Are there other ways you can think of to evaluate the use of text messaging?

VISUAL DESIGN

Letters of Appeal

LETTER OF APPEAL

DOCTORS WITHOUT BORDERS/MÉDECINS SANS FRONTIÈRES (MSF)

Doctors Without Borders/Médecins Sans Frontières (MSF) delivers emergency medical care to people in crisis in nearly 80 countries worldwide. An independent, international humanitarian organization, MSF was awarded the Nobel Peace Prize in 1999.

Analysis: The Visual Design of Letters of Appeal

This letter from Doctors Without Borders, along with an enclosed report on epidemics in Indonesia, Somalia, and Sudan, is typical of the letters of appeal that humanitarian and advocacy groups rely on to bring their work to public attention. The letter includes such standard features as the organization name and logo on the letterhead, a salutation (the familiar "Dear Friend"), a signature, and a P.S. Notice also how selective underlining adds a sense of urgency to the letter. The accompanying report is a brochure that describes mass vaccination campaigns and emergency responses to epidemic outbreaks by Doctors Without Borders. Included here is one of the six pages, with information on yellow fever in Sudan.

■ **FOR CRITICAL INQUIRY**

1. Logos are symbols that identify organizations. Think, for example, of the Nike swoosh or the CBS eye. What does the Doctors Without Borders logo seem to represent? What does it suggest about the organization? Consider, too, how the logo is used.

MÉDECINS SANS FRONTIERES
DOCTORS WITHOUT BORDERS

Awarded the 1999
Nobel Peace Prize

333 Seventh Avenue, 2nd Floor
New York, NY 10001

Tel: (212) 679-6800
Fax: (212) 679-7016

Web: www.doctorswithoutborders.org

Dear Friend,

Doctors Without Borders/Médecins Sans Frontières (MSF) is working to halt the spread of epidemics in many areas vulnerable to outbreaks.

Speed, experience, and breadth of response are critical in the race to reach those who need to be immunized or require medical attention. The presence of our teams in many of the areas most susceptible to outbreaks means we are able to respond at the first sign of an approaching crisis, and carry out prevention and treatment necessary to save lives.

Our pre-assembled disaster relief kits enable us to get medicines, vaccines, cold chain (the transport system for delivering temperature-sensitive vaccines into remote areas) materials, and other supplies to affected areas quickly. Certain epidemic diseases such as cholera are worsened by contaminated water and unsanitary living conditions, so Doctors Without Borders logistical volunteers complement the response with a focus on sanitation facilities and clean water.

Doctors Without Borders doctors and nurses treat infected patients and perform vaccination campaigns that can require fanning out to remote regions with small teams and mobile clinics. In a yellow fever epidemic, for example, containment is as important as treatment since 20 percent of the infected patients do not survive. So in the current yellow fever epidemic in Sudan, our medical teams set out urgently to vaccinate hundreds of thousands of people in only a few weeks. (See the enclosed report.)

Thanks to our quick response and experience, we are saving thousands of lives. Thanks to the generosity of supporters like you, we have the logistical capacity, advance preparedness, and medical protocols to respond to these urgent outbreaks. Yet, we are responding to many epidemics and threats at the same time, so your continued support is very important. Please help us today. Thank you.

Sincerely,

Nicolas de Torrenté
Executive Director

P.S. The enclosed report highlights four current outbreaks of Cholera, Kala Azar, Measles, and Yellow Fever where our medical and logistical teams are racing against time to save lives. Please help us and be as generous as you can.

Printed on Recycled Paper
R62A-1

2. Notice that the actual appeal for contributions appears at the bottom of the letter. Why do you think it is located there? Explain how the writing that precedes it sets up the appeal.

3. What sort of relationship does this letter want to establish with readers? What assumptions about intended readers does the letter seem to make?

4. How does the enclosed report support the letter's appeal?

YELLOW FEVER IN SUDAN

DECEMBER 2005: To halt a yellow fever epidemic in central Sudan's Kordofan province, a region of 1.7 million people, Doctors Without Borders medical teams, working with health officials, led a mass vaccination campaign in Abu Gebeiha and Rashad, two of the province's large towns. **The Doctors Without Borders team in Kordofan overcame a very large challenge: the need to vaccinate 200,000 people against yellow fever in two weeks, working in a desert region, using vaccines that must be maintained at between 35 and 46 degrees Fahrenheit.**

"Organizing such a large-scale campaign in a very short time is a real challenge," says Coralie Léchelle of the Doctors Without Borders emergency department, who returned from Kordofan. "The major difficulty was organizing the cold chain so that we could transport and maintain the effectiveness of the vaccine doses." Fleury Girard, a Doctors Without Borders logistician, added, **"That means 1,300 pounds of ice has to be produced, packaged, and transported every day!"**

Because there is no specific treatment for yellow fever, a highly contagious viral illness, treating symptoms is the only option. Even those whose symptoms are treated remain in grave danger as nearly 25 percent die. To prevent the disease from spreading, the vaccination campaign targeted practically everyone: adults as well as children over nine months old. The vaccine provides immunity for 10 years.

Organizing the vaccination teams is also critical. "For the city of Abu Gebeiha, with a population of 40,000, and for the surrounding towns, we set up three two-person teams composed of a logistician and a nurse," Girard said. "Each pair supervised four vaccination teams."

"During the first few days, each vaccinator immunized 1,200 people per day," Girard said. The teams also treated people already infected with yellow fever. In all, nearly 200,000 people were vaccinated in fewer than two weeks.

> The vaccine for yellow fever must be kept between 35 and 46 degrees Fahrenheit at all times to maintain its effectiveness. This is a real challenge to medical teams traveling across desert regions where temperatures routinely exceed 90 degrees. Doctors Without Borders designed an intricately planned "cold chain" of refrigerated storage and transportation that keeps all vaccines at a precise temperature from the factory to the field.

ETHICS OF WRITING

USING THE INTERNET

One of the most exciting aspects of the Internet is its capacity to open up new public forums for the exchange of ideas. A posting from an individual to a mailing list or message board can connect him or her to people all over the world with an immediacy that promotes rapid feedback and response. But precisely because email offers such exciting possibilities for transmitting information and ideas, it is important to use it properly—to understand what can be sent to whom under what conditions.

❑ **Author's permission:** Communicating on the Internet requires the same attention to copyright and intellectual property as print communication. In other words, you need to cite your sources, and if you want to forward a message written by someone else, you need to secure permission first.

❑ **Reader's permission:** Don't just assume that people will want to be added to a regular mailing list or newsgroup. You need to secure people's permission before adding their names. Readers are likely to resent unsolicited email and feel imposed upon. Be careful not to flood cyberspace with junk email. ■

FURTHER EXPLORATION: LETTERS

■ GENRE CHOICES

Like letters, email, chat rooms, newsgroups, and listservs are forms of correspondence that enable writers to stay in touch and exchange views. Despite this similarity, there are also significant differences between letters and these new electronic genres. Draw on your own experience to examine the similarities and differences between print letters and electronic correspondence. Take into account the occasions when it makes sense to use one or the other. When, for example, is it better to write a letter than email? Or, given something urgent to say, when would you write a letter to the editor, to a politician, or to an organization, and when would you post your views online?

■ WORKING TOGETHER

Designing a Letter of Appeal

Design a letter of appeal. As a group, you will need first to identify an issue, a cause, or an organization you want your readers to support. Then you need to decide exactly what you will ask your readers to do. If you wish, you can design a two-sided letter, using the Doctors Without Borders letter as a model. Here are some possibilities:

■ You could write a fund-raising letter for a worthy organization or a particular cause (such as a fund for victims of a recent flood, hurricane, or earthquake).

■ You could call on your readers to write to government, business, or education officials, asking them to change a policy or implement a new one, to release a prisoner who has been unjustly jailed (as appeals from Amnesty International do), or to support or oppose impending legislation.

- You could call on readers to donate their time to a project worth supporting (such as mentoring at-risk teenagers, volunteering in a soup kitchen or food pantry, or attending a demonstration or rally).

Once you have determined the purpose of your letter, consider to whom you will send the letter. Who is most likely to respond to your appeal? Based on your sense of who your readers will be, consider what arguments are most likely to persuade them to take the action you call for. What information will prove persuasive? What appeals to shared values? Use this information to design the letter of appeal. Part of the letter's persuasiveness, of course, will depend on its design. How do you want the letter to look? What features of document design will make it more likely that the letter will get a sympathetic reading?

WRITING ASSIGNMENT

Composing a Letter

Online Study Center

For this writing assignment, compose a letter. In the pages that follow, you will find exercises and ideas for deciding the kind of letter you'll write, what the letter will be about, to whom you will send it, and how your letter should be presented. There are many possibilities. You can write to someone you know, to the editor of a newspaper, to a politician, to a college official, or to a local community group concerning an issue of public concern. Here are some other letters you might find yourself called to write:

- An open letter to a public official, organization, or company arguing for policy change.

- A letter to your parents or to a friend explaining the impact of a public event on you personally, how you make sense of it, and, if appropriate, what you have done or plan to do.

- A letter to the editor of a newspaper or magazine responding to a news story, feature article, editorial, or column that particularly moved you. Or you might raise an issue that's important to you but hasn't yet appeared in the press.

- A letter to a younger relative or student. You might use James Baldwin's letter to his nephew as a model here. That is, speak directly to the younger person but include a public audience as your intended readers. You might explain what it takes to survive in college or how to handle particular kinds of peer-group pressures such as drinking, drugs, and sex. Or you might explain what it's like to be a scholarship athlete, a woman, an African American, a gay or lesbian, a Latino, or a working-class student in a middle-class college.

- A letter of appeal, calling on readers to support a cause, take an action, or make a contribution. You can identify an organization or cause that you believe deserves support, and design a letter that presents the aims and activities of the organization and that calls on readers to do something—to become a member, to send a donation, to write a letter. You may want to design this letter of appeal for the Internet.

- A posting to an electronic discussion group.

Alternative Assignments

Online Study Center

■ RHETORICAL ANALYSIS

Analyze the writer's argument in one of the letters included in this chapter. Pay particular attention to how the writer establishes a rhetorical stance that combines the persuasive appeals of ethos, pathos, and logos. See guidelines and a sample rhetorical analysis of an argument in Chapter 3.

■ WORKING WITH SOURCES

Use Mark Patinkin's "Commit a Crime, Suffer the Consequences" and the Letters to the Editor as a model to assemble your own sources to write a letter to the editor (as Michael Brody has done in Writer's Workshop). Look at the letters to the editor section in newspapers and magazines for an issue that interests you. Then find the article, editorial, or op-ed commentary that prompted the letters to the editor. Write your own letter that responds to both the article and the letters.

Invention

Identifying the Call to Write

The first thing you need to do is identify something that moves you to write. Obviously, one thing that is calling on you to write is that you've just been given a writing assignment in a composition course. But to write a letter that you can be proud of, you'll need to find your own reasons and your own motivation to write. Make this assignment work for you.

- Has a particular subject been making you curious or angry?
- Are you learning something in one of your courses that you want to tell someone about?
- Have you recently read something in a newspaper or magazine that you'd like to respond to?
- Is there a public issue in your community, on campus, at home, or on the national or international scene that has captured your interest?
- Throughout this chapter there have been examples of different kinds of letters people have written. As you can see, there is a broad range of types of letters. Is there a subgenre of letters that you would like to try writing? Do any of those subgenres make you think of something you have been meaning to do? If so, you can choose to do it now.

■ **EXERCISE**

Writing a Statement of Purpose

Write a statement of purpose, using these questions to guide you:

1. To whom are you writing?
2. What calls on you to write?
3. What are you going to say?
4. What do you want to accomplish in your letter?
5. How do you want your reader to respond?

Understanding Your Readers

How successful you will be in eliciting the response you want from your readers depends in part on how well you understand them and your relationship to them. If you are appealing for something—whether it's money from your parents or donations to a cause you believe in—you need to figure out what might persuade your readers. If you want to irritate them or get under their skin, you need to know what buttons to push. To influence a politician, you need to know his or her interests and how you can tap into them.

To gather ideas about how you can most effectively address your reader, respond to these questions:

1. On what terms do you know your reader: family, personal, institutional? Describe your relationship to the person. Is it formal or informal? How does this relationship affect what you can and cannot say in your letter? If you are writing online, how does the electronic forum of the Internet affect your relationship to your reader?
2. What is an effective way to present yourself to your reader? What will it take to establish the credibility and authority of what you have to say? What kind of personality or attitude is your reader likely to respond to?
3. What attitude is your reader likely to have toward your letter? What is your reader's interest in what you have to say? Will your reader care personally or read your letter as part of work?
4. What is your reader likely to know about the message you are sending? How much shared information is involved? How much do you need to explain?
5. What values and beliefs do you think your reader might hold about the subject of your letter? What common ground can you establish? What shared values can you appeal to?

Background Research: Finding Models

To determine how to communicate with your readers, find some models of the type of letter you want to write.

1. How long do these types of letters tend to be?

2. How do readers address one another? Do they use first names only, last names only, or some other way?

3. Do paragraphs tend to be short or long? Or do they vary greatly?

4. What level of formality do these writers tend to use?

5. If the writers are giving someone else credit for a quote or an idea, how do they handle the citation (if there is one)?

Planning

Establishing the Occasion

Letters often begin by establishing their timeliness: why they're written at that moment, in response to what call to write, to what person or people, on the basis of what relationship. Notice the ways in which writers establish the occasion in the reading selections:

- Explaining the writers' professional credentials ("Meth Science Not Stigma")

- Establishing authority to speak and familiarity with the topic (Kristin Tardiff, regular reader of Mark Patinkin's column)

- Characterizing an opponent's position, expressing sense of outrage (John N. Taylor, "whiny, moralizing claptrap")

- Invoking family ties as the right to speak (James Baldwin)

The need to establish the occasion of a letter—the grounds for writing it in the first place—is also true of business letters, job application letters ("I am interested in applying for the position you have advertised . . ."), letters to politicians and public officials ("I write to urge you to . . ."), letters of sympathy and condolence ("I know this is a difficult time, and I wanted you to know . . ."), letters of congratulations ("Congratulations, you really deserve . . ."), and letters of gratitude ("Thanks for the birthday present . . ."). In some instances, writers will make explicit their relationship to the reader—as in letters to politicians ("I have been a registered Democrat in the Third Ward for thirty years, and like my neighbors I am concerned about . . .") or letters of complaint ("I bought one of your products and . . ."). In letters where the reader knows you personally, relationships are often implied rather than stated.

In your letter, you need to design an opening that treats the occasion of the letter and your relationship to the reader. How explicitly you do this will depend on what your reader needs to hear. Politicians, businesspeople, government officials, and newspaper editors all appreciate letters that get right to the point. In letters home and other personal letters, staying in touch (as much as or more than the letter's content) may be the main point of writing.

Arranging Your Material

List the points you want to make and the information you want to include in your letter. Arrange the material in an outline that consists of three sections:

1. **Opening:** To establish occasion, relationship, and the point of the letter.
2. **Main body:** To explain and develop the point of the letter, whether that means concentrating on one main topic or including a number of separate topics.
3. **Closing:** To reiterate the main point of the letter, whether that involves calling for action, firing a final salvo, reaffirming your relationship to the reader, sending regards, or thanking the reader for his or her time.

Working Draft

Once you have a list of the main points you want to make, the next step is to write a working draft. As you write, new ideas may occur to you. That's only natural. Don't censor them by trying rigidly to follow your list of points. Instead, try to incorporate new points by connecting them to the ones you have already listed. If you can connect them, the new points probably belong in the letter. If you can't, then you'll need to think carefully about whether they really fit your letter. As you write your working draft, keep in mind the overall movement you want in your letter—from an opening that sets the occasion, to a main body that explains your key points, to a closing that wraps things up for the reader.

Beginnings and Endings: Using an Echo Effect

One effective way to begin and end your letter may be to use an echo effect by looping back in the ending to issues raised in your opening. This echo effect can provide a satisfying sense of closure because it reminds readers of the major themes you introduced earlier.

Nicolas de Torrente uses an echo effect in his letter on behalf of Doctors Without Borders. In the opening paragraph, he describes the situation in Afghanistan:

> All across Afghanistan, people are picking up the pieces of their shattered lives. Whether they are returning to looted homes and bombed-out villages, crowding into camps for displaced people, or searching in the countryside for family and loved ones, the situation remains dire.

Then, after detailing the work of Doctors Without Borders, de Torrente returns to the overall situation, describing how "the survival needs of hundreds of thousands of Afghans remain in the balance." This echo effect gives the ending a sense of urgency to "act immediately to avert a major health crisis."

You may want to try this echo effect in your own writing. Take a look at your opening and see if you find a theme that you would like to have recur in your closing. Or think about adding a theme to your introduction that you will return to at the end of your letter.

Using Topic Sentences

Topic sentences help to guide readers by establishing a paragraph's focus and by explaining how the paragraph is linked to earlier ones. The most common type of topic sentence appears at the beginning of a paragraph and thereby enables readers to anticipate what is to come in the rest of the paragraph. When writers stick to the topic they've announced in the opening topic sentence, paragraphs are easier to follow. They unify the letter, since they don't digress or run off the point. Notice how Mark Patinkin uses a topic sentence in the following paragraph from his column about the Michael Fay caning. The first sentence (which we have italicized in the example) establishes the focus of the paragraph; then the rest of the sentences explain it more fully:

> *All of this is just part of the new American game of always saying, "It's not my fault."* No one, when caught, seems ready to admit having done anything wrong anymore. They just whine and appeal. As in: "Your honor, the stabbing was not my client's fault. He had a bad childhood. And was caught up in a riot at the time. In fact, he's not a criminal at all, he's one of society's victims."

Topic sentences also link paragraphs together. To keep readers oriented to the train of thought as it moves from paragraph to paragraph, writers often show how a particular paragraph's focus is linked to the paragraphs that precede and follow.

Sometimes topic sentences appear at the end of a paragraph instead of the beginning. Building toward the topic sentence can give a paragraph a powerful dramatic structure. James Baldwin uses this type of dramatic structure in the second paragraph of his letter by moving from the personal toward a general point about the "crime of which I accuse my country and my countrymen":

> I have known both of you all your lives, . . . I know what the world has done to my brother and how narrowly he has survived it. And . . . this is the crime of which I accuse my country and my countrymen, and for which neither I nor time nor history will ever forgive them, that they have destroyed and are destroying hundreds of thousands of lives and do not know it and do not want to know it. One can be, indeed one must strive to become, tough and philosophical concerning destruction and death, for this is what most of mankind has been best at since we have heard about man. (But remember: most of mankind is not all of mankind.) But it is not permissible that the authors of devastation should also be innocent. *It is the innocence which constitutes the crime.*

By the end of this paragraph, Baldwin has worked his way from a loving tribute about his brother to a painful critique of society's destruction. The topic sentence at the end of the paragraph (which we have italicized here for emphasis) sets Baldwin up to make a transition that links his "countrymen's" crime of innocence to the next paragraph:

> Now, my dear namesake, these innocent and well-meaning people, your countrymen, have caused you to be born under conditions not very far removed from those described for us by Charles Dickens in the London of more than a hundred years ago.

Peer Commentary

Exchange working drafts with a classmate. Depending on your teacher's direction, you can do this peer commentary electronically via email or a class listserv. In classes without computer access, you will probably want to write your comments either on your classmate's paper itself or on a separate sheet of paper. Comment on your partner's draft by responding to these questions:

1. Whom is the writer addressing? What is the occasion of the letter? Where in the letter did you become aware of the writer's purpose? Be specific— is there a particular phrase, sentence, or passage that alerted you to the writer's purpose? If not, where would you like this information to be?

2. What kind of relationship does the writer seem to want to establish with the reader? How does the writer seem to want the reader to respond? How can you tell? Are there places where you think the writer should make the relationship or the desired response more explicit?

3. Does the writer address the reader in a way that makes a positive response likely or possible? Explain your answer. What could the writer do to improve the chances of making the impression he or she wants?

4. Describe the tone of the letter. What kind of personality seems to come through in the letter? What identity does the writer take on in the letter? Do you think the intended reader will respond well to it? If not, what might the writer change?

Revising

Review the peer commentary you received about your letter. Based on the response to your working draft, consider the following points to plan a revision:

1. Have you clearly defined the occasion and your purpose?

2. Does the letter establish the kind of relationship with your reader that you want?

3. Do you think your reader will respond well to the way you present yourself?

4. Do you think you accomplished your purpose with your letter?

Once you are satisfied with the overall appeal of your letter, you can fine-tune your writing. You might look, for example, at your topic sentences to see if they establish focus and help the reader see how ideas are linked in your letter.

Strengthening Topic Sentences for Focus and Transition

The following two paragraph excerpts show how one student, Michael Brody, worked on his letter to the editor (the final version appears below in Writers' Workshop). Notice how he clarifies the focus of the third paragraph by rewriting the topic sentence so that it emphasizes what "readers need to understand" about the Singapore government's use of the Michael Fay case. Clarifying the focus in paragraph 3's topic sentence also strengthens the transition between paragraphs and makes it easier for readers to see how the ideas in the two paragraphs are linked.

2   . . . As readers point out, the crime rate in Singapore is low, the streets are safe, and there are no drive-by shootings. While this picture of Singapore may appear to be reassuring to some readers, it hides the fact that beneath a polished, secure, and business-like facade Singapore is ruled by a brutal dictatorship that keeps its people in fear by punishing not only vandalism and spraypainting but chewing gum as antisocial crimes.

3   . . . *Readers need to understand how the Michael Fay case is being used by the Singapore government as a lesson to its own people about the decadence of American ways* Michael Fay's actions were [admittedly immature and illegal], calling for some official response. But this should not blind us to the problems in Singapore and how the government is using the Michael Fay case. The leaders of Singapore are portraying Michael Fay as a living illustration of all that's flawed about American values of freedom and individual rights, *and his admittedly immature and illegal actions are held up as a direct consequence of the American way of life.* Mark Patinkin and his supporters have failed to see . . .

WRITERS' WORKSHOP

Michael Brody wrote the following letter to the editor in a first-year writing class after he read Mark Patinkin's column "Commit a Crime, Suffer the Consequences," which appeared in the *Providence Journal-Bulletin* on April 19, 1994 (he then followed with two more letters to the editor on May 3 and May 9, 1994). As you will see, entering the caning debate at this point enables Brody to summarize positions people have already taken as a way to set up his own main point. The letter to the editor is followed by a commentary Brody wrote to explain his approach to the issue.

MICHAEL BRODY, LETTER TO THE EDITOR

To the Editor:

Mark Patinkin's column "Commit a crime, suffer the consequences" (4/19) has generated heated responses from readers and understandably so. For some, the sentence of six strokes of the cane, at least by American standards, does indeed seem to be "cruel and unusual punishment," no matter what Patinkin writes about Michael Fay's "whining." On the other hand, Patinkin and those readers who side with him are right that Michael Fay is the criminal in this case, not the victim, and that he deserves to suffer the consequences of his actions.

I happen to agree with readers who argue for leniency. Let Michael Fay pay for his crime by fines and a jail sentence. It worries me that some readers are willing to tolerate or even endorse caning. Obviously, these sentiments show how fed up Americans are with the problem of crime in our society. But there is a tendency in some of the pro-Patinkin letters to idealize Singapore's strong measures as a successful get-tough solution to crime. As readers point out, the crime rate in Singapore is low, the streets are safe, and there are no drive-by shootings. While this picture of Singapore may appear to be reassuring to some readers, it hides the fact that beneath a polished, secure, and business-like facade Singapore is ruled by a brutal dictatorship that keeps its people in fear by punishing not only vandalism and spraypainting but chewing gum as antisocial crimes.

Readers need to understand how the Michael Fay case is being used by the Singapore government as a lesson to its own people about the decadence of American ways. The leaders of Singapore are portraying Michael Fay as a living illustration of all that's flawed about American values of freedom and individual rights, and his admittedly immature and illegal actions are held up as direct consequences of the American way of life. Mark Patinkin and his supporters have failed to see how the Michael Fay incident is more than a matter of whether America, unlike Singapore, is soft on crime, coddles law breakers, and ignores the true victims. For the Singapore government, the caning of Michael Fay is a stern warning to the people of Singapore against the dangers of American democracy.

What is ironic about this attempt to use Michael Fay for anti-American purposes is the fact that caning is itself not a traditional Singapore means of punishment. It's tempting to think of caning as the barbaric practice of cruel Asian despots, but in reality Singapore learned about caning from the British colonial powers who once ruled the country. The British Empire, as I'm sure Mark Patinkin is well aware, took a tough stand on law and order in the colonies and routinely crushed native movements for freedom and independence. I wish Mark Patinkin and others who are properly concerned about crime would consider the lessons Singapore leaders learned from their former masters about how to control and intimidate those they rule. Caning is not a matter of different national customs, as some people make it out to be. Nor is it an extreme but understandable response to crime in the streets. In Singapore, caning is part of both a repressive judicial system and a calculated propaganda campaign to discredit democratic countries and silence dissent.

Michael Brody
Worcester, MA

MICHAEL BRODY'S COMMENTARY

When I read Mark Patinkin's column, I got angry and wanted to denounce him as a fascist. Then I read the letters readers had written opposing or supporting Patinkin's point of view, and they made me realize that I didn't want to follow them because they all seemed to be too emotional, just gut responses. I wanted to find a different approach to the whole caning incident so that I could raise an issue that was different or had been overlooked.

Now I must admit that when I first heard about the sentence of caning, I thought it was barbaric, probably something typical of Asian dictatorships. I thought of the massacre at Tiananmen Square, and I dimly recalled what I had heard when I was young about how the Chinese Communists tortured Catholic missionaries, stuff like bamboo slivers under the fingernails. Then I read somewhere that caning was brought to Singapore by the British in colonial days, and I started to think along new lines. It occurred to me that maybe the caning wasn't just about crime but had something to do with how governments ruled their people.

As I read more in the newspapers, *Time,* and *Newsweek* about the incident, I was shocked to discover how Michael Fay was being used by Singapore leaders to build up anti-American sentiment, to paint America as a permissive society that coddled its criminals. I decided that I'd try to write something that looked at how the case was being used by Singapore's rulers. The more I thought about it, this seemed to give me an angle to go beyond agreeing or disagreeing with Patinkin's column and still have something interesting to say.

When I was getting ready to write, I made a quick outline of my points. I wanted to sound reasonable so I decided to concede that both sides, for or against caning, had some valid points. I decided to show this in my opening and wait until the second paragraph to indicate where I was coming from. I wanted to create the effect that there's this debate going on, which I figured readers would know about and already have their own opinions about, but that I had an angle people maybe hadn't thought about. So I tried to get this point to emerge in the second paragraph and then drive it home at the beginning of the third paragraph with the sentence that starts "Readers need to understand . . . "

That sentence set me up to give my own analysis of the incident and of how Patinkin and the pro-caning people failed to see the full political picture. I decided to leave the idea that caning came from British colonial powers until the end as my clincher. I figured this would do two things. First, it would surprise people, who like me thought caning was a barbaric Asian punishment. Second, it would have an emotional charge because I assumed most people would be against colonialism, especially British colonialism, given that America had to fight England for our independence. Besides I'm Irish, and I know a lot of people where I live are against the British in Ireland, and I knew they'd be against anything associated with the British empire.

I'm not totally sure the irony I talk about in the opening line of the last paragraph works. I remember learning about irony in English class in high school, and how funny or odd it is when things don't turn out the way you expected. So I wanted to throw that in, to make readers feel, well I thought it was one way but when you look at it again, it's another way. I thought this might work in the very end to show that caning is not just this (a barbaric national custom) or that (an extreme form of punishment) but also a form of political intimidation.

■ WORKSHOP QUESTIONS

1. When you first read Michael Brody's letter to the editor, at what point did you become aware of his perspective on the caning debate? Is it just a matter of being for or against caning? Note the sentence or passage that enabled you to see where Brody is coming from.

2. Brody devotes considerable space in the first two paragraphs to presenting positions people have already taken on the caning debate. What

kind of relationship does he seem to want to establish with his readers by doing so?

3. Describe the tone Brody uses in the letter. How does it compare to the tone in Mark Patinkin's column and in the letters to the editor from Kristin Tardiff and John N. Taylor? Do you think Brody's tone works well? Explain your response.

4. Reread Brody's commentary. If you could talk to him, how would you respond to what he says about composing his letter? ■

REFLECTING ON YOUR WRITING

Use the commentary Michael Brody wrote as a model for writing your own account of how you planned and composed the letter you wrote. Explain how you defined the call to write and how you positioned yourself in relation to your readers, your topic, and what others had already said about your topic (if that applies to your letter). Notice that Brody explains how he developed his own position by considering what others had said and reading newspapers and magazines on the Michael Fay incident. Explain, as Brody does, in a step-by-step way how you composed your letter, what effects you were trying to achieve, and what problems or issues emerged for you along the way. Indicate any aspects of the letter that you're not certain about. Add anything else you'd like to say.

chapter 5

memoirs: recalling personal experience

THINKING ABOUT THE GENRE

Writing a *memoir,* as the word itself suggests, involves memory work. Memoirists draw on their pasts, looking back at events, people, and places that are important to them, in order to re-create, in written language, moments or episodes of lived experience. This re-creation of particular experiences distinguishes memoir from the genre of autobiography, which seeks to encompass an entire life. But memoirists don't just re-create moments of experience—they seek to imbue them with a significance readers will understand.

The call to write memoirs comes in part from the desire people have to keep track of the past and to see how their lives have intersected with public events. This impulse to remember is what leads people to take photographs, compile scrapbooks, and save letters and keepsakes of all sorts. Long after a particular experience is over, these objects help remind us of how things were at that moment. They also help remind us of how we were.

This sense of connection between present and past is at the center of memoir writing. By re-creating experiences from the past and exploring their significance, memoirists identify the continuities and discontinuities in their own lives. Writing memoirs is at least in part an act of self-discovery, of clarifying where the writer has come from and what he or she has become. The memoir writer is both participant and observer. On the one hand, the writer often appears as a character in the memoir, a participant in the events that unfold. On the other hand, the writer is also an observer who comments on and interprets these unfolding events, giving them a shape and meaning for the present.

Successful memoirs make personal experiences significant to others. Memoir writers often focus on details that reveal deeper meanings to themselves and to readers. Memoirist Patricia Hampl records details such as a "black boxy Ford" in a photograph, a "hat worn in 1952," an aunt polishing her toenails, and the "booths of the Gopher Grill" at the University of Minnesota. Such details can move writers to recover and convey to readers what might otherwise be overlooked in their pasts—the "intimate fragments

Online Study Center

. . . that bind even obscure lives to history." Memoir writers take incidents from childhood or adolescence—such as visiting grandparents, going on a first date, moving to a new town, or going away to college—and bring out new and unsuspected meanings. Writers may focus on moments of revelation, showing how crises and insights have challenged and changed their perceptions, expectations, and values.

Another strategy that writers use in memoirs is to put their experiences into a larger historical or cultural context. They present their pasts in part as exemplifying and shedding light on something larger—what it meant, say, to grow up during the 1960s or to experience the attacks on September 11, 2001. The point here is that as detailed, specific, and filled with sensory impressions as successful memoirs typically are, it is the larger context that gives these details their significance. Memoirs offer writers a way to show how the details of everyday life take on wider meanings.

Ultimately, people are called on to write memoirs not only to establish a connection to the past and to inform and entertain readers about the past but also from a sense of responsibility to the past, from a desire to bear witness to things that might otherwise be overlooked or forgotten. In many respects, memoirs derive their unique power to move readers from the way writers position themselves in the present in order to bear witness to the past, thus revealing the secrets and unsuspected meanings of ordinary lives that turn out to be not so ordinary after all.

■ WRITING FROM EXPERIENCE

Consider Patricia Hampl's point that memories are stored in the details of photos, a particular hat, and the booths at a campus hangout. Write a list of things that somehow capture an important moment or period in your life—such as photos, popular songs, hairstyles, articles of clothing, movies, posters, stuffed animals, toys, letters, cards, newspaper clippings, school or team uniforms, art objects, or souvenirs. Compare your list with your classmates' lists. What generalizations can you make about the capacity of things to hold and evoke memories?

READINGS

FROM *AN AMERICAN CHILDHOOD*
ANNIE DILLARD

Annie Dillard is a poet, novelist, essayist, and memoirist. She won the Pulitzer Prize in 1975 for Pilgrim at Tinker Creek, *an account of the year she spent observing nature in the Roanoke Valley of Virginia. The following selection is a chapter from* An American Childhood, *her memoir of growing up in Pittsburgh.*

1

Some boys taught me to play football. This was fine sport. You thought up a new strategy for every play and whispered it to the others. You went out for a pass, fooling everyone. Best, you got to throw yourself mightily at someone's running legs. Either you brought him down or you hit the ground flat out on your chin, with your arms empty before you. It was all or nothing. If you hesitated in fear, you would miss and get hurt; you would take a hard fall while the kid got away, or you would get kicked in the face while the kid got away. But if you flung yourself wholeheartedly at the back of his knees—if you gathered and joined body and soul and pointed them diving fearlessly—then you likely wouldn't get hurt, and you'd stop the ball. Your fate, and your team's score, depended on your concentration and courage. Nothing girls did could compare with it.

2

Boys welcomed me at baseball, too, for I had, through enthusiastic practice, what was weirdly known as a boy's arm. In winter, in the snow, there was neither baseball not football, so the boys and I threw snowballs at passing cars. I got in trouble throwing snowballs, and have seldom been happier since.

3

On one weekday morning after Christmas, six inches of new snow had just fallen. We were standing up to our boot tops in snow on a front yard on trafficked Reynolds Street, waiting for cars. The cars traveled Reynolds Street slowly and evenly; they were targets all but wrapped in red ribbons, cream puffs. We couldn't miss.

4

I was seven; the boys were eight, nine, and ten. The oldest two Fahey boys were there—Mikey and Peter—polite blond boys who lived near me on Lloyd Street, and who already had four brothers and sisters. My parents approved of Mikey and Peter Fahey. Chuckie McBride was there, a rough kid, and Billy Paul and Mackie Kean too, from across Reynolds, where the boys grew up dark and furious, grew up skinny, knowing, and skilled. We had all drifted from our houses that morning looking for action, and had found it here on Reynolds Street.

5

It was cloudy but cold. The cars' tires laid behind them on the snowy street a complex trail of beige chunks like crenellated castle walls. I had stepped on some earlier; they squeaked. We could have wished for more traffic. When a car came, we all popped it one. In the intervals between cars we reverted to the natural solitude of children.

6

I started making an iceball—a perfect iceball, from perfectly white snow, perfectly spherical, and squeezed perfectly translucent so no snow remained all the way through. (The Fahey boys and I considered it unfair actually to throw an iceball at somebody, but it had been known to happen.)

7

I had just embarked on the iceball project when we heard tire chains come clanking from afar. A black Buick was moving toward us down the street. We all spread out, banged together some regular snowballs, took aim, and, when the Buick drew nigh, fired.

8   A soft snowball hit the driver's windshield right before the driver's face. It made a smashed star with a hump in the middle.

9   Often, of course, we hit our target, but this time, the only time in all of life, the car pulled over and stopped. Its wide black door opened; a man got out of it, running. He didn't even close the car door.

¶s 9–14:
* describes
the chase

10   He ran after us, and we ran away from him, up the snowy Reynolds sidewalk. At the corner, I looked back; incredibly, he was still after us. He was in city clothes: a suit and tie, street shoes. Any normal adult would have quit, having sprung us into flight and made his point. This man was gaining on us. He was a thin man, all action. All of a sudden, we were running for our lives.

** notice
the chrono-
logical
order*

11   Wordless, we split up. We were on our turf; we could lose ourselves in the neighborhood backyards, everyone for himself. I paused and considered. Everyone had vanished except Mikey Fahey, who was just rounding the corner of a yellow brick house. Poor Mikey, I trailed him. The driver of the Buick sensibly picked the two of us to follow. The man apparently had all day.

12   He chased Mikey and me around the yellow house and up a backyard path we knew by heart: under a low tree, up a bank, through a hedge, down some snowy steps, and across the grocery store's delivery driveway. We smashed through a gap in another hedge, entered a scruffy backyard and ran around its back porch and tight between houses to Edgerton Avenue; we ran across Edgerton to an alley and up our own sliding woodpile to the Hall's front yard; he kept coming. We ran up Lloyd Street and wound through mazy backyards toward the steep hilltop at Willard and Lang.

13   He chased us silently, block after block. He chased us silently over picket fences, through thorny hedges, between houses, around garbage cans, and across streets. Every time I glanced back, choking for breath, I expected he would have quit. He must have been as breathless as we were. His jacket strained over his body. It was an immense discovery, pounding into my hot head with every sliding, joyous step, that this ordinary adult evidently knew what I thought only children who trained at football knew: that you have to fling yourself at what you're doing, you have to point yourself, forget yourself, aim, dive.

** notice
descriptive
detail*

14   Mikey and I had nowhere to go, in our own neighborhood or out of it, but away from this man who was chasing us. He impelled us forward; we compelled him to follow our route. The air was cold; every breath tore my throat. We kept running, block after block; we kept improvising, backyard after backyard, running a frantic course and choosing it simultaneously, failing always to find small places or hard places to slow him down, and

** notice
action
verbs*

discovering always, exhilarated, dismayed, that only bare speed could save us—for he would never give up, this man—and we were losing speed.

15
¶s 15–19:

He chased us through the backyard labyrinths of ten blocks before he caught us by our jackets. He caught us and we all stopped.

16

* climax
of the
story

We three stood staggering, half blinded, coughing, in an obscure hilltop backyard: a man in his twenties, a boy, a girl. He had released our jackets, our pursuer, our captor, our hero: he knew we weren't going anywhere. We all played by the rules. Mikey and I unzipped our jackets. I pulled off my sopping mittens. Our tracks multiplied in the back-yard's new snow. We had been breaking new snow all morning. We didn't look at each other. I was cherishing my excitement. The man's lower pants legs were wet; his cuffs were full of snow and there was a prow of snow beneath them on his shoes and socks. Some trees bordered the little flat backyard, some messy winter trees. There was no one around: a clearing in a grove, and we the only players.

17

It was a long time before he could speak. I had some difficulty at first recalling why we were there. My lips felt swollen; I couldn't see out of the sides of my eyes; I kept coughing.

18

"You stupid kids," he began perfunctorily.

19

* moment
of revela-
tion

We listened perfunctorily indeed, if we listened at all, for the chewing out was redundant, a mere formality, and beside the point. The point was that he had chased us passionately without giving up, and so he had caught us. Now he came down to earth. I wanted the glory to last forever.

20

But how could the glory have lasted forever? We could have run through every back-yard in North America until we got to Panama. But when he trapped us at the lip of the Panama Canal, what precisely could he have done to prolong the drama of the chase and cap its glory? I brooded about this for the next few years. He could only have fried Mikey Fahey and me in boiling oil, say, or dismembered us piecemeal, or staked us to anthills. None of which I really wanted, and none of which any adult was likely to do, even in the spirit of fun. He could only chew us out there in the Panamanian jungle, after months or years of exalting pursuit. He could only begin, "You stupid kids," and continue in his ordinary Pittsburgh accent with his normal righteous anger and the usual common sense.

Ending:
* reflects
on mean-
ing of the
chase

21

* echoes
last
sentence
of ¶2

If in that snowy backyard the driver of the black Buick had cut off our heads, Mikey's and mine, I would have died happy, for nothing has required so much of me since as be-ing chased all over Pittsburgh in the middle of winter—running terrified, exhausted—by this sainted, skinny, furious redheaded man who wished to have a word with us. I don't know how he found his way back to his car.

Analysis: Re-creating Experience

At their best, memoirs re-create experience so that readers can actually feel what it was like to be alive at that moment in the writer's life. In this chapter from *An American Childhood*, Annie Dillard isn't just recalling the time she and some friends were out throwing snowballs and this guy stopped and chased them around the neighborhood. Instead she takes us with her as she flees from the man pursuing her. To make the chase come alive, Dillard has re-created the young girl she was at the age of 7. Accordingly, as readers, we experience what takes place from the young girl's perspective and share her sense of excitement and exhilaration. In many respects, this memoir hinges on Dillard's ability to shape the person she once was into a believable character.

■ FOR CRITICAL INQUIRY

1. In the opening paragraphs, Dillard talks about playing football and baseball. What does this reveal about the character of Dillard as a 7 year-old? How does this information prepare readers for what's to come?

2. Dillard doesn't just tell a story about something that happened. She invests the experience with meaning: "I got in trouble throwing snowballs, and have seldom been happier since." What made her so happy? Point to particular words, sentences, and passages where she develops the meaning of the experience.

3. In the final paragraph, Dillard describes the man who chased her as "this sainted, skinny, furious redheaded man who wished to have a word with us." How do the adjectives *sainted, skinny, furious,* and *redheaded* go together in her description? Why does she use the word *sainted?*

4. One could argue that throwing snowballs is dangerous and irresponsible behavior. In fact, that is probably what the man who chased Dillard and her friends was thinking. Dillard avoids the issue, however, and puts the emphasis instead on her "immense discovery." What assumptions about readers' reactions does she seem to count on in doing so?

BLACK HAIR

GARY SOTO

Gary Soto, poet, fiction writer, and essayist, is the author of many collections for adults and young readers, including A Summer Life *(1990),* Baseball in April *(1990), and* Buried Onions *(1997). The following selection appears in his book of essays* Living Up the Street *(1985).*

1   There are two kinds of work: One uses the mind and the other uses muscle. As a kid I found out about the latter. I'm thinking of the summer of 1969 when I was a seventeen-year-old runaway who ended up in Glendale, California, working for Valley Tire Factory. To answer an ad in the newspaper I walked miles in the afternoon sun, my

stomach slowly knotting on a doughnut that was breakfast, my teeth like bright candles gone yellow.

2   I walked in the door sweating and feeling ugly because my hair was still stiff from a swim at the Santa Monica beach the day before. Jules, the accountant and part owner, looked droopily through his bifocals at my application and then at me. He tipped his cigar in the ashtray, asked my age as if he didn't believe I was seventeen, but finally, after a moment of silence, said, "Come back tomorrow. Eight-thirty."

3   I thanked him, left the office, and went around to the chain-link fence to watch the workers heave tires into a bin; others carted uneven stacks of tires on hand trucks. Their faces were black from tire dust, and when they talked—or cussed—their mouths showed a bright pink.

4   From there I walked up a commercial street, past a cleaners, a motorcycle shop, and a gas station where I washed my face and hands; before leaving I took a bottle that hung on the side of the Coke machine, filled it with water, and stopped it with a scrap of paper and a rubber band.

5   The next morning I arrived early at work. The assistant foreman, a potbellied Hungarian, showed me a time card and how to punch in. He showed me the Coke machine and the locker room with its slimy shower, and also pointed out the places where I shouldn't go: the ovens where the tires were recapped and the customer service area, which had a slashed couch, a coffee table with greasy magazines, and an ashtray. He introduced me to Tully, a fat man with one ear who worked the buffers that resurfaced the whitewalls. I was handed an apron and a face mask and shown how to use the buffer: Lift the tire and center it, inflate it with a foot pedal, press the buffer against the white band until cleaned, and then deflate and blow off the tire with an air hose.

6   With a paintbrush he stirred a can of industrial preserver. "Then slap this blue stuff on." While he was talking a coworker came up quietly behind him and goosed him with the air hose. Tully jumped as if he had been struck by a bullet and then turned around cussing and cupping his genitals in his hands as the other worker walked away calling out foul names. When Tully turned to me, smiling his gray teeth, I lifted my mouth into a smile because I wanted to get along. He has to be on my side, I thought. He's the one who'll tell the foreman how I'm doing.

7   I worked carefully that day, setting the tires on the machine as if they were babies, because it was easy to catch a finger in the rim that expanded to inflate the tire. At the day's end we swept up the tire dust and emptied the trash into bins.

8   At five the workers scattered for their cars and motorcycles while I crossed the street to wash at a burger stand. My hair was stiff with dust and my mouth showed pink against the backdrop of my dirty face. I ordered a hotdog and walked slowly in the direction of the abandoned house where I had stayed the night before. I lay under the trees and within minutes was asleep. When I woke my shoulders were sore, and my eyes burned when I squeezed the lids together.

9   From the backyard I walked dully through a residential street, and as evening came on, the TV glare in the living rooms and the headlights of passing cars showed against the blue drift of dusk. I saw two children coming up the street with snow cones, their tongues darting at the packed ice. I saw a boy with a peach and wanted to stop him but felt embarrassed by my hunger. I walked for an hour, only to return and discover the house lit brightly. Behind the fence I heard voices and saw a flashlight poking at the garage door. A man on the back steps mumbled something about the refrigerator to the one with the flashlight.

10   I waited for them to leave but had the feeling they wouldn't because there was a commotion of furniture being moved. Tired, even more desperate, I started walking again with a great urge to kick things and tear the day from my life. I felt weak and my mind kept drifting because of hunger. I crossed the street to a gas station where I sipped at the water fountain and searched the Coke machine for change. I started walking again, first up a commercial street, then into a residential area where I lay down on someone's lawn and replayed a scene at home—my mother crying at the kitchen table, my stepfather yelling with food in his mouth. They're cruel, I thought, and warned myself that I should never forgive them. How could they do this to me?

11   When I got up from the lawn it was late. I searched out a place to sleep and found an unlocked car that seemed safe. In the backseat, with my shoes off, I fell asleep but woke up startled about four in the morning when the owner, a nurse on her way to work, opened the door. She got in and was about to start the engine when I raised my head to explain my presence. She screamed so loudly when I said "I'm sorry" that I sprinted from the car with my shoes in hand. Her screams faded, then stopped altogether, as I ran down the block, hid behind a trash bin, and waited for a police siren to sound. Nothing. I crossed the street to a church where I slept stiffly on cardboard in the balcony.

12   I woke up feeling tired and greasy. It was early and a few streetlights were still lit, the east growing pink with dawn. I washed myself from a garden hose and returned to the church to break into what looked like a kitchen. Paper cups, plastic spoons, a coffee pot littered on a table. I found a box of Nabisco crackers and ate until I was full.

13   At work I spent the morning at the buffer, but was then told to help Iggy, an old Mexican who was responsible for choosing tires that could be recapped without the risk of exploding at high speeds. Every morning a truck would deliver used tires, and after I unloaded them Iggy would step among the tires to inspect them for punctures and rips on the sidewalls.

14   With yellow chalk he marked circles and Xs to indicate damage and called out "junk." Tires that could be recapped got a "goody" from Iggy, and I placed them on my hand truck. When I had a stack of eight I kicked the truck at an angle and balanced off to another work area, where Iggy again inspected the tires, scratching Xs and calling out "junk."

15   Iggy worked only until three in the afternoon, at which time he went to the locker room to wash and shave and to dress in a two-piece suit. When he came out he glowed with a bracelet, watch, rings, and a shiny fountain pen in his breast pocket. His shoes sounded against the asphalt. He was the image of a banker stepping into sunlight with millions on his mind. He said a few low words to workers with whom he was friendly and none to people like me.

16   I was seventeen, stupid because I couldn't figure out the difference between an F78 14 and a 750 14 at sight. Iggy shook his head when I brought him the wrong tires, especially since I had expressed interest in being his understudy. "Mexican, how can you be so stupid?" he would yell at me, slapping a tire from my hands. But within weeks I learned a lot about tires, from sizes and makes to how they are molded in iron forms to how Valley stole from other companies. Now and then we received a truckload of tires, most of them new or nearly new, and they were taken to our warehouse in the back, where the serial numbers were ground off with a sander. On those days the foreman handed out Cokes and joked with us as we worked to get the numbers off.

17   Most of the workers were Mexican or black, though a few redneck whites worked there. The base pay was a dollar sixty-five but the average was three dollars. Of the black workers, I knew Sugar Daddy the best. His body carried 250 pounds and armfuls of scars, and he had a long knife that made me jump when he brought it out from his boot without warning. At one time he had been a singer and had cut a record in 1967 called *Love's Chance,* which broke into the R & B charts. But nothing came of it. No big contract, no club dates, no tours. He made very little from record sales, only enough for an operation to pull a steering wheel from his gut when, drunk and mad at a lady friend, he slammed his Mustang into a row of parked cars.

18   "Touch it," he smiled at me one afternoon as he raised his shirt, his black belly kinked with hair. Scared, I traced the scar that ran from his chest to the left of his belly button, and I was repelled but hid my disgust.

19   Among the Mexicans I had few friends because I was different, a pocho [outsider] who spoke bad Spanish. At lunch they sat in tires and laughed over burritos, looking up at me to laugh even harder. I also sat in tires while nursing a Coke and felt dirty and sticky because I was still living on the street and had not had a real bath in over a week. Nevertheless, when the border patrol came to round up the nationals, I ran with them as they scrambled for the fence or hid among the tires behind the warehouse. The foreman, who thought I was an undocumented worker, yelled at me to run, to get away. I did just that. At the time it seemed fun because there was no risk, only a good-hearted feeling of hide-and-seek, and besides, it meant an hour away from work on company time. When the police left we came back, and some of the nationals made up stories of how they were almost caught—how they outraced the police. Some of the stories were so convoluted and unconvincing that everyone laughed and shouted "mentiras" [lies], especially when one described how he overpowered a policeman, took his gun away, and sold the patrol car. We laughed and he laughed, happy to be there to make up such a story.

20   If work was difficult, so were the nights. I still had not gathered enough money to rent a room, so I spent the nights sleeping in parked cars or in the church balcony. After a week I found a newspaper ad for a room for rent, phoned, and was given directions. Finished with work, I walked the five miles down Mission Road looking back into the traffic with my thumb out. No rides. After eight hours of handling tires I was frightening to drivers, I suppose, since they seldom looked at me; if they did, it was a quick glance. For the next six weeks I would try to hitchhike, but the only person to stop was a Mexican woman who gave me two dollars to take the bus. I told her it was too much and that no bus ran from Mission Road to where I lived, but she insisted that I keep the money and trotted back to her idling car. It must have hurt her to see me day after day walking in the heat and looking very much the dirty Mexican to the many minds that didn't know what it meant to work at hard labor. That woman knew. Her eyes met mine as she opened the car door, and there was a tenderness that was surprisingly true—one for which you wait for years but when it comes it doesn't help. Nothing changes. You continue on in rags, with the sun still above you.

21   I rented a room from a middle-aged couple whose lives were a mess. She was a schoolteacher and he was a fireman. A perfect setup, I thought. But during my stay there they would argue for hours in their bedroom.

22 When I rang at the front door both Mr. and Mrs. Van Deusen answered and didn't bother to disguise their shock at how awful I looked. But they let me in all the same. Mrs. Van Deusen showed me around the house, from the kitchen and bathroom to the living room with its grand piano. On her fingers she counted out the house rules as she walked me to my room. It was a girl's room with lace curtains, scenic wallpaper of a Victorian couple enjoying a stroll, a canopied bed, and stuffed animals in a corner. Leaving, she turned and asked if she could do laundry for me. Feeling shy and hurt, I told her no; perhaps the next day. She left and I undressed to take a bath, exhausted as I sat on the edge of the bed probing my aches and my bruised places. With a towel around my waist I hurried down the hallway to the bathroom where Mrs. Van Deusen had set out an additional towel with a tube of shampoo. I ran water into the tub and sat on the closed toilet, watching the steam curl toward the ceiling. When I lowered myself into the tub I felt my body sting. I soaped a washcloth and scrubbed my arms until they lightened, even glowed pink, but I still looked unwashed around my neck and face no matter how hard I rubbed. Back in the room I sat in bed reading a magazine, happy and thinking of no better luxury than a girl's sheets, especially after nearly two weeks of sleeping on cardboard at the church.

23 I was too tired to sleep, so I sat at the window watching the neighbors move about in pajamas, and, curious about the room, looked through the bureau drawers to search out personal things—snapshots, a messy diary, and high-school yearbook. I looked up the Van Deusen's daughter, Barbara, and studied her face as if I recognized her from my own school—a face that said "promise," "college," "nice clothes in the closet." She was a skater and a member of the German Club; her greatest ambition was to sing at the Hollywood Bowl.

24 After a while I got into bed, and as I drifted toward sleep I thought about her. In my mind I played a love scene again and again and altered it slightly each time. She comes home from college and at first is indifferent to my presence in her home, but finally I overwhelm her with deep pity when I come home hurt from work, with blood on my shirt. Then there was another version: Home from college she is immediately taken with me, in spite of my work-darkened face, and invites me into the family car for a milkshake across town. Later, back at the house, we sit in the living room talking about school until we're so close I'm holding her hand. The truth of the matter was that Barbara did come home for a week but was bitter toward her parents for taking in boarders (two others besides me). During that time she spoke to me only twice: Once, while searching the refrigerator, she asked if we had any mustard; the other time she asked if I had seen her car keys.

25   But it was a place to stay. Work had become more and more difficult. I worked not only with Iggy but also with the assistant foreman, who was in charge of unloading trucks. After they backed in I hopped on top to pass the tires down, bouncing them on the tailgate to give them an extra spring so they would be less difficult to handle on the other end. Each truck was weighted down with more than two hundred tires, each averaging twenty pounds, so that by the time the truck was emptied and swept clean I glistened with sweat and my T-shirt stuck to my body. I blew snot threaded with tire dust onto the asphalt, indifferent to the customers who watched from the waiting room.

26   The days were dull. I did what there was to do from morning until the bell sounded at five; I tugged, pulled, and cussed at tires until I was listless and my mind drifted and caught on small things, from cold sodas to shoes to stupid talk about what we would do with a million dollars. I remember unloading a truck with Hamp, a black man.

27   "What's better than a sharp lady?" he asked me as I stood sweaty on a pile of junked tires. "Water. With ice," I said.

28   He laughed with his mouth open wide. With his fingers he pinched the sweat from his chin and flicked at me. "You be too young, boy. A woman can make you a god."

29   As a kid I had chopped cotton and picked grapes, so I knew work. I knew the fatigue and the boredom and the feeling that there was a good possibility that you might have to do such work for years, if not for a lifetime. In fact, as a kid I had imagined a dark fate: to marry Mexican poor, work Mexican hours, and in the end die a Mexican death, broke and in despair.

30   But this job at Valley Tire Company confirmed that there was something worse than fieldwork, and I was doing it. We were all doing it, from the foreman to the newcomers like me, and what I felt heaving tires for eight hours a day was felt by everyone—black, Mexican, redneck. We all despised those hours but didn't know what else to do. The workers were unskilled, some undocumented and fearful of deportation, and all struck with uncertainty at what to do with their lives. Although everyone bitched about work, no one left. Some had worked there for twelve years; some had sons working there. Few quit; no one was ever fired. It amazed me that no one gave up when the border patrol jumped from their vans, batons in hand, because I couldn't imagine any work that could be worse—or any life. What was out there, in the world, that made men run for the fence in fear?

31   Iggy was the only worker who seemed sure of himself. After five hours of "junking," he brushed himself off, cleaned up in the washroom, and came out gleaming with an elegance that humbled the rest of us. Few would look him straight in the eye or talk to him

in our usual stupid way because he was so much better. He carried himself as a man should—with Old World "dignity"—while the rest of us muffed our jobs and talked dully about dull things as we worked. From where he worked in his open shed he would now and then watch us with his hands on his hips. He would shake his head and click his tongue in disgust.

32   The rest of us lived dismally. I often wondered what the others' homes were like; I couldn't imagine that they were much better than our workplace. No one indicated that his outside life was interesting or intriguing. We all looked defeated and contemptible in our filth at the day's end. I imagined the average welcome at home: Rafael, a Mexican national who had worked at Valley for five years, returned to a beaten house full of kids dressed in mismatched clothes and playing kick the can. As for Sugar Daddy, he returned home to a stuffy room where he would read and reread old magazines. He ate potato chips, drank beer, and watched TV. There was no grace in dipping socks into a washbasin where later he would wash his cup and plate.

33   There was no grace at work. It was all ridicule. The assistant foreman drank Cokes in front of the newcomers as they laced tires in the afternoon sun. Knowing that I had a long walk home, Rudy, the college student, passed me waving and yelling "Hello" as I started down Mission Road on the way home to eat out of cans. Even our plump secretary got into the act by wearing short skirts and flaunting her milky legs. If there was love, it was ugly. I'm thinking of Tully and an older man whose name I can no longer recall fondling one another in the washroom. I had come in cradling a smashed finger to find them pressed together in the shower, their pants undone and partly pulled down. When they saw me they smiled with their pink mouths but didn't bother to push away.

34   How we arrived at such a place is a mystery to me. Why anyone would stay for years is an even deeper concern. You showed up, but from where? What broken life? What ugly past? The foreman showed you the Coke machine, the washroom, and the yard where you'd work. When you picked up a tire, you were amazed at the black it could give off.

Analysis: A Moment of Revelation

Much of the power of memoirs, as Gary Soto's "Black Hair" illustrates, is their capacity to bring to life a moment of personal experience. Notice that Soto provides little information about why he was a runaway or how his experience at the Valley Tire Factory ended. Instead, he concentrates the reader's attention on the physical experience of work—the dirt, the noise, the smells, the sweat and bodily exhaustion of a day's labor. Soto seems to want us as readers to feel this remembered moment as intensely as he does. But he also wants the intensity of his recalled experience to unlock its significance—for readers and for himself. As the best memoirs do, Soto's "Black Hair" turns a moment of personal experience into a moment of revelation. Looking back on himself as a 17-year-old, Soto uses his account of this moment in the past to explain what he found out about work.

■ FOR CRITICAL INQUIRY

1. In the opening lines of his memoir, Gary Soto explains that there are "two kinds of work" and that he found out about work that "uses muscle" when he was a 17-year-old runaway. When you reach the end of the memoir, do you feel he has adequately explained his point? How does Soto's account of his experience develop the point about work with which he begins?

2. The final six paragraphs seem to offer Soto's closing evaluation of his experience. Explain the conclusions he appears to reach at the end. Do they seem justified based on his account of his experience?

3. Soto does not tell us why he was a runaway or how his experience working at the Valley Tire Factory ended. Why do you think he has decided not to provide this information? How does it affect the way you read his memoir?

4. Consider the title of the memoir "Black Hair." What are the various meanings this title might hold?

TEENAGE ANGST IN TEXAS

GAIL CALDWELL

Gail Caldwell is the chief book critic at the Boston Globe. *Caldwell adapted this short piece of writing from her memoir* A Strong West Wind *(2006). "Teenage Angst in Texas" appeared in the* New York Times Magazine *on January 29, 2006.*

In the mid-1960's, the wind-swept plains of the Texas Panhandle could be a languid prison for an adolescent girl with a wild spirit and no place to go. I buried myself in Philip Roth novels and little acts of outrage, and on lonesome afternoons, I would drive my mother's Chevrolet out onto the freeway and take it up to 90 m.p.h., smoking endless cigarettes and aching with ennui. I was bored by the idea of mainstream success and alienated from what the world seemed to offer—one of my poems from those days weighs heavily on the themes of coffins, societal hypocrisy and godlessness. And yet I cannot locate the precise source of my anger. For years I thought all teenagers were fueled by a high-octane mix of intensity and rage; I only know that what sent me onto the highways and into my own corridors of gloom was inexplicable to others and confusing to me.

Around this time my father began what I dismally thought of as our

Sunday drives. As kids, my sister and I were bored but tolerant when we had to tag along on his treks, which were always aimless. But now his itinerary was to chart the path of my dereliction, and that meant getting me alone in the car so that we could "talk": about my imminent doom, about my mother's high blood pressure. Thus incarcerated, slouched in the shotgun seat with my arms folded against my chest, I responded to his every effort by either staring out the window or yelling back. I don't remember a word I said. What I still feel is the boulder on my heart—the amorphous gray of the world outside the car window, signaling how trapped I felt, by him and by the hopeless unawareness of my age.

My father, far more than I, seemed to sense that the country was raging, that it was a bad time to surrender your daughters to strange lands. But these things—a war somewhere far away, a civil rights movement over in the Deep South—belonged to the evening news, not to the more intimate treacheries of car rides and deceits and disappointments, and so were rarely addressed on any personal level, not yet. Instead we fought about curfews or bad boyfriends; we fought about straightening up and flying right. We fought about everything but the truth, which was that I would be leaving soon.

I had already seen two casualties claimed by history, men who were lighting out for the territory to avoid the 1-A draft notices they had just received. The first was a boy who stopped by the house to say goodbye a few days before leaving for Toronto. When the other young man disappeared, the federal authorities came sniffing around my high school, and I covered for him without a shred of hesitation. I told them I thought he went east, to his mother's in Missouri, when I knew it was the one place he would never go.

These losses and the lies they demanded frightened me, in vague and then inarticulate ways, about just who was in charge—about the dangers posed by the institutions that were supposed to keep you safe. It was difficult in those days to care much about the College Boards, or to think that the path in front of me would hold the traditional landscapes of marriage and family. In some ways the tempests of my adolescence had set me against myself; I'd found that introspection couldn't buy you love, that poetry helped only momentarily, that straight A's and spelling bees were no guarantee of knowing where to turn. Worse and more pervasive, I was maturing under the assumption that you should never let men know how smart you were, or how mouthy—a girl's intelligence, brazenly displayed, was seen as impolite, unfeminine and even threatening.

So I kept quiet; when I dated a boy who liked George Wallace, I rolled my eyes and looked out the window. The smarter you were, the more subversive you had to be. Girls could excel in English, say, or languages, as long as they didn't flaunt it or pretend to be superior to males.

But God forbid, they should try to carve a life out of such achievements. God forbid they display a pitcher's arm, or an affinity for chemistry or analytic prowess in an argument with a man.

In the end, my own revisionism was unconscious but thorough. I neglected anymore to mention the mysterious test, taken at age 7, that resulted in my skipping second grade. Toward the end of high school, I began lying to my peers about my high scores on placement exams, and I blew admission, with half-intention and private relief, into the National Honor Society. The summer before college, in 1968, I had to declare a major; I took a deep breath and wrote "mathematics" on my admission forms. And when friends asked me what I'd chosen, I lied about that too.

Analysis: Using Episodes

Instead of telling a story from her past in chronological order, from start to finish, Gail Caldwell brings together a series of episodes to re-create a sense of what her life was like as a teenager in the Texas Panhandle during the mid-1960s. Notice how she moves from one episode to another—driving 90 miles an hour, the rides with her father, the two young men fleeing the military draft, how she lied about the major she wrote on her college admissions forms. Notice also how the episodes are arranged to work together, creating a moment in time that enables readers to see an individual life in the midst of historical events (the Vietnam War, the civil rights movement, the presidential campaign in 1968 of the segregationist George Wallace) and the cultural realities of the day (parent-child relations, pressures on young women).

■ FOR CRITICAL INQUIRY

1. How does Gail Caldwell establish her situation in the opening paragraph? Notice she says it was "inexplicable to others and confusing to me." By the time you get to the end of this brief memoir, what light has been shed on this confusion? How would you describe the arc of the memoir, from where it begins to where it ends?

2. How do the various episodes contribute to the memoir? How does Caldwell put them together? Examine the order she uses and the amount of explanation.

3. How does your experience of reading Caldwell's episodes compare to the chronological order in Annie Dillard and Gary Soto?

4. As is typical of memoirs, the writer is very much in the present looking at the past. What does Caldwell's attitude toward her past seem to be? How does this attitude compare to her state of mind in the past? How do these past and present perspectives shape the reader's experience of Caldwell's memoir?

WRITING IN A DIGITAL WORLD

Social Networking Web Sites

Web sites like Friendster, MySpace, and Facebook have taken the idea of the college facebook online, where individuals create and link personal home pages, thereby creating social networks of old friends and new acquaintances. According to Duncan Watts, a sociologist who studies social networks, these Web sites are places you can cruise or hang out, see people and be seen, like the mall or a campus coffee shop. By 2005, MySpace had over 80 million members and more page views than Google.

The personal home pages in part resemble individual scrapbooks, with photos and lists of favorite music and movies. In that sense, like memoirs, they capture a person at a point in time. But these home pages are also links in online social networks, connecting individuals in virtual communities.

■ FOR CRITICAL INQUIRY

1. Consider what people include in their personal home pages. Like memoirs, these are self-presentations. What seems to determine individuals' choices about how they want to be seen?

2. What functions do online social networks like Friendster, MySpace, and Facebook serve for people? Why would individuals want to be a part?

3. Facebook has a more restrictive policy than MySpace or Friendster by limiting its users to the home pages of other students at their college or, with permission, adding students at other schools to their list of friends. What issues about privacy and safety are involved in online social networks?

VISUAL DESIGN

Graphic Novels

PERSEPOLIS

MARJANE SATRAPI

Marjane Satrapi was born in 1969 in Iran. She has written several children's books but is best known for *Persepolis: The Story of a Childhood* (2003), *Persepolis 2: The Story of a Return* (2004), and *Embroideries* (2005). This brief excerpt comes from the opening chapter of *Persepolis: The Story of a Childhood*, Satrapi's memoir of growing up in Iran during the Islamic revolution.

From *Persepolis: The Story of a Childhood* by Marjane Satrapi; translated by Mattias Ripa & Blake Ferris, Translation copyright © 2003 by L'Association, Paris, France. Used by permission of Pantheon Books, a division of Random House, Inc.

Analysis: Mixing Genres

Marjane Satrapi is one of the leading writer/illustrators who have developed the visual conventions of the comic book into the graphic novel or, more accurately in her case, the graphic memoir. This hybrid form uses the panels of a comic book, a limited number of words, and stylized drawings of people and places to narrate events from Satrapi's years growing up in Iran after the Islamic revolution of 1979. Notice in this selection how you as a reader move from one panel to the next. Sometimes the shift is a relatively small one, as in the movement from the first panel to the second. Other times, however, it is much more significant, involving leaps in time and space, as in the movement from the second panel to the third and then to the fourth. In any case, part of what makes graphic novels and graphic memoirs work is the involvement of the reader filling in meanings and connecting one panel to the next.

■ FOR CRITICAL ANALYSIS

1. Look closely at the panels. What information is provided in words? What in drawings? How do you as a reader draw on the words and drawings to put the meaning together? What are you filling in from your own knowledge and experience that is not on the page?

2. Notice how Marjane Satrapi uses panels of different sizes and, in some cases, uses a black background. What do these techniques contribute to the overall design? How do they help create emphasis?

3. Compare the graphic memoir to the print memoir. How are they alike? How do they differ? How do these differences shape the reader's experience?

4. Imagine you are going to turn Gail Caldwell's "Teenage Angst in Texas" into a graphic novel. Turn the opening three paragraphs into panels. How many would you need? What drawings and words would you put in them? How would you set up the transition from one panel to the next?

FURTHER EXPLORATION: MEMOIRS

■ GENRE CHOICES

Gary Soto's "Black Hair" and the Justice for Janitors ad in Chapter 7 both provide accounts of life in the workplace, though one is a memoir and the other an appeal to support a union campaign. Compare them in terms of what each brings to light about the nature of work. What, if anything, do they have in common? How might their differences as genres of writing affect readers?

■ WORKING TOGETHER

Creating a Time Capsule

Time capsules contain items that are meant to represent a particular moment or period of history. The term *time capsule* was coined in 1938 for a cylinder the Westinghouse

Electrical Company filled with more than one hundred articles used for scientific, industrial, or everyday purposes, along with microfilms and newsreels. It was buried on the grounds of the New York World's Fair of 1939, to be opened in 6939.

- Work together in groups of four or five to create a time capsule that can serve to capture the present moment in history. To do this, select twenty-five things that, in your judgment, best represent what it means to be alive in the first decade of the twenty-first century.

- Write a list of the items with brief explanations of why you have included each one. Make enough copies of the list for the other members of your class or circulate it on a class listserv.

- Compile the items on each group's list in a master list. Now work together as a class to narrow the items down to twenty-five that the majority can agree on. Provide a rationale for each item: what does it represent about the present culture that would help future generations (or aliens) understand current ways of life?

ETHICS OF WRITING

BEARING WITNESS

Part of a memoirist's authority derives from the fact of his or her having been an eyewitness to the events recounted. Memoirists are participants as well as observers. For these reasons, memoirists face some important ethical issues concerning their responsibility as witnesses to the past. How does the memoirist represent the other people involved? What are the memoirist's responsibilities to these people? What is the memoirist entitled to divulge about his or her private life? What are the memoirist's loyalties to those he or she writes about? Might such loyalties conflict with obligations to readers? What impact will the memoir have on the writer's relationship with others in the present, and does this potential impact affect the retelling? In cases where the memoirist feels hurt, angry, or offended by what took place, can he or she nonetheless be fair?

These are questions that memoirists invariably struggle with, and there are no easy answers, especially when a memoir treats situations that are difficult or painful. The memoir, don't forget, is an act of self-discovery, and yet memoirs are written for the public to read. As witnesses to the past, memoirists can handle their responsibility to others in an ethical way by seeking to understand the motives and character of those involved, including themselves. ■

WRITING ASSIGNMENT

Writing Memoir

Online Study Center

Recall a person, place, or event from your past and write a memoir. You will want to use detail and sensory impression to re-create the moment for your readers. Remember that the point of a memoir, as you have seen, is to reveal the meaning of the past so that readers can understand the significance your memories hold for the present. Since memoirs function to help both writers and their readers understand the past, this assignment can be a good time for you to probe significant times in your life, revisiting them now that you have some distance from them.

- Consider the tensions or conflicts you experienced in high school, as Gail Caldwell does.

- Focus on a job you have held at some time in the past, as Gary Soto does.

- Pick a photograph that holds memories and emotional associations. Focus on a particular detail that recalls a particular moment in the past to explore how your family's history intersects larger social and historical forces.

- Recall a particular family ritual, such as visits to grandparents, Sunday dinners, summer vacations, holiday celebrations, weddings, and so on, as a way to focus on an event or a person that is especially significant to you.

- Consider some aspect of your own cultural ancestry—whether it is the language your ancestors spoke, a kind of food or music, a family tradition, an heirloom that has been passed down from generation to generation—to explain how the past has entered your life and what it reveals about your relationship to the culture of your ancestors.

- Focus on a childhood incident, as Annie Dillard does, to re-create the event and your own perspective as a younger person.

- Look through an old diary or journal, if you have kept one. Look for moments when you faced an occasion that challenged your values or where you had a difficult decision to make, experienced a situation that turned out unexpectedly, or were keenly disappointed. Consider using these memories as the starting point for your memoir, in which you can reflect upon the experience and put it in a larger context.

Alternative Assignments

 **Online Study Center**

■ RHETORICAL ANALYSIS

Consider the writers' ethos in the memoirs you've just read. You can focus on one memoir or compare them. How do the writers construct their characters? Take into account the role each author plays as a character in the memoir and the relationship between the writer's present-day self and as a character in the memoir. How have the writers handled their ethical responsibility to others involved in the memoir? What kind of relationship do they want to establish with their readers?

■ **WORKING WITH SOURCES**

For this assignment, write an essay that relates your personal experience to the experience in a published memoir. You'll need to find a memoir that has something in common with your life. The memoir might, for example, be located in the same town, city, or region of the country where you grew up, or take place in a middle-class suburb, working-class neighborhood, inner city, or rural area. Or the point in common could be that the writer is like you in some key way—say a Muslim or a Jew, African American or Asian American, gay or lesbian. In any case, the purpose of the essay is not simply to compare experiences point by point but to explain how reading the memoir caused you to reflect on your own experience and what the results are.

Invention

Sketching

Consider what moves you to write. The call to write often begins with the memory of a single detail or an image from everyday life. The seemingly mundane memory of an old bicycle, the refrain from a song, or the smell of your grandparents' kitchen can unlock a series of emotional associations worth exploring. To see what such memories hold for you, do some sketching of scenes or memories from the past.

Just as artists often sketch as preliminary work, you can use sketching as a form of exploratory writing to recall the details, sensory impressions, emotional associations, and social allegiances that moments in the past contain for you. Here's an example of what a sketch might look like:

> It was a green ten-speed Schwinn bike that I remember, a gift for my eleventh birthday. It was sleek and racy-looking, with handbrakes that could stop you on a dime and the exotic-sounding derailleur with its levers to change gears. This was no child's bike; this was an instrument of speed and effortless motion. When I rode this ten-speed, I felt weightless and free, an anonymous blur of cycling energy zooming through my neighborhood and beyond. I could go, and the bike brought me a mobility I had never imagined before. I named my bike "The Green Wind" and rode out of my childhood and into the adventure of adolescence and parts of town my parents would have been horrified to know I visited. The Green Wind took me many places and I learned to be silent about my travels.

Guidelines for Sketching

- **Visualize the moment** in the past. Imagine you are photographing or videotaping. What exactly do you see? List as many specific items and details as you can. Think about the time of day, the season of the year, and what the weather was like. If your memoir is located mostly indoors, try to recall what particular rooms looked like—the furniture, the color of the walls or the design of wallpaper, anything hanging, such as pictures, posters, photographs, and so on. Recall, too, the movement of people. How do they move through the physical space in which your memoir is located? What are they doing?

- **Note other sensory perceptions**, such as sounds, smells, tastes, and textures. What do you hear in the physical space you're writing about? What produces the sounds—people's voices, people's work, animals, machines, city traffic, the wind? Are there characteristic smells associated with the place? If there is a meal or food involved in your memoir, what do various dishes taste like? Are there particular textures to objects that you can recall?

- **Describe the people involved** in your memoir. What do they look like? How do they move? What are they doing? What are they wearing? Recreate conversation among the people in your memoir. What are they talking about? Can you capture particular ways of speech? Can you use snatches of dialogue to define people and issues?

■ WORKING TOGETHER

Creating a Sketch

1. Using the guidelines above, sketch a scene, memory, event, or incident from the past—something you can recall in reasonable detail that has important associations for you.

2. Exchange your sketch with a classmate. Read your partner's sketch.

3. Take turns interviewing each other. Ask your partner about the sketch you wrote: What does your partner think is most interesting about the sketch? What would your partner like to know more about? What themes or issues does he or she see in the sketch?

Past and Present Perspectives

To clarify the purpose of your memoir and what you want it to mean to readers, consider what your feelings were at the moment things were taking place in the past and what they are now as you look back from the perspective of the present.

In the sketch about the ten-speed bicycle, the writer has re-created the excitement and sense of adventure he felt as an 11-year-old. However, as the writer reflected on and wrote about the importance of the bike from the perspective of the present, he realized that his travels to the "wrong side" of town not only opened up a whole new world of class and cultural differences but also created a barrier of silence between him and his parents. Some of the work ahead for this writer is to decide how much he wants to emphasize the physical freedom, mobility, and new knowledge he acquired and how much he wants to emphasize what the consequences of his silence have been for his relationship with his parents.

Considering the memory you're writing about from past and present perspectives can help you to clarify the double role of the memoir writer—as a participant and as an observer—and to decide what relative emphasis each of the two perspectives will take on in your memoir.

■ **EXERCISE**

Exploring Past and Present Perspectives

Past perspective: Recall in as much detail as possible what your feelings were at the time you are writing about in your memoir. Spend five minutes or so responding to these questions in writing:

1. What was your initial reaction to the moment in the past you're writing about? What did you think at the time? How did you feel? What did other people seem to think and feel?

2. Did you share your reaction with anyone at the time? If so, how did they respond?

3. Did your initial reaction persist or did it change? If it changed, what set of feelings replaced it? What caused the change? Were other people involved in this change?

Present perspective: Now think about your present perspective. Write for another five minutes or so in response to these questions:

1. Looking back on the moment in the past, how do the feelings you experienced at the time appear to you today? Do they seem reasonable? Why or why not?

2. If you were in the same situation today, would you act the same way? Why or why not? If you would act differently, what would you change? How? Why?

3. What are your present feelings about the event you're describing? Have your feelings changed? Do things look different from the perspective of the present? If so, how would you explain the change?

4. As you compare your feelings from the past and your feelings in the present, what conclusions can you draw about the significance the memory has for you? Are your feelings resolved, or do they seem unsettled and changing? In either case, what do you think has shaped your current perspective?

Review the two writings: Use them to write a third statement that defines what you see as the significance of the memory you're writing about and what your purpose is in re-creating it for your readers. What does the memory reveal about the past? How do you want to present yourself in relation to what happened in the past? If there is conflict or crisis, what are your loyalties toward the people and the events?

Background Research: Putting Events in Context

As Gail Caldwell's memoir "Teenage Angst in Texas" shows, placing your memories and experiences in a larger cultural and historical context can add layers of meaning to the event or events you are telling. In this way, you can link your life with social trends and political events happening around you at the time.

You may want (or need) to look in the library and on the Internet for more help in responding to these questions. Check, for example, *The New York Times Index* for that particular year, or the *Facts on File Yearbook*. Weekly periodicals such as *Time, Newsweek,* and *U.S. News & World Report* have an end-of-year issue that can help provide both cultural and historical perspectives.

Isolate the year in which your chosen event happened. If you are examining a ritual that occurred many times, pick one such instance and focus only on that. In answering the following questions, you might need to ask family members or friends for their impressions, insights, and suggestions.

- Was there anything remarkable about that year in the context of national and world events? Is that year "famous" for anything?
- What was the "news story" of the year? What was the "success story" of the year? Who were the "heroes" that year?
- What were the major social conflicts that year? Were there important political demonstrations or social movements in any part of the country? If so, what were they about? Were there any natural disasters that captured national attention that year?
- Is there a generation associated with that year (World War II veterans, baby boomers, Generation X)?
- What kind of music was most popular? What TV shows and movies?

Review your responses. What links, if any, can connect your own experience and the experiences of others at the historical moment you are considering? What cultural and historical contexts might be illuminating in your memoir?

Planning

Arranging Your Material

Memoir writers sometimes tell a story in chronological order, from beginning to end, as Gary Soto and Annie Dillard do. Notice how Soto begins many of the paragraphs so that readers can easily keep track of the events as they unfold over time:

¶ 5: "The next morning, I arrived early at work."

¶ 8: "At five the workers scattered . . . "

¶ 9: "From the backyard I walked dully through a residential street, and as evening came on . . . "

¶11: "When I got up from the lawn it was late."

¶13: "At work I spent the morning at the buffer . . . "

On the other hand, Gail Caldwell presents a sequence of episodes to create a dominant impression of her teenage years in Texas:

¶ 1: Driving mother's car 90 miles an hour.

¶ 2–3: Rides with her father and "talks."

¶ 4: Two young men Caldwell knows flee to Canada to avoid the military draft.

¶ 6: Caldwell keeps quiet about George Wallace.

¶ 7: Caldwell blows admission to National Honor Society and lies about her major.

Here are some questions to help you design a working draft:

- **How will you begin?** Do you want to ease into the moment from the past or state it outright? How can you capture your readers' interest?

Do you need to establish background information? How will you present yourself—as a participant in the past or as an observer from the perspective of the present?

- **What arrangement best suits your material?** If you are telling a single story, how can you keep the narrative crisp and moving? Do you need to interrupt the chronology with commentary, description, interpretation, asides? If you are using selected incidents, what order best conveys the point you want them to make? Do the separate incidents create a dominant impression?

- **How will you set up the moment of revelation** that gives your memoir its meaning and significance? Do you want to anticipate this moment by foreshadowing, which gives readers a hint of the revelation that is to come? Or do you want it to appear suddenly?

- **How will you end your memoir?** Do you want to surprise readers with an unsuspected meaning? Or do you want to step back from what has taken place to reflect on its significance? Is there a way in which you can echo the opening of the memoir to make your readers feel they have come full circle?

Based on your answers to these questions, make a working outline of your memoir. If you're planning to tell a story from start to finish, indicate the key incidents in the event you're remembering. If you're planning to use a sequence of memories, block out the separate events. Then you can consider the best order to present them.

Working Draft

Review the writing you have done so far. Draw on the sketching you have done, the writing that compares past and present perspectives, and your analysis of cultural and historical contexts. Consider the tentative decisions you've made about how to arrange your material—in chronological order or as a related sequence of events. As you begin composing a working draft of your memoir, you'll need to think about how you can best bring out the significance of your memories.

Beginnings and Endings: Framing Your Memoir

Notice how the writers frame their memoirs to highlight the revelations that make these writings meaningful. For example, in his opening paragraph Gary Soto introduces the idea that there are "two kinds of work," and then, after telling about his experience at the tire factory, he returns in the last six paragraphs to explore what he found out about work that "uses muscle."

Annie Dillard also uses this strategy to frame her essay. In the opening passage she anticipates the larger significance of the event she is about to recreate: "I got in trouble throwing snowballs, and have seldom been happier since." Then she tells the story of the man who chased her and of her "immense discovery." At the end of the memoir, Dillard extends the meaning of the opening lines: "If in that snowy backyard the driver of the black Buick had cut off our heads, Mikey's and mine, I would have died happy, for nothing has required so much of me since as being chased all over Pittsburgh in the middle of winter—running terrified, exhausted."

Selecting Detail

Memoirists often use techniques you can find in fiction: scene-setting, description of people, action, and dialogue. These techniques enable memoirists (like fiction writers) to re-create the past in vivid and convincing detail. Designing a memoir (like fiction writing) involves decisions about the type and amount of detail you need to make your re-creation of the past memorable to readers.

- **Scene-setting:** Use vivid and specific description to set the scene; name particular objects; give details about places and things; use description and detail to establish mood.

- **Description of people:** Use descriptions of people's appearances to highlight their personalities in your memoir; describe the clothes they are wearing; give details about a person's physical presence, gestures, facial features, and hairstyle; notice personal habits; use description and detail to establish character.

- **Dialogue:** Put words in your characters' mouths that reveal their personalities; invent dialogue that is faithful to people's ways of speaking (even if you don't use their exact words); use dialogue to establish relationships between characters.

- **Action:** Put the characters in your memoir in motion; use narrative to tell about something that happened; use narrative to develop characters and reveal the theme of your memoir.

Peer Commentary

Once you've written a working draft, you are ready to get feedback from others. Before exchanging papers, work through the following exercise. Then, you can guide your partner or group members in how to best help you.

■ EXERCISE

Analyzing Your Draft

1. Write an account of your working draft.

   a. What made you want to write this memoir? Describe in as much detail as you can what you experienced as the call to write.

   b. What is your purpose in the working draft? What are you trying to reveal about the moment in the past? What significance does this moment hold for you?

   c. What problems or uncertainties do you see in your working draft? Ask your readers about particular passages in the draft so that you can get specific feedback.

2. Your readers can offer you feedback, either oral or written, based on your working draft and the commentary you have written. Here are questions for your readers to take into account.

a. Does the writer's purpose come across clearly? Are you able to see and understand the significance of the moment in the writer's past? If the significance of the moment is not revealed clearly enough, what suggestions can you offer?

b. Is the memoir organized effectively? Does the moment of revelation appear in the best place? Does the essay begin with sufficient background information and scene-setting? Comment on the ending of the memoir. Does the writer pull things together in a way that is satisfying to the reader?

c. Is the writing vivid and concrete in re-creating particular scenes and moments from the past? Point to passages that are particularly vivid. Are there passages that are too vague, obscure, or abstract? Do the narrative passages move along crisply or do they seem to drag?

Revising

Use the commentary you have received to plan a revision.

1. Do you re-create the experience you're remembering, as opposed to just telling your readers what happened?

2. Can readers easily follow what you're remembering?

3. Will readers be able to see clearly how you experienced the events in the past and how you think about them now?

4. Are the events and people in the memoir vivid? Do you need more detail?

5. What, if anything, should you cut? What do you need to add?

6. Is there a moment of revelation that gives the memoir significance?

From Telling to Showing

Jennifer Plante revised the opening paragraphs of her memoir (a complete draft of the memoir is included in the Writers' Workshop below) to move from a summary of Sunday afternoons at her grandparents' house to a much fuller scene-setting. Her revision is a good example of the difference between telling and showing. Plante said she wanted to begin by just telling about these family gatherings. Telling about them helped her to bring her memories to consciousness. At the same time, however, she wasn't satisfied that the first version really captured the feeling of those afternoons. There's more she wanted to show about what those afternoons were really like. Notice how the memories in one paragraph of the early draft generate two paragraphs.

Early Draft

When I was ten years old, my family used to go to my grandparents' house every Sunday for dinner. It was a kind of ritual. My grandmother would cook a pot roast—I should say she overcooked it—and at the dinner table, my grandfather would carry forth on his political views. He was an intimidating, opinionated man. Nonetheless, this was a special time for me. As a ten-year-old, I didn't really understand the politics but I did know I was a special granddaughter. After dinner, my grandfather and I would watch the New England Patriots if they were on TV that week. He was the kind of hardcore fan who shouted at the Patriots players as if he were the coach, and I imitated him.

Revised version

The smell of over-cooked pot roast still magically carries me back to Sunday afternoons at my grandparents' house. I was all of ten years old; a tom-boyish, pig-tailed girl who worshiped the ground that her elders walked on. Back then, my grandfather seemed like an enormous man, every bit as intimidating as he was loving. He knew what he wanted, what he believed in, he thought that President Reagan was a demigod, and he thought that his only granddaughter was one of the biggest joys of his life. I remember that every time my family went over to my grandparents' humble home, I would run into my grandfather's warm arms and get swallowed up in a loving hug. Then, he'd sweep me off of my feet and twirl me around in the air until I was giggling so hard that I could no longer breathe.

After we ate the charcoaled roast, I would follow my grandfather into the living room. Light always seemed to radiate from the huge picture window spreading warmth into the living room; it never seemed to rain while I was at my grandparents' house. I would proceed to sit on my grandfather's lap while he stretched out in his La-Z Boy and flipped through the T.V. channels to find the New England Patriots' football game. He would often shout at the players as if he was their coach, and trying to emulate him, I would shout equally as loud not knowing what the hell I was talking about (face-masking means nothing to a ten-year-old girl). This is how every Sunday afternoon of my childhood was spent; the sequence of events was very ritualistic, and the only thing distinguishing one Sunday from another was which meal my grandmother would decide to burn. ∎

W WRITERS' WORKSHOP

Jennifer Plante wrote the following two pieces in response to an assignment in her composition class that called on students to write a memoir. The first piece is Plante's commentary on an early working draft of a short memoir based on her recollections of Sunday afternoon visits to her grandparents' house. In this commentary, she describes the call to write that got her started on the piece in the first place and her own sense of both the potential and the problems of her work in progress. You'll notice that she wrote her commentary as a kind of interim report—to explain what she was trying to do and to request feedback, constructive criticism, and suggestions from her readers.

The second piece of writing is the working draft itself, before Jennifer went on to revise it. As you read, remember that Jennifer's memoir is a work in progress. Try to read it through her commentary, to see what advice or suggestions you would give her concerning revision.

JENNIFER PLANTE'S COMMENTARY

What got me started on this piece of writing is exactly what I begin with—the smell of over-cooked pot roast. For some reason, when I was thinking about a memoir I might write, this smell suddenly seemed to leap out at me and bring me back to the Sunday afternoons we spent at my grandparents. In one way, I wanted to remember these days because I loved them so much. I felt so safe and secure and loved, with not only my parents but my grandparents surrounding me. I tried to find images of warmth, light, and enclosure to re-create this feeling. I wanted the opening to have a Norman Rockwell-like, almost sentimental feel to it—of the "typical" American family living out the American dream of family gatherings. A ritualistic feel.

But I also wanted the paragraphs to serve as a set-up for what was to come, which is really the point of the memoir. It was on a typical Sunday when I was ten that my father and grandfather argued, and my grandfather made these incredibly racist and homophobic comments. I didn't understand at the time exactly what my grandfather meant but I did understand the look on my father's face—and that something had happened that was going to change things.

I think I've done a decent job of setting this scene up, but I don't think it fully conveys what I want it to. So I had to add the final section reflecting back on it and how I now feel betrayed by my grandfather. I think this last part is probably too obvious and maybe even a little bit preachy or self-righteous, though I try to explain how my grandfather is a product of his upbringing. I want readers to understand how my feelings toward my grandfather went from completely adoring to totally mixed and contradictory ones. I don't think this is coming out clearly enough and I would appreciate any suggestions about how to do it or to improve any other parts of the essay.

JENNIFER PLANTE, SUNDAY AFTERNOONS

The smell of over-cooked pot roast still magically carries me back to Sunday afternoons at my grandparents' house. I was all of ten years old; a tom-boyish, pig-tailed girl who worshiped the ground that her elders walked on. Back then, my grandfather seemed like an enormous man, every bit as intimidating as he was loving. He knew what he wanted, what he believed in, he thought that President Reagan was a demigod, and he thought that his only granddaughter was one of the biggest joys of his life. I remember that every time my family went over to my grandparents' humble home, I would run into my grandfather's warm arms and get swallowed up in a loving hug. Then, he'd sweep me off of my feet and twirl me around in the air until I was giggling so hard that I could no longer breathe.

After we ate the charcoaled roast, I would follow my grandfather into the living room. Light always seemed to radiate from the huge picture window spreading warmth into the living room; it never seemed to rain while I was at my grandparents' house. I would proceed to sit on my grandfather's lap while he stretched out in his La-Z Boy and flipped through the T.V. channels to find the New England Patriots' football game. He would often shout at the players as if he was their coach, and trying to emulate him, I would shout equally as loud not knowing what the hell I was talking about (face-masking means nothing to a ten-year-old girl). This is how every Sunday afternoon of my childhood was spent; the sequence of events was very ritualistic, and the only thing distinguishing one Sunday from another was which meal my grandmother would decide to burn.

One Sunday afternoon, my grandfather and I had assumed our normal positions on the brown, beat-up chair and found our Patriots losing to some random team. I'm not exactly sure how the subject came up, but my grandfather and my dad began discussing politics and our society. My grandfather and my dad held different opinions about both topics, so as usual, the debate had gotten pretty heated. I began feeling a bit uncomfortable as the discussion wore on; they talked for what seemed like hours and they must have discussed every issue that was of importance to our society. To numb my discomfort, I became focused on the T.V. screen—Steve Grogan had just completed a 30-yard touchdown pass, but the referee had called that "face-masking" thing on the offense, sending Patriot fans into a frenzy. Then, just as quickly as it had started, the debate ended in dead silence. My father sat, open-mouthed, in disbelief at what he'd just heard; my grandfather had finally spoken his mind.

"What is this interracial marriage garbage? Decent white people shouldn't be marrying those blacks. And what is this perverted gay business? All the gays should go back into the closet where they belong!"

I didn't understand what my grandfather had said at the time, but I did notice the look on my father's face. It was as if my grandfather had just slapped him, only I somehow knew that what he'd said had hurt my father much more than any slap ever could have. And I did notice that, for the first time ever, a hard rain began to fall outside.

I look back on that day now and I understand why my father looked so hurt. I also understand now what my grandfather had said, and can't help but feel betrayed that a man that I admired so much had managed to insult over half of the population in one breath. I do feel bitter towards my grandfather, but I can't really blame him for his ignorance; he is a product of his time, and they were taught to hate difference. But ever since that day, I have vowed that, when my grandchildren come to visit me on Sunday afternoons, they will never see a hard rain falling outside of my picture window.

■ WORKSHOP QUESTIONS

1. Do you agree with Jennifer Plante that she has done a "decent" job of scene-setting in the opening sections of her memoir? Does the memoir's opening effectively re-create the "ritualistic feel" of family gatherings? Does it become too sentimental? Explain your responses to these questions and make any suggestions you might have for strengthening the opening.

2. Plante's memoir relies on a moment of revelation—when her grandfather makes racist and homophobic remarks and these remarks have an effect on her father. Does this moment have the dramatic value and emotional force it needs as the pivotal point in the memoir—the moment that "changed things"? What suggestions, if any, would you offer to strengthen this crucial point in the memoir?

3. Plante seems dissatisfied with the final section of the memoir, in which she writes from the perspective of the present, reflecting back on a moment in the past. She worries about seeming "obvious," "preachy," and "self-righteous" in describing her sense of betrayal. Do you think this is a problem in the draft? What advice would you offer to strengthen this section of the memoir? ■

REFLECTING ON YOUR WRITING

Write an account that explains how you handled the dual role of the memoir writer as a participant and as an observer. How did you re-create yourself as a character in your memoir? What is the relationship between your self in the past and the perspective of your present self? If memoirs are in part acts of writing that bear witness to and thereby take responsibility for the past, how do the selves you have created and re-created express loyalties and social allegiances?

chapter 6

public documents:
codifying beliefs
and practices

THINKING ABOUT THE GENRE

People in contemporary society rely on public documents to organize and carry out a wide range of social activities. Public documents serve to codify the beliefs and practices of a culture, a community, an organization—any group of people who share a mutual concern. Unlike many of the genres of writing in this textbook, public documents derive their authority from collective sources instead of from the individual who wrote them. Public documents speak on behalf of a group of people to articulate the principles and procedures that organize their purposes and guide their way of life.

Some public documents, such as the Ten Commandments or the Declaration of Independence, have taken on a sacred or nearly sacred character because they codify principles of morality and political liberty that are considered fundamental to a whole way of life. Their power resides in the authority people have invested over time in these documents as basic accounts of what they believe and hold most dear.

Other public documents serve to codify customary behavior and legal arrangements. Marriage vows, contracts, wills, and other agreements commit parties to binding relationships that are publicly and legally recognized. Government documents of all types—from laws and passports to driver's license applications and tax forms—establish relationships between the state and citizens.

Still other documents charter the mission and activities of voluntary associations people have formed to respond to particular needs—organizations such as student clubs, neighborhood associations, trade unions, and nonprofits. Writing a constitution for such a group literally constitutes it as a public entity by giving the group a name and a statement of purpose. Not only does this establish an identity for members of the group, but it also enables them to be heard on the public record and to shape public opinion. Citizen organizations, advocacy groups, and professional associations routinely issue petitions calling for change and policy statements addressing public concerns.

Public documents can tell us a lot about the culture we're living in. The encounters people have with public documents reveal how writing links individuals to social institutions. Just as important, you can write and use documents on your own behalf to accomplish your ends—to establish new voluntary associations and their purposes, to define policies and procedures you're willing to live by, to recruit sympathizers to a cause you believe in, to articulate new social identities, and to define new directions for the future.

■ WRITING FROM EXPERIENCE

List as many documents from your college or university as you can that involve students. Pick one that in your view reveals something interesting about students' relationship to others. It could be your college's honor code or its policy on sexual harassment, a student loan form, or a job description. Analyze the relationship the document seeks to establish between the individual student and others. Describe what the document covers. What rights and responsibilities does it assign to the individual student? What rights and responsibilities does it assign to others? What beliefs does the document attempt to put into practice?

READINGS

DECLARATION OF INDEPENDENCE

By July 4, 1776, when the Continental Congress approved the Declaration of Independence written by Thomas Jefferson, fighting had already broken out between American patriots and the British military. The Declaration of Independence is a manifesto that marks the decisive moment when severing ties to England and establishing a new nation become the goals of the struggle.

Establishes the occasion

Gives a reason why declaration was written and identifies audience

IN CONGRESS, July 4, 1776

The unanimous Declaration of the thirteen United States of America,

When in the Course of human Events, it becomes necessary for one People to dissolve the Political Bands which have connected them with another, and to assume among the Powers of the Earth, the separate and equal Station to which the Laws of Nature and of Nature's God entitle them, a decent Respect to the Opinions of Mankind requires that they should declare the causes which impel them to the Separation.

We hold these truths to be self-evident, that all Men are created equal, that they are endowed by their Creator with certain unalienable Rights, that among these are Life,

Sets out
funda-
mental
premises

Claims a
right
based on
premises

Qualifies
right

Establishes
grounds
for inde-
pendence

Presents
evidence of
tyranny

Lists
king's
oppressive
acts

Liberty and the pursuit of Happiness.—That to secure these Rights, Governments are instituted among Men, deriving their just Powers from the Consent of the Governed, That whenever any Form of Government becomes destructive of these ends, it is the <u>Right of the People to alter or to abolish it</u>, and to institute new Government, laying its Foundation on such Principles and organizing its Powers in such Form, as to them shall seem most likely to effect their Safety and Happiness. Prudence, indeed, will dictate that Governments long established <u>should not be changed for light and transient Causes</u>; and accordingly all Experience hath shewn, that Mankind are more disposed to suffer, while Evils are sufferable, than to right themselves by abolishing the Forms to which they are accustomed. But <u>when a long Train of Abuses and Usurpations</u>, pursuing invariably the same Object evinces a Design to reduce them under absolute Despotism, it is Right, it is their Duty, to throw off such Government, and to provide new Guards for their future security. Such has been the patient Sufferance of these Colonies; and such is now the Necessity which constrains them to alter their former Systems of Government. The history of the present King of Great-Britain is a history of repeated Injuries and Usurpations, all having in direct Object the Establishment of an absolute Tyranny over these States. To <u>prove this, let Facts be submitted</u> to a candid World.

He has refused his Assent to Laws, the most wholesome and necessary for the public Good.

He has forbidden his Governors to pass Laws of immediate and pressing importance, unless suspended in their Operation till his Assent should be obtained; and when so suspended, he has utterly neglected to attend to them.

He has refused to pass other Laws for the Accommodation of large Districts of People, unless those People would relinquish the Right of Representation in the Legislature, a Right inestimable to them and formidable to Tyrants only.

He has called together Legislative Bodies at Places unusual, uncomfortable, and distant from the Depository of their public Records, for the sole Purpose of fatiguing them into Compliance with his Measures.

He has dissolved Representative Houses repeatedly, for opposing with manly Firmness his invasions on the Rights of the People.

He has refused for a long Time, after such Dissolutions, to cause others to be elected; whereby the Legislature Powers, incapable of Annihilation, have returned to the People at large for their exercise; the State remaining in the mean time exposed to all the Dangers of Invasion from without, and Convulsions within.

He has endeavoured to prevent the Population of these States; for that Purpose obstructing the Laws for Naturalization of Foreigners; refusing to pass others to encourage their Migrations hither, and raising the Conditions of new Appropriations of Lands.

He has obstructed the Administration of Justice, by refusing his Assent to Laws for establishing Judiciary Powers.

He has made Judges dependent on his Will alone, for the Tenure of their Offices, and the Amount and Payment of their Salaries.

He has erected a Multitude of New Offices, and sent hither Swarms of Officers to harass our People, and eat out their Substance.

He has kept among us, in Times of Peace, Standing Armies without the Consent of our Legislatures.

He has affected to render the Military independent of and superior to the Civil Power.

He has combined with others to subject us to a Jurisdiction foreign to our Constitution, and unacknowledged by our Laws; giving his Assent to their Acts of pretended Legislation:

For quartering Large Bodies of Armed Troops among us:

For protecting them, by a mock Trial, from Punishment for any Murders which they should commit on the Inhabitants of these States:

For cutting off our Trade with all Parts of the World:

For imposing Taxes on us without our Consent:

For depriving us in many Cases, of the Benefits of Trial by Jury:

For transporting us beyond Seas to be tried for pretended Offences:

Lists oppressive acts of colonial government

For abolishing the free System of English Laws in a neighbouring Province, establishing therein an arbitrary Government, and enlarging its Boundaries so as to render it at once an Example and fit Instrument for introducing the same absolute Rule into these Colonies:

For taking away our Charters, abolishing our most valuable Laws, and altering fundamentally the Forms of our Governments:

For suspending our own Legislatures, and declaring themselves invested with Power to legislate for us in all Cases whatsoever.

He has abdicated Government here, by declaring us out of his Protection and waging War against us.

He has plundered our Seas, ravaged our Coasts, burnt our Towns, and destroyed the Lives of our People.

Lists further actions by king

He is, at this Time, transporting large Armies of foreign Mercenaries to compleat the Works of Death, Desolation and Tyranny, already begun with circumstances of Cruelty & perfidy scarcely paralleled in the most barbarous Ages, and totally unworthy the Head of a civilized Nation.

He has constrained our fellow Citizens taken Captive on the high Seas to bear Arms against their Country, to become the Executioners of their Friends and Brethren, or to fall themselves by their Hands.

He has excited domestic Insurrections amongst us, and has endeavoured to bring on the Inhabitants of our Frontiers, the merciless Indian Savages, whose known Rule of Warfare, is an undistinguished destruction of all Ages, Sexes and Conditions.

In every stage of these Oppressions <u>We have Petitioned</u> for Redress in the most humble Terms: Our repeated Petitions have been answered only by repeated Injury. A Prince, whose character is thus marked by every act which may define a Tyrant, is unfit to be the Ruler of a free People.

Explains efforts to remedy situation

<u>Nor have We been wanting in Attentions</u> to our British Brethren. <u>We have warned</u> them from Time to Time of Attempts by their Legislature to extend an unwarrantable Jurisdiction over us. We have reminded them of the Circumstances of our Emigration and Settlement here. <u>We have appealed</u> to their native Justice and Magnanimity, and <u>we have conjured</u> them by the Ties of our common Kindred to disavow these Usurpations, which, would inevitably interrupt our Connections and Correspondence. They too have been deaf to the Voice of Justice and of Consanguinity. We must, therefore, acquiesce in the Necessity, which denounces our Separation, and hold them, as we hold the rest of Mankind, Enemies in War, in Peace Friends.

Declares independence as only logical conclusion

We, therefore, the Representatives of the united States of America, in General Congress, Assembled, appealing to the Supreme Judge of the World for the Rectitude of our Intentions, do, in the Name, and by Authority of the good People of these Colonies, solemnly Publish and Declare, That these United Colonies are, and of Right ought to be Free and Independent States; that they are Absolved from all Allegiance to the British Crown, and that all political Connection between them and the State of Great Britain, is and ought to be totally dissolved; and that as Free and Independent States, they have full Power to levy War, conclude Peace, contract Alliances, establish Commerce, and to do all other Acts and Things which Independent States may of right do.—And for the support of this Declaration, with a firm reliance on the Protection of divine Providence, we mutually pledge to each other our Lives, our Fortunes, and our sacred Honor.

Lists
Signers

Declaration of Independence (Stone engraving of original document)

Analysis: Self-evident Truths

One of the key tasks Thomas Jefferson faced in writing the Declaration of Independence was presenting persuasive grounds for dissolving the political ties between the American colonies and the British Empire. It was not enough, for example, to say that the rights of Englishmen had been violated (as American colonists had been arguing), for that could be corrected within the framework of the empire. Instead, Jefferson appeals to "the Laws of Nature and of Nature's God" to justify rebellion and independence. These natural rights to life, liberty, and the pursuit of happiness, as Jefferson puts it, are held to be "self-evident," something that all reasonable people will recognize. In turn, these "self-evident" truths become the enabling assumptions of independence. By shifting political authority from the king or the empire to the consent of the governed, the Declaration of Independence argues that when the people's natural rights have been abridged, they are empowered to overthrow their ruler and establish new forms of government.

■ FOR CRITICAL INQUIRY

1. How does the opening paragraph establish the occasion for the Declaration of Independence? What is the call to write?

2. Consider the organization of the second paragraph. It begins with Jefferson's famous statement "We hold these Truths to be self-evident," which, as just noted, establishes the grounds for independence. Notice, however, the concession that follows, namely that "Prudence" dictates that governments "should not be changed for light and transient Causes." What role does this concession play in the unfolding argument? How is it linked to the final passages in the paragraph?

3. Describe the overall organization and movement of the Declaration of Independence. Consider how the enabling assumptions connect the main claim of the document to the evidence it brings forward.

ENCOUNTERS WITH PUBLIC DOCUMENTS

The following two reading selections offer accounts of how ordinary people encounter public documents and glimpses of what is at stake in these encounters. The first reading is taken from Abraham Verghese's book *My Own Country,* an account of his experience as a doctor working with HIV-positive and AIDS patients in Johnson City, Tennessee. This selection recounts a medical emergency where Verghese had to determine whether to put a patient on life support machines. As you will see, legal documents concerning both the patient's wishes and who will make the decision play prominent roles in shaping the outcome.

The second reading is from Ellen Cushman's *The Struggle and the Tools,* a study of how African Americans in an inner-city neighborhood negotiate with various public institutions. This selection focuses on how a particular individual, Lucy Cadens, makes sense of the forms to apply for the Home Emergency Assistance Program (HEAP) that provides help to offset high utility costs.

FROM *MY OWN COUNTRY*

ABRAHAM VERGHESE

1. Bobby Keller called me in the office as I was about to leave for home. He sounded shrill and alarmed.

2. "Doc? Ed is very sick! He is very, very short of breath and running a fever. A hundred and three. Dr. Verghese, he's turning blue on me."

3. "Bobby, call the emergency ambulance service—tell them to bring you to the Johnson City Medical Center."

4. Ed Maupin, the diesel mechanic, had had a CD4 count of 30 the previous week when I had seen him in clinic; Bobby Keller's was 500. At that visit, Ed's oral thrush had cleared up but he was still feeling tired and had been missing work. When I had examined Ed, the lymph nodes in his neck, which had been as big as goose eggs, had suddenly shrunk: I had thought to myself that this was either a good sign or a very bad sign; his immune system had either given up the fight or successfully neutralized the virus. The latter was unlikely.

5. Bobby, at that visit, had looked well and continued to work in the fashion store. I hoped now that Bobby's description of the gravity of the situation was just histrionics.

6. I was at the Miracle Center well ahead of the ambulance. Soon it came roaring in, all its lights flashing. When the back door opened, I peeked in: Ed's eyes were rolled back in his head, and he was covered with a fine sheen of sweat. Despite the oxygen mask that the ambulance crew had on, his skin was the color of lead. His chest was making vigorous but ineffective excursions.

7. Bobby, who had ridden in the front, was scarcely able to stand up. His face was tremulous; he was on the verge of fainting.

8. "Don't put him on no machines, whatever you do," Bobby begged me. "Please, no machines."

9. "Why?"

10. "Because that's what he told me. He doesn't want it."

11. "When did he tell you? Just now?"

12. "No. A long time ago."

13. "Did he put it in writing? Does he have a living will?"

14. "No . . ."

15. In the emergency room, I stabilized Ed as best I could without intubating him. I took his oxygen mask off momentarily and looked at his mouth. His mucous membranes were loaded with yeast again—it had blossomed in just a week. But I was examining his

mouth to try to decide how difficult it would be to intubate him. His short, receding lower jaw, which the beard concealed well, could make this a tricky intubation. I asked him to say "aaah." He tried to comply; his uvula and tonsils just barely came into view, another sign that he would be a tough intubation.

16 Ideally, an anesthetist would have been the best person to perform intubation. But I didn't want to call an anesthetist who, given the patient, might or might not be willing to do this procedure. Time was running out.

17 Ed was moaning and muttering incomprehensibly; his brain was clearly not getting enough oxygen. His blood pressure was 70 millimeters of mercury systolic over 50 diastolic. This was extremely low for him, because he had baseline hypertension. His cold, clammy extremities told me that the circulation to his arms and legs had shut down in an effort to shunt blood to the brain; even so, what blood got to the brain was not carrying enough oxygen. Ed's chest sounded dull in the bases when I percussed it; on listening with my stethoscope, he was wet and gurgly. The reason he was not oxygenating his blood was clear: his lungs were filled with inflammatory fluid. I ordered a stat chest x-ray and arterial blood gases. I had only a few minutes before I had to either breathe for him, or let him go. I needed more guidance from Bobby as to Ed's wishes.

18 I had an excellent nurse assisting me; she had already started an IV and brought the "crash cart." The respiratory therapist was administering oxygen and had an Ambu bag ready. I asked them to get goggles and masks in addition to their gloves, and to get a gown, mask and gloves ready for me. They were to put theirs on and wait for me. The curtains were pulled and Ed's presence was largely unnoticed in the bustle of the ER. An orthopedist was putting a cast on an individual in the next room, and patients were waiting in the other cubicles.

19 I came out to the waiting room, but Bobby was not there!

20 I hurried outside.

21 Bobby and three other men and one woman were near the ambulance entrance, smoking. The men bore a striking resemblance to Ed Maupin—the same sharp features, the slightly receding chin. One of them, the oldest, wore a green work uniform. I recognized his face as a familiar one, someone who worked in an auto parts store where I had ordered a replacement bumper for the rusted one that had fallen off my Z. Bobby Keller, still trembling, introduced me to Ed's brothers, all younger than Ed. The woman was the wife of one of the brothers.

22 "Bobby," I asked, "can I tell them what's going on?"

23   "Tell them everything," Bobby said, the tears pouring down uncontrollably, his body shaking with sobs.

24   I addressed the brothers: "Ed is very sick. A few months ago we found out he has AIDS." (There was no point in trying to make the distinction between HIV infection and AIDS. If Ed had not had AIDS when I saw him in the clinic, he most certainly did now.) "Now he has a bad pneumonia from the AIDS. I need to put him on a breathing machine in the next few minutes or he will die. I have a feeling that the pneumonia he has can be treated. If we put him on the breathing machine, it won't be forever. We have a good chance of getting him off. But Bobby tells me that Ed has expressed a desire not to be put on the machine."

25   The assembled family turned to Bobby who nodded vigorously: "He did! Said he never wanted to be on no machines."

26   The family was clear-eyed, trying to stay calm. They pulled hard at their cigarettes. The smoke rose quietly around their weathered faces. They looked like a Norman Rockwell portrait—small-town America's citizens in their work clothes in a hospital parking lot, facing a family crisis. But this situation was one that Norman Rockwell hadn't attempted, one he had never dreamed of. I felt they were fond of their oldest brother, though perhaps disapproving of his relationship with Bobby. Yet judging by how they had all been standing around Bobby when I walked out, I didn't think they had any strong dislike for Bobby—it was almost impossible to dislike him. They had had many years to get used to the idea of Bobby and Ed, the couple, and it was only the idea, I sensed, that they had somehow not accepted.

27   "We need to discuss this," the older brother said.

28   "We have no time, I need to go right back in," I said.

29   They moved a few feet away from Bobby and me. I asked Bobby, "Do you have power-of-attorney or anything like that to make decisions for Ed?" Bobby shook his head.

30   We looked over to where the family was caucusing. The oldest brother was doing all the talking. They came back.

31   "We want for you to do everything you can. Put him on the breathing machine, if you have to."

32   At this a little wail came out of Bobby Keller and then degenerated into sobs. I put my hand on Bobby's shoulder. He shook his head back and forth, back and forth. He wanted to say something but could not find a voice.

33   The oldest brother spoke again. His tone was matter-of-fact and determined:

34 "We are his family. We are legally responsible for him. We want you to do everything for him."

35 We are his family. I watched Bobby's face crumble as he suddenly became a mere observer with no legal right to determine the fate of the man he had loved since he was seven years old. He was finally, despite the years that had passed and whatever acceptance he and Ed found together, an outsider.

36 I took him aside and said, "Bobby, I have to go on. There is no way for me not to at this point. There's a really good chance that I can rescue Ed from the pneumonia. If I thought it would only make Ed suffer, I wouldn't do it. If this is Pneumocystis, it should respond to treatment."

37 Bobby kept sobbing, shaking his head as I talked, fat tears rolling off his eyes onto the ground, onto his chest. He felt he was betraying Ed. He could not deliver on his promise.

38 I had no time to pacify Bobby or try to convince him. I rushed back in. Ed looked worse. As I went through the ritual of gowning and masking (it was reassuring to have rituals to fall back on, a ritual for every crisis), it struck me that the entire situation had been in my power to dictate. All I had to do was to come out and say that the pneumonia did not look good, that it looked like the end. I mentioned the respirator, I offered it as an option. I could have just kept quiet. I had, when it came down to the final moment, given Ed's brothers the power of family. Not Bobby.

39 But there was no time to look back now.

FROM *THE STRUGGLE AND THE TOOLS*

ELLEN CUSHMAN

1 Community members often interpreted the demeaning attitudes of institutional agents by assessing the oral and literate language used in day-to-day proceedings of public service organizations. The first example shows typical forms required to access programmatic services. Whether a DSS, Medicaid, or HUD application, they all came with a list of documents required in order to validate the completed form, an information sheet describing the program, and the actual application. Applicants completed the Home Emergency Assistance Program (HEAP) forms when they needed to offset their high utility costs. In

January of 1996, Lucy Cadens picked up a HEAP application when she received a notice of termination of service from her utility company. Although she paid $45 or more a month on her bill, the high costs of gas and electric heat for a poorly insulated three-bedroom apartment continued to add up over the cold months. Her bill for January alone was close to $400, bringing her total owed to just over $960 for the winter of 1996. Lucy had heard about HEAP from a neighbor. Working on a limited budget of state funds, the HEAP office was opened only through January and mid-February before its funding ran out. Lucy and I looked over the ten pages of the application materials in my car.

2   "Jesus, these things are long," I flipped through my copies before I started the car. We were headed to our favorite buffet.

3   "They try to scare you out of applying. Try to discourage you. And it do for some folks. They see all these forms and all the shit you got to bring with you and they think, 'Hell, it gonna take me four or five hours just to pull this shit together.' And they don't do it. You spend all that time and what do you get in return?" We reached the buffet, parked in the slushy snow and buttoned our coats against the wind and flurries. I brought the application with me hoping she would talk more about it. We got our first round of food, chicken and rice soup, salads, and rolls, and we sat in a booth. Lucy took the "documentation requirements" sheet off the top of the stack and shook her head.

4   "Look at the hoops they make us jump through. Like we got nothing better to do than give them 'One or more of the following'" she read from the sheet. "Why would they need more than my Social Security card anyways?" She shook her head, poked at her pasta salad, and checked off the listed items she already had. She decided she needed to make more photocopies of everyone's birth certificates, but resented the assumptions behind the application: "They think we give up easy. Or that if we really need it, then we better be willing to work for it. That's why they need two verifications of my address. They think all poor people be tryin' to get a free ride. Or, we poor so we got to be watched, you know? They be doublechecking us all the time." She sucked on her teeth in disgust and pushed her soup and salad dishes away. Turning to the application, she glanced over the first page. "I can go through this whole thing and tear it up. Every bit of it bullshit."

5   Lucy interprets the class-based prejudices permeating the language of this application. She understands that this public service organization views her as an unethical, shifty person by virtue of her having to complete the application in the first place. While many bureaucracies have long and involved forms to complete, community members attached significance to this length. The number of documents indicates to Lucy that the institution has hidden agendas. With the length of the form alone, the institution daunts the applicants ("They try to scare you out of applying. Try to discourage you."). The application as a whole places high demands on those seeking services.

PAGE 3

LDSS-3421 (Rev. 7/99)

SECTION 4: HOUSEHOLD INCOME

CHECK (✓) YES OR NO FOR EVERY QUESTION. REPORT ANY INCOME FOR ALL HOUSEHOLD MEMBERS. ATTACH ADDITIONAL SHEETS IF NECESSARY.

INDICATE IF YOU OR ANYONE WHO LIVES WITH YOU GETS MONEY FROM:

TYPE OF INCOME	CHECK ONE (✓)	WHO RECEIVES?	SOURCE OF INCOME	IF YES, GIVE AMOUNT
1. SOCIAL SECURITY/SOCIAL SECURITY DISABILITY including direct deposit	☐ NO ☐ YES			MONTHLY AMT. $

2. SUPPLEM

3. PENSION

4. VETERAN

5. DISABILIT

6. CONTRIB

7. CHILD SU

8. ALIMONY

9. RENTAL I

10. ROOM/BC

11. WORKER'

12. UNEMPLC

13. TAP, PELI

14. INTEREST etc.

15. DIVIDEND

16. Does anyc

If yes, sub

IS THERE ANY (

I understand
not be requi
awareness c
agency to v
requirements
If you apply
information |
Line Teleph(

I swear and
Misrepresen
assistance p
obtaining as
understand t
any other inv

SIGN HERE
NAME OF PERS

LDSS-3421 (Rev. 7/99)

PAGE 4

PERSONAL PRIVACY LAW - NOTIFICATION TO CLIENTS

The State's Personal Privacy Protection Law, which took effect September 1, 1984, states that we must tell you what the State will do with the informa

Assistance
21 of the S
we check v

• We m
of Ta:

• We m

• We m

Besides us
Home Ene
State to m
payments
assistance
Support In

Comments
expedited

LDSS-3421 (Rev. 7/99)

PAGE 2

IS THERE ANYONE LIVING IN YOUR HOME/APARTMENT, INCLUDING YOURSELF, WHO IS:

BLIND OR DISABLED   ☐ NO ☐ YES   IF YES, WHO? _____

60 YEARS OR OLDER   ☐ NO ☐ YES   IF YES, WHO? _____

UNDER 8 YEARS OLD   ☐ NO ☐ YES   IF YES, WHO? _____

DO YOU OR

☐ N

DO YOU OR

☐ N

LDSS-3421 (Rev. 7/99)

SECTION

☐ HOMEO

☐ HOMEO

☐ CO-OPA

☐ RENTEI

2. MY MON(

3. IF APPLIC

4. DO YOU (

SECTION

IF YO

My main

☐ Fuel C

☐ Coal c

Is the hea
If "No," t

NO.   STF

☐ Applica   Relations
Your heat
(if you ha

CITY

MY MAILING
NO.   STR

☐ PE   Your heat

HAVE YOU A

MY MAIDEN I
FIRST

STREET AD

CITY/TOWN

Do you a
cooking

Your utilit
(if you ha

Your utilit

Is electri

CD	LN
1	01
1	02
1	03
1	04
1	05
1	06
1	07
1	08

TOTAL NUME
BESIDES MY:

FUEL/UTILITY

OFFICE

CASE NAME

SECTION

CD LN   MY NJ

1 01

FIRST

TOTAL INCC
CERTIFYING

WORKER'S SI

SUPERVISOR

HOME ENERGY ASSISTANCE PROGRAM APPLICATION

(HEAP)
Home Energy Assistance Program

IMPORTANT NOTICE

YOU SHOULD BE AWARE THAT THERE IS LIMITED MONEY AVAILABLE FOR HEAP BENEFIT PAYMENTS. ONCE AVAILABLE MONEY IS USED UP, NO BENEFITS WILL BE ISSUED AND THE PROGRAM WILL CLOSE. THEREFORE, IT IS STRONGLY RECOMMENDED THAT YOU COMPLETE AND RETURN YOUR APPLICATION AS SOON AS POSSIBLE. BE AWARE THAT IN PAST YEARS THE PROGRAM HAS CLOSED DOWN AS EARLY AS MARCH 12.

APPLICANT NAME	DATE

DSS-3431 (Rev. 6/93) FACE

(HEAP)
Home Energy Assistance Program

HOME ENERGY ASSISTANCE PROGRAM
(HEAP)

DOCUMENTATION REQUIREMENTS

☐ WHEN YOU APPLY FOR HEAP ASSISTANCE IN PERSON, YOU **MUST** PROVIDE PROOF FOR **ALL** ITEMS LISTED BELOW.

☐ IF YOU HAVE ALREADY APPLIED FOR HEAP ASSISTANCE, YOU **MUST** PROVIDE PROOF OF THE ITEMS CIRCLED. BRING THESE STATEMENTS NO LATER THAN _____ OR YOUR APPLICATION **MAY BE DENIED.**

ADDRESS (Where you now live)

You must provide **one or more** of the following:

- Current rent receipt with name and address
- Copy of lease with address
- Water, sewage, or tax bill
- Mortgage payment books/receipts with address
- Homeowners insurance policy
- Deed

ALL PEOPLE IN YOUR HOUSEHOLD

You must provide **one or more** of the following for **each** person in your household:

- Birth certificate
- Baptismal certificate
- School records
- Social Security card
- Driver's license
- Marriage certificate

FUEL/UTILITY BILLS

- If you pay a fuel or utility bill, bring a copy of your most recent fuel/utility bill.
- If you pay for **neither** heat **nor** utilities, bring a statement from your landlord that indicates heat and utilities are included in your rent.
- If you have a utility emergency, bring your utility termination notice.

INCOME

You must provide proof of **income** for all household members who receive any type of income, earned or unearned, including but not limited to:

- Pay stubs for the most recent four weeks
- If self-employed or have rental income, business records for the most recent three months
- Child support or alimony checks
- Bankbook/dividend or interest statement
- Statement from roomer/boarder
- Other _____

COPY OF MOST RECENT CHECK OR AWARD LETTER:

- Social Security/Supplemental Security Income (SSI)
- Veteran's Benefits
- Pensions
- Worker's Compensation/Disability
- Verification of Unemployment Insurance Benefit amount
- Educational Grants/Loans

RESOURCES (For emergency applications only)

- Statement claiming zero resources
- Bank Statement showing current balance for checking, savings, and credit union accounts, IRA's, etc.
- Stocks, bonds, dividends

Depending on your circumstances, additional documentation may be required.

If you have any questions, please call _____

First, the demand is on time and energy and can be seen in the number of hours it takes to complete these forms ("it gonna take me four or five hours just to pull this shit together"). Second, the demands are on literate skills. To make this application successful, individuals selected only information they could convincingly support. Without certain verifications, such as one or more forms of identification, community members' applications would not present a compelling display of need. Residents understood that these demands were shaped from the belief that poor people need to "work" (read: appease gatekeepers) for their public assistance. "Look at the hoops they make us jump through," Lucy says. In order to receive their "awards," residents had to fill numerous institutional requirements.

6   Lucy also perceives the ways the institutions mistrust those they serve. Public service agencies view community members as often trying to manipulate the system of benefits in order to receive more ("they think all poor people be tryin' to get a free ride"). Because poor people are presumably unscrupulous, they will resort to illegal means more quickly, and therefore need to be policed ("We poor so we got to be watched, you know? They be doublechecking us all the time"). These forms often asked for the same information to be presented in different ways. So verifications must accompany what the applicant lists, and when applicants handed in these forms, they often were asked verbally to recount what appears on the application. The caseworker would ask the applicant to recall specific lines of information (i.e., "so do you receive disability payments?") and doublecheck the verbal answers against the written. While one could argue that caseworkers are merely checking the internal consistency of the application, their verifications and questions indicated to residents that the institution perceives applicants as typically unethical and needing to be kept under surveillance.

7   My point here isn't so much that this literacy artifact represents the insidious values it does, but that Lucy critically reads this artifact, locates these insidious assumptions, and analyzes the politics imbued in this form. As she says, "I can go through this whole thing and tear it up. Every bit of it bullshit." She understands how public service institutions degrade those they seek to serve. She knows how institutional representatives view her using their own classist presumptions. She understands too that despite how much she balks at the institutions present throughout this application, she will still apply because she needs to keep her apartment warm. She did apply for this program, and did receive the aid she sought—four months after she submitted the application.

Analysis: Encountering Public Documents as Literacy Events

We can analyze these two reading selections as describing literacy events in which public documents—or their absence—play a key role in how people interact with each other and make sense of things.

In the excerpt from *My Own Country,* the absence of two crucial public documents shapes the outcome of this event. There is no "living will" to express Ed's wishes about medical treatment. Nor is there a marriage license or power of attorney, entitling Bobby legally to make decisions on Ed's behalf. Instead, as Ed's oldest brother tells Abraham Verghese, "We are his family. We are legally responsible for him." It is precisely because the brothers' relationship to Ed can be documented in the public record that they have the legal right to make decisions. Family ties can be verified, while Bobby and Ed's relationship remains private and unofficial, neither legally recognized nor culturally sanctioned.

The selection from *The Struggle and the Tools* explores a case where a public document—the six-page HEAP application—is a source of mutual suspicion between public assistance workers and poor people seeking help. As Lucy Cadens points out, the sheer length of the application can discourage people from applying. Just as telling, Cadens reads the application as one that expresses mistrust of the applicants—that, in effect, assumes the worst about them.

■ FOR CRITICAL INQUIRY

1. Describe how the decision to put Ed on the respirator was made. Why is Abraham Verghese conflicted by the decision? Do you think he could or should have acted differently given the circumstances?

2. Here is the main text of a sample "living will," which Ed Maupin did not have on record. What protections does it offer a patient?

   Declaration

   If I should have an incurable and irreversible condition that has been diagnosed by two physicians and that will result in my death within a relatively short time without the administration of life-sustaining treatment or has produced an irreversible coma or persistent vegetative state, and I am no longer able to make decisions regarding my medical treatment, I direct my attending physician, pursuant to the Natural Death Act of California, to withhold or withdraw treatment, including artificially administered nutrition and hydration, that only prolongs the process of dying or the irreversible coma or persistent vegetative state and is not necessary for my comfort or to alleviate pain.

   If Ed had had a signed living will, do you think Verghese's decision about putting him on a respirator would have been different? Why or why not?

3. Notice how Lucy Cadens identifies assumptions that public assistance agencies make about poor people and how these assumptions are reflected in their application forms. What are these assumptions? What must Cadens assume in order to identify the attitudes expressed in forms such as the HEAP application?

4. What experience, if any, have you had filling out application forms? How does it compare to Cadens's experience? How would you explain differences and similarities?

5. Explain how the two readings could be analyzed as literacy events. In Chapter 1, literacy events are defined as "ways to think about how reading and writing enter people's lives and shape their interactions with others." Apply the definition to the two readings. How does the presence and absence of public documents influence how the literacy event takes place?

PETITIONS

Petitions are an indispensable part of a democratic society, offering citizens the means to express their views and call for changes in public policy. The gallery of petitions presented here offers typical examples of how individuals and advocacy groups call on people to support their aims. The first petition comes from Amnesty International, while the second was circulated online by an individual, Jason Pierce. Notice that each petition is addressed to a particular individual who is capable of bringing about the change called for.

CALL FOR HUMAN RIGHTS IN RUSSIA
AMNESTY INTERNATIONAL

Accountability for human rights abuses and justice for victims of such abuses in the Russian Federation remains an abstract. The state is rarely held accountable for these abuses, and avenues of redress available to the victims are dysfunctional. People have no confidence that state or judicial institutions will right the wrongs, and those who violate human rights do so with confidence that they have every chance of getting away with it. In view of this disturbing situation, Amnesty International is launching a worldwide campaign with an aim to end the cycle of impunity for human rights abuses in Russia. President Putin, we call on you to:

- Show a clear political commitment to promote and protect fundamental human rights for everybody and to give an unequivocal message that violations of these rights will not be tolerated.

- Ensure that prompt, impartial, independent and thorough investigations of complaints relating to human rights abuses are carried out and that those responsible are brought to justice in line with international human rights standards.

- Protect ethnic minorities from arbitrary detention, particularly in the context of checking residence permits or "propiska," and from torture and ill-treatment by police. Steps to be taken should include bringing to justice the officers involved in such abuses and instituting training and monitoring programs to ensure that police do not act in a racist or discriminatory way.

- Change current practice so that children are held in detention only as a measure of last resort, and introduce training for all law enforcement officials on the special needs and rights of children in custody, as spelled out in the UN Convention on the Rights of the Child.

- Make domestic violence a distinct criminal offence and introduce training for law enforcement officials to recognize and prosecute violence against women, including domestic violence and trafficking of women. Furthermore, amend legislation to ensure that medical reports from all qualified medical personnel are accepted as evidence in cases related to allegations of torture, including rape and ill-treatment.

TIGER WOODS—STAND UP FOR EQUALITY—AUGUSTA NATIONAL GOLF CLUB

JASON PIERCE

Dear Tiger Woods,

1   We, the undersigned, request that you stand up for Equal Rights by boycotting the Masters golf tournament this coming April [2003] unless the all-male Augusta National Club admits women members.

2   As the world's most famous golfer, like it or not, you have unique power and the responsibility that goes with it. You are well aware, particularly given the tremendous public outcry against the all-male club, that your decision to participate in the Augusta tournament will effectively be an endorsement of that club's policies.

3   You've been a wonderful inspiration for young golfers, your dedication and hard work are admirable, but please, do not now send the message that you support sexism.

4   William W. "Hootie" Johnson, chairman of the Augusta National Golf Club, would like us to believe the issue is about the rights of a private club. And while the club does have a legal "right" to discriminate (its first black member was only admitted in 1990, and the 300 CEOs and other wealthy men who belong are invited to join by invitation only)—why would you want to support that?

5   Your decision to play or not to play at Augusta will be a strong statement. That is a given, and it is one of the prices of fame. Please make the right decision.

Analysis: Looking at Voice in Petitions

These two petitions are similar in that each is calling on someone to do something, whether it's ending human rights abuses or boycotting the Masters golf tournament. Each of the petition writers clearly feels a sense of urgency about an existing situation that calls on them to write. Notice, however, that the tone of voice in the petitions differs dramatically. "Call for Human Rights in Russia" is measured and formal. On the other hand, "Tiger Woods—Stand Up for Equality—Augusta National Golf Club" is warm and personal.

One of the main questions people who write petitions have to grapple with is how to fashion an appropriate tone that will best accomplish their purposes. This is not a simple matter because petition writers are involved in a dual act of persuasion: to persuade readers to sign the petition and the recipient of the petition to take an action.

■ FOR CRITICAL INQUIRY

1. Analyze the tone of voice in each of the petitions. We have already characterized the tone in each briefly, but you can add your own thoughts and insights to those characterizations or propose altogether different terms. Look closely at the petitions. What creates the tone of voice in each? Cite particular words, phrases, and passages.

2. The main claim in each petition is quite clear—end human rights abuses, and boycott the Masters. Consider how the evidence offered in each petition is linked to the claim. What enabling assumptions would someone have to accept to be persuaded by the claim? Do you think this might differ in the case of readers called on to sign the petition and recipients called on to take action?

3. Evaluate the effectiveness of each petition. Do you think one is more effective than the other? If so, why?

POLICY STATEMENTS

WPA OUTCOMES STATEMENT FOR FIRST-YEAR COMPOSITION
COUNCIL OF WRITING PROGRAM ADMINISTRATORS

The WPA Outcomes Statement for First-Year Composition was approved in 2000 by the Council of Writing Program Administrators, the leading professional association of college writing programs.

Introduction

This statement describes the common knowledge, skills, and attitudes sought by first-year composition programs in American postsecondary education. To some extent, we seek to regularize what can be expected to be taught in first-year composition; to this end the document is not merely a compilation or summary of what currently takes place. Rather, the following statement articulates what composition teachers nationwide have learned from practice, research, and theory. This document intentionally defines only "outcomes," or types of results, and not "standards," or precise levels of achievement. The setting of standards should be left to specific institutions or specific groups of institutions.

Learning to write is a complex process, both individual and social, that takes place over time with continued practice and informed guidance. Therefore, it is important that teachers, administrators, and a concerned public do not imagine that these outcomes can be taught in reduced or simple ways. Helping students demonstrate these outcomes requires expert understanding of how students actually learn to write. For this reason we expect the primary audience for this document to be well-prepared college writing teachers and college writing program administrators. In some places, we have chosen to write in their professional language. Among such readers, terms such as "rhetorical" and "genre" convey a rich meaning that is not easily simplified. While we have also aimed at writing a document that the general public can understand, in limited cases we have aimed first at communicating effectively with expert writing teachers and writing program administrators.

These statements describe only what we expect to find at the end of first-year composition, at most schools a required general education course or sequence of courses. As writers move beyond first-year composition, their writing abilities do not merely improve. Rather, students' abilities not only diversify along disciplinary and professional lines but also move into whole new levels where expected outcomes expand, multiply, and diverge. For this reason, each statement of outcomes for first-year composition is followed by suggestions for further work that builds on these outcomes.

Rhetorical Knowledge

By the end of first-year composition, students should

- Focus on a purpose
- Respond to the needs of different audiences
- Respond appropriately to different kinds of rhetorical situations
- Use conventions of format and structure appropriate to the rhetorical situation
- Adopt appropriate voice, tone, and level of formality
- Understand how genres shape reading and writing
- Write in several genres

Faculty in all programs and departments can build on this preparation by helping students learn

- The main features of writing in their fields
- The main uses of writing in their fields
- The expectations of readers in their fields

Critical Thinking, Reading, and Writing

By the end of first-year composition, students should

- Use writing and reading for inquiry, learning, thinking, and communicating
- Understand a writing assignment as a series of tasks, including finding, evaluating, analyzing, and synthesizing appropriate primary and secondary sources
- Integrate their own ideas with those of others
- Understand the relationships among language, knowledge, and power

Faculty in all programs and departments can build on this preparation by helping students learn

- The uses of writing as a critical thinking method
- The interactions among critical thinking, critical reading, and writing
- The relationships among language, knowledge, and power in their fields

Processes

By the end of first-year composition, students should

- Be aware that it usually takes multiple drafts to create and complete a successful text
- Develop flexible strategies for generating, revising, editing, and proof-reading
- Understand writing as an open process that permits writers to use later invention and re-thinking to revise their work
- Understand the collaborative and social aspects of writing processes
- Learn to critique their own and others' works
- Learn to balance the advantages of relying on others with the responsibility of doing their part
- Use a variety of technologies to address a range of audiences

Faculty in all programs and departments can build on this preparation by helping students learn

- To build final results in stages
- To review work-in-progress in collaborative peer groups for purposes other than editing
- To save extensive editing for later parts of the writing process
- To apply the technologies commonly used to research and communicate within their fields

Knowledge of Conventions

By the end of first-year composition, students should

- Learn common formats for different kinds of texts
- Develop knowledge of genre conventions ranging from structure and paragraphing to tone and mechanics
- Practice appropriate means of documenting their work
- Control such surface features as syntax, grammar, punctuation, and spelling

Faculty in all programs and departments can build on this preparation by helping students learn

- The conventions of usage, specialized vocabulary, format, and documentation in their fields
- Strategies through which better control of conventions can be achieved

Analysis: Policy Statements

The WPA Outcomes Statement for First-Year Composition is a good example of the way professional associations, nonprofit organizations, task forces, government agencies, and panels of experts issue policy statements. In this case, by considering what students should learn in composition classes, the WPA Outcomes Statement establishes standards to guide the professional work of writing teachers and writing programs. What students should learn cannot, of course, be separated from what they are taught, and one of the balances this statement must find is a clear articulation of common purposes that does not prescribe a rigid uniformity. Without a shared sense of standards, the document can have little meaning or influence. But if the document is too prescriptive it can infringe on teachers' autonomy, curtail their creativity, and undermine its own purposes. The ideal is to provide teachers with a set of standards they can use to think about and refine their own writing courses and programs.

■ FOR CRITICAL INQUIRY

1. How does the Introduction establish the call to write this outcomes statement? What need does it seek to fulfill?

2. Compare the WPA Outcomes Statement to your expectations when you began your writing course. What goals did you have for yourself? Have you modified these expectations? To what extent do your goals overlap with those of the WPA outcomes? Are there outcomes listed in the statement that you find surprising? Do you have goals not listed by the WPA statement?

3. In each of the four main areas, the statement lists how "faculty in all programs and departments can build on this preparation." Consider the writing you are called to do in your other courses. In what ways does this writing fit with WPA outcomes? Are there other aims not listed in the statement?

WRITING IN A DIGITAL WORLD

Posting a Memorandum on Torture

On June 14, 2004, the *Washington Post* posted a memorandum from August 1, 2002, on the use of torture in interrogating suspected al Qaeda detainees, prepared for Alberto R. Gonzales, legal counsel to President George W. Bush at that time, at the request of the CIA. You can find the memo, along with links to a number of other documents, including a 2003 Pentagon report on the interrogation of detainees at Guantanamo which was posted by the *Wall Street Journal*, the Taguba Report on prisoner abuse at Abu Ghraib, and sections of the U.S. Code and the Geneva Conventions on torture and the treatment of prisoners, at www.washingtonpost.com/wp-dyn/articles/A38894-2004 Jun13.html

Analysis: Leaked Documents

The memorandum on torture of August 2, 2002, as well as the Pentagon report on detainee interrogation of March 6, 2003, raise important questions about the public's right to see the documents that shape government policy. Before the *Washington Post* and the *Wall Street Journal* made them available on their Web sites in June 2004, Attorney General John D. Ashcroft had already refused a request on the part of the Senate Judiciary Committee to release the two documents, citing the principle of confidentiality in executive branch discussions of policy. By posting the documents they had obtained from anonymous sources, the *Washington Post* and the *Wall Street Journal* are making, in effect, the counterargument—namely, that the public does have the right to know the line of reasoning by government officials that torture may be justified under certain circumstances.

■ FOR CRITICAL INQUIRY

1. Visit the *Washington Post* Web site www.washingtonpost.com/wp-dyn/articles/A38894-2004Jun13.html. Read the five paragraphs in the opening section of the August 1, 2002, memorandum for Alberto R. Gonzales, which provides a summary of the main findings. Consider the definition of torture. Compare it to the definitions in the U.S. Code and the Geneva Conventions. What do you see as the main differences? What implications do these differences have for policy in interrogating detainees?

2. One of the arguments in the memorandum is that international laws barring torture may not apply in the Bush administration's war on terrorism. What is the line of reasoning at work here? What enabling assumptions distinguish the war on terrorism from other types of war?

3. When is it justified for newspapers to publish documents that the government will not release? What criteria do you think newspapers should use in making such a decision?

U.S. Department of Justice

Office of Legal Counsel

Office of the Assistant Attorney General   Washington, D.C. 20530

August 1, 2002

Memorandum for Alberto R. Gonzales
Counsel to the President

Re: Standards of Conduct for Interrogation under 18 U.S.C. §§ 2340–2340A

You have asked for our Office's views regarding the standards of conduct under the Convention Against Torture and Other Cruel, Inhuman and Degrading Treatment or Punishment as implemented by Sections 2340–2340A of title 18 of the United States Code. As we understand it, this question has arisen in the context of the conduct of interrogations outside of the United States. We conclude below that Section 2340A proscribes acts inflicting, and that are specifically intended to inflict, severe pain or suffering, whether mental or physical. Those acts must be of an extreme nature to rise to the level of torture within the meaning of Section 2340A and the Convention. We further conclude that certain acts may be cruel, inhuman, or degrading, but still not produce pain and suffering of the requisite intensity to fall within Section 2340A's proscription against torture. We conclude by examining possible defenses that would negate any claim that certain interrogation methods violate the statute.

In Part I, we examine the criminal statute's text and history. We conclude that for an act to constitute torture as defined in Section 2340, it must inflict pain that is difficult to endure. Physical pain amounting to torture must be equivalent in intensity to the pain accompanying serious physical injury, such as organ failure, impairment of bodily function, or even death. For purely mental pain or suffering to amount to torture under Section 2340, it must result in significant psychological harm of significant duration, e.g., lasting for months or even years. We conclude that the mental harm also must result from one of the predicate acts listed in the statute, namely: threats of imminent death; threats of infliction of the kind of pain that would amount to physical torture; infliction of such physical pain as a means of psychological torture; use of drugs or other procedures designed to deeply disrupt the senses, or fundamentally alter an individual's personality; or threatening to do any of these things to a third party. The legislative history simply reveals that Congress intended for the statute's definition to track the Convention's definition of torture and the reservations, understandings, and declarations that the United States submitted with its ratification. We conclude that the statute, taken as a whole, makes plain that it prohibits only extreme acts.

In Part II, we examine the text, ratification history, and negotiating history of the Torture Convention. We conclude that the treaty's text prohibits only the most extreme

VISUAL DESIGN

Defective Equipment: The Palm Beach County Ballot

PAULA SCHER

Paula Scher is a graphic designer and partner at Pentagram Design in New York City. Her visual analysis "Defective Equipment: The Palm Beach County Ballot" appeared as op-art in the *New York Times* four days after the 2000 presidential election. As you no doubt recall, the presidential election was not decided until a month later, when the U.S. Supreme Court refused to allow the recount of contested ballots, thereby making George W. Bush the next president. Al Gore and others raised a number of issues about voting irregularities in Florida. In the case of the now infamous Palm Beach County "butterfly" ballot, it's hard to forget the frustration of many voters who thought they were voting for Al Gore but, due to the design of the ballot, voted for Pat Buchanan instead.

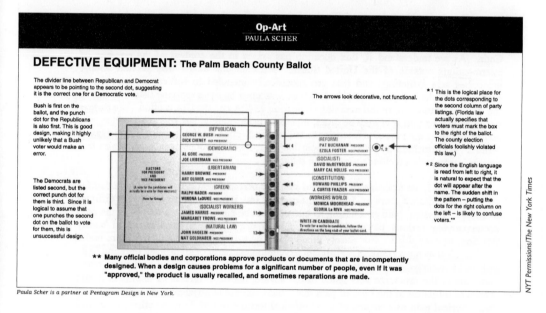

Paula Scher is a partner at Pentagram Design in New York.

NYT Permissions/The New York Times

Analysis:
Breaking Visual Design Conventions

The Palm Beach County ballot shows how the design of public documents can have very real consequences. No one knows for sure how many people in Palm Beach County intended to vote for Al Gore but, confused by the design of the ballot, voted for Pat Buchanan instead. Some go so far as to argue that the design of the ballot actually cost Gore the election. This may be, but let's leave that question aside for a moment to look more closely at how the ballot confused voters.

As Paula Scher's analysis points out, the ballot's design violated a number of visual conventions we as readers typically take for granted. We expect, that is, to follow documents from top to bottom and left to right. This is the normal reading path of written English, and any departure from it can cause confusion. Notice that the Palm Beach County ballot does not read consistently from top to bottom. Instead, although the Democratic candidates are listed second, the punch dot for them is third. This confusion, in turn, is caused by the fact that the ballot does not read consistently from left to right (as specified by Florida law). Instead, in the first column of candidates, voters read from the names of candidates on the left to the punch dots on the right, while the second column reverses direction, with the names on the right and the punch dots to the left.

■ FOR CRITICAL INQUIRY

1. Notice the design of Paula Scher's op-art piece "Defective Equipment: The Palm Beach County Ballot." Scher reproduces the section of the ballot in dispute and then uses arrows and written commentary to point out design flaws. Did you find her analysis easy to follow and understand? Why or why not?

2. Imagine that only written text was available for the analysis. What would you have to say in writing to make the points that Scher does? What would be lost to the analysis?

3. Scher's analysis develops an argument that is presented in the double asterisked (**) two sentences in bold that appear underneath the ballot. Explain how the analysis leads visually to this point. How do the asterisks link the line of reasoning? Do the two sentences at the bottom seem to follow logically and persuasively from Scher's analysis?

4. The Palm Beach County ballot was designed and approved by Democrats. No one is suggesting that it was intended to rig the election for George W. Bush, though clearly it helped him. Instead, the ballot appears to be a simple design error. What do you think should have been done immediately following the elections? Do you agree with those who argued that the design flaw literally (though not intentionally) disenfranchised voters—and that new elections should have been held with new ballots?

5. Redesign the ballot to eliminate confusion.

FURTHER EXPLORATION: PUBLIC DOCUMENTS

■ GENRE CHOICES

Under what circumstances do individuals or groups turn to the manifesto as a public declaration of a position, belief, or plan? What are the advantages and disadvantages of a manifesto as compared to a commentary, proposal, or other genre?

■ WORKING TOGETHER

Writing a Class Charter

For this assignment, you will be working together as a whole class to design and produce a charter for the writing course you are currently taking. One way to do this assignment is to break the class into working groups of four to six, depending on the size of the class, with each group responsible for drafting one section of the charter. Here is one possible way of dividing the charter into sections. Your class, however, may decide to modify this plan.

- **Preamble:** The preamble to a charter explains the purposes and goals of an organization or, in this case, of a writing course.

- **Teacher's rights and responsibilities to the students:** This section explains the role of the teacher in the writing course and what students can legitimately expect from the teacher.

- **Students' rights and responsibilities to the teacher:** This section explains the role of students in their relationship to the teacher in a writing class and what teachers can legitimately expect from them.

- **Students' rights and responsibilities to each other:** This section explains the relationship among students in a writing class and what students can legitimately expect from each other.

- **Bylaws governing classroom life:** While the first four sections will be somewhat general in their explanations of the goals of the course and individuals' roles within it, this section should be more specific, presenting the policies that will govern classroom life. Bylaws often appear in charters as numbered points. Here are some things you will likely want to consider in the bylaws section: attendance, timely completion of work, how to ensure that everyone is heard in class discussion, how to handle differences of opinion, and how to make group work productive. There are probably other things, depending on the circumstances, that you will want to cover in this section.

The class as a whole will need to discuss collectively what it wants in each of the sections. Then the working groups can draft sections, make sufficient copies, and bring them to class for revision. Or the class can work on and respond to the sections electronically through a listserv or Web page.

WRITING ASSIGNMENT

Public Documents

Online Study Center

The focus on public documents in this chapter can lead to a number of different writing assignments. The following list ranges from writing about public documents to designing your own documents. Your instructor will let you know which possibilities to consider for this assignment, or you may be assigned to write a class charter with your classmates.

- **Analysis of encounters with public documents as literacy events:** Analyze an encounter you have had with a public document. Explain how the document shaped roles, relationships, and outcomes. Consider how your encounter can be understood as a literacy event (as explained in the Chapter 1 Writing Assignment: Analyzing a Literacy Event).

■ **Rhetorical analysis:** Analyze one (or more) of the documents in this chapter or a public document of your choice, such as the Communist Manifesto, or the Freedom Charter of the African National Congress in South Africa. You could analyze the rhetorical situation (as explained in the Chapter 2 Writing Assignment: Rhetorical Analysis), the argument (as explained in the Chapter 3 Writing Assignment: Analyzing Arguments), or you could combine the two.

■ **Manifesto:** Write a manifesto that explains what calls on you to publicly proclaim a new identity, mission, and purpose. Consider the persona you are inventing in the manifesto and on whose behalf the manifesto is speaking. Explain why the current situation needs to be changed and what you are calling on like-minded people to do. (See "Declaration of Independence" in this chapter.)

■ **Petition:** Write a petition that calls on a public official or figure to do something. Explain an existing problem and what should be done about it. Consider the tone of voice you want to use and how you will need to persuade readers to sign the petition and the recipient to take action.

■ **Policy Statement:** Write a statement of policy that takes a position on a public concern or sets standards of practice. (See WPA Outcomes Statement and the Warehouse State Honor Code in this chapter.)

Invention

Chapters 1, 2, and 3 provide guidelines to analyze an encounter with a public document as a literacy event, to analyze the rhetorical situation, and to analyze arguments, so we'll focus in this section on writing manifestos and petitions.

Clarifying Purpose and Genre

People write manifestos and petitions out of a sense of urgency that their voices need to be heard—that new identities need to be asserted and that changes need to take place. As you've probably noticed, however, manifestos and petitions differ considerably in their scope. Manifestos take broad views of the current state of affairs, while petitions focus on specific issues or problems. If you're considering writing one or the other, the following questions can help you clarify your purpose and determine which of the two genres to use.

1. Consider who you are, the people you hang out with, and groups that you identify with—whether Goths, geeks, alternative, straight-edge,

jocks, preps, or whatever. What gives your group its particular identity? What are its values and its relationship to other groups? How are that identity and those values represented publicly—by members of your group or others? Is there a need for someone to speak out on behalf of the group, to explain what it's really all about? If so, you may want to write a manifesto on behalf of your group.

2. Consider the problems and issues that concern you personally— whether global warming, the occupation of Iraq, domestic violence, or the dorm rules on your campus. Has a new law or public policy been proposed that you're concerned about? Is there something specific that you think should be changed? Or something that the people in charge could be doing that they're not? In these cases, you may have an idea to write a petition to a particular public official or figure, calling for some new course of action.

Background Research: Understanding the Rhetorical Situation

If you're planning to write a manifesto or a petition, you may well need to do some background research to clarify the rhetorical situation that is calling on you to write. For one thing, you'll need a good grasp of the existing state of affairs and, in the case of petitions, the specific issue or problem you're addressing. In either case, consider who is involved in the situation and what interests are at stake. You can do background reading and talk to people who know about the situation. For petitions, you'll need to determine the appropriate person to whom you'll send the petition.

Planning

Public documents often follow a set pattern, making them easily recognizable to readers and easily reproducible by writers to account for new situations. Different genres—whether a manifesto, a petition, or an organization's charter—have their own typical design. If you are designing a document, a good way to begin is to find one or more examples of a document like it to identify its typical features. If you are analyzing an existing document, you will also want to pay attention to its design features.

As you can see from the examples in this chapter, manifestos tend to have an open form, while petitions typically state the problem or issue and then present their demand or demands. Charters almost always have a preamble that explains an organization's mission and goals, followed by clearly defined sections and often a list of bylaws.

Readability and the Visual Design of Public Documents

Here are some considerations to take into account, whether you're designing or analyzing a public document. These visual design features enhance the readability of a document by helping readers mentally organize the material presented.

See Chapter 19, "Visual Design," for more on white space, page layout, headings, and fonts.

- **Title and logo:** How is the document titled? Does it use a logo or other identifying graphic feature?

- **Preamble or background section:** Does the document have a preamble or a background section that explains the occasion that called for it and its general principles? If not, how does it begin?

- **White space:** Does the document use white space to separate sections in the document and to emphasize key points?

- **Headings and subheadings:** Does the document use headings and subheadings to denote separate sections? How do such divisions make the document easier to read?

- **Bullets:** Does the document use bullets to emphasize key points? Notice, for example, how Amnesty International's "Call for Human Rights in Russia" uses a list of bulleted points to present its demands.

- **Fonts:** Does the document use capital letters, italics, boldface, underlinings, or designer fonts to emphasize key words or phrases?

- **Parallelism:** Does the document use parallel grammatical structures? Here are some of the most commonly used structures:

  Infinitives: Notice how the Preamble to the United Nations charter uses infinitive phrases, such as "to save" and "to reaffirm":

  > We the People of the United Nations Determined
  >
  > to save succeeding generations from the scourge of war, which twice in our lifetime has brought untold sorrow to mankind, and
  >
  > to reaffirm faith in fundamental human rights, in the dignity and worth of the human person, in the equal rights of men and women and of nations large and small, and
  >
  > to establish conditions under which justice and respect for the obligations arising from treaties and other sources of international law can be maintained, and
  >
  > to promote social progress and better standards of living in larger freedom,

  Noun phrases: "Rhetorical Knowledge," "Critical Thinking, Reading, and Writing," "Processes," and "Knowledge of Conventions" (from WPA Outcomes Statement)

> *Repeated phrases:* "By the end of first-year composition, students should . . . " "Faculty in all programs and departments can build on this preparation by helping students learn . . . " (from WPA Outcomes Statement)

> *Imperatives*: "Show," "Ensure," "Protect," and "Change" (from "Call for Human Rights in Russia")

- **Signature:** Is the document signed? If so, by whom? What does signing commit people to?

Working Draft

Whether you are analyzing a document or designing one of your own, you will want to consider the tone of the writing—the voice readers hear in the written text.

Tone and Rhetorical Distance

A writer's tone of voice is one key way of establishing his or her relationship to readers. Notice how the following examples of informal, standard, and official tone put the writers into quite different relationships to readers:

- **Informal:** Writing that speaks in the first person singular, addresses readers as "you," uses colloquialisms and contractions, poses rhetorical questions, and generally strives to sound like spoken language creates an informal tone that reduces the distance between the writer and readers. "Hacker's Manifesto," for example, seeks to involve readers and create a sense of intimacy:

  > But did you, in your three-piece psychology and 1950s techno-brain, ever take a look behind the eyes of the hacker?

  > I am a hacker, enter my world . . .

  Notice also how the petition to Tiger Woods uses a personal tone.

- **Standard:** The tone of voice readers hear in many instances of professional communication, journalism, textbooks, and other forms of nonfiction prose can be characterized as "standard" because it relies on a plain, relatively formal (but not elevated or pretentious) style. This tone does not usually call attention to the writer's personality, as is often the case with an informal tone, or address readers intimately as "you." Instead, it seeks to establish a relationship with readers based on shared interests and the mutual respect of reasonable persons exchanging views. The opening paragraph of Amnesty International's "Call for Human Rights in Russia" is a good example of such a tone:

  > Accountability for human rights abuses and justice for victims of such abuses in the Russian Federation remains an abstract. The

state is rarely held accountable for these abuses, and avenues of redress available to the victims are dysfunctional. People have no confidence that state or judicial institutions will right the wrongs, and those who violate human rights do so with confidence that they have every chance of getting away with it. In view of this disturbing situation, Amnesty International is launching a worldwide campaign with an aim to end the cycle of impunity for human rights abuses in Russia. President Putin, we call on you to:

■ **Official:** An official tone creates the most distance between the written document and readers. The voice that readers hear is not that of an individual writer but of an institution or collective body speaking. The style of writing tends to have a certain bureaucratic or legalistic tone. The controversial Proposition 215 to legalize medical uses of marijuana that appeared on the California state ballot—and passed—in 1996 is a typical example:

> The people of the State of California hereby find and declare that the purposes of the Compassionate Use Act of 1996 are as follows:
>
> To ensure that seriously ill Californians have the right to obtain and use marijuana for medical purposes where that medical use is deemed appropriate and has been recommended by a physician. . . .
>
> This measure amends state law to allow persons to grow or possess marijuana for medical use when recommended by a physician.

Peer Commentary

Exchange drafts with a classmate. Depending on whether you have analyzed or designed a public document, use the appropriate guidelines.

For Manifestos, Petitions, Policy Statements, and Class Charters

1. Is the purpose of the document clear and easy to find? Explain where you became aware of its purpose. Will readers understand what, if anything, it calls on them to do?

2. What suggestions can you offer to improve or strengthen the format of the document? Consider its layout, organization, use of numbered or bulleted items, and other design features.

3. Is the language of the document precise and easy for readers to understand? Underline words, phrases, or passages that might be written more clearly. Explain why you marked them. Is the tone appropriate for the type of document your partner has designed? Why or why not?

Circle words, phrases, or passages where you think the tone does not work well. Explain.

For Analysis of a Document

1. Explain what you see as the writer's purposes—analyzing a personal encounter with a public document, doing a rhetorical analysis, or something else? Is the main point of the analysis clearly stated and easy to find?
2. Describe how the writer develops an analysis. Does the analysis fulfill the writer's purposes or some other purposes? What suggestions can you offer to extend or deepen the analysis?
3. Do you agree with the analysis? If so, explain why. If not, explain why.

Revising

Review the peer commentary you have received and then consider these questions, depending on whether you've designed or analyzed a document:

For Manifestos, Petitions, Policy Statements, and Class Charters

1. Is the purpose of your document easy for the reader to identify?
2. Have you ordered your points in a way that is easy to follow? Check at this point to make sure similar points are parallel in structure.
3. Is each point clearly separate from other points? Consider the feedback you have received on the tone of the document.

For Analysis of a Document

1. Is the purpose your reader identified what you intended?
2. What suggestions about your analysis does your reader offer? Why do you think your reader made these suggestions?
3. What assumptions about your analysis does your reader seem to be making in agreeing or disagreeing with it? How do these assumptions compare to assumptions you make in the draft?

Locating Common Ground

Public documents such as laws, contracts, and codes are agreements about the way we will conduct ourselves and our relations with others. Because of this, documents rely on consent—through advocacy, voting in elections, and other forms of participation in decision making. When individuals and groups believe their views have not been represented in shaping the policies outlined in public documents, they are less likely to invest authority in or abide by these documents.

An interesting case in point occurred at Warehouse State College recently. The Ad Hoc Committee on Academic Honesty, consisting of students, faculty, and administrators, issued a draft version of an academic honor code which, if approved, all members of the Warehouse State community would be expected to sign and to follow. (The complete draft appears below in Writers' Workshop.) The following section caused a particular controversy among students:

> As a member of the Warehouse State community, I shall not intentionally or knowingly violate the bonds of academic trust among us, nor shall I tolerate violations of this trust.

A later section in the draft specified students' responsibilities:

> Upon witnessing any act of academic dishonesty, a student must:
>
> a. Communicate either verbally or in writing, either directly or anonymously, with the student or students who have committed the act of academic dishonesty, informing this or these students that an act of academic dishonesty has been observed. A student must also:
> b. Give prompt notification to the Academic Honor Council that a violation has occurred. The student reporting the violation must identify him or herself and the name(s) of the violator(s).

These provisions in the honor code draft quickly became known as the "rat rule," sparking a heated discussion. Some students argued that they went to Warehouse State to be educated, not to "spy" on other students. Some worried that if they observed cheating during an exam, the responsibility to report violations would interfere with their own academic performance. Others supported the proposed code. Seeking to preserve the spirit of the honor code and, at the same time, to satisfy objections and establish a common ground, the committee revised the two sections. Changes are in italics.

> As a member of the Warehouse State community, I shall not intentionally or knowingly violate the bonds of academic trust among us. *I recognize that protecting academic integrity is the collective responsibility of students, faculty, and staff at Warehouse State.*
>
> Upon witnessing any act of academic dishonesty, *a student will be guided by conscience whether to report the act or to take other appropriate action.*

Whether removing the "rat rule" waters down the original intention or provides a common ground all can agree to is an open question. ■

W R I T E R S ' W O R K S H O P

Here is the complete draft, before the revision you've just seen, of the proposed academic honor code for Warehouse State College.

THE WAREHOUSE STATE HONOR CODE

Ad Hoc Committee on Academic Honesty

Proposal for an Academic Honor Code

February 21, 2001

Preamble

At Warehouse State, the bonds of academic trust among all members of the academic community are paramount. Establishing and maintaining these bonds require a unified commitment to the principles of academic integrity and honesty in all educational interactions. To this end, Warehouse State students, faculty, and administrators affirm the following pledge.

I.   **Honor pledge**

As a member of the Warehouse State community, I shall not intentionally or knowingly violate the bonds of academic trust among us, nor shall I tolerate violations of this trust.

II. **Definition of Academic Trust**

Academic trust is the assurance that teacher and student will faithfully abide by the rules of intellectual engagement established between them. This trust can exist only when students adhere to the standards of academic honesty and when faculty test and evaluate students in a manner that presumes that students are acting with academic integrity.

III. **Definition of Academic Dishonesty**

Any willful act that either interferes with the process of evaluation or misrepresents the relation between the work evaluated and the student's actual state of knowledge is an act of academic dishonesty and a violation of academic trust. The following are some examples of dishonesty:

a. *Cheating.* Misrepresentation of the work of another as one's own; use of purchased term papers; copying on exams; submission of homework, programs, projects, and take-home exams with portions done by another; use of unauthorized materials or sources of information, such as "crib sheets" or unauthorized storing of information in calculators; assistance of another person in cases where prohibited.

b. *Fabrication.* Alteration of grades or official records; changing of exam answers after the fact; falsifying or inventing laboratory data.

c. *Facilitating Academic Dishonesty.* Assisting or facilitating any act of academic dishonesty.

d. *Academic Sabotage.* Sabotage of another student's work or academic record.

e. *Plagiarism.* Representing the work or ideas of another as one's own without giving proper credit.

IV. **Responsibilities**

A. Student Responsibilities

1. Know and uphold the Honor Pledge.

2. Do not commit any acts of academic dishonesty.

3. Upon witnessing any act of academic dishonesty, a student must:

a. Communicate either verbally or in writing, either directly or anonymously, with the student or students who have committed the act of academic dishonesty, informing this or these students that an act of academic dishonesty has been observed. A student must also:

    b. Give prompt notification to the Academic Honor Council that a violation has occurred. The student reporting the violation must identify him or herself and the name(s) of the violator(s).

4. When in doubt about classroom or project rules, ask the professor.

B. Faculty Responsibilities

1. Know and uphold the Honor Pledge.

2. Foster an educational environment that is consistent with the definition of academic trust.

3. Communicate to students individual policies concerning evaluation procedures and expectations pertaining to academic integrity and trust.

4. Report any act of academic dishonesty to the Academic Honor Council.

5. Recognize that judgments about academic dishonesty are the sole responsibility of the Academic Honor Council. If a student is found not guilty on a charge of academic dishonesty, the instructor will not penalize the student in any way.

C. Institutional Responsibilities

1. Disseminate annually the Academic Honor Code to all students, faculty, and staff.

2. Through Faculty and New Student Orientation, promote discussion of the Academic Honor Code and the value Warehouse State places on integrity.

3. Have new students sign the Academic Honor Pledge upon joining the institution.

4. Give administrative support to the Academic Honor Council to ensure ongoing implementation of the Academic Honor Code.

5. Maintain appropriate confidential mechanisms for reporting honor code violations.

V. **Acceptance of the Academic Honor Pledge**

Students sign a pledge they will uphold the principles of academic trust and that they will fulfill their responsibilities concerning the Academic Honor Code as part of their admission to the institution. A student's placing his or her name on an exam, paper, or project shall be understood as a reaffirmation of the student's pledge to abide by the Academic Honor Code. Faculty are expected to conduct classes according to the spirit of academic trust and to follow academic honor code procedures concerning violations.

■ **WORKSHOP QUESTIONS**

1. Imagine that the Ad Hoc Committee on Academic Honesty at Warehouse State College has asked you to review its draft of the Academic Honor Code. How would you respond? Does the Preamble clearly articulate the purpose of the document? Are the definitions of terms and of student, faculty, and institutional responsibilities clearly stated? Are there things not included that you think the document should contain?

2. Evaluate the revision of the two sections of the honor code that appear in the preceding section. Consider student objections to the "rat rule." Do you think they are valid? Do you think an academic honor code should require students to report violations?

3. Does your college or university have an honor code? If so, what does it commit students, faculty, and administrators to do? How is it similar to or different from the Warehouse State draft? What revisions, if any, do you think it needs? If your school does not have an honor code, do you think there should be one? What should it cover?   ■

REFLECTING ON YOUR WRITING

Write a short account of your experience analyzing or composing a public document. Take into account the authority you drew on to write the document or the source of authority the document you analyzed drew on. On whose behalf did you write the document or was the document written? What problems or issues did you encounter in your writing? Explain how you dealt with them.

chapter 7

profiles: creating a dominant impression

THINKING ABOUT THE GENRE

Talking about people and places amounts to a sizeable component of conversation—whether you're telling your parents what your new roommate is like or describing to friends the neighborhood where you grew up. This impulse to describe, to analyze, and to understand seems to grow out of a genuine need to come to terms with our social experience, the places we live, and our relationships with others.

It's not surprising, then, that a genre of writing—the profile—is devoted to describing and analyzing people and places. Profiles are a regular feature in magazines such as *Rolling Stone, Sports Illustrated, Ebony*, and *Ms.*, as well as in newspapers. Many profiles are of well-known people, and the call to write profiles undoubtedly has a lot to do with writers' and readers' fascination with the famous and the powerful. The allure of such profiles is that they can offer us a behind-the-scenes look at people we've heard so much about.

But profiles can also focus on ordinary people. When an issue moves to the forefront of the public's attention, ordinary people often become the subject of profiles that describe, say, the lives of undocumented workers or the plight of a corporate executive laid off by downsizing. Such profiles of ordinary people supplement statistical and analytical treatments of issues, making concrete and personal what would otherwise remain abstract and remote. These profiles can take readers beyond their preconceptions to explore the remarkable variety of people, backgrounds, lifestyles, and experiences that are frequently reduced to a single category such as "the elderly" or "blue-collar workers." There are profiles of places, as well as of people. The travel section of newspapers, for example, profiles places to visit, while feature articles may look at the fate of the Ninth Ward in New Orleans or why Modesto, California, has become the car-theft capital of the United States.

Sometimes, profiles seem to take place in real time. They may tell what a person does over the course of a day or during characteristic activities. Such profiles create a sense of immediacy and intimacy, as though the reader were there on the spot, watching and listening to what's going on. Readers of profiles have come to expect that they will be able to visualize the person (What does she look like? What is she wearing? What are her surroundings?), to hear the person's voice (What does she sound like? How does she talk to the people around her?), and to witness revealing incidents (What is she doing? How and why does she do it? What does this show about her?).

To convey this sense of immediacy and intimacy, writers of profiles often rely on interviewing and observation. This doesn't mean, of course, that library research isn't involved. On the contrary, consulting written sources can supplement interviewing and observation and make them much more effective.

In any case, one point to keep in mind is that no matter how immediate or persuasive a profile seems to be, we are not seeing a person or a place directly but rather through the eyes of the writer. The way a person appears in a profile—and the impact his or her story has on readers—depends as much on the writer as on the person profiled. Profiles express, explicitly or implicitly, the author's point of view or dominant impression. No profile will really work for its readers unless it creates this dominant impression—a particular and coherent sense of its subject.

■ WRITING FROM EXPERIENCE

We talk about other people all the time. We tell stories about what others do and comment on what they are like. Think about the conversations you have with others—friends, relatives, coworkers, neighbors, acquaintances, or strangers. In these conversations, what kinds of stories and comments about people come up? List four or five occasions when you or someone else told a story or made a comment about another person. What was the purpose?

Compare your list with the lists of your classmates and see whether any patterns emerge. Are there, for example, any differences between men's and women's stories and comments? Can you classify these examples—by purpose or by who is speaking or whom the stories or comments are about?

READINGS

INSURGENT IMAGES: MIKE ALEWITZ, MURALIST

PAUL BUHLE

Paul Buhle is a historian of labor and popular arts at Brown University. His books include The New Left Revisited *(2003),* Tender Comrades: A Backstory of the Hollywood Blacklist *(1999), and* C.L.R. James' Caribbean *(1992). The following profile is of Mike Alewitz, one of the most prominent American muralists in the last twenty years, an art teacher at Central Connecticut State, and a noted social activist. Buhle and Alewitz collaborated on the book* Insurgent Images: The Agitprop Murals of Mike Alewitz *(2002), which features examples of Alewitz's murals, including those that appear here.*

Si Se Puede, Oxnard, California, 1993

1   A large outside wall of Cesar Chavez High School in Oxnard, California, carries the portrait of the famed Latino labor leader and social visionary, "the Chicano Martin Luther King, Jr.," against a background of grape fields and a foreground of the message "Si se puede! Yes! It can be done!" Chavez is seen holding up a book, open to facing pages in English and Spanish, with the text: "We need a meaningful education, not just about the union, but about the whole idea of the cause. The whole idea of sacrificing for other people . . . " Not himself Chicano, not even a Californian, muralist Mike Alewitz was (as actor Martin Sheen pronounced at the 1993 dedication ceremony) the natural choice of artists.

2   Alewitz is happiest in a small crowd of amateur painters and community members who meet to discuss with him what kind of mural would best suit the purposes of the community and the building. Artistic choices are important, but this is public art, its role in some ways better understood in the past than today: art that becomes part of the daily life of ordinary people by picturing their aspirations and struggles in cartoons, murals, posters, and banners. Beginning with the tumultuous labor conflicts in the decades after

Opening
* describes
an Alewitz
mural
* puts
Alewitz
and
murals in
historical
context

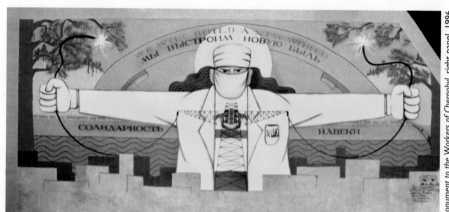

Monument to the Workers of Chernobyl, right panel, 1996

the Civil War, a public art grew out of union-organizing, agitation against war, and the radical dreams of the American left for women's liberation, racial equality, and social justice. Like many of his artistic predecessors, Alewitz was a factory or office worker for most of his working life, until he became a full-time painter.

3

gives biographical details

Born in 1951 and growing up in Wilmington, Delaware and Cleveland, Alewitz was barely aware that his Cleveland neighborhood had produced the creators of Superman, and was about to bring forth such noted popular artist-creators as Harvey Pekar (subject of an award-winning 2003 film, *American Splendor*) and Peter Kuper (current artist of *Mad* magazine's feature, "Spy Versus Spy"). These artists all shared a sense for the vernacular: the art that almost never reaches gallery walls, but captures the attention of young people in particular. He almost didn't make it to college, and dropped out after a year. That college was Kent State.

4

By an accident of fate, he had landed on the most explosive campus in North America. At President Richard Nixon's announcement of the US invasion of Cambodia in May 1970, enlarging the Vietnam War dramatically, peace demonstrators took over the grounds of universities and colleges for days, and police and National Guardsmen moved in to halt the demonstrations. At Kent State, guardsmen shot into the crowd, killing students and prompting the most provocative rock music hit of the season, "Four Dead in Ohio" by Crosby, Stills, Nash and Young. Alewitz, a central leader of the Kent antiwar movement,

Monument to the Workers of Chernobyl, left panel, 1996

dropped out of school to coordinate the Committee of Kent State Eyewitnesses and to help explain the events and their importance to the national student strike then in progress.

5   Mike Alewitz found a second home in the college town and state capital, Austin, Texas, where he ran for local office as a peace candidate. He began painting signs again, for the growing antiwar activity among GIs in basic training at nearby Fort Killeen. He was locally famous (or notorious) for his visual sense of humor, aimed at the clichés of activists, politicians and the military alike.

6   For most of the next twenty years, he worked on railroad lines, at printshops, and most happily as a billboard and sign painter. He painted his first murals in Central America, during the regional conflicts of the 1980s, but received his first major commission almost accidentally in 1984 while visiting a historic packinghouse not far from the twin cities of St. Paul/Minneapolis, in Austin, Minnesota. There, a committee of strikers in local P-9, United Food and Commercial Workers (UFCW) asked him to paint a large wall on the side of their union hall. With the help of strikers and local sympathizers, Alewitz created a panorama of labor dignity, assaulted by corporate mismanagement. The mural was dedicated to Nelson Mandela, then-imprisoned leader of the African National Congress and destined to be the black president of a future South Africa. Widely recognized as one of labor's most important artistic statements in decades, it was destroyed at the orders of national union officials who had decided to end the strike and take control of the union local.

7   Many similar adventures followed in strikes, Labor Day parades, demonstrations for the rights of working people, women, immigrants and minorities. Alewitz became a

*describes some of Alewitz's murals

widely-recognized artist for unions like the Oil, Chemical and Atomic Workers and the United Brotherhood of Carpenters, the movement for a Labor Party (for which he served as Chair of the Cultural Workers and Artists Caucus), but also for many local causes in his adopted New Jersey, and for school buildings. He also traveled abroad, painting for the endangered atomic-plant workers in Chernobyl, Ukraine, site of the world's worst nuclear energy disaster, to the Middle East and to Mexico.

8

*explains how Alewitz's style emerged

The last was very much like coming home in an artistic sense. The foremost muralists of the Americas in the twentieth century, along with the Works Progress Administration public artists during the 1930s, were the giants of Mexican muralism, especially Diego Rivera, David Alfaro Siqueiros, Jose Clemente Orozco. These artists, with some of their outstanding 1930s work painted in the U.S., more than anyone else restored painting to its public role in conjunction with social movements whose participants best understood what art might become once again. From them, Alewitz learned purpose. But he had to develop his own style.

9

Everything under the sun is suitable for reworking as an Alewitz image. From comic strips to earth-shaking events like revolutions and wars, labor leaders and ordinary workers, social heroes and martyrs, nature scenes, factories and neighborhoods, funny and tragic lessons alike. Perhaps most continuous and vividly expressed, though, is the reality of working for a living in hundreds of different ways, old style factories to new style computer terminals—and the overwhelming importance of education.

10

*explains how Alewitz works

All this goes into the making of the mural. Painters and assorted volunteers help to procure materials, erect scaffolding, repair and prime walls for painting, and often block in large areas of color as well. He has also developed methods of providing space for casual or symbolic contributions to the painting by a larger group of supporters. Artists, poets, musicians and activists of all sorts are invited to create work around the project, at concerts, dedication ceremonies and other public events.

11

Alewitz himself meanwhile takes strong and direct control of the imagery. He does not believe that his role is to attempt to paint "as if" someone else might, but rather to express those events, struggles and personalities through his own experiences as worker, artist and activist. He has learned that art by committee usually fails because art cannot be negotiated without being homogenized. That said, he works out a final design after thorough discussion. He prefers, for the most part, to work with young assistants who will go through the experience and learn skills that will help them create mural art of their own.

12

Ending
* *uses a*
particular
mural to
make
closing
point

One of Alewitz's most revealing murals stands on the Highlander Center in New Market, Tennessee, a historic center of civil rights activity and craft training. On one side, leading to a loaf of bread and sumptuous tomatoes (because Highlander is famous for its own produce), is Dr. Martin Luther King, Jr., and on the other side, Highlander's founder, the late Myles Horton, with multiracial working people marching underneath, and the banner-message, "Sin accion, no hay conocimiento/Without action, there is no knowledge."

13

Democracy, Alewitz's paintings boldly insist, demands active citizens, proud of themselves for what they produce, educated to take responsibility for their history and the better future that America may hold.

Analysis: Using Cultural and Historical Background

The two profiles that follow capture their subjects at a particular moment in time. Paul Buhle's profile, on the other hand, emphasizes Mike Alewitz's work as a muralist in many places, from Cesar Chavez High School, where the profile opens, to Austin, Minnesota, where Alewitz painted one of his most important murals, to Alewitz's travels to Chernobyl, the Middle East, and Mexico, to the closing scene at the Highlander Center in Tennessee. To create a dominant impression that conveys the signficance of Alewitz's wide-ranging work, Buhle provides crucial cultural and historical background.

Notice how Buhle skillfully integrates information and commentary into his profile at a number of key points: by defining the function of public art in the second paragraph; by describing in the third paragraph Alewitz's Cleveland neighborhood as the home of Superman's creators and other popular artists; by recounting the events of May 1970 at Kent State in the fourth paragraph; and by explaining in the eighth paragraph the muralist traditions of Mexican painters and public artists of the Works Progress Administration in the 1930s.

■ FOR CRITICAL INQUIRY

1. In the last sentence of the opening paragraph, Paul Buhle says that Mike Alewitz was the "natural choice of artists" to paint the mural at Cesar Chavez High School, but he doesn't explain why this is so. Consider whether a satisfactory answer emerges for readers by the end of the profile. What is the effect of letting the question of why Alewitz was the "natural choice" float throughout the profile? Do you think it's a good opening strategy?

2. Use the annotations to consider how (or whether) the profile creates a dominant impression of Mike Alewitz. Trace how this impression develops from the opening scene to the end of the profile. List some of the words, phrases, and sentences that are central to conveying a dominant impression.

3. The single-sentence final paragraph is an eloquent commentary on what "Alewitz's paintings boldly insist." What exactly is Buhle's evaluation of Alewitz's

work? Do you think the profile has prepared readers to understand and perhaps to share the sentiments of the last sentence? Why or why not?

A SURGEON'S WAR ON BREAST CANCER

MOLLY O'NEILL

Molly O'Neill is a staff writer for the New York Times, *where her profiles, feature stories, and food columns appear regularly. The following profile, from 1994, is of Dr. Susan M. Love, a prominent surgeon, biomedical researcher, and activist.*

A Surgeon's War on Breast Cancer

MOLLY O'NEILL

Three mammography films were clipped to the light box on the wall of a sleek conference room at the U.C.L.A. Breast Center. The different perspectives of a woman's breast looked like black-and-white photographs of the earth taken from a satellite. From each angle, the dark shadow of a tumor hovered like a storm cloud near the center of the gray sphere.

A woman born 50 years ago had, on the day of her birth, a 1 in 20 chance of being diagnosed with breast cancer in her lifetime. A woman born today has a 1 in 9 chance, partly due to a longer life expectancy. The U.C.L.A. Breast Center, part of the U.C.L.A. Medical Center, is one of about a dozen clinics in the country that both treat and research the disease. And Dr. Susan M. Love, the director of the U.C.L.A. program, is a leading crusader in the war against breast cancer.

A radiologist used a pointer to outline the tumor for a group of radiologists, oncologists, pathologists and surgeons. Dr. Love stood in the back of the conference room, rocking in her bone-colored pumps. Her brown eyes were narrowed behind red-frame glasses.

The lab coat she wore was a bulletin board of buttons. "Keep abreast," read one, "Get a second opinion." On another: "T.G.I.F. (Thank God I'm Female)." Under the string of fat white pearls around her neck was a gold chain with an ankh, an ancient symbol of life. Above one of the gold Chanel-style earrings was a tiny labrys, the mythical double-bladed ax used by Amazons.

Dr. Love is not without contradictions.

She is a traditionally trained surgeon; yet, she believes political action, not surgery, is the only real hope for stemming the increase in breast cancer. She is a feminist, but is skeptical of self-help techniques like breast self-examinations. She was raised Irish Catholic, at one point entered a convent and is now a lesbian mother.

With patients, she is funny, warm and accessible. With peers, "Dr. Love constantly challenges dogma," said Dr. Jay Harris, a radiation oncologist and professor at Harvard University, who has known and worked with Dr. Love since her residency at Beth Israel Hospital in Boston nearly 15 years ago. "Surgeons aren't supposed to do that. Susan makes many surgeons uncomfortable."

Even the staff of Dr. Love's clinic say that the surgeon's approach is not for every patient. "Some women want to be

told what to do," said Sherry Goldman, a nurse practitioner at the U.C.L.A. center. "Options make them nervous."

Even before she published *Dr. Susan Love's Breast Book* (Addison Wesley, 1990), a down-to-earth guide that has become the bible of women with breast cancer, she stirred controversy. In Boston, where she practiced before accepting the U.C.L.A. appointment in 1992, Dr. Love questioned the necessity of radical mastectomies and was an early champion of conservative surgeries like lumpectomies and partial mastectomies.

She is critical about what she sees as condescending and paternalistic attitudes among traditional breast surgeons. She is indefatigable in raising money—and political consciousness—for breast cancer research and prevention.

In 1991, Dr. Love helped found the National Breast Cancer Coalition, a federation of nearly 200 support and advocacy groups that helped raise the national budget for breast cancer research and prevention from $90 million to $420 million. "Thanks to Anita Hill," she likes to say. "After that debacle, congressmen were all looking for a nice, noncontroversial women's issue."

Dr. Love, who is 46, is known as a brilliant surgeon. She is also known for her bluntness.

She grins puckishly when she describes conventional breast cancer treatment, as "slash, poison and burn." She hopes that hers will be the last generation of surgeons to treat breast cancer with radical and invasive methods. Meanwhile, she performs surgery eight times a week.

The woman whose mammogram she was regarding would probably wind up in her operating room.

Her tone is kindly, forever big sister. The faint arc of freckles across her nose seems to expand as she smiles. Hers is the sort of open, guileless face that is hard to refuse. But as she rattled off studies, statistics and personal experience to support her recommendations for treating patients, she sounded indomitable.

A minute later, as she was entering another examining room, however, her tone was alternately jovial and intimate. "Is it lethal?" asked the 32-year-old patient. The surgeon laughed, pulled up a chair, plunked down and leaned toward the patient, elbows resting on her knees.

"Driving in L.A. is lethal," she said. "Your mammogram doesn't say anything about death. We're not talking doom."

For the next 40 minutes, using her own left breast to demonstrate each point, Dr. Love discussed the basic purpose of a breast ("it's like a milk factory"), how, under certain circumstances, cells build up on the wall of the duct, "like rust in a pipe," she said, "reversible."

The patient was laughing by the time Dr. Love told her: "When those cells break out into the surrounding fatty tissue, that's cancer. It is not reversible. We need to find out where you are on this continuum before we can really talk about options. But there are options. And you have time to think about it."

"And you'll take care of me?" the patient asked as they stood.

"I will take good care of you," said the surgeon, hugging the patient.

In the last 50 years, one-third of women diagnosed with breast cancer died of breast cancer. Dr. Love doesn't claim a better sur-

vival rate. She claims to take better care of women, and her patients generally agree.

Born in Long Branch, N.J., the oldest of five children, Susan Margaret Love was raised to change the world by doing good work. After two years as a pre-med student at the College of Notre Dame of Maryland in Baltimore, Dr. Love joined a convent but left after four months.

"I wanted to save the world," she said, "but they wanted to save their own souls." She enrolled at Fordham University and continued her pre-med studies. In 1970, she applied to medical school.

She wasn't fazed by the quota that limited women to 10 percent of the student body in most medical schools. "I wasn't political, I was a nerd," she said. "I've always been mainstream, pretty conservative."

After graduating fourth in her class from the State University of New York, Downstate Medical Center, in Brooklyn, she entered the surgical residency program at Beth Israel Hospital in Boston. "The program was modeled after the military," she said. "Most women who survived paid a price. They lost their marriages, or their minds. I did it by being totally out of touch with myself, a good old Irish Catholic."

Besides, she loved surgery. "It's so pragmatic, so tactile," she said. "You can fix things."

Breast surgery, though, isn't a sure-fire fix. And initially, it didn't interest Dr. Love. "I didn't want to be ghettoized in a women's specialty," she said. But when she established her practice in Boston, doctors referred breast cancer patients to her. "I started to see that this was an area where I could make a difference." Within two years, she had become the breast surgeon for the Dana Farber Cancer Institute in Boston.

At the same time, she said, after mounting a "massive find-a-man campaign," she faced her own sexuality. For years, she had avoided another surgeon, Dr. Helen Cooksey, who was gay. "I thought it might be catching," Dr. Love said. "It was."

The couple have been together for 13 years. Five years ago, by artificial insemination, Dr. Love had a daughter, Katie Love Cooksey. Dr. Cooksey left surgery to stay home with the child. Last September, the couple won a legal battle that allowed Dr. Cooksey to adopt Katie. "Helen and I have money and privilege, so it's our obligation to pave the way," Dr. Love said.

The noblesse oblige theme also rises when she discusses the move from private practice to U.C.L.A.

"I was this little person in private practice, and now I have a whole medical school behind me," Dr. Love said. "Of course that means a huge responsibility. I have to get this clinic up and running and then build an equally serious research effort."

At 7 a.m. every weekday, Dr. Love takes her daughter to preschool and goes to the hospital, where she performs any surgeries by 10 a.m. She then dashes down one flight of stairs to the Breast Center to confer, teach and work on grants before patients arrive. One patient was worried. Her aunt had died of breast cancer. "Not close enough to worry," Dr. Love said briskly. She examined the patient, found nothing and said, "Now, what else can I do for you?"

"Can you, uh, show me how to do, uh, one of those things?" the patient asked.

"Breast self-exam?" Dr. Love responded. "Sure, but it's an overrated activity. The medical establishment would like you to believe that breast cancer starts as a grain of sand, grows to be the size of a pea and on and on until it becomes a grapefruit. Breast cancer doesn't work like that. It grows slow and it's sneaky. You could examine yourself every day and suddenly find a walnut."

A 55-year-old patient with a small tumor had been advised by another surgeon to have a complete mastectomy, immediately. "Give me a break," Dr. Love told the patient. "Using a mastectomy to treat a lesion like yours is like using a cannon to shoot a flea."

Yet another patient, a 48-year-old woman, had an aggressive cancer but was hesitant to have a mastectomy. Was it possible to save her breast?

"Look, breast cancer is like mental health," Dr. Love said. "The early forms are neurotic and can be treated. The later forms are psychotic, and it's more difficult. You have a lot of pre-cancer, a little bit that's crossed the line. I can probably go in and take a wedge out of your breast; it's sort of like taking a dart.

"I think I could do it, but I may not get it all. You'll have a 50–50 chance of having to come back for a mastectomy. Go home, sleep on it. The good news is this is not an emergency."

The next patient was not so lucky. A 64-year-old who had had a partial mastectomy 10 years previously and had been cancer-free since had found a new lump. Subsequent tests found cancerous lesions in the chest wall, the stomach, the liver, the kidneys and the skull. "It doesn't make any sense," Dr. Love said to the team in the conference room. "Where have these cells been for 10 years?"

"Quiescent," said Dr. Dennis Slamon, the chief of oncology.

"Why can't we make them all quiescent?" Dr. Love asked. She repeated the question several times as she packed a bulging briefcase, exchanged her lab coat for a smart silk jacket and, after a typical 13-hour workday, walked down the long, cool hall and headed home.

The Breast Center is one of a handful of such centers that offer an interdisciplinary approach, using medical specialists and psychologists to care for patients from diagnosis through treatment. The force of Dr. Love's personality is the glue that holds the staff of 30 together. Still, Dr. Love is impatient.

"Research is the only way we are going to solve this thing, and I don't mean research into new chemo formulas, I mean research into the cause of breast cancer," she said, as she walked through an empty parking lot to a new Volvo station wagon.

"And we're so close," she said. "We know it's genetic. Some people are born with the gene, others develop the gene. We don't know what causes the gene to change. Pesticides? Pollution? Food additives? They are all possibilities. All we know is that a gene is involved. And we are very close to finding it. Unbelievably close."

Sliding behind the steering wheel, she distilled the latest breast cancer research with the same kind of down-to-earth similes that she uses to explain the disease to patients.

"You see, the gene is like a robber in the neighborhood," she said. "We have the neighborhood roped off. Now all we have to do is knock on every single door."

Analysis: Open Form to Create a Dominant Impression

Molly O'Neill never directly indicates what she wants readers to think of Dr. Susan M. Love. The profile doesn't state and then support a main idea; this isn't the basis of its organization. Nonetheless, the profile effectively conveys a dominant impression of Dr. Love because the information, description, scenes, conversations, and quotes vividly and consistently contribute to this impression.

Moreover, the information, description, and other elements are carefully organized into sections. Each section clusters together a particular kind of information or discussion, contributing to the dominant impression in a specific way. If, as in this profile, sections are carefully designed, they can resonate with each other, suggesting connections a reader can make so that the dominant impression created by the whole is that much stronger. If the sections are not carefully designed, readers will likely experience the piece as incoherent and frustrating.

The pattern of organization used in this profile is called *open form*, characterized as having an implicit center of gravity around which parts revolve, rather than an explicit main point that the parts develop.

If you reread the profile, you can see that it divides into the following sections:

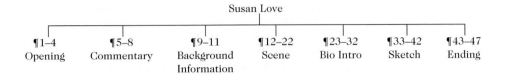

Susan Love

| ¶1–4 | ¶5–8 | ¶9–11 | ¶12–22 | ¶23–32 | ¶33–42 | ¶43–47 |
| Opening | Commentary | Background Information | Scene | Bio Intro | Sketch | Ending |

To see how a section can contribute to a dominant impression, consider the opening scene of the profile (¶1–4). Effective profiles usually rely on a powerful opening that establishes a perspective for readers. This profile begins in a conference room where a radiologist is showing mammography films to a group of doctors. Readers are immediately immersed in Dr. Love's world. Love herself is initially at the back of the room, and O'Neill takes her time in introducing her.

First O'Neill describes the mammography films, using metaphorical language (they "looked like black-and-white photographs of the earth taken from a satellite" and "the dark shadow of a tumor hovered like a storm cloud") to put what may be unfamiliar to readers into more familiar terms, and then she quickly sketches in statistics on the rising incidence of breast cancer.

It is only after this extended scene that Love appears, "a leading crusader in the war against breast cancer," as though O'Neill were using a camera to zoom in on her subject. Love is seen "rocking in her bone-colored pumps. Her brown eyes were narrowed behind red-frame glasses." The opening concludes with a description of Love. As in most successful profiles, this is by no means a full description. Instead, O'Neill describes only a couple of details—the buttons Love has on her lab coat and the jewelry she wears. Note that these are key details, revealing something important about Dr. Love. Like Dr. Love's posture and gaze, they point to characteristics that are part of the dominant impression the profile goes on to establish.

■ FOR CRITICAL INQUIRY

1. Reread the profile, paying attention to how your perceptions of Dr. Susan Love develop over the course of the profile. Annotate the profile by indicating what your impression of Love is in the opening scene, at three or four points in the middle, and at the end. Now read back over your annotations to see how your impression of Love has developed. Is your final impression basically similar to your initial one? Are there any changes or shifts along the way? Explain why you think your impressions developed as they did.

2. What dominant impression does the profile seem to create? How do you think O'Neill wants readers to see Love? How does O'Neill establish such a perspective for readers?

3. Point to words (nouns, verbs, adjectives, adverbs), phrases, sentences, and passages that indicate the perspective O'Neill offers to readers.

4. Focus on a particular passage that you think is especially revealing about the kind of person Love is. What is it about the passage that you find effective in characterizing Dr. Love? Compare the passage you have selected with those chosen by other students in class. Use these comparisons to develop a list of effective strategies for characterizing people in profiles.

I JUST WANNA BE AVERAGE

MIKE ROSE

Mike Rose is a teacher, poet, and professor of education at UCLA. The following selection, which in effect contains three profiles, was taken from his award-winning book Lives on the Boundary (1989).

1   Students will float to the mark you set. I and the others in the vocational classes were bobbing in pretty shallow water. Vocational education has aimed at increasing the economic opportunities of students who do not do well in our schools. Some serious programs succeed in doing that, and through exceptional teachers—like Mr. Gross in *Horace's Compromise*—students learn to develop hypotheses and troubleshoot, reason through a problem, and communicate effectively—the true job skills. The vocational track, however, is most often a place for those who are just not making it, a dumping ground for the disaffected. There were a few teachers who worked hard at education; young Brother Slattery, for example, combined a stern voice with weekly quizzes to try to pass along to us a skeletal outline of world history. But mostly the teachers had no idea of how to engage the imaginations of us kids who were scuttling along at the bottom of the pond.

2   And the teachers would have needed some inventiveness, for none of us was groomed for the classroom. It wasn't just that I didn't know things—didn't know how to simplify algebraic fractions, couldn't identify different kinds of clauses, bungled Spanish translations—but that I had developed various faulty and inadequate ways of doing algebra and making sense of Spanish. Worse yet, the years of defensive tuning out in elementary school had given me a way to escape quickly while seeming at least half alert. During my time in Voc. Ed., I developed further into a mediocre student and a somnambulant problem solver, and that affected the subjects I did have the wherewithal to handle: I detested Shakespeare; I got bored with history. My attention flitted here and there. I fooled around in class and read my books indifferently—the intellectual equivalent of playing with your food. I did what I had to do to get by, and I did it with half a mind.

3   But I did learn things about people and eventually came into my own socially. I liked the guys in Voc. Ed. Growing up where I did, I understood and admired physical prowess,

and there was an abundance of muscle here. There was Dave Snyder, a sprinter and half-back of true quality. Dave's ability and his quick wit gave him a natural appeal, and he was welcome in any clique, though he always kept a little independent. He enjoyed acting the fool and could care less about studies, but he possessed a certain maturity and never caused the faculty much trouble. It was a testament to his independence that he included me among his friends—I eventually went out for track, but I was no jock. Owing to the Latin alphabet and a dearth of *R*s and *S*s, Snyder sat behind Rose, and we started exchanging one-liners and became friends.

4   There was Ted Richard, a much-touted Little League pitcher. He was chunky and had a baby face and came to Our Lady of Mercy as a seasoned street fighter. Ted was quick to laugh and he had a loud, jolly laugh, but when he got angry he'd smile a little smile, the kind that simply raises the corner of the mouth a quarter of an inch. For those who knew, it was an eerie signal. Those who didn't found themselves in big trouble, for Ted was very quick. He loved to carry on what we would come to call philosophical discussions: What is courage? Does God exist? He also loved words, enjoyed picking up big ones like *salubrious* and *equivocal* and using them in our conversations—laughing at himself as the word hit a chuckhole rolling off his tongue. Ted didn't do all that well in school—baseball and parties and testing the courage he'd speculated about took up his time. His textbooks were *Argosy* and *Field and Stream*, whatever newspapers he'd find on the bus stop—from the *Daily Worker* to pornography—conversations with uncles or hobos or businessmen he'd meet in a coffee shop, *The Old Man and the Sea*. With hindsight, I can see that Ted was developing into one of those rough-hewn intellectuals whose sources are a mix of the learned and the apocryphal, whose discussions are both assured and sad.

5   And then there was Ken Harvey. Ken was good-looking in a puffy way and had a full and oily ducktail and was a car enthusiast . . . a hodad. One day in religion class, he said the sentence that turned out to be one of the most memorable of the hundreds of thousands I heard in those Voc. Ed. years. We were talking about the parable of the talents, about achievement, working hard, doing the best you can do, blah-blah-blah, when the teacher called on the restive Ken Harvey for an opinion. Ken thought about it, but just for a second, and said (with studied, minimal affect), "I just wanna be average." That woke me up. Average?! Who wants to be average? Then the athletes chimed in with the clichés that make you want to laryngectomize them, and the exchange became a platitudinous melee. At the time, I thought Ken's assertion was stupid, and I wrote him off.

But his sentence has stayed with me all these years, and I think I am finally coming to understand it.

6   Ken Harvey was gasping for air. School can be a tremendously disorienting place. No matter how bad the school, you're going to encounter notions that don't fit with the assumptions and beliefs that you grew up with—maybe you'll hear these dissonant notions from teachers, maybe from the other students, and maybe you'll read them. You'll also be thrown in with all kinds of kids from all kinds of backgrounds, and that can be unsettling—this is especially true in places of rich ethnic and linguistic mix, like the L.A. basin. You'll see a handful of students far excel you in courses that sound exotic and that are only in the curriculum of the elite: French, physics, trigonometry. And all this is happening while you're trying to shape an identity, your body is changing, and your emotions are running wild. If you're a working-class kid in the vocational track, the options you'll have to deal with this will be constrained in certain ways: You're defined by your school as "slow"; you're placed in a curriculum that isn't designed to liberate you but to occupy you, or, if you're lucky, train you, though the training is for work the society does not esteem; other students are picking up the cues from your school and your curriculum and interacting with you in particular ways. If you're a kid like Ted Richard, you turn your back on all this and let your mind roam where it may. But youngsters like Ted are rare. What Ken and so many others do is protect themselves from such suffocating madness by taking on with a vengeance the identity implied in the vocational track. Reject the confusion and frustration by openly defining yourself as the Common Joe. Champion the average. Rely on your own good sense. Fuck this bullshit. Bullshit, of course, is everything you—and the others—fear is beyond you: books, essays, tests, academic scrambling, complexity, scientific reasoning, philosophical inquiry.

7   The tragedy is that you have to twist the knife in your own gray matter to make this defense work. You'll have to shut down, have to reject intellectual stimuli or diffuse them with sarcasm, have to cultivate stupidity, have to convert boredom from a malady into a way of confronting the world. Keep your vocabulary simple, act stoned when you're not or act more stoned than you are, flaunt ignorance, materialize your dreams. It is a powerful and effective defense—it neutralizes the insult and the frustration of being a vocational kid and, when perfected, it drives teachers up the wall, a delightful secondary effect. But like all strong magic, it exacts a price.

Analysis: Claim and Evidence

Mike Rose's profiles of three students are part of a larger piece: they are the third through fifth paragraphs in a selection with seven paragraphs, which is itself an excerpt from a book. Notice that the first two paragraphs in the selection establish a main idea, or claim, that the three profiles then support. In the final two paragraphs, the author in effect generalizes from the profiles and draws conclusions related to the main point. In contrast to O'Neill's piece, which uses open form, this selection uses an organization familiar from argumentative writing: *claim and evidence.*

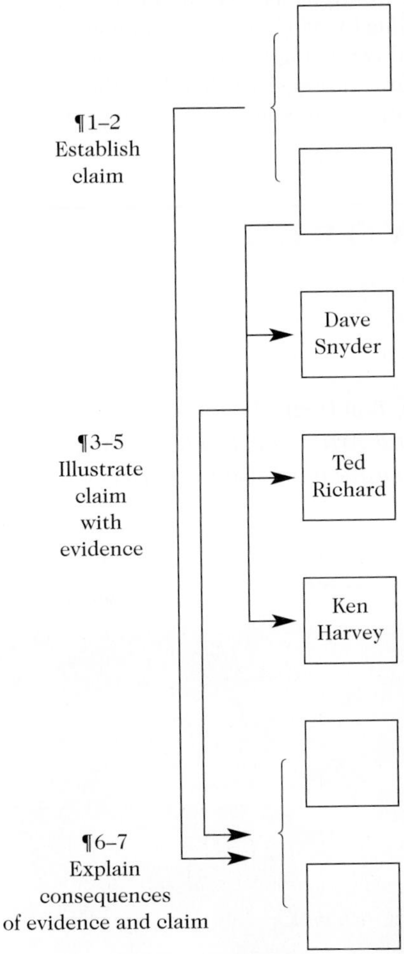

Whereas the success of O'Neill's article comes from the way sections establish a dominant impression, the success of a piece with claim and evidence organization comes from the way the evidence supports the claim and serves as a basis for conclusions that say something significant. If these parts and their relationships to one another aren't clear, readers will find the piece hard to follow.

Notice that Rose's piece is just as effective as O'Neill's but in a way that is appropriate to the type of organization he uses. He begins with two memorable sentences that help establish the main idea: "Students will float to the mark you set. I and the others in the vocational classes were bobbing in pretty shallow water."

Notice also that the high school students Rose then profiles are much more than just evidence to support this main idea. He sketches Dave Snyder, Ted Richard, and Ken Harvey in vivid detail. Each appears to the reader as a unique individual, with his own characteristics and idiosyncrasies. Yet there is also a sort of shared dominant impression that emerges, an impression that is linked to Rose's main idea. For Rose is showing us, through their experience, a central problem in American schooling: it produces students who, in Ken Harvey's unforgettable words, "just wanna be average." Interpretation on the part of the author, inevitable in any profile, is made explicit in a piece like this one, occurring from the beginning sentences quoted above to the final judgment that the "powerful and effective defense" that vocational education students develop, "like all strong magic, . . . exacts a price."

Diagram labels (left margin):

¶1–2 Establish claim

¶3–5 Illustrate claim with evidence

Dave Snyder

Ted Richard

Ken Harvey

¶6–7 Explain consequences of evidence and claim

■ FOR CRITICAL INQUIRY

1. What is the main idea (or claim) that Rose introduces in the two opening paragraphs? How do the profiles of the three students provide evidence for the claim? What enabling assumptions connect this evidence to the claim?

2. Rose wants his profiles of the three students to serve as evidence for his claim, but he also wants to capture the individuality of each student. How does he do this? Point to particular passages, sentences, or words in the text that provide revealing characterization.

3. In the final two paragraphs of this selection, Rose wants to generalize from the experience of the three students he has profiled—to develop further his controlling theme about the effects of schooling by making some final points. What points exactly is Rose making in the final two paragraphs? Do they seem to be justified and to flow naturally from the three profiles? Explain how these points seem to grow logically from the profiles (or why in your view they don't).

WRITING IN A DIGITAL WORLD

Soundmap

FOLK SONGS FOR THE FIVE POINTS

Folk Songs for the Five Points was created by Alastair Dant, Tom Davis, Victor Gama, and David Gunn for the Lower East Side Tenement Museum's Digital Artists in Residence Program in response to an invitation for "works that explore contemporary immigrant experience in New York City."

Analysis: Using Sound to Profile a Place

The Lower East Side in New York City was one of the places immigrants from southern and eastern Europe settled during the great migrations of 1880 to 1924. It is still a place of great cultural diversity, as Folk Songs for the Five Points reveals. This soundmap includes street sounds, interviews, local music (African American spirituals, a Chinese opera rehearsal, Puerto Rican bomba), and folk songs written and performed by Victor Gama.

You can visit Folk Songs for the Five Points at www.tenement.org/folksongs/client. Notice how you can make and save your own mixes of the various sounds the Web site documents. Notice too how much information about the Lower East Side as a place is available by clicking on various points on the map.

■ FOR CRITICAL INQUIRY

1. List all the sounds that are available at Folk Songs for Five Points. Taken together, what does this range of sounds tell you about the place? Does it create a dominant impression or does it work in other ways, as a profile of the Lower East Side?

2. Make your own sound mix. Compare the mix you've made to those of your classmates. How do differences in the combinations reveal various sides to the Lower East Side?

3. Compare this soundmap of the Lower East Side to the photo essay "Cancer Alley," which follows. What does each bring to light about the place it is profiling? What do you see as the main differences and similarities?

4. Design your own soundmap for a place with which you are familiar. What kind of sounds would you include? How would these sounds work together?

ETHICS OF WRITING

RESPONSIBILITY TO THE WRITER'S SUBJECT

What is a writer's responsibility to his or her subject? How does this responsibility interact with the writer's responsibility to readers? What potential conflicts are there between the two responsibilities? These are questions profile writers invariably grapple with.

Profiles, after all, are meant to inform readers and offer them the writer's honest perspective—not to serve as publicity or public relations for the person or place profiled. If profile writers are to have an independent voice and fulfill their responsibilities to readers, they must be able to make their own judgments about what is fit to print. But an important basis for these judgments is a sense of responsibility toward the subject. ■

VISUAL DESIGN

Photo Essay

CANCER ALLEY: THE POISONING OF THE AMERICAN SOUTH

RICHARD MISRACH, PHOTOGRAPHS, AND JASON BERRY, ESSAY

Richard Misrach is a photographer whose work has often focused on the American desert, including studies of former nuclear testing sites and bombing ranges. Jason Berry is a writer and documentarian who lives in New Orleans. His novel *Last of the Red Hot Poppas* explores the politics of pollution. His investigative books include *Lead Us Not Into Temptation* and *Vows of Silence: The Abuse of Power in the Papacy of John Paul II*. This is an excerpt from a photo essay that originally appeared in *Aperture* (Winter 2001). It includes the full text of Jason Berry's essay and three of the twelve photographs by Richard Misrach.

Analysis: How Photographs and Texts Go Together

Photo essays consist of a series of photographs that work together by telling a story, describing a place, portraying individuals or groups of people, or otherwise evoking emotions in order to create a dominant impression. Some photo essays rely on photographs alone. Others, like "Cancer Alley," combine photographs and texts. In this excerpt, you can see two common features of the photo essay—the two-page spread and the use of captions—that join words and images together. Notice in "Cancer Alley" that the photographs do not simply illustrate ideas in the written text, nor does the written text simply explain what the photographs are showing. Instead, the relationship between photographs and text is dynamic and reciprocal.

WITNESS

CANCER ALLEY
THE POISONING OF THE AMERICAN SOUTH

PHOTOGRAPHS / RICHARD MISRACH
ESSAY / JASON BERRY

"Baton Rouge was clothed in flowers, like a bride—no, much more so; like a greenhouse. For we were in the absolute South now," wrote Mark Twain of the vistas from a riverboat in his 1883 classic *Life on the Mississippi*. "From Baton Rouge to New Orleans," he continued, "the great sugar-plantations border both sides of the river all the way, and stretch their league-wide levels back to the dim forest of bearded cypress in the rear. The broad river lying between the two rows becomes a sort of spacious street."

Twain caught the ninety-mile river corridor between the old Capitol and New Orleans at a poignant moment. Plantations still harvested profits in cotton and sugarcane; the black field workers, no longer slaves, were sharecroppers or virtual serfs. The river flowed through a land riddled with injustice. Yet there was beauty in the waterway and surrounding landscape, and beauty—although burdened with an unsavory history—in those old houses of "the absolute South," with their porticoes and pillared balconies.

By the 1940s, when Clarence John Laughlin trained his lens upon the area, some of the mansions had been torn down and others lay in ruins. The wrecked buildings riveted his eye as much as the several dozen that were still preserved (then starting to shift from farming to tourist sites, which most remain today). A haunting sense of loss suffuses the black-and-white surrealism in Laughlin's remarkable book *Ghosts Along the Mississippi*.

Between the time of Twain's reportage and Laughlin's elegiac photographs from the mid-twentieth century, oil and petrochemical

ABANDONED TRAILER HOME

West Bank Mississippi River, near Dow Chemical plant, Plaquemine, Louisiana, 1998

no. 162 Aperture / 31

REVETMENT SIGN AND HALE-BOGGS BRIDGE, WEST BANK, MISSISSIPPI RIVER

Luling, Louisiana, 1998. The Mississippi is the dominant river basin in North America and drains more than 1.2 million square miles, or about 40 percent of the continental United States. It provides 18 million people with drinking water, 1.5 million in Louisiana alone. In a recent study of pollutants discovered in the drinking water of a single Louisiana parish, over 75 toxins were found, including the carcinogens carbon tetrachroride, chloroform, 0-chloronitrobenzene, p-chloronitrobenzene, 1,4-dichlorobenzene, DDT, DDE, and DDD, dichloromethane, alachlor, atrazine, dieldrin, heptachlor epoxide, hexachlorobenzene, and pentachlorobenzene. The thirteen Louisiana parishes that depend on the Mississippi as a source of drinking water have some of the highest mortality rates in the United States from several forms of cancer.

NORCO CUMULUS CLOUD, SHELL OIL REFINERY

Norco, Louisiana, 1998. Norco, twenty-five miles upriver from New Orleans, is the site of a massive Shell Oil Refinery. Throughout the day, natural-looking clouds, nicknamed "Norco cumulus," hover over the site, created by the comingling of moisture and volatile hydrocarbons originating in the refinery process of gasoline, jet fuel, cooking oil, and other products. Louisiana ranks second in the nation, behind Texas, in the amount of toxic substances released into the air and water: 183 million tons of toxic chemicals were emitted in 1997.

no. 162 Aperture / 41

■ FOR CRITICAL INQUIRY

1. Consider how the two-page spread opens the photo essay. How does Richard Misrach's photograph of the abandoned trailer establish the mood of the photo essay? What terms would you use to describe the dominant impression the photo essay makes?

2. How do the captions and the photographs work together? What would it be like if just text or just photographs appeared without the other?

3. As you can see, Misrach's photographs of pollution and environmental devastation are quite beautiful. What is the relationship between this beauty and the damage the photos document?

FURTHER EXPLORATION: PROFILES

■ GENRE CHOICES

Profiles and biographies are both genres of writing that inform readers about people, but they do so in different ways. To understand what distinguishes profiles and biographies, read one or two short biographies in a standard reference source, such as an encyclopedia, the *Dictionary of American Biography,* or *Current Biography.* Note the information that is included in—and excluded from—the two writings. Note also the arrangement of information. How do the profile and the biographical entry differ? What do the differences between the two writings tell you about the two genres?

■ WORKING TOGETHER

Analyzing Profiles in Documentary Films

Many notable documentary films profile well-known public figures (Bob Dylan in *Don't Look Back*, the comic artist R. Crumb in *Crumb*, the rapper Tupac Shakur in *Tupac: The Resurrection*, and Secretary of Defense during the Vietnam War Robert McNamara in *The Fog of War*) as well as ordinary people (including Amish youth in *The Devil's Playground*, Seattle street kids in *Streetwise*, and young basketball players in *Hoop Dreams*). Working with a group of three or four, locate a documentary film in your library or local video store that profiles an individual or a group of people. Develop an oral presentation on the film that analyzes the filmmaker's portrait of the person or group of people. Use clips to illustrate the filmmaker's attitude and how he or she wants viewers to see the person being profiled.

WRITING ASSIGNMENT

Creating a Profile

Online Study Center

Choose a person, a group of people, or a place to write a profile about. The point of this assignment is to bring that person or place to life in writing so that you can learn more about your subject while helping your readers to see and understand what makes your subject worth reading about.

The subject you choose for your profile may teach you something about yourself; for instance, you may be able to clarify why this person or place has had an influence on your life and the culture around you. Likewise, you may find that a particular group of readers may have an interest in learning about a subject that interests you; in that case, your call to write a profile can grow from your readers' need to know.

Often profiles are based on observing and interviewing, but as the reading selections indicate, profiles can also be drawn from memory, as in the case of Mike Rose's "I Just Wanna Be Average," or from the public record, as in the case of Richard Misrach and Jason Berry's "Cancer Alley." Here are some possibilities to help you think about whom you might profile:

- Pick a place to profile. It could be somewhere you hang out, a neighborhood, a park, or as in "Cancer Alley," an industrial site.

- Choose someone whose profile will illustrate a larger social issue—a recent immigrant to the United States, a senior citizen, an environmental activist, a consumer advocate, a community organizer, a gang member. Consider submitting this profile to a paper or newsletter interested in addressing such social issues.

- Choose a local personality—a politician, writer, musician, artist, athlete, or newspaper editor or columnist—or someone prominent on your own campus—a coach, administrator, distinguished teacher, or well-known scholar. Your community or campus newspaper might publish your profile if you write it with your local readership in mind.

- Follow Mike Rose's example in "I Just Wanna Be Average" and compose a series of personality sketches, from memory or from interviews, that illustrates some larger point or controlling theme.

- Choose a public figure, living or dead, and write a profile that makes a judgment about the meaning of that person's life.

Alternative Assignments

Online Study Center

■ RHETORICAL ANALYSIS

Compare the writer's purposes in two of the profiles in this chapter. Take into account the context of issues, the writer's intended audience, and the relationship the writer is trying to establish with readers. How do the writer's purposes influence the presentation of the subject or subjects? How do these purposes influence the amount of description and interpretation in the profile?

■ WORKING WITH SOURCES

Use Jason Berry's profile of "Cancer Alley" to explain the significance of a place. Notice the sources Berry draws on to examine how the land between New Orleans and Baton Rouge has been portrayed by earlier writers and photographers. Pick a place where you can find such sources. Use those sources to explain how and why the place has changed.

Invention

Finding a Subject

Take some time to decide on the person (or persons) you want to profile. Don't limit yourself to people or places that are familiar to you. Writing a profile offers an opportunity to learn about something new, and it will allow you to bring a fresh perspective to that subject.

■ EXERCISE
Developing Your Topic

1. **Make a list:** Make a list of people or places that, for one reason or another, interest you. Try to come up with at least ten. This will give you some choices.

2. **Talk to others:** Meet with two or three other students in your class and share the lists each of you has developed for feedback and advice about the most promising subjects. Ask the other students to tell you which people or places are most interesting to them, why, and what they would like to know about them.

3. **Decide tentatively on a subject:** Use the feedback you have received to help you make a tentative decision about which subject you will profile. Take into account your partners' reasons for being interested in a person or place.

4. **Contact your subject:** If you are planning an interview, you will need to contact your subject. Explain that you're a student working on an assignment in a writing course. You'll be amazed—and reassured—by how helpful and gracious most people will be. If they don't have time, they'll tell you so, and then you can go back to your list and try your second choice. Most likely, however, you'll be able to schedule a time to meet and talk with the person. Ask if he or she can suggest anything you might read or research as background information before the interview to help you prepare for it.

At this point it may also be helpful for you to sketch out a schedule for yourself. To write this profile, you will need to allow time for the several stages of both research and writing.

Clarifying Your Purpose

Write a brief statement of purpose. This can be helpful preparation for an interview or as exploratory writing for a profile from memory or based on research.

■ EXERCISE

Developing a Statement of Purpose

Take fifteen minutes to answer the following questions:

- Why are you interested in the particular person or place you're profiling? What is your attitude toward the subject?

- What do you already know about the person and his or her job, hobby, political or community activity, or social role? If you are profiling a place, what do you know about its history, culture, and current issues?

- What do other people think about the person or place you're writing about? Do you share these views? What makes your perspective unique?

- What do you expect to find out by interviewing a person or observing a place?

- What is your purpose in profiling this particular person or place?

Background Research: Deciding What Information You Need

Whether you're planning an interview, writing from memory, or profiling a place, you'll need to determine the type of information called for by your profile. The nature of this research, of course, will vary depending on whom you're profiling and what your purpose is. Here are some questions to help you make appropriate decisions:

1. How much information do you need? Are there key moments or periods that you should focus on? How is this information pertinent to your profile? Is this information readily available or do you need to find ways to get it?

For more information about how to conduct interviews, see the "interviewing" section in *Chapter 15.*

2. If you are profiling a person, how much do you need to know about the person's field of work? How much do you already know? How can you find out more, if needed? If you're doing an interview, can your subject suggest things you could read before you meet?

3. Are there relevant social, cultural, or political issues you need to know about for the profile? Do you need to understand the historical context? If so, what's important to understand?

4. What, if anything, has already been written about the person or the place? What would be useful to read?

Planning

Deciding on the Dominant Impression

As you have seen from the reading selections in this chapter, the purpose of a profile is to capture your subject at a particular moment in time and to take your readers into your subject's world. In these ways, profiles offer readers a dominant impression of the person (or persons) being profiled. In a profile, you need to inform your readers about the person in question, but you also need to provide your readers with a point of view—a way of seeing and understanding the significance of the person being profiled.

Here are some questions to help you determine the dominant impression you want to create:

- What is the most interesting, unusual, or important thing you have discovered about your subject?

- What are your own feelings about your subject?

- What do others say about your subject? Are these responses to your subject consistent, or do people differ?

- Can you think of two or more dominant impressions you could create to give readers a way of understanding your subject?

Use your answers to these questions to refine your sense of purpose. It may help at this point to talk to a friend or classmate. Explain the different ways in which you might portray your subject. Ask how the dominant impressions you are considering affect the way your classmate or friend understands your subject.

Arranging Your Material

Inventory the material you have to work with. Look over your notes and notice how many separate items about your subject you have. These are the building blocks of your profile, the raw material that you will put together to construct it. Label each item according to the kind of information it contains—such as physical description, biographical background, observed actions and procedures, revealing incidents or anecdotes, direct quotes, things you have read, and things other people have told you.

Once you have inventoried your material, your task is to sketch a tentative plan for your profile. The arrangement of your material will depend, of course, on your purpose in writing the profile. As you have seen, Molly O'Neill and Mike Rose use quite different arrangement patterns in their profiles. O'Neill uses open form to present clusters of information about Dr. Susan Love, while Rose uses claim and evidence to present a main point and then illustrate it with individual profiles. Reread the two profiles. Do you want to use open form to create a dominant impression of your subject by presenting loosely arranged clusters of information? If so, what order will best enable you to establish a perspective for your readers? Or do you want to use your profile to illustrate a main point? If so, how can you make sure to present the main point clearly and then show how the profile meaningfully illustrates it?

When you have decided your purpose and form, arrange the items of information you have labeled in your inventory and create a working outline. You are likely to have more material than you can use, so don't worry if you can't fit everything in.

Working Draft

By this time you have organized a lot of material from your research, and you have probably gained some new insight into the person or group you are profiling. Now that you have learned something new, your challenge is to teach your readers what is interesting, unusual, and important about the person or group. Use your working outline to write a working draft.

Beginnings and Endings: Using Figurative Language

As you write your draft, consider whether *figurative language* can make your profile more vivid and interesting. The use of figurative language such as *similes* and *metaphors* implies a comparison by describing one thing in terms of another. The main difference between similes and metaphors is that similes use a linking term such as *like.* The profile of Dr. Susan Love, for example, has a powerful ending that makes good use of figurative language:

> "You see, the gene is like a robber in the neighborhood," she said. "We have the neighborhood roped off. Now all we have to do is knock on every single door."

Susan Love, of course, is not asking us to believe genes are really robbers. Rather, the simile asks us to think of how genes are like robbers in one sense. Love then extends the comparison by using a metaphor that makes cancer researchers into detectives who have the "neighborhood roped off" and are going to "knock on every single door." This use of figurative language gives the search for breast cancer genes a dramatic character and enables readers to visualize Love's appraisal of current breast cancer research.

Mike Rose uses metaphor to begin and end the first paragraph of his profile. The paragraph starts with this sentence:

> Students will float to the mark you set. I and the others in the vocational classes were bobbing in pretty shallow water.

The paragraph ends by returning to the metaphor:

> But mostly the teachers had no idea of how to engage the imaginations of us kids who were scuttling along at the bottom of the pond.

By using figurative language in these ways, you can help readers understand the points you want to make in your profile.

Peer Commentary

Exchange drafts with a partner. Respond in writing to these questions about your partner's draft:

1. Describe what you see as the writer's purposes. Does the working draft create a dominant impression? Does it imply or state a main point? Explain how and where the draft develops a dominant impression (and main point, if pertinent).

2. Describe the arrangement of the working draft. Divide the draft into sections by grouping related paragraphs together. Explain how each section contributes to the overall impression the profile creates. Do you find the arrangement easy to follow? Does the arrangement seem to suit the writer's purposes? If there are rough spots or abrupt shifts, indicate where they are and how they affected your reading.

3. How effective are the beginning and ending of the draft? What suggestions would you make to strengthen the impact, increase the drama, or otherwise improve these two sections of the draft? Should the writer have used a different strategy?

4. Do you have other suggestions about how the writer could enhance the profile? Are there details, reported speech, descriptions, or incidents that the writer could emphasize? Are there elements the writer should cut?

Revising

Use the peer commentary to do a critical reading of your draft.

1. Consider first how your reader has analyzed the arrangement of your profile. Notice in particular how the commentary has divided the draft into sections. Do these sections correspond to the way you wanted to arrange the profile? Are there ways to rearrange material to improve its overall effect?

2. If you are using open form, are the clusters of information clear to your reader? Are there ways to enhance the presentation?

3. If you are presenting a claim and evidence, was this pattern of organization clear to your reader? Are there ways to enhance its presentation?

4. Does the draft create the kind of dominant impression you intended?

5. What did your writing partner suggest? Evaluate specific suggestions.

Establishing Perspective from the Beginning

The beginning of your profile is a particularly important place to establish a perspective on the person, place, or group you're writing about. The strategy you use to design an opening will depend both on your material and on the attitude you want your readers to have toward your subject. Notice how Richard Quitadamo revised the opening paragraph of his profile. (The full draft is included in Writers' Workshop, below.) The early draft reads more like a paragraph from a biography of Edward Sweda, while the revised version takes us into Sweda's world.

Early Draft of "A Lawyer's Crusade Against Tobacco"

Edward Sweda began his career as an anti-smoking activist over twenty years ago, when he became involved as a volunteer in a campaign to provide non-smoking sections in restaurants. He is currently the senior staff attorney for the Tobacco Product Liability Project (TPLP) at Northeastern University. Since 1984, when TPLP was established, Sweda and his associates have battled the powerful tobacco interests.

Revised Version of "A Lawyer's Crusade Against Tobacco"

The office of the Tobacco Product Liability Project (TPLP) at Northeastern University in Boston is decorated with anti-smoking propaganda. One poster shows the damage that smoking has done to someone's lungs. The office secretary sat at her desk and typed busily, while Edward Sweda, senior attorney of the TPLP, conversed on the phone with Stanton Glantz, author of the well-known exposé of the tobacco industry Cigarette Papers.

Here is a list of techniques for establishing perspective at the beginning of a profile:

1. **Set the scene:** Describe the place where you encounter your subject; give details about the physical space; describe other people who are there; explain what the people are doing; set the stage for your subject's entrance.

2. **Tell an anecdote:** Narrate an incident that involves your subject; describe how your subject acts in a revealing situation.

3. **Use a quotation:** Begin with your subject's own words; use a particularly revealing, provocative, or characteristic statement.

4. **Describe your subject:** Use description and detail about your subject's appearance as an opening clue to the person's character.

5. **Describe a procedure:** Follow your subject through a characteristic routine or procedure at work; explain the purpose and technical details; use them to establish your subject's expertise.

6. **State your controlling theme:** Establish perspective by stating in your own words a key theme that will be developed in the profile. ■

W WRITERS' WORKSHOP

Richard Quitadamo wrote the following profile, "A Lawyer's Crusade Against Tobacco," for a course that focused on the politics of public health. Quitadamo plans on becoming a lawyer, and he wanted to find out more about the kind of work lawyers do in the public interest, particularly in the area of product liability. What appears here is Quitadamo's working draft, followed by his questions for a peer commentary. Read the draft, keeping in mind that it is a work in progress. Then consider how you would respond to the questions Quitadamo raises in his note.

RICHARD QUITADAMO, A LAWYER'S CRUSADE AGAINST TOBACCO [WORKING DRAFT]

The office of the Tobacco Product Liability Project (TPLP) at Northeastern University in Boston is decorated with anti-smoking propaganda. One poster shows the damage that smoking has done to someone's lungs. The office secretary sat at her desk and typed busily, while Edward Sweda, senior attorney of the TPLP, conversed on the phone with Stanton Glantz, author of the well-known exposé of the tobacco industry Cigarette Papers.

Sweda seemed fixated on one subject, the recent banning of RJ Reynolds' "Joe Camel" cartoon character from Camel cigarette advertisements. He felt it was a small victory in the ongoing war against smoking. "Look, Stanton, Joe is gone and that's great, but that really doesn't affect the foreign market. It seems the percentage of people outside the US who smoke has risen dramatically.

There's got to be something we can do." They talked for a few more moments, and then Sweda hung up the phone.

Edward Sweda, a tall, slender man, with graying hair, turned in his office chair. A button on his sweater read "No Smoking." He began to discuss the history of the war on tobacco and the part he has played in it.

Sweda began his career in 1979 as a local volunteer against cigarette smoking in Massachusetts. "I hated smoking from day one. It was disgusting, and besides it can kill you." In the late 1970s, the dangers of smoking were a novel concept, and industry leaders were quick to cover up the ill effects of smoking. It was also at this time that medical professionals, political activists, and health care advocates began pushing for stronger regulation of tobacco products.

In 1980, Sweda worked in Newton, MA, for regulations that would require restaurants to provide at least 15% of its seating to non-smokers. "People have to breathe, and if other people are smoking in close proximity to you, then they are infringing on your right to breathe fresh air. That's a crime. I as a non-smoker really feel strongly about this issue."

Sweda has also worked to stop free samples of cigarettes from being dispersed. "It reminded me of drugs. The first time was free, but after that, you had to pay. I figured I could stop this vicious cycle before it got a chance to start. That's why we eventually formed the TPLP, to use litigation as a tool to make the tobacco industry take responsibility for its actions."

TPLP was established in 1984, and since then Sweda and his associates have battled the tobacco industry. "Tobacco industry knew smoking was bad long before TPLP ever showed up. The first report of the Surgeon General on smoking in 1964 proved that cigarette smoking could have harmful effects on human health." But, Sweda continued, the only thing that the anti-smoking campaign got out of the Surgeon General's report was the Fanning Doctrine, which stated that there must be a comparable number of anti-smoking public service announcements (PSAs) to the number of cigarette advertisements. This doctrine, Sweda said, may or may not have led to the drop off of cigarette sales noticeable between 1966 and 1970.

However, on January 1, 1971, cigarette advertising was banned from TV, and along with them, the antismoking PSAs. "At first, I was overjoyed," Sweda said, smiling. "What a fool I was. The tobacco industry used other methods to lure potential smokers to their products, the PSAs were gone, and the levels of smoking increased nationwide. It seemed they could sidestep every regulation we imposed."

As Sweda spoke, his secretary called attention to the flashing computer screen. Sweda rose from his chair and observed the screen. "You see this? This is something I'm working on right now." Sweda was looking at the next date scheduled for hearings of the Massachusetts State Public Health Council on new proposed legislation to force the tobacco industry to disclose their secret ingredients. "What we want to do at this hearing is to make the industry sweat. They failed to block the hearing and were forced to appear. They didn't even testify on their own behalf, and I just kept talking about the list of secret ingredients and the falsified tests. You should have seen their faces."

Yet, Sweda is cautious with his optimism about the future of anti-smoking initiatives. He has seen things go wrong before. The tobacco industry has many influential lobbyists on their side, along with the political backing of tobacco state politicians. They are able to hide information and falsify reports to government officials. This makes the industry virtually untouchable at the federal level. Nonetheless, Sweda said he was more confident this time around. "Things are different in this day and age. People are more educated about the dangers of smoking. With the banning of Joe Camel and the Liggett case of 1996, we seem to be gaining ground on them. The Liggett case is probably the biggest breakthrough in our struggle because it's the first time a tobacco manufacturer cracked and admitted what we've known all along about the health hazards of smoking. And it actually resulted in a settlement."

Sweda paused, then sighed. "But there is still the problem of youth. They seem more susceptible to smoking. Maybe it's the age, maybe it's a rebellion thing, or maybe it's the advertisements. The ads seem to target youth. That's why I'm glad Joe Camel is gone."

The TPLP has been working with the Federal Drug Administration on a game plan that focuses specifically on the youth smoking problem. The plan centers on keeping youth from smoking through education and other programs. "I hate to admit it, but it seems our best bet for beating smoking and the industry is to forget adult smokers. They've made their decisions, and it's their choice to continue smoking. Cessation programs and medical help groups exist for those who want to quit. But by focusing on youth, we are taking away the customers of the future. This is important because as the older generation of smokers fades away, the tobacco industry will be looking to recruit new smokers."

As Sweda stepped away from the computer, he said, "We'll get them, the industry, that is," and stepped to his desk, picked up the phone, and began to dial a number. This is all in a day's work for Edward Sweda and his TPLP group. They exist to promote public health and stop the growth of the tobacco industry, or as Sweda refers to them, "the merchants of death."

RICHARD QUITADAMO'S COMMENTARY

I think I do a pretty good job in this draft of setting the scene and showing Sweda at work. The guy was a great interview, and I got a lot of good quotes to use. Do these seem effective? Are they easy to understand? Do you need more information at points? Is it clear, for example, what happened in the Liggett case and why anti-smoking people consider it such a huge victory? Any suggestions in this regard would be greatly appreciated.

Another thing I'm not certain about is whether I should give more information about Sweda himself. I don't provide much background information on him or talk about his personal life. I wanted to focus on him mainly as an anti-smoking activist and felt too much biographical detail would distract from this. What do you think?

My last question involves the notorious "dominant impression" we've been talking about in class so much. Do you feel that this draft gives you a strong perspective on the person? I wasn't sure whether I should provide more commentary on my own. I want readers to see Sweda as an embattled crusader but not a fanatic. Does this come across?

■ WORKSHOP QUESTIONS

1. Consider Richard Quitadamo's first set of questions concerning the information in the draft. Are there places where you needed more information to understand the issues? If so, indicate the passage or passages in question and explain what's not clear to you.

2. Quitadamo's second question focuses on whether he should give more background on Sweda. What is your opinion? To answer this question, take into account what Quitadamo's purpose seems to be in this profile. Would more biographical detail further his purpose or, as he worries, distract from it? Explain your response.

3. One mark of a successful profile is that it creates a dominant impression of the subject. Explain in your own words the impression of Sweda this draft created for you. Given what you've read here, what kind of person does he seem to be? How well does the impression you've formed match Quitadamo's goals in portraying Sweda? How could Quitadamo strengthen or enhance his portrayal? ■

REFLECTING ON YOUR WRITING

Write an account of how you put your profile together. Explain why you selected your subject. Then describe the interview, if you did one. Explain whether your final version confirmed or modified your initial preconceptions about your subject. Finally, explain how writing a profile differs from other kinds of writing you have done. What demands and satisfactions are there to writing profiles?

chapter 8

reports: informing and explaining

THINKING ABOUT THE GENRE

Reports are a genre of writing that presents the results of research to inform and explain. Reports can be as simple as the morning weather report or as complex as an in-depth explanation of climate change. Sometimes the writer's task is just to organize information in a useful and accessible way. Other times, report writers analyze the research and draw conclusions.

Writers typically turn to the genre of reports when they believe there exists a need or a desire to know on the reader's part. The form of report writing varies, though, depending on the writer's setting and purposes. News reports and feature articles in newspapers and magazines, research articles in academic journals, briefings and fact sheets, brochures, informational Web sites, studies from government agencies and advocacy groups, community newsletters, corporations' annual reports—all these are instances of writers reporting to inform and explain.

As these examples show, reports appear in many spheres of life. It is likely, for example, that you have been writing reports since elementary school, whether book reports, lab reports, or term papers. But you may also have reported information in other ways. You may have designed a poster for a science fair or history class or given an oral report on a famous artist.

As you can see, report writing takes many forms. Nonetheless, there are some characteristic features. First, as noted already, reports are based on *research*. Report writers typically begin with a question they want answered. They identify a need to know that might call on them to find out what happened at the city council meeting last night, what the latest data suggest about the consequences of welfare reform, or why students choose the majors they do.

A second feature that characterizes the genre of reports is the writer's *purpose*. The point of doing research for most reports is to inform and explain. For this reason, the focus in a report tends to be placed on the subject rather than on the writer's experience and perceptions. Unlike, say, a memoir, where the reader is asked to share an important moment with the writer, a report writer's relationship to readers tends to be more formal, distanced, and impersonal. And unlike in other genres, such as commentary, proposals, and reviews, where the writer's argument is usually introduced early in a prominent position and then supported by evidence, in report writing the evidence normally comes first, followed by the writer's analysis, interpretation, and conclusions. Writers often take positions in reports. But by presenting their main claims after the evidence, report writers create the impression that their conclusions have been suggested by the data.

This focus on the data leads to a third characteristic feature of report writing, the writer's *tone of voice*. In reports, writers typically strive to sound objective in their presentation of information and conclusions. The use of an objective tone does not mean, of course, that writers are simply transferring information to readers. Report writers are always sifting through and selecting information according to their sense of what is notable and significant. Reports deliver the writer's version of what is most pertinent given the circumstances, the writer's understanding of readers' needs, and the writer's own values.

From this perspective, the objectivity in the writer's voice has to do with the credibility readers invest in the writer as a reliable, honest, and responsible source of information and analysis. If the writer's own views figure prominently, then readers will sense they are encountering a commentary and not a report. But if the writer is successful in maintaining a focus on the subject and an objective tone, readers are likely to take the data and conclusions seriously, even as they realize that the writer may have taken a strong role in shaping the presentation of the material.

■ WRITING FROM EXPERIENCE

When you need to know something, where do you turn? What are your main sources of information, both in and out of school, and what are your purposes in using them? (For example, you may have used an encyclopedia to prepare a written report for a class, read a pamphlet about date rape, or checked the Web for sports scores or movie and music reviews.) Compare your list with those of your classmates. Next, pick three or four information sources to analyze in some detail, choosing sources that differ from each other. Analyze the way each source makes information available. What is the purpose of the information source? How does the source select information to include? How does the source organize the information? What uses do people make of the information?

READINGS

NEWS REPORTS

The following two news reports on a study of the relationship of mental illness and violence appeared on the same day in 1995. The first comes from the Associated Press and was published in many local newspapers. The second was written for the *New York Times* by Fox Butterfield, one of its staff reporters at the time. Both provide accurate reports of the findings published in *The Archives of General Psychiatry* by a team of researchers. The question remains, though, what kind of impression the two reports created in the minds of their readers.

Providence Journal   May 14, 1995

Mentally Ill People Aren't More Violent, Study Finds

CHICAGO (AP)—*Mentally ill people who do not abuse alcohol or drugs are no more violent than their neighbors, a study has found.*

Mental-health advocates and former patients say the finding could help chip away at the stereotypes that have provoked unnecessary fear and driven misguided public policy for years.

Discharged mental patients with substance-abuse problems are five times as likely to commit acts of violence as people without drug problems, according to the study, published in this month's edition of the *Archives of General Psychiatry*.

Non-patients with substance abuse problems had three times the violence rate of the general population. But the violence rate was about the same for patients and non-patients who were drug-free.

The study followed 951 acute psychiatric patients in the year after their discharge in 1994 from hospitals in Pittsburgh, Kansas City and Worcester, Mass. Researchers compared the findings with a sample of 519 non-patients who lived in the same neighborhoods as the patients discharged in Pittsburgh.

John Monahan, one of the study's authors, says several recent surveys, including some conducted at Columbia University, have shown that most Americans believe mentally ill people are prone to violence.

"I think the public's fears are greatly exaggerated," said Monahan, a psychologist at the University of Virginia School of Law.

Margin annotations:

Headline:

Lead: main event findings of study

¶2: Consequences of main event

¶s 3–5: Details of main event

¶5: Detail of how study was conducted

¶6: Comment from author of study

Analysis: Organization of Information in a Newspaper Report: The Inverted Pyramid

Newspaper stories report the information with the highest value first. The assumption is that busy readers, skimming the newspaper, may not read the entire news report. Accordingly, a condensed version of the most important information needs to be frontloaded, with other information following.

- **Headline:** this tells in a very brief way what the main event is (in the case of this news report, what the "study finds").

- **Lead:** the opening paragraph or two present in capsule form the most important information about the main event ("mentally ill people . . . are no more violent").

- **Details of the main event:** this provides further information on what happened, who was involved, where, how, and why.

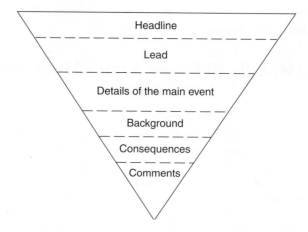

- **Background:** sometimes reporters will fill in background information about the main event.

- **Consequences:** this explains the larger significance of the main event (in this case, "the finding could help chip away at stereotypes").

- **Comments:** this provides insights and opinions ("'I think the public's fears are greatly exaggerated,' said Monahan").

The headline and lead always appear first. After that, the order may vary. Consider in the next news report—on the same study of violence and mental illness—how the order of information is organized.

STUDIES OF MENTAL ILLNESS SHOW LINKS TO VIOLENCE

FOX BUTTERFIELD

New York Times   May 14, 1995

Studies of Mental Illness Show Links to Violence
New Finding Cites Role of Subtance Abuse

BOSTON, May 14—After a generation of believing that the mentally ill are no more violent than other people, psychiatrists and advocates for the emotionally disturbed are wrestling with studies that show that the mentally ill may indeed be more violent in some circumstances.

Their difficulty was underscored today in a report of the latest of these studies in *The Archives of General Psychiatry*, a publication of the American Medical Association. The studies found that mental patients discharged from a hospital stay are no more violent than other members of their community, unless they have been abusing alcohol or drugs. Substance abuse increased the rates of violence by mental patients by up to five times, the study concluded, while it tripled the rate of violence by other people.

The finding about substance abuse is particularly important because the mentally ill are almost twice as likely as other people to be alcoholics or on drugs, the report said.

The study, paid for by the MacArthur Foundation, is part of a broad effort by researchers to find out why recent reports have found higher levels of violence among the mentally ill than in the general population, contradicting previous research dating from the 1950's and 1960's.

The relationship between mental illness and violence is an extremely sensitive subject because the public has long believed that the emotionally disturbed are more dangerous, despite the experts' views, and this popular perception has helped stigmatize the mentally ill.

To complicate the situation, with the closure of most state hospitals in recent years an increasing number of the mentally ill have been sent to jail or prison, where they receive little treatment, then are released only to be arrested again.

"We wanted to find some factors that distinguished which patients were at higher risk of violence, and substance abuse turned out to be a key distinction," said John Monahan, an author of the report who is a psychologist and a law professor at the University of Virginia. "We hope this will lead people not to tar everybody who is discharged from the hospital with the same brush."

The study also found that the types of violence committed by the mentally ill were largely the same that other people committed and that more than 85 percent of the violence committed by the mentally ill was directed at family members or friends, with only 14 percent of the attacks involving strangers.

"These findings clearly indicate that public fears of violence on the street by discharged patients who are strangers to them are misdirected," Professor Monahan said.

The study was conducted on 1,000 patients discharged from hospitals in Pittsburgh, Kansas City, Mo., and Worcester, Mass.

Another recent study, by Bruce Link, a professor at the Columbia University School of Public Health, found that the mentally ill are more violent if they are suffering from paranoia or from certain delusions and hallucinations.

Still another new study, by Jeffrey Swanson, an assistant professor of psychiatry at Duke University Medical Center, showed an increased risk of violence for mentally ill patients who are substance abusers and who stop taking their antipsychotic drugs a frequent problem.

As an indication of how sensitive the issue of mental illness and violence is, the authors of the MacArthur Foundation study conducted focus groups before writing their report. "Language is important, and we wanted to cast things in the least inflammatory way," Professor Monahan said.

As a further indication of this sensitivity, the report immediately produced different reactions from the two major advocacy groups.

Mike Faenza, president of the National Mental Health Association, the nation's oldest and largest mental health organization, said: "This study's findings counter the fictional and highly stigmatizing images propagated by Hollywood movie studios and New York ad men. It is time we kill our cultural fantasy of deranged psychotic killers on the loose. The public's fear is out of time with reality."

Mr. Faenza said the report also underscored the need to "bring mental health and substance abuse treatment services together." He maintained that because of the ingrained habits of mental health professionals and the way government money is allocated, people now tend to be treated for either mental illness or for substance abuse but not jointly for both. This practice, he said, lets many patients fall through the cracks.

But Dr. E. Fuller Torrey, a psychiatrist affiliated with the National Alliance for the Mentally Ill, an advocacy group made up of family members of the emotionally disturbed, said the authors of the report had failed to draw the most important conclusion from their own data. These were data showing that mentally ill people who underwent hospitalization had a 50 percent reduction rate in violent acts in the year after their release, and people who were both mentally ill and abused drugs or alcohol had a 54 percent reduction rate in violent behavior.

"This is the first time that anyone has shown what we have long suspected, that if you treat mental illness, you can reduce the violence," said Dr. Torrey, who is executive director of the Stanley Foundation research programs in Washington.

Dr. Torrey's point was echoed in an editorial in *The Archives of General Psychiatry* by Professor Link of Columbia, who said that the most important finding in the MacArthur study is that the mentally ill tend to be violent when they are "symptomatic" in the period before hospitalization, and that after treatment, when their symptoms wane, "the risk for violence declines to the point where it is no different from the base level in the community."

Dr. Torrey is an outspoken critic of the restrictive laws against involuntary hospitalization of the mentally ill, believing that many disturbed people do not understand their disease and therefore resist attempts to treat them. This can sometimes result in untreated mentally ill people harming themselves or others.

Laurie Flynn, executive director of the National Alliance, said, "This violence is preventable." But she added that the lack of access to treatment "is a direct contributor to the criminalization problem," the growing number of mentally ill people who are sent to jail or prison rather than a clinic or hospital.

Trying not to tar every discharged mental patient with the same brush.

The situation is especially hard on family members who care for the mentally ill, Ms. Flynn said, since, as the new study found, it is relatives and friends who are most likely to be the victims of violence.

"People end up telling us it is easier to get your relative arrested than to get them treatment," she said "It is a kind of family secret."

Dr. Torrey said he believes the amount of violence by the mentally ill has been increasing because of the closing of state hospitals and with financial pressures resulting in shorter stays for those patients who are hospitalized. Dr. Torrey estimates that the mentally ill are responsible for about 1,000 homicides a year in the United States.

But Professor Swanson said that in an earlier study he conducted in five cities, he found that the mentally ill were responsible for only about 4 percent of overall violence. Mental illness, he found, is a much smaller risk factor for violence than is being young, male, poor or addicted to alcohol or drugs.

Analysis: Framing the Story

News reports seem to be among the most straightforward forms of writing because they appear simply to inform readers about something that happened. In this case, an important study was published in *The Archives of General Psychiatry* on a question of great public interest, namely the relationship between mental illness and violence, and accordingly both the Associated Press and the *New York Times* decided to cover the story. As you can see, the two reporters' accounts of the study's findings are very similar—and yet, if you were to read just the two headlines, you might think otherwise.

It's not only the headlines that seem to create two different and perhaps divergent accounts. News reporting is never simply a matter of telling what happened. The news has to be produced—put into intelligible shape by the reporter's writing. One of the key devices reporters use to produce the news is the technique of *framing*. Notice how the headlines contribute to two quite different ways of framing the story. For the Associated Press news report, the study, as mental health advocates and former patients say, may "chip away" at "stereotypes," "unnecessary fear," and "misguided public policy." For Fox Butterfield, on the other hand, his longer news report enables him to frame the story by putting it in the context of an ongoing debate over the "extremely sensitive subject" of the relationhip between mental illness and violence and what to do about it.

■ FOR CRITICAL INQUIRY

1. What was your immediate reaction when you read the two headlines? Was this reaction modified or changed as you read the two news reports?

2. Notice who is quoted in each of the news reports. How do these quotes shape the way readers are likely to understand the study? What differences, if any, do you see in the use of quotes?

3. Describe what you see as the two news reporters' purposes. To what extent are they similar? How do they differ? How would you account for these differences?

4. Work in a group with two other students. Choose a recent event that all know something about and that interests you. By yourself, write a headline and one or two opening paragraphs, just enough to frame the event. Now compare your versions. How do they differ? How is each likely to influence readers' understanding of the event?

FACT SHEETS

FACTS ABOUT PRISONS AND PRISONERS

NEW INCARCERATION FIGURES: GROWTH IN POPULATION CONTINUES

THE SENTENCING PROJECT

The Sentencing Project is a nonprofit organization that promotes reduced reliance on incarceration and increased use of alternatives to deal with crime. It is a nationally recognized source on criminal justice policy analysis, data, and program information.

514 TENTH STREET NW, SUITE 1000
WASHINGTON, DC 20004
TEL: 202.628.0871 • FAX: 202.628.1091
STAFF@SENTENCINGPROJECT.ORG
WWW.SENTENCINGPROJECT.ORG

THE SENTENCING PROJECT

FACTS ABOUT PRISONS AND PRISONERS

The Growing Corrections System

- The number of inmates in state and federal prisons has increased more than six-fold from less than 200,000 in 1970 to 1,421,911 by yearend 2004. An additional 713,990 are held in local jails, for a total of more than 2.1 million.

- The state and federal prison population grew by more than 28,000 persons (1.9%) between 2003 and 2004, while the jail population increased by more than 22,000 inmates (3.3%).

- As of 2004, 1 of every 138 Americans was incarcerated in prison or jail.

- The number of persons on probation and parole has been growing dramatically along with institutional populations. There are now 6.9 million Americans incarcerated or on probation or parole, an increase of more than 275 percent since 1980.

- One in eight (12.6%) black males aged 25-29 was in prison or jail in 2004 as were 1 in 28 (3.6%) Hispanic males and 1 in 59 (1.7%) white males in the same age group.

- Nationally, 64 females per 100,000 women are serving a sentence in prison; 920 males per 100,000 men are in prison.

- The 2004 United States' rate of incarceration of 724 inmates per 100,000 population is the highest reported rate in the world, well ahead of the Russian rate of 532 per 100,000.

Who is in our Prisons and Jails?

- 93% of prison inmates are male, 7% female.

- As of 2004, there were more than 190,000 women in state and federal prison or local jail.

- 41% of prison inmates in 2004 were black and 19% were Hispanic.

- 60% of jail inmates in 2004 were unconvicted and awaiting trial, compared to 51% in 1990.

- 76% of those sentenced to state prisons in 2002 were convicted of non-violent crimes, including 31% for drug offenses, and 29% for property offenses.

- 1 in 4 jail inmates in 2002 was in jail for a drug offense, compared to 1 in 10 in 1983; drug offenders constituted 20% of state prison inmates and 55% of federal prison inmates in 2001.

- Black males have a 32% chance of serving time in prison at some point in their lives; Hispanic males have a 17% chance; white males have a 6% chance.

Source: Bureau of Justice Statistics.

10/05

514 10th Street NW, Suite 1000
Washington, DC 20004
Tel: 202.628.0871 • Fax: 202.628.1091
Staff@Sentencingproject.org
WWW.Sentencingproject.org

NEW INCARCERATION FIGURES:
GROWTH IN POPULATION CONTINUES

Bureau of Justice Statistics figures for 2004 indicate that there were more than 2.1 million inmates in the nation's prisons and jails, representing an increase of 2.6% (54,300) over the previous twelve months.

The new figures represent a record 32-year continuous rise in the number of inmates in the U.S. The current incarceration rate of 724 per 100,000 residents places the United States first in the world in this regard. Russia had previously rivaled the U.S., but substantial prisoner amnesties in recent years have led to a decline of the prison population, resulting in a current rate of incarceration of 564 per 100,000. Rates of incarceration per 100,000 for other industrialized nations include Australia - 120, Canada - 116, England/Wales - 145, France - 88, and Japan - 60.

The continued growth in incarceration comes despite the fact that the last decade has witnessed a sustained, falling crime rate that has reduced crime to levels last experienced in the 1960s. In addition, a number of states have implemented reforms in sentencing and corrections policy with the intent of diverting more people from prison and increasing the use of parole. Despite these developments, the prison and jail population has continued to grow to unprecedented levels, with 1 in every 138 U.S. residents incarcerated. This has had profound consequences for racial and ethnic minorities and women. These and other factors relating to the current prison figures are assessed below:

Rising Incarceration Despite Falling Crime Rates – Despite falling crime rates since 1991, the rate of incarceration in prison has increased by more than 50% since that time. These dynamics suggest that the rise in imprisonment is due to changes in policy that have increased the amount of time that offenders are serving in prison, and not crime rates. An examination of the rise of imprisonment from 1992 to 2001 concluded that the *entire* increase was a result of changes in sentencing policy and practice.[1] These include such measures as "three strikes," mandatory sentencing, and "truth in sentencing." From 1995 to 2001, the average time served in prison rose by 30%.

Federal Prison System Leads Growth – The federal prison system continues to grow at an unprecedented rate, increasing 4.2% during 2004 to a total of 180,328 prisoners. The number of federal prisoners in custody has increased by 90% in the last decade. More than one-quarter (26%) of the national growth in the prison population in the past year is attributable to the federal prison system, contributing to an overcrowding level of 140%. This expansion has come about primarily as a result of the incarceration of non-violent offenders. More than half (55%) of

---

[1] Jennifer C. Karberg and Allen J. Beck, "Trends in U.S. Correctional Populations: Findings from the Bureau of Justice Statistics," presented at the National Committee on Community Corrections, Washington, D.C., April 16, 2004.

federal prisoners are serving time for a drug offense, while only 11% are incarcerated for a violent offense.

Sentencing Reform Impacts – In the past several years, at least half the states have enacted some type of sentencing or drug policy reform, largely motivated by the need to cut corrections costs. These include such policies as reducing the length of low-level drug terms in Kansas and Washington state, granting judges more discretion in school-drug zone cases in Connecticut, and scaling back mandatory minimums in Michigan. While this trend represents a significant shift from the "get tough" policies that have characterized the last three decades, the overall scale of reform has not been sufficient to control prison growth.

For example, in the wake of the passage of Proposition 36 in California in 2000, a measure designed to divert low-level drug offenders into treatment, there were predictions that this practice would result in a decline in the overall prison population. The combination of Proposition 36 and fewer parole revocations led corrections analysts to predict that by 2004 the prison population would decline to 156,000 before stabilizing. However, an unexpected increase in admissions offset any gains that had been forecast to emerge from diversion and parole changes.

While modifications in the parole release system in Texas had resulted in a significant reduction in the state prison population, a sustained rise in admissions and parole revocations erased any benefits of this policy change. The cases of California and Texas illustrate the difficulty of enacting long-term, sustainable sentencing reform. Despite policy changes targeted at addressing problematic areas of growth in the correctional system, in practice the implementation of reform can be imprecise and the continued existence of punitive sentencing laws serves as a continuous engine of growth through new prison admissions.

Sentencing Policy Changes – Counterbalancing the sentencing reforms intended to reduce incarceration, policies enacted at the federal and state levels during the 1980s and 1990s continue to exert significant upward pressure on the prison system, even as crime rates decline. These include "truth in sentencing" laws enacted by 30 states that mandate that offenders serve at least 85% of their time, "three strikes and you're out" laws enacted by half the states since 1993, and a variety of mandatory sentencing policies that apply to drug and other offenses.

California's "three strikes" law is by far the broadest in the nation, with 7,716 persons now serving terms of 25 years to life under its provisions. The third "strike" of more than half (56%) of these persons is for a non-violent offense. An initiative to reduce the number of non-violent offenders serving a third strike sentence, Proposition 66, was narrowly defeated in November 2004 after heavy lobbying from Governor Schwarzenegger in the final weeks of the election.

Female Prison Population Continues to Grow – The number of women in prison first exceeded 100,000 in 2003, and currently there are 104,848 female prisoners. In addition, there are 87,583 women in local jails. The rapid growth of women's incarceration – at nearly double the rate for men over the past two decades – is disproportionately due to the war on drugs. Women in prison are more likely than men (32% vs. 21%) to be serving a sentence for a drug charge.

2

Aging Prison Population – One of every 23 inmates in prison today is age 55 or older, an 85% increase since 1995. A significant contributor to this growth has been the fact that persons sentenced to prison today are serving more time those in past decades. A 2004 report by The Sentencing Project found an 83% increase in the number of prisoners serving a life sentence from 1992 to the present, yielding a total of 127,000 lifers today.[2] Of this total, one-quarter are serving terms of life without parole. The average time to be served by newly admitted lifers has also increased substantially, rising from 21 years in 1991 to 29 years by 1997.

Jail Dynamics Changing – Along with prison populations, the number of persons in local jails has been rising steadily throughout this period. Of particular note is that the proportion of persons held in jail awaiting trial has risen considerably, from 51% in 1990 to 60% in 2004, with nearly half of that growth occurring in the last three years. These dynamics are likely due to inadequacy of defense counsel representation at early stages of justice system processing and limited access to pretrial release programs in some jurisdictions. Research has demonstrated that persons detained prior to trial have a greater likelihood of conviction and sentencing to prison.

Racial Dynamics Persist – The new imprisonment figures document the continuing dramatic impact of incarceration on African American communities. One of every eight black males in the age group 25-29 is incarcerated on any given day. In historical perspective, the 910,000 African Americans incarcerated today are more than nine times the number of 98,000 in 1954, the year of the *Brown v. Board of Education* decision.

Policies to Control Prison Growth – As states grapple with the increasingly expensive costs of imprisonment and its effects on vital public services, a comprehensive strategy is needed if policymakers are to be able to control the rise in incarceration. Such a framework should be developed with the goal of public safety, by using funds saved through unnecessary incarceration to targeted approaches for reducing crime and supervising offenders in the community. The elements of such a framework include:

- Reconsideration of sentence lengths by judges, sentencing commissions, and legislatures;
- Enhance drug offender diversion to treatment through drug court and other mechanisms;
- Increased development of alternatives to incarceration that can provide services and supervision that meet the needs of individual offenders;
- Reconsideration of policies that result in unnecessarily lengthy incarceration, such as "three strikes" laws, "truth in sentencing," mandatory sentencing, and life without parole;
- Enhanced use of judicial discretion through increasing the range of factors that can be taken into account at sentencing and providing options to mandatory sentencing;
- Reconsideration of parole revocation policies, particularly for technical violations, that have increasingly contributed to prison admissions;
- Reallocate justice system funds to support greater investments in "community justice" programs that can target services pro-actively to communities heavily affected by both crime and incarceration.

---

[2] Marc Mauer, Ryan S. King, and Malcolm C. Young, *The Meaning of "Life": Long Prison Sentences in Context*, The Sentencing Project, May 2004.

514 TENTH STREET NW, SUITE 1000
WASHINGTON, DC 20004
TEL: 202.628.0871 • FAX: 202.628.1091
STAFF@SENTENCINGPROJECT.ORG
WWW.SENTENCINGPROJECT.ORG

TEN LEADING NATIONS IN INCARCERATION RATES

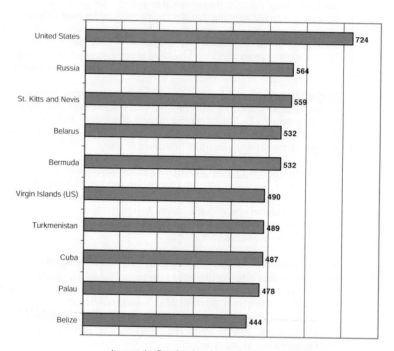

Incarceration Rate (number of people in prison per 100,000 population)

Source: Rate for the US from *Prisoners in 2004*; for all other nations, International Centre for Prison Studies available online at www.prisonstudies.org. Incarceration data were collected on varying dates and are the most current data available as of 2005.

514 TENTH STREET NW, SUITE 1000
WASHINGTON, DC 20004
TEL: 202.628.0871 • FAX: 202.628.1091
STAFF@SENTENCINGPROJECT.ORG
WWW.SENTENCINGPROJECT.ORG

RATE OF INCARCERATION IN SELECTED NATIONS

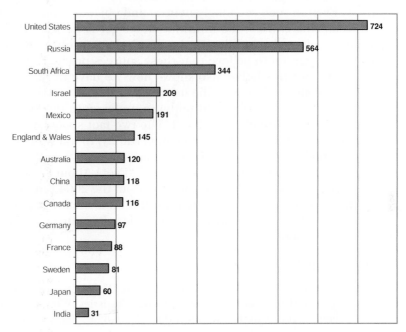

Incarceration Rate (number of people in prison per 100,000 population)

Source: Rate for the US from *Prisoners in 2004*; for all other nations, International Centre for Prison Studies available online at www.prisonstudies.org. Incarceration data were collected on varying dates and are the most current data available as of 2005.

11/05

Analysis: Information and Persuasion

The idea that information exists independently of the people who gather, organize, distribute, and use it is an old one. There is a profound—and understandable—wish that if we could only get all the information, we would know what is true and what decisions we should make about private and public affairs. For better or for worse, however, from a rhetorical perspective, such a wish is just that—wishful thinking. Information doesn't come to us innocently. It comes through the intentions of other people, organizations, and institutions. Even in such seemingly neutral and objective forms as news articles or encyclopedia entries, the information we get is not the whole picture but a version, selected according to the best judgment of the writer. We may well have good reason to believe that these sources provide accurate and reliable accounts, but this belief also shows how we have been persuaded to invest credibility and authority in the information the writer presents.

This point is worth mentioning to underscore the fact that information and persuasion are closely linked. The two fact sheets prepared by the Sentencing Project campaign are meant, certainly, to inform readers. Much of the information comes from Bureau of Justice Statistics, a federal agency that reports on the criminal justice system; "Facts About Prisons and Prisoners" appears to summarize key information from the 2004 report on incarceration. At the same time, however, the information is meant to persuade readers to take prison issues seriously and to consider alternatives to the current system of incarceration.

■ FOR CRITICAL INQUIRY

1. Consider the information presented in "Facts About Prisons and Prisoners." Notice the source is Bureau of Justice Statistics. What effect on the credibility and authority of the fact sheet does this have?

2. In visual design, "Facts About Prisons and Prisoners" is a bulleted list of statistics. What overall picture emerges? How does the order of information influence your understanding of the current situation of prisons and prisoners?

3. Compare "Facts About Prisons and Prisoners" to "New Incarceration Figures: Growth in Population Continues." The two fact sheets present some of the same information, but "New Incarceration Figures" offers discussion and not just bulleted points. What does this discussion add to the information? What purposes does each of the fact sheets serve?

REPORTS ON GRAPHIC DESIGN

The two selections that follow come from Steven Heller and Karen Pomeroy's book *Design Literacy: Understanding Graphic Design* (1997). Heller has written numerous books on graphic design and is a senior art director at the *New York Times* and editor of *AIGA Journal of Graphic Design*. Pomeroy is a graphic designer and writer in Los Angeles whose books include *Designing with Illustration*. *Design Literacy* was written, as the authors say, to present "object lessons" that explain the history and design principles of memorable examples of graphic design.

I SHOP THEREFORE I AM—BARBARA KRUGER

STEVEN HELLER AND KAREN POMEROY

"Untitled" (I shop therefore I am) by Barbara Kruger, 1987. Photographic silkscreen/vinyl, 112" x 112". Courtesy of Mary Boone Gallery, New York.

1   A shopping bag with the words *I shop therefore I am* might be mistaken for a promotion by some tony retail store. But seen in a museum as a nearly nine-foot-square photographic silkscreen on vinyl with a red enamel frame, this work assumes a different meaning. Is it advertising or art, design or propaganda?

2   Barbara Kruger (b. 1945) ignores these distinctions. She makes graphic work that expresses political and social folly through the traditional venues of both art and advertising: museums, art galleries, billboards, posters, book covers, matchbooks, shopping bags, and even covers for such mainstream magazines as *Newsweek, Ms.*, and *Esquire*. She rejects the terms design or advertising to describe her work stating, "I'm someone who works with pictures and words, and people can take that to mean anything they like." In 1990 the large-scale silkscreened version of *I Shop Therefore I Am* was exhibited in Cologne at the Kölnischer Kunstrerein; the printed shopping bag was given away free with the purchase of the show catalog.

3   *I Shop Therefore I Am*, like most of her work, was designed with economy. An enlarged black-and-white photograph of a single hand, tightly cropped, palm forward, fills the visual field. A red block almost perfectly proportional to a credit card appears to

balance between the thumb and third finger in an act of optical trickery. The "card" is not actually held by the hand, but is instead mechanically positioned and appears to be pushed forward. The typeface, Futura Bold, reinforces the blunt declarative statement in what at once reads like advertising exhortation and philosophical pontification.

4   Kruger's art emerged in the milieu of 1970s feminism. Feminists argued that gender was not an innate condition, but rather a construct created by adaptation to societal norms and expectations. They contended that in a visual culture, the masculine eye objectifies and masters, casting women as objects of the male gaze. In his 1972 edition of *Ways of Seeing*, the British writer John Berger observed, "Men look at women. Women watch themselves being looked at." Kruger's early imagery combined stereotypical images of women borrowed from fashion magazines and advertising with text in a contrapuntal dialog. An untitled work from 1983 contrasts a photograph of a woman's manicured hands underwater pulling the stopper from a drain (an ad for dishwashing soap?) with the text "Now you see us, now you don't."

5   In 1984 Kruger expanded her targets with a series of posters attacking money and consumption as even more pervasive tools of masculine power. *I Shop Therefore I Am* is not only a parody of Descartes's *cogito ergo sum*, "I think therefore I am," but also an exposé of a culture so dominated by consumerism that it substitutes acquisition for thinking as the apotheosis of human existence. Shopping is no mere dalliance, but a crucial quest for an identity capable of being created, not just honed, through the acquisition of appropriate things.

6   In typical editorial or advertising design, words reinforce or support the visual message. Conversely, Kruger creates a vigorous dialogue between word and image, trapping the viewer somewhere in between. She instigates questions and encourages doubt. Kruger's strength lies in the tension and contrast: the images are anti-individual, stereotypical photographs appropriated from the cultural collective, old photographic albums, instruction manuals, and magazines; her statements use the personal textual pronouns, I, we, you, and speak to the spectator directly. The mixed messages make provocative alchemy.

7   Kruger draws inspiration from her earlier jobs. As an editorial designer at *Harper's Bazaar* she worked under art director Marvin Israel, who convinced her to assemble a professional art portfolio and introduced her to photography. Later she worked under art director Roger Schoening at *Mademoiselle*, and when the senior designer left six months after her arrival, twenty-two-year-old Kruger was given the job. Her rapid rise in the commercial art world was matched by an equal rise in disillusionment. After four years of full-time employment she took refuge in the darkroom doing work that allowed her to

stay connected to the world as a freelance picture editor and designer. She continued commercial freelancing for almost eleven years.

8   Kruger's work has been compared to the polemical photomontages of German dadaist John Heartfield. She denies any conscious link; she didn't even know of Heartfield's political work for the Berlin-based communist newspaper *AIZ* until 1980, well after her own signature style was developed. "Critics always focus on the fine art/constructivism end of my work, rather than thinking that this was somebody who had a job, who had training in cropping photographs and who pasted words over them." She sees her work as a logical evolution from that framework, turning the word/image apposition into a socially meaningful device.

9   As Kruger has co-opted the tools of design and advertising, likewise the design field has borrowed from her. It should come as no surprise that the commercial world Kruger assails has reclaimed her methods. She doesn't seem to mind though, for when her style is stripped of its meaning and taken out of context—used only for its graphic vocabulary—it validates her critique of the system.

DYLAN—MILTON GLASER
STEVEN HELLER AND KAREN POMEROY

1   Bob Dylan arrived in New York in January 1961 at the age of twenty-one. In five years he produced seven albums and came to symbolize a generation caught between the unprecedented consumer prosperity that followed World War II and the Cold War's chilling rhetoric of mutually assured destruction. The 1960s generation adopted Dylan, projecting onto him its collective hope and cynicism. On July 29, 1966, it was reported that while riding his motorcycle on the back roads in Woodstock, New York, the back wheel locked, and Bob Dylan was thrown over the handlebars and seriously injured. Rumors abounded. Some thought he was dead, and some thought it was a ruse to cover up a recovery from an overdose. Whatever the truth, the words and the music stopped.

2   After six months without any new Dylan material, Columbia Records was in a nervous panic. To fill the gap, Columbia unilaterally decided to issue a greatest hits album pieced together from previous album cuts. Creative director Bob Cato and art director John Berg had a dramatic, backlit photo by Roland Scherman of a closely cropped profile of Dylan playing the harmonica, his wild hair bathed in a corona of light. Dylan had previously rejected it as cover art. But because he was in breach of contract, Dylan could no longer control what his recording studio did.

3   It was further decided to include a free poster in each new greatest hits album. Columbia decided to use the Scherman photographic profile on the album cover, but needed someone to design the poster. The Scherman profile triggered Berg's memory of Milton Glaser's (b. 1929) playful and inventive silhouettes that captured the essence of gesture and content through minimal means.

4   The hallmark of Glaser's work was an aggressive mining of visual artifacts and archetypes from diverse and unexpected sources. In addition to silhouettes, Glaser was working with black-ink contour lines, creating flat shapes and enriching them with adhesive color films, echoing the simple iconography and directness of comic books. He was interested in Islamic miniatures and was intrigued by the psychedelia emerging from the West Coast. Long before postmodernism, Glaser understood that design is essentially a vernacular language, and he delighted in discovering obscure typographic forms. On a trip to Mexico City he was so captivated by the letterforms on a small advertisement for a tailor that he photographed the sign and returned home to invent the remainder of the alphabet, which became the typeface Baby Teeth.

5   When the request came from Berg to design the poster of Dylan along with a package of pictorial reference, including copies of the Scherman photograph, it didn't strike

6   First, the memory of a powerful icon surfaced, a self-portrait by Marcel Duchamp—a profile torn from a single piece of colored paper and placed on a black background. Dylan's hair became an inductive mélange of Persian-like forms. Dylan's name, executed in Glaser's own Baby Teeth typeface, rested in the bottom right corner of the poster, a warm brown against a black background, unusual in its subtlety. The geometric letterforms contrasted sharply with the mellifluous hair and sinuous profile. Glaser admitted to being consciously intrigued by the notion of opposites; the hard, reductive edge of Dylan's profile contrasts with the expressive nature of the hair; bright, whimsical color reverberates off the dense, solid black.

7   In the original sketch (his only sketch), Glaser positioned a harmonica in front of Dylan's mouth, as in Scherman's photograph. When Berg saw the sketch, Glaser recalled, he said "Simplify, simplify." What he meant was, "Get rid of the harmonica." Eliminating the harmonica created a white negative space nearly equal to the black silhouetted profile. This increased the visual vibration of the whole piece and focused more attention on the "coastline" of Dylan's profile. Glaser went directly to finish. Six million *Dylan* posters were printed and included in the album, making it the single most reproduced image Glaser ever created, aside from his I ♥ NY™ Campaign.

Analysis: Object Lessons

Steven Heller and Karen Pomeroy chose ninety-three examples of graphic design as "object lessons" for their book *Design Literacy*. The term "object lessons" reveals the writers' purpose of enabling interested readers to learn about the history of graphic design and the contributions of individual designers. Reading the two selections is in many ways like listening to a good lecture that informs and explains.

Notice, for example, how Heller and Pomeroy use historical background and details about the lives and works of Barbara Kruger and Milton Glaser to explain their significance. Heller and Pomeroy are working with limited space for each designer, so they have to select information carefully to advance their aim of explaining why each work of graphic design is noteworthy. Notice, too, that the writers weave in brief but telling explanations of design principles: "The typeface, Futura Bold, reinforces the blunt declarative statement in what at once reads like advertising exhortation and philosophical pontification" (about Barbara Kruger's "I Shop Therefore I Am") and "Dylan's name, executed in Glaser's own Baby Teeth typeface, rested in the bottom right corner of the poster, a warm brown against a black background, unusual in its sub-tlety. The geometric letterforms contrasted sharply with the mellifluous hair and sinuous profile" (in the case of Milton Glaser's Dylan poster).

■ FOR CRITICAL INQUIRY

1. Graphic design uses a visual language that combines words and images. One of the challenges of analyzing graphic design is to devise a written language that explains how it works. How do Heller and Pomeroy go about doing this? Pick a phrase or passage that you found particularly clarifying in explaining each of the two works of graphic design.

2. Consider how Heller and Pomeroy combine background information and expla-nation. How does informing contribute to their goal of explaining?

3. These selections, as noted, are meant to be "object lessons." What did you learn from each? What made that learning possible?

4. Bring to class an example of graphic design that you find especially striking. It could be the cover of a magazine or book, a CD cover, an ad, a poster, or what-ever. To use it as an "object lesson," as Heller and Pomeroy do with their examples of graphic design, consider what you would need to know. What back-ground information would you need? How might you go about doing an explanation of its design features?

REPORT ON SCIENTIFIC RESEARCH

Daniel Pauly is the principal investigator and Reg Watson is a senior scientist at the Sea Around Us Project based at the Fisheries Center at the University of British Columbia. Pauly and Watson are fisheries researchers who study the effect of commercial fishing on marine ecosystems. Their article "Counting the Last Fish," which appeared in the July 2003 issue of *Scientific American*, is based in part on research studies Pauly and Watson had already published in scientific journals. Thus, one of their tasks as writers was to translate these findings for a general readership.

Analysis: Explaining Scientific Research

As you can see from the three bulleted points under the heading "Overview/Fish Declines," the main findings of Daniel Pauly and Reg Watson's report can be stated in a fairly simple and straightforward manner. But Pauly and Watson's purposes go beyond just informing readers that there is an overfishing crisis and suggesting ways to deal with it. Their aim is also to explain, first, how sci-entists have determined that there has been a slow decline in the tons of fish landed since the late 1980s and, second, how the notion of "fishing down the food web" enabled them to estimate the damage fishing has done to marine ecosystems. To do this, Pauly and Watson have to explain how scientists do re-search. In particular, notice how they define and explain their use of the idea "trophic levels" (TL) to calculate by numerical values the reduction in com-plexity of food chains caused by "fishing down." To understand the results of

COUNTING

THE Last Fish

OVERFISHING HAS SLASHED STOCKS—ESPECIALLY OF LARGE PREDATOR SPECIES—TO AN ALL-TIME LOW WORLDWIDE, ACCORDING TO NEW DATA. IF WE DON'T MANAGE THIS RESOURCE, WE WILL BE LEFT WITH A DIET OF JELLYFISH AND PLANKTON STEW

By Daniel Pauly and Reg Watson

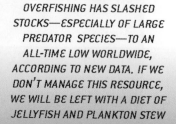

Georges Bank—the patch of relatively shallow ocean just off the coast of Nova Scotia, Canada—used to teem with fish. Writings from the 17th century record that boats were often surrounded by huge schools of cod, salmon, striped bass and sturgeon. Today it is a very different story. Trawlers trailing dredges the size of football fields have literally scraped the bottom clean, harvesting an entire ecosystem—including supporting substrates such as sponges—along with the catch of the day. Farther up the water column, longlines and drift nets are snagging the last sharks, swordfish and tuna. The hauls of these commercially desirable species

An Example of "Fishing Down"

FOOD WEBS contain fewer steps, or trophic levels, when overfishing occurs. After fishers have taken the largest members of a slow-growing predatory species—such as saithe—they must turn to smaller individuals that have not yet achieved full size. Unlike older saithe, these younger fish are not large enough to catch cod, which normally consume whiting, which in turn usually eat krill-grazing haddock (left). Instead the small saithe must eat even smaller fish, such as herring, which feed directly on krill (right). Wiping out larger saithe therefore shortens the food web to four levels instead of six, disrupting ecosystems. Note that actual trophic levels rarely reach six because large fish eat a variety of other fish.

are dwindling, and the sizes of individual fish being taken are getting smaller; a large number are even captured before they have time to mature. The phenomenon is not restricted to the North Atlantic but is occurring across the globe.

Many people are under the mistaken impression that pollution is responsible for declines in marine species. Others may find it hard to believe that a shortage of desirable food fish even exists, because they still notice piles of Chilean sea bass and tuna fillets in their local fish markets. Why is commercial fishing seen as having little if any effect on the species that are being fished? We suspect that this perception persists from an-

Overview/Fish Declines

- New analyses show that fisheries worldwide are in danger of collapsing from overfishing, yet many people still view the ocean as a limitless resource whose bounty humanity has just begun to tap.
- Overfishing results from booms in human populations, increases in the demand for fish as a nutritious food, improvements in commercial fishing technology, and global and national policies that fail to encourage the sustainable management of fisheries.
- Solutions to the problem include banning fishing gear such as dredges that damage ecosystems; establishing marine reserves to allow fisheries to recover; and abolishing government subsidies that keep too many boats on the seas chasing too few fish.

other age, when fishing was a matter of wresting sustenance from a hostile sea using tiny boats and simple gear.

Our recent studies demonstrate that we can no longer think of the sea as a bounteous provider whose mysterious depths contain an inexhaustible resource. Over the past several years we have gathered and analyzed data on the world's fisheries, compiling the first comprehensive look at the state of the marine food resource. We have found that some countries, particularly China, have overreported their catches, obscuring a downward trend in fish caught worldwide. In general, fishers must work farther offshore and at greater depths in an effort to keep up with the catches of yesteryear and to try to meet the burgeoning demand for fish. We contend that overfishing and the fishing of these distant stocks are unsustainable practices and are causing the depletion of important species. But it is not too late to implement policies to protect the world's fisheries for future generations.

The Law of the Sea

EXPLAINING HOW THE SEA got into its current state requires relating a bit of history. The ocean used to be a free-for-all, with fleets flying the flags of various countries competing for fish thousands of miles from home. In 1982 the United Nations adopted the Convention on the Law of the Sea, which allows countries bordering the ocean to claim exclusive economic zones reaching 200 nautical miles into open waters. These areas include the highly productive continental shelves of roughly 200 meters in depth where most fish live out their lives.

The convention ended decades—and, in some instances, even

centuries—of fighting over coastal fishing grounds, but it placed the responsibility for managing marine fisheries squarely on maritime countries. Unfortunately, we cannot point to any example of a nation that has stepped up to its duties in this regard.

The U.S. and Canadian governments have subsidized the growth of domestic fishing fleets to supplant those of now excluded foreign countries. Canada, for instance, built new offshore fleets to replace those of foreign nations pushed out by the convention, effectively substituting foreign boats with even larger fleets of more modern vessels that fish year-round on the same stocks that the domestic, inshore fleet was already targeting. In an effort to ensure that there is no opportunity for foreign fleets to fish the excess allotment—as provided for in the convention—these nations have also begun to fish more extensively than they would have otherwise. And some states, such as those in West Africa, have been pressured by others to accept agreements that allow foreign fleets to fish their waters, as sanctioned by the convention. The end result has been more fishing than ever, because foreign fleets have no incentive to preserve local marine resources long-term—and, in fact, are subsidized by their own countries to garner as much fish as they can.

The expansion made possible by the Convention on the Law of the Sea and technological improvements in commercial fishing gear (such as acoustic fish finders) temporarily boosted fish catches. But by the late 1980s the upward trend began to reverse, despite overreporting by China, which, in order to meet politically driven "productivity increases," was stating that it was taking nearly twice the amount of fish that it actually was.

In 2001 we presented a statistical model that allowed us to examine where catches differed significantly from those taken from similarly productive waters at the same depths and latitudes elsewhere in the world. The figures from Chinese waters—about 1 percent of the world's oceans—were much higher than predicted, accounting for more than 40 percent of the deviations from the statistical model. When we readjusted the worldwide fisheries data for China's misrepresentations, we concluded that world fish landings have been declining slowly since the late 1980s, by about 700,000 metric tons a year. China's overreporting skewed global fisheries statistics so significantly because of the country's large size and the degree of its overreporting. Other nations also submit inaccurate fisheries statistics—with a few overreporting their catches and most underreporting them—but those numbers tend to cancel one another out.

Nations gather statistics on fish landings in a variety of ways, including surveys, censuses and logbooks. In some countries, such as China, these data are forwarded to regional offices and on up through the government hierarchy until they arrive at the national offices. At each step, officials may manipulate the statistics to meet mandatory production targets. Other countries have systems for cross-checking the fish landings against import/export data and information on local consumption.

The most persuasive evidence, in our opinion, that fishing is wreaking havoc on marine ecosystems is the phenomenon that one of us (Pauly) has dubbed "fishing down the food web." This describes what occurs when fishers deplete large preda-

Hot Spots of Overfishing

Trophic Level Decline   0   0.5   1.0   >1.0

OVERFISHING caused the complexity of the food chains in important fisheries to drop by more than one trophic level between the years 1950 and 2000. The open ocean usually has few fish.

tor fish at the top of the food chain, such as tuna and swordfish, until they become rare, and then begin to target smaller species that would usually be eaten by the large fish [see illustration on opposite page].

Fishing Down

THE POSITION A PARTICULAR ANIMAL occupies in the strata of a food web is determined by its size, the anatomy of its mouthparts and its feeding preferences. The various layers of the food web, called trophic levels, are ranked according to how many steps they are removed from the primary producers at the base of the web, which generally consists of phytoplanktonic algae. These microscopic organisms are assigned a trophic level (TL) of 1.

Phytoplankton are grazed mostly by small zooplankton—mainly tiny crustaceans of between 0.5 and two millimeters in size, both of which thus have a TL of 2. (This size hierarchy stands in stark contrast to terrestrial food chains, in which herbivores are often very large; consider moose or elephants, for instance.) TL 3 consists of small fishes between 20 and 50 cen-

THE AUTHORS

DANIEL PAULY and REG WATSON are fisheries researchers at the Sea Around Us Project in Vancouver, where Pauly is the principal investigator and Watson is a senior scientist. The project, which was initiated and funded by the Pew Charitable Trusts, is based at the Fisheries Center at the University of British Columbia and is devoted to studying the impact of fishing on marine ecosystems. Pauly's early career centered on formulating new approaches for fisheries research and management in tropical developing countries. He has designed software programs for evaluating fish stocks and initiated FishBase, the online encyclopedia of fishes of the world. Watson's interests include fisheries modeling, data visualization and computer mapping. His current research focuses on mapping the effects of global fisheries, modeling underwater visual census techniques and using computer simulations to optimize fisheries.

NINA FINKEL

POPULAR FISH—including many of the fillets and steaks that can be found in piles at fish markets (*above*)—have been decimated by overfishing. Fishers must use increasingly complex technology and fish farther offshore and at greater depths to catch such fish. The National Audubon Society and other organizations have issued wallet cards (*right*) so that consumers can avoid overfished species (*red*) or those whose status is cause for concern (*yellow*). The entire card can be downloaded at www.audubon.org/campaign/lo/seafood/cards.html

timeters in length, such as sardines, herring and anchovies. These small pelagic fishes live in open waters and usually consume a variable mix of phytoplankton and both herbivorous and carnivorous zooplankton. They are caught in enormous quantities by fisheries: 41 million metric tons were landed in 2000, a number that corresponds to 49 percent of the reported global marine fish catch. Most are either destined for human consumption, such as canned sardines, or reduced to fish meal and oil to serve as feed for chickens, pigs and farmed salmon or other carnivorous fish.

The typical table fish—the cod, snapper, tuna and halibut that restaurants serve whole or as steaks or fillets—are predators of the small pelagics and other small fishes and invertebrates; they tend to have a TL of between 3.5 and 4.5. (Their TLs are not whole numbers because they can consume prey on several trophic levels.)

The increased popularity in the U.S. of such fish as nutritious foods has undoubtedly contributed to the decline in their stocks. We suggest that the health and sustainability of fisheries can be assessed by monitoring the trends of average TLs. When those numbers begin to drop, it indicates that fishers are relying on ever smaller fish and that stocks of the larger predatory fish are beginning to collapse.

In 1998 we presented the first evidence that "fishing down" was already occurring in some fishing grounds, particularly in the North Atlantic, off the Patagonian coast of South America and nearby Antarctica, in the Arabian Sea, and around parts of Africa and Australia. These areas experienced TL declines of 1 or greater between 1950 and 2000, according to our calculations [*see map on preceding page*]. Off the west coast of New-

foundland, for instance, the average TL went from a maximum of 3.65 in 1957 to 2.6 in 2000. Average sizes of fish landed in those regions dropped by one meter during that period.

Our conclusions are based on an analysis of the global database of marine fish landings that is created and maintained by the U.N. Food and Agriculture Organization, which is in turn derived from data provided by member countries. Because this data set has problems—such as overreporting and the lumping of various species into a category called "mixed"—we had to incorporate information on the global distribution of fishes from FishBase, the online encyclopedia of fishes pioneered by Pauly, as well as information on the fishing patterns and access rights of countries reporting catches.

Research by some other groups—notably those led by Jeremy B. C. Jackson of the Scripps Institution of Oceanography in San Diego and Ransom A. Myers of Dalhousie University in Halifax—suggests that our results, dire as they might seem, in fact underestimate the seriousness of the effects that marine fisheries have on their underlying resources. Jackson and his colleagues have shown that massive declines in populations of marine mammals, turtles and large fishes occurred along all coastlines where people lived long before the post–World War II period we examined. The extent of these depletions was not recognized until recently because biologists did not consult historians or collaborate with archaeologists, who study evidence of fish consumption in middens (ancient trash dumps).

JASON NOSITO-ESKENAZI (*photograph*); LIVING OCEANS PROGRAM, AUDUBON (*wallet card*)

Myers and his co-workers used data from a wide range of fisheries throughout the world to demonstrate that industrial fleets generally take only a few decades to reduce the biomass of a previously unfished stock by a factor of 10. Because it often takes much longer for a regulatory regime to be established to manage a marine resource, the sustainability levels set are most likely to be based on numbers that already reflect population declines. Myers's group documents this process particularly well for the Japanese longline fishery, which in 1952 burst out of the small area around Japan—to which it was confined until the end of the Korean War—and expanded across the Pacific and into the Atlantic and Indian oceans. The expansion decimated tuna populations worldwide. Indeed, Myers and his colleague Boris Worm recently reported that the world's oceans have lost 90 percent of large predatory fish.

Changing the Future

WHAT CAN BE DONE? Many believe that fish farming will relieve the pressure on stocks, but it can do so only if the farmed organisms do not consume fish meal. (Mussels, clams and tilapia, an herbivorous fish, can be farmed without fish meal.) When fish are fed fish meal, as in the case of salmon and various carnivores, farming makes the problem worse, turning small pelagics—including fish that are otherwise perfectly fit for human consumption, such as herring, sardines, anchovies and mackerels—into animal fodder. In fact, salmon farms consume more fish than they produce: it can take three pounds of fish meal to yield one pound of salmon.

One approach to resolving the difficulties now besetting the world's fisheries is ecosystem-based management, which would seek to maintain—or, where necessary, reestablish—the structure and function of the ecosystems within which fisheries are embedded. This would involve considering the food requirements of key species in ecosystems (notably those of marine mammals), phasing out fishing gear that destroys the sea bottom, and implementing marine reserves, or "no-take zones," to mitigate the effects of fishing. Such strategies are compatible with the set of reforms that have been proposed for years by various fisheries scientists and economists: radically reducing global fleet capacity; abolishing government subsidies that keep otherwise unprofitable fishing fleets afloat; and strictly enforcing restrictions on gear that harm habitats or that capture "bycatch," species that will ultimately be thrown away.

Creating no-take zones will be key to preserving the world's fisheries. Some refuges should be close to shore, to protect coastal species; others must be large and offshore, to shield

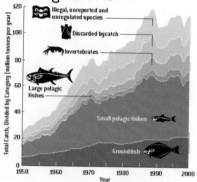

Catching More Fish

AMOUNT OF FISH LANDED has more than quintupled over the past 50 years. As the world's population has grown, commercial fishing technology has advanced, and demand for fish in some countries has surged.

oceanic fishes. No-take zones now exist, but they are small and scattered. Indeed, the total area protected from any form of fishing constitutes a mere 0.01 percent of the ocean surface. Reserves are now viewed by fishers—and even by governments—as necessary concessions to conservationist pressure, but they must become management tools for protecting exploited species from overfishing.

A major goal should be to conserve species that once maintained themselves at deeper depths and farther offshore, before fishers developed improved gear for going after them. This type of fishing is similar to a nonrenewable mining operation because fishes are very vulnerable, typically long-lived, and have very low productivity in the dark, cold depths. These measures would enable fisheries, for the first time, to become sustainable. PM

MORE TO EXPLORE

Effect of Aquaculture on World Fish Supplies. Rosamond L. Naylor, Rebecca J. Goldburg, Jurgenne H. Primavera, Nils Kautsky, Malcolm C. M. Beveridge, Jason Clay, Carl Folke, Jane Lubchenco, Harold Mooney and Max Troell in *Nature*, Vol. 405, pages 1017–1024; June 29, 2000.

Historical Overfishing and the Recent Collapse of Coastal Ecosystems. Jeremy B. C. Jackson et al. in *Science*, Vol. 293, pages 629–638; July 27, 2001.

Systematic Distortion in World Fisheries Catch Trends. Reg Watson and Daniel Pauly in *Nature*, Vol. 414, pages 534–536; November 29, 2001.

In a Perfect Ocean: The State of Fisheries and Ecosystems in the North Atlantic Ocean. Daniel Pauly and Jay Maclean. Island Press, 2003.

Rapid Worldwide Depletion of Predatory Fish Communities. Ransom A. Myers and Boris Worm in *Nature*, Vol. 423, pages 280–283; May 15, 2003.

More information on the state of world fisheries can be found on the Web sites of the Sea Around Us Project at www.saup.fisheries.ubc.ca and of FishBase at www.fishbase.org

NINA FINKEL (*graph*) AND CLEO VILETT (*illustrations*)

NATIONAL GEOGRAPHIC CHANNEL

A segment based on this article will air June 26 on *National Geographic Today*, a program on the National Geographic Channel. Please check your local listings.

scientific research, Pauly and Watson seem to assume, readers also need to understand something about the methods and ways of thinking that scientists employ to get the results.

■ FOR CRITICAL INQUIRY

1. "Counting the Last Fish" consists of four major sections: the opening three paragraphs and the sections "The Law of the Sea," "Fishing Down," and "Changing the Future." Describe the function of each section. What does the writers' strategy seem to be in each section? How do the sections contribute to the whole report?

2. How do Pauly and Watson explain the decline in tons of fish landed since the late 1980s? What evidence do they provide? What difficulties do they note in estimating the fish catch?

3. One of the central ideas Pauly and Watson present is that of "fishing down the food chain." How do they explain it? What do they see as its consequences? How do the illustrations help them get their ideas across?

4. Consider the concluding recommendations Pauly and Watson make. Do they seem to follow from the description of the problem?

WRITING IN A DIGITAL WORLD

An Informational Web Site

THE TRIANGLE FACTORY FIRE

KHEEL CENTER FOR LABOR-MANAGEMENT DOCUMENTATION
AND ARCHIVES, CORNELL UNIVERSITY

The Triangle Factory Fire is an informational Web site about one of the worst industrial disasters of the twentieth century, the fire of 1911 that killed 146 immigrant workers in a clothing factory in New York City. The Web site gives background on the history of sweatshops, tells the story of the fire and the resulting investigation, and contains original documents and secondary sources housed in the Kheel Center for Labor-Management Documentation and Archives at Cornell University's School of Industrial and Labor Relations.

Analysis: Information Design

The Triangle Factory Fire of 1911 is a pivotal event in United States labor history because it brought the dangerous working conditions in the needle trades and other factories dramatically to the public's attention. The 146 workers who died, largely Italian and Eastern European Jewish women as young as 15, had been trapped in a locked building. The unnecessary tragedy of their deaths prompted official investigations and significant reforms of workplace safety.

The Triangle Factory Fire Web site (http://www.ilr.cornell.edu/trianglefire) presents a wealth of information about the fire and the events that took place in

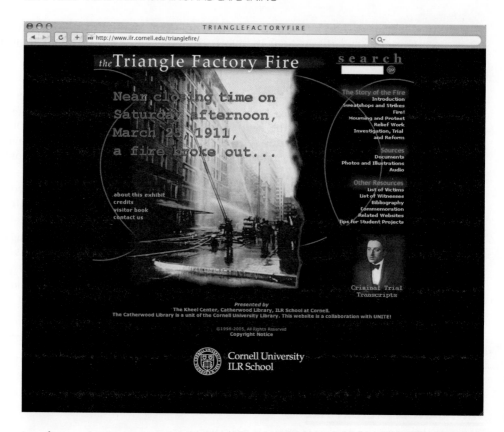

its aftermath. As anyone who's ever browsed the Web knows, good information design makes the navigation of a Web site intuitive and user-friendly so that information appears where it makes sense and is easy to find. Notice in this regard how the Web site uses horizontal organization to tell "The Story of the Fire" as a chronological sequence, with the "Introduction" giving a brief overview, the "Sweatshops and Strikes before 1911" page providing historical background, and then the four pages—"Fire!" "Mourning and Protest," "Relief Work," and "Investigation, Trial, and Reform"—recounting the cause of the fire and its consequences in roughly the order things happened. Notice next how the information on the six main pages is organized vertically, to display types of information that enable visitors to go into greater depth on various aspects of the fire.

■ FOR CRITICAL INQUIRY

1. Do a quick tour through the "The Triangle Factory Fire" Web site at http://www.ilr.cornell.edu/trianglefire Browse it in any way you want. Based on this initial browsing, how would you describe the purpose of the Web site and the information it makes available? Compare your answers to those of classmates.

2. Now click systematically through the six pages that tell "The Story of the Fire"—"Introduction," "Sweatshops and Strikes Before 1911," "Fire!" "Mourn-

ing and Protest," "Relief Work," and "Investigation, Trial, and Reform." What do you learn? How does dividing the information into six separate pages help you understand the fire and its aftermath?

3. Next, spend some time investigating a number of the six pages. What type of information do the links on each of the six pages make available? How does this information add to what you've learned? In what circumstances would this archival material be useful to you? When would it be enough just to read the six main pages?

4. Compare "The Triangle Factory Fire" with other informational Web sites you have visited in the past. What do you see as the main differences and similarities? What generalizations might you draw about the features of information design that make Web sites effective?

VISUAL DESIGN

PowerPoint

POWERPOINT IS EVIL

EDWARD R. TUFTE

Edward R. Tufte is professor emeritus of political science, computer science and statistics, and graphic design at Yale University. He is also the author, designer, and publisher of three highly influential books on information design *The Visual Display of Quantitative Information* (1983), *Envisioning Information* (1990), and *Visual Explanation* (1997). "PowerPoint Is Evil" was published in *Wired* in September 2003.

PowerPoint Is Evil
Power Corrupts.
PowerPoint Corrupts Absolutely.

Imagine a widely used and expensive prescription drug that promised to make us beautiful but didn't. Instead the drug had frequent, serious side effects: It induced stupidity, turned everyone into bores, wasted time, and degraded the quality and credibility of communication. These side effects would rightly lead to a worldwide product recall.

Yet slideware—computer programs for presentations—is everywhere: in corporate America, in government bureaucracies, even in our schools. Several hundred million copies of Microsoft PowerPoint are churning out trillions of slides each year. Slideware may help speakers outline their talks, but convenience for the speaker can be punishing to both content and audience. The standard PowerPoint presentation elevates format over content, betraying an attitude of commercialism that turns everything into a sales pitch.

Of course, data-driven meetings are nothing new. Years before today's slideware, presentations at companies such as IBM and in the military used bullet lists shown by overhead projectors. But the format has become ubiquitous under PowerPoint, which was created in 1984 and later acquired by Microsoft. PowerPoint's pushy style seeks to set up a speaker's dominance over the audience. The speaker, after all, is making power points with bullets to followers. Could any metaphor be worse? Voicemail menu systems? Billboards? Television? Stalin?

Particularly disturbing is the adoption of the PowerPoint cognitive style in our schools. Rather than learning to write a report using sentences, children are being taught how to formulate client pitches and infomercials. Elementary school PowerPoint exercises (as seen in teacher guides and in student work posted on the Internet) typically consist of 10 to 20 words and a piece of clip art on each slide in a presentation of three to six slides—a total of perhaps 80 words (15 seconds of silent reading) for a week of work. Students would be better off if the schools simply closed down on those days and everyone went to the Exploratorium or wrote an illustrated essay explaining something.

In a business setting, a PowerPoint slide typically shows 40 words, which is about eight seconds' worth of silent reading material. With so little information per slide, many, many slides are needed. Audiences consequently endure a relentless sequentiality, one damn slide after another. When information is stacked in time, it is difficult to understand context and evaluate relationships. Visual reasoning usually works more effectively when relevant information is shown side by side. Often, the more intense the detail, the greater the clarity and understanding. This is especially so for statistical data, where the fundamental analytical act is to make comparisons.

Consider an important and intriguing table of survival rates for those

AP/Wide World Photos

Tufte satirizes the totalitarian impact of presentation slideware.

with cancer relative to those without cancer for the same time period. Some 196 numbers and 57 words describe survival rates and their standard errors for 24 cancers.

Applying the PowerPoint templates to this nice, straightforward table yields an analytical disaster. The data explodes into six separate chaotic slides, consuming 2.9 times the area of the table. Everything is wrong with these smarmy, incoherent graphs: the encoded legends, the meaningless color, the logo-type branding. They are uncomparative, indifferent to content and evidence, and so data-starved as to be almost pointless. Chartjunk is a clear sign of statistical stupidity. Poking a finger into the eye of thought, these data graphics would turn into a nasty travesty if used for a serious purpose, such as helping cancer patients assess their survival chances. To sell a product that messes up data with such systematic intensity, Microsoft abandons any pretense of statistical integrity and reasoning. Presentations largely stand or fall on the quality, relevance, and integrity of the content. If your numbers are boring, then you've got the wrong numbers. If your words or images are not on point, making them dance in color won't make them relevant. Audience boredom is usually a content failure, not a decoration failure.

At a minimum, a presentation format should do no harm. Yet the PowerPoint style routinely disrupts, dominates, and trivializes content. Thus PowerPoint presentations too often resemble a school play—very loud, very slow, and very simple.

GOOD. *A traditional table: rich, informative, clear.*

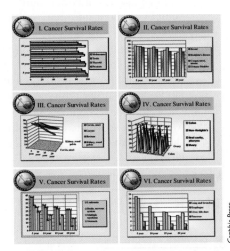

BAD. *PowerPoint chartjunk: smarmy, chaotic, incoherent.*

The practical conclusions are clear. PowerPoint is a competent slide manager and projector. But rather than supplementing a presentation, it has become a substitute for it. Such misuse ignores the most important rule of speaking: Respect your audience.

Analysis: Information Design

As Edward R. Tufte notes, PowerPoint presentations are everywhere. They have become a standard feature in business, government, and education. If anything, people have come to expect PowerPoint presentations. It is easy enough to account for PowerPoint's appeal. As a softward package that produces and displays slides, PowerPoint has much clearer visual resolution than the old overhead transparencies and is much simpler to use than the old way of making individual slides. To get high-quality visuals, all you have to do is download files or scan images. It is quite likely that have seen PowerPoint presentations in classes, and you may have produced your own PowerPoint presentations. Still, for however ubiquitous PowerPoint has become, there are serious questions about how it helps or hinders what Tufte calls "visual reasoning."

■ FOR CRITICAL INQUIRY

1. Edward R. Tufte says that PowerPoint has a particular "cognitive style" that is "disturbing" in schools. How would you define the "cognitive style" Tufte is pointing to? What does he see as the problem? How do the examples of "good" and "bad" PowerPoint design illustrate Tufte's point?

2. Compare Tufte's sense of "good" and "bad" PowerPoint design to Ellen Lupton's "Do's and Don'ts of PowerPoint" in Chapter 21. Do they seem to share similar assumptions about information design? What do you see as main similarities and differences?

3. Consider Tufte's assertion that "PowerPoint's pushy style seeks to set up the speaker's dominance over the audience." Explain what Tufte is getting at. Take into account how he reinforces his point with the visual satire of the "totalitarian impact of presentation software."

4. Use Tufte's ideas, Lupton's advice, and your own sense of what PowerPoint can do well and not so well to design your own examples of "good" and "bad" PowerPoint slides. Imagine you are making a presentation to your class on a topic you know a lot about. Explain what makes the "good" slides "good" and the "bad" slides "bad."

FURTHER EXPLORATION: REPORTS

■ GENRE CHOICES

Pick a reading in one of the other chapters on a topic you find particularly interesting. Consider how you could present the information in that reading in the form of a fact sheet or brochure. What would your purposes be for doing so? Who would your intended readers be? What would you imagine them doing with the information? When would it make sense to choose a genre of informative writing, as presented in this chapter, and a genre in another chapter?

■ WORKING TOGETHER

Designing an Informational Web Site

Work together in a group of three or four. Your task is to design an informational Web site. You can use "The Triangle Factory Fire" as a model, but you don't necessarily have to focus on a historical event. The point is to use the principles of information design for your own Web site. You might, for example, use the information you find in Daniel Pauly and Reg Watson's *Scientific American* article "Counting the Last Fish" and elsewhere to design a Web site on the problems of commercial fishing. You don't have to put the Web site online, though you may decide to. Instead, your group could design Web pages on paper and plan the architecture to navigate them. (For information on the architecture of Web sites, see Chapter 20, "Web Design.") In any case, pick something you're interested in and that readers have a need to know about.

WRITING ASSIGNMENT

The Report

For this assignment, write a report that presents information on a subject that interests you and that you think your intended readers have a need to know about. Your work here will involve determining the purpose of your informative writing and deciding what information is relevant to your readers. How much research you do will depend on time and your teacher's instructions. Here are some preliminary ideas about how to approach this assignment.

- **News report:** You may want to report on a recent event in the news—whether on campus, in your local community, or on the national or international scene.

- **Fact sheet:** Fact sheets are particularly suitable if you want to introduce readers to a subject or issue they may not know much about. You could, for example, design a fact sheet such as the "Facts About Prisons and Prisoners" and "New Incarceration Figures" on a current issue to give readers a quick understanding of what is at stake concerning, say, the use of medical marijuana, U.S. military support of the Colombian government, same-sex marriage, or bird flu.

- **Explanatory essay:** Short explanatory essays, like Steven Heller and Karen Pomeroy's "object lessons" in graphic design, inform readers about things such as the significance of a work, the meaning of a concept, or the importance of an event. You might, for example, explain a concept you've learned in one of your classes or elucidate the importance of a musician, writer, or artist.

- **Article:** Articles such as "Counting the Last Fish" and Michael Crouch's "Lost in a Smog" (below, in Writers' Workshop) typically report the current state of knowledge about a particular topic or issue. They require research to report on subjects such as increases in employers' use of temporary contracts, the incidence of caesarian births, or proposed changes to the Social Security system.

- **Brochure:** Like fact sheets, brochures are good means of introducing readers to a subject. You might want to design a brochure to present information about, say, the dangers of lead paint in older houses, or a walking tour of notable sites on your campus or in your town. (See Chapter 19, "Visual Design," for information about designing brochures.)

- **Web site:** Web sites have become one of the prime sources of information. You may want to design a Web site to inform readers about a particular topic or issue that concerns you. As noted in the Working Together section, you don't have to have the technical ability to put up a Web site online to design one on paper. See the directions there and also see Chapter 20, "Web Design."

Alternative Assignment

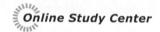

Online Study Center

■ RHETORICAL ANALYSIS

Pick one (or more) of the examples of informative writing in this chapter. Write a rhetorical analysis that explains what called on the writers to produce it. Take into account how the example defines its readers' need to know and what it wants them to do. How would you describe the relationship the report seeks to establish with its readers?

Invention

One of the first things you need to do for your writing assignment is identify situations that call for the kind of informative writing featured in this chapter. Make a list of topics that interest you. Think about information people could use and issues that involve you and others.

Subjects	Needed Information	Issues
Bicycling	What are good bike rides?	When is the city going to develop more bike paths?
Resident assistants	What is their role?	Should RAs be required to turn in students for drinking?
NAFTA	How does it work?	Has NAFTA led to loss of U.S. jobs?
Late-term abortions	What are they?	Should they be allowed?

As you can see, the chart helps you visualize needed information and issues. If you are a weekend bicyclist, for example, you could design a brochure of easy, moderate, and difficult bike rides. On the other hand, you might find the situation calls on you to write a fact sheet that explains the current status of public bike paths in your city or town and how and why they should be extended. Or you might write an article on the debate about requiring RAs to report underage students for drinking.

Clarifying Your Purpose and Your Readers' Need to Know

Once you have some tentative ideas about information people could use and issues facing you and others, you can begin to ask what gives these topics an urgency or importance that would make them worth writing about. You need to consider why readers need or want information about the subject and how this information will help them learn or do something new, important, or otherwise worthwhile. At the same time, you need to ask what is at stake for you as a writer and a person in informing your readers—to make sure your purposes match what your readers need.

■ **EXERCISE**

Getting Started

Pick one (or more) of the subjects of interest on your chart. Then write on each subject for five minutes or so:

1. What interests you about this subject? Why is it important to you?

2. Who are your intended readers? Why do they need information about your subject? What are they likely to know already about it? What information do you think they need? What should they be able to do with this information?

3. Read over what you have just written. What do you now see as the purpose of informing your readers about the subject? Do you want to help them understand something, show them how to do something, persuade them about an issue, identify something of interest, or do you have some other purpose? Assess whether this purpose is consistent with what you see as your readers' need to know. What genre appears most suitable? Why?

Background Research: Surveying the Information at Hand

Once you have determined your purpose and what your readers need to know, the next step is to assess your current state of knowledge—to determine whether the information you already have available is adequate to your purposes or whether you need to do more research.

1. Write a list of questions that cover what you think your readers need to know. Here, for example, is a list concerning the status of public bike paths that you can use as a model:

   a. What is the current status of the bike path system?

   b. What actions or land acquisitions are pending?

   c. How do such acquisitions generally take place?

   d. What local action is needed to support additional acquisitions?

   e. How have other communities responded?

   f. What has been done in this community in the past?

   g. What are the greatest obstacles to getting more land for this project?

2. Use your list of questions to survey the information you have. Can you answer the questions with the information at hand? Is your information up-to-date, reliable, and authoritative? Is it relevant to your readers' needs? If you need more information, where can you get it?

3. Take into account the information you have at hand, the information you need to get, and the amount of time you have to complete this assignment. Will you be able to find what you need in the time available? If not, consider whether the scope of your project is too broad. How can you set priorities based on your sense of purpose and of what your readers need to know?

Planning: Organizing the Information

Whether you're designing a Web site or writing a fact sheet, an explanatory essay, or an article, the organization of information you provide readers is crucial to the way they navigate your work. Notice how Daniel Pauly and Reg Watson's "Counting the Last Fish" led readers step by step:

¶ 1–3: Introduces the problem of commercial overfishing.
¶ 4–9: Describes how the problem came about.
¶ 5–11: Gives a scientific explanation of the problem.
¶ 12–15: Offers a possible solution.

■ **EXERCISE**

Organizing Your Report

To help determine how you'll organize your report, respond to the following directions:

1. Write a list of all the information you have about your topic. Make it as complete as possible.
2. What items of information can be combined? Revise your list by grouping closely related topics into clusters.
3. If there are items that don't seem to fit, put them aside for the moment.
4. Number the revised list according to the order in which the items might appear in your report. Then label the function of each cluster of information. What will they do in the report you're planning?
5. Does any of the information you've set aside now seem to fit into your planning? What purpose will it serve?

Drafting: Introducing the Topic

Readers justifiably expect that the kind of reports featured in this chapter will cue them right away to the topic at hand. There are various ways to create this focus. Here are some options.

You can be direct and focus right away on the information you are reporting and its significance, as in "Mentally Ill People Aren't More Violent, Study Finds."

Or you can use a question, as Heller and Pomeroy do in the case of Barbara Kruger:

A shopping bag with the words *I shop therefore I am* might be mistaken for a promotion by a tony retail store. But seen in a museum as a nearly nine-foot-square photographic silkscreen on vinyl with a red enamel frame, this work assumes a different meaning. Is it advertising or art, design or propaganda?

Or you could put things in historical and geographical perspective, as Daniel Pauly and Reg Watson do in "Counting the Last Fish":

> Georges Bank—the patch of relatively shallow ocean just off the coast of Nova Scotia, Canada—used to teem with fish. Writings from the 17th century record that boats were often surrounded by huge schools of cod, salmon, striped bass and sturgeon. Today it is a very different story. Trawlers trailing dredges the size of football fields have literally scraped the bottom clean—including supporting substrates such as sponges—along with the catch of the day. Farther up the water column, longlines and drift nets are snagging the last sharks, swordfish and tuna. The hauls of these commercially desirable species are dwindling, and sizes of individual fish being taken are getting smaller; a large number are even captured before they have time to mature. The phenomenon is not restricted to the North Atlantic but is occurring across the globe.

Peer Commentary

Exchange your working draft with a classmate and then answer these questions in writing:

1. Explain to the writer what you knew about the subject before you read the working draft, what you learned from reading it, and what (if anything) surprised you.

2. Explain to the writer whether you found the working draft easy to understand. Point to sections that are especially clear or interesting. Also point to any parts you found confusing.

3. What questions, if any, does the draft raise in your mind that you believe are not adequately answered? Are there points in the draft where you wanted more information from the writer? If so, explain.

4. Comment on the design. Is the purpose clear at the outset? Does the draft break the information into manageable chunks? Is the order of information easy to follow?

5. What suggestions do you have for revision?

Revising

Use the peer commentary to do a careful critical reading of your working draft.

1. Did your reader find the purpose clear?

2. Are the amount and type of information adequate? Is the information easy to understand?

3. Is the information presented in the best possible order?

4. Does the design enable your reader to move easily from point to point?

Getting the Right Order

Thinking about the order in which you present information can help you see whether one item leads to the next, what you have left out, and what you can combine.

Here are the questions on a student's working draft of a fact sheet about the herpes simplex virus:

Is there a cure for herpes?

How contagious is the virus?

Besides the unappealing sores, does the virus pose any other health risk?

What can be done to prevent it?

How does herpes really spread?

What about the possibility of herpes being spread by a toilet seat?

How often do the symptoms recur?

How is herpes treated?

What can I do to prevent herpes?

After getting a peer commentary, the student revised the order by combining information, adding further information, and developing a new set of questions:

What is herpes?

What are the symptoms?

How does it spread?

What are the health risks?

How is herpes treated?

How can I prevent herpes? ■

W WRITERS' WORKSHOP

Michael E. Crouch's draft-in-progress of the article "Lost in a Smog" is modeled on the kind of writing that appears in *Scientific American*. Crouch emulates the page layout of *Scientific American* by including a headline, photos, sidebars, and information boxes.

Lost in a SMOG

By Michael E. Crouch

TRAFALGAR SQUARE [above] thickly shrouded in the Great Smog of 1952. Similarly, the Canary Wharf skyline [right] obscured by a blue cloud of ozone during the heat wave of summer 2003. Even 50 years after the environmental disaster, London's skies are susceptible to choking smogs that pose serious health threats to its citizens.

The nights come on fast during a London December, but when the sun was not visible by midday on December 6, 1952, something was obviously wrong. This was no solar eclipse; the combination of a harsh cold front and a cityís dependency on coal produced the greatest peace-time disaster in London's long history: a cloud of thick, impenetrable pollution that covered the city and everything within a 20-mile radius for three days.

Provoked by a particularly harsh winter, a large portion of London's 8.3 million citizens fired up their coal stoves and hid away in the warmth of their homes to avoid the bitter cold. Their reaction to the chilly weather was intuitive; the unfortunate outcome was not. Millions of chimneys unleashed sooty, sulphurous smoke, a by-product of coal-burning, into the atmosphere. A weak winter sun, the cold front, and low winds gave the smoke nowhere to go. A well-intentioned population had no idea about the disaster they were in the process of unleashing.

When the Londoners emerged, the sight was – well, there was no sight. Visibility had dropped to near zero, and the air was thick with acrid coal smoke. The sun could scarcely penetrate the massive cloud of haze, a condition with which Londoners were all too familiar. So frequent were the hazes that in 1905, Dr. HA Des Vouex created the term 'smog,' a word combined of 'smoke' and 'fog,' two of London's most common wintertime occurrences. Most smogs proved only an inconvenience, and a scant few even approached the death tolls seen in 1952. The Great Smog, however, was suffocating, and for a few harrowing days, London found itself completely enveloped in its pollutants.

When the smog had cleared on December 9, the people of London saw more than they were ready to. The death toll was disturbingly high: nearly 4,000 Londoners had succumbed to the elements of the deadly poison and its after-effects from December 5 until Christmas. In one week alone, 4,703 people met their ends, though in truth, not all of those who died that week expired because of the smog. In 1951, the number of Londoners who had died in the same time span equaled 1,852 people, mean-

ing that the death toll was up by more than 150% in 1952. The smog-related deaths did not cease with the exit of the cloud. Two recent publications in *Environmental Health Perspectives*, one by Michelle L. Bell and Devra Lee Davis and the other from Andrew Hunt and a team of researchers, suggest that lingering effects of the smog killed more than 8,000 Londoners within the next year. In all, they contend the Great Smog claimed approximately 12,000 lives.

What bearing does this have on the lives of 8 million Londoners today? A trio of Clean Air Acts, the first of which the British government passed in 1956 as a response to the Great Smog of 1952, has insured that London's skies are free from the excess sulfur dioxide (SO_2) and particulate matter that accompanied coal burning. The three laws instituted smokeless zones around London – effectively stopping the use of coal domestically – and forced industries to utilize large smoke stacks so that pollution would be released higher in the air and more easily dispersed by the wind. Furthermore, coal itself – replaced by cleaner burning fuels – is no longer such a popular source of heat and energy in the famed city. Knowing all this, one might be tempted to write off disasters like the

Great Smog and insist that they cannot happen today. Doing so, however, would be a grave mistake.

Today coal-burning chimneys pollute the skies above London much less frequently, but motor-vehicle emissions pump out air toxins that are just as harmful, if not worse. Millions of cars and buses add to a wealth of air pollution, much of which is nearly invisible. Coal smoke contributed mainly sulfur dioxide (SO_2) and particulate matter (PM) to the atmosphere; motor vehicles pump out carbon monoxide (CO), nitrogen dioxide (NO_2), and PM. This deadly mix, a poisonous cocktail that can lead to the creation of harmful ground-level ozone (O_3), kills thousands of Londoners prematurely every year. To say that skies above London are in the clear just because they are seldom overcast with a sickening mixture of smoke and fog is to ignore the fact that the city, and much of the rest of the world, has a lot to learn about air pollution.

Microscopic Killers

THESE DAYS, it is widely understood that inhaling smog or smoke is a health risk, yet few actually understand why this is. Still fewer even know what smog is, whether it is the smog that enveloped London in 1952 or the smog that we are more familiar with in the 21st century. Understanding these facts is an important step in learning that modern air pollution, too, presents a serious threat.

Smogs that killed prior to 1952 were not without precedence in London, but most posed smaller health risks

The days of oppressive killer smogs are gone, but pollution lingers on in a new form

than the Great Smog. Londoners died with great frequency during the smogs of December 1813, January 1880, February 1882, December 1891, December 1892 (1,000 dead), and November 1948 (700-800 dead). Smogs continued to plague London even after 1952 and the passage of the first Clean Air Act, which created for the first time in London smokeless zones where only clean fuels could be burned. The last large-scale smog occurred in 1962 and claimed 750 lives. Inferring from these disasters, it seems simple to think polluted air could kill, but how does it do so?

Let us look to 1952 for an example. Precipitating the disaster, fog formed. On December 5, the air near the ground was thick with moisture, and the ground itself was cool. The two conditions together caused condensation, and all the water vapor that formed settled onto unseen dust particles that always inhabit the air, thus creating the relatively harmless condition of fog. The naturally occurring fog trapped in its midst all the coal smoke released from countless London chimneys. Aided by the winter sun, which could neither warm the air enough to get it moving nor penetrate the smog to shed light on the dismal situation, the pollution became even thicker between December 6 and December 8. Visibility was at times only a few meters; at others, pedestrians could not even see their feet. The air, thick and humid, was an irritant to both the eyes and respiratory systems of Londoners.

Coal smoke fills the air with acids containing free ions of hydrogen. These ions can create acid rain that is strong enough to kill plants. Today one can still see the remnants of the acidic smogs of London on the city's older buildings, a shade darker than they were when the architects of the past built them.

The unpleasant smog reeked havoc on the throats and lungs of Londoners. In humans, the acid irritates the throat and bronchial tubes, causing them to become inflamed and produce excess mucus. Thusly, smog adversely affects those with existing lung and heart conditions. Cases of asthma, pneumonia, bronchitis, and tuberculosis all flare up under these conditions. As one would imagine, the dead in London were comprised mostly of the people afflicted with these conditions, the elderly, and the very young. The smog also hit hard those with heart disease. Inhaling mostly coal smoke limited the amount of oxygen they took into their systems, and many died because of low levels of the compound in their blood.

Several new studies suggest that the Great Smog also affected the long-term health of those who lived through it. Along with releasing sulfur dioxide, coal smoke burns off small, sooty particles covered in moisture, called PM. Michelle L. Bell of Johns Hopkins Bloomberg School of Public Heath and Devra Lee Davis, acclaimed author and a researcher at Carnegie Mellon University, suggest that "the true scope and scale of the health effects linked with London's lethal smog extended over a longer period than originally estimated." The team, which waded through and analyzed piles of 50-year-old data to come to its conclusions, contends that illnesses in January and February of 1953 had a strong correlation to both the sulfur dioxide and PM levels during the Great Smog. Bell and Davis believe this correlation means that the excess deaths were due to a lagged effect of exposure to PM.

Picking up where Bell and Davis' research left off, Andrew Hunt and a team of researchers from the State University of New York Upstate Medical University and the Royal London Hospital studied archived lung tissues from 16 Londoners who perished in the Great Smog in order to determine how PM affected their deaths. The team found high concentrations of PM in the tissue samples. Particu-

Overview/Troubling Pollutants

- Recent reviews of London's Great of Smog of 1952 indicate that particulate matter (PM) can have both severe short and long-term effects on the human cardiac and respiratory systems.
- Coal smoke is no longer the most dangerous toxin that occupies London's air. Motor vehicles are the main source of pollution in the modern day capital. Their toxins do as much, if not more, harm to humans as coal smoke does.
- Although PM and sulfur dioxide levels in London are lower than they were 50 years ago, carbon monoxide, nitrogen dioxide, and ground-level ozone levels are now much higher. It is estimated that, along with PM, these three chemical compounds cause 1,600 to 2,000 Londoners to die prematurely every year.

CHANGE OF SEASONS

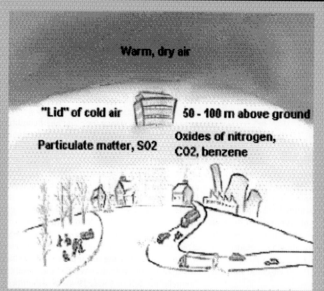

Warm, dry air

"Lid" of cold air   50 - 100 m above ground

Particulate matter, SO2   Oxides of nitrogen, CO2, benzene

Summer Smog (Below)

While London must now endure summer smogs, or photochemical smogs, they are not alone in such an experience. Virtually every urban area in the world has to deal with this sort of pollution thanks to the advent and proliferation of the automobile.

Summer smogs, unlike their winter counterparts, contain very little smoke, so the term smog is somewhat misleading. However, the mixture of pollutants in summer smogs varies greatly; seven ingredients make up a summer smog: ozone, carbon monoxide, nitrogen dioxide, hydrocarbons, lead, PM and sulfur dioxide. Hydrocarbons – of which VOC are a subgroup – react with the sun's solar energy and nitrogen dioxide to produce ozone. As is the case in the winter, the formation of smog is aided by low winds. When the sun is not visible, summer smog is not a problem.

Winter Smog (Above)

London particulars, another phrase for the city's frequently occurring smogs, are a part of the mystique of London, but they are by no means particular to the capital city. Donora, Pennsylvania, saw 20 of its residents die and nearly half of its population of 14,000 became ill when a smog settled overhead in October 1948. In December 1930, over 60 residents of the Meuse Valley in Belgium succumbed to a five-day smog.

How did all these disasters occur? They begin with the arrival of an anticyclone, a weather system marked by low wind speeds and moist air near ground level. Colder air remains further up in the atmosphere while warmer air stays near the ground, allowing the cooler earth to cause condensation-forming fog. Any pollutants released into the air mingle with the fog, trapped in place by the anticyclone's high pressure. Thick smog then slowly poisons anyone unfortunate enough to be lost amidst its cloudy form.

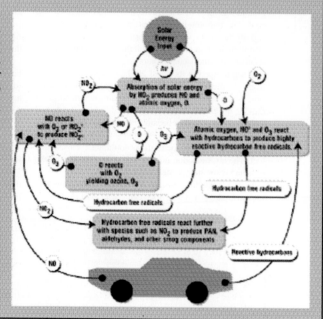

COVER-UPS AND BLUNDERS

ONLY AFTER A GREAT push from the public and the media did the British government decide to take action to curb more smog disasters. Even then, the official reaction was lukewarm at best. "Today everybody

A PROPOSAL for an air cannon that would blast away London's pollution woes.

expects the government to solve every problem. It is a symptom of the welfare state. For some reason or another 'smog' has captured the imagination of the press and people.... Ridiculous as it appears, I suggest we form a committee. We cannot do very much, but we can be seen to be very busy, and that's half the battle nowadays," wrote Harold Macmillan, then Minister of Housing, in a secret memo shortly after the Great Smog of 1952. Unfortunately, his attitude was typical of most government officials of the time.

England had mounted a war debt of over £31 billion, and the government was hesitant to add new expenditures to its budget. Britain took drastic measures, such as the selling of horsemeat for food, to overcome its deficit. Most shocking, however, is that the country sold all its cleaner-burning coal to foreign industries in order to make a larger profit. Those inside the country received the leftovers: sooty coal whose smoke filled the London sky for five days in 1952.

Actions originally taken by the government to battle the fog were wholly ineffective. The National Health Service distributed over three

late matter inhabited two different areas of the lung tissues: those associated with short-term storage (lung airways) and those associated with long-term storage (situated around the vessels and bronchioles of the lung and in the lymph nodes). Carbonaceous PM, synonymous with the combustion of coal and diesel fuel, was found in both retention compartments, suggesting that the people of London were not only hit hard by the Great Smog, but they were exposed to these kinds of PM over long periods of time.

Neither group purports to know exactly how PM causes deaths. A plethora of studies since the early 1990s, however, have tried to establish the link. Among the many possibilities are that PM causes decreased red blood-cell counts, increased blood viscosity, heart rate changes, increased arrhythmias, and increased defibril-

lator discharges. None of these hypotheses have been established. All that is known is that in smog incidents, elevated PM concentration is highly correlated with increased death rates. Understanding of the PM problem is crucial to populated cities where pollution levels are much higher than those found here in America.

A New Danger

THANKS TO the first Clean Air Act, homes in London can no longer burn coal as a means to generate heat. Londoners instead turned to the cleaner systems of electric and gas-powered heating. Thus, the days of oppressive killer smogs are gone, but pollution lingers in a new form. The vehicles that Londoners rely on are slowly poisoning the city's air.

Diesel fuel, when burned, gives off nearly the same carbonaceous PM that coal burning does. The trucks, buses, and taxis that rely on this fuel spit out cancer-causing chemicals, such as benzo-a-pyrenes, while they transport citizens and goods about the city.

These vehicles and others also subject the city to carbon monoxide. Carbon monoxide is undetectable by humans, being both colorless

THE AUTHOR

MICHAEL E. CROUCH is in his final year of study at Worcester Polytechnic Institute in Massachusetts, where he majors in Technical, Scientific, and Professional Communication. This article is a portion of his MQP, the WPI senior project, which he is completing abroad in the city of London. Crouch has written about health communication on the Internet and researched ancient Near Eastern artifacts for the Higgins Armory Museum of Worcester, MA.

million face masks made of gauze to the people of London. The masks did nothing to prevent the harmful effects of the smog, something Health Minister Iain Macleod knew even before the NHS gave them out. One American tobacco company offered to donate to the British government 100,000 masks that employed a filtering technique designed for cigarettes. The ministers refused the offer in order to curb advertising.

London had a history of eccentric fixes to its smog problem. A plan from 1925 proposed that several giant air cannons be placed around the city. When smog rolled in, the cannons would fire several blasts of powerful winds until the acrid haze was dispersed. Nothing like this was ever constructed. London post-1952 had no shortage of these unique "solutions." Anti-fog lozenges gave the consumer a false sense of security against the poisonous air. Fog flares, designed to guide buses through the premature darkness that smogs brought during the day, proved that the government had no hope – or perhaps no intention – of preventing more deadly clouds of pollution.

When none of these solutions proved helpful, government officials, eager to take the onus off themselves, explained that 5,655 of the deaths which occurred in the months following the Great Smog were due to a bout of influenza. This explanation was widely accepted until 2001, when Michelle Bell and Devra L. Davis published their study of the fatalities. In order for the number of reported influenza deaths to fit the average number of people who succumb to the disease (0.2%), almost one in every three Londoners would have to have contracted the illness. There is simply no evidence that such a widespread epidemic occurred.

There is no telling whether the British government could have saved lives if they had taken action against London's pollution problems sooner than it did. Four major smog events took place between 1956 and 1962, killing another 2,700 people. Not until 1956 did the Clean Air Act put an end to coal burning in homes and some industrial settings. Perhaps legislation in 1952 could have prevented some of these later disasters; perhaps not. What is clear is that a government must tackle the issue of pollution and environmental health in order to better the lives of its citizens.

and odorless. When inhaled, the gas attaches itself to human red blood cells, preventing the distribution of carbon monoxide and oxygen to and from the lungs. A large amount of carbon monoxide can lead to asphyxiation, the consequence of sitting in an idling car without proper ventilation for too long.

Another byproduct of fuel combustion, nitrogen dioxide is visible as reddish-brown gas and has a pungent and irritating acrid odor. Nitrogen dioxide, like coal smoke, is associated with acid rain. In humans, it can aggravate cases of asthma and other lung conditions.

Though it is directly attributed to automobiles, ground-level ozone is not emitted from any vehicle. Instead, nitrogen dioxide reacts with Volatile Organic Compounds (VOC) – organic chemicals commonly found in household cleaners and some fuels – and sunlight to form the gas, which in its pure form is bluish and has a penetrating odor. Studies have shown ozone at ground level to be harmful to those with lung ailments, and it has the ability to damage crops and forests. Some believe it also causes asthma.

The combination of these three gases and PM makes air hazardous to breath and prematurely kills between 1,600 to 2,000 Londoners every year. Surges in the levels of these pollutants send people to hospitals with respiratory ailments in great numbers. This is no surprise as England's relaxed standards on motor vehicle emissions means that the country has higher concentrations of carbon monoxide, nitrogen dioxide, and ground-level ozone than the US and many countries in Europe.

London has begun to experience more smog in the summertime. Increased global warming and automobile emissions are combining to make summers unbearable on the historically cold island. The summer of 2003 saw the first ever temperatures above 100° F in England. The season's harsh sun not only caused heat exhaustion, but also increased ozone levels in the air, creating a deadly trio of extreme heat, humidity, and smog. An estimated 2,045 people died from exposure to all three. Clearly, problems with pollution are not over for England, and much still needs addressing.

A Grim Future

IF LONDONERS have anything to look forward to in the next century, it is that their winters will likely become warmer, and the feared smogs that accompany the season will be a thing of the past. That may be where the hope ends, though. Projections suggest that global warming will increase summertime temperatures, too. High temperatures could consistently reach 100° F and above. Summer smogs, the air full of ozone, would be the new concern for Londoners.

Other predictions foretell a future much less desirable. A group of scientists who make up the Intergovernmental Panel on Climate Change (IPCC) have predicted that the combination of global warming and pollution will prove so overwhelming by the year 2100 that the entire northern hemisphere will be enveloped in an impenetrable smog. Summon up what it would be like to live the title to Devra Davis' acclaimed book, *When Smoke Ran Like Water*. Much of the population would have to escape to the southern hemisphere, as the north would no longer be hospitable to animals or plants.

This horrible scenario is, of course, only a prediction. Whether or not it will come to pass remains to be seen. The world has nearly ten decades to prevent or prepare for this outcome. In the meantime, most countries are moving forward with stricter air pollution regulations.

The search for a new fuel source to power automobiles is surging forward. London already has three hydrogen-powered buses in its fleet. With no carbon in their fuel source, the buses produce much less pollution. Other buses in the city are being retrofitted with pollution filtering devices to bring down PM and nitrogen dioxide emissions.

Instead of pushing expensive cars with alternative fuel systems onto its citizens, London is trying to promote a better public transportation system. City officials also encourage Londoners to use their vehicles only when necessary, such as when going to work. The campaign has been successful; the last year has seen a 30 percent increase in the number of cyclists in the city.

Despite the many attempts to clean up London's historically polluted air, both the government and the public have much to do in order to prevent more smog disasters. If no one takes action on this issue, Londoners may want to start hoping that their government plans to join the US in occupying the moon within the next century because instead of premature darkness, their city could be experiencing perpetual darkness.

SA

MORE TO EXPLORE

The Big Smoke: A History of Air Pollution in London since Medieval Times. Peter Brimblecombe. Methuen, 1987.

Toxicologic and Epidemiologic Clues from the Characterization of the 1952 London Smog Fine Particulate Matter in Archival Autopsy Lung Tissues. Andrew Hunt, Jerrold L. Abraham, Bret Judson, and Colin L. Berry in *Environmental Health Perspectives*, Vol. 111, No. 9, pages 1209-1214; July 2003.

When Smoke Ran Like Water: Tales of Environmental Deception and the Battle Against Pollution. Devra Lee Davis. Basic Books, 2002.

London Air Quality Network Homepage: **www.erg.kcl.ac.uk/london/asp/home.asp**

■ WORKSHOP QUESTIONS

1. How do the photos on the first page of Michael E. Crouch's "Lost in a Smog" help you visualize the topic he's writing about?

2. Crouch's article is divided into four sections. Describe the function each section seems intended to perform. Do you think the order of information works well?

3. What do the diagram "Change of Season," the sidebar "Cover-Ups and Blunders," and the "Overview" information box add to Crouch's presentation of information?

4. What advice would you give Crouch to revise this work? ■

REFLECTING ON YOUR WRITING

Think about how you wrote and revised the informative writing you did as this chapter's work. What did you discover along the way about informative writing that you didn't know before?

chapter 9

commentary:
identifying patterns
of meaning

THINKING ABOUT THE GENRE

Commentary is a genre of writing that uses analysis and interpretation to find patterns of meaning in events, trends, and ideas. The purpose of commentary is not simply to report on things but to give readers a way to make sense of them.

This purpose should be clear if you think about the commentaries you've heard on radio and television and read in newspapers and magazines. For example, when television news commentators such as Chris Matthews or Bill O'Reilly present their remarks, you don't see news footage on the television screen—just the commentator speaking directly to you. Thus, the focus has shifted away from the news itself to the commentator's analysis and interpretation of the news. The same is true of commentaries by newspaper and magazine columnists such as Mollie Ivens or George Will.

Whether commentaries are on TV or in print, we expect them to give us something to react to, to think about, and to use to make sense of contemporary experience. We have this expectation because of the feature that most clearly distinguishes the commentary from news reports and articles: commentary doesn't use the objective tone and neutral stance of reporting but instead is written from a particular perspective. Commentary takes a position and presents an interpretation that the writer hopes readers will find persuasive.

In contemporary society, in which new ideas emerge and trends and events occur at a dizzying pace, commentators perform several crucial functions. For one thing, they perform a *labeling* function, identifying current trends and giving readers labels for these trends (for example, "metrosexuals," "outsourcing," "gentrification," "the network society"). For another, by seeking to find patterns of meaning in events, trends, and ideas, commentators call on readers to think about the causes and consequences of what is happening in the world today (for example, "Bush's tax cuts unfairly favor the rich," or "The drop in reading scores results from the neglect of phonics instruction").

Online Study Center

Finally, in the process of explaining, commentators often apportion praise and blame and take a moral stance on events—whether of solidarity, indignant reaction, or ironic distance (for example, "Canada has taken the right stand by recognizing gay marriage," or "It's amusing to watch the baby boomers of the psychedelic sixties tell their children not to use drugs").

Commentary is by no means limited to print and broadcast journalism. It is also an important genre in academic writing, where books and articles seek to provide persuasive explanations of issues in a particular field—whether it is the meaning of Hamlet's melancholia, the causes of slavery in the New World, the nature of human–computer interactions, the role of trade in Paleolithic economies, or the results of new AIDS therapies. In academic commentaries, the issues are often more technical and specialized than the issues commentators treat in the popular media. But in many respects, it is the same desire to go beyond the given facts—to find patterns of meaning, identify underlying causes, explain consequences, and make judgments—that drives academic inquiry.

Whatever the context may be, the call to write commentary grows in part out of this desire to analyze and explain what happens around us—to have satisfying accounts of our experience and to find patterns of meaning that can make the world cohere. In conversation, we routinely offer commentary on events, trends, and other people. We want to get a handle on the local scene at work, in school, in our neighborhood, and so we talk about what is going on, analyzing the motives for actions and the reasons for events. A good deal of everyday talk, in fact, serves as a kind of social analysis that shapes how we negotiate our relationships with others.

■ WRITING FROM EXPERIENCE

Think of a place where you routinely talk with others. It could be your workplace, the family dinner table, your dormitory, or any place you hang out. What topics come up in conversations—events, trends, ideas, people? What makes these topics of interest to the people involved? Characterize the kinds of comments people make. What role does such talk play in the particular setting? Use your findings to see if you can form any tentative generalizations about how people use conversation to find patterns of meaning and manage their lives.

ETHICS OF WRITING

IN WHOSE INTEREST?

Commentators often seek to persuade an audience that their commentaries represent the best interests of the public and the common good. By speaking on behalf of the public, commentators play a vital role in a democracy, holding accountable those in positions of power and explaining what the public's stake is in events, trends, and ideas.

Speaking in the name of the public, however, is rarely a simple matter, and it brings with it ethical responsibilities that writers need to take into account. Since commentary offers explanations, it presumes, for example, to represent other people's motives. Commentators therefore need to avoid falling into stereotyped representations of groups of people ("Gay men are promiscuous," "Young people today don't have a social conscience"). Such stereotypes not only characterize groups unfairly but also turn these groups into "them" who are different from "us," and often present the interests of these groups as incompatible with the public interest.

Writers need to be aware that speaking in the name of the public may in fact amount to speaking on behalf of some people or groups and distancing themselves from others. Writers need to examine their own assumptions about who is included in the public and try to understand how the people they write about perceive themselves and their experience. ■

READINGS

REMEMBER WHEN PUBLIC SPACES DIDN'T CARRY BRAND NAMES?
ERIC LIU

Eric Liu is a regular commentator on MSNBC. A second-generation Chinese American, Liu has written a memoir, The Accidental Asian: Notes on a Native Speaker *(1998), that raises questions about assimilation, ethnicity, and race. His commentary on "branding" appeared in* USA Today.

Opening:
* uses example to identify issue
* reveals his perspective

In a few weeks, when the world champion New York Yankees open their home season, will they take the field at Trump Stadium? Time Warner Park? Maybe AT&T Arena?

Chances are the park will still be called Yankee Stadium. But it won't be that way for long. Quietly, and with strikingly little protest, the Yankees have announced that they are planning to sell the "naming rights" to their Bronx homestead. By the time the 2000 season arrives, some lucky corporation may well have bought the sign outside the House that Ruth Built. And frankly, that turns my stomach.

* generalizes from example to wider trend

It's not just that Yankee Stadium is a national treasure. It's not just that allowing the highest bidder to rename this 76-year-old icon feels like an insult—to New Yorkers, to tradition and to the memory of Yankees past, such as Joe DiMaggio. It's also that what is about to happen to Yankee Stadium is part of a deeper, accelerating trend in our society, the relentless branding of public spaces.

The sports world gives us piles of examples. San Francisco's fabled Candlestick Park is now 3Com Park. The selling of bowl names has reached sublimely ridiculous levels. (Remember the Poulan/Weed Eater Independence Bowl?) And the trend is hardly confined to sports. Branding—the conspicuous marking of places and things with corporate names and logos—is now everywhere in the civic square.

Consider the public schools, some of which are flooded with advertising for merchandise and fast food. Districts around the country are raising money by making exclusive deals with Pepsi or Coke or with credit card companies or banks. In one Texas district, Dr. Pepper recently paid $3.45 million in part to plaster its logo on a high school roof to attract

¶s 3–7:
* Provides examples as evidence of trend

¶s 8–9:
* Makes qualification and explains his promise about public space

¶s 10–14:
* Explains consequences of branding

Ending:
* uses rhetorical question to shift to closing section
* projects possible counter tendencies
* ends on note of caution

the attention of passengers flying in and out of Dallas.

Other efforts to turn public spaces into commercial vessels are no less corrosive. Rollerblade now hawks its wares in Central Park under the banner "The Official Skate of New York City Parks." Buses in Boston and other cities don't just carry ad placards anymore; some of them have been turned into rolling billboards.

How far can this go? Over in England, the legendary white cliffs of Dover now serve as the backdrop for a laser-projected Adidas ad. Here in America, we haven't draped Mount Rushmore with a Nike "swoosh." But things are heading in that general direction.

You might say at this point, "What's the big deal? America is commercialized—get over it!" And I admit my views may sound a bit old-fashioned. But this isn't a matter of priggishness or personal nostalgia.

Public spaces matter. They matter because they are emblems, the physical embodiments, of a community's spirit and soul. A public space belongs to all who share in the life of a community. And it belongs to them in common, regardless of their differences in social station or political clout. Indeed, its very purpose is to preserve a realm where a person's worth or dignity doesn't depend on market valuations.

So when a shared public space, such as a park or a schoolhouse, becomes just another marketing opportunity for just another sponsor, something precious is undermined: the idea that we are equal as citizens even though we may be unequal as consumers.

What the commercialization of public spaces also does, gradually and subtly, is convert all forms of identity into brand identity.

We come to believe that without our brands, or without the right brands, we are literally and figuratively no-names. We question whether we belong in public, whether we are truly members.

We forget that there are other means, besides badges of corporate affiliation, to communicate with one another.

It could, of course, be said, with a place like Times Square in mind, that brands, logos, and slogans are now our most widely understood public language. It could be said that in this age of cultural fragmentation, the closest thing we have in common is commerce.

But is this the best vision of American life we can muster?

In the military, they worry about "mission creep." In civilian life, the problem is "market creep." And the question now is how to stem this creeping sickness. We know that there is some limit to what people will accept: a 1996 April Fools announcement that the Liberty Bell had been purchased and rechristened the "Taco Liberty Bell" provoked a storm of angry calls. Drawing the line there, though, isn't protecting an awful lot.

Maybe the renaming of Yankee Stadium will shame some legislators or zoning czars into action. Maybe the "corporatization" of our classrooms will spark some popular protest. Maybe the licensing away of Central Park will awaken us to the disappearance of public space—and to the erosion of the public idea.

Then again, maybe not. In which case, we'd better keep a close eye on Mount Rushmore.

Analysis: Conversing with Readers

Eric Liu's commentary is typical in many respects of the kind of commentary you'll find in newspapers and on television. The tone is informal and the paragraphs are short; though the topic is serious, Liu treats it with a good deal of humor. As readers, we feel Liu is a person of goodwill who wants to engage us in a conversation about something he's noticed (not unlike the way we talk about things with friends).

Liu's breezy presentation, however, does not just make his commentary inviting to readers and easy to read. Notice at two key points how he incorporates what readers might be thinking. In the eighth paragraph, after he has substantiated the reality of the "branding" by giving a series of examples, Liu addresses readers directly and says, "You might say at this point, 'What's the big deal?'" Next, after acknowledging that he "may sound old-fashioned," Liu pinpoints the main issue of his commentary, namely that public spaces belong to everyone and that branding threatens to "convert all forms of identity into brand identity." Then, in the fourteenth paragraph, Liu anticipates his readers again, this time by imagining that people might say that brands "are now our most widely understood public language" and the "closest thing we have in common is commerce." By conversing with his readers at two pivotal points in his commentary, Liu establishes the groundwork for readers to join him in asking the question "Is this the best vision of American life we can muster?"

■ FOR CRITICAL INQUIRY

1. Almost half of Liu's commentary—the first seven paragraphs—is devoted to establishing the reality of the branding phenomenon. As you read, when did you become aware of Liu's perspective on this trend? What cued you to Liu's point of view?

2. What exactly is Liu's argument against branding? Is there a sentence or sentences anywhere that express his main claim? What evidence does Liu offer to support his claim? What enabling assumptions connect the evidence to the claim? Are these assumptions stated explicitly or implied?

3. As noted, Liu anticipates what readers might be thinking at two key points in the commentary—at the beginnings of paragraphs 8 and 14. How does Liu handle these possible differing views? How successful do you think he is in countering or negotiating such differences?

HOW TO FIGHT THE NEW EPIDEMICS

LUNDY BRAUN

Lundy Braun teaches pathology to medical students and courses on the biological and social origins of disease to undergraduates at Brown University. Braun wrote this commentary in response to public fascination with media accounts of "killer viruses" and other epidemic diseases.

One of the hottest topics in the news these days seems to be "killer" viruses. With the outbreak of bird flu and the popular accounts of epidemics of virus infection in feature films, made-for-television movies and best-selling nonfiction, the public has been captivated by the apparent power of microorganisms to sweep through towns and villages unfettered.

But hidden behind our fascination with these real and fictional epidemics is a profound feeling of betrayal, stemming from the widely held view that science had won the war against microbial infections.

The recent outbreaks have taken us by surprise, threatening our carefully nurtured sense of health and well-being. We diet, consume vitamins and exercise vigorously to ward off heart disease and cancer. But infectious diseases strike in a seemingly unpredictable pattern, leaving us feeling unprotected and vulnerable. With the re-emergence of tuberculosis as a significant public health problem in the United States, cholera in Latin America, the plague epidemic in India last year and the Ebola virus infection in Zaire, HIV infection, formerly considered an isolated occurrence confined to marginalized populations, now seems a harbinger of ever more terrifying microbial agents.

Yet, the reasons for the re-emergence of infectious diseases are not particularly mysterious. In reality, infectious diseases never were conquered, and the recent epidemics are quite predictable. For centuries, infectious diseases have been the major cause of death in the developing world. Moreover, even in the developed world, successful management relies on active disease surveillance and public health policies.

In 1966, the eminent Australian immunologist Sir MacFarlane Burnet declared, "In many ways one can think of the middle of the 20th Century as the end of one of the most important social revolutions in history, the virtual elimination of infectious disease as a significant factor in social life." Shared by most of the scientific community, this view is rooted in the rise of the germ theory in the late 19th and early 20th centuries that associated specific microbial agents with particular diseases.

The germ theory took hold not only because of the spectacular technical achievements represented by the isolation of the microorganisms, but also because infectious disease, once seen as divine retribution for past sins, now appeared potentially controllable. The discovery of antibiotics and the development of vaccines lent further support to this notion of control. Thus, the germ theory effectively replaced disease prevention policies based on sanitary reforms, including improvement in sewage systems and better housing conditions, which were primarily responsible for the dramatic decline in the death rates from infectious disease.

The possibility of control over these great afflictions of humankind became even more appealing in the post–World War II period when a sense of endless optimism about the future was fueled by economic expansion in industrialized countries. Unfortunately, during this period, we also began to rely exclusively on science to solve the problems of disease. Throughout this century the role of the natural and social environment in the development of disease has been largely ignored by the scientific and medical communities and policy-makers.

Yet, the obstacles to management of many infectious diseases are social as well as scientific, and disease prevention policies based exclusively on science leave us ill-prepared to respond effectively to the current epidemics.

In the case of tuberculosis, we know how the bacterium is transmitted, how it causes disease and until recently, we had drugs that were relatively effective in reducing transmission and the development of disease. Despite this wealth of medical knowledge, tuberculosis continues to thrive, primarily in marginalized groups with minimal or no access to medical care. Without a concerted effort to improve access to the health care system, tuberculosis will remain a formidable challenge irrespective of the development of new drug treatments or more effective vaccines.

In the case of AIDS, basic scientific research coupled with education, public health measures and the political will to address difficult social issues are essential to managing this epidemic.

There are many other examples of microbial diseases where the failure to integrate scientific knowledge with social programs has hampered the development of sound disease prevention policies. Cervical cancer, for example, is the second most common cause of cancer-related mortality in women worldwide. Over a decade ago, sexually transmitted human papillomaviruses were linked to this cancer. Yet years later, we still know relatively little about the mechanisms by which human papillomaviruses contribute to the development of cervical cancer. To reduce the morbidity and mortality associated with this infection we need to develop more precise ways of identifying women at increased risk of progression to cancer.

An investment in basic microbiological research will be required to answer these questions. Meantime, however, we have more than sufficient scientific information to begin to educate the population most at risk of contracting the disease, namely adolescents. Again, the failure to implement such programs is fundamentally a political issue, reflecting our reluctance as a society to deal with adolescent sexuality.

Effective management of infectious diseases is achievable. Many of the agents associated with recent outbreaks are not new microbes but rather newly recognized ones that have appeared in human populations as a consequence of social disorganization and ecological disruption. To be successful, disease-prevention policies must be based on more than technical solutions. They must be firmly rooted in an ecological perspective of disease that does not separate scientific knowledge from an understanding of the influence of the natural environment on disease and a commitment to social justice.

There are no magic bullets. We will have little impact on infectious diseases without addressing the living conditions of large segments of our society and rebuilding our public health infrastructure. In the absence of such a policy, however, future outbreaks will continue to be viewed with the mixture of fascination, fear, helplessness and misdirected social policy that has characterized our response to the recent epidemics.

Analysis: Explaining Causes and Effects

"How to Fight the New Epidemics" opens by noting the public's "fascination" when new and mysterious "killer diseases" became hot topics in the news. As you can see, Lundy Braun felt called on to address the fascination with these epidemics and the "profound feeling of betrayal" that science had not won the war against infectious diseases. For Braun, the purpose of characterizing this public mood goes beyond simply labeling a trend in the popular mind. As her commentary unfolds, readers quickly become aware that this public mood is only an occasion for her to explain the limits of the germ theory of disease and the failure of scientific and medical policy-making to take social conditions into account in preventing and controlling disease. Accordingly, Braun is asking her readers to reconsider the dominant theory of disease causation and to see that disease prevention and control relies on integrating scientific knowledge with social programs.

■ FOR CRITICAL INQUIRY

1. How does Braun use the hot news topic of "killer viruses" to frame her commentary?

2. Braun is addressing general readers, but she is also positioning her commentary in relation to the scientific community's understanding of modern medicine. What are the main issues involved? What are the main points of agreement and disagreement?

3. Consider how Braun uses examples of diseases such as tuberculosis and cervical cancer as evidence. How does she link these examples to specific claims? What do her enabling assumptions seem to be?

4. Do you find Braun's argument about disease causation, prevention, and control persuasive? Explain your reasoning.

MARILYN MONROE'S SAD, LONELY CRY FOR HELP

AYN RAND

Ayn Rand (1905–1982) was a philosopher and writer whose ideas about individualism and rational self-interest can be found in the novels The Fountainhead *(1943) and* Atlas Shrugged *(1957). This commentary was originally published two weeks after Marilyn Monroe died in 1962 as "Through Your Most Grievous Fault." It was reprinted widely in 2002 to mark the fortieth anniversary of Monroe's death, appearing under this title in the* Providence Journal.

The death of Marilyn Monroe shocked people with an impact different from their reaction to the death of any other movie star or public figure. All over the world, people felt a peculiar sense of personal involvement and of protest, like a universal cry of "Oh, no!"

They felt that her death had some special significance, almost like a warning which they could not decipher—and they felt a nameless apprehension, the sense that something terribly wrong was involved.

They were right to feel it.

Marilyn Monroe on the screen was an image of pure, innocent, childlike joy in living. She projected the sense of a person born and reared in some radiant utopia untouched by suffering, unable to conceive of ugliness or evil, facing life with the confidence, the benevolence, and the joyous self-flaunting of a child or a kitten who is happy to display its own attractiveness as the best gift it can offer the world, and who expects to be admired for it, not hurt.

In real life, Marilyn Monroe's probable suicide—or worse: a death that might have been an accident, suggesting that, to her, the difference did not matter—was a declaration that we live in a world which made it impossible for her kind of spirit, and for the things she represented, to survive.

If there ever was a victim of society, Marilyn Monroe was that victim—of a society that professes dedication to the relief of the suffering, but kills the joyous.

None of the objects of the humanitarians' tender solicitude, the juvenile delinquents, could have had so sordid and horrifying a childhood as did Marilyn Monroe.

To survive it and to preserve the kind of spirit she projected on the screen—the radiantly benevolent sense of life, which cannot be faked—was an almost inconceivable psychological achievement that required a heroism of the highest order.

Whatever scars her past had left were insignificant by comparison.

She preserved her vision of life through a nightmare struggle, fighting her way to the top. What broke her was the discovery, at the top, of as sordid an evil as the one she had left behind—worse, perhaps, because incomprehensible. She had expected to reach the sunlight; she found, instead, a limitless swamp of malice.

It was a malice of a very special kind. If you want to see her groping struggle to understand it, read the magnificent article in the August 17, 1962, issue of *Life* magazine. It is not actually an article, it is a verbatim transcript of her own words—and the most tragically revealing document published in many years. It is a cry for help, which came too late to be answered.

"When you're famous, you kind of run into human nature in a raw kind of way," she said. "It stirs up envy, fame does. People you run into feel that, well, who is she—who does she think she is, Marilyn Monroe? They feel fame gives them some kind of privilege to walk up to you and say anything to you, you know, of any kind of nature—and it won't hurt your feelings—like it's happening to your clothing. . . . I don't understand why people aren't a little more generous with each other. I don't like to say this, but I'm afraid there is a lot of envy in this business."

"Envy" is the only name she could find for the monstrous thing she faced, but it was much worse than envy: it was the profound hatred of life, of success and of all human values, felt by a certain kind of mediocrity—the kind who feels pleasure on hearing about a stranger's misfortune. It was hatred of the good for being the good—hatred of ability, of beauty, of honesty, of earnestness, of achievement and, above all, of human joy.

Read the *Life* article to see how it worked and what it did to her:

An eager child, who was rebuked for her eagerness—"Sometimes the [foster] families used to worry because I used to laugh so loud and so gay; I guess they felt it was hysterical."

A spectacularly successful star, whose employers kept repeating: "Remember you're not a star," in a determined effort, apparently, not to let her discover her own importance.

A brilliantly talented actress, who was told by the alleged authorities, by Hollywood, by the press, that she could not act.

An actress, dedicated to her art with passionate earnestness—"When I was 5—I think that's when I started wanting to be an actress—I loved to play. I didn't like the world around me because it was kind of grim—but I loved to play house and it was like you could make your own boundaries"—who went through hell to make her own boundaries, to offer people the sunlit universe of her own vision—"It's almost having certain kinds of secrets for yourself that you'll let the whole world in on only for a moment, when you're acting"—but who was ridiculed for her desire to play serious parts.

A woman, the only one, who was able to project the glowingly innocent sexuality of a being from some planet uncorrupted by guilt—who found herself regarded and ballyhooed as a vulgar symbol of obscenity—and who still had the courage to declare: "We are all born sexual creatures, thank God, but it's a pity so many people despise and crush this natural gift."

A happy child who was offering her achievement to the world, with the pride of an authentic greatness and of a kitten depositing a hunting trophy at your feet—who found herself answered by concerted efforts to negate, to degrade, to ridicule, to insult, to destroy her achievement—who was unable to conceive that it was her best she was punished for, not her worst—who could only sense, in helpless terror, that she was facing some unspeakable kind of evil.

How long do you think a human being could stand it?

That hatred of values has always existed in some people, in any age or culture. But a hundred years ago, they would have been expected to hide it. Today, it is all around us; it is the style and fashion of our century.

Where would a sinking spirit find relief from it?

The evil of a cultural atmosphere is made by all those who share it. Anyone who has ever felt resentment against the good for being the good and has given voice to it, is the murderer of Marilyn Monroe.

Analysis: Making Interpretive Judgments

Ayn Rand's commentary on Marilyn Monroe begins by noting that people seemed to feel her death had a "special significance." Accordingly, Rand takes her work to be exploring what that significance might be. As you can see, Rand devotes most of the space here to presenting a vivid dominant impression of the suffering and frustrations in Monroe's life. Nonetheless, her commentary differs from a profile in important ways. It's not just to capture a person at a moment in time but to use the sad trajectory of that life to comment on a society that, in Rand's words, "kills the joyous." In the final four paragraphs, Rand reveals her purposes. Rand's explanation of Monroe's death sets her up to deliver a withering condemnation of what she calls a "hatred of values" that has become "the style and fashion of our century."

■ FOR CRITICAL ANALYSIS

1. Examine how Ayn Rand establishes the focus of her commentary in the opening three paragraphs. Notice how she describes certain feelings and views that she says are widely shared. How does this shape her relationship to readers?

2. As just noted, most of Rand's commentary is devoted to an analysis of Marilyn Monroe's life and what went "terribly wrong." What exactly is the judgment Rand is making in this section, from paragraph 4 to 13? When did you become aware of the judgment? What evidence does Rand use to support it?

3. Consider how Rand ends the commentary. Notice how the analysis of Monroe's life and death turns in the final four paragraphs into a condemnation. Who or what is the target of Rand's blame here as the "murderer of Marilyn Monroe"? Does the language Rand uses—"hatred," "evil," "murderer"—seem justified?

4. How does this commentary differ from a profile? To what extent do the two genres overlap in this case?

WRITING IN A DIGITAL WORLD

Blogs

BAGHDAD BURNING: GIRL BLOG FROM IRAQ

RIVERBEND

In August 2003, just a few months after the invasion and occupation of Iraq, a 25-year-old Iraqi woman in Baghdad began a blog, using the name Riverbend, to conceal her identity. Riverbend's riveting accounts of life in an occupied city and her political analyses have made her blog a source of insight and information not available through the mainstream media. Her blogs have been collected in the book Baghdad Burning: Girl Blog from Iraq *(2005). Here are two of the earliest blogs Riverbend posted. You can find her current blogs, as well as a complete archive, at riverbendblog.blogspot.com/*

Baghdad Burning

. . . I'll meet you 'round the bend my friend, where hearts can heal and souls can mend.

Sunday, August 24, 2003
About Riverbend

A lot of you have been asking about my background and the reason why my English is good. I am Iraqi—born in Iraq to Iraqi parents, but was raised abroad for several years as a child. I came back in my early teens and continued studying in English in Baghdad—reading any book I could get my hands on. Most of my friends are of different ethnicities, religions and nationalities. I am bilingual. There are thousands in Iraq like me—kids of diplomats, students, ex-patriots, etc.

As to my connection with Western culture . . . you wouldn't believe how many young Iraqi people know so much about American/British/French pop culture. They know all about Arnold Schwarzenegger, Brad Pitt, Whitney Houston, McDonalds, and M.I.B.s . . . Iraqi tv stations were constantly showing bad copies of the latest Hollywood movies. (If it's any consolation, the Marines lived up to the Rambo/Terminator reputation which preceded them.)

But no matter what—I shall remain anonymous. I wouldn't feel free to write otherwise. I think Salam and Gee are incredibly brave . . . who knows, maybe one day I will be too. You know me as Riverbend, you share a very small part of my daily reality—I hope that will suffice.

—posted by river @ 11:33 PM

Thursday, August 21, 2003
My New Talent

Suffering from a bout of insomnia last night, I found myself in front of the television, channel-surfing. I was looking for the usual—an interesting interview with one of the council, some fresh news, a miracle . . . Promptly at 2 am, the electricity went off and I was plunged into the pitch black hell better-known as "an August night with no electricity in Iraq". So I sat there, in the dark, trying to remember where I had left the candle and matches. After 5 minutes of chagrined meditation, I decided I would 'feel' my way up the stairs and out onto the roof. Step by hesitant step, I stumbled out into the corridor and up the stairs, stubbing a toe on the last step (which wasn't supposed to be there).

(For those of you who don't know, people sleep up on the roof in some of the safer areas because when the electricity goes off, the houses get so hot, it feels like you are cooking gently inside of an oven. The roof isn't much better, but at least there's a semblance of wind.)

Out on the roof, the heat was palpitating off of everything in waves. The strange thing is that if you stand in the center, you can feel it emanating from the walls and ground toward you from all directions. I stood there trying to determine whether it was only our area, or the whole city, that had sunk into darkness.

A few moments later, my younger brother (we'll call him E.) joined me—disheveled, disgruntled and half-asleep. We stood leaning on the low wall enclosing the roof watching the street below. I could see the tip of Abu Maan's cigarette glowing in the yard next door. I pointed to it with the words, "Abu Maan can't sleep either . . ." E. grunted with the words, "It's probably Maan". I stood staring at him like he was half-wild—or maybe talking in his sleep. Maan is only 13 . . . how is he smoking? How can he be smoking?

"He's only 13." I stated.

"Is anyone only 13 anymore?" he asked.

I mulled the reality of this remark over. No, no one is 13 anymore. No one is 24 anymore . . . everyone is 85 and I think I might be 105. I was too tired to speak and, in spite of his open eyes, I suspected E. was asleep. The silence was shattered a few moments later by the sound of bullets in the distance. It was just loud enough to get your attention, but too far away to be the source of any real anxiety. I tried to determine where they were coming from . . .

E: How far do you think that is?

Me: I don't know . . . 'bout a kilometer?

E: Yeah, about.

Me: Not American bullets—

E: No, it's probably from a . . .

Me: Klashnikov.

E (impressed): You're getting good at this.

No—I'm getting great at it. I can tell you if it's 'them' or 'us'. I can tell you how far away it is. I can tell you if it's a pistol or machine-gun, tank or armored vehicle, Apache or Chinook . . . I can determine the distance and maybe even the target. That's my new talent. It's something I've gotten so good at, I frighten myself. What's worse is that almost everyone seems to have acquired this new talent . . . young and old. And it's not something that anyone will appreciate on a resume . . .

I keep wondering . . . will an airplane ever sound the same again?

—posted by river @ 3:15 PM

Analysis: The Popularity of Blogs

Since the late 1990s, Web logs (or blogs for short) have proliferated dramatically, with over 40 million blogs now in existence and the numbers growing. Technorati estimates that 75,000 new blogs appear daily. Part of the popularity of blogs, of course, is the relative ease with which individuals can publish their ideas and comment on others' blogs. In turn, blogs have become increasingly influential as alternative sources of opinion and information, with 50 million daily readers, about the same number that newspapers have. For these reasons, political and business consultants are paying increasing attention to what people are saying; the established media—radio, television, and newspapers—are setting up their own blogs; and whether blogs will become more mainstream or stay alternative seems an open question. Nonetheless, Riverbend's *Baghdad Burning: Girl Blog from Iraq* shows how in at least one case blogs can link writers in isolated and difficult circumstances to readers all over the world.

■ FOR CRITICAL INQUIRY

1. At first glance, Riverbend's blog seems to resemble a diary with its dated entries and personal accounts of life in occupied Baghdad. But it's clear that the blog is meant to be more than the private record of a life. Examine the blog postings here—and if you wish, further postings at Riverbend's blog site. How would you describe the voice you hear in the blog and its approach to readers? Are there other forms of writing, such as a diary, that it reminds you of? If so, how is a blog similar to and different from other forms?

2. Visit Technorati at www.technorati.com, where you'll find a list of the top 100 blogs. Check out a sample of these blogs. Examine them with the idea of determining what makes a blog popular.

3. You can search blogs at blogsearch.google.com. Use keywords (such as *Lost* final episode, Barry Bonds, Guantanamo) to get a list of blog postings. Read five or six to see what range of opinion and information you can find on blogs.

VISUAL DESIGN

Parody

Visual commentary often uses humor to get its point across—to poke fun at the rich and famous, to expose hypocrisy in public life, and to underscore the foibles of contemporary society. The two examples here parody advertising to make wider political and cultural points. The iRaq series, based on iPod ads, were designed by Forkscrew Graphics to post in public places. The Prozac parody appeared in *Adbusters* magazine.

Analysis: Rewriting Ads

As parodies (or satirical imitations), these visual commentaries rely on readers' recognition of Apple's advertising campaign for iPods and Tide's trademark whirlpool design. The humor—and the insight—of the parodies plays off this knowledge by imitating the original in order to present unsuspected meanings. Reworking visual designs that have become so familiar causes readers to stop for a moment, as the differences between the original and the rewritten sink in.

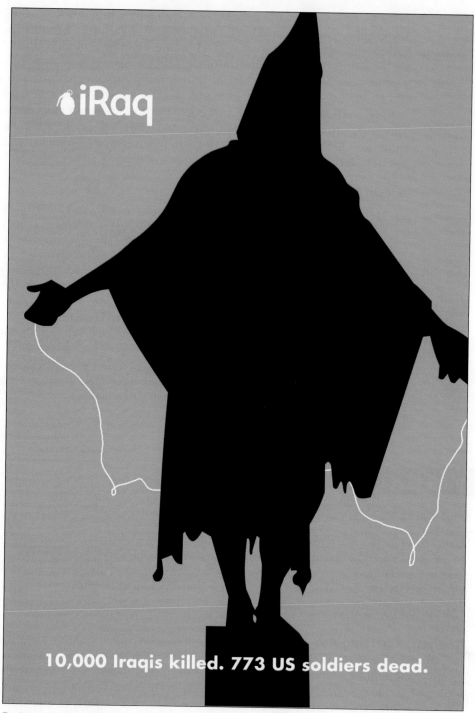

Forkscrew Graphics

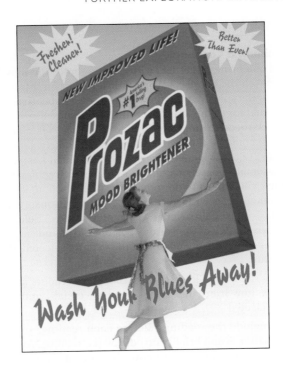

■ FOR CRITICAL INQUIRY

1. What design features make the original iPod ads and Tide trademark immediately recognizable? How do the parodies rework the originals to elicit new responses?

2. Put together a group of editorial cartoons that offer commentary on a recent event or issue in the news. (*Newsweek*, the Sunday edition of the *New York Times*, and the Saturday edition of the *Washington Post* all feature cartoons from the past week.) Notice how the cartoons use parody that exaggerates or simplifies the appearances of public figures. What effects does this use of parody have?

3. Choose an image to rework—an ad, a detergent box or other packaged product, a magazine or book cover, a poster, or a sign. Rework the image in a way that clearly imitates the original and at the same time brings to the surface a new perception.

FURTHER EXPLORATION: COMMENTARY

■ GENRE CHOICES

Compare Riverbend's blog *Baghdad Burning* to Marjane Satrapi's graphic memoir *Persepolis*. How easy or difficult is it to divide memoir and commentary as distinct genres? To what extent is there overlap? Explain how the text/picture integration of graphic novels differs from blogs. What is gained and lost in each genre?

■ WORKING TOGETHER

Assembling a Casebook

A casebook brings together writings on a topic. You may have used casebooks in other courses—on the causes of World War I, say, or on interpretations of *The Scarlet Letter*. A casebook typically organizes a range of perspectives on a topic so that readers can reconstruct for themselves the context of issues surrounding the topic.

Work together in groups of two or three. Pick a current issue that has generated debate. It could be the U.S. Patriot Act, affirmative action, immigration, eligibility standards for college athletes, or any other issue that has provoked a good deal of commentary. Assemble a casebook on the issue for high school students.

First you'll need to do some library research, to search newspapers and magazines for commentaries written from different positions. (Don't assume that there are just two sides—most controversies have many sides.) Select five or six commentaries that are representative of the various positions you find.

After rereading the commentaries you've selected, design your casebook in the following way:

1. Write a brief introduction that gives readers an overview of the issue—what it is, how it began, why it is controversial—and mentions the articles you have selected.

2. Include the readings. Before each reading, give a headnote that tells who the writer is and briefly introduces the reading. After each reading, provide discussion questions to promote thinking about it. (You can use the headnotes and discussion questions in this book as models.)

3. At the end of the casebook, include several questions that pull together the various readings to make sure the students have understood the overall issue.

WRITING ASSIGNMENT

Writing Commentary

Online Study Center

For this assignment, write a commentary that addresses a topic of interest to you. As you have noticed throughout the readings in this chapter, writing a commentary involves making an argument about an issue circulating in your culture. To help you get ideas for this assignment, consider what has called on the writers represented in this chapter's reading selections to write commentary.

- **Trends:** Labeling trends is a strategy commentators use to give readers a handle on what is taking place around them. Trends are not objective phenomena waiting to be discovered, like some new species of animal. Rather, they rely on the interpretive powers of commentators to name what's happening, thereby giving a series of events a distinct identity and making it available as a topic for public discussion. The idea of "branding" in Eric Liu's commentary is a good example of how identifying and labeling trends can bring an issue into focus. There are plenty of other trends as well—body-piercing, tattooing, cybercafes, nostalgia for the 1970s, the growth of microbreweries, and corporate downsizing are just a few. You might write about the significance of a particular trend that is already well-known, or you can invent a new label to characterize a trend that has not been noticed before.

- **Policy issues:** Commentators often address issues of public policy. For example, Lundy Braun's commentary, "How to Fight the New Epidemics," analyzes the causes of infectious disease and the adequacy of the "germ theory" to control disease. You might write a commentary that focuses on the causes of an issue that interests you and the implications for public policy. Accounting for why things happen is often the first step in explaining what should be done—to endorse, alter, or control the situation.

- **Current events:** Stories that break in the news, such as the Abu Ghraib prison scandal or the death of a celebrity, seem to call for a swift response to coalesce readers' feelings and influence public reaction. Here is writing at the point of opinion making, shaping the public mood and sense of issues. You might draw on a recent event to serve as the springboard for your commentary, something current that your readers are likely to know about but where the meaning is still up for grabs.

- **Historical events:** You could comment on a historical event—the Civil War, the Great Depression, the dropping of the atomic bomb, the beginning of rock and roll. Commentators often analyze past events and point out implications that would otherwise go unnoticed. You could write a commentary about the significance of a historic event, an invention, a social movement, or an everyday occurrence.

- **Satire and humor:** As you have seen, visual commentaries often use satire to bring out the unstated logic of an event or situation. Satire and humor can be used effectively to question conventional ideas. You might write a satirical commentary that uses humor to rework existing ways of thinking. Or, if your instructor is agreeable, you might design and produce a poster, a cartoon, or a comic strip to comment on a current event, issue, or idea. Or write and perform a comic skit either as a monologue or with others.

- **Responses to readings:** Another strategy for finding issues for your commentary is to respond to one of the reading selections in this book or to something you have read recently in another course. You can frame your commentary by agreeing or disagreeing with another writer, or you can use that writer's presentation of an issue as a jumping-off point to develop your own perspective and position.

Alternative Assignments

■ RHETORICAL ANALYSIS

Pick one of the commentaries (or two for comparison) and analyze the rhetorical situation. Pay particular attention to how the writer identifies the key issue and how this perspective on the topic shapes the commentary. See the guidelines and sample rhetorical analysis in Chapter 2.

■ WORKING WITH SOURCES

Use Ayn Rand's "Marilyn Monroe's Sad, Lonely Cry for Help" to write a commentary on a celebrity. It could be on someone like Marilyn Monroe who died young, such as Janis Joplin, Jimi Hendrix, James Dean, or Kurt Cobain. Or it could be on someone who lived to old age. Notice how Rand makes use of the *Life* magazine interview as source material. You will need to find background information, interviews, or interpretive books or essays. Draw on your research to write a commentary that interprets the meaning of the person's life.

Invention

As you have seen, the reading selections in this chapter offer perspectives after the fact—after events have taken place, personalities have emerged in the media, or ideas, styles, fads, and moods have started floating around in the public consciousness. The point of commentary is to name a topic, identify an important issue, and explain its significance. Commentators, in effect, are asking their readers to consider one possible way of making sense of what has happened in the past and what is going on in the present.

Naming the Topic

Corporate branding, the new epidemics, and the lives (and deaths) of movie stars are topics because they refer to things your readers are likely to have read about in the news or observed in their personal experience—events, situations, trends, ideas, conflicts, or debates that people are talking about.

Topics are forms of knowledge, the facts and information that have acquired public recognition and that you can assume your readers will recognize and be familiar with. Topics have names—whether those of individuals (George W. Bush, Kobe Bryant), historical and political events (slavery, the Vietnam War), social and cultural trends (increase in two-career families, video games, animal rights advocacy), or concepts (natural selection, Einstein's theory of relativity, the germ theory of disease). You can look up a topic and find information on it in the library. Your topic is the source of your commentary, the information whose significance you want to explore.

Background Research: Assessing Your Knowledge of the Topic

To write an effective commentary, writers often begin by assessing their knowledge of the topic they're writing about in order to make decisions about further research they might need to do. Here are some steps to help you assess your knowledge. State your topic in the form of a noun phrase (the Protestant Reformation, conversation patterns between men and women, global warming). Then, to identify what you already know and what you need to find out about the topic, respond to the following questions in writing:

1. What do you know about the topic at this point? How do you know what you know about it? What is the source of your knowledge? List as

many sources as you can. Which of these sources are available to you? Which might it be helpful to reread?

2. What do you think other people know about the topic? Is it widely known, or is it likely to be of interest to a more limited readership? How are other people likely to have learned about the topic? Which of these sources might be useful to you?

3. As far as you know, are there conflicting views or a range of opinion on the topic? If you're not aware of opposing views, consider whether they exist and how you could find them. If you do know, how would you describe the conflict or difference of opinion? Are there readily distinguishable sides involved? If so, do you tend to have allegiances to one side rather than the other? Explain how you align yourself to the topic and to what others have said about it.

4. Based on your answers to these questions, what further research might you do to research your topic?

Identifying the Issue

An *issue* refers to how the writer focuses attention on what he or she thinks is important about the topic. This is where the function of commentary comes in. Commentators establish issues to explain some meaningful aspect of the topic according to their own perspective.

Let's say, for example, that you want to write a commentary about video games. There are a number of issues you could use to focus your commentary. Here is a list of possible issues, phrased as questions:

- Do video games promote violent behavior?
- What role do video games play in youth subcultures?
- How have video games changed over time?
- Do video games neglect the interests of girls and women?

After you have identified an issue, you can begin to explain its particular urgency. Why should your readers be concerned and interested? Why is the issue being raised in the first place? Or, if you're writing about an issue that has not received attention, why has the issue been ignored and why do you want to raise it?

■ EXERCISE

Finding an Issue

1. Locate three readings (from newspapers, magazines, journals, or books) on the topic you are planning to write about. List as many issues as you can. You don't have to agree with the sense of the issue or be interested in writing about it just yet. The point at this stage is to get as wide a picture as possible of available issues. For now, just brainstorm for all the issues you can; you will pare the list down to the most interesting ones later.

2. Circle the three or four issues that interest you most. Consider what, if any-thing, they have in common with one another. Do they overlap in any way? How do they differ? Does one bring to light something that the others don't? If you notice a connection between the issues you've circled, that connection may well be worth writing about in your commentary.

3. Decide tentatively on one issue to write about. What would you say about the issue in a commentary? What do you imagine as your main point? How does this perspective align you with some people and positions? What common ground do you share?

4. Consider the position of people who differ with you. What are the key points of dif-ference? What objections might people have to your commentary? Are any valid? Are there any points of agreement or common values? How can you use these in your commentary? What differences need to be addressed in your statement?

5. Think about the implications of your commentary. If people were persuaded by your position, what would happen? How would this be an improvement over the present condition of things? If your readers take your commentary seriously, what would you hope to achieve? Is there something you would like them to do?

Planning

Framing the Issue

Like the frame of a painting, the frame of a commentary goes on the outside to give it boundaries and a focus of attention. Commentaries typically open by framing an issue—defining it, explaining its relevance to readers, and using it to set up the writer's position. Framing, then, has two main purposes.

First, it focuses readers' attention on a particular aspect of the topic. It es-tablishes a perspective for readers to see significant features of a topic they al-ready know something about. Framing the issue often begins with the familiar and then seeks to add a new or different angle or way of analyzing and ex-plaining what is known.

Second, framing the issue sets up the writer to present the main point of his or her commentary. Depending on how the writer frames the issue, he or she will enter into one or another relationship to the topic and to what other people have said about it.

Planning the Introduction

Commentary writers use various techniques in their introductions to name the topic and frame the issue. Here are a few:

- **Describe an event or an existing situation:** The point is to establish what is known in order to set yourself up to explain what new perspec-tive you are going to bring to the issue. The amount of detail will de-pend on how familiar you think your readers will be with your topic.

- **Describe the sides of a controversy, conflict, or debate:** On issues where people differ or find themselves on opposing sides, commentary writers often briefly sketch the different views in order to explain what they believe is at stake. By analyzing and evaluating the sides that already exist, you can set yourself up to present your own perspective and to show how it allies you with some people and positions but not with others.

- **Explain the causes or origins of an issue:** Giving readers accounts of how something got started raises underlying issues of cause and effect: Why does something occur in the first place? What causes things to happen over a period of time? What are the results? Who is affected? Who is responsible? By explaining the causes or origins of an issue, you can set yourself up to show readers how something came to have the shape and importance it does.

- **Explain how you became aware of the issue:** Writers draw on what through reading, observation, or experience brought a particular issue to their attention—how something hit home for them. This technique can help set up writers to explain an event, a situation, a conflict, or a debate by showing why and on what terms the writer is invested in the issue.

- **Explain points and principles you have in common with readers:** Writers often join with others on certain shared points or principles. Affirming common values and attitudes gains you consideration for your views, which can help set you up to introduce ideas that may not fit in readily with the thinking of others.

- **Use examples or personal anecdotes:** Begin with an example or anecdote that illustrates the issue you are writing about. More importantly, draw explicit connections between the example or anecdote and the larger issue. Is the example or anecdote representative of the situation your position addresses, or is it an exception? Make this clear in your framing of the commentary.

Planning the Ending

Endings apply the final frame to the writer's position. They give the writer the chance to have the last word, to leave readers with a closing sense of the issue and the writer's stand. Here are some ways writers design endings:

- **Point out the consequences of your position:** What would happen if your position were taken up? How would that improve the current situation?

- **Reaffirm shared values and beliefs:** What common values and beliefs does your commentary draw on? How does your position express these values and beliefs?

- **Make recommendations:** What would your commentary look like if it were carried through in practice? What concrete proposals does it lead to?

- **Call on readers to take action:** What steps can readers take, assuming they agree with you? What changes in thinking, personal habits, or public policy follow from your commentary?

Working Draft

Write a page or two as quickly as you can. Write as if you were warming up to write the "real" first draft. Begin by identifying the topic and the issue you're writing about. Explain your perspective on the issue, and quickly sketch an ending. Now you can use this writing as a discovery draft to clarify your own perspective on the issue you are writing about, to explore your own sympathies, and to understand on whose behalf you want to speak and with whom you differ. Use this draft to produce a working draft of your commentary.

Emphasizing Your Main Point and Distinguishing Your Perspective

Readers of commentary expect a writer to give them something to think about. They assume that the point of reading a commentary is not just—or even primarily—to be informed about an issue but to consider what the writer has to say about it. For this reason, it is important that the writer's main point be easy to find.

One way to make sure readers can readily see your perspective is to distinguish it from another perspective. This is a widely used technique in commentary, as we can see in Lundy Braun's "How to Fight the New Epidemics":

> To be successful, disease-prevention policies must be based on more than technical solutions. They must be firmly rooted in an ecological perspective of disease.

It's easy enough to see in this passage where Braun is coming from, in part because she shows how her perspective differs from the germ theory as a way of managing disease.

Peer Commentary

Exchange working drafts and respond in writing to these questions about your partner's draft:

1. Identify the topic of the draft. How does the writer frame the main issue? Point to a phrase or sentence. Where did you become aware of what the writer has to say about the issue? Point to a phrase or sentence where you first got the writer's point. If you can't point to particular phrases or sentences, what answers does the writer seem to imply to these questions?

2. Who is likely to agree with the writer's commentary? What beliefs and values does the commentary appeal to? Does the commentary seem to choose sides? If so, who else is on the writer's side? Who is excluded?

3. Do you share the writer's perspective on the issue? If so, does the writer make the most effective case in presenting that perspective? Can you offer suggestions about ways to improve it? If you don't share the writer's perspective, explain why. Describe your own perspective.

Revising

Read the peer remarks on your working draft. Use them to take the following questions into account:

1. Does the introduction frame the issues and forecast the main point and the direction of your commentary?

2. Is the main point located at an effective place in the commentary? How much background or context is necessary for your main point to take on significance? When it does appear, is the main point stated as clearly as possible?

3. Are details, facts, and other information about the topic clearly related to your main point? If you use examples, is it clear what point or points they are intended to illustrate?

4. Do your explanations develop the main point of the commentary, or do they raise other issues? If they do, is this intended on your part, or are you starting to jump from issue to issue? Can you point out the connection between issues so that readers will be able to follow your line of thought?

5. Does the ending offer a satisfying sense of closure? Will readers find it easy to see how you arrived at your final point? Does the ending help to emphasize the main point or lesson of the commentary?

Maintaining a Reasonable Tone

One of the appeals of writing commentary is that the genre offers writers the opportunity to stake out a position on issues they are passionate about. Commentators often want to make sense of things because they are invested and believe there is really something that matters. For this reason, commentators typically pay attention to the tone of their writing so that their readers, whether they share the writer's perspective or not, will at least take the commentary seriously as a reasonable effort to explain and analyze.

To see how a student worked on the tone of her commentary, go to the next section, Writers' Workshop. ■

WRITERS' WORKSHOP

Below you will find the first draft of a commentary "Socially Acceptable Discrimination" that Rachel Smith wrote for her first-year writing course, the revised version of the essay, and an interview with the writer.

I am so sick of the way born-again Christians are portrayed in the media. What's wrong with people? Do they think all born-agains are narrow-minded, Bible-waving bigots?

Is the desire for sensationalism so strong that the media have to make every born-again a Bible-waving fanatic who chains herself to abortion-clinic doors and supports the madmen who shoot the doctors that perform abortions? It is so unfair to focus on the extremist fringe and ignore all the normal people who are born-again Christians.

This movie is only one example of the way that born-again Christians are portrayed in the media. America's most popular image of a born-again Christian is a narrow-minded, Bible-waving bigot who doesn't know how to have fun.

Now, don't get me wrong; I'm not saying that we don't sometimes wave our Bibles around. There are people who call themselves born-again Christians who find it absolutely imperative that they shove their beliefs down everyone's throat, "waving their Bible" all the while. They chain themselves to abortion-clinic doors and support the madmen who shoot the doctors that perform abortions.

In this draft, as a peer reviewer suggested to Rachel, her anger, though arguably justified, was getting in the way of her analysis of how born-again Christians are portrayed in the media. The peer reviewer thought Rachel was calling too much attention to her own feelings ("I am so sick" and "It is so unfair") and blaming others ("What's wrong with these people?") when she should have been explaining the issue and its significance. The peer reviewer also mentioned that the rhetorical questions at the end of the opening paragraph and beginning of the second made her feel that Rachel was trying to strong-arm her readers instead of persuading them. Notice in the revised version how Rachel turns the sequence of questions into analytical statements that explore the issue at hand instead of assuming agreement on the reader's part. Rachel also enhances the reasonable tone of the commentary by making the rhetorical question in the second paragraph into a concession on her part that it's true some born-agains are extremists.

REVISED VERSION

Smith 1

Rachel Smith
Writing 1
Prof. Thesen
1 October 2000

Socially Acceptable Discrimination?

I looked up at the billboard as we drove home from church one Sunday and saw the advertisement for the newest Steve Martin movie, Leap of Faith. Martin stood in the center of the board, arms raised above him, his suitcoat gaudy and sparkling. His face was tilted upwards. A slight smile on his lips, his eyes were squinted. His stance suggested religious worship. Lights shone down from behind him, and the words Leap of Faith were pasted on the board over his head. At first glance, the picture looked sincere; here was a man worshipping God. However, when I noticed the overdone clothes and the pious look on his face, I knew that this was not a picture of a man praising his God. This was an advertisement for a movie whose sole purpose was to make a "hilarious" comedy out of the life of a television evangelist. Later, when I saw the preview trailers for Leap of Faith on television, I saw Steve Martin pushing fat, sweating women to the floor in a cheap imitation of what sometimes happens at real evangelical tent meetings. He had this look of intense pleasure on his face, his body language wide and over-the-top, almost as if he was getting a sexual kick out of what he was doing. The character was described as being "a born-again, Spirit-filled, holy-rollin' Christian," and often spouted "Well, Peraaaise God!" This movie is only one example of the way that born-again Christians are portrayed in the media. America's most popular image of a born-again Christian is a narrow-minded, Bible-waving bigot who doesn't know how to have fun.

Now, don't get me wrong; I'm not saying that we don't sometimes wave our Bibles around. There are people who call themselves born-again Christians who find it absolutely imperative that they shove their beliefs down everyone's throat, "waving their Bible" all the while. They chain themselves to abortion-clinic doors and support the madmen who shoot the doctors that perform abortions. There are people in every group, whether it is feminists, African Americans, those of Middle Eastern descent, or teenagers, who are the "black sheep," so to speak, of the group. They are the radicals and therefore are sensational. They get the publicity and portray their group as being as radical and unbalanced as they are. Not all African Americans harbour deep, hateful grudges against whites. Actually, a large majority of them don't. Often, in movies, they are portrayed in the stereotype that they all hate whites, as in Malcolm X. This portrayal is the most sensational, and therefore the most newsworthy. Why hasn't anyone made a major, widely released movie about the life of Martin Luther King Jr.? Because he didn't have a checkered past, his life wasn't filled with violence and anger (on his part, at least), and he preached a message of forgiveness. Those things aren't sensational. They aren't as newsworthy as the radical, insane things that the media prefer to focus on.

Because of the media's attraction to the sensational, often groups are represented erroneously. What's sensational about the rest of the born-again Christians? They don't attack doctors and plant explosives in office buildings. They don't all go around condemning everyone they meet to hell. They live just like everyone else. Granted, they don't frequent too many bars and brothels, they tend to spend more time in church than most Americans, and they live, very strictly, by the Bible. Because of this last point, many believe that Christians don't have any fun. That is one of the main reasons movies like Leap of Faith were made. The media say that underneath that "good" image, Christians are probably really warped human beings, following some long-dead cult that says the world will come to an end pretty soon, so all the rest of us had better join up or we'll be in lots of trouble. Leap of Faith just gives people a laugh and helps relieve them of the little suspicion that those crazy, born-again Christians just might have something. When a prominent televangelist is

Smith 3

exposed, the media jump into the fray and triumphantly hold up the tattered pieces, flaunting the fall of someone supposed to be "good." This concentration on the negative side of Christianity lends itself to making the public see born-again Christians as completely unbalanced, non-rational, bigoted people. We are portrayed in only the worst ways.

My intent in writing on this subject is not to whine about injustice and the liberal media, but to bring out the other side of the issue. To put it plainly, every special interest group in America has gained a lot of publicity for fighting discrimination, except for the born-again Christians. Politically correct speech is the newest fad; everyone is careful about what they say. More movies are being released that center on the lives of homosexuals, there is a rise in the frequency of African American sitcoms, Greenpeace gets news coverage every time they try to sue a lumber company, and whenever there is a story on abortion, a majority of the personal interviews come from the pro-choice side. In all this "political correctness," born-again Christians are invariably left out by the media because the beliefs that we hold do not embrace all the personal preferences that people have. We live by a definite standard of right and wrong, and because people do not want to be told that something they are doing is wrong, they invent their own morality: situation ethics. Born-again Christians do not fit into that jelly-mold of American society. When a movie like Leap of Faith came out, the only protests against such discrimination were in Christian magazines and books. We fight the currents, and yes, we do make people uncomfortable sometimes, but why is discrimination against us more culturally acceptable?

Interview with Rachel Smith

Q: *What prompted you to write "Socially Acceptable Discrimination"?*

A: I have felt for a long time that people unfairly judge born-again Christians like myself. If you go by the newspapers, born-agains are narrow-minded bigots, madmen who kill abortion doctors, or hypocrites like Jim Bakker. I know this isn't the real story, but it seemed that these stereotypes of born-agains are just something I had to live with—that I couldn't really do anything about it. Then I saw the Steve Martin movie, *Leap of Faith*, and I began to think that this might give me an occasion to try to correct perceptions.

Q: *How did you decide to focus on the particular issues you explore in "Socially Acceptable Discrimination"?*

A: I knew I wanted to change the way people perceive born-again Christians but I also knew I couldn't just say, "Hey, you've got it all wrong. That's not the way we really are." I'd be asking people to accept my personal experience, and I was pretty sure this wasn't going to work. So I thought that if I focused on how the media portrayed born-again Christians, and tied this to the idea that the media love to sensationalize things, I might get a different response from readers. I figured most people think the media are sensationalistic and that by using this as a kind of common ground with readers, I could introduce my own point of view in a way that might get a hearing.

Q: *What conflicts, if any, did you experience writing this commentary?*

A: It's hard because movies like *Leap of Faith* and all the media coverage of crazed evangelicals really gets me angry. I know it's a false picture and totally unfair to me and other born-agains, who are just normal people who happen to believe in God and want to follow the Bible. I wanted to make this point, but I also knew that if I let my anger come out too strongly, I was going to lose readers—or maybe even confirm their impression that we're all nuts. So I definitely experienced this conflict of wanting to be loyal to other believers and to get their real story out and, at the same time, knowing that I had to write in a reasonable tone. That's where the Steve Martin movie and the idea of media sensationalism were so helpful to me. By analyzing them (instead of screaming at people, which is what I felt like doing), I think I got some critical distance and could still be true to what I wanted to say.

■ WORKSHOP QUESTIONS

1. As Rachel Smith notes in the interview, her main purpose is to "correct perceptions" of born-again Christians. What was your attitude toward born-again Christians before you read "Socially Acceptable Discrimination"? Did reading her commentary confirm, modify,

change, or otherwise affect the attitude you began with? Given your experience reading the essay, what suggestions would you offer Smith to help achieve her purpose?

2. Smith says that she realized she couldn't persuade people solely on the basis of her personal experience as a born-again Christian. Instead, she focuses on how the media portray born-agains. Evaluate this strategy. To what extent does it offer the common ground with readers that she hopes to find? Are there ways she could strengthen this appeal?

3. Smith notes a conflict between her loyalty to other believers and her desire to reach out to her readers. One way this conflict manifests itself is in the tension between the anger she feels about being portrayed unfairly and the need she acknowledges to maintain a reasonable tone in her writing. How well do you think she handles this tension? What suggestion would you offer about how to manage this conflict? ■

REFLECTING ON YOUR WRITING

Use the following questions from the interview with Rachel Smith to interview someone who has recently written a commentary. It could be a classmate, but also consider interviewing columnists of your student or local newspaper.

1. What prompted you to write the commentary?
2. How did you decide to establish the focus of the piece?
3. What conflicts, if any, did you experience when you wrote it?

Compare the writer's experience writing the commentary with your own.

proposals: formulating and solving problems

THINKING ABOUT THE GENRE

Proposals put forth plans of action and seek to persuade readers that those plans should be implemented. Like commentary, proposals involve analyzing issues, taking a position, and making an argument. However, proposals go beyond commentaries by recommending a course of action, often a solution to a problem that has been identified as needing attention. Like commentaries, proposals use arguments to influence readers' beliefs, but they do so with the aim of advancing a new program or policy.

This difference between commentaries and proposals is not an absolute one but a matter of emphasis. After all, the positions writers take in commentaries have consequences. Whether writers make it explicit or not, their positions imply certain policies, courses of action, and ways of living. But proposals emphasize this dimension of making policy, devising courses of action, and negotiating the demands of everyday life. The focus of attention shifts from the statement and explanation of the writer's position to what we ought to do about it. Thus, in proposals, a writer's position has a practical or applied dimension in that it involves identifying problems and offering solutions.

Many proposals involve problems and solutions in matters of public policy. For example, private foundations and government agencies commission bodies of experts to study problems in their fields—education, the environment, civil rights, international trade, labor relations—and to issue reports with proposals for change. By the same token, citizens' organizations and advocacy groups of all sorts—from neighborhood and church associations to local preservationist and environmental groups to national organizations such as Greenpeace, the National Organization for Women (NOW), and the National Rifle Association (NRA)—also study problems, consider alternatives, and make recommendations to appropriate government bodies. Their proposals seek to gain public support and influence government policy.

In order to explore the main features shared by these different kinds of proposals, let's look at a situation that might call for a written proposal. A local community group thinks that a vacant lot the city owns could be converted

Online Study Center

into a neighborhood park. The group knows that there's strong support for local parks and recreation among city residents and municipal officials. But it also knows that the city's resources are limited, so any proposal involving spending would need ample justification—to show that the proposed park would solve a problem of some urgency and consequence. For example, the group might show that, compared to other areas of the city, the neighborhood lacks recreational facilities. Or, if the lot has given rise to other problems—if, for example, it is becoming a site for drug dealing or vandalism—the group might argue that a park could simultaneously solve those problems. For the proposal to be persuasive, it would require a clear and convincing statement of the problem and of the general goals and specific objectives being proposed.

In its proposal, the group would need to show that the proposed solution will have the intended effects. If the group claims that drug dealing is part of the problem, then its proposal needs to explain exactly how turning the lot into a park can, in fact, get rid of the dealers. But this isn't enough. The group would also need to show that the solution deals with the problem in the best, most appropriate way, given the alternatives available and the needs and values of the people affected (perhaps drug dealing could be dealt with more cheaply and effectively through increased police surveillance; perhaps the lot is too small to serve all age groups, and the neighborhood and city would be better off expanding a park in an adjoining neighborhood). A proposal that is both capable of solving the problem and suitable for doing so is said to be *feasible.* To have a chance of being implemented, a proposal needs to establish that it passes the *feasibility test*—that its solution will have the intended effects and that it fits the situation.

Proposals often require research. The community group proposing the park could strengthen its case considerably, for example, by showing that the proposed park fits the needs of the neighborhood, given the age and interests of its residents. This information could be obtained by surveying households, as could specifics about the kinds of recreational facilities to include in the park. By comparing the parks in their neighborhood to those elsewhere in the city, the group could argue that their neighborhood needs to be brought up to the city standard.

Proposals need to convince readers—to fund a project, to implement a solution, to change a policy. Proposals are a form of persuasive writing, and clear statements of problems and solutions, demonstrations of feasibility, documentation through research, and careful organization can all help make a proposal persuasive to readers.

■ WRITING FROM EXPERIENCE

In our daily lives, as just noted, we are constantly making proposals. Analyze one such proposal by describing an instance in which you encountered a situation, defined it as a problem, and proposed a solution. Explain the steps you followed to define the problem, consider alternatives, anticipate objections, and formulate a feasible solution—even though you probably did not experience the problem solving you engaged in as a series of steps. Looking back on this experience, what made your solution successful or unsuccessful? Were there any unforeseen consequences?

READINGS

RX FOR AN AILING PLANET

ROSS GELBSPAN

Ross Gelbspan was a reporter for thirty-one years and won the Pulitzer Prize at the Boston Globe *in 1984. His books on climate change include* The Heat Is On: The High Stakes Battle Over Earth's Threatened Climate *(1997) and* Boiling Point: How Politicians, Big Oil and Coal, Journalists, and Activists are Fueling the Climate Crisis—and What We Can Do to Avert Disaster *(2004). His proposal for a 3-point clean energy transition appeared in the* Boston Globe *on April 22, 2003.*

Opening:
* defines health problems caused by climate change
* links to other problems
* proposes a common solution

¶5: Quali-fies scope of proposed solution

¶6: Pre-sents main ob-jective

Rx for an Ailing Planet

ROSS GELBSPAN

THE CLIMATE-PROPELLED spread of diseases of humans, animals, and ecosystems constitutes yet another emerging crisis in this period of proliferating crises.

Many of the new and recurring epidemics are fueled by a warming atmosphere, which is accelerating the disappearance of species, spawning weather extremes, and driving shifts in biological systems. Intensifying climate change portends increased mortality from heat, especially in urban areas, more disease from increasing insect populations, destruction of food crops from extreme weather events and pests, and the increasing scarcity of drinking water.

Developing countries are especially vulnerable because they lack resources for coping and for providing adequate health services.

The alarms about the deteriorating health of the planet follow preoccupations about our newfound vulnerability to international terrorism, distortions in our foreign policy from our dependency on oil, and persisting concerns about global economic stagnation. What joins all these challenges is that they may well be susceptible to a common solution—a rapid worldwide program to rewire the planet with clean energy.

Allowing the climate to restabilize would not solve all these health problems. But if such a global public works program to change the world's energy systems were structures to promote poverty alleviation in the developing world, it would go a long way toward making the world a healthier place.

Climate stabilization, according to more than 2,000 scientists from 100 countries reporting to the Intergovernmental Panel on Climate Change, requires a worldwide cut of 70 percent in our use of fossil fuels.

Moreover, a properly framed program to rewire the world with clean energy would achieve more than climate stabilization. It would allow developing economies to grow without regard to atmospheric limits and, in many instances, without the budgetary burden of imported oil.

Development economists tell us that every dollar invested in energy in poor countries creates far more jobs and wealth than the same dollar invested in any other sector.

A successful worldwide energy transition could begin to transform impoverished and dependent countries into robust trade partners. Increased living standards in poor countries would provide the resources to strengthen and expand public health services.

Transforming the world's energy system requires bold steps. One policy package—a set of three interacting strategies—could reduce emissions by 70 percent while creating millions of jobs, especially in developing countries. The strategies include:

- Withdrawing government subsidies in industrial nations from fossil fuels and putting equivalent subsidies behind renewable energy sources. The United States spends more than $20 billion a year to subsidize fossil fuels. Industrial countries as a whole spend about $200 billion. If those subsidies were invested in renewable technologies, they would provide the incentive for major oil companies to retool and retrain their workers to become aggressive developers of fuel cells, wind farms, and solar systems. (A portion of these US subsidies would have to be used to retrain or buy out the nation's 50,000 coal miners, but that would leave more than enough money for its intended purpose.)

- Creating a fund on the order of $300 billion a year to transfer clean energy to developing countries. Virtually all poor countries would love to go solar; virtually none can afford it. The world's most air-polluted cities are in Asia, Latin America, and other developing areas. The money could come from a variety of sources—a carbon tax in industrial countries, a tax on travel, a small levy on international currency transactions. The fund would be directed specifically to finance wind farms in India, solar assemblies in El Salvador, fuel cell factories in South Africa, and vast solar-powered hydrogen farms in the Middle East.

- Incorporating into the Kyoto process a progressively more stringent fossil fuel efficiency standard. Under this standard, every country would begin at its current base line to raise its fossil fuel efficiency by 5 percent a year (i.e., it would produce the same output next year with 5 percent less fossil fuel or produce 5 percent more goods with the same amount of fossil fuel) until the 70 percent reductions were attained. Countries would be able to use verifiable carbon trading as a tool to help achieve the 5 percent annual increase in carbon efficiency.

¶s 14–15:
Explains
what
results
might be

Ending:
Sums up
possible
result of
proposed
solution

For the first few years, most nations would meet the progressive annual goal by implementing low-cost—even profitable—efficiencies with short payback periods. After the cheap efficiencies were captured, countries would then meet the progressive efficiency goal by deriving increasing amounts of energy from renewable sources. This, in tandem with the fund, would create the mass markets for solar, wind, and hydrogen energy technologies that would bring down their costs and make them economically competitive with fossil fuels.

Under such a plan, the subsidy switch would propel the metamorphosis of oil companies into energy companies. The progressive fossil fuel efficiency standard would harmonize the transformation of national energy structures, create a level field of predictable regulation for the major energy corporations, and jump renewable energy into a global industry. The competition for the new $300 billion-a-year market in clean energy would power the whole process.

It is just possible that an authentic solution to climate change—one that is appropriate to the scale and urgency of the crisis—has the potential to begin to create a wealthier, more peaceful and, ultimately, healthier world.

Analysis: Problems and Solutions

In the opening four paragraphs, Ross Gelbspan quickly sketches a host of problems (what he calls "challenges") that result from climate change. He seems to assume that readers will recognize theses problems as familiar ones and, accordingly, they do not require extensive explanation. Instead, the central focus in this short proposal is on the solution Gelbspan offers ("to rewire the planet with clean energy") and the three interconnected steps to reduce emissions by 70 percent. Notice that part of the persuasiveness of Gelbspan's proposal is the projected consequences of this plan and its potential not only to restabilize the climate but also to have wider benefits.

■ FOR CRITICAL INQUIRY

1. Do you think Ross Gelbspan's decision to sketch the problem in broad strokes and devote more attention to the solution is a reasonable one?

2. Discussions of environmental issues are often polarized into economic development, on one hand, and preservation of the natural world, on the other. How does Gelbspan handle the relationship between economy and environment?

3. Describe Gelbspan's ethos. How does he go about establishing his credibility and goodwill?

A FIELDWORK PROPOSAL

Lucia Trimbur was a graduate student in sociology and African American studies at Yale when she wrote this proposal for funding for a fieldwork project.

Training Fighters, Making Men: A Study of Amateur Boxers
and Their Trainers at Gleason's Gym

Lucia Trimbur

Background

Significant research has been devoted to the sport of boxing, the majority of which has concerned itself with the economic achievements and careers of professional fighters (Dudley, 2002; Wacquant, 1998, 1995a, 1995b, 1992; Early, 1996; Sugden, 1987; Gorn, 1987; Evans, 1985; Hare, 1971; Weinberg & Arond, 1957). Yet the sport of boxing is pursued not only by professional pugilists but also by amateur and recreational boxers, for whom economic success and fame are not necessarily the primary motivation. Rather, for a substantial number of athletes, boxing affords a set of possibilities that may not be available elsewhere. In a time of deindustrialization, changing social circumstances, and transformation of urban space (Davis, 1999), pugilism may enable the formation of identity accessible in few other social spaces. With declining employment opportunities, especially for inner-city men of color, the workplace is not always available as a site for young men to construct masculine selves. Thus, the boxing gym may offer one of the last social realms for the construction of identity, the expression of masculinity, and the negotiation of violence and aggression.

Objectives

Mention the terms "manly art" and "sweet science of bruising," or merely the word boxing, and gender is implicit. Yet in order to understand the forms of masculinity implicit in the sport, gender must be analyzed explicitly. The research I propose examines the formation of identity in a boxing gym to understand how competitive amateur fighters use the culture of training and bodily discipline to create forms of masculinity. Michel Foucault suggests that discipline is a form of power that takes the body as its object; in institutions such as prisons, schools, the military, and, as I would contend, the gym, bodies are manipulated, trained, and thus transformed (Foucault, 1977). I would like to understand how the discipline demanded in the gym facilitates the production and transformation of masculinities and attendant forms of incorporated identity[1] (Connerton, 1989).

Understanding the formation of identity requires apprehending the social relations cultivated in the boxing gym. For this reason, my research examines the relationships developed between trainers and their boxers. Coaches and fighters characterize their relationships as those of life mentoring and deep social trust rather than as merely athletic. As coaches consider it their responsibility to provide both athletic and life guidance, I would like to understand the experiences that inform and shape the advice they impart and how they disseminate such information. Many trainers have, in their pasts, participated in criminal activity, been incarcerated, and engaged in a process of rehabilitation. I would like to discern how trainers simultaneously coach their athletes and discourage them from partaking in similar criminal activity. Thus my project seeks to examine the effect trainer-knowledge has on their athletes in relation to crime and life choices.

Finally, I want to understand the connections between the identities constructed in the gym and those produced in other social institutions, such as the workplace, family, and prison. For instance, many amateur athletes have been incarcerated, and the gym is frequently sought out by boxers recently released from prison, a phenomenon that might suggest boxing offers a way to re-enter society after prison. I would like to analyze the practices and techniques of training and discipline that allow athletes to regroup after the trauma of prison life.

---

[1] In his work *How Societies Remember,* Paul Connerton makes the distinction between "assigned" and "incorporated" identities. Whereas assigned identities are largely non-negotiable, incorporated identities, such as forms of masculinity, are those individuals seek to produce or attempt to transform (Connerton, 1989).

Focusing on trainers and amateur athletes, my specific research questions are: (1) what identities are created and performed in the boxing gym? What are the practices and techniques of the sport's training and regimen that facilitate this identity formation? (2) how is violence managed in the gym? For example, violence is inherent to the sport yet its management is crucial; what are the practices that control violence? How does this management relate to identity? And what does engaging in boxing enable and/or preclude that other sports may not? and (3) how do trainers influence life choices? How do trainers train their boxers in extra-athletic ways?

Research Plan and Methodological Approaches

My research will be conducted at Gleason's Gym in New York City. I have chosen this gym because, founded in the lower Bronx in 1937, it is the oldest and one of the most famous gyms in the United States. Pugilists such as Jake LaMotta, Mike Belloise, Jimmy Carter, and Muhammad Ali, trained at Gleason's Gym, cultivating the gym's reputation as a producer of highly-ranked contenders and unbeatable world champions. Today the gym, which relocated to Brooklyn in 1984, boasts 78 trainers, who work with 850 athletes. Because of its reputation, Gleason's draws some of the most talented amateur and professional boxers in the world, all of whom have a deep investment in their participation in the sport. This investment amplifies the intensity of the gym and creates a rigorous sporting climate.

To examine the process by which identity is constructed and social relations between trainers and their athletes forged, I will employ two methods: participant observation and interviewing. Participant observation will allow me to document the patterns of social interaction in Gleason's Gym and to examine the multiple ways identity is formed and trainer guidance delivered (Emerson, Fretz, & Shaw, 1995). Interviewing will allow me to investigate the dynamics of the relationships among boxing, identity formation, masculine selfhood, and life choices.

Participant Observation

Over the course of one year, I will follow a group of 25–30 amateur athletes, who train for the Golden Gloves of New York City, the most prestigious annual amateur event in boxing, and their trainers. I will recruit my sample based upon 5 trainers with whom I have established a close working relationship and who have agreed to collaborate with me. I plan to observe these athletes and their mentors beginning in September 2003, when training typically commences, and through the course of the tournament, which runs January through May. I also plan to observe the group after the tournament has finished—over the summer months—to study how the fighters use the gym and interact with their trainers when competition is not imminent. Over this year, I will examine the mundane daily activities and regimens of boxers and their trainers in the gym five days a week. I will also accompany them to the tournament in order to observe their extraordinary experiences of competition, talking with them before and after the fights. As they prepare for the Golden Gloves, I plan to analyze the social relations between the amateurs and their trainers, examining how homosocial bonding develops and shapes the process of training. I plan to study how the athlete-coach relationship emerges and influences the decisions boxers make about labor, leisure, and crime.

Interviewing

In addition to participant observation, I will also conduct 25–30 extensive, open-ended interviews with the amateur boxers and their trainers. One goal of the interviews is to identify the range of recurring themes associated with identity, mentoring, violence, and life choices. These interviews will focus on the meanings that informants attach to their participation in the sport, the range of experiences they have had with boxing, and the alternatives boxing may offer to street crime. In structuring and conducting these interviews, I am particularly interested in fighters' own expectations of training and competition: why they became involved and how they assess their progress. Of crucial importance is how they conceptualize violence and corporeal harm in the sport and how they envision their participation in this dynamic of physical conflict. I will also examine the connections between their activities in the gym and other aspects of their lives, such as labor, leisure, education, and family.

Based upon these open-ended interviews, I will then re-interview the group of boxers and trainers with a structured battery of questions about the factors involved in their senses of identity, their connection with boxing and with the mentor-mentee relationship. I will standardize my list of questions in order to facilitate a comparison of my respondents' answers. Together, these methods will enable an understanding of how identity and masculinity are formed, contested, or perhaps exposed as unstable. They will also provide an elucidation of how trainers intervene, inform and shape this process.

References

Connerton, P. (1989). *How societies remember.* New York: Cambridge University Press.

Davis, A., & Gordon, A. (1999). Globalization and the prison industrial complex: An interview with Angela Davis. *Race and Class, 2-3,* 145–157.

Dudley, J. (2002). Inside and outside the ring: Manhood, race, and art in the literary imagination. *College Literature, 29,* 53–82.

Early, G. (1996). Mike's brilliant career. *Transition, 71,* 46–59.

Emerson, R. M., Fretz, R. I., & Shaw, L. L. (1995). *Writing Ethnographic Fieldnotes.* Chicago: University of Chicago Press.

Evans, A. (1995). Joe Louis as key functionary: White reactions toward a black champion. *Journal of Black Studies, 16,* 95–111.

Foucault, M. (1977). *Discipline and punish: The birth of the prison.* New York: Pantheon Books.

Gorn, E. (1987). *The manly art: Bare-knuckle prizefighting in America.* Ithaca, NY: Cornell University Press.

Hare, N. (1971). A study of the black fighter. *Black Scholar, 3,* 2–8. *Slavery to Freedom.* New York: Oxford University Press.

Sugden, J. (1987). The exploitation of disadvantage: The occupational sub-culture of the boxer. *Sociological Review Monograph, 33,* 187–209.

Wacquant, L. (1992). The social logic of boxing in black Chicago: Toward a sociology of pugilism. *Sociology of Sport Journal 9,* 221–254.

Wacquant, L. (1995a). The pugilist point of view: How boxers think and feel about their trade. *Theory and Society, 24,* 489–535.

Wacquant, L. (1995b). Pugs at work: Bodily capital and bodily labour among professional boxers. *Body and Society, 1,* 63–93.

Wacquant, L. (1998). A fleshpeddler at work: Power, pain, and profit in the prizefighting economy. *Theory and Society, 27,* 1–42.

Weinberg, S. K., & Arond, H. (1952). The occupational culture of the boxer. *American Journal of Sociology, 57,* 460–469.

Analysis: Research Proposals

Research proposals are similar in many respects to other types of proposals, whether to change a policy or improve a service. The same task of defining a problem and then proposing a satisfactory solution is common to all. What distinguishes a research proposal is that the problem is one of understanding something—the structure of DNA, the effects of asbestos on the health of South African miners, or the legacy of slavery in the United States—and the solution is to design a workable research plan to investigate the subject and produce new insights. Most research proposals seek to persuade the reader about the merit of the research and the researcher's ability to carry it out. In the case of these two fieldwork proposals, the goal is that the graduate students will secure funding to carry out their research.

The research question or questions in a proposal are crucial. As you can see in these two proposals, the research plan follows from the questions the two graduate students want to answer. Explaining the central research questions accomplishes two things in the proposal. First, it tells readers why the research is meaningful. Second, it enables them to judge whether the proposed plan of action is in fact well-suited to answer the questions.

■ FOR CRITICAL INQUIRY

1. Consider the first two sections of "Training Fighters, Making Men." How does the Background section identify a neglected area of study? How does the Objectives section raise specific questions about amateur boxers?

2. Evaluate the match between the research questions and the research plan in the proposal. Does the research plan seem capable of providing answers to the questions each of the fieldwork proposals raises? Why or why not?

3. What do you see as the strengths and weaknesses of each of the fieldwork proposals? Would you approve them? What suggestions would you offer to modify or refine the proposed research?

LET TEENAGERS TRY ADULTHOOD

LEON BOTSTEIN

Leon Botstein is the president of Bard College and author of Jefferson's Children: Education and the Promise of American Culture. *The following proposal appeared on the Op-Ed page of the* New York Times *in May 1999, shortly after the school shootings in Littleton, Colorado.*

Let Teenagers Try Adulthood
LEON BOTSTEIN

The national outpouring after the Littleton shootings has forced us to confront something we have suspected for a long time: the American high school is obsolete and should be abolished. In the last month, high school students present and past have come forward with stories about cliques and the artificial intensity of a world defined by insiders and outsiders, in which the insiders hold sway because of superficial definitions of good looks and attractiveness, popularity, and sports prowess.

The team sports of high school dominate more than student culture. A community's loyalty to the high school system is often based on the extent to which varsity teams succeed. High school administrators and faculty members are often former coaches, and the coaches themselves are placed in a separate, untouchable category. The result is that the culture of the inside elite is not contested by the adults in the school. Individuality and dissent are discouraged.

But the rules of high school turn out not to be the rules of life. Often the high school outsider becomes the more successful and admired adult. The definitions of masculinity and femininity go through sufficient transformation to make the game of popularity in high school an embarrassment. No other group of adults young or old is confined to an age-segregated environment, much like a gang in which individuals of the same age group define each other's world. In no workplace, not even in colleges or universities, is there such a narrow segmentation by chronology.

Given the poor quality of recruitment and training for high school teachers, it is no wonder that the curriculum and the enterprise of learning hold so little sway over young people. When puberty meets education and learning in modern America, the victory of puberty masquerading as popular culture and the tyranny of peer groups based on ludicrous values meet little resistance.

By the time those who graduate from high school go on to college and realize what really is at stake in becoming an adult, too many opportunities have been lost and too much time has been wasted. Most thoughtful young people suffer the high school environment in silence and in their junior and senior years mark time waiting for college to begin. The Littleton killers, above and beyond the psychological demons that drove them to violence, felt trapped in the artificiality of the high school world and believed it to be real. They engineered their moment of undivided attention and importance in the absence of any confidence that life after high school could have a different meaning.

Adults should face the fact that they don't like adolescents and that they have used high school to isolate the pubescent and hormonally active adolescent away from both the picture-book idealized innocence of childhood and the more accountable world of adulthood. But the primary reason high school doesn't work anymore, if it ever did, is that young people mature substantially earlier in the late 20th century than they did when the high school was invented. For example, the age of first menstruation has dropped at least two years since the beginning of this century, and not surprisingly, the onset of sexual activity has dropped in proportion. An institution intended for children in transition now holds young adults back well beyond the developmental point for which high school was originally designed.

Furthermore, whatever constraints to the presumption of adulthood among young people may have existed decades ago have now fallen away. Information and images, as well as the real and virtual freedom of movement we associate with adulthood, are now accessible to every fifteen- and sixteen-year-old.

Secondary education must be rethought. Elementary school should begin at age four or five and end with the sixth grade. We should entirely abandon the concept of the middle school and junior high school. Beginning with the seventh grade, there should be four years of secondary education that we may call high school. Young people should graduate at sixteen rather than eighteen.

They could then enter the real world, the world of work or national service, in which they would take a place of responsibility alongside older adults in mixed company. They could stay at home and attend junior college, or they could go away to college. For all the faults of college, at least the adults who dominate the world of colleges, the faculty, were selected precisely because they were exceptional and different, not because they were popular. Despite the often cavalier attitude toward teaching in college, at least physicists know their physics, mathematicians know and love their mathematics, and music is taught by musicians, not by graduates of education schools, where the disciplines are subordinated to the study of classroom management.

For those sixteen-year-olds who do not want to do any of the above, we might construct new kinds of institutions, each dedicated to one activity, from science to dance, to which adolescents could devote their energies while working together with professionals in those fields.

At sixteen, young Americans are prepared to be taken seriously and to develop the motivations and interests that will serve them well in adult life. They need to enter a world where they are not in a lunchroom with only their peers, estranged from other age groups and cut off from the game of life as it is really played. There is nothing utopian about this idea; it is immensely practical and efficient, and its implementation is long overdue. We need to face biological and cultural facts and not prolong the life of a flawed institution that is out of date.

Analysis: Facing the Facts

Leon Botstein's proposal to abolish high school as we currently know it is likely to come as a surprise to many readers. After all, high school is one of those institutions we take for granted, and we think of it, whether fondly or not, as a stage of life that everyone goes through. Botstein wants to change all that. In his view, high school has such serious problems that we should rethink the whole schooling system instead of trying to reform it.

Notice that Botstein is assuming that his intended readers will recognize the problems of high schools that he details in the opening paragraphs (cliques, the dominance of athletics, recruitment and training of teachers). To get his readers to take seriously his proposal to abolish high schools, however, Botstein needs to take them further—to "face the fact" that American high schools are obsolete because they've been used to isolate biologically and culturally mature young people from the world of adulthood. Whether readers will agree that Botstein's proposal is a feasible one, of course, remains to be seen. Nonetheless, by defining the problem of high school as that of an obsolete system of age segregation, Botstein is able to show how his proposal "faces the fact" that teenagers are ready to be taken seriously and to join the adult world.

■ FOR CRITICAL INQUIRY

1. What are the reasons Botstein gives to support his view that "high school doesn't work anymore"? Notice that he reserves the "primary reason" for the sixth paragraph. Consider the effect on readers of the way he has arranged his reasons.

2. What assumptions about high schools and American teenagers is Botstein counting on his intended readers to share with him? How do these shared assumptions help to establish the grounds for Botstein's proposal?

3. What are the "facts" Botstein thinks we need to "face"? How does Botstein's call to "face the facts" appeal to his readers?

4. How feasible is Botstein's proposal? What differing views would have to be addressed to establish the proposal's feasibility?

WRITING IN A DIGITAL WORLD

Public Campaigns

2006 NATIONAL STUDENT LABOR WEEK OF ACTION

STUDENT LABOR ACTION PROJECT

The Student Labor Action Project is af-filiated with Jobs with Justice, a na-tional organization whose mission is to improve working people's standard of living, fight for job security, and protect workers' right to organize.

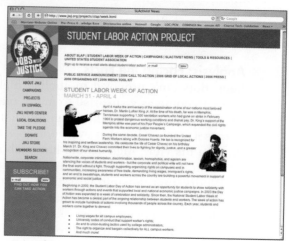

Analysis: Organizing on the Internet

In the mid-1990s, the Zapatistas in Chiapas, Mexico, were among the first to use the Internet as a political tool, to overcome their geographical and media isolation, communicate their struggle for social justice, and establish an inter-national support network. Since then, political groups, from antiglobalization activists to conservative Christians, have relied on the Internet to recruit members and sympathizers, to disseminate their ideas, and to organize events. The 2006 National Student Labor Week of Action is just one example of how groups are using the Internet to organize.

A public campaign is a way of disseminating a group's proposals and goals. Visit the National Student Labor Action Project Web site at www.jwj.org/projects/slap/week.html and click on Tools and Resources. Notice the genres of writing included—fact sheets, news advisories, public service announce-ments, and letters to the editor.

■ FOR CRITICAL INQUIRY

1. A public campaign like the 2006 National Student Labor Week of Action is, in the broadest sense of the term, a proposal. It identifies a problem and proposes solutions. What does the problem seem to be in this instance? What solutions does the Student Labor Action Project propose?

2. Consider the variety of writing genres that go into a public campaign like the National Student Labor Week of Action. What particular role do two or three of the genres play?

3. What public campaigns do you know about? How are they organized to get a mes-sage before the public? What types of writing are associated with the campaigns?

VISUAL DESIGN

Proposals

PROPOSAL FOR A NEIGHBORHOOD STREET TREE PROGRAM

THE BE GREEN NEIGHBORHOOD ASSOCIATION

Proposals by neighborhood associations and community organizations are familiar means of participating in public policy by making known the needs and interests of ordinary people. Often such proposals, as in the case here, involve allocation of resources—for a child care center, an after-school youth program, a literacy program for recent immigrants, or a street tree program. As you can see, the following proposal uses four main headings—Problem, Solution, Benefits, and Conclusion—to make visible its underlying argument.

THE BE GREEN NEIGHBORHOOD ASSOCIATION
"Creating a Sustainable, Healthy Community For All"

BE GREEN NEIGHBORHOOD ASSOCIATION

Proposal for a Neighborhood Street Tree Program

1   The Be Green Neighborhood Association proposes a street tree program to enhance the environmental, aesthetic, and social aspects of our community.

Problem

2   Our neighborhood suffers from a lack of green space. Environmentally, large areas of concrete and pavement exacerbate already high temperatures in summer months. A lack of trees and shaded spaces on our streets means higher pollution levels, higher home cooling costs, and greater strain on electric utility already over-taxed in the summer. Aesthetically, long stretches of road, concrete sidewalks, paved driveways and parking lots create an eyesore and depress property values.

Solution

3   Neighborhood associations in cities such as Berkeley, Chicago, Sacramento, Seattle, Charlotte, Los Angeles, and Providence have implemented street tree programs to address, at the local level, the effects of climate change, pressures on city electricity grids, and high pollution levels as well as to beautify their neighborhoods. The US Forest Service estimates "for a planting cost of $250–6000 one street tree returns over $90,000 of direct benefits in the lifetime of the tree" (Burden). In addition, street trees can be planted in all climates.

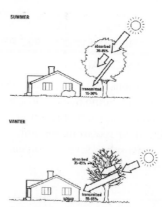

Figure 1   Street trees cool in summer and heat in winter.

4   The Be Green Neighborhood Association proposes the creation of a tree-planting program in our community. The city's already-existing Urban Forest will provide the trees to the neighborhood association free of charge, and the citizens of our association agree to be involved in the planting of the trees and to water and maintain them (weeding and mulching). The president of the neighborhood association will submit a request, in writing, for each tree to the director of the Urban Forest by November 1 of each year. If the request is approved, street trees will be delivered and planted on a Saturday in the spring of the following year.

5   Street trees in our community will be planted 4 to 8 feet from the curb so as not to obscure traffic lights, signposts, streetlamps, or driveways. We will adopt trees of an uneven age distribution, as a combination of young and mature trees is essential for a successful street tree program. Where possible, we will promote species diversity, which is also important for the long-term health of the trees.

Benefits

6   The planning, planting, and maintenance of street trees promote environmental, social, and financial wellbeing of communities.

Environmental

7   Trees catch air pollution particles on their leaves and help remove pollutants such as nitrogen oxides, sulphur, ammonia, and dust particles (Benefits of Trees). Street trees also absorb and store carbon, the main ingredient of smog, removing it from the atmosphere. The US Forest Service explains that "trees in

Figure 2   Street trees provide environmental, social, financial, and aesthetic benefits.

street proximity absorb 9 times more pollutants than more distant trees, converting harmful gasses back into oxygen and other useful and natural gasses" (Burden). According to the Street Tree program in Los Angeles, one tree can produce enough oxygen for a family of four in one year (Bureau of Street Services). Street trees also absorb storm water, which decreases runoff and soil erosion. Street trees lower indoor air temperatures by shading houses and residential buildings. One urban forest program estimates that energy savings can be up to 25% per year. In addition, street trees block UV rays harmful to the eyes and skin, and provide protection from rain and sun that extends pavement life (City of St. Louis).

Social

8   Studies have shown that people drive at lower and more reasonable speeds because "urban street trees create vertical walls framing streets and a defined edge, helping motorists guide their movement and assess their speed." Street trees also make walking areas safer "by forming and framing visual walls and providing distinct edges to sidewalks so that motorists better distinguish between their environment and one shared with people" (Burden). Street trees can reduce noise pollution, which reduces stress, lowers blood pressure, dissipates road rage, and provides a connection to the natural world.

Financial and Aesthetic

9   Studies show that businesses surrounded by street trees bring in 20% more revenue than businesses in areas without street trees (Burden). Street trees increase residential property values by up to 20% (Bureau of Street Services). Aesthetically, street trees beautify streets and parking and walking areas.

Conclusion

10   The Be Green Neighborhood Association believes that a street tree program in our community would greatly improve life in an environmentally sustainable manner. In partnership with the city's Urban Forest department, we can plant and maintain a number of trees that will add important environmental, social, aesthetic, and financial value to our neighborhood for a modest start-up cost.

Works Cited

Benefits of Trees. www.streettree.org/BenefitsofTrees/tabid/258/Default.aspx.

Burden, Dan. "22 Benefits of Urban Street Trees." http://www.ufei.org/files/pubs/22BenefitsofUrbanStreetTrees.pdf.

Bureau of Street Services, Street Tree Division, City of LA. http://www.cityofla.org/BOSS/streettree/UrbanForest.htm

City of St. Louis. http://stlouis.missouri.org/citygov/parks/forestry_div/TreeProgram.pdf.

Analysis: Making Purposes Visible

Some proposals take the form of an essay, as is the case with the pieces of writing in this chapter by Ross Gelbspan and Leon Botstein, which appeared originally on op-ed pages in newspapers. In other cases, however, such as Lucia Trimbur's fieldwork proposal or proposals like this one from the Be Green Neighborhood Association, proposal writers rely on conventions of visual design to make the purposes of their proposal visible to readers. The Be Green Neighborhood Association uses a familiar pattern of organizing proposals:

¶ 1: Introduction: goal of the proposal

¶ 2: Problem

¶ 3–5: Solution

¶ 6–9: Benefits

■ Environmental

■ Social

■ Financial and aesthetic

¶ 10: Conclusion

The Proposal for a Neighborhood Street Tree Program is meant to be read as a plan of action that responds to a felt need. By identifying the structure of its argument through familiar headings and subheadings, the proposal enables readers to easily follow its line of reasoning.

■ FOR CRITICAL INQUIRY

1. Notice how the four main sections of the "Proposal for a Neighborhood Street Tree Program" display the steps in the proposal's reasoning. Consider what each section contributes to the development of the argument to start a street tree program. What is the persuasive effect of the order in which the sections appear?

2. In terms of the proportion of space devoted to it, the section "Problem" is by far the shortest in the proposal. Consider the neighborhood association's rhetorical decision to keep this section brief. What is the overall effect of emphasizing the "Solution" and "Benefit" sections? What assumptions do the proposal writers seem to be making about their intended audiences and those audiences' need to know? Take into account here the various audiences who might read this proposal and their various perspectives that make them stakeholders in the proposed program.

3. Notice how the proposal writers draw on authorities, including two municipalities and the U.S. Forestry Service, to make their case for a street tree program. What gives these authorities their persuasive force in this proposal? What, in turn, does this reveal about the beliefs of readers in the reliability of sources?

FURTHER EXPLORATION: PROPOSALS

■ GENRE CHOICES

Think of a current problem—campuswide, local, national, or international. Imagine a feasible solution to the problem. You could write a formal proposal to solve the problem, as the students who proposed a campus coffee house did—see the Writers' Workshop section, later in this chapter. Let's assume you're really serious about getting your proposal implemented. What other genres of writing might you use to publicize your proposal? What do you see as the purpose of those genres?

■ WORKING TOGETHER

Advocacy Group Proposals

Advocacy groups do a wide range of writing to publicize their proposals: advertisements in newspapers and magazines and on radio and television, flyers, letters of appeal, posters, bumper stickers, articles in the opinion pages of newspapers, petitions, and proposals.

Work together in a group of three or four to write two pieces of different types. Follow these steps:

1. Choose an issue that could interest an advocacy group. What is a key problem connected with the issue? What might be a feasible solution to the problem? As a group, come to a consensus about a problem and feasible solution.

2. Once you have defined the problem you want to address, think about the types of writing listed above that might be most relevant for presenting your solution, and choose two. What will the specific purpose of each piece be? Who is the likely audience for each piece and how can you most effectively address this audience?

3. When you are finished, write an introduction to the project, explaining the problem you defined and the solution you proposed, why you chose the types of writing you chose, how audience and purpose were reflected in what you wrote, and what you did to make the visual design of the pieces effective.

ETHICS OF WRITING

PROBLEMS AND CONFLICTS

Understanding the situations that confront us in everyday life and in public affairs as problems that can be solved is a powerful way of making reality more manageable. Once you have defined a problem, it then becomes possible to think in terms of a solution.

However, problems take shape according to the way people define them. Depending on how the problem is defined, particular solutions seem more—or less—logical than others. Yet, underlying many definitions of problems are real conflicts about values and beliefs. And genuine differences in beliefs lead to very different statements of the problem and thus to different proposed solutions.

Formulating a problem invariably means taking a position in relation to what others think and believe—aligning yourself with particular values and beliefs and distancing yourself from others. If you assume that you can simply define a problem objectively, you might well wind up ignoring the underlying conflicts in the situation and interpretations and in the needs of others. Such ethical issues arise with other genres, but they become especially important with proposals because proposals are focused on action and in many cases influence decisions about the use of limited resources. ■

WRITING ASSIGNMENT

Proposing a Problem Solution

 *Online Study Center*

For this assignment, write a proposal that formulates a problem and offers a solution. You will need to think of an existing situation that calls for attention, whether it is on campus or at the local, national, or international level. Something may be wrong that needs to be changed or corrected. Something may be lacking that needs to be added. Something worthwhile may not be working properly and therefore needs to be improved. Or it may be that a situation needs to be redefined in order to find new approaches and solutions.

Here are some specific possibilities:

- **Proposals for new or improved services:** Proposals call on government agencies, professional associations, educational institutions, and private foundations to provide new or improved services—for example in health care, education, and recreation. The student "Proposal for a Campus Coffee House" (see Writers' Workshop) is a good example of such a proposal for a college campus. You might write a proposal based on a situation you see on campus—to improve residential life, food service, social climate, advising, or academic programs. Or you may want to write a proposal for new or improved services in your local community or at the state or federal level.

- **Public policy proposals:** These range from editorials in newspapers and journals of opinion to actual legislation that proposes to do things such as change immigration laws, recognize gay and lesbian relationships, require a balanced budget, or devise a national health care plan. Leon Botstein's proposal to abolish American high schools, as well as the National Urban League's proposal to improve the recruitment, training, and supervision of police officers or FAIR's call for a moratorium on immigration, offer examples of short public policy proposals that seek to influence public opinion and create a favorable political climate for the writer's plan.

- **Research proposals:** Lucia Trimbur's "Training Fighters, Making Men" offers an example of a research proposal. You might draw on one of the classes you're taking right now to write a research proposal. What is an interesting and important problem or issue that has emerged in readings, lectures, and discussions? How would you go about researching it?

Alternative Assignments

Online Study Center

■ RHETORICAL ANALYSIS

Analyze the argument in one (or more) of the proposals in this chapter. Pay particular attention to the enabling assumptions that connect the claim (the writer's proposal) and the evidence. What backing of these assumptions is offered explicitly or assumed implicitly? Consider how the shape of the writer's argument is likely to influence readers' evaluations of whether the proposal is feasible or not.

■ WORKING WITH SOURCES

As you can see in the fieldwork proposal earlier in this chapter, the researcher locates the work she is proposing in relation to work that has already been done. Notice in "Training Fighters, Making Men," Lucia Trimbur opens her proposal by explaining that previous research has focused largely on professional boxers, leaving a gap in understanding that she intends to fill by researching amateur boxing. Use this section of the proposal as a model. Identify 4–5 sources on a topic or issue that interests you. Use these sources to explain further research you might do by filling in a gap or extending existing work.

Invention

To think more systematically about proposals you might be called to write, try working through the following exercises. Your proposal may well grow out of a situation you are currently in, or it may stem from an experience you have had in the recent past.

1. Start by taking an inventory of the issues around you that might call for a solution. As you could tell from the readings, there is a wide range of possibilities open to you. Begin by thinking small and local. Make a list of those positions in which you have the most power to enact change. Are you an officer of any groups, clubs, or organizations? Are you in any classes where the teacher allows the students to carry a lot of responsibility? Are you a leader or captain on a team? If so, write down each example where you find yourself speaking from a position of authority. Then think through the issues that confront those groups, and keep track of them as possibilities.

2. Next, identify those positions where you would be listened to as a fellow member rather than as a leader. What other groups are you a part of? What are the issues that circulate in each of those groups? Do any of these issues call you to propose a solution (even if you haven't thought of one yet)? If so, write them down as good possibilities.

3. Now broaden your thinking to national and international issues. Which do you identify as real problems? Which do you care enough about to spend time thinking of and proposing a solution to? What kind of a power position are you in when you talk about these types of issues? Who might listen to you? What is the best forum for getting people to hear your proposal?

4. Once you have created your list of possibilities, narrow it down to the three most promising options, beginning with the ones you care most about or that have the potential to make your life (or that of someone you know) markedly better. Then try the exercises in the sections that follow on formulating a problem, assessing alternatives, and matching problems and solutions. After you have thought about your potential proposals from all those directions, you should be able to tell which one will make the best proposal.

5. Decide tentatively on the audience. Who can realistically make changes happen? To whom do you have realistic access? With whom do you have credibility? Is there a specific person or governing body in a position to enact the changes you will present? Create a list of at least three

possible audiences and consider the implications each audience holds for the successful implementation of your proposal. Notice how your definition of the problem may change depending on your audience. Do these shifts in definition hold any consequences for you or for those you are trying to help?

Background Research: Formulating the Problem

As you have seen, problems don't just come in prepackaged form, calling on us to solve them. They first have to be defined. By formulating problems, writers take situations that already exist and point out what aspects call for urgent attention and action. In this sense, problem formulation is always in part an interpretation—a way of establishing the relevance of a problem to readers. This is a powerful move, since, as a writer, you are taking a group of people and defining them (and their problems) in a particular way. As a proposal writer, you establish criteria for deciding what is good and normal and what is bad and in need of some sort of repair. There are, of course, many ways to define problems, so part of your job is to do so responsibly and ethically.

Illegal drugs are a good example of how problems can be defined in a number of ways. If you ask most Americans about the problems that currently beset American society, many will quite likely name "drugs." But what exactly is the problem with drugs? There is little question that millions of Americans use illegal drugs and that there is a flourishing criminal drug trade. To say as much, however, only describes an existing situation in the broadest sense. What, if anything, should we do about illegal drugs? To propose solutions to the issue, you will have to define more precisely what you see as the problem raised by drugs.

Depending on the writer's perspective, the problem can vary considerably and lead to very different proposals. For example, some would say that the problem with drugs is that illegal drug trade results in police corruption and powerful underworld drug cartels. Others would argue that drugs are causing social decay and destroying the moral fiber of a generation of American young people. Still others would hold that Americans and drug laws haven't distinguished adequately between recreational drugs like marijuana and addictive drugs like heroin and cocaine. In the following chart, notice how different problem formulation leads to different proposals. Notice, too, how each solution growing from the problem formulation will impact a different community.

Issue	Illegal drug use		
Problem	Underworld drug trade	Social decay	Need for redefinition
Proposed Solution	Step up war against major drug dealers.	Education, jobs programs.	Decriminalize marijuana.

| Cut off drugs at point of distribution. | Eliminate conditions of drug use, such as poverty and hopelessness. | Make legal distinctions that recognize differences between kinds of drugs (recreational versus addictive). |

Use the chart as a guide to analyze an existing situation by breaking it down into a number of problems. You will probably not be able to address in one proposal all the aspects of the situation that you identify as problems. In fact, you may find that the proposed solutions suggested by the various problems are contradictory or mutually exclusive. The idea at this point is to see how many different problems you can formulate so that you will be able to decide which seems most pressing or important.

Assessing Alternatives

Once you have identified a number of possible solutions to the problems you've defined, you can then assess the relative strengths and weaknesses of proposals. One way to do this is to test the feasibility of proposed solutions—their capability and suitability to solve problems. Again this can be done by using a chart:

Problem	What policy on international drug trade should the government follow?	
Proposed Solution	Legalize drug trade under state control.	Step up the war against international drug trade.
Capability	Unknown. Costs and benefits uncertain. Would require considerable administration. What about possible black market?	Could reduce amount of illegal drugs to enter the U.S. However, very costly to have widespread effect. What about domestic trade?
Suitability	Politically unpopular. Voters would interpret as a state endorsement of drug use.	Foreign policy implications need to be carefully considered.

Planning

Relative Emphasis on the Problem and the Solution

As the readings in this chapter show, the amount of space devoted to formulating the problem and to explaining the solution may vary considerably, depending on the writer's situation and purposes. Look, for example, at the relative emphasis on the problem and on the solution in Lucia Trimbur's research proposal "Training Fighters, Making Men" and in Leon Botstein's "Let Teenagers Try Adulthood."

"Training Fighters, Making Men"

¶ 1: Gives background

¶ 2–5: States objectives of study and research questions (the problem)

¶ 6–10: Presents research plan and methods (the solution)

¶ 9: Indicates significance of research

Notice in this case that 50 percent of the proposal (¶¶ 1–5) is concerned with formulating the problem in the Background and Objectives sections, while the second half of the proposal (¶¶ 6–10) consists of explaining the solution in the Research Plan. This makes sense, for a research proposal needs to indicate how a researcher plans to answer her research question. On the other hand, Leon Botstein devotes the first seven paragraphs to formulating the problem (almost 2/3) and only four to presenting solutions.

"Let Teenagers Try Adulthood"

¶ 1–2: Defines current situation in high school

¶ 3–7: Explains the problems with the current situation

¶ 8–10: Proposes a solution

¶ 11: Comments on efficacy of the proposed solution

Botstein assumes that his readers need more analysis of the problem of high school in order to propose a new way of thinking about the issue. As you begin to sketch a working outline of your proposal, take into account your readers' needs. Is a quick sketch of the problem adequate, or should you go into greater detail? Your answer will depend in large part on the situation you're facing and what your purposes are.

Developing a Working Outline

Review the writing and thinking you've done so far. Use the following guidelines to sketch a working outline of your proposal. The guidelines indicate the main issues that writers typically address to design persuasive proposals. As you have just seen, the relative proportion of space devoted to the problem statement and to your explanation of the solution is something you must determine.

1. **Statement of the problem:** Decide how readily readers will recognize the problem and how much agreement already exists about how to solve it. Your first task is to establish the relevance of the problem to your intended audience. Who does the problem affect? What makes it urgent? What will happen if the problem is not addressed?

2. **Description of the solution:** Since effective proposals present both general goals that appeal to shared values and attitudes and the specific solution to be accomplished, you need to state the goals you have identified and then state clearly how and why your proposed solution will work. Describe the solution and the steps needed to implement it. Decide on the level of detail required to give readers the necessary information to evaluate your proposal.

3. **Explanation of reasons:** Identify the best reasons in support of your proposal. Consider the available alternatives and to what length you need to address them. Finally, think about what counterarguments are likely to arise and to what length you need to deal with them.

4. **Ending:** Some proposals have short endings that reinforce the main point. Others, such as the advertisements commonly found in magazines and newspapers, end by calling on readers to do something.

Working Draft

Use the working outline you have developed to write a draft of your proposal.

Matching Problems and Solutions

Perhaps the most important feature of a persuasive proposal is the match between the problem as the writer defines it and the solution as the writer describes and explains it. Unless the two fit together in a logical and compelling way, readers are unlikely to have confidence in the proposal.

Proposal writers often link solutions to problems in two ways—in terms of long-term, overall goals and in terms of objectives that specify the outcome of the proposal.

Objectives normally tell who is going to do what, when they are going to do it, what the projected results will be, and (in some instances) how the results will be measured.

As you design your proposal, consider how you can effectively present your goals and objectives. Your goals will give readers a sense of your values and offer common ground as the basis for readers' support, while your objectives will help convince readers you have a concrete plan of action that can succeed.

Peer Commentary

Once you have written a draft proposal, exchange drafts with a classmate. If you are working in a group, exchange drafts between groups. Write a commentary to the draft, using the following guidelines.

1. How does the proposal establish the need for something to be done—by defining a problem, describing a situation, using an example, providing

facts and background information? Is the need for action convincing? Who is likely to recognize and want to address the main issue of the proposal? Who might feel excluded? Is there any way to include more potential supporters?

2. Where does the proposal first appear? Is it clear and easy to find? Put the proposal in your own words. If you cannot readily paraphrase it, explain why. What is the objective of the proposal? Is it clear who is going to do what, when, how much, and (if appropriate) how the results will be evaluated? Do you think the proposal will have the results intended? Why or why not? What other results might occur?

3. What reasons are offered on behalf of the proposal? Do you find these reasons persuasive? Why or why not? Are these the best reasons available? What other reasons might the writer use?

4. Does the solution appear to be feasible? Why or why not? Does the writer need to include more information to make the proposal seem more feasible? What would it take to convince you that this proposal would work?

5. Is the proposal addressed to an appropriate audience? Can the audience do anything to support the actions suggested in the proposal? If not, can you suggest a more appropriate audience? If so, does the way the proposal is written seem suitable for that audience? Point to specific places in the text that need revision. What kinds of changes would make the proposal work better for the audience?

Revising

Now that you have received feedback on your proposal, you can make the revisions you think are necessary—to make sure that the solution you propose follows logically and persuasively from the problem as you have defined it. To help you assess the relationship between your problem formulation and the solution you propose, consider this early draft of the problem and solution sections of the "Proposal for a Campus Coffee House." Notice two things. First, this proposal devotes approximately equal space to the problem and to the solution. Second, the early draft does not clearly separate the problem statement from the solution statement. In fact, as you can see, the problem is initially defined as the lack of a solution—a logical confusion that will make readers conclude that the reasoning is circular (the reason we need X is because we don't have it), which is not likely to be very persuasive. To see how the writer straightened out the relationship between problems and solutions, compare this early draft to the revised version that appears in Writers' Workshop.

Early Draft

The Problem: Drinking on Campus

The absence of an alcohol-free social life has become a major problem at Warehouse State. Because there are no alternatives, campus social life is dominated by the fraternities, whose parties make alcohol easily available to minors. Off campus, local bars that feature live bands are popular with students, and underage students have little difficulty obtaining and using fake IDs.

The Student Counseling Center currently counsels students with drinking problems and has recently instituted a peer counselor program to educate students about the risks of drinking. Such programs, however, will be limited and largely reactive unless there are alcohol-free alternatives to social life on campus.

The Solution: Campus Coffee House

The Student Management Club proposes to operate a campus coffee house with live entertainment on Friday and Saturday nights in order to provide an alcohol-free social environment on campus for 200 students (capacity of auxiliary dining room in Morgan Commons when set up cabaret-style).

Such a campus coffee house would have a number of benefits. It would help stop the high levels of drinking on campus by both legal and underage students (Martinez & Johnson, 1998), as well as the "binge drinking" that has increased the number of students admitted to the student infirmary for excessive drinking by almost 50% in the last four years. It would serve as a public endorsement of alcohol-free social life, enhance student culture by providing low-cost alcohol-free entertainment on campus, and support current ongoing alcohol abuse treatment and prevention programs. ■

W WRITERS' WORKSHOP

A group of three students wrote the following "Proposal for a Campus Coffee House" in response to an assignment in a business writing class that called on students to produce a collaboratively written proposal to deal with a campus problem. Their commentary on the decisions they made formulating problems and solutions and designing the format appears after the proposal.

PROPOSAL

Proposal for a Campus Coffee House

To meet the problem of excessive drinking on campus, we propose that a coffee house, open on Friday and Saturday nights with live entertainment, be established in the auxiliary dining room in Morgan Commons and operated by the Student Management Club to provide an alcohol-free alternative to undergraduate social life.

The Problem: Drinking on Campus

A recent study by the Student Health Center indicates high levels of drinking by undergraduates on campus (Martinez & Johnson, 1998). Both legal and underage students drink frequently (Fig. 1). They also increasingly engage in unhealthy "binge drinking" to the point of unconsciousness. The number of students admitted to the student infirmary for excessive drinking has increased almost 50% in the past four years (Fig. 2). These patterns of drinking conform to those observed in a recent national study (Dollenmayer, 1998). Like many

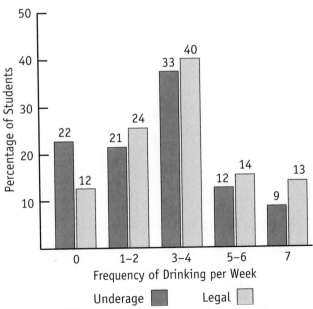

Fig. 1   Frequency of Drinking Per Week, Underage and Legal.

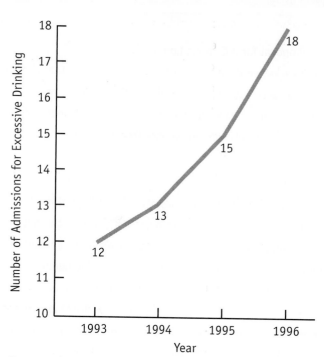

Fig. 2   Admissions to Student Infirmary for Excessive Drinking

other colleges and universities, Warehouse State is faced with a serious student drinking problem (Weiss, 1997).

Currently there are few alternatives for students seeking an alcohol-free social life. Campus social life is dominated by the fraternities, whose parties make alcohol easily available to minors. Off campus, local bars that feature live bands are popular with students, and underage students have little difficulty obtaining and using fake IDs.

The Solution: Campus Coffee House

The Student Management Club proposes to operate a campus coffee house with live entertainment on Friday and Saturday nights in order to provide an alcohol-free social environment on campus for 200 students (capacity of auxiliary dining room in Morgan Commons when set up cabaret-style).

Such a campus coffee house would have a number of benefits. It would serve as a public endorsement of alcohol-free social life, enhance student culture by providing low-cost alcohol-free entertainment on campus, and support current ongoing alcohol abuse treatment and prevention programs. The Student Counseling Center currently counsels students with drinking problems and has recently instituted a promising peer counselor program to educate students about the risks of drinking. Such programs, however, will be limited and largely reactive unless there are alcohol-free alternatives to social life on campus.

Organizational Capability

The Student Management Club has the experience and expertise needed to run the proposed coffee house. Since 1991, it has successfully run a coffee counter in Adams Union, open five days a week from 8 to 3:30. Management majors are interested in expanding their work into the areas of arts programming and publicity.

Budget

The proposed campus coffee house will require initial funding of $1,250 to begin operations. See cost breakdown in Table 1, Initial Expenditure. We believe, however, that such expenditures are one-time only and that the campus coffee house should become self-supporting. See projected budget in Table 2.

Table 1   Initial Expenditures

Supplies (mugs, plates, spoons, forks, paper products, etc.)	$ 750
Coffee, tea, milk, pastries	250
Publicity	250
Total	$1,250

Table 2   Projected Budget

Per evening of operation

Income		Expenses	
(estimated)	$400	Entertainment (band or singer)	$100.00
		Staff (2 persons, 5 hrs each @$5.35)	53.50
		Supplies	75.00
		Food	100.00
		Publicity	25.00
		Total	$353.50

References

Dollenmayer, L. C. (1998). Patterns of alcohol use among American college students. *Journal of the American Medical Association, 275*(16), 223–229.

Martinez, M., & Johnson, R. (1998). Alcohol use and campus social life. Livingston, NM: Student Health Center, Warehouse State University.

Weiss, I. (1997, December 2). Drinking deaths prompt concern on campus. *New York Times,* pp. 1, 7.

WRITERS' COMMENTARY

Following are excerpts from a group meeting, which the participants taped. Here are some passages from the transcript where the three group members, Kathy, Andrea, and Bruce, talk about why they got involved in the coffee house project and how they went about writing the proposal.

KATHY: One of the things that has been interesting about working in this group is that the members come to it from different perspectives. Andrea and I see the coffee house more as a crusade against drinking, which we've watched do a lot of damage to some people we know. So that's a pretty big motivation to get involved, to provide alternatives. Bruce, I think, is into it more out of his interest in folk music and running coffee houses.

BRUCE: Yeah, I mean I do support the idea of having alcohol-free alternative places for students to go. That makes sense to me. But, I agree, definitely. My main thing is arts programming and administration, that whole business. If I can, that's what I want to do when I graduate.

BRUCE: Some of that came up when we were trying to think of reasons for the coffee house, and I was into how it would help promote the arts on campus. We ended up not using that stuff.

ANDREA: Right, but I think Kathy and I became more aware of how we had to make sure the proposal didn't sound moralistic. Remember at first we defined the problem as "drinking on campus" and only later changed it to "excessive drinking." We wanted the proposal to sound positive—that a coffee house would enhance student life.

BRUCE: Exactly. We didn't want it to sound like punishment. And you're right, the proposal doesn't really come out against drinking as the problem but against excessive drinking, binge drinking. I mean alcohol is legal for people over 21. Besides it's unrealistic to think a campus coffee house or anything else for that matter is going to end drinking on campus.

ANDREA: Another thing I felt we tried to do in the proposal was link the coffee house concept to other campus anti-drinking programs. I thought we did a pretty good job of listing benefits in the solution section.

■ WORKSHOP QUESTIONS

1. Consider how well the proposed solution matches the problem defined in this proposal. Is the problem well-defined and substantiated by adequate evidence? Does the proposed solution seem to offer a feasible approach to excessive drinking on campus? Are there other important factors the writers have not taken into account?

2. The writers, as you may have noticed, are reasonably concerned that their proposal doesn't sound moralistic, even though Kathy and Andrea were initially interested in the idea because of their strong feelings about drinking. Do you think they have been successful in presenting their proposal as a "positive" step to "enhance student life"? If so, what is it about the proposal that creates this impression? If not, why?

3. Imagine that you are on a campus committee that reviews proposals and decides which ones to support. There are more worthy proposals than there are funds available, so you will have to make some hard decisions. The proposal for a campus coffee house is one of the finalists, and the committee plans to meet each group of proposers before making its decision. Draw up a list of questions you would ask Kathy, Andrea, and Bruce to help you make a decision. ■

REFLECTING ON YOUR WRITING

If you did a group proposal, when you have finished, hold a meeting to look back and evaluate the experience of working together.

1. Explore the reasons each member was drawn to the problem the proposal addresses. To what extent do these reasons overlap? How are they distinct from each other? How did they combine in the group? What influence did this have on writing the proposal?

2. Describe how the group went about writing the proposal. What parts went smoothly? What problems, if any, did the group have? How did individual members and the group deal with problems in the writing?

If you wrote an individual proposal, ask similar questions: What called you to the problem you address? What made it important or urgent? How did you go about writing the proposal? What was easy about it? What problems, if any, did you have? How did you deal with these problems?

reviews: evaluating works and performances

THINKING ABOUT THE GENRE

Reviews are a genre of writing people turn to when they are called on to make evaluations. Of course, reviewers normally describe and analyze whatever they are reviewing—whether it is a movie, a CD, an employee's performance, or a government program. Still, as readers are aware, reviewers provide this background information and analysis as evidence for the evaluation they are making.

Reviews take place informally all the time in everyday life. Part of daily conversation is talking about what people need, what they have seen and done, and what kinds of judgments they make about their experience: What kind of lawn mower should I buy? Is the psychology course you're taking any good? Is the latest Spike Lee movie worth seeing? Do you like your new car? Where's a good place to get a cheap meal?

At times the informal judgments that result from such questions can spark extended debate. Sports fans, for example, can argue endlessly about everything from who was the best quarterback of the 1990s to which team is going to win the game on Saturday. In these debates, individuals not only make claims—"Babe Ruth was the greatest baseball player of all time"—but must also be able to state the criteria these claims are based on—"No one else has been able to hit the way Babe Ruth did." And, if necessary, they have to justify these criteria. After all, someone might respond that Willie Mays was the greatest because he was the best all-around player. Then the first person would have to justify using hitting as the main criterion. Making evaluations based on justified criteria is at the heart of these informal reviews—and of their formal, written counterparts as well.

Perhaps the most familiar written reviews are newspaper and magazine reviews of the arts—reviews of books, music, film, art, architecture, television, and dance. But newspapers and magazines also feature other kinds of reviews. For example, *Consumer Reports* reviews a broad range of products, and specialized magazines like *Runner's World* and *Wired* routinely assess the particular products that interest their readers. Most newspapers review local restaurants, and most have a travel section that reviews tourist attractions and vacation spots, often with tips on what to see and do and where to stay. In addition, Web sites of various sorts feature reviews of music, films, television shows, books, and consumer products. As these examples suggest, readers use reviews in a variety of ways: to get information, to get advice from experts, and to compare their judgments to the reviewer's.

You've probably written book reviews in school. Sometimes students think the point of book reviews is to prove to teachers they've read the book, but it's important to understand the role that reviewing plays in academic work. Like newspapers and magazines, scholarly journals feature reviews that assess the contribution of new books to a field of study. Just as key, though, is the way scholars and researchers are persistently reviewing the literature in their field to frame their own intellectual projects and explain the significance of their work. One of the standard features of an academic article is a literature review that locates the work being presented in relation to previous work, whether by applying an established concept to a new case, tackling a neglected topic, or offering a counter-interpretation.

At the center of all these reviews are the criteria used to make evaluations. The criteria reviewers use may be explicit or implicit. *Consumer Reports*, for example, uses explicit criteria based on quantitative data. Readers can find them listed and explained on the page. Often, however, the criteria are far less explicit. In movie reviews, for example, readers must frequently figure out the criteria from the critic's discussion and analysis of the film.

The way readers respond to a review and whether they find its evaluation persuasive will depend to a large extent on whether they believe the criteria used are justifiable. At times, of course, readers may accept the criteria used and yet not agree with how the criteria are applied. For example, a film critic and readers might share the belief that the leading actress's performance is crucial to the success of a film but disagree nonetheless about the performance of a particular actress in a particular movie. In other cases of evaluation, however, people disagree not because they apply shared criteria in different ways but because their criteria of evaluation differ altogether. In a heterogeneous society such as our own, it is virtually inevitable that people's evaluations—whether in politics, academic work, the arts, or other areas—and the criteria and assumptions that underlie them will differ considerably.

■ WRITING FROM EXPERIENCE

How do you and the people you know find out about movies, CDs, television shows, live music, books and magazines, restaurants, plays, dance performances, concerts, and Web sites? Do you read reviews that appear in newspapers, magazines, or online? How often do you hear and make use of informal, word-of-mouth reviews from family, friends, or coworkers? Think of a discussion you had in which people's evaluations differed. What was being reviewed? What did people say? Why did their evaluations differ? Did they seem to be using the same criteria but applying them differently, or were they using different criteria? How did the discussion end? Did anyone modify his or her views?

READINGS

REVIEWS

1979; THE CASE AGAINST COLDPLAY

Sasha Frere-Jones is the pop music critic at the New Yorker, *where "1979" appeared in the November 1, 2004, edition. Jon Pareles is a pop music critic at the* New York Times, *where "The Case Against Coldplay" appeared in the Sunday Arts and Leisure section on June 5, 2005.*

POP MUSIC

1979

The year punk died, and was reborn.

SASHA FRERE-JONES

Opening: Describes situation the Clash faced in 1979

In 1979, The Clash were experiencing some pressure. Whether they wanted it or not, punk rock had become their responsibility. In New York, the Ramones had come up with the musical idea of reducing rock to three chords, doubling the volume, and accelerating songs until they sounded like Morse code. In London, the Sex Pistols had turned disgust into an ideology and made punk a historical moment, inspiring teen-agers across England to start bands. But by March of 1979 the Ramones had become more interested in being themselves than in changing the world, the Sex Pistols had disbanded, and The Clash, feeling burned out, had fired the manager who helped put the band together, in 1976. Yet they still owed CBS a record.

¶2: looks at first two albums

The Clash were able to fit more music and faith through the keyhole of punk than anyone else. Their début album, "The Clash," was a brick in flight, fourteen songs, half of them under two minutes long. The lyrics talk about the riots the band members want to start, the American imperialism they want to stop, and England's general lack of "career opportunities." It is an act of political resistance and pure pleasure. Their second album, "Give 'Em Enough Rope," was criticized for having an allegedly American sheen, but you'd have trouble hearing that now. The music is hard and echoey, barking but sweetly melodic. Actually, no—the hierarchy is more specific than that. Someone is singing sweetly way in the back, behind the loud guitars, and there's a very loud singer in the front who sounds like he's going to die if he doesn't get to sing *right now*. The one in the back is Mick Jones, the guitarist, who wrote most of The Clash's music, and the one in the front is Joe Strummer, who wrote and sang most of the lyrics, if singing is the right word. Strummer delivered words as if there were no such things as amplification and he would have been willing to run around town singing through a tube if he had to.

Strummer's moral authority, coupled with Jones's ability to synthesize decades of rock music without seeming too clever, made people care about The Clash, personally, intensely, and totally. When the band, not yet a year old, signed with CBS in 1977, the London fanzine writer Mark Perry said, "Punk died the day The Clash signed to CBS." Perry was only taking the band as seriously as they took themselves. Strummer, especially, believed that punk should be available to all, and felt inherently hostile to authority. Paradoxically, it was the corporate paymaster CBS that eventually ran ads for The Clash with the tagline "The only band that matters." In March of 1979, everyone, including The Clash, knew that the hype might be more than hype. But how could a rock band possibly live up to those expectations?

By releasing "London Calling," sixty-five minutes of rock music that never goes wrong. Without self-importance, the music covers huge amounts of ground. The stories hang together with the weight of command-

ments and the serendipitous grace of a pile of empty bottles. Montgomery Clift becomes a folk hero ("The Right Profile"), the myth of Stagger Lee is resurrected for a new audience ("Wrong 'Em, Boyo"), and London burns. Nothing sounds forced or insincere, not the breezy cover of an obscure English rockabilly song ("Brand New Cadillac") or fantasies of being a Jamaican bad boy ("Revolution Rock"). Hyperbole itself cannot diminish this record. Each of us is invincible when it's playing.

Now reissued in a new boxed set, "London Calling" comes with a bonus CD of rehearsals and a DVD documentary about the making of the album and original promo clips. This generosity would have pleased Strummer, who died in 2002, but he likely would have been less thrilled that the set lists for $29.98. When the album was originally released, as a two-LP set, the band felt that their records had to be priced for punks and insisted that CBS sell it for $9.98.

The documentary and the rough rehearsal demos make the same point: The Clash worked fiendishly hard to be magical. In an on-camera interview, Strummer says, "For some reason, we weren't night-clubbing people. All I can remember is writing and rehearsing and recording. A real intensity of effort." The rehearsals are evidence that the songs on "London Calling" were almost entirely worked out before the record's producer, Guy Stevens, was even hired. The only remaining task was to record the music.

¶3: Describes the Clash's position in music world

¶3: Poses key question review seeks to answer

¶4: Gives answer

¶4: Provides examples as evidence

¶4: Restates answer

¶5: Describes the reissue of "London Calling"

¶6: Explains how the Clash worked

How Stevens, who died of an overdose of an anti-alcohol medication two years later, helped do this is unclear; thanks to this DVD, history will remember him as the guy who threw chairs and swung ladders about while The Clash recorded.

On "London Calling," Strummer remakes his major points: the police are on the wrong side, wage labor will crush your soul, and sometimes people need to destroy property to be heard. His sense of righteousness is enhanced by the album's sequencing, which feels Biblically logical and begins with one of the best opening songs of any record ever, the title track. The song starts cold. Two guitar chords ring on the downbeats, locked in step with the drums, marching forward with no dynamic variation. A second guitar introduces difference, coming toward us like an ambulance Dopplering into range. The bass guitar, sounding like someone's voice, heralds everybody over the hill and into the song. If you can listen to it without getting a chilly burst of immortality, there is a layer between you and the world. Joe Strummer simultaneously watches the riots and sloughs off his role as de-facto punk president: "London calling, now don't look to us / All that phony Beatle-mania has bitten the dust / London calling, see we ain't got no swing / 'Cept for the ring of that truncheon thing." The chorus forms a keystone for the whole album: "A nuclear error, but I have no fear / London is drowning and I, I live by the river." The Clash are laughing at Margaret Thatcher and will be dancing long after the police have come and gone.

And what can you call this generous mountain of music, this sound that levitates around its own grievances like a plane on fire? Is it chopped-up rock? Very loud reggae? Some kind of devotional punk? The sensation of hearing several kinds of music at once runs through the album. Reggae is a force that permeates much of it, both as a source of topical songwriting and as a sound, but nothing on the album is strictly reggae. A song like the massive "Clampdown" shifts naturally through three sections: the four huge, descending chords big enough to open a season at Bayreuth; the dancing, pendulous rock of the verses; and the taunting funk of the bridge. The song fades away in a vamp that sounds like disco, so light you might get the impression the band had forgotten everything they'd just sung about: institutional racism, political brainwashing, and the creeping compromise of working life. "You start wearing the blue and brown / You're working for the clampdown / So you got someone to boss around / It makes you feel big now." The hectoring is never so simple that you don't wonder if they're directing it partly at themselves.

The album's soul might be found in "The Guns of Brixton," by the group's bassist, Paul Simonon. It's reggae thickened up and filtered by musicians who don't exactly know how to play reggae but love it completely. Their heavy hands make it something new. Simonon is a croaky and

¶7: Uses first track "London Calling" to describe the album's main theme

¶8: Poses question about the music

¶8: Gives answer

¶8: Provides example

¶8: Notice attention to music and lyrics

¶9: Another key example of music and lyrics

Ending: Final evaluation and the Clash's legacy

untrained singer, and this only enhances his convictions: "When they kick at your front door / How you gonna come? / With your hands on your head / Or on the trigger of your gun?" Threatening your rivals and writing scatological lyrics is one way to be "controversial." Staring down the riot police is another.

If Strummer's instincts were not his alone, then somewhere right now a kid is throwing a fancy, overpriced package of twenty-five-year-old material across the room and pledging to reinvent punk rock once and for all, doubting her heroes while carrying their astonishing music in her whole body.

JON PARELES

The Case Against Coldplay

The grandiose, calculated self-pity of the decade's most insufferable band.

THERE'S nothing wrong with self-pity. As a spur to songwriting, it's right up there with lust, anger and greed, and probably better than the remaining deadly sins. There's nothing wrong, either, with striving for musical grandeur, using every bit of skill and studio illusion to create a sound large enough to get lost in. Male sensitivity, a quality that's under siege in a pop culture full of unrepentant bullying and machismo, shouldn't be dismissed out of hand, no matter how risible it can be in practice. And building a sound on the lessons of past bands is virtually unavoidable.

But put them all together and they add up to Coldplay, the most insufferable band of the decade.

This week Coldplay releases its painstakingly recorded third album, "X&Y" (Capitol), a virtually surefire blockbuster that has corporate fortunes riding on it. (The stock price plunged for EMI Group, Capitol's parent company, when Coldplay announced that the album's release date would be moved from February to June, as it continued to rework the songs.)

"X&Y" is the work of a band that's acutely conscious of the worldwide popularity it cemented with its 2002 album, "A Rush of Blood to the Head," which has sold three million copies in the United States alone. Along with its 2000 debut album, "Parachutes," Coldplay claims sales of 20 million albums worldwide. "X&Y" makes no secret of grand ambition.

Clearly, Coldplay is beloved: by moony high school girls and their solace-seeking parents, by hip-hop producers who sample its rich instrumental sounds and by emo rockers who admire Chris Martin's heart-on-sleeve lyrics. The band emanates good intentions, from Mr. Martin's political statements to lyrics insisting on its own benevolence. Coldplay is admired by everyone—everyone except me.

It's not for lack of skill. The band proffers melodies as imposing as Romanesque architecture, solid and symmetrical. Mr. Martin on keyboards, Jonny Buckland on guitar, Guy Berryman on bass and Will Champion on drums have mastered all the mechanics of pop songwriting, from the instrumental hook that announces nearly every song they've recorded to the reassurance of a chorus to the revitalizing contrast of a bridge. Their arrangements ascend and surge, measuring out the song's yearning and tension, cresting and easing back and then moving toward a chiming resolution. Coldplay is meticulously unified, and its songs have been rigorously cleared of anything that distracts from the musical drama.

Unfortunately, all that sonic splendor orchestrates Mr. Martin's voice and lyrics. He places his melodies near the top of his range to sound more fragile, so the tunes straddle the break between his radiant tenor voice and his falsetto. As he hops between them—in what may be Coldplay's most annoying tic—he makes a sound somewhere between a yodel and a hiccup. And the lyrics can make me wish I didn't understand English. Coldplay's countless fans seem to take comfort when Mr. Martin sings lines like, "Is there anybody out there who / is lost and hurt and lonely too," while a strummed acoustic guitar telegraphs his aching sincerity. Me, I hear a passive-aggressive blowhard, immoderately proud as he flaunts humility. "I feel low," he announces in the chorus of "Low," belied by the peak of a crescendo that couldn't be more triumphant about it.

In its early days, Coldplay could easily be summed up as Radiohead minus Radiohead's beat, dissonance or arty subterfuge. Both bands looked to the overarching melodies of 1970's British rock and to the guitar dynamics of U2, and Mr. Martin had clearly heard both Bono's delivery and the way Radiohead's Thom Yorke stretched his voice to the creaking point.

Unlike Radiohead, though, Coldplay had no interest in being oblique or barbed. From the beginning, Coldplay's songs topped majesty with moping. "We're sinking like stones," Mr. Martin proclaimed. Hardly alone among British rock bands as the 1990's ended, Coldplay could have been singing not only about private sorrows but also about the final sunset on the British empire: the old opulence meeting newly shrunken horizons. Coldplay's songs wallowed happily in their unhappiness.

"Am I a part of the cure / Or am I part of the disease," Mr. Martin pondered in "Clocks" on "A Rush of Blood to the Head." Actually, he's contagious. Particularly in its native England, Coldplay has spawned a generation of one-word bands—Athlete, Embrace, Keane, Starsailor, Travis and Aqualung among them—that are more than eager to follow through on Coldplay's tremulous, ringing anthems of insecurity. The emulation is spreading overseas to bands like the Perishers from Sweden and the American band Blue Merle, which tries to be Coldplay unplugged.

A band shouldn't necessarily be blamed for its imitators—ask the Cure or the Grateful Dead. But Coldplay follow-throughs are redundant; from the beginning, Coldplay has verged on self-parody. When he moans his verses, Mr. Martin can sound so sorry for himself that there's hardly room to sympathize for him, and when he's not mixing metaphors, he fearlessly slings clichés. "Are you lost or incomplete," Mr. Martin sings in "Talk," which won't be cited in any rhyming dictionaries. "Do you feel like a puzzle / you can't find your missing piece."

Coldplay reached its musical zenith with the widely sampled piano arpeggios that open "Clocks": a passage that rings gladly and, as it descends the scale and switches from major to minor chords, turns incipiently mournful. Of course, it's followed by plaints: "Tides that I tried to swim against / Brought me down upon my knees."

On "X&Y," Coldplay strives to carry the beauty of "Clocks" across an entire album—not least in its first single, "Speed of Sound," which isn't the only song on the album to borrow the "Clocks" drumbeat. The album is faultless to a fault, with instrumental tracks purged of any glimmer of human frailty. There is not an unconsidered or misplaced note on "X&Y," and every song (except the obligatory acoustic "hidden track" at the end, which is still by no means casual) takes place on a monumental soundstage.

As Coldplay's recording budgets have grown, so have its reverberation times. On "X&Y" it plays as if it can already hear the songs echoing across the world. "Square One," which opens the album, actually begins with guitar notes hinting at the cosmic fanfare of "Also Sprach Zarathustra" (and "2001: A Space Odyssey"). Then Mr. Martin, never someone to evade the obvious, sings about "the space in which we're traveling."

As a blockbuster band, Coldplay is now looking over its shoulder at titanic predecessors like U2, Pink Floyd and the Beatles, pilfering freely from all of them. It also looks to an older legacy; in many songs, organ chords resonate in the spaces around Mr. Martin's voice, insisting on churchly reverence.

As Coldplay's music has grown more colossal, its lyrics have quietly made a shift on "X&Y." On previous albums, Mr. Martin sang mostly in the first person, confessing to private vulnerabilities. This time, he sings a lot about "you": a lover, a brother, a random acquaintance. He has a lot of pronouncements and advice for all of them: "You just want somebody listening to what you say," and "Every step that you take could be your biggest mistake," and "Maybe you'll get what you wanted, maybe you'll stumble upon it" and "You don't have to be alone." It's supposed to be compassionate, empathetic, magnanimous, inspirational. But when the music swells up once more with tremolo guitars and chiming keyboards, and Mr. Martin's voice breaks for the umpteenth time, it sounds like hokum to me.

Analysis: Good and Bad Reviews

Reading these two reviews together offers an opportunity to think about the criteria music critics like Sasha Frere-Jones and Jon Pareles use to review recent and reissued CDs. Both critics look at the CD under review in the context of the band's earlier work. Both draw comparisons to other rock groups. And both look in some detail at one or more of the tracks, paying attention to both the music and the lyrics. But not much could be further apart than Frere-Jones's evaluation of the Clash's *London Calling* as "sixty-five minutes of music that never goes wrong" and Pareles's disdain for Coldplay as "the most insufferable band of the decade." Behind these judgments are beliefs about what rock and roll should be, what it should stand for, and how it should sound. These enabling assumptions are never quite articulated in the reviews, but nonetheless guide the critics and provide the unstated grounds to engage their readers.

■ FOR CRITICAL INQUIRY

1. Sasha Frere-Jones opens by locating the Clash in 1979, when they were about to record *London Calling*. In part, the band owed CBS a record, but for Frere-Jones, there is more involved. What is at stake for the Clash? How does this opening set the tone for the rest of the review?

2. Jon Pareles opens by saying "There's nothing wrong with self-pity." How does this concession set him up to make the rather devastating judgment in the second paragraph?

3. Identify moments where Frere-Jones praises *London Calling* and Pareles condemns *X&Y*. Pay particular attention to the language each uses, making a list of key phrases. Consider what these phrases reveal about each critic's criteria of judgment.

AFTER 20 YEARS, IT STILL COMES OUT SWINGING

STEPHEN HOLDEN

Stephen Holden is a film and music critic for the New York Times. *His review of* Raging Bull *appeared in August 2000, when a new 35-millimeter print was released to mark the twentieth anniversary of the film. Starring Robert De Niro in an Academy Award–winning performance as the boxer Jake La Motta and directed by Martin Scorsese,* Raging Bull *was a critical success when it first came out in 1980. As you read, notice that Holden's review amounts to a critical reassessment of* Raging Bull *to put the film in perspective and to see how it holds up to viewing twenty years later.*

STEPHEN HOLDEN

After 20 Years, It Still Comes Out Swinging

Raging Bull is not simply the greatest boxing movie ever made; Martin Scorsese's 1980 masterpiece is arguably the finest American film released in a decade when Hollywood retreated from the tragic realist vision of American life enshrined in Francis Ford Coppola's first two *Godfather* films.

It may also have been the last movie to embody an ascendant cinematic vision that stretched neo-realist aesthetics to fit epic Hollywood ambitions. If *Raging Bull* is much closer in look and spirit to Rossellini than Mr. Coppola's films are, it is also an extremely self-conscious masterwork that forces us to feel the metaphorical weight of every bead of sweat, hallway shadow and camera angle.

On one level, the black-and-white film (augmented with a short-grainy color home movie sequence), which Film Forum is showing to celebrate the picture's 20th anniversary, is a grim, realistic biography of the boxing legend Jake La Motta. But the 1940's middleweight champion who is its real-life antihero is also emblematic of larger forces. He is the ultimate screen embodiment of raw Italian-American machismo at a certain moment in the ever-shifting melting pot of New York City. Blindly fighting his way to the top, then falling and stumbling into a shabby middle age, undone by the same forces by which he rose, he is a potent tribal symbol who ultimately embarrasses his tribe.

The wonder of Mr. Scorsese's vision and of Robert De Niro's Academy Award–winning portrayal of Jake is that we feel any compassion for this flailing, instinctual beast who abuses his wife and, in a fit of paranoia, beats up his brother. Yet by the end of the movie, when Jake is a bloated, chest-puffing stand-up comic pathetically mouthing off in a dive for a few extra dollars, the character has achieved a certain embattled nobility. Encased in rolls of flesh (Mr. De Niro put on 50 pounds to play the older Jake) and flashing an ugly, porcine grin, he is still lunging and punching at life as aggressively (and as blindly) as ever.

Raging Bull, like no movie before, personalizes the *Godfather* films' Darwinian vision of an immigrant urban culture muscling its way up the lower rungs of the social ladder. But where Mr. Coppola celebrated a shadow aristocracy with its own grand, quasi-royal pecking order, rituals and traditions, Mr. Scorsese imagined a world unencumbered by majesty. Even the Copacabana, the legendary

Manhattan nightclub, is remembered as a boisterous roughneck dive peopled with fight promoters and Mafiosi dolled up in their Saturday night best. Few movies have so indelibly captured the gritty squall of New York's mean streets in the 1940's and 50's, a world of streetwise men in sweat-stained undershirts in unair-conditioned tenements.

The boxing sequences, with their gorgeous images of sweat and blood flying from smashed heads and the thuds of body blows (made by squashing melons and tomatoes) echoing in a concentrated silence, are among the most visceral fight scenes ever filmed. They are matched in intensity by an unforgettable scene in which Jake, finally forced into a corner, turns on himself as he would on an opponent. Dragged into a prison cell after being convicted of selling alcohol to minors in his nightclub, he violently butts his head against the wall and howls and screams in pain and frustration.

Raging Bull brought Joe Pesci to the screen in what remains his greatest role as Jake's devoted, protective brother, who nurtures the fighter until Jake turns on him. As Jake's teenage wife, Vickie, who stoically endures his pathologically jealous tirades and brutal manhandling until the lid blows off, Cathy Moriarty is the essence of sullen, smoldering sexuality. Think of Lana Turner in *The Postman Always Rings Twice*, stripped of genteel Hollywood airs and with a tough New York accent.

Raging Bull is showing in a glistening new 35-millimeter print. It should be seen in a theater. It's one American classic without a misstep.

Analysis: Creating a Classic

The main point of Stephen Holden's review of *Raging Bull* comes out clearly enough in the title "After 20 Years, It Still Comes Out Swinging." Notice how the words in the title alert readers to two key aspects of the review. First, they tell us we are revisiting a highly acclaimed film twenty years after it initially secured its critical reputation, and second, the title lets us know the reviewer thinks the film holds up to scrutiny. If anything, the passage of time, Holden suggests, has clarified the achievement of the film. In retrospect, he claims in the opening paragraph, we can see that *Raging Bull* is not only the "greatest boxing movie ever made" but also "arguably the finest American film" released in the 1980s.

From the first paragraph, where Holden describes *Raging Bull* as "Martin Scorsese's 1980 masterpiece," to the final paragraph, where he calls the film "one American classic without a misstep," he is lavish in his praise. In many respects, Holden seems to assume that his readers already know the film and will readily accept his characterization of it as a "masterwork." The real issue in the review concerns why the film is a classic— the reasons and evidence Holden presents to support and explain his evaluation. Notice in particular how Holden discusses *Raging Bull* in relation to the first two *Godfather* films as a way of explaining what is distinctive about it. In a larger sense, the review raises the question about what we mean when we call a film (or a song, TV show, live performance, play, or novel) a "classic." What exactly is invested in the term *classic* that gives a work such a special standing?

■ FOR CRITICAL INQUIRY

1. Notice that Holden's purposes in this review go beyond simply offering an evaluation of a film. He is also ranking the film in a larger sense, as an "American classic" and "arguably the finest American film" of the 1980s. What does it mean to call something a "classic"? How does the term distinguish a work?

2. How does Holden go about justifying his claim that *Raging Bull* is a "classic"? What do his criteria of evaluation seem to be? What reasons does he offer to support his evaluation?

3. In paragraphs 1 and 2 and again in paragraph 5, Holden compares *Raging Bull* to the first two *Godfather* films. What does this comparison and contrast accomplish in the review? What does it enable Holden to highlight that might not be so clear otherwise?

4. In the third paragraph, Holden looks at the film on two levels—as a "grim, realistic biography" and as "emblematic of larger forces." What are these "larger forces"? How are they connected to the realistic details of biography in the film? What do these two levels enable readers to see about the film?

ETHICS OF WRITING

REVIEWING AS A PARTISAN ACTIVITY

Reviewers are by no means neutral observers. On the contrary, they are in the business of being partisan. After all, even the more quantitative and objective reviews, such as the product ratings in *Consumer Reports*, require that criteria for evaluation be chosen and weighted.

Reviewers have a responsibility to their readers because something of consequence is at stake: a consumer wants to spend money on the best available product; an employer wants to know which workers to promote; a business or government agency needs to know what changes in the system are needed.

For precisely this reason, reviewers have a responsibility to those whose products and performances are being reviewed. Even if unfair, negative reviews can kill a play or cost an employee his or her job.

As you begin considering what kind of review you might write, these issues of partisanship and responsibility will inevitably arise. On whose behalf will you be writing? What are the potential consequences of the evaluations you will make? What responsibilities does this bring to you as a reviewer? ■

GRAND THEFT AUTO: SAN ANDREAS

SCOTT JONES

Scott Jones is a reviewer for GameCritics.Com, where this review appeared at www.gamecritics.com/review/gtasa/main.php.

> Grand Theft Auto: San Andreas
> Platform: PS2
> Developer: Rockstar North (DMA Design)
> Publisher: Rockstar
>
> Review By Scott Jones
> Consumer Advice
> ESRB Rating: Mature (17+) Strong Language, Severe Violence,
>   Blood and Gore

1   It's without a doubt the most clichéd of all hardboiled crime story clichés: the low down, dirty double-cross. The two previous games in the Grand Theft Auto series each began with a double-cross—my girlfriend referring to me as "small time," then shooting me during a bank heist in GTA III; Tommy Vercetti taking the blame for a bad drug deal in Vice City. San Andreas, the third game since the series went 3D (and launched the GTA-ification of the industry, for better or worse), doesn't open with a double-cross, but starts in a darker, more mature place: with the death of the protagonist's mother.

There's even a funeral scene, complete with some nasty bickering among the surviving family members.

2   That funeral scene, along with a touching moment when a grieving son walks into his now empty childhood home and looks at his dead mother's photograph, are surprisingly emotional moments, moments that had me checking the disc to make sure that I'd loaded up the right game. Has GTA gone all Dr. Phil on me? I wondered. Both scenes are landmark moments for the series because they're indicative of a subtle, yet all-important content shift away from the caricature and cartoonish-ness that plagued the previous games. Indeed, San Andreas has something that GTA III and Vice City sorely lacked: a touch of emotional gravitas. There's less satire here, more heart. While the game still revels in thrill-kill missions and its trademark Mad magazine aesthetic—one of the betting parlor ponies is named Air Biscuit (oh, what a knee-slapper!)—I'm happy to report that there's evidence in San Andreas that the GTA series is finally starting to grow up.

3   Carl Johnson, a.k.a. C.J., returns to his hometown "hood" of San Andreas (a fictional early '90s hybrid of L.A., San Francisco, and Las Vegas) to bury his dead mother and quickly finds himself involved in a burgeoning neighborhood gang war. It's the usual GTA Horatio Alger-style set-up: C.J., like his predecessors in GTA III and Vice City, is a nobody who wants to be a somebody—only this time around the star of the game isn't a mobbed-up white guy, but a West Coast "homie," more accustomed to drive-bys than whackings.

4   Playing as C.J., I started the game penniless, living in my mother's house, sleeping in my childhood bedroom. In this rags-to-riches narrative, I found myself literally in rags, unable to even shop at Binco, the crummy discount clothing store down the street. Earning money in the early stages of the game is surprisingly difficult, thanks to the fact that the first missions rewarded me not with cash but with "Respect" (more on this later). I drove taxicabs and ambulances, and even worked as a bike messenger just to put a few dollars in my bank account. Haircuts, tattoos, sneakers—no matter what I wanted or needed, San Andreas made me hustle for it.

5   Of course, this being a Grand Theft Auto game, instead of driving a cab I could have simply mowed down hundreds of pedestrians, then collected the little bundles of cash that hovered eerily above their corpses (and risked peeving the cops, who are much more tenacious in San Andreas than they were in Vice City). But I've never approached the GTA games in this fashion; only a sociopath would. I learned long ago that I get more—much more—by

respecting the game world, by treating the city like I would a real city. I try to drive carefully, taking pride in my ability to avoid getting into accidents. I dislike running over people (though it's inevitable at times). Depending on my mood, I might even stop at a traffic light and fiddle around with the radio, looking for a good song.

6   I started the game the same way I started the previous GTA games: hopelessly lost. San Andreas is easily the largest, most detailed, and most confusing GTA landscape yet. But after spending countless hours meticulously exploring the city (and countryside) block by block and acre by acre, I began recognizing familiar landmarks. After about a week, a change had come over me; I suddenly knew every back-alley, every shortcut, every nuance of the game world. I wasn't lost anymore. What was once overwhelmingly confusing now made perfect sense to me. That transition from being hopelessly lost to knowing where I was at all times is probably the most gratifying aspect of any Grand Theft Auto game for me. On a more abstract level, it's a real-time transformation from "foreigner" to "resident," an experience that only a GTA game can give me.

7   Unfortunately, the missions are still my least favorite part of the game. They're basically of the drive-someplace/shoot-something/drive-someplace-else variety, and after most of them, when the words "Mission Passed" appeared on screen, I usually felt only a sense of relief that I didn't have to ever do them again. The true allure of a GTA game, in my opinion, can be found between the missions. Routines develop naturally in San Andreas. Here's a typical San Andreas day for me: go to the gym, pick up cash from one of my assets, stop by the Inside Track Betting parlor to gamble, take my girlfriend out dancing, get something to eat at a restaurant, stock up on bullets at Ammu-Nation, drive to my usual secret spot for body armor (because I'm too cheap to spend $200 for armor at Ammu-Nation), sign up for one of the low-rider races, defend my territory from a take-over attempt from a rival gang, etc. Rhythms and habits get established in the game—rhythms and habits that have very little to do with furthering the core narrative, and everything to do with simply reveling in the verisimilitude of the game world. Indeed, all of these day-to-day activities, when taken together, add up to a kind of virtual lifestyle.

8   San Andreas has made one revolutionary advancement in the gameplay department: it's now a full-blown role-playing game (RPG). I can customize C.J. to my liking, buying clothes, hats and sneakers for him. I can get him tattooed, and even give him cornrows or a goatee. If I eat too many fast food meals and don't hit the gym often enough, C.J. will visibly

gain weight. My "progress" is tracked via a series of meters; "experience" is gained simply by doing things. Driving skills, for example, are improved by spending more time wheeling around the city. If I used the shotgun for the duration of a few fire fights, my skills with the shotgun were automatically upgraded. And Respect is earned by conquering territories occupied by rival gangs. Sure, it's a relatively crude system by traditional RPG standards, but it's a step in the right direction for the series. Not only does it make me feel like the story being told is my story, but the RPG dynamic also impacts gameplay in an interesting fashion. If I was having trouble with a particular mission, I simply spent time improving whatever skills were relevant to that mission (driving, shooting, etc.), then took another crack at it.

9   When Vice City was released two years ago, I stood in line at my local EBGames anxious to get my hands on the game. I certainly didn't feel that same level of excitement for San Andreas. (I pre-ordered, but actually forgot to pick it up on release day.) Maybe I was still a little burned out from my marathon nights with Vice City. Or maybe it was the fact that the San Andreas previews didn't impress me much; it looked like more of the same, nothing more than a West Coast version of Vice City. But after spending only an hour or two with the game, San Andreas managed to pull me in into its orbit and has held me there for a couple of weeks now. This is arguably the most important videogame this year—yes, even more important than Halo 2—not only because it's a superbly crafted videogame, but because it's also a bona fide sociological artifact, one that manages to effectively evoke a specific time and place in American history—in this case, a hot and hazy California during the nascent days of hip-hop culture. San Andreas is also one of the few videogames to boldly feature an African-American as a hero (or, more appropriately, an anti-hero). Beyond that, the GTA series continues to function as a gathering place for A-list artists, writers, musicians, and actors. Only a GTA game can bring together Samuel L. Jackson, Peter Fonda, and Chris Penn; only a GTA game would dare to mix Dr. Dre, Kiss, and Merle Haggard on the same soundtrack. Indeed, this is more than a videogame; this is a great confluence of mediums and talents, a veritable pop culture divining rod that makes me imagine a future where GTA-caliber games are commonplace, where videogames are no longer marginalized, but like film and television, have become the medium of choice. And for this glimpse of the future, we should all be grateful.

RATING: 9.5
Published: December 1, 2004

Analysis: A Gamer's Review

At its Web site, GamesCritic.Com describes itself as "an independently owned videogame webzine," dedicated to the following principles: (1) providing "consumers with insightful, useful, and entertaining content on videogames"; (2) presenting "a diverse range of perspectives and opinions from writers of different backgrounds": and (3) redefining "the grammar of game criticism and mainstream perception of videogames." We learn further that Scott Jones "spends his days working as an editor at a men's sophisticate magazine and his nights playing games." Notice in his review, how Jones combines an understanding of "hard-boiled crime story clichés" in the opening paragraph and cultural commentary about how *Grand Theft Auto: San Andreas* evokes "a hot and hazy California during the nascent days of hip-hop culture" in the last paragraph, with an experienced gamer's evaluation of play in between.

■ FOR CRITICAL INQUIRY

1. Consider the organization of this review. As just noted, the opening and ending paragraphs put *Grand Theft Auto: San Andreas* in a broad perspective, while the paragraphs in the main body explain Jones's experience playing the game. How do these parts go together?

2. What do Jones's criteria for evaluating video games seem to be? Does he make these criteria explicit? Does it seem reasonable that the criteria would be widely shared by gamers? What about people who don't play video games?

3. How does Jones's review compare to the CD reviews by Sasha Frere-Jones and Jon Pareles? Are they asking the same questions or different ones?

WRITING IN A DIGITAL WORLD

Monitoring the Media

GRAND THEFT AUTO: SAN ANDREAS

COMMON SENSE MEDIA

Common Sense Media is a nonprofit organization that reviews the media, including TV shows, movies, video games, books, and music. Its goal is to provide families with "trustworthy information to manage their kids' media lives." You can find the complete review of Grand Theft Auto: San Andreas at www.commonsensemedia.org/game-reviews/Grand-Theft-Auto-San_2.html

Analysis: The "Other Parent"

Common Sense Media believes that the media have become, in effect, "the other parent" in children's lives. Accordingly, parents need to be informed about movies, television shows, and video games in order to shape their childrens' media habits. *Grand Theft Auto: San Andreas* was a wildly successful new installment of a wildly popular video game. Given this popularity, it is not unreasonable for parents to wonder if the video game is an appropriate one for their children and, more broadly, what criteria they should use in determining what games their children play. Common Sense Media is not, of course, the only Web site reviewing video games for parents. But its concerns for "media sanity, not censorship" and its commitment to "diversity of programming and media ownership" make it an interesting one to analyze.

■ FOR CRITICAL INQUIRY

1. Consider the variety of evaluations offered by the Common Sense Media Web site. Notice the chart about Content, the Common Sense Note, and the Common Sense Review by Jeremy Gieske. What seem to be the criteria of evaluation? To what extent are the criteria presented as self evident? To what extent are they explained?

2. Visit the About Us page at the Common Sense Media Web site www. commonsensemedia.org/about_us/, where you will find the Ten Common Sense Beliefs. How are these beliefs applied in the case of *Grand Theft Auto: San Andreas*?

3. Aside from the criteria Common Sense Media uses to review *Grand Theft Auto*, are there other perspectives you might bring to bear in reviewing the video game?

4. Compare the Common Sense Media review to Scott Jones's review at Games Critic.Com. Notice the Consumer Advice box at the online review.

VISUAL DESIGN

Travel Guides

FROM SAN FRANCISCO

DK EYEWITNESS TOP 10 TRAVEL GUIDES

San Francisco *is part of a series,* DK Eyewitness Top 10 Travel Guides. *The two-page spread reproduced here appears at the beginning of the guide with the city's top ten highlights.*

Analysis: Guides and Lists

Travel guides often list the not-to-be-missed highlights of a city. That's part of the information a visitor wants from a travel guide— and one of the key ways that travel guides resemble other types of reviews. They depend on the evaluations of knowledgeable experts. DK Eyewitness Top 10 Travel Guides have taken the list of tourist attractions a step further, using it as a visual and verbal organizing scheme for the entire

TOP 10 San Francisco's Highlights

San Franciscans will, rather candidly, admit that they are the most fortunate people on earth, the occasional earthquake notwithstanding; and most visitors, after a few days of taking in the sights and sounds of this magnificent city, will agree. Ask anyone who has been here and they will tell you it's their favorite US city. The geographical setting evokes so much emotional drama, the light seems clearer, the colors more vivid, the cultural diversity of the ethnic neighborhoods so captivating and inviting, that it's a place almost everyone can fall in love with at first sight.

Golden Gate Bridge 1
The much-loved symbol of the city and of California's place on the Pacific Rim, the Golden Gate Bridge is the third-largest single span bridge in the world, connecting San Francisco to Marin County *(see pp8–9).*

2 Cable Cars
San Francisco's little troopers have endured technological progress, and are now the only system of the kind in the world that still plays a daily role in urban life *(see pp10–11).*

3 Fisherman's Wharf
Despite rampant tourism and commercialization, the saltiness and authenticity are still to be found here if you take time to look. The views of the bay are unmatched, and you'll have an opportunity to sample some great seafood *(see pp12–13).*

4 Alcatraz
Although it was a federal prison for just under 30 years, the myth of "The Rock" continues to capture the imagination of visitors. Even if exploring prison life holds no appeal, the ferry ride makes it well worth a visit *(see pp14–17).*

5 Chinatown
The exotic feel of one of the world's largest Chinese communities outside of Asia makes this a magnet for locals and visitors alike *(see pp18–19).*

6 Golden Gate Park
The city boasts one of the largest public parks in the world, with natural beauty and fine museums *(see pp20–23).*

7 Grace Cathedral
Dominating Nob Hill with its timeless beauty, San Francisco's favorite cathedral offers a host of awe-inspiring and historic treasures, including Italian Renaissance masterpieces and stained-glass windows *(see pp24–5).*

8 San Francisco Museum of Modern Art
Second only to New York City's Museum of Modern Art, San Francisco's newest architectural landmark houses 20th-century masterworks of painting, sculpture, and photography, and the edgiest digital installations *(see pp26–9).*

9 Mission Dolores
The city's oldest building is also the only intact chapel among the 21 California missions that Father Junipero Serra founded in the late 18th century. Its founding just days before the Declaration of Independence makes San Francisco older than the US *(see pp30–31).*

10 The Wine Country
So internationally recognized have the wines from this region become that French, Italian, and Spanish winemakers have all established vineyards here. A day trip or a longer stay shouldn't be missed *(see pp32–5).*

guide. As you can see here, the guide uses the convention of the top ten list to map San Francisco's highlights for visitors. In fact, in subsequent pages, each of the ten highlights appears in a two-page spread with its own top ten features displayed. Likewise, the sections on restaurants, hotels, bars and clubs, beaches, shopping, and so on are all organized as top ten lists. The consistent appearance of this top ten device gives the travel guide a unified and authoritative look, marking it as well designed and trustworthy.

■ FOR CRITICAL INQUIRY

1. Consider the information this two-page spread makes available. Take into account the overall layout and the integration of text and graphics.

2. Design a similar presentation of top ten highlights for your college or university, neighborhood, town or city, local region, or state—any identifiable geographical unit will work. This can be a simple sketch or a more elaborate production. Take into account who will use your guide.

3. Top ten lists are a familiar feature of the cultural landscape, whether the ten best movies of the year, the ten greatest quarterbacks of all time, or the ten worst political blunders in U.S. history. Typically such lists have brief explanations following each entry. Consider your own interests and knowledge. Make a top ten list for one area of interest with your explanations. Then consider how you might design the list into a two-page spread using visuals as well as text.

FURTHER EXPLORATION: REVIEWS

■ GENRE CHOICES

There are a number of Web sites devoted to Martin Scorsese, including an "unofficial fan site" at http://www.scorsesefilms.com and a "God Among Directors" site http://www.godamongdirectors.com/scorsese/index/shtml. Visit these sites to see how the people present Scorsese and his films on the Web. Notice in particular what's written about *Raging Bull*. Compare this to Stephen Holden's treatment in his review of *Raging Bull*. What do you see as the main differences and similarities between the Web sites and the *New York Times* review? How would you describe the call to write in these cases? How is a Web site or review an appropriate response to the call?

■ WORKING TOGETHER

Course Review

Work together as a class to review your writing course. The review will require planning questions and methods, conducting research, compiling and analyzing the information obtained, and finally, evaluating the course based on that information. Here is a basic procedure, which you may want to modify, depending on the size of your class and the scope of your review:

■ Working together in groups of five or six, think about criteria for evaluating the course. What is important in a writing course: interesting readings, lively discussions, group activities, engaging and varied writing assignments, the teacher's presentations and instructions, classroom atmosphere? What about the results: improvement in writing, preparation for writing in other classes or at work, changed attitudes toward writing and a greater understanding of its usefulness? These are, of course, only some criteria you might use.

■ Make a list of specific questions that would give you information related to the criteria you're using. Once you have a list, decide which questions seem the most important and useful. Compile a final list of questions, and make enough copies of the list for everyone in class. Have each group present its questions. As a class, synthesize the questions into a master list.

■ With your questions in mind, decide how you will get answers—what forms of research you want to use. You could, for example, use surveys, written evaluations, interviews, or discussion groups. Decide which methods would be practical as well as most useful for getting the information you need.

■ Conduct the research and compile the results. How you compile results will, of course, depend on the method of gathering information you used. For example, survey responses can be tallied, whereas interviews would have to be analyzed.

■ The two final steps are to analyze and interpret the results of your research and to prepare a final evaluation based on this analysis. You can begin by having the groups that conducted the research report to the class. A group can be given the responsibility of writing the review, or different groups can write sections, but the entire class should read and approve the final course review.

WRITING ASSIGNMENT

Writing a Review

Online Study Center

For this assignment, write a review. Pick something to review that you know well or that you find interesting and would like to learn more about. You will write this review for a particular group of readers, so you might target a particular publication, such as a student or local newspaper or one of the national magazines you are familiar with. This will help you anticipate what your readers already know, what they value, and what criteria they accept as a basis of evaluation.

The subject of your review can be drawn from many spheres of life. Here are some common types of reviews:

■ **Live performances:** Attend a musical concert, a play, or a club with live music and write a review of the performance.

■ **Media:** Television programs, radio shows, movies, and musical recordings are all possible subjects for reviews.

■ **The Web:** As the Internet grows more crowded, people can use help finding which sites are worth visiting and which are not. Gather an assortment of related Web sites and write a comparative review of them. Or just focus on one site and review it in depth.

- **Exhibitions:** Local museums, on and off campus, may be featuring special art, historical, or scientific exhibitions that you could review.

- **Books:** You could review a best-seller, a recent book in an academic field that interests you, a controversial book, a book that is particularly popular with college students, or an older book that invites a revisit.

- **Sports:** Write a preview of an upcoming season of a college or professional sport, or make a prediction about an important game.

- **Leisure and entertainment:** Write a restaurant review, a guide to entertainment on campus, or an evaluation of backpacking routes you have taken. Visit historical places, local parks, or parts of a city, and write an evaluation of what they have to offer.

- **Education:** Write a review of a course you have taken, a textbook, or a program you have been involved in (such as an orientation for first-year students or a summer program).

- **Letters of recommendation:** You may be in a position to write a letter of recommendation for somebody you know. Such letters, in fact, are reviews of the person you are recommending (they are, by nature, generally positive). If you have a friend applying to college or for a position such as orientation leader, peer counselor, or resident assistant that requires recommendations, you can consider the writing you do for that person for this assignment. Likewise, if you have worked with somebody who is searching for a job, consider writing that person a recommendation that he or she can take to interviews.

- **Politics and the public sphere:** Write a review of the Bush presidency, a particular elected official, a candidate for office, a proposed law, an ongoing program, or a controversial event.

- **Rating systems:** Design a rating system for reviewing consumer products, musical recordings, movies, restaurants, or some other product or service.

- **Greatest or best lists:** You could list the top ten (or twenty-five or hundred) rap songs, punk bands, teenage movies, game shows, actresses, hockey players, or presidents and explain your criteria of evaluation. Some lists focus on the best of the year, while others identify the all-time greatest.

- **Paired reviews:** Work with a partner to write paired reviews that offer differing judgments about a CD, movie, upcoming sports event, or who is going to win an Academy Award.

Alternative Assignments

■ RHETORICAL ANALYSIS

Pick one or two of the reviews in this chapter. Identify the main criteria of evaluation. Notice that in each review's argument, the criteria of evaluation play the role of enabling assumptions. Explain how the criteria enable the reviewer to connect the evidence provided to the review's central claim. Consider how widely shared the criteria of evaluation are likely to be on the readers' part. What does the reviewer's assumption seem to be? Does the reviewer appear to assume that the criteria can be taken for granted as something most readers already believe, or do the criteria seem to require explanation and justification?

■ WORKING WITH SOURCES

Identify a book, recording, film, play, TV show, or other work that interests you and that has been reviewed widely. Find three or four reviews that bring different perspectives to bear on the work. Your task is to write a review of the reviews. To do this, you'll need to go beyond simply summarizing what each reviewer says. Explain what is at stake in how and why the reviewers hold differing and similar views. Use your own evaluation of the significance of the work to analyze what others have said.

Invention

Exploring Your Topic

To get started thinking about your topic and how you might approach it in a review, assess what you already know and what further information you need.

■ EXERCISE

Assessing What You Know

Write about your topic using the following points of departure. Write what you know, and don't worry if your response is incomplete or you have little or no information. The following questions can help you determine whether you need to do further research.

1. **Describe your subject:** Tell as much as you know about it. If it's a book or movie, identify the genre (for example, coming-of-age novel, action-adventure movie, biography, or political analysis), and write a brief summary. If you're reviewing a musical performance or recording, identify the style (for example, classical, modern jazz, urban blues, heavy metal, or country and western), the musicians and instruments, and the tunes or scores they play.

2. **State your current feelings and opinions:** Do you like or dislike what you are reviewing? Everything or just aspects? Do you think it is a good, average, mediocre, or poor example of its kind? Have you always had the same feelings and opinions, or have your views changed? Are there similar works you prefer? If so, why? Are there similar works you think are inferior to your subject? If so, why?

3. **Describe your readers:** Who is likely to be interested in your subject? Why? What values and attitudes are they likely to hold? How knowledgeable are your readers likely to be about your subject and other subjects of similar type? What kinds of judgments have they made in the past? What are they likely to think about your opinion? Do you think they will agree or disagree, be surprised, shocked, amused, or angry? At this point, you might want to look carefully at the readers who tend to read the publication to which you are hoping to submit your review. What kinds of reviews have appeared there before? What kinds of values do the readers of that publication seem to have?

Background Research: Looking at a Body of Work

A common feature of reviews is to explain how a particular book, film, or recording fits into a larger body of work ("*London Calling* is the Clash masterpiece that pulls together the range of musical sources in their earlier work") or a particular genre ("James Ellroy's *LA Confidential* belongs on the same shelf as the great *noir* novels of Dashiell Hammett, Raymond Chandler, and Jim Thompson"). Such explanations help readers see the significance of the work in question and establish the credentials of the reviewer as a knowledgeable person. Here are some questions to identify background information you can use in your review:

1. What do you know about the author of the book, the director of the film, the composer or musical leader? What other works do you know by the same person? How is this work like or different from those other works?

2. How would you describe the genre of the work? What do you know about the history of the genre? What other examples can you think of?

3. What is the critical evaluation of the writer, director, or composer? Do you know of reviews, articles, or books on your subject? Do the critics and reviewers seem to agree, or are there debates, differences, or controversies? If so, what's at stake?

Establishing Criteria of Evaluation

Criteria are the standards critics and reviewers use to justify their evaluations. They will vary, depending on what you are reviewing and who your audience is. For example, the criteria you would use to judge suitable movies for eight-year-olds will quite likely differ in at least some important respects from the criteria you would use to judge what is suitable for college students or other adults. You might recommend the Disney/Pixar collaboration *Cars* or one of the *Lion King* movies for an eight-year-old but rule out a Quentin Tarantino bloodbath like the two *Kill Bill* films.

To put it another way, one of your criteria in this example would be age appropriateness. Applying this criterion of evaluation might lead to assertions such as these:

- I think children (not to mention most adults) will enjoy *Cars* because it has great animation, memorable characters, and a reassuring lesson about the value of family and friendship.

- Quentin Tarantino may indeed put his vast knowledge of film history to good cinematic use in *Kill Bill*, but it's not a movie for children or the squeamish.

Notice in this case that the assertions are based on the same criterion, namely age appropriateness. Readers who accept this criterion are likely to agree with your assertions, or at least give them a sympathetic reading.

As a review writer, then, part of your job is to identify the criteria that make for the most appropriate and compelling review. Depending on your purpose and audience, you may not be concerned about age appropriateness. You, as the writer, need to decide which criteria will matter; you also need to identify the criteria to your readers so that they know whether or not to accept your evaluation.

■ **EXERCISE**

Identifying Criteria

To identify criteria that may help you in your evaluation, respond to the following questions.

1. What qualities do you look for in a good example of the type of item you are reviewing? List at least seven qualities. Rank them from most to least important.

2. What qualities seem to be acceptable to most people? What qualities seem to be the most attractive? Again, list as many qualities as you can, and rank them in order of importance.

3. What makes a particularly bad example? When you write this list, don't simply write the opposite of the "good" qualities listed above. Instead, think of several specific bad examples, and try to identify what made them really stand out as inferior. List these and rank them.

4. What criteria do your friends, family members, or coworkers use to form evaluative judgments? Ask others about their criteria of evaluation.

Applying Your Criteria of Evaluation

Once you have identified criteria of evaluation, the next step is to apply them to whatever you are reviewing. Keep in mind readers may accept your criteria but not how you apply them. You need to make a persuasive case by explaining how and why the criteria you're using lead to a particular evaluation.

■ **EXERCISE**

Assessing Your Criteria

1. Write down a series of assertions you want to make about what you are reviewing. Use this form of sentence: "X is significant because Y" or "What made X a great movie is Y."

2. Analyze the assertions. What criteria are you applying in each instance? Do you think readers are likely to accept these criteria as reasonable ones? Why or why not?

3. How might people apply the same criteria but come up with a different evaluation? Are there criteria of evaluation people might use that differ from those you use? How would these criteria influence a reviewer's evaluation?

Criteria of evaluation in a review can also be described as the enabling assumptions by which reviewers link their claim (the movie was good, bad, disappointing, sensationalistic, and so on) to the available evidence (the movie itself). To justify their criteria, reviewers offer backing.

Planning

Considering the Relation Between Description and Evaluation

One issue reviewers face is how much they need to describe what they are reviewing. How much detail should you give? Should you summarize the plot of the movie or book? If so, where and in what detail? How can you best combine such description with your evaluation?

Answers to these questions will depend in part on what your readers are likely to know about the topic. Their level of familiarity will shape how much you are called on to provide as background information and description.

These are very real considerations. At the same time, however, it is important to see description and evaluation not as separate writing strategies that require separate space in a review but as strategies that are related to each other.

Stephen Holden's review of *Raging Bull* offers a good example of how writers integrate description and evaluation. In the third paragraph, Holden describes *Raging Bull* as a "grim, realistic biography of the boxing legend Jake La Motta." But then, instead of giving an extended summary of the plot, Holden uses the plot to analyze the film and explain his evaluation.

Notice, for example, in the following sentence, how Holden begins with a description of *Raging Bull*'s plot,

> Blindly fighting his way to the top, then falling and stumbling into a shabby middle age,

but then shifts in the main clause to analysis and evaluation:

> undone by the same forces by which he rose, he [Jake La Motta] is a potent tribal symbol who ultimately embarrasses his tribe.

Similarly, notice how Holden combines description and evaluation, using the final scenes of the film to illustrate his assessment of Robert De Niro's performance. The "wonder" of De Niro's portrayal of Jake La Motta, Holden says, "is that we feel any compassion for this flailing, instinctual beast." In the next two sentences, Holden takes readers to the end of the film,

> Yet by the end of the movie, when Jake is a bloated, chest-puffing stand-up comic pathetically mouthing off in a dive for a few extra dollars,

to see the culmination of De Niro's performance,

> the character has achieved a certain embattled nobility.

Holden then consolidates his point with a description of De Niro's physical appearance and the sheer energy and physical force of his acting style:

> Encased in rolls of flesh (Mr. De Niro put on 50 pounds to play the older Jake) and flashing an ugly, porcine grin, he is still lunging and punching at life as aggressively (and as blindly) as ever.

Using Comparison and Contrast

Comparison and contrast are good strategies to put what you are reviewing in perspective by seeing how it stacks up to something similar. For example, comparing a record album, movie, book, or live performance to others of its kind can help readers get a handle on what you are reviewing.

Stephen Holden, for example, uses comparison and contrast to explain what *Raging Bull* and the *Godfather* films have in common and how they differ. First, Holden identifies their common ground:

> *Raging Bull*, like no movie before, personalizes the *Godfather* films' Darwinian vision of an immigrant urban culture muscling its way up the lower rungs of the social ladder.

Then he points out the main difference:

> But where Mr. Coppola celebrated a shadow aristocracy with its own grand, quasi-royal pecking order, rituals and traditions, Mr. Scorsese imagined a world unencumbered by majesty.

Working Draft

Use the writing you have already done to get started. Consider how your opening can characterize what you're reviewing and make your evaluation clear to readers. Reviewers do not necessarily point out the criteria of judgment they are using. Nonetheless, to engage your readers, you need to make sure the criteria are easy to identify, even if they are only implied. Consider, too, how you can weave description and other background information into your review. Are there comparisons and contrasts worth making?

Engaging Others

Reviews do not take place in a vacuum. In many cases, reviewers not only tell readers their evaluation of a work or performance but also locate that evaluation in relation to evaluations others have made. Doing so enables them to distinguish their views from what others have said or written and thereby clarify exactly where they are coming from and what criteria they are using.

Take, for example, the fifth paragraph of Jon Pareles's review "The Case Against Coldplay":

> Clearly Coldplay is beloved: by moony high school girls and their solace-seeking parents, by hip hop producers who sample its rich instrumental sounds and by emo rockers who admire Chris Martin's heart-on-sleeve lyrics. . . . Coldplay is admired by everyone—everyone except me.

Peer Commentary

Exchange the working draft of your review with a classmate. Respond to the following questions in writing:

1. Is the subject defined clearly? Does the review give the reader enough details and background information to understand the reviewer's evaluation?

Are there things you wanted to know that the writer left out? Are there things the writer mentions but that you would like to know more about?

2. Does the reviewer's evaluation come across clearly? As you read the draft, where did you become aware of the reviewer's evaluation? Point to the sentence or passage. Do you understand what the reviewer's criteria are? Do they need to be stated more clearly? Are they reasonable criteria? Are there other criteria you think the writer should take into account?

3. Does the review seem balanced? How does the reviewer combine description and evaluation? Does the reviewer talk about good and bad points, positive and negative aspects? Is the tone appropriate?

4. Does the reviewer use comparisons? If so, where and for what purposes?

5. What suggestions would you make to strengthen the review?

Revising

Use the peer responses to revise your working draft. Consider these issues:

1. Do you bring the work or performance into focus for your readers by using strategies such as describing it, characterizing what type or genre it is, explaining how it is similar to or differs from others of its kind, and providing adequate background information?

2. Is your evaluation clear and easy to understand, or are you hedging in one way or another?

3. Does it make sense in your review to engage what others have already written or said about the work or performance? If so, how can you distinguish your own perspective from others'?

4. Do you attend to both good and bad points, positive and negative features? Remember, being balanced does not mean being objective or neutral. To make an evaluation you have to commit yourself and explain how, given the good and the bad, you have made a judgment based on criteria.

Options for Meaningful Endings

The ending of your review should do more than just summarize what you have already said. Look at the ending as an opportunity to leave your readers with something further to think about regarding the significance of the work or performance you've reviewed.

Notice, for example, the strategy for ending that Denise Sega uses in her working draft "More Than Just Burnouts," a review of Donna Gaines's book *Teenage Wasteland* (the full text appears in Writers' Workshop, below). In this case, Denise ends her review by indicating who would be interested in the book and why.

Working Draft

In conclusion, I believe this is an important book that should be read by anyone interested in finding out more about the "gritty underside of white teen life in the suburbs" (cover notes). Compared to the sensationalistic stories in the press that blame teenage suicide on drugs or heavy metal, Donna Gaines has taken the time to listen—and to hear what the kids have to say.

The strategy Sega has chosen, of course, is not the only possible way to end her review meaningfully. Here are two other strategies reviewers commonly draw on.

1. Anticipate a possible objection.

Some readers may think that Donna Gaines identifies too much with the "burnouts"—and that her research is thereby "contaminated" by her personal allegiances. Gaines's partisanship, however, gives the book its unique authority. By gaining the trust of Bergenfield's heavy metal kids, Gaines is able to give their side of things and to show how they make sense of their world. After reading *Teenage Wasteland*, it's hard not to think these kids need an advocate who can speak on their behalf.

2. Connect to a larger context of issues.

Youth-bashing has become a popular spectator sport in recent years, and events such as the school shootings in Littleton, Colorado, and elsewhere have fueled adult fears and anxieties about teenagers. Perhaps the most important achievement of *Teenage Wasteland* is that it cuts through the moral panic and the sensationalistic stories in the press and on TV about young people. Instead, Gaines gives us an understanding of how alienated teenagers experience their lives. ■

W WRITERS' WORKSHOP

Written for a sociology course on youth culture, the following is a working draft of a review of Donna Gaines's book *Teenage Wasteland*. The assignment was to draft a four-page review that evaluated the book, to exchange it with a classmate for peer commentary, and to revise. The writer, Denise Sega, had a number of concerns she wanted her partner to address in the peer commentary. Here's the note she wrote:

I'm worried that I spend too much time summarizing the book and not enough explaining my evaluation of it. What do you think? Do I say too much about the author and the book's contents? Is my evaluation clear to you? Do you think I give enough explanation of why I liked the book so much? Any other suggestions are also appreciated. Thanks.

As you read, keep in mind what Denise asked her partner. When you finish reading the working draft, consider how you would respond.

DENISE SEGA, MORE THAN JUST BURNOUTS (WORKING DRAFT)

Youth culture. Teenagers have devised many different ways of growing up. From jocks and preps to neo-Beatnicks and hip-hop kids, most high schools contain a range of distinctive social groupings. In Teenage Wasteland, Donna Gaines looks at a group of "burnouts" and heavy metal teens in suburban New Jersey, the "dead end" working-class kids who are alienated from school and community. The opening paragraphs explain the situation that led Gaines to write this book:

> When I heard about the suicide pact it grabbed me in the solar plexus. I looked at the pictures of the kids and their friends. I read what reporters said. I was sitting in my garden apartment looking out on Long Island's Jericho Turnpike thinking maybe this is how the world ends, with the last generation bowing out first.
>
>   In Bergenfield, New Jersey, on the morning of March 11, 1987, the bodies of four teenagers were discovered inside a 1977 Chevrolet Camaro. The car, which belonged to Thomas Olton, was parked in an unused garage in the Foster Village garden apartment complex, behind the Foster Village Shopping Center. Two sisters, Lisa and Cheryl Burress, and their friends, Thomas Rizzo and Thomas Olton, had died of carbon monoxide poisoning. (3)

The remainder of the introduction reveals the rationale and research plan for Gaines's investigation of the suicides. What began as an assignment for the Village Voice, for which Gaines writes regularly, her investigation eventually became her doctoral work as well as the book in review.

Besides providing more details about the instigating event, the Bergenfield suicide pact, the introductory pages also provide autobiographical details about the author which are essential to understanding Gaines's devotion to her task, as well as her informed frame of reference. Gaines, too, in many ways, was a "burnout." She describes her growing up years and habits. She explains that "like many of [her] peers, [she] spent a lot of [her] adulthood recovering from a personal history of substance abuse, family trauma, school failure, and arrests" (4). To put this life behind her, Gaines turned to social work, first as a "big sister" with junior high students in Brooklyn and then as a helper on a suicide prevention hotline. After becoming a New York State certified social worker, Gaines worked in the special adoptions and youth services divisions and as a street worker providing services for troubled teens. Eventually she moved into research and program evaluation and finally returned to school to complete her doctorate in sociology.

In the introduction, Gaines also explains the need for the book. Initially, she was reluctant to write about suicidal teens because she felt that "if I couldn't help them, I didn't want to bother them" (6). She did not like the idea of turning vulnerable people like the Bergenfield teens into "research subjects" by getting them to trust her with their secrets. Despite these qualms, however, she did decide to go to Bergenfield and ultimately spent two years hanging out with the "burnouts" and "dropouts" of suburban New Jersey, talking to them about heavy metal music, Satanism, work, school, the future, and many other things. Gaines was angry because these teens had been classified by adults as "losers" and never allowed to tell their side of the story. The press had explained the suicides as the result of the individual problems of troubled teens and failed to see, as Gaines does so clearly in her book, how the suicides "symbolized a tragic defeat for young people" (6) and a wider pattern of alienation.

Teenage Wasteland reveals the sense of sadness among the teens in Bergenfield. "By nineteen," Gaines writes, "you've hit the brick wall and you really need something. Because there is nothing to do here and there is nowhere to go" (78). Young people hanging out seems to annoy and even frighten adults. Nevertheless, for these teens, there does not seem to be anything else to do. According to Gaines, they have been neglected by society for so long, experienced so much lack of care in so many ways, that they see no alternatives. They see no hope for anything better.

The only "ticket out" these teens see is to be like Jon Bon Jovi or Keith Richards. The chances of becoming a rock star, of course, is one in a million. The dream breaks down, the kids realize their limitations, and they feel they have run out of choices for the future. There seem to be no alternatives to their bleak situations:

> At the bottom are kids with poor basic skills, short attention spans, limited emotional investment in the future. Also poor housing, poor nutrition, bad schooling, bad lives. And in their bad jobs they will face careers of unsatisfying part-time work, low pay, no benefits, and no opportunity for advancement.
>
> There are the few possibilities offered by a relative—a coveted place in a union, a chance to join a small family business in a service trade, a spot in a small shop. In my neighborhood, kids dream of making a good score on the cop tests, working up from hostess to waitress. Most hang out in limbo hoping to get called for a job in the sheriff's department, or the parks, or sanitation. They're on all the lists, although they know the odds for getting called are slim. The lists are frozen, the screening process is endless. (155)

According to Gaines, these are "America's invisible classes," the "unseen and unheard . . . legions of young people who now serve the baby boom and others, in fancy eateries, video stores, and supermarkets" (157). Given this situation, it is no surprise that Bergenfield's teens turn to Satanism and heavy metal to give them a sense of power and a refuge in a world over which they feel they have no control. There are no good jobs, and the social programs for these teens only label them as "troubled" or "deviant" or "burnouts" and do not work.

One truly fascinating part of the book involves Gaines's etymology of the term "burnout." Besides providing at least twenty-five synonyms for the term, she also explains its evolution. Furthermore, she differentiates between "burnouts" and "dirtbags"—a subtle yet significant distinction. Her discussion of how these terms reflect teens feeling "powerless, useless, and ineffectual" is, in itself, powerful, useful, and effectual in helping readers understand the deep sense of alienation afflicting the "teenage wasteland."

In conclusion, I believe this is an important book that should be read by anyone interested in finding out more about the "gritty underside of white teen life in the suburbs" (cover notes). Compared to the sensationalistic stories in the press that blame teenage suicide on drugs or heavy metal, Donna Gaines has taken the time to listen—and to hear what the kids have to say.

■ WORKSHOP QUESTIONS

1. In her note to her partner, Denise Sega raises a number of issues about her working draft. One of these concerns the amount of description and evaluation that appear in the draft. She seems worried that she spends too much time summarizing the book and talking about the author and not enough on evaluation. How would you respond to this concern? What suggestions would you offer?

2. It is obvious that Sega admires *Teenage Wasteland*, but she raises the question of whether the criteria of evaluation she uses come across clearly enough. Reread the draft and mark those passages that make an evaluation or imply one. What seem to be the criteria Sega uses in each case? If the criteria are not stated explicitly, express in your own words what they seem to be. What advice would you give Sega about presenting her criteria of evaluation more explicitly?

3. In the third paragraph, Sega compares the treatment of the Bergenfield suicide pact by the press to Gaines's treatment in *Teenage Wasteland*. What is the point of this comparison? Do you think Sega could do more with it? If so, how could the comparison be extended and strengthened? Do other comparisons appear in the draft? If so, are they effective, or could they use more work? Are there other comparisons you can think of that Sega might use?   ■

REFLECTING ON YOUR WRITING

The assignments throughout the chapter have put you in the role of a reviewer and shown how you might evaluate a performance, a program, or a policy. For your portfolio, shift focus to discuss how you have been reviewed by others— by teachers in school, supervisors at work, judges at performances, and peer commentators in your writing course.

First, give a little background on your experiences of being evaluated in and out of school. What were the circumstances of the evaluations? Why were you being evaluated? What criteria were used? What was your response to the evaluations? Were these experiences helpful to you? Explain why or why not.

Second, use this background to reconstruct your attitude toward evaluation when you entered your writing course. Has your attitude changed? Why or why not? What has been the effect on you as a writer, a student, and a person of receiving reviews from both your teacher and your peers? What differences, if any, do you see between teachers' and peers' evaluations? What suggestions would you offer for improving the process of evaluation in your writing course?

part three

writing and

research projects

INTRODUCTION: DOING RESEARCH AND THE NEED TO KNOW

People do research in one form or another all the time, perhaps without even being aware of it.

■ Many students do considerable research to decide which colleges to apply to. People who want to buy a new car often consult *Consumer Reports* and talk to friends to find the best deal. If you are planning a vacation, you might look at travel guides.

■ Many types of research take place in the workplace—for example marketing research, product development, and productivity studies. The professions, such as law and medicine, are defined in many respects by the kind of research practitioners in those fields do to deal with clients' legal situations or to diagnose patients' conditions and recommend treatment.

■ Public opinion polling has become a common feature of politics and journalism, a way to keep track of the public's attitudes about the issues of the day. Public advocacy groups often conduct their own research on questions that matter to them—whether it's the impact of mining on national lands, the effect of outsourcing on American jobs, or drunk driving.

■ Research is a familiar part of academic life. You may recall some of the research assignments you encountered in elementary school and high school—term papers, book reports, science fair projects, history posters, oral presentations—and you will almost certainly do research in your college courses.

One thing the examples of research have in common is that they are all motivated by the need to know. In each case, something is calling on a person or a group of people to do research—to get the information needed, to investigate a problem, to provide a new way of seeing things. To put it another way, research begins when people have questions they need answers to: What kind of computer should I buy? How are consumers likely to respond to a new product or service? What does the public think about immigration reform? what causes breast cancer?

Researchers in different fields of study, of course, have different ways of asking questions and different ways of answering them. Take the AIDS epidemic, for example. Scientific researchers have been asking questions about the nature and behavior of the human immunodeficiency virus (HIV) and about the kinds of treatment that can alter the course of infection. Psychologists and sociologists, in contrast, have studied the effect of AIDS on the identities of HIV-negative gay men and the benefits and drawbacks of needle-exchange programs. Economists have calculated the financial impact of AIDS on medical institutions, health insurance companies, government programs, and employers.

Researchers, as you can see, do not just think of a topic and start to investigate it. They turn the general topic of AIDS into specific questions that concern people in their field of study. This gives them an angle on the problem and a way of starting their research.

In the following chapters, you will learn more about how to carry out research. As you will see, the focus of these chapters is on academic research, the kind of assignments you are likely to get in college courses. Nonetheless, the information is just as pertinent to research in other spheres. Chapter 12 explains how to organize a research project. Chapter 13 discusses how to work with sources, while Chapter 14 provides a guide to print, electronic, and other sources. Chapter 15 discusses field research. (We do not include research that involves experimental work in laboratories, a specialized topic better handled in a science or social science course devoted to research design.)

the research process: critical essays and research projects

Research begins when people need to know something and have important questions to answer. In college, of course, the call to do research most often comes from teachers, in the form of a writing assignment. For this reason, it's worth considering what faculty are looking for when they ask students to do research. Most faculty believe that an important part of a college education is learning how to pose a meaningful problem to investigate, then research and analyze what leading authorities have said about it, and finally, form your own judgment about it. Faculty are interested certainly in the correct citation form and document design. In college, however, doing research and working with sources are first of all intellectual work. Research is not just a matter of reporting information in proper formats but of grappling with the ideas of others.

In the first part of this chapter, we'll look at two of the most familiar writing assignments that call on you to work with sources: the critical essay and the research paper. We'll look at them as genres of writing in order to identify how they position writers in relation to the context of issues, the sources they're working with, and their readers. In the second part of the chapter, we'll take an overview of the research process and follow one student, Amira Patel, as she designs and carries out a research project in an American history course.

UNDERSTANDING THE GENRE: CRITICAL ESSAYS AND RESEARCH PROJECTS

As we just noted, the critical essay and the research paper are two of the most common writing tasks in college.

- *Critical essays* for a college assignment are usually short papers—3 to 7 pages in length—that tackle a question or issue in a field of study.

Online Study Center

Often the sources of critical essays are assigned readings in the course, perhaps supplemented by additional research.

■ *Research papers* tend to be longer projects than critical usage, both in terms of page length—ranging from 8 to 20 or more pages—and in the amount of sources and the amount of time devoted to the research and writing.

WHAT ARE FACULTY LOOKING FOR? UNDERSTANDING ACADEMIC WRITING

Faculty assign short critical essays and longer research papers because they want students to act like members of a field of study, whether drama critics, literary scholars, design theorists, or historians. Those writing assignments call on the students to enter into an ongoing discussion and to position themselves in relation to what the experts have already said. Faculty know, of course, that students are novices in the field. But that's why faculty ask students to gain some experience of what it means to engage with the questions and issues in a field of study.

To understand critical essays and research papers as genres of academic writing, it can help to consider these faculty expectations:

■ **Faculty expect you to work with your sources**—to create an interplay of perspectives and interpretations instead of just summarizing what the authorities have said. For example, it's not enough to report on the causes of the French Revolution in 1789. The real question is, what have historians *said* about the causes of the French Revolution and how do these interpretations differ and why?

■ **Faculty expect you to create you own research space.** A critical essay or research paper does not simply convey information from reliable sources. It uses these sources to establish a problem or issue that has some significance. Even in cases where an instructor assigns the problem or issue to examine—how, say, does futurism embody modernist design—it's still up to you to explain why and how this question is worth investigating and what makes it meaningful.

■ **Faculty expect you to identify the central discussions, debates, and controversies in a field**—and to use them to locate your own thinking in relation to what the authorities have said. In academic writing, it is rare that problems or issues have been settled once and for all and there's nothing left to say. Usually, there are discussions, debates, and controversies taking place, in which scholars argue for a particular interpretation or way of understanding the matter at hand. Your task as a researcher is to understand these ongoing controversies and figure out where you stand in relation to them.

SAMPLE STUDENT PAPERS FOR ANALYSIS

In the three examples of student writing that follow, we'll look more closely at how students have responded to these faculty expectations. The first paper is a sample critical essay, which uses American Psychological Association (APA) citation style. The second paper was prepared using the style of the Modern Language Association (MLA), and the third paper uses APA style.

SAMPLE CRITICAL ESSAY

This short critical essay, "The Dilemma of Empire," was written for a course on international relations. The writing assignment called on students to analyze a set of class readings about American power after 1989 and explain key differences. As you read, notice how Jacqueline Perkins works with her sources to create an interplay of voices.

Dilemma of Empire 1

The Dilemma of Empire

Jacqueline Perkins

International Relations 201

March 4, 2005

With the fall of the Soviet Union and the end of the Cold War in 1989, the political landscape of international relations changed dramatically. The balance of power between two camps, the communist and the free world, that had dominated world politics since the end of World War II became suddenly a thing of the past, and the United States emerged as the single, uncontested global

Introduction:
*Establishes
context of
issues

power. This shift from a bipolar to a unipolar world system has raised many questions about how the United States should use its unparalleled military and economic power. This question has become even more complicated since the attacks on the World Trade Center and the Pentagon on September 11, 2001.

With the invasions and occupations of Afghanistan and Iraq and an ongoing war on terrorism that seems to have no fixed boundaries, the United States has become embroiled in military operations and nation-building that no one could have anticipated in 1989. In the eyes of many here and abroad, the

Dilemma of Empire 2

United States is no longer just a superpower but an imperial power. For the first time since the Spanish-American war, political commentators are talking frankly and approvingly of American empire, often making comparisons between the United States today and the British Empire of the nineteenth century. In fact, the British historian Niall Ferguson (2003) has gone so far as to ask whether the United States has the political and moral stamina to embark "on a new age of empire" (p. 54) by picking up the legacy of the British Empire which America has now, for better or worse, inherited.

In a speech at West Point in June 2002, President George W. Bush said plainly that "America has no empire to extend" (cited in Ignatieff p. 23). Nonetheless, despite Bush's disclaimer, "empire" may be a word that fits what Michael Ignatieff describes as "the awesome thing that America is becoming":

> It is the only nation that polices the world through five global military commands; maintains more than a million men and women at arms on four continents; deploys carrier battle groups on watch at every ocean; guarantees the survival of countries from Israel to South Korea; drives the wheels of global trade and commerce; and fills the hearts and minds of an entire planet with its dreams and desires. (p. 23)

As President Bush's speech indicates, there is a deep-rooted ambivalence in the United States about the idea of empire. Americans like to think of their country as a freedom-loving liberator of the oppressed and a foe of the nineteenth-century European colonialist. Still, growing numbers of liberals and conservatives see empire as an unavoidable fact that has been thrust upon us instead of an option we can choose or reject. The question, then, is not whether the United States should be an empire but how its imperial power should be used. In making sense of America's unrivaled power and of the opposition and even hatred this power elicits in many corners of the world, foreign policy strategists are united by the shared goal of maintaining the United States' global domination but divided over the means to do so. In this paper, I will use Joseph S. Nye Jr.'s notions of "hard" and "soft" power to show

Margin annotations:

* Identifies key focus of the paper

Presents question to be examined

Introduces debate

Introduces two key terms and states purpose

Dilemma of Empire 3

how these two ways of thinking about power have shaped our understanding of the new American empire.

Defines "hard" power

According to Nye (2002), "hard" power consists of "inducements" and "threats" to get others to change their positions (p. 8). One of the most influential statements of "hard" American power comes from Project for the New American Century (PNAC). This is a group of conservative foreign policy officials and scholars associated with the Reagan and the first Bush administration. Some, such as Donald Rumsfeld and Paul Wolfowitz, are now key figures in the second Bush administration, while others, such as Richard Perle, are influential policy advisors. In its founding "Statement of Principles" in 1997, PNAC criticized the "incoherent policies of the Clinton administration" and argued that "American foreign and defense policy are adrift." According to PNAC, the United States "cannot safely avoid the responsibilities of global leadership. . . . The history of the 20th century should have taught us that it is important to shape circumstances before crises emerge, and to meet threats before they become dire. The history of this century should have taught us to embrace the cause of American leadership" (1997).

Gives examples

Although PNAC does not use the politically loaded term "empire," its 2000 report "Rebuilding America's Defenses: Strategy, Forces and Resources for a New Century" does link the need for increased defense spending, heightened military readiness, and modernization of the armed services to a global *Pax Americana*. For PNAC, embracing the "cause of American leadership" means building up and using "hard" military power, both preemptively as well as defensively. To preserve and extend American interests, which, in classic imperial style, PNAC identifies with peace and security at home and abroad, the United States must be willing to act as a global "constabulary," to intervene in regional conflicts, to deter the rise of great-power competitors, and to remove existing regimes when necessary.

Acting "to meet threats before they become dire" has become a key point for the current Bush administration's foreign policy and a central justification for the invasion and occupation of Iraq. Bush's willingness to act unilaterally

Dilemma of Empire 4

Transition
from
"hard" to
"soft"
power

and preemptively and to use overwhelming and even excessive military force is
very much in keeping with PNAC's "hard" version of power. We turn now to
foreign policy strategists who are equally intent on meeting "threats before
they become dire" but argue the United States should do so by exercising
"soft" power, either alone or in conjunction with "hard" power.

Defines
"soft"
power

As Nye defines it, "soft" power means attracting other countries to the
American way of life instead of forcing them to change through military or
economic coercion. "Soft power," Nye says, "rests on the ability to set the
political agenda in a way that shapes the preferences of others." Soft power
results from the values that "are expressed in our culture, in the policies we
follow inside our country, and in the way we handle ourselves internationally"
(p. 9). It means setting a good example at home, using American prosperity
and openness, standing up for human rights internationally, and thereby
persuading other nations to follow our lead. In its crassest form, "soft" power
refers to Hollywood glitz, fast food, and the consumerism of the shopping mall.
Nye does not dismiss the "hard" power of military and economic threats. But
he says it should be used to reinforce "soft" power.

Gives
example

Paul Berman's *Terror and Liberalism* (2003) is a good example of "soft"
power in its purest form. According to Berman, the main conflict in the "war
on terrorism" is an ideological one between open and free societies such as
the United States and political movements such as Saddam Hussein's Baathist
Party, Al Qaeda, and other Islamist fundamentalists. For Berman, this
amounts to a replay of the conflict between the totalitarianism of Stalin and
Hitler and the liberal democracies of the West in the 1930s and during the
Cold War. Berman supports the invasion and occupation of Iraq, just as he
supported the Persian Gulf War of 1991, but on different grounds than "hard"
power advocates like PNAC and the two Bush administrations. For Berman,
the issue is not "vital interests" such as the oil supply in the Middle East or
the "credibility" of American power "to scare its enemies" (p. 4). Instead, he
sees the two wars against Iraq as a way to enhance America's moral authority

Dilemma of Empire 5

by overthrowing a dictator and instituting democracy. In this way, Berman uses the idea of "soft" power to argue for a "concerted mobilizing of liberal thinkers and writers" and an anti-totalitarian "war of ideas" (p. 185).

Berman would probably deny that his support of the Iraq wars has bolstered a new American empire and a foreign policy devoted to global domination. Another liberal foreign policy strategist, Michael Ignatieff (2003), is more honest when he says that he believes empire "has become, in places like Iraq, the last hope for democracy and stability alike" (p. 54). Ignatieff is quite straightforward when he explains hows "hard" and "soft" power go together in the "21st century imperium," where "free markets, human rights and democracy" are "enforced by the most awesome military power the world has ever known" (p. 24). Unlike Berman, who seems committed mainly to a "mental war" of ideological struggle in his support of the Iraq invasion, Ignatieff is more realistic. Ignatieff quotes the theologian Reinhold Niebuhr's words that the United States likes to think it has a mission to free the rest of the world from tyranny, while "frantically avoiding recognition of the imperialism that we now in fact exercise" (p. 24). Advocates of "soft" power, such as Berman, should not forget that invasions of other countries involve the very real use of "hard" military power that kills people in the interest of liberating them.

The debate about the relative merits of "hard" and "soft" power and their relation to each other should not hide the fact that the United States is using both to further its global and imperial aims. Some will argue that we should use more "soft" power and pursue a policy of multilateralism, diplomacy, and containment, while others argue for the use of "hard" power, preemptive wars, economic coercion, and regime change. What is critical in this debate, as I see it, is the growing realization of America's undisputed economic and military power and its effect on the rest of the world. In this sense, as Ignatieff says, September 11 can be seen as an "awakening, a moment of reckoning with the extent of American power and the avenging hatreds it arouses" (p. 23). This is the dilemma of empire the United States is only beginning to face. No matter

Gives example of combining "hard" and "soft" power

Explains significance of debate

Gives writer's own opinion

whether America uses "soft" or "hard" power or a combination, the United States can expect the same kind of resentment and rebellion that has been directed against all the empires of the past.

References

Berman, P. (2003). *Terror and liberalism*. New York: Norton.

Ferguson, N. (2003, April 27). The empire slinks back. *New York Times Magazine*, 52–57.

Ignatieff, M. (2003, January 5). The burden. *New York Times Magazine*, 23–27, 50–54.

Nye, J. (2002). *The paradox of American power: Why the world's only superpower can't go it alone*. New York: Oxford UP.

Project for the New American Century. (2002 September). Rebuilding America's defenses: Strategy, forces and resources for a new century. Retrieved February 2, 2005 from http://www.newamericentury.org.

Project for the New American Century. (1997, June 3). Statement of principles. Retrieved February 2, 2005 from http://www.newamericentury.org.

Analysis: Working with Sources

As noted, for this writing assignment, the sources were already at hand, and the task Jacqueline Perkins faced was that of turning the assigned class readings into the makings of a critical essay. Notice two strategies she has used to organize her sources in such a way that they seem to speak to each other.

First, in the opening three paragraphs, she establishes a context of issues to discuss the question of American power after 1989. She does this by suggesting that whether we like it or not, the United States has become not just the single superpower but a new kind of empire. (Notice how she uses references to Niall Ferguson and Michael Ignatieff and plays off President Bush's denial of empire to set up the context of her critical essay.)

Second, in the fourth paragraph, she introduces the notion of "hard" and "soft" power as the terms she will use in the rest of the essay to analyze her sources. Then, she explains that the purpose of her essay is to see what light the idea of "hard" and "soft" power can shed on the new American empire. As you can see from the rest of the essay, these two terms provide the conceptual framework to organize her sources so that they seem to speak to each other. Notice that Perkins is not simply summarizing what the various thinkers have said. Instead, it's as though she is orchestrating an interplay of voices that resonate and bounce off each other.

■ FOR CRITICAL INQUIRY

1. Consider how Jacqueline Perkins sets up the context of issues in the opening paragraphs of her essay. How does she move from the fall of the Soviet Union and the end of the Cold War to the emergence of a new American empire? What evidence does she use to establish the reality of such an empire? What enabling assumptions would readers need to share with her to accept her line of reasoning?

2. Consider how Perkins works with her sources. Pick one or two passages where she has effectively created an interplay of voices. How does this interplay contribute to the essay overall? Are there other passages where she is less successful in working with her sources? Explain your answer.

3. Consider the ending of the essay. What is the final point Perkins is making? Does it seem to flow logically from the discussion in the rest of the essay?

SAMPLE RESEARCH PAPER IN MLA FORMAT

Andy Mgwanna wrote this research paper for a first-year composition class. As you read, consider how Andy establishes the purpose of the paper and how he uses his research as evidence.

Mgwanna 1

Andy Mgwanna

Professor Chisolm

Writing 101

5 November 2006

The Prison Privatization Debate: The Need for a New Focus

In 1976, the state of Florida hired a private company to operate the Weaversville Intensive Treatment Unit for Juvenile Delinquents. In 1982, the state privatized a second facility, the Okeechobee School for Boys (Young 12).

Mgwanna 2

Several years later, federal, state, and local government began privatizing a range of prison services and entire correctional facilities in order to cut costs and accommodate a rapidly expanding number of inmates. This recent wave of privatization in corrections can mean several things. First, it can mean that private companies contract with local, state, and federal governments to provide such services in public prisons as medical care, counseling, mental health, and drug treatment, education and vocational training, laundry and food services, and staff training. Second, privatization can mean that prison labor is contracted out to private companie such as Chevron, Victoria Secret, and Best Western who hire prisoners to enter data, make products, and take telephone reservations (Davis 102). Third, privatization can mean that a private company owns and operates a correctional facility as a for-profit enterprise.

Almost as soon as the ink from these new contracts had dried, a heated debate about the ethics, economics, and administration of prisons-for-profit erupted. In this paper, I examine the debate about privatization of prisons and prison services in order to identify the issues it raises for prison policy. First I provide some background on privatization. Second, I investigate the arguments for private prisons and the arguments against private prisons. Finally, I suggest that the debate about privatization has reached an impasse and needs to be broadened to include a stronger emphasis on rehabilitation and recidivism.

Background on the Privatization of Prisons and Prison Services

Privatization dates back to the mid-1800s when private companies were given contracts to run Louisiana's first prison, Auburn Prison, Sing Sing in New York, and San Quentin in California. As the use of private companies to run jails and prisons increased, a number of groups protested. Businesses and labor advocates objected to the free labor many private prisons contracted out because it was "'unfair' competition." Reformers cited whippings, malnourishment, overwork, and overcrowding as evidence of prisoner abuses in private facilities. By the end of the nineteenth century, states had largely stopped using private companies and assumed full management of correctional facilities themselves (Young 8).

By the mid 1980s, however, federal, state, and local governments once again were allowing private companies to run their jails, prisons, and detention centers. Phil Smith attributes this decision to the intersection of the "ideological imperatives of the free market; the huge increase in the number of prisoners; and the concomitant increase in imprisonment costs" (4). The American Federation of State, County, and Municipal Employees (AFSCME), the largest public service employees union in the country, which counts prison employees among its members, says that the trend of privatization at the end of the twentieth century can be attributed to Thomas Beasley, the Tennessee Republican Party chairman, who founded the Corrections Corporation of America (CCA) in 1983, with help from Jack Massy, who started Kentucky Fried Chicken. Since the CCA's inception and with help from Wall Street firms such as Goldman Sachs and Merrill Lynch, the private prison industry has expanded dramatically in scope (Parenti 14).

Today private companies operate juvenile detention centers, county jails, work farms, state and federal prisons, and INS holding camps all over the United States. The Corrections Corporation is the largest private prison operator. In 2003, it managed 58,732 beds in 59 jails, detention centers, and prisons in 20 states and the District of Columbia. One third of CCA's revenue comes from the federal government, while the remaining two thirds come from state and local government. The CCA's largest clients are Wisconsin, Georgia, Texas, Tennessee, Florida, and Oklahoma. Although the CCA tried to operate facilities overseas, after a series of setbacks, it now works primarily in the United States. It is the sixth largest prison system in the United States with only Texas, California, the Federal Bureau of Prisons, New York, and Florida managing more prisoners (Smith 9). The CCA owns 49% of U.S. prison beds under private operation, while Wackenhut Corrections, an offshoot of the

Wackenhut Corporation, a private security and investigation firm founded by former FBI agent George Wackenhut, controls 21% (Lyon).

Arguments for Prison Privatization

Proponents of privatization present two main points when they argue that private companies can maintain low-cost and high-quality prisons and prison services while generating a profit for investors. First, they argue that private prisons offer significant savings over government-run prisons. Geoffrey Segal of The Reason Foundation reviewed 23 articles by government officials and academics and found that private prisons are, on average, 10 to 15% cheaper than government prisons (2). Taxpayers are also saved the expenses and risk of building new facilities ("Prison Privatization a Boon to Taxpayers"). Alexander Tabarrok says private prisons offer 15 to 25% savings on construction and 10 to 15% on administration. These savings, in turn, pressure public prisons to lower their costs. He writes:

> States with a greater share of prisoners in private prisons have lower costs of housing public prisoners. Perhaps more tellingly, from 1999 through 2001, states without any private prisons saw per-prisoner costs increase by 18.9 percent, but in states where the public prisons competed with private prisons, cost increases were much lower, only 8.1 percent. (6)

Another economic reason supporters offer for privatization is that although most prisoners come from urban areas, many new prisons are located in rural areas, providing jobs where there are few employment opportunities (Huling 98). And finally, according to Dana Joel of the Heritage Foundation, wages earned by staff in private prisons are equal to or higher than those earned in public prisons (5).

Second, proponents of privatization point to the high quality of private prisons. Segal cites four reasons why quality in private prisons matches or exceeds the quality in public prisons. First, the results of six independent studies, which focused specifically on quality, indicate that private prisons are

Mgwanna 5

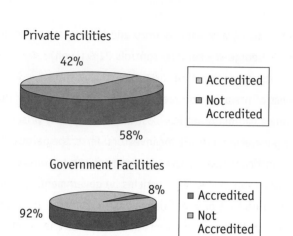

Fig. 1   Facilities with ACA accreditation, from "Prison Privitazation and the Use of Incarceration."

equal to if not better than government prisons. Second, 44% of private prisons have been accredited by the American Correctional Association, which provides standards for quality, management, and maintenance, while only 10% of government prisons have been accredited (see fig. 1). Third, almost all contracts with private prisons are renewed. Fourth, no private facilities have been placed under court order for issues of quality.

Others argue that high standards within private prisons are likely to be maintained and even improved upon as more companies enter the market. Frequent rebidding will likely force companies to maintain high quality in order to retain contracts. To preempt the argument that the economic goals of running a prison for profit conflict with the operational objectives, which is providing services, Joel writes:

> The contracting process significantly reduces such dangers. Contractors must abide by state laws, regulations, and policies and are held accountable for fulfilling these obligations. If the state is dissatisfied, it can refuse to renew the contract. Some states, such as New Mexico and Tennessee, also include termination clauses within

contracts in the event a contractor provides inadequate services. In
addition, contractors are watched very closely by the courts, the
press, civil-rights groups, and prison-reform groups. Such close
scrutiny forces the contractor to maintain adequate standards. (5)

Arguments Against Prison Privatization

Those who oppose prison privatizations are a heterogeneous group, and
they oppose privatization for several reasons: ethical, financial, and
administrative. Those who oppose prison privatization on ethical grounds argue
that punishment and profit are not compatible (Smith 13). Fundamentally the
goal of for-profit corporations is to make as much money as possible, and in
the case of prisons, profits depend on people being incarcerated. Accordingly,
AFSCE objects to privatization on the grounds that it allows private companies
to profit from crime. Along similar lines, Mattera, Khan, and Nathan note that
the "existence of an industry based on incarceration for profit creates a
commercial incentive in favor of government policies that keep more people
behind bars for longer periods of time" (15).

Second, opponents assert that private prisons do not save money. AFSCME
asserts that there is no indication that private prisons demonstrate cost
savings, while The Sentencing Project writes, "Research to date has concluded
that there is little evidence that privatization of prisons results in significant
public savings." The General Accounting Office (GAO) conducted a study in
1996, which found that private and public correctional facilities cost the same
amount of money (Parenti 154). In addition, the finances of private prisons are
often in disarray. Mattera, Khan, and Nathan point out that CCA nearly went
bankrupt in the 1990s after borrowing $1 billion to build speculative prisons
and undergoing a troubled corporate restructuring (11). In 2000, the CCA's
chief executives lost his job, and the company settled a series of lawsuits from
shareholders to the tune of $120 million. CCA today "is weighed down by debt.
It also continues to face weak demand for new private prisons at the state and

Mgwanna 7

local level" (Mattera, Khan, and Nathan 21). Wackenhut has not fared much better. The corporation has been charged with squeezing money out of rehabilitation programs, counseling, and literacy courses. In 1995, for example, investigators accused Wackenhut of diverting almost three quarters of a million dollars from a drug treatment program in a Texas facility ("Wackenhut"). Opponents also argue that whatever money may be saved in private prisons is the result of the low wages and substandard benefits staff are given (AFSCME 2000). In discussing the CCA, Mattera, Khan, and Nathan write:

> The CCA has sought to depress its labor costs by keeping wages low and by denying its employees traditional (defined-benefit) pension plans. There have been reports of understaffing and high rates of turnover at some of its facilities. For example, the annual turnover rates at several CCA facilities in Tennessee have been more than 60 percent. (16)

Third, opponents of private prison facilities charge that CCA and other private companies poorly manage their facilities, allowing prisoner abuse, violence, medical maltreatment, and escapes ("Lock Up Private Prisons"). Mattera, Khan, and Nathan found that CCA routinely failed to give prisoners adequate medical care, create an environment where inmates were safe from harm—both from other prisoners and from correctional staff—and control the drug activities of both prisoners and CCA employees (17). Further, as Christian Parenti shows, in a 15-month period, the privately-operated Northeast Ohio Correctional Center in Youngstown, Ohio experienced six escapes, 44 assaults, 16 stabbings, and two murders (234). At the same time, prisoners have protested and rioted against substandard conditions. In 1995, North Carolinian prisoners, who were living in overcrowded conditions in a Tennessee prison, burnt their dorms in a several-hour riot (Parenti 173).

Sexual abuse has been one of the chief allegations against Wackenhut. In 1999, Wackenhut lost a $12 million a year contract with Texas after several correctional officers were indicted for having sexual relations with female prisoners. Wackenhut fired five guards in a work-release facility in Fort Lauderdale, Florida, after learning they were having sex with inmates. After the U.S. Justice Department found Wackenhut subjected inmates to "excessive abuse and neglect," the state of Louisiana reassumed operations of a juvenile prison (The Sentencing Project).

CCA and other private prison companies have been plagued by escapes and inadvertent releases of violent inmates. Judith Greene writes that 37 inmates escaped custody from private prisons in 1999 alone (97). Mattera, Khan, and Nathan estimate that at least a dozen inmates have been mistakenly released from custody (25). In some situations, the mistakes are administrative. For example, after one month of operation, an employee at the David L. Moss Criminal Justice Center permitted an inmate to post bond after registering the wrong offense. But in other situations, CCA employees have been fooled by inmates passing as other prisoners, who are eligible for release. Some prisoners are never recaptured. At the same time, important security positions in a facility in Georgia went unfilled for 8-hour shifts 20 times in one month ("Lock Up Private Prisons").

After chronicling dozens of incidents of abuse, violence, and murder in private prisons, Greene summarizes the case of opponents of prison privatization:

> Industry executives will tell you that the prison management disasters catalogued here are just isolated events, confined to a handful of 'underperforming' facilities. But evidence is mounting that a number of key structural deficiencies—high staff turnover, defective classification and security procedures, inadequate program services—are found in many private prisons (112).

Conclusion: A New Focus?

The debate between supporters and opponents of private prisons and the privatization of prison services has reached a stalemate. Supporters argue that

Mgwanna 9

well-documented studies of financial savings demonstrate the logic of the market and the superiority of privatization. Opponents argue that privatization amounts to an abdication of government responsibility that has produced systematic abuses. As we have seen, the sides in the debate are deeply divided by their assumptions and beliefs. One of the problems with this impasse, as Thomas O'Brien of the Horizon Institute for Policy Solutions suggests, is that the key issues of rehabilitation and recidivism, which have significant implications for the cost of the prison industrial complex, have been lost in a polarized debate. O'Brien argues that rather than becoming bogged down in the pros and cons of privatization, we should focus on incentives to both private and public prisons to prevent recidivism:

> If private competition can find the keys to making young offenders become productive citizens rather than career criminals, government will save far more money than the typical 10 to 25 percent savings now found with privatization. Two out of three released convicts are now rearrested. Preventing a young offender from coming back for 20 years can save $400,000 per head (at $20,000 per year in incarceration expenses).

O'Brien helps to redefine the debate about privatization by shifting the measure of success from short-term financial savings to the long-term outcomes of prisoners. This should please opponents of privatization because it makes rehabilitation, instead of profits, the central function of the prison system. At the same time, O'Brien should please supporters of privatization because he does not give up on "private competition" but rather challenges it to develop guidelines and programs that promote rehabilitation and thereby reduce long-term recidivism. In any case, by focusing on outcomes rather than ownership, O'Brien offers at least a starting point to move beyond the current impasse.

Works Cited

American Federation of State, County and Municipal Employees. "The Evidence is Clear, Crime Shouldn't Pay." Spring 2000 <http://www.afscme.org/private/evidtc.htm>.

Davis, Angela Y. Are Prisons Obsolete? New York: Seven Stories, 2003.

Greene, Judith A. "Entrepreneurial Corrections: Incarceration As a Business." Invisible Punishment: The Collateral Consequences of Mass Imprisonment. Ed. Marc Mauer and Meda Chesney-Lind. New York: New York P, 2002. 95-113.

Huling, Tracy. "Building a Prison Economy in a Rural Area." Invisible Punishment: The Collateral Consequences of Mass Imprisonment. Ed. Marc Mauer and Meda Chesney-Lind. New York: New York P, 2002. 197-213.

Joel, Dana. "A Guide to Prison Privatization." The Heritage Foundation. 24 May 1988 <http://www.heritage.org/Research/Crime/BG650.cfm>.

"Lock Up Private Prisons: Chronic Problems Demonstrate Why Incarceration Should be Left to the State." The Atlanta Constitution 6 Oct. 1999. Lexis-Nexis. Warehouse State Lib. 19 Oct. 2006 <http://lexis-nexis.com>.

Lyon, Juliet. "Open Debate Needed Over Private Sector Impact on Prison System." The Financial Times 3 Feb. 2005. Lexis-Nexus. Warehouse State Lib. 24 Oct. 2006 <http://lexis-nexis.com>.

Mattera, Philip, Mafruza Khan, and Stephen Nathan. "Corrections Corporation of America: A Critical Look at Its First Twenty Years." A Report by the Grassroots Leadership, the Corporate Research Project of Good Jobs First, and Prison Privatisation International. Dec. 2003 <www.soros.org/initiatives/justice/articles_publications/cca_20_years_20031201/ CCA_Report.pdf>.

O'Brien, Thomas. "Letter to the Editor." The Washington Post 26 Jan. 1998. Lexis-Nexus. Warehouse State Lib. 22 Oct. 2006 <http://lexis-nexis.com>.

Parenti, Christian. Lockdown America: Police and Prisons in the Age of Crisis. New York: Verso, 1999.

"Prison Privatization a Boon for Taxpayers." The Atlanta Constitution 24 Apr. 1996. Lexis-Nexus. Warehouse State Lib. 1 Nov. 2006 <http://lexis-nexis.com>.

Segal, Geoffrey. "Corporate Corrections? Frequently Asked Questions About Prison Privatization." The Reason Foundation. Nov. 2002 <http://www.reason.org/corrections/faq_private_prisons.shtml>.

Sentencing Project. "Prison Privatization and the Use of Incarceration." Sept. 2004. <http://www.sentencingproject.org/pdfs/1053.pdf>.

Smith, Phil. "Private Prisons: Profits of Crime." Covert Action Quarterly Fall 1993. <http://mediafilter.org/caq/Prison.html>.

Tabarrok, Alexander. "Private Prisons Have Public Benefits." Pasadena Star News, North County Times 23 Nov. 2004. Lexis-Nexus. Warehouse State Lib. 17 Oct. 2006 <http://lexis-nexis.com>.

"Wackenhut." Wikipedia. June 8, 2006 <http://en.wikipedia.org/wiki/Wackenhut>.

Young, Marc Tafolla. "Prison Privatization: Possibilities and Approaches to the Privatization of Prisoner Security and Services." Criminal Justice Working Papers 27 Jan. 2006. <www.law.stanford.edu/programs/academic/criminaljustice/workingpapers/MTafollaYoung_05.pdf>.

Analysis: Finding a Place in a Debate

Andy Mgwanna establishes the purpose of his research paper at the end of the second paragraph, when he says that he will (1) give background information on prison privatization, (2) analyze the positions for and against, and (3) explain how the debate has reached an impasse. Notice how the paper builds toward the conclusion it has already anticipated in the introductory section.

¶1–2: Introduction

■ Establishes trend toward privatization

■ Defines privatization

■ Explains purpose of the paper

¶3–7: Background on the Privatization of Prisons and Prison Services

■ Provides reasons for the emergence of privatization

■ Explains the scope of privatization

¶8–10: Arguments for Prison Privatization

- Economic
- Quality

¶11–16: Arguments Against Prison Privatization

- Ethical
- Economic
- Administrative

¶17–18: Conclusion: A New Focus?

- Concludes debate has reached an impasse
- Suggests a way to refocus

As you can see, one of the important features of this paper is that it does not simply describe the debate about privatization but presents a position on it. Readers may sense that the writer sympathizes with one side in the debate. Opponents of privatization, after all, get twice the space as supporters. However, Mgwanna's main point is that the pro-con debate itself has reached an impasse and that the terms of the debate need to be changed. And, in this way, he goes beyond merely reporting research findings to draw an arguable conclusion about the prison privatization debate.

■ FOR CRITICAL INQUIRY

1. A question readers are entitled to ask about a research paper is whether its conclusions are justified by the evidence presented. Explain the conclusion Andy Mgwanna reaches at the end of the paper. Consider whether the background section and analysis of the privatization debate provide adequate grounds to draw such a conclusion. When you first read the conclusion, did Mgwanna's position seem adequately prepared for?

2. One feature of this paper is that it promises to give a balanced account of the privatization debate. Consider how the writer goes about that in the sections for and against prison privatization. Does the analysis of the debate seem to be a fair and accurate one? Explain your answer by pointing to particular passages in the two sections.

3. How does Mgwanna use his sources? Pick passages in the paper to analyze what the writer is seeking to accomplish by citing sources from his research. Try to identify at least three distinct purposes his sources are meant to serve.

CHECKLIST FOR MLA AND APA STYLE

The two main styles of citation and manuscript preparation in academic research were developed by the Modern Language Association (MLA) and the American Psychological Association (APA). You can find details in Chapter 13, "Working with Sources," about using each style to set up in-text citations and Works Cited or References pages. Here is information about manuscript preparation.

Features Common to Both MLA and APA Style

❑ Manuscript should be double-spaced, including block quotations and Works Cited or References pages. Do not add extra spacing.

❑ Format a one-inch margin all around, top and bottom, left and right.

❑ Indent five spaces to begin a paragraph.

❑ Use ragged right margins.

❑ Don't end the line at the bottom of a page with a hyphen.

❑ Number pages consecutively, including Works Cited or References pages.

Special Features Called for by MLA Style

❑ Unless your teacher tells you to, do not include a separate cover sheet. Type the following information, double-spaced, at the top left corner of the manuscript, in this order: your name, your professor's name, course number, and date. Double-space and center the title of your paper. Follow conventional rules of capitalizing words in a title. Don't use quotation marks, italics, boldface, underlining, all capitals, or showy fonts. Double-space and begin the text.

❑ Insert page numbers in the upper right corner, flush with the right margin, one-half inch from the top of the page. Precede the page number with your last name. Begin the text one inch from the top.

❑ Begin your bibliography on a separate page, titled "Works Cited." Center the title one inch from the top, without any quotation marks, underlining, boldface, or italics. Include in the Works Cited only those works you have cited in the text of the paper. It is not a comprehensive bibliography (you may have used other works which are not cited).

Special Features Called for by APA Style

❑ Unless your teacher directs otherwise, use a separate cover page. Center your title approximately one-third from the top of the page. Type the title double-spaced if it has more than one line. Follow usual capitalization conventions. Don't use all caps, boldface, quotation marks, underlining, or italics. Double-space and type your name. Double-space again and type the course number, and then, following another double space, type the date.

❑ On the page immediately following the cover sheet, include a one-paragraph "Abstract" of no more than 120 words that summarizes the content of your paper.

❑ Begin the text on the third page. Don't repeat the title. Number all the pages, beginning with the cover sheet as page 1 and the Abstract as page 2. Type a running head (the first two or three words of the title) before the page number.

❑ APA style research papers are much more likely than MLA style papers to use section headings. Some research papers use the conventional headings—"Introduction," "Methods," "Results," and "Discussion"—but others use headings based on the content of the paper. Notice the section headings Jennie Chen uses in her paper.

❑ Begin your References section on a separate page, following the text. Center the word "References" one inch from the top, without any underlining, italics, quotes, boldface, or other special treatment.

SAMPLE RESEARCH PAPER IN APA FORMAT

Jennie Chen wrote "Defining Disease: The Case of Chronic Fatigue Syndrome" as a term paper for a public health course on the social contexts of disease. Because she is using APA style, Chen included an abstract at the beginning of her paper.

As you read Chen's complete paper, notice how she uses an existing controversy to focus her research project.

Defining Disease 1

Defining Disease

The Case of Chronic Fatigue Syndrome

Jennie Chen

English 101

November 20, 2005

Defining Disease 2

Abstract

The current controversy about whether chronic fatigue syndrome (CFS) is an illness with an organic basis or an imaginary condition poses important questions about how the medical profession defines disease and contains important consequences for treatment. CFS affects predominantly white, middle-class women. Literary critic Elaine Showalter has claimed that CFS is a contemporary version of nineteenth-century neurasthenia or nervous exhaustion and should be treated by psychotherapy. Others argue that treating CFS as a psychological disorder stigmatizes CFS patients and causes conflicts between patients and doctors. Some physicians have proposed that the biomedical model of disease is too rigid and that the medical profession and the public need to understand how the physical and psychological operate simultaneously in patients' illness.

Defining Disease 3

The publication of Elaine Showalter's *Hystories: Hysterical Epidemics and Modern Media* (1997) has intensified the debate over chronic fatigue syndrome (CFS) and how it should be defined as a medical condition. According to the Centers for Disease Control (2005), CFS has been recognized since the early 1980s as an illness whose cause is unknown. No diagnostic tests have been developed. CFS patients are predominantly white middle-class women. The "illness is diagnosed primarily on the basis of symptoms and signs reported by the patient and exclusion of other possible causes of prolonged, debilitating fatigue" (Reyes & Luciano, p. 2).

In Showalter's view, CFS is a psychogenic condition, a modern-day form of nineteenth-century neurasthenia or nervous exhaustion. For Showalter, CFS has no physical basis but results from repressed and unarticulated psychological conflicts that manifest themselves in such flu-like symptoms as sore throat, tired and achy feeling, low-grade fever, and swollen lymph nodes. The appropriate treatment is psychotherapy.

One of the things that makes Showalter's book so controversial is that she groups CFS, as well as gulf war syndrome and multiple personality syndrome, with other contemporary "hysterical epidemics" such as alien abductions, satanic ritual abuse, and recovered memory. In Showalter's account, people "learn" the symptoms of these disorders from the media, telecommunications, and e-mail: "Infectious epidemics of hysteria spread by stories circulated through self-help books, articles in newspapers and magazines, TV talk shows and series, films, the Internet, and even literary criticism" (p. 5). For her critics, however, lumping illnesses such as CFS and gulf war syndrome together with UFOs and satanic cults trivializes real suffering. By defining "illness as a story instead of a physical condition (with the CFS sufferer acting out, say, the narrative of the bored and frustrated housewife), Showalter diverts our attention from real suffering" (M. Richardson, personal communication, October 21, 2005).

Defining Disease 4

The controversy over Showalter's new book is not just an academic one. CFS presents an interesting and important case study of how medical conditions are categorized and how they acquire legitimacy. Skepticism concerning CFS is not limited to literary critics such as Showalter. It is also widespread within the medical profession. Whether CFS is an illness with an organic basis or an imaginary condition is a question that carries important implications for treatment. Should CFS be treated by a physician or a psychiatrist? Answers to this question depend on assumptions about how illness is defined.

Background on CFS

Chronic fatigue syndrome began to draw national attention in the early 1980s. In 1984, the outbreak of a mysterious illness in Incline Village, a small town of 6,000 inhabitants near Lake Tahoe, manifested a number of symptoms subsequently associated with CFS—dizziness, sore throats, headaches, diarrhea, shortness of breath, rapid heartbeat, and overall weakness. Within a year, there were over one hundred cases reported, and the Centers for Disease Control (CDC) sent a team to investigate. CDC officials concluded that the Epstein-Barr virus, suspected at the time of being the source of chronic fatigue symptoms, could not be established as the cause of the mysterious illness (Johnson, 1996, pp. 33–51).

The Lake Tahoe outbreak is emblematic in many respects of the state of knowledge about CFS. Many of the patients were affluent young professionals, the majority were women, and their condition became known in the media in the 1980s as "Yuppie Flu." At the time, some physicians believed the cause of fatigue might be stress or overwork that led to immunological and neurological dysfunction.

Nonetheless, no causal agent could be established. Lake Tahoe patients were no more likely than the general population to show evidence of infection with Epstein-Barr virus (Reyes & Luciano, 1997, p. 2), and other studies have eliminated a host of chemicals, bacteria, and viruses as suspected causes (Showalter, 1997, p. 125).

Defining Disease 5

Since the outbreak at Lake Tahoe, epidemiological studies have complicated our understanding of the demographics of CFS. An initial four-city study (Reyes & Luciano, 1997) seemed to confirm the media's picture of "Yuppie flu," with findings that 98% of CFS patients were white, 85% were female, 80% had advanced education, and one-third were in upper income brackets and that the average age of onset was 30 years. Subsequent studies, however, suggested that these percentages reflect those who are under care for CFS, rather than its prevalence throughout society. A study in Seattle, for example, (CDC, 2005) found women represented 59% of CFS sufferers, while a San Francisco study (Steele, et al., 1998) found CFS was most prevalent among black and Native American women whose income was below $40,000. A recent study in Wichita, Kansas (Reyes, et al., 2003) found that CFS was four times more common among women, but the average age of CFS sufferers was 50 to 59.

At present, the etiology of CFS is unknown. While there is no established cause, there are nonetheless a cluster of symptoms that seem to be associated. The persistence of these symptoms led the CDC in 1988 to classify chronic fatigue as a syndrome and publish a case definition of CFS. According to CDC guidelines (2005), the diagnosis of CFS depends on two major criteria, namely the exclusion of other clinical conditions (such as cancer, AIDS, or multiple sclerosis) and the persistence of four or more of the following symptoms over a period of six months or more: Substanial impairment in short-term memory or concentration, sore throat, tender lymph nodes, muscle pain, multi-joint pain without swelling or redness, headaches of a new type, pattern, or severity, unrefreshing sleep, and post-exertional malaise lasting more than 24 hours.

To put it in other words, the CDC classification of chronic fatigue as a syndrome establishes CFS as a medical condition that can be diagnosed as a cause of illness. CFS does not have the status of disease. Instead, it is

Defining Disease 6

considered a syndrome, or cluster of associated symptoms whose causes are unknown.

Defining Illness

As Simon Wessely (1994) says,

> Worrying about whether or not CFS exists . . . is hardly the issue. It
> exists in the real world. . . . What lies behind CFS is neither a virus,
> nor psychiatry, but our idea of what constitutes a real illness, what
> doesn't, and what we do to make something real. (p. 29)

Although Showalter argues that people should not be ashamed of hysteria, there is nonetheless a strong stigma attached to imaginary illnesses. As Arthur Kleinman and Stephen Straus (1993) write, "In much of biomedicine, only a tangible or laboratory abnormality justifies the imprimatur of a 'real' disease" (p. 3).

Often if the organic cause of an illness is not known, the illness is dismissed as a "real" disease and the sufferer is not entitled to sympathy from doctors or society. According to Charles Rosenburg (1992), "For many Americans, the meaning of disease is the mechanism that defines it" (p. 312). For patients with cancer, tuberculosis, multiple sclerosis, and other diseases with established etiologies, an identity and a social role are available to patients based on diagnosis by the medical profession. Naming a patient's disease in effect gives him or her "permission" to be sick and offers validation to the patient's complaints.

Such diagnosis, as Hans Selye writes, can have direct benefit to the patient: "It is well-established that the mere fact of knowing what hurts you has an inherent curative value" (cited in Berne, 2003, p. 53). Rosenburg makes a similar point when he says that even "a bad prognosis can be better than no prognosis at all; even a dangerous disease, if it is made familiar and understandable, can be emotionally more manageable than a mysterious and unpredictable one" (p. 310).

Defining Disease 7

Moreover, there are very real legal and financial consequences to the diagnosis of disease. Health benefits from insurance companies normally cover only those medical conditions that are considered legitimate and well established. Similarly, eligibility for disability benefits and other social services is based on medical diagnosis. Employers' policies concerning medical leave, job responsibilities, special accommodations, and so on likewise depend on definitions of illness and disease.

Defining and Treating CFS

The popular press and medical journals discuss CFS in very different terms. According to a study of all the articles published in the British scientific, medical, and popular press between 1980 and 1994, only 31% of articles in medical journals believed the cause of CFS to be organic rather than psychological, while 69% of the articles in newspapers and magazines held to an organic explanation for the illness (MacLean & Wessely, 1994). This division between journalism and biomedicine is a troubling one because it points to divisions between patients and physicians concerning the origins and treatment of CFS.

In newspapers and magazines, CFS is often portrayed as a mystery disease which has yet to be conquered by modern medicine. The idea that the cause of CFS is out there to be found is reassuring to CFS patients, in part because it tells the familiar story of the march of scientific progress and its victories over disease. In this sense, CFS patients have their own stake in desiring that the causes of CFS are organic. Such a view of causation, where a pathogenic agent causes a pathological effect, is the basis for a potential cure in store—the magic bullet that can knock out the illness.

An organic cause of the illness not only makes CFS more treatable. It would also lift feelings of guilt and stigma from patients and clear them of charges of laziness, malingering, depression, and deceit. As David Bell (2004) writes, "Patients are angry and frustrated, interpreting the debate over emotions as trivializations of their illness and as the explanation for why so

Defining Disease 8

little is done for them" (p. 53). In many of the magazine articles, especially in personal accounts of CFS, patients express deep and abiding anger that physicians routinely describe their illness as psychological in origin. Part of the conflict between patients and doctors stems from the fact that defining CFS as a psychological syndrome, as most physicians do, appears to disqualify the patient's experience as a proper illness and portray it as a moral failing instead.

The most sympathetic physicians, on the other hand, respond that patients and the public at large need to recognize that psychological illness is just as real as illness that has a somatic basis. Anthony Komaroff (1994) says that CFS "may become a paradigmatic illness that leads us away from being trapped in the rigidity of the conventional biomedical model and leads us toward a fuller understanding of suffering" (52). Komaroff's sentiments are important ones, and there seems in principle to be growing agreement, in the words of the British Royal College of Physicians, Psychiatrists, and General Practitioners, that "CFS cannot be considered either 'physical' or 'psychological'—both need to be considered simultaneously to understand the syndrome" (cited in Brody, 1996, p. C14).

Nonetheless, the paradigm shift that Komaroff talks about has yet to take place, and the world of medicine continues to hold to a traditional biomedical model of illness in which patients with organic illness are treated by physicians and patients with psychological problems are treated by psychiatrists. So the basic problem of legitimate and illegitimate illness remains, marked by the presence or absence of organic causes. Perhaps the best solution, as Kleinman (1993) suggests, is to have physicians, not psychiatrists, treat CFS patients:

> One can affirm the illness experience without affirming the attribution for it; in other words, we can work within a 'somatic' language and do all the interventions . . . from the psychosocial side, but in such a way to spare patients the . . . delegitimization of their experience. (p. 329)

Defining Disease 9

References

Bell, D. S. (2004). *The doctor's guide to chronic fatigue syndrome*. Boston: Addison-Wesley.

Berne, K. H. (2003). *Running on empty: A complete guide to chronic fatigue syndrome*. Alameda, CA: Hunter House.

Brody, J. E. (1996, October 9). Battling an elusive foe: Fatigue syndrome. *The New York Times,* p. C14.

Centers for Disease Control (2005). Chronic fatigue syndrome. Retrieved October 9, 2005, from http://www.cdc.gov/ncidod/diseases/cfs/index.htm

Johnson, H. (1996). *Osler's web*. New York: Crown Books.

Kleinman, A. (1993). CFS and the illness narrative. In A. Kleinman & S. Straus (Eds.), *Chronic fatigue syndrome* (pp. 318–332). London: Wiley.

Kleinman, A., & Straus, S. (1993). Introduction. In A. Kleinman & S. Straus (Eds.), *Chronic fatigue syndrome* (pp. 3–25). London: Wiley.

Komaroff, A. K. (1994). Clinical presentation and evaluation of fatigue in CFS. In S. Straus (Ed.), *Chronic fatigue syndrome* (pp. 47–64). New York: Marcel Dekker.

MacLean, G., & Wessely, S. (1994). Professional and popular views of chronic fatigue syndrome. *British Medical Journal,* 308, 773–786.

Reyes, M., Simons, L., & Luciano, P. (1997, February 21). Surveillance for chronic fatigue syndrome: Four U.S. cities, September 1989 through August 1993. *Morbidity and Mortality Weekly Report, 46* (SS-2), 1–13.

Reyes, M., Nisenbaum, R., Hoaglin, D.C., Unger, E.R., Emmons, C., Randall, B., et al. (2003). Prevalence and incidence of chronic fatigue syndrome in Wichita, Kansas. *Archives of Internal Medicine* 163 (2003): 1530–1536. Retrieved April 2, 2004, from American Medical Association database.

Rosenburg, C. (1992). *Explaining epidemics and other studies in the history of medicine*. New York: Cambridge University Press.

Showalter, E. (1997). *Hystories: Hysterical epidemics and modern media*. New York: Columbia University Press.

Wessely, S. (1994). The history of chronic fatigue syndrome. In S. Straus (Ed.), *Chronic fatigue syndrome* (pp. 11–34). New York: Marcel Dekker.

Analysis: Identifying a Central Controversy

The academic disciplines acquire their identities in part by the kinds of questions participants in the field ask and by the kinds of answers that count as reasonable ones. The question in Jennie Chen's research, namely is chronic fatigue syndrome (CFS) a disease, seems like a simple and direct one. As you have seen, however, the question of how to define disease can in fact be quite complex and controversial, with people sharply divided over what counts as a persuasive answer.

In the opening section of this term paper, Chen has used the appearance of an especially controversial book, Elaine Showalter's *Hystories: Hysterical Epidemics and Modern Media,* to identify the central issues and focus her research project. Notice, for example, how Chen gives a brief summary of Showalter's line of reasoning in the first three paragraphs and then, in the fourth paragraph, generalizes Showalter's skepticism about CFS to the medical profession and points out how the controversy over CFS has important consequences for treatment.

By identifying a central controversy, Chen accomplishes a number of things: She establishes her credibility as someone who is knowledgeable about current issues in the field of study; she creates a space for her own research project within the ongoing debate; and she sets up a conceptual framework to organize the interplay of her sources.

■ FOR CRITICAL INQUIRY

1. Unlike Andy Mgwanna's research paper, which has an explicit statement of purpose in the opening paragraph, Jennie Chen's opening section isn't as plain about the purposes of the paper. Consider whether this is a limitation. Rewrite the fourth paragraph to include a more explicit statement of purpose. What is gained? What, if anything, is lost?

2. Consider the overall organization of the paper. Following the introduction, there are three further sections. What function does each perform? Can you imagine an alternative arrangement of the material?

3. How does Chen locate herself in the controversy over CFS? When do you first become aware of where she stands on the issue? Where in the paper do you see her developing further a sense of her own position and perspective? How does she use her sources to do so?

THE RESEARCH PROCESS: AN OVERVIEW

In this section, we'll be following Amira Patel as she works on a research paper for her American immigration history course. First, though, we present an overview of the research process—to identify the main steps in responding to the call to write a research paper and some of the key tasks involved at each point.

1. **Defining a research question:** Do preliminary research to get an overview of your topic. Start to focus your reading to develop a research question. Evaluate your research question and revise or modify it, if necessary. Write a proposal to clarify the purpose of your research.

2. **Finding sources:** Use your library's card catalog, indexes, bibliographies, and other databases to identify print and electronic sources. Browse sites on the Internet. Keep a working bibliography.

3. **Evaluating sources:** Take notes. Photocopy sources. Assess the relevance and credibility of the sources. Look for assumptions and biases. Keep an open mind. Be prepared to revise or modify your own thinking in light of what you've read.

4. **Making an argument:** Take into account all you have read. Determine where you stand in debates and controversies. Develop an argument that answers your research question.

5. **Planning and drafting:** Develop a working outline of your paper. Start drafting. Reread sources and find additional information as needed. Revise or modify your outline if necessary.

DEFINING A RESEARCH QUESTION

Research depends in part on knowing what you are looking for. This will depend, of course, on the research assignment. In some cases, the assignment will provide specific directions; in others, it will be open-ended. If you have questions about what the assignment is calling on you to do, make sure you consult with your instructor.

Here is the research assignment Amira Patel was given in her American immigration history course.

> The final writing assignment of this course is a term paper, 12 to 15 pages, that researches any topic of your interest in American immigration history, 1880 to present. You should begin by clearly defining your research question and writing a proposal. The paper should establish the importance of the problem you are researching and offer an interpretation. You should not simply report what happened or summarize what you have read. You are expected to read sources from the period you have chosen along with scholarly accounts.

ANALYZING THE ASSIGNMENT

Analyzing the assignment means identifying what it is calling on you to do so that you can clarify your own purposes and determine how you will work with your sources. As we've seen, some assignments provide the purpose for you— for example, to explain why or why not Willie Loman is a tragic hero in *Death of a Salesman*. In other cases, you'll have to figure out what you need to do and what your stance will be in relation to the context of issues, the sources, and your readers.

Here are some common ways that researchers position themselves:

- **To provide an overview of the current thinking of experts:** The purpose in this case is largely an informative one—to report on what experts in the field think about an important issue. You might, for example, explain the current views of experts on the extinction of dinosaurs or report on the latest results of drug treatment of HIV-positive people.

- **To review the arguments in a controversy:** Your purpose is largely informative—to explain to readers the positions people have taken in a current debate. You might, for example, report on the legal controversy prompted by the prosecution of pregnant women for doing harm to their fetuses by drinking or taking drugs.

- **To pose and answer an important question or solve a problem:** In this case, your purpose is not simply to report on what is known but to put forward your own analysis and interpretation. You might, for example, explain the causes of a resurgence of tuberculosis or the consequences of deregulation in the telecommunications industry.

- **To position your own interpretation in relation to what others have said:** In this case, your purpose is similar to that of answering an important question. The key difference is that instead of simply using what others have written as evidence for your interpretation, you also explain how your analysis or interpretation relates to the views of others—how and why it differs, how and why it shares common ground. You might, for example, explain how your analysis of Martin Luther King's "I Have a Dream" speech differs from and is similar to the analyses of others.

- **To take a stand on a controversy:** Here your purpose is not simply to report and analyze but also to persuade. In this case, you have an argument to make. You might claim, for example, that there should (or should not) be mandatory HIV testing. Or you could argue that the United States should (or should not) adopt more stringent limits on commercial fishing in the North Atlantic.

Following a Research Path: Analyzing the Assignment

Amira's First Reaction

This is exactly what I was afraid of. I hate these kind of open-ended writing assignments where the teacher doesn't give you any idea of what you should write about. I have no idea.

Amira's Reaction After Talking to Other Students

OK, I have calmed down a little. I know I've got to get an angle on the assignment. What we were reading about American nativism and negative attitudes toward immigrants between 1880 and 1920 was interesting to me. Maybe I can find something in that. It seems like the important thing is to find a good research question and then explain how to answer it.

PRELIMINARY RESEARCH

Sometimes you know right away what you want to research. In other cases, especially when the topic you're researching is new to you, you'll need to do some preliminary research to develop a research question. The following sources offer good places to start:

- **The Web:** Web sites can offer helpful starting places for research projects. See "Following a Research Path: Preliminary Research," on page 423, for an example of how a student used the Web to do preliminary research and develop a research question.

- **Encyclopedias:** You can find an overview of many topics in general encyclopedias. It can also be helpful to consult specialized encyclopedias that cover a particular field of study and often include bibliographies for each entry. See the list of general and specialized encyclopedias in Chapter 14.

- **Recent books:** Skim a recent book on your topic, looking in particular at its introduction to see how the writer describes the issues the book addresses. Notice, too, what the book seems to cover by reading the table of contents. And don't forget to see whether it has a bibliography.

- **Recent articles:** Find a recent article in a scholarly journal or a popular magazine on your topic. Read the article, noticing what question or questions the writer poses and (in the case of academic articles) what sources are listed in the references.

- **Classmates, librarians, teaching assistants, faculty members:** Talk to other people who know something about your topic and the current questions people are asking about it. They can help you understand what the issues are and what sources you might look for.

Your preliminary research should give you some ideas about the ways others have approached the topic you're interested in, the kinds of questions they raise, and the differences of opinion and interpretation that divide them. This research should also help you identify other books and articles on the subject that you may want to consult.

Following a Research Path: Preliminary Research

Amira's Reflections on Getting Started

I thought I'd see what I could find about nativism on the Web and if that would give me any ideas about the paper.

I used "American Nativism" as a key word on Google, and after looking at a couple of sites that didn't seem that helpful, I found the Wikipedia page and a pdf "Cycles of Nativism in U.S. History." I read these and learned that nativism was wider than just 1880 to 1920. Both talked about the English Only movement as a kind of nativism that surfaced in the 1990s. Maybe I should use that as my topic. I think I'd rather do something about recent immigration.

Next, I typed in "English Only" and found a ton of information on English Only at James Crawford's "Language Policy Web Site and Emporium." Crawford seems to be a pretty prominent writer about language issues, and the site has articles and sections of his books. It also gives links to other Web sites so that I could read what supporters of English Only had to say about the issue. [See Fig. 1.]

By this point, I was beginning to feel I had found a good topic in "English Only." I just wasn't sure what my research question should be.

DEVELOPING A RESEARCH QUESTION

Once you've done some preliminary research, answer the following questions to refine your own sense of the research question you want to investigate:

1. What questions, issues, and problems appear repeatedly? Why do people think they are important?

2. Are there arguments, debates, or controversies that appear in what you've read? What positions have others taken? What seems to be at stake in these arguments? Do you find yourself siding with some people and disagreeing with others?

3. Is there some aspect of your topic that people don't seem to pay much attention to? Why do you think this is so? Are they neglecting questions or issues that could provide a good focus for research?

4. Given what you've read so far, what questions, issues, arguments, and controversies do you find most interesting? What, in your view, makes them important?

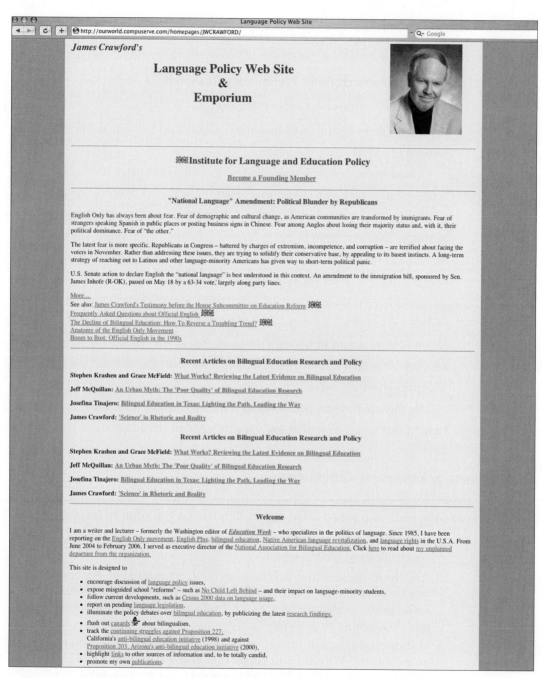

Fig. 1   James Crawford. Language Policy Web Site

Following a Research Path: Defining the Research Question

Amira's Further Thoughts About a Research Question

It's interesting that so many Americans in the 1990s started thinking English should be the official language and that bilingual education should be banned. It's almost as though the whole English Only thing just came out of the blue, when organizations like US English started getting together and sponsoring legislation to make English the official language. But that can't be true. There's got to be some reason it happened in the 1990s, when so many new immigrants from Asia and Latin America were coming into the country.

WRITING A PROPOSAL

Some teachers ask students to write a proposal that defines the purpose of their research and indicates their research plan. Even if your teacher does not require a proposal, writing one can be a useful exercise to help you clarify your purpose.

A research proposal typically does three things:

1. Identifies the general topic or problem of the research and explains its significance.

2. Presents the specific issue and the research question you are addressing.

3. Sketches briefly the research plan, indicating how it will answer the research question.

Following a Research Path: Writing a Proposal

Amira's Research Proposal

American nativism goes back as far as the Alien and Sedition Acts of 1798 and anti-Catholic agitation in the 1830s and 1840s, directed toward recent immigrants from Ireland. According to many historians, the period of 1880 to 1920 witnessed virulent outbursts of nativism against the waves of new immigrants arriving in the United States. It seems that every time large numbers of people immigrate to this country, American nativism arises. For my research project, I am interested in American attitudes toward the new immigrants who have been coming to the United States since the 1990s, from Asia, Central and Latin America, and the Caribbean. I plan to focus specifically on the English Only movement as a response to this immigration. The question I'm researching asks why American nativism emerged in this form in the 1990s. My plan is to do some background research on earlier forms of nativism but to focus mainly on what the English Only movement is and what it believes. I will also research the conditions in the country in the 1990s so I can explain how this movement took root.

FINDING SOURCES

Once you have established a direction for your research project, the next step is in-depth research. You will find detailed information on a wide range of research sources in Chapter 14, "A Guide to Print, Electronic, and Other Sources." In this section, we look first at what the Web and the library have to offer you as a researcher. Then we follow Amira on her research path.

THE WEB AND THE LIBRARY: WHAT THEY OFFER RESEARCH PROJECTS

Part of doing research is understanding what you can expect from the various sources available and which are considered credible for academic research projects. Let's look at what the Web and your college library can offer.

What the Web Is Good For

Web pages such as the Wikipedia entry on American nativism or "Cycles of American Nativism" can offer general background information and useful bibliography, but they are not considered authoritative scholarly sources in their own right. Most teachers would question a research paper that relied very heavily on them.

The Web is very good for getting public documents, reports, studies, and policy statements from government agencies, professional associations, universities, and nonprofits. It is very good at answering specific questions (if, say, you want to know how many people immigrated to the United States between 1965 and 1990 or how many households speak Spanish as the first language). It's also good for finding information about institutions or organizations such as U.S. English, to see how it presents itself and the case for English Only.

You may find sources such as James Crawford's Language Emporium that can be considered credible and authoritative. Crawford is widely recognized as an important writer on language policy, and so the articles and the sections of his books at the Web site are good sources for academic research. You may find such reliable sources at Web sites associated with universities, museums, research institutes, or other organizations. But you can't count on it.

Conclusions: Use the Web for background and specific information. Don't expect to write a research paper based exclusively or primarily on Web sources. The Web can be complementary to library research, but it can't substitute for it.

What the Library Is Good For

College and university libraries provide a number of ways to find appropriate scholarly and popular books and articles, in both print and electronic form.

Searchable library catalogs can be used to make subject searches, which will identify books on a particular topic in the library's holdings. Some books may be available in electronic form.

Searchable online databases and library subscription services such as JSTOR, Project Muse, PubMed, and LexisNexis can identify articles on your topic in scholarly journals, popular magazines, and newspapers, with access to abstracts or the complete text. Note, however, that not all scholarly and popular periodicals are included in these services. For this reason, don't count on finding all the readings you need online. It's quite likely you will need to look up articles in print form in the library stacks.

In fact, it can be rewarding to browse the shelves where books and journals on your topic are kept. Use the call number of a book that looks promising and see what other books are nearby. (You can also do this on many online library catalogs.)

Finally, libraries have knowledgeable librarians who can answer your questions and help guide you in the research process.

Conclusions: Expect that even with the best available online databases and library subscription services, you will not be able to find all the books and articles you need online. Plan to make use of the library in person. Browse the stacks. Consult with librarians.

HOW TO IDENTIFY RELEVANT SOURCES

How you read depends on your purposes and where you are in the research process. Once you have identified a research question, you are probably reading to gather information and to understand what others have said about the question you're investigating. As you're reading a source, ask yourself how relevant it is for your research question:

- Does it provide useful background information?

- Does it review previous research on the question?

- Could it help explain differences of opinion on the question?

■ Can you use it as supporting evidence for your analysis and interpretations?

■ Does it present evidence or ideas that run counter to your perspective? How should you take these into account?

KEEPING A WORKING BIBLIOGRAPHY

As you identify key research sources, make sure you take down the information you need to find the source as well as the information you'll need for your Works Cited or References section.

Books

Call number
Author, editor, translator
Title and subtitle
Place of publication, name of publisher, date of publication

Articles

Author(s)
Title and subtitle
Periodical name
Volume and issue numbers
Date
Page numbers
Name of electronic resource, date of access, URL (if applicable)

Online sources

Author (if available)
Title
Site name
Page numbers (if available)
Paragraph numbers (if available)
Date of publication or posting
Name of sponsoring organization or institution (if available)
Date of access
URL

Following a Research Path: Finding Relevant Sources

Let's look at Amira's notes as she looks for useful sources.

Using the Library Catalog

I already had the title of some books from browsing the Web, but I wanted to do a systematic search of the university library.

First, I tried "English Only movement" as a subject heading but only got three books. When I looked up one of them, <u>Nativism Reborn?</u>, I noticed the catalog entry listed other subjects: "Language policy—United States," "English language—Political aspects," and "English language—Social aspects—United States." I tried all these, and the best by far was "Language policy—United States." It turned up 30 references. I printed the search and headed for the stacks. [See Fig. 2 and Fig. 3.]

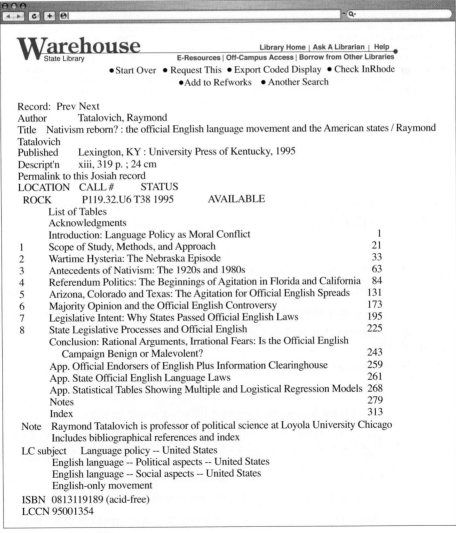

Fig. 2   Book entry in online catalog

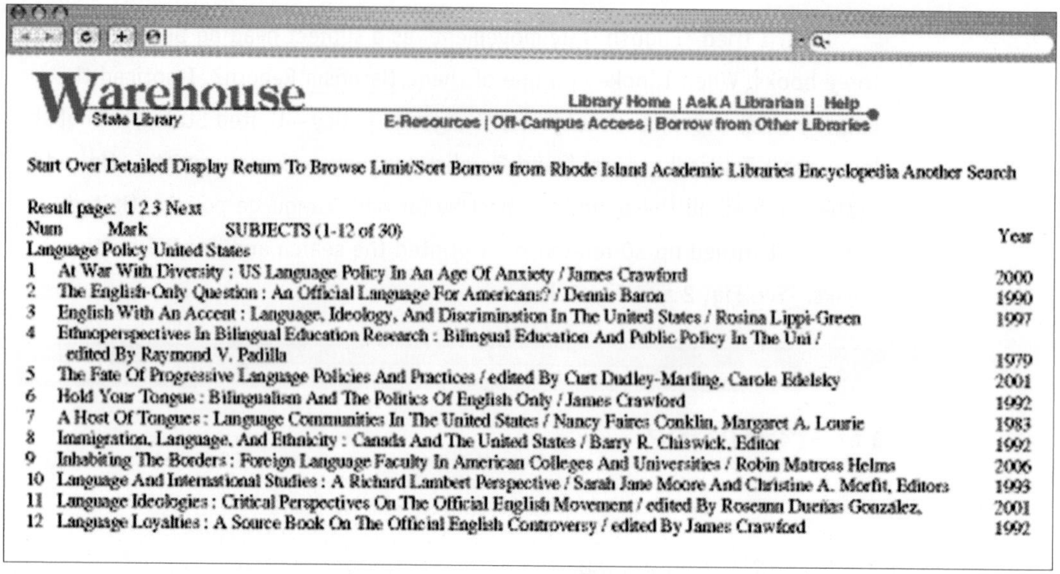
Warehouse
State Library
Library Home | Ask A Librarian | Help
E-Resources | Off-Campus Access | Borrow from Other Libraries

Start Over Detailed Display Return To Browse Limit/Sort Borrow from Rhode Island Academic Libraries Encyclopedia Another Search

Result page: 1 2 3 Next

Num	Mark	SUBJECTS (1-12 of 30)	Year
		Language Policy United States	
1		At War With Diversity : US Language Policy In An Age Of Anxiety / James Crawford	2000
2		The English-Only Question : An Official Language For Americans? / Dennis Baron	1990
3		English With An Accent : Language, Ideology, And Discrimination In The United States / Rosina Lippi-Green	1997
4		Ethnoperspectives In Bilingual Education Research : Bilingual Education And Public Policy In The Uni / edited By Raymond V. Padilla	1979
5		The Fate Of Progressive Language Policies And Practices / edited By Curt Dudley-Marling, Carole Edelsky	2001
6		Hold Your Tongue : Bilingualism And The Politics Of English Only / James Crawford	1992
7		A Host Of Tongues : Language Communities In The United States / Nancy Faires Conklin, Margaret A. Lourie	1983
8		Immigration, Language, And Ethnicity : Canada And The United States / Barry R. Chiswick, Editor	1992
9		Inhabiting The Borders : Foreign Language Faculty In American Colleges And Universities / Robin Matross Helms	2006
10		Language And International Studies : A Richard Lambert Perspective / Sarah Jane Moore And Christine A. Morfit, Editors	1993
11		Language Ideologies : Critical Perspectives On The Official English Movement / edited By Roseann Dueñas Gonzalez.	2001
12		Language Loyalties : A Source Book On The Official English Controversy / edited By James Crawford	1992

Fig. 3 Subject search in online catalog

Using Electronic Databases: Readers' Guide Abstracts

I had used Readers' Guide to Periodical Literature in print form many times in high school, so I decided to try the online Readers Guide Abstracts because I know they list a lot of popular magazines and I wanted to get a sense of what people were saying about English only legislation in the 1990s. I used English-Only as a keyword and set dates from 1990 to 2000. That turned up 26 helpful sources that included abstracts. [See Fig. 4.]

Finding Full Text Articles Through Electronic Databases

I knew the library had all these full-text subscription services, but I had never used them before. So I asked a librarian where to start, and he suggested InfoTrac, JSTOR, and Project Muse would be good for my topic. Each of these works a little differently and what you get depends on the keywords you use. Sometimes it's overwhelming, and I had to sort through a lot to find what I was looking for on the English Only movement of the 1990s. Using English-Only as a keyword, I found 76 articles at InfoTrac. What's great is that they give you the whole article online, and you can download it. [See Fig. 5.]

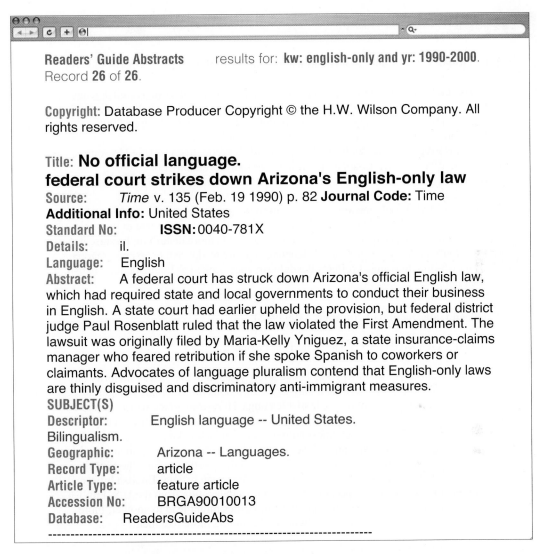

Fig. 4   Results from Readers' Guide Abstracts

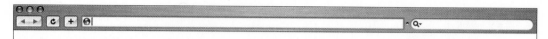

Lingo jingo: English only and the new nativism. (English language in US society)

Nunberg, Geoffrey. "Lingo jingo: English only and the new nativism. (English language in US society)." *The American Prospect* n33 (July-August 1997 n33): 40(8). *Expanded Academic ASAP*. Thomson Gale. Worcester Polytechnic Institute. 16 June 2006 <http://find.galegroup.com/ips/infomark.do?&contentSet=IAC-Documents&type=retrieve&tabID=T002&prodId=IPS&docId=A19939424&source=gale&srcprod=EAIM&userGroupName=mlin_c_worpoly&version=1.0>.

Abstract:

The current English-only movement has focused the public eye on the question of the continued status of English as the common language of public discourse in the society. The movement is not only insulting to immigrants but is more disturbing because it reflects doubt in the ability of English-language culture to flourish in an open market. The English-only movement reflects the defensiveness linked to linguistic nationalism in other countries.

Thomson Gale Document Number:A19939424

Full Text:COPYRIGHT 1997 The American Prospect, Inc.

Since Slovakia became an independent state a few years ago, the Slovak majority has been imposing increasingly stringent language restrictions on the ethnic Hungarian minority, whom they suspect of irredentist leanings. Hungarian place-names must be changed to accord with Slovak spellings, all official business must be transacted in Slovak even in districts that are almost entirely Hungarian-speaking, and so forth. It's a familiar enough pattern in that part of the world, where antique ethnic policies are in fact thoroughly modern--even American. By way of demonstrating this, the Slovak State Language Law of 1995 cites the example of American official-English bills, and the drafters of the law made a point of entertaining a delegation from the U.S. English organization. In American eyes, though, the similarities might lead to another, more disquieting conclusion: What if it's we who are becoming more like them?

Fig. 5   Downloadable, full-text. InfoTrac.

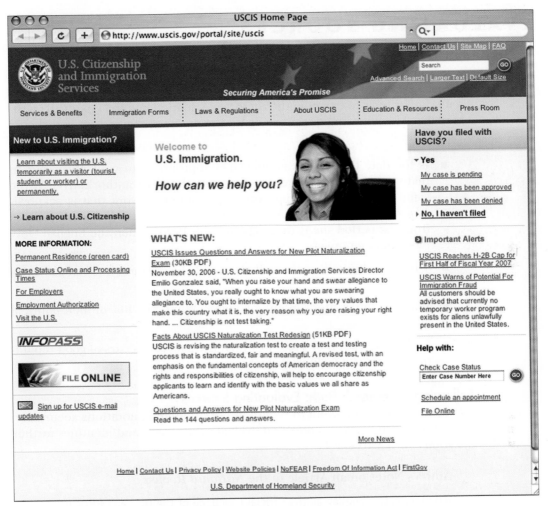

Fig. 6   Office of Immigration Statistics

Finding Immigration Statistics

As I got deeper into my research, I realized that the English Only movement emerged as immigration to the United States increased after the immigration law changed in 1965. I wanted to get some statistics on the patterns of immigration—where people came from, how many there were, where they settled. I remembered looking at the U.S. Citizenship and Immigration Services Web site when I was getting started, so I decided to go back and see what they had. I found the Office of Immigration Statistics that had the information I was looking for. [See Fig. 6.]

EVALUATING SOURCES

As you continue your research, keep in mind that you can't accept what your sources say at face value. Chapter 2, "Reading Strategies of Academic Purposes," and Chapter 3, "Persuasion and Responsibility: Analyzing Arguments," offer tools to examine the rhetorical situation and the arguments writers make. The following questions distill the main considerations you should keep in mind:

- Is the date the work was published appropriate to your purposes? In many cases, the most recent source is the most authoritative. At the same time, it may be appropriate to read older work that is acknowledged as important. In Amira's case, it makes sense to read sources from the period she is investigating, the 1990s, when the English Only movement emerged.

- What credibility does the writer have? Is he or she acknowledged as an authority?

- What is the writer's point of view? What are his or her political allegiances?

- Is the publication or press in which the source appears of good reputation? What is its editorial slant?

Following a Research Path: Evaluating Sources

Notice how Amira is careful to record information and quotations accurately. She follows with her own notes that evaluate the source and identifies further questions for her research.

Amira's Notes on an Article in the *National Review*

O'Beirne, Kate. "English as the Official Language of the U.S. and Bilingual Education." National Review 1 July 1996:21.

Cites opinion polls:

- In a 1996 Gallup Poll, 82% favored making English the official language.
- A 1993 poll by the Tarrance Group found 78% registered voters favored official English laws and over 60% favored it strongly.
- A 1993 poll by the San Francisco Chronicle found that 90% of Filipinos, 78% of Chinese, and nearly 70% of Latino immigrants in California favored official English.

Gives details on the Republican Party position on official English and bilingual education, ballots, and health care. Argues that given popular support for official English, Republicans should take stronger stand.

Key quote:

"We must stop the practice of multilingual education as a means of instilling ethnic pride or as a therapy for low self-esteem, or out of elitist guilt over a culture built on the tradition of the west." Bob Dole, in a speech to the American Legion.

Notes: Great find. National Review is an important conservative magazine, and Kate O'Beirne seems to be a prominent conservative commentator. Helps explain ideas of English Only movement.

Check San Francisco Chronicle poll. I may need to explain high support of official English among immigrant groups. May be a sign of desire to assimilate and could be used to argue that official English is unnecessary.

MAKING AN ARGUMENT

Doing research is learning new things and encountering new perspectives. Research involves you in a conversation with other people, who may influence what you think and believe. Stay open to these influences. It's not unusual for researchers to modify their initial ideas in light of what they find in their research.

At the same time, you need to assess what you've been reading so that you can make your own argument about the issues you've been examining. Here are some questions to help you determine the argument you want to make:

- Given what you've read so far, what sources have made the strongest impression on you, whether you agree with them or not?

- How have your sources influenced your thinking? Do you see your research question in the same way as when you started researching? What changes have occurred?

- What new perspectives or questions have you encountered? How do you plan to deal with them?

- Given all this, how can you put an argument together?

Following a Research Path: Making an Argument

Amira's Statement of Purpose

A lot of what I've read about the English Only movement (like James Crawford's Hold Your Tongue and Raymond Tatalovich's Nativism Reborn?) see it as an anti-immigrant backlash. The articles I've read by supporters of English

Only don't come right out and say they are anti-immigrant, but they do talk about how the U.S. is losing its national identity because of immigration and multiculturalism. They use terms like "balkanization" to create the impression that America is fragmenting into separate ethnic groups. They seem to think that the English language can hold everything together.

The feeling I get is that people are afraid that they are going to be overwhelmed by Spanish-speaking immigrants, if not now, then in the near future. Crawford's idea of "Hispanophobia" makes a lot of sense to me as a way to explain the English Only movement. That's what I think I want to say in my paper.

PLANNING AND DRAFTING YOUR PROJECT

There's always more to read, and it may seem that the research process could continue indefinitely. In certain respects, of course, this is true. Individuals have devoted their lives to research and never really reached the end of what they could learn. That's why deadlines are so useful—to remind writers that they need to emerge from the research process and start writing.

An important point here is that you need to make sure you're not using research to procrastinate and avoid writing. As already mentioned, when you're reading and evaluating your sources, you should also be making tentative plans about how to use these materials in your paper. Moreover, you can begin drafting well before you end your research. In fact, many researchers find that drafting helps them refine the focus of their research and directs them to issues they need to investigate further. To put it another way, you don't have to stop your research when you begin writing. But you do have to begin writing.

Following a Research Path: Making an Outline

Amira's First Outline

Set up the issue of English Only

> background information on states with English Only laws

> public opinion polls

emergence of U.S. English and English first in the 1990s

present basic positions and arguments of English Only

State purpose of paper: to explain the emergence of English

Only movement in the 1990s as "hispanophobia" resulting from new

patterns of immigration and cultural anxiety

Historical background

relation of language policy and nativism/Americanization

Anti-Irish literacy requirements for voting (1850s)

American Protective Association's campaign vs. German-language instruction

in parochial schools (1880s)

U.S. Bureau of Americanization (early 1900s)

1965 Immigration Reform Act

ended racial quotas

"new immigration"

demographic shifts increase in Latino population

Analysis of English Only movement

familiar sources of nativism in the 1990s:

economic stagnation (California)

widening gap between rich and poor

distrust of public institutions

breakdown of community

"hispanophobia" in California and the Southwest

historical roots

present manifestations

explain focus on language as symbol of imagined lost community

A CLOSING NOTE

As you can see from Amira Patel's sketch of her outline for her research paper on the English Only movement, she has listed topics and points of analysis that will be central to drafting her paper. Her task now is to begin writing so that she can see how the information and ideas from her research connect to each other.

You'll no doubt reach a similar point in your own research—when it's time to start writing. Remember that you know a lot by this point. You will have information, evidence, and arguments from others that may not be widely available to your readers. Don't assume that just because you know something, everyone else must know it too. You're the authority who is immersed in the topic and issues of your research, and it's your job to explain how it all fits together. Keep in mind what your purpose is in writing your research paper. To what extent do you need to inform, explain, evaluate, or argue about the issues that have come up in your research? What sources are likely to persuade your readers to take your point of view seriously? How can you make the best use of what you've found in the research process?

In the next chapter, we'll look at some of the options for incorporating your sources into critical essays and research papers.

chapter 13

working with sources

As noted already, academic writing does more than simply present the results of research. More importantly, it shows how the writer's research grows out of issues and problems in a particular field of study, and it explains the significance of the research to this ongoing discussion. Integrating and citing sources in a research paper lets your readers know how your work fits into a larger conversation.

Students sometimes think that using sources weakens their writing—that readers will think the important ideas in a paper come from others instead of from them. In college, however, readers expect writers to use and acknowledge sources. Readers want to understand what others have said about the issue you've researched, who has influenced your thinking, and how you stand in relation to the analyses, interpretations, and arguments others have offered. In fact, these expectations define in many respects what it means to work with sources.

In this chapter, we look first at some of the ways academic researchers work with their sources. Next, we present information on what plagiarism is and how to avoid it by properly integrating your sources. Finally, we cover how to document your sources in MLA and APA formats.

WORKING WITH SOURCES TO ANSWER YOUR RESEARCH QUESTION

In academic writing, you want to demonstrate how you are using your sources to create a meaningful answer to your research question. Here are some of the common ways to work with sources in college:

■ **To support a position, analysis, or interpretation:** Notice, for example, how Salim Muwakkil uses a study by the Sentencing Project and a quote from its executive director to establish his analysis of the "incarceration epidemic" in the United States:

> According to the Sentencing Project, a research group that advocates alternatives to prison, these rates of incarceration have increased

Online Study Center

439

despite sharp drops in violent crime since 1994. The relentless increase in inmates "can best be explained as the legacy of an entrenched infrastructure of punishment that has been embedded in the criminal justice system over the last 30 years," says Malcolm C. Young, the project's executive director.

■ **To assess the uses and limits of an analysis or interpretation:** Jennie Chen brings up the controversy over Elaine Showalter's book *Hystories: Hysterical Epidemics and the Modern Media* to point out an important issue in Showalter's interpretation of chronic fatigue syndrome. Notice how she uses Showalter's critics to explain the limits of the notion of "hysterical epidemic":

> One of the things that makes Showalter's book so controversial is that she groups CFS, as well as gulf war syndrome and multiple personality syndrome, with other contemporary "hysterical epidemics" such as alien abductions, satanic ritual abuse, and recovered memory. . . . For her critics, however, lumping illnesses such as CFS and gulf war syndrome with UFOs and satanic cults trivializes real suffering. By defining "illness as a story instead of a physical condition (with the CFS sufferer acting out, say, the narrative of a bored and frustrated housewife), Showalter diverts our attention from real suffering."

■ **To apply a concept to a new case or situation:** In her critical essay "The Dilemma of Empire," Jacqueline Perkins uses Joseph S. Nye Jr.'s concepts of "hard" and "soft" power to identify where foreign policy strategists stand since 9/11. After explaining what Nye means by "soft" power, Perkins then says:

> Paul Berman's *Terror and Liberalism* is a good example of "soft" power in its purest form. According to Berman, the main conflict in the "war on terrorism" is an ideological one between open and free societies such as the United States and political movements such as Saddam Hussein's Baathist Party, al Qaeda, and other Islamist fundamentalists.

■ **To change the terms of a debate:** In his research paper, "The Prison Privatization Debate: The Need for a New Focus," Andy Mgwanna shows how the arguments for and against the privatazation of prisons have reached an impasse. Then he explains what has been neglected by the debate and points to a new focus:

> One of the problems with this impasse, as Thomas O'Brien of the Horizon Institute for Policy Solutions suggests, is that the key issues of rehabilitation and recidivism, which have significant implications for the cost of the prison industrial complex, have been lost in a polarized debate. O'Brien suggests that rather than becoming bogged

down in the pros and cons of privatization, we should focus on incentives to both private and public prisons to prevent recidivism.

■ **To uncover an enabling assumption and its consequences:** In "How to Fight the New Epidemics," Lundy Braun first cites a well-known scientist to establish the dominant view of infectious diseases:

> In 1966, the eminent Australian immunologist Sir MacFarlane Burnet declared, "In many ways one can think of the middle of the 20th Century as the end of one of the most important social revolutions in history, the virtual elimination of infectious disease as a significant factor in social life." Shared by most of the scientific community, this view is rooted in the rise of the germ theory in the late 19th and early 20th centuries that associated specific microbial agents with particular diseases.

Then she explains the consequences of the germ theory's assumptions about disease causation:

> Thus, the germ theory effectively replaced disease prevention policies based on sanitary reforms, including improvement in sewage systems and better housing conditions, which were primarily responsible for the dramatic decline in the death rates from infectious disease.

WHAT IS PLAGIARISM?

Plagiarism is taking the words or ideas of someone else and presenting them as your own, without properly acknowledging their source in another's work. There are different ways in which plagiarism occurs.

■ **Cheating:** Buying a research paper, paying someone else to write a paper for you, or turning in someone's old paper is academic dishonesty, plain and simple, and is obviously intentional.

■ **Copying:** Reproducing sentences or passages from a book or article without citation may be intentional or may be due to a lack of understanding how properly to acknowledge sources.

■ **Copying patterns:** Plagiarism includes copying sentence structures, even if you change some of the words.

You can see how copying patterns works in a recent example, where Kaavya Viswanathan says that she "accidentally borrowed" sections from *Sloppy Firsts,* a book by Megan McCafferty, for her novel *How*

Opal Mehta Got Kissed, Got Wild, and Got a Life. Because of the plagiarism, her publishers withdrew the novel. Below are the examples of similar passages in the two books.

McCafferty's novel, page 7:

"Bridget is my age and lives across the street. For the first twelve years of my life, these qualifications were all I needed in a best friend. But that was before Bridget's braces came off and her boyfriend Burke got on, before Hope and I met in our seventh grade Honors classes."

Viswanathan's novel, page 14:

"Priscilla was my age and lived two blocks away. For the first fifteen years of my life, those were the only qualifications I needed in a best friend. We had bonded over our mutual fascination with the abacus in a playgroup for gifted kids. But that was before freshman year, when Priscilla's glasses came off, and the first in a long string of boyfriends came on."

McCafferty, page 6:

"Sabrina was the brainy Angel. Yet another example of how every girl had to be one or the other: Pretty or smart."

Viswanathan, page 39:

"Moneypenny was the brainy female character. Yet another example of how every girl had to be one or the other: smart or pretty."

- **Failure to cite properly:** The most common form of unintentional plagiarism results from not understanding how to use and cite sources properly. For this reason, to avoid plagiarism you need to be aware of the conventions of citation and the various options you have in integrating sources into your writing.

AVOIDING PLAGIARISM: HOW TO CITE PROPERLY

Here is a passage from Alan M. Kraut's chapter "Plagues and Prejudice: Nativism's Construction of Disease in Nineteenth- and Twentieth-Century New York" that appears on page 67 in *Hives of Sickness: Public Health and*

WHAT DO I HAVE TO CITE?

A reliable rule of thumb is that you should cite the source of any information, analysis, interpretation, or argument that is not common knowledge. It is common knowledge, for example, that William Shakespeare was a playwright in Elizabethan England, the Earth travels around the sun, and Darwin formulated the theory of natural selection. This is information so widely known that it doesn't really belong to anyone. On the other hand, a literary critic's interpretation of Hamlet, *an analysis of how Darwin developed his idea of natural selection, or an argument about the consequences of climate change is not considered common knowledge because it belongs to a particular person or group.*

Epidemics in New York City, the type of source you're likely to be working with in academic writing:

> As early as the 1830s, Irish immigrants who lived in rundown shanties and tenements along New York's rivers were being blamed for importing the cholera epidemic (from which they suffered disproportionately). Fear of cholera, especially after the epidemic of 1832, stimulated public demand for inspection of emigrants prior to departure. Soon, those who left from Western European ports began to receive an exam from a physician employed by the country of departure, lest shiploads of emigrants be annihilated by cholera during the voyage.

Problem 1: Copying and Failing to Cite Properly

Notice the following student-written passage plagiarizes (probably unintentionally) by copying sentences and failing to identify the source.

Copied Phrases Are Highlighted

During the 1830s, there was widespread concern about the danger of cholera being brought to the United States by immigrants. Prime suspects were the Irish, who lived in rundown shanties and tenements along New York's rivers and who suffered a high rate of cholera. Following the cholera epidemic of 1832, public pressure mounted to examine emigrants before they left Europe. Physicians hired by the European countries inspected departing passengers, lest shiploads of emigrants be annihilated by cholera during the voyage.

Revised Version

According to Alan M. Kraut, during the 1830s, there was widespread concern about the danger of cholera being brought to the United States by immigrants. Prime suspects were the Irish, "who lived in rundown shanties and tenements along New York's rivers" and who suffered a high rate of cholera. Following the cholera epidemic of 1832, public pressure mounted to examine emigrants before they left Europe. Physicians hired by the European countries inspected departing passengers, "lest shiploads of emigrants be annihilated by cholera during the voyage" (67).

Notice how the revised version (1) turns the source "on" by attributing the ideas to the author ("According to Alan M. Kraut") and then turns it "off" with the page citation (67) at the end of the passage, and (2) carefully puts direct quotes in quotation marks.

Problem 2: Copying Sentence Structure and Failing to Cite Properly

Notice in this example how the student copies sentence structure and does not cite the source of the ideas.

Alan M. Kraut (original source)	Student
Soon, those who left from Western European ports began to receive an exam from a physician employed by the country of departure, lest shiploads of emigrants be annihilated by cholera during the voyage.	Before long, those departing from Western European ports were examined by doctors hired by the country of departure, so that boatloads of emigrants would not die from cholera during the trip.

Revised Version

Following the cholera epidemic of 1832, public pressure mounted to examine emigrants before they left Europe. Physicians in European ports of departure inspected passengers in an effort to prevent the spread of cholera (Kraut 67).

Notice how the revised version (1) integrates ideas into the student's own sentence structure, and (2) includes citation of the author's name and the page number at the end of sentence.

OPTIONS FOR INTEGRATING SOURCES

The three basic methods of integrating sources are *paraphrasing*, *summarizing*, and *quoting*. Whichever you use, be sure to cite properly. Turn your source "on" by citing the author with a phrase like "According to Alan M. Kraut" or "Kraut points out" and "off" by citing the page number in parentheses. When you do not identify the author with one of these phrases, include the author's last name and the page number (Kraut 67).

- **Paraphrasing** means restating in your own words and sentence structure. A paraphrase is typically about the same length as the original and is used when you want to explain the details in the original source:

    According to Alan M. Kraut, during the 1830s, there was widespread concern about the danger of cholera being brought to the United States by immigrants. Prime suspects were the Irish, who suffered a high rate of cholera. Following the cholera epidemic of 1832, public pressure mounted to examine emigrants before they left Europe. In order to prevent devastating outbreaks of disease onboard the ships, physicians hired by the European countries inspected departing passengers (67).

- **Summarizing** means selecting main ideas from the original and presenting them in your own words and sentence structure. Summaries can range from a sentence to a paragraph or more, depending on the amount of detail you need. Notice in this example, how details are omitted to emphasize a single point:

> During the 1830s the fear that immigrants were bringing cholera with them to the United States led to health inspections of departing passengers in the European ports (Kraut 67).

- **Quoting** means duplicating the exact words as they appear in the original. In general, use direct quotations selectively. Quotations are best suited when you want to capture something in the original you would lose by paraphrasing, or when a direct quotation from an expert will lend authority. Short quotes, even a key word or phrase, are often more effective than longer ones.

SHORT QUOTATIONS

Words

Writers typically quote single words to emphasize important points and represent key concepts in their discussion. Often the quoted word is a term that someone has coined for analytical purposes, as in these two instances:

> The ceremonial suspension of normal identities by World Wrestling Federation stars offers spectators a way to participate in what Victor Turner calls a "liminal" moment, when ordinary time and everyday human affairs come briefly to a halt and the extraordinary takes over.
>
> Stuart Hall's notion of "encoding/decoding" in media communication enables us to see how messages are transformed as they circulate from production to reception.

Notice in these two examples that the key terms "liminal" and "encoding/decoding" appear in quotes and that in each case the author is noted. There are no page numbers, however, because the terms appear throughout the original sources, which are then acknowledged in Works Cited.

Phrases

You can integrate phrases as elements in sentences of your own construction:

> Alan M. Kraut explains how the growing fear that immigrants were bringing cholera to the United States "stimulated public demand for inspection of emigrants prior to departure" from Europe (67).

Sentences

You can use a complete sentence or two from your source:

> According to Alan M. Kraut, "Fear of cholera, especially after the epidemic of
> 1832, stimulated public demand for inspection of emigrants prior to departure" (67).

LONG QUOTATIONS

Use an indented block for long quotations. MLA identifies long quotations as more than four lines, while APA uses 40 words. Indent one inch (or ten spaces) from the left margin if you are using MLA style, or a half-inch (or five spaces) from the left margin if you are using APA style, and in both cases double-space the passage with no extra space above or below the block. Using this block form tells readers that the material is quoted directly from the original, so you don't need quotation marks. The page citation goes in parentheses after the punctuation at the end of the quote. The example below uses MLA style—indenting ten spaces to form the block. For single paragraphs or portions of a paragraph, do not indent the first line. If you quote two or more paragraphs, indent three additional spaces (one-quarter inch) at the beginning of each successive paragraph.

> Public health historian Alan M. Kraut points out how Americans have long
> viewed immigrants as carriers of disease:
>
> > As early as the 1830s, Irish immigrants who lived in rundown shanties and tenements along New York's rivers were being blamed for importing the cholera epidemic (from which they suffered disproportionately). Fear of cholera, especially after the epidemic of 1832, stimulated public demand for inspection of emigrants prior to departure. Soon, those who left from western European ports began to receive an exam from a physician employed by the country of departure, lest shiploads of emigrants be annihilated by cholera during the voyage. (67)

FITTING QUOTATIONS TO YOUR SENTENCES

Under certain circumstances, you may modify the material you're quoting. The two basic techniques for modifying the original passage are ellipses and brackets. You use ellipses to omit something in the original and brackets to add or change something. Here are examples of typical uses of each.

Ellipses

Use ellipses when you want to omit part of the original passage. If you are omitting material in the middle of a sentence, use a set of three spaced periods, with a space before and after.

> "As early as the 1830s," Alan M. Kraut notes, "Irish immigrants . . . were
> being blamed for importing the cholera epidemic" (67).

When you quote single words or phrases, you don't need to use ellipses because readers can see you're quoting only part of a passage. If the material you're omitting occurs between sentences, include a fourth period to mark the end of the first sentence.

> Alan M. Kraut notes similarities between the official response to cholera, polio, and tuberculosis in the nineteenth and early twentieth centuries and to AIDS in the 1990s:
>
>> In the early 1990s, the federal government continued to pursue institutional means of epidemic control to stop AIDS at the border, a means that stigmatizes immigrants of all nationalities. . . . As in earlier crises, the federal government had sought to use exclusion to control the epidemic; immigrants were subjected to mandatory testing for no clear epidemiological reason other than foreign birth. (83)

Brackets

Brackets are used to make small changes in the original passage so that it fits grammatically into your sentences.

> According to Alan M. Kraut, the federal government's use of mandatory AIDS testing repeats a pattern that can be found in earlier public health crises, "stigmatiz[ing] immigrants of all nationalities" (83).

Brackets can also be used to add clarifying material.

Original

> Wealthy New York City merchants and uptown landowners, who in the early 1850s proposed the creation of Central Park, hoped to create a refined setting for their own socializing. But seeking to establish the public value of their project, they also invoked the language of the English sanitary reformers and claimed the park would improve the health and morals of the city's working people.
>
> *(Alan M. Kraut, "Plagues and Prejudice," p. 57)*

Use of Brackets

> Alan M. Kraut shows how the proposal to create Central Park drew on themes from the public health movement: "seeking to establish the public value of their project, they [wealthy New York City merchants and uptown landowners] also invoked the language of the English sanitary reformers and claimed the park would improve the health and morals of the city's working people" (57).

Quotations Within Quotations

The passage you want to quote may at times contain quoted material. If the passage is long enough to use block form, then keep the quotation marks as they are in the original. If, however, you are going to incorporate a quotation that includes a quotation into your own sentence, then change the double quotation marks in the original into single quotation marks.

Original

Against this backdrop of economic depression, the physician and city inspector John Griscom launched a new phase of sanitary reform in his 1842 report when he singled out "the crowded conditions, with insufficient ventilation" of dwellings as "first among the most serious causes of disordered public health."

(Alan M. Kraut, "Plagues and Prejudice," p. 54)

Quotations Within a Quotation

Alan M. Kraut claims that "John Griscom launched a new phase of sanitary reform in his 1842 report when he singled out 'the crowded conditions, with insufficient ventilation' of dwellings as 'first among the most serious causes of disordered public health'" (54).

CHECKLIST FOR USING QUOTES EFFECTIVELY

The following questions offer further guidelines as you review your work and consider needed revisions.

DO YOU NEED THE QUOTE?

Quoted material should be chosen carefully to advance the line of thinking in a research project. It should emphasize main ideas, not just be used decoratively or as proof that you've read a number of sources.

The plot of Wuthering Heights puts the death of the heroine in the middle of the novel. Although she has died in childbirth, Catherine Earnshaw relentlessly haunts Heathcliff until eighteen years later he too finally rests by her side in a grave "on the edge of the churchyard" (Frank 219).

The quoted phrase does not really contain an idea that matters to the discussion. Quotes like this one should be scrutinized closely to see if they are needed.

IS IT CLEAR WHERE SOURCES START AND STOP?

One of the keys to avoiding plagiarism is marking clearly where quoted material starts and stops. In the example below, notice how the first two quotes—the highlighted sentence and phrase—seem to be floating in the paragraph, and how the in-text citation (219) confusingly appears before the writer has finished quoting from the source.

> Wuthering Heights uses subtle psychological portrayals of its main characters, Catherine Earnshaw and Heathcliff, to turn them into mythic figures. "They are driven, tormented, violent lovers, and there are no wedding bells for them in the final chapter." In the grip of a titanic passion, their love can only be realized in death. Before his death, Heathcliff arranges to have the sides of his and Catherine's adjoining coffins dismantled "so that in death they might finally achieve the consummation of their love" (219). This is the "perfect and irrevocable union," Katherine Frank says, "which had tormented and eluded them when they were alive."

All the quoted material is from Katherine Frank's book *A Chainless Soul*, but readers will have to guess the source of the first two quotes. This problem can easily be fixed, as you can see by the highlighted revisions:

> Wuthering Heights uses subtle psychological portrayals of its main characters, Catherine Earnshaw and Heathcliff, to turn them into mythic figures. "They are driven, tormented, violent lovers," Katherine Frank says, "and there are no wedding bells for them in the final chapter." In the grip of a titanic passion, their love can only be realized in death. Before his death, Heathcliff arranges to have the sides of his and Catherine's adjoining coffins dismantled "so that in death they might finally achieve the consummation of their love." According to Frank, this is the "perfect and irrevocable union—which had tormented and eluded them when they were alive" (219).

ARE SOURCES USED PURPOSEFULLY OR JUST STRUNG TOGETHER?

Make sure your sources are set up so that readers will see how each quoted and paraphrased idea fits into your writing. Sources that are strung together, as in the following example, resemble research notes transcribed directly into a paper. As you can see, the writing seems to ramble from quote to quote without any sense of purposeful direction:

> The musical label "soul" is associated with Motown and Memphis in the 1960s, but the term has been in use much longer. According to gospel singer

Mahalia Jackson, "What some people call the 'blues singing feeling' is expressed by the Church of God in Christ. . . . The basic thing is soul feeling. The same in blues as in spirituals. And also with gospel music. It is soul music" (qtd. in Ricks 139). "Soul assumes a shared experience, a relationship with the listener . . . where the singer confirms and works out the feelings of the audience. In this sense, it remains sacramental" (qtd. in Guralnick 3). "As professions, blues singing and preaching seem to be closely linked in both the rural or small town settings and in the urban ghettos" (Keil 143). Nonetheless, "Ray Charles's transformation of dignified gospel standards into cries of secular ecstasy came in for a good deal of criticism at first, mostly from the pulpit" (Guralnick 2).

A revision of this paragraph would require unpacking each quote by explaining the ideas and connecting them to the main points in the paper. Each quote may need its own paragraph, or the writer might combine two or more quotes in a paragraph. In any case, the quotes need space to breathe.

Do You Provide Commentary Where It Is Needed?

Quotes don't speak for themselves. As you've just seen in the example with the string of quotes, you need to connect your sources to the main points in your paper so that readers can see how and why the sources are significant. Your commentary is crucial to making these connections explicit. In the following example, notice how the quote leaves us hanging because it is not followed up by commentary from the writer:

Wuthering Heights is partially based on the Gothic tradition, a quasi-horror writing that features haunting imagery, desolate landscapes, and supernatural encounters. Bronte draws on the Gothic to turn her main characters, Catherine Earnshaw and Heathcliff, into mythic figures in the grip of a titanic passion. Catherine marries Edgar Linton, and Heathcliff marries Edgar's sister Isabella, but these marriages have no impact on Catherine and Heathcliff's passionate love. Nor does death. Although she dies in childbirth in the middle of the novel, Catherine relentlessly haunts Heathcliff until eighteen years later he too finally rests by her side. As Katherine Frank explains:

> Before he dies, Heathcliff makes a ghoulish arrangement with the sexton to knock out the adjoining sides of his own and Catherine's coffins so that in death they might finally achieve the consummation of their love—a perfect and irrevocable union—which had tormented and eluded them when they were alive. (219)

In earlier Gothic novels, the central narrative is often approached by way of a frame tale that uses diaries, letters, and other documents, which are transcribed or edited by the narrator. Similarly, the reader approaches the narrative of <u>Wuthering Heights</u> via an outsider, Lockwood.

A few lines of commentary from the writer would not only consolidate the point in the paragraph but also set up a smoother transition into the next paragraph, as shown in the example that follows.

> . . . the consummation of their love—a perfect and irrevocable union— which had tormented and eluded them when they were alive (219).

In true Gothic style, Bronte blurs the line between life and death to create an imaginary world of haunted and uncontrollable passions.

This imaginary world is typically both verified and kept at a mysterious distance in Gothic novels by a frame tale that uses diaries, letters, and other documents, which are transcribed or . . .

DOCUMENTING SOURCES: MLA AND APA STYLE

The two main styles of citation—MLA and APA—use parenthetical citations within the text. Information about the source is included in the text and keyed to a list of sources at the end of the paper—*Works Cited* in MLA style and *References* in APA. The information called for by MLA and APA in the parenthetical citation differs somewhat. MLA uses author and page, while APA uses author, year, and page.

The following pages describe MLA and APA systems for citing sources within the text and for listing sources at the end of the paper. For further information, you can consult *MLA Handbook for Writers of Research Papers* (6th ed., 2003) or the MLA Web site www.mla.org and *Publication Manual of the American Psychological Association* (5th ed., 2001) or the APA website on documenting electronic sources www.apastyle.org/elecref.html.

IN-TEXT CITATIONS

The following list shows how MLA and APA styles set up parenthetical in-text citations for many types of sources.

SOURCES WITH ONE AUTHOR

In many instances, you'll be citing the author in the sentence that uses the source material.

MLA

> According to Daniel J. Czitrom, following the Civil War, there appeared the "first rush of literature on the pathology of mass communication, with which we are so familiar today" (19).

Note that you do not repeat the author's name when you give the page number at the end of the quotation.

APA

> According to Daniel J. Czitrom (1982), following the Civil War, there appeared the "first rush of literature on the pathology of mass communication, with which we are so familiar today" (p. 19).

Note that in APA style, the date of publication appears immediately after the author's name.

If you don't cite the author in the sentence, then use these forms:

MLA

> Following the Civil War, there appeared the "first rush of literature on the pathology of mass communication, with which we are so familiar today" (Czitrom 19).

MLA style notes the author and the page number, with no punctuation in between or "p." before the page.

APA

> Following the Civil War, there appeared the "first rush of literature on the pathology of mass communication, with which we are so familiar today" (Czitrom, 1982, p. 19).

APA style includes the author's name, the date of publication, and the page number, with commas in between and "p." before the page number.

Notice that for both MLA and APA styles, the final period comes after the citation.

MLA

> Following the Civil War, there appeared the "first rush of literature on the pathology of mass communication, with which we are so familiar today" (Czitrom, Media 19).

When you have more than one source by an author, MLA style uses the author's name, a shortened version of the title (the full title is *Media and the American Mind: From Morse to McLuhan*), and the page number.

APA

> Following the Civil War, there appeared the "first rush of literature on the pathology of mass communication, with which we are so familiar today" (Czitrom, 1982, p. 19).

APA style remains the same because the work is already noted by the year. However, if you are citing in APA style more than one work published by an author in the same year, add a letter to the date (1982a, 1982b) and key these to your references at the end of the paper. For example, if you cited a second work Czitrom published in 1982, the first work would be cited as:

(Czitrom, 1982a, p. 19)

and the second would look like this:

(Czitrom, 1982b, p. 43)

SOURCES WITH MULTIPLE AUTHORS

MLA and APA use different systems to cite sources having more than one author.

MLA

If the work has two or three authors, cite all:

Despite the claims made for it, literacy "is not in itself a panacea for social inequity" (Lunsford, Moglen, and Slevin 2).

If the work has more than three authors, use the first author's name followed by "et al."

What we know of Indian cultures prior to 1700 has mostly been gleaned from the evidence of various artifacts, such as pottery, weapons, and stories passed down from generation to generation (Lauter et al. 5).

APA

If the source you are citing has two authors, include both last names in the reference, separated by an ampersand (&).

Nigeria home-video movies "are turning out the Nigerian story in a no-holds-barred fashion which leaves no room for anybody to hide" (Ofeiman & Kelani, 2005, p. 245).

For sources with three to five authors, list all of the authors' last names the first time you cite the source, separating each name by a comma and putting an ampersand before the final name.

Despite the claims made for it, literacy "is not in itself a panacea for social inequity" (Lunsford, Moglen, & Slevin, 1990, p. 2).

For subsequent citations, include simply the last name of the first author followed by "et al." and the year and the page. If a source has six or more authors, use the last name of the first author and "et al." in every citation:

Despite the claims made for it, literacy "is not in itself a panacea for social inequity" (Lunsford et al., 1990, p. 2).

SOURCES WITH NO AUTHOR LISTED

If no author is listed on the work, both MLA and APA use a shortened version of the title.

MLA

A 1996 study found that men who frequent prostitutes or have many sexual partners may increase their wives' risk of cervical cancer ("Man's Sex Life").

Note that if your source appears on a single page, MLA does not require you to list the page number.

APA

A 1996 study found that men who frequent prostitutes or have many sexual partners may increase their wives' risk of cervical cancer ("Man's Sex Life," 1996, p. 15).

The MLA and APA citations use a shortened version of the title of the article, "Man's Sex Life and Cancer in Wife Linked."

ELECTRONIC SOURCES

Sources you have accessed on the Web or through electronic databases are handled in much the same way as print sources.

MLA

Hurricane Katrina revealed "some of the blank spots and overlooked inequities in race relations that were shocking to many whites but lived realities for most blacks" (Carpenter 2).

If no author is listed, use the title of the document. If the document has numbered paragraphs rather than pages, use the number following a comma and the abbreviation par. (e.g., McKenzie, par. 4). For documents with no numbered pages or paragraphs, no number is listed.

APA

Hurricane Katrina revealed "some of the blank spots and overlooked inequities in race relations that were shocking to many whites but lived realities for most blacks" (Carpenter, 2006, p. 2).

If no date of publication is given, use "n.d." If no author is listed, use a shortened version of the title. When there are no page numbers, use paragraph numbers to document quotes:

The marketing of race-specific drugs such as Bi-Dil has raised "troubling questions about the reinstitution of race as a biological category in medicine" ("Return of Race," n.d., para. 4).

INDIRECT QUOTATIONS

For cases when you want to quote something that appeared as a quote in one of your sources, use "qtd. in" (MLA) or "cited in" (APA). In the following two examples, the writer is quoting the blues musician Son House from an interview that appeared originally in Pete Welding's book *The Living Blue* and then was quoted by Greil Marcus's in his book *Mystery Train*.

MLA

"He sold his soul to the devil to get to play like that," House told blues historian Pete Welding (qtd. in Marcus 32).

APA

"He sold his soul to the devil to get to play like that," House told blues historian Pete Welding (cited in Marcus, 1975, p. 32).

WORKS CITED (MLA) AND REFERENCES (APA)

Every source that appears in the text should be listed in a separate section at the end of your paper. Don't include works that you read but did not cite. MLA calls the list "Works Cited," while APA uses "References." Both systems alphabetize by author's last name or the first word in the title of a work with no author.

BOOKS

Here is the basic format for MLA and APA. Notice how they differ.

MLA

Gilroy, Paul. <u>Postcolonial Melancholia</u>. New York: Columbia UP, 2005.

MLA style uses the complete first name of the author, capitalizes major words in the title, lists the date at the end of the citation, and indents the second line five spaces. The period following the book title is not underlined or italicized. In MLA style, use the abbreviation "UP" for university presses, as in Columbia UP.

APA

Gilroy, P. (2005). *Postcolonial melancholia*. New York: Columbia University Press.

APA style uses the author's first initial, lists the date right after the author's name, capitalizes only the first word in the title and after a colon (plus any proper nouns), spells out "University Press," and indents the second line five spaces.

Both systems double-space throughout.

Notice in the examples that the place of publication is well known. In these cases, don't add the state. In APA citations where the place of publication is not well known, do add the state: e.g., Thousand Oaks, CA: Sage.

Two Listings by One Author
MLA

> Gilroy, Paul. Postcolonial Melancholia. New York: Columbia UP, 2005.
> ---. "There Ain't No Black in the Union Jack": The Cultural Politics of Race and Nation. Chicago: U of Chicago P, 1987.

When you're listing two or more works by the same author, use alphabetical order according to title. For the second title, type three hyphens and a period in place of the author's name.

APA

> Gilroy, P. (1987). *"There ain't no black in the Union Jack": The cultural politics of race and nation*. Chicago: University of Chicago Press.
> Gilroy, P. (2005). *Postcolonial melancholia*. New York: Columbia University Press.

APA style uses chronological order to list works, beginning with the earliest. When an author has more than one work published in the same year, list them in alphabetical order by title and add lowercase letters to the year—e.g., 1977a, 1977b:

> Gould, S. J. (1977a). *Ontogeny and phylogeny*. Cambridge, U.K.: Cambridge University Press.
> Gould, S. J. (1977b). Sociobiology: The art of storytelling. *New Scientist, 80,* 530–533.

Books with Multiple Authors
MLA

For two or three authors, list them in the order in which they appear on the book's title page. Invert only the first author's name.

> Current, Richard Nelson, Marcia Ewing Current, and Loie Fuller. Goddess of Light. Boston: Northeastern UP, 1997.

If there are more than three authors, you may list them all or list only the first author followed by "et al."

> Anderson, Daniel, Bret Benjamin, Christopher Busiel, and Bill Parades-Holt. Teaching On-Line: Internet Research, Conversation, and Composition. New York: Harper, 1996.

or

> Anderson, Daniel, et al. Teaching On-Line: Internet Research, Conversation, and Composition. New York: HarperCollins, 1996.

APA

For works with two to six authors, list the authors in the order in which they appear on the title page, using last name and initials. Use an ampersand before the last author's name.

> Anderson, D., Benjamin, B., Busiel, C., & Parades-Holt, B. (1996). *Teaching online: Internet research, conversation, and composition.* New York: HarperCollins.

Books by a Corporate Author or Organization

Give the name of the corporate or organizational author as it appears on the title page.

MLA

> NOW Legal Defense and Educational Fund. Facts on Reproductive Rights: A Resource Manual. New York: NOW Legal Defense and Educational Fund, 2004.

APA

> NOW Legal Defense and Educational Fund. (2004). *Facts on reproductive rights: A resource manual.* New York: Author.

Books by an Anonymous Author

In MLA style, if no author is listed or the author is anonymous, begin with the title of the publication.

MLA

> Primary Colors: A Novel of Politics. New York: Random, 1996.

APA

> *Primary colors: A novel of politics.* (1996). New York: Random House.

In APA style, begin the entry with the title if no author is listed. If a work's author is designated as "Anonymous," however, use the word "Anonymous" at the beginning of the entry.

An Edition of an Original Work
MLA

> Melville, Herman. Moby-Dick. 1851. Ed. Alfred Kazin. Boston: Houghton, 1956.

APA

> Melville, H. (1956). *Moby-Dick* (A. Kazin, Ed.). Boston: Houghton Mifflin. (Original work published 1851)

An Introduction, Preface, Foreword, or Afterword
MLA

> Kazin, Alfred. Introduction. Moby-Dick. By Herman Melville. Ed. Alfred Kazin. Boston: Houghton, 1956. v-xiv.

APA

> Kazin, A. (1956). Introduction. In H. Melville, *Moby-Dick* (A. Kazin, Ed.) (pp. v–xiv). Boston: Houghton Mifflin.

Edited Collections
MLA

> Grumet, Robert S., ed. <u>Northeastern Indian Lives</u>. Amherst: U of Massachusetts P, 1996.

APA

> Grumet, R. S. (Ed.). (1996). *Northeastern Indian lives*. Amherst: University of Massachusetts Press.

Works in Collections and Anthologies
MLA

> Fitzgerald, F. Scott. "Bernice Bobs Her Hair." <u>The Short Stories of F. Scott Fitzgerald: A New Collection</u>. Ed. Matthew J. Bruccoli. New York: Scribner, 1989. 25–47.
> Ochs, Donovan J. "Cicero's Rhetorical Theory." <u>A Synoptic History of Classical Rhetoric</u>. Ed. James J. Murphy. Davis: Hermagoras, 1983. 90-150.

APA

> Fitzgerald, F. (1989). Bernice bobs her hair. In M. J. Bruccoli (Ed.), *The short stories of F. Scott Fitzgerald: A new collection* (pp. 25–47). New York: Scribner.
> Ochs, D. J. (1983). Cicero's rhetorical theory. In J. J. Murphy (Ed.), *A synoptic history of classical rhetoric* (pp. 90–150). Davis, CA: Hermagoras.

Translations
MLA

> Sartre, Jean-Paul. <u>The Age of Reason</u>. Trans. Eric Sutton. New York: Bantam, 1959.

APA

> Sartre, J. P. (1959). *The age of reason* (E. Sutton, Trans.). New York: Bantam Books.

Books in a Later Edition
MLA

> Woloch, Nancy. <u>Women and the American Experience</u>. 3rd ed. New York: McGraw, 1999.

APA

> Woloch, N. (1999). *Women and the American experience* (3rd ed.). New York: McGraw-Hill.

Dictionary Entries and Encyclopedia Articles
MLA

> "Australia." The Concise Columbia Encyclopedia. 3rd ed. 1995.
> "Freeze-etching." Merriam-Webster's Collegiate Dictionary. 11th ed. 2003.
> Jolliffe, David A. "Genre." Encyclopedia of Rhetoric and Composition. Ed. Theresa Enos. New York: Garland, 1996.

In MLA style, for familiar reference works such as *Merriam-Webster's Collegiate Dictionary* and *The Concise Columbia Encyclopedia,* you can omit listing the editors and publication information. For less familiar or more specialized sources, however, you should include all the information. Page numbers are not needed as long as the work is arranged alphabetically.

APA

> Australia. (1995). *The concise Columbia encyclopedia* (3rd ed.). New York: Columbia University Press.
> Freeze-etching. (2003). *Merriam-Webster's collegiate dictionary* (11th ed.). Springfield, MA: Merriam Webster.
> Jolliffe, D. A. (1996). Genre. In Theresa Enos (Ed.), *Encyclopedia of rhetoric and composition*. New York: Garland.

Government Documents
MLA

> United States. Dept. of Commerce. International Trade Administration. A Guide to Financing Exports. Washington: GPO, 2005.

APA

> Department of Commerce, International Trade Administration. (2005). *A guide to financing exports* (Monthly Catalog No. 85024488). Washington, DC: U.S. Government Printing Office.

APA includes the catalog number of the publication.

Unpublished Doctoral Dissertations
MLA

> Herzong, Mary Lucinda. "Living and Dying: Accommodating AIDS into Autobiography (Immune Deficiency)." Diss. U of California, 1995.

APA

Herzong, M. L. (1995). *Living and dying: Accommodating AIDS into autobiography (immune deficiency)*. Unpublished doctoral dissertation, University of California, Berkeley.

ARTICLES IN PERIODICALS

Here are examples of the basic MLA and APA formats for listing articles that appear in periodicals such as scholarly journals, magazines, and newspapers.

MLA

Bangeni, Bongi and Rochelle Kapp. "Identities in Transition: Shifting Conceptions of Home among 'Black' South African University Students." African Studies Review 48.3 (2005): 110-31.

MLA style uses the author's full name, marks article titles by using quotation marks and capitalization, and lists both volume 48 and issue 3 for journals that page each issue separately. Notice that MLA separates page numbers with a hyphen and shortens the second number 110-31.

For journals with continuous pagination, drop the issue number:

Lu, Min-Zhan. "Living-English Work." College English 68 (2006): 605-18.

APA

Bangeni, B., & Kapp, R. (2005). Identities in transition: Shifting conceptions of home among "black" South African university students. *African Studies Review, 48*(3), 110–131.

APA style uses abbreviations for first and middle names, and the date follows the author's name. APA does not use quotation marks or capitalization for article titles (except for the first word of the title and any subtitle, and any proper nouns and proper adjectives). In APA style, the name of the journal, the volume number (48), and the comma that follows it are all underlined or italicized, and the issue number is included in parentheses (3) for journals that page issues separately. Notice that APA uses a dash to separate page numbers and does not shorten the second number.

For journals with continuous pagination, drop the issue number:

Lu, M-Z. (2006). Living-English work. *College English, 68*, 605–618.

Magazine Articles

The first two examples show how to list magazines that appear monthly or bimonthly and weekly or biweekly. The third example is an article without an author listed.

MLA

Augustine, Pablo. "Irrawaddy River Dolphins." Scientific American Sept. 2005: 26–30.

"Pleas from Prison." <u>Newsweek</u> 24 Nov. 1997: 44.

Pollitt, Katha. "No Presents Please." <u>Nation</u> 14 Aug. 2006: 10.

APA

Augustine, P. (2005, September). Irrawaddy River dolphins. *Scientific American,* 26–30.

Pleas from prison. (1997, November 24). *Newsweek,* 44.

Pollitt, K. (2006, August 14). No presents please. *The Nation,* 10.

Notice that APA style capitalizes "the" in the title of magazines and newspapers such as *The Nation* and *The New York Times,* while MLA style does not use "the" in these cases.

Newspaper Articles
MLA

"AMA Plans Seal of Approval for Physicians." <u>Providence Journal-Bulletin</u> 19 November 1997: A5.

Morrow, David J. "Attention Disorder Is Found in Growing Number of Adults." <u>New York Times</u> 2 Sept. 1997: A1.

APA

AMA plans seal of approval for physicians. (1997, November 19). *The Providence Journal-Bulletin,* p. A5.

Morrow, D. J. (1997, September 2). Attention disorder is found in growing number of adults. *The New York Times,* p. A1.

Editorial
MLA

"Lessons from Prudhoe Bay." Editorial. <u>New York Times</u> 6 Aug. 2006: A30.

APA

Lessons from Prudhoe Bay [Editorial]. (2006, August 6). *The New York Times,* p. A30.

Review
MLA

Ewald, Paul W. "Pedigree of a Retrovirus." Rev. of <u>Viral Sex: The Nature of AIDS,</u> by Jaap Goudsmit. <u>Natural History</u> June 1997: 8-9.

APA

Ewald, P. W. (1997, June). Pedigree of a retrovirus [Review of the book *Viral sex: The nature of AIDS*]. *Natural History,* 8–9.

If there is no author listed for the review, begin with the title of the review. If there is no title, use "Rev. of <u>Title</u>" for MLA format and "[Review of the book

Title]" for APA. In this case, alphabetize under the title of the book being reviewed.

Letter to the Editor
MLA

> Daniels, John. Letter. <u>Sacramento Bee</u> 8 Mar. 2003: A30.

APA

> Daniels, J. (2003, March 8). [Letter to the editor]. *Sacramento Bee,* p. A30.

ONLINE AND ELECTRONIC SOURCES

For online sources, MLA and APA guidelines call for much of the same information you use for print sources, such as document title and author's name (if it is available). In addition, MLA and APA also call for two special items of information:

- **Date of posting and retrieval:** Online sources can change quickly, so you need to provide dates that identify which version of a source you are citing. If it is available, provide the date of publication or update when the source you consulted was posted online. You can always give the date you retrieved the source.

- **Uniform resource locator (URL):** So readers can find online sources, give each source's exact and complete electronic address or URL. The easiest way to make sure the URL is accurate is to copy it from your browser's address window and paste it in your paper. If you have to break up an address at the end of a line, do not use a hyphen. Make the break only after a slash (/).

Web Sites
MLA

> Crawford, James. <u>Language Policy Web Site & Emporium</u>. 8 Feb. 2001
> <http://ourworld.compuserve.com/homepages/jwcrawford>.
> <u>Kheel Center for Labor-Management Documentation and Archives</u>. 2006. Cornell
> University School of Industrial and Labor Relations. 14 July 2006
> <http://www.ilr.cornell.edu/library/kheelcenter/default.html?page+home>.
> <u>U.S. English Only</u>. Home page. 19 Jan. 2006. 8 Feb. 2006
> <http://www.us-english.org>.

The order of information for MLA: Name of author, creator, or site owner, if available; title of document, if named; date of last posting, if available; name of any institution or organization associated with the date; date of retrieval; URL enclosed in angle brackets < >.

In the first example above, no posting date is given, only the date of retrieval. The second example includes both posting and retrieval dates. Notice in the U.S. English Only example, where the Web site is not titled, you add the description "home page" without underlining or putting it in quotes.

APA

Crawford, J. (n.d.). *Language policy web site and emporium.* Retrieved February 8, 2001, from http://ourworld.compuserve.com/homepages/ jwcrawford

Kheel Center for labor-management documentation and archives. (2006). Retrieved July 14, 2006, from Cornell University School of Industrial and Labor Relations Web site: http://www.ilr.cornell.edu/library/kheelcenter/ default.html?page+home

Upstate Economic Development Council. (2005, March 15). *Prospects for rural revitalization: New crops and new markets.* Retrieved July 7, 2006, from http:www.upecodev.gov/html

The order of information for APA: Name of author, creator, or site owner, if available; date of last posting; title of document, if named; date of retrieval and URL in one sentence, without using angle brackets or a period at the end.

As is true with print sources, APA uses an initial for an author's first and middle names and capitalizes only the first word in a document title and the first word following a colon. Notice in the second example that you use "n.d." (no date) if there is no date of posting available.

Web Sites: Secondary Pages
MLA

de Ferranti, David. "Innovative Financing Options and the Fight against Global Poverty: What's New and What Next?" Brookings Institute. July 2006. 29 July 2006 <http://www.brook.edu/index/papersarticles.htm>.

"The Triangle Factory Fire." Kheel Center for Labor-Management Documentation and Archives. 24 Mar. 2005. Cornell University School of Industrial and Labor Relations. 14 Oct 2005 <http://www.ilr.cornell.edu/trianglefire/>.

Notice that the URL links to the Web page cited, not to the home page of the Brookings Institute or the Kheel Center.

APA

de Ferranti, D. (2006, July). *Innovative financing options and the fight against global poverty: What's new and what next?* Retrieved 29 July, 2006, from the Brookings Institute Web site: http://www.brook.edu/index/ papersarticles.htm

The triangle factory fire. (2005, March 24). Retrieved October 14, 2005, from Cornell University of Industrial and Labor Relations, Kheel Center for Labor-Management Documentation and Archives Web site: http://www.ilr.cornell.edu/trianglefire/

Notice that the Brookings Institute and the Kheel Center Web sites are included in the retrieval statement.

Online Books and Reports
MLA

Ginsburg, Allen. Howl and Other Poems. San Francisco: City Lights, 1956. 14 Sept. 2006 <http://php.indiana.edu/~avigdor/poetry/ginsburg.html>.

APA

Harrison Rips Foundation. (2000). *Creating underdevelopment: Capital flight and the case for debt reduction in South Africa.* Retrieved August 5, 2001, from http://www.ripsfoundation.org/southafrica.report.html

Online Scholarly Articles
MLA

Foster, George. "Language Policy in Namibia." Southern Africa Review 7 (2004). 18 June 2006 <http://www.soafricarev.org/foster7.01>.

Rodriguez-Alegria, Enrique. "Eating Like an Indian: Negotiating Social Relations in the Spanish Colonies" Current Anthropology 46 (2005). 29 Sept. 2006 <http://www.journals.uchicago.edu/CA/>.

Warren, William. "Allergies and Spatio-Temporal Disorders." Modern Psychology 6.3 (1997): 15 pars. 13 Nov. 2000 <http://www.liasu.edu/modpsy/warren6(3).html>.

Online journals may give page numbers (as in the first example); number paragraphs (as in the second example); or not use page or paragraph numbers at all (as in the third example).

APA

Rodriguez-Alegria, E. (2005). Eating like an Indian: Negotiating social relations in the Spanish colonies. *Current Anthropology,* 46. Retrieved September 29, 2006, from University of Chicago Web site: http://www.journals.uchicago.edu/CA/

Warren, W. (1997). Allergies and spatio-temporal disorders. *Modern Psychology,* 6(3). Retrieved November 13, 2000, from http://www.liasu.edu/modpsy/warren6(3).html

Online Magazine or Newspaper Articles
MLA

Morrow, David J. "Attention Disorder Is Found in Growing Number of Adults." New York Times 2 Sept. 1997. 15 Oct. 2006 <http://archives.nytimes.com/archives/search/fastweb?search>.

Schiff, Stacy. "Know It All: Can Wikipedia Conquer Expertise?" <u>New Yorker</u> 24 July, 2006. <http://www.newyorker.com/fact/content/articles/060731fa_fact>.

APA

Morrow, D. J. (1997, September 2). Attention disorder is found in growing number of adults. *The New York Times*. Retrieved October 15, 2006, from http://www.nytimes.com/archives/search/fastweb?search

Schiff, S. (2006). Know it all: Can Wikipedia conquer expertise? *The New Yorker*. Retrieved July 24, 2006 from http://www.newyorker.com/fact/content/articles/060731fa_fact

Sources Accessed Through Online Subscription Service
MLA

"Lock Up Private Prisons: Chronic Problems Demonstrate Why Incarceration Should Be Left to the State." <u>Atlanta Constitution</u> 6 Oct. 1999. Lexis-Nexis. Warehouse State Lib. 19 Oct. 2006 <http://lex-nexis.com>.

Online Posting to Electronic Forum
MLA

Lopez, Arsenio. "Globalization or Imperialism as the Highest Stage of Capitalism?" Online posting. 18 November 2004. Black Flag Forum. 31 June 2001 <http://www.blackflag.org/openforum/mail-archive111800>.

Marshall, Richard. "The Political Economy of Cancer Research." Online posting. 21 Apr. 2003. H-Net List on the History of Science, Medicine, and Technology. 28 Sept. 2005 <h-sci-med-tech@h-net.msu.edu>.

Murphy, Christian. "Irish FAQ: The Famine." Online posting. 5 Apr. 1998. 1 May 2005 <news:soc.culture.irish/Irish_FAQ_The_Famine>.

Notice that for Usenet newsgroups, as in the third example, the name of the news group appears in the URL.

APA

Lopez, A. (2004, November 18). Globalization or imperialism as the highest stage of capitalism? Message posted to Black Flag Forum, archived at http://www.blackflag.org/openforum/mail-archive111800

In general, only cite in References those postings that have been archived and thus can be retrieved. See note on APA in next section.

Email
MLA

Chaney, Ryan. Email to the author. 25 Feb. 2006.

Dever, Elizabeth. "Re: Eddie Vetter's Conversion." Email to the author. 4 May 2006.

For email, list the title (if there is one) from the email's subject heading.

APA

APA style treats email, as well as any nonarchived postings on electronic forums, as a nonretrievable source. Cite emails and other nonretrievable sources in the text as personal communications, but do not list them in the References section. For example:

> Medical historians have challenged Elaine Showalter's view of chronic fatigue syndrome (L. Braun, personal communication, February 25, 2005).

MISCELLANEOUS SOURCES

Films and Videocassettes
MLA

> <u>Citizen Kane</u>. Screenplay by Orson Welles. Dir. Orson Welles. RKO, 1941.
> <u>Star Wars</u>. Dir. George Lucas. Perf. Mark Hamill, Harrison Ford, Carrie Fisher, and Alec Guinness. Videocassette. CBS Fox, 1992.

APA

> Lucas, G. (Director). (1992). *Star wars* [Videocassette]. Hollywood: CBS Fox.
> Welles, O. (Writer-Director). (1941). *Citizen Kane* [Film]. Hollywood: RKO.

The amount of information to include about films and videocassettes depends on how you have used the source. In addition to title and director, you may cite the writer and performers as well.

Television and Radio Programs
MLA

> "Tuskegee Experiment." <u>Nova</u>. WGBH, Boston. 4 April 2005.

APA

> Tuskegee experiment. (2005, April 4). *Nova*. Boston: WGBH.

Records, Tapes, and CDs
MLA

> Ellington, Duke. <u>The Far East Suite</u>. Bluebird, 1995.
> Verdi, Giuseppe. <u>La Traviata</u>. London Symphony Orchestra. Cond. Carlo Rizzi. Teldec, 1992.
> White Stripes. <u>Get Behind Me Satan</u>. V2, 2005.

APA

> Ellington, D. (Composer). (1995). *The far east suite* [Record]. New York: Bluebird.

Verdi, G. (Composer). (1992). *La Traviata* [With C. Rizzi conducting the London Symphony Orchestra] [CD]. New York: Teldec.

White Stripes. (2005). *Get behind me Satan* [CD]. New York: V2.

Interviews
MLA

Haraway, Donna. "Writing, Literacy, and Technology: Toward a Cyborg Literature." By Gary A. Olson. <u>Women Writing Culture</u>. Ed. Gary A. Olson and Elaine Hirsch. Albany: SUNY, 1995. 45-77.

Press, Karen. Personal interview. 27 Apr 2003.

Sole, Kelwyn. Interview with Anita Amirault. <u>Cape Town Poetry Newsletter</u> 20 Mar. 2001: 30-34.

MLA cites interviews by listing the person being interviewed first and then the interviewer. Note that the first two interviews are published and the third is unpublished.

APA

Amirault, A. (2001, March 20). Interview with Kelwyn Sole. *Cape Town Poetry Newsletter,* 30–34.

Olson, G. A. (1995). Writing, literacy, and technology: Toward a cyborg literature [Interview with Donna Haraway]. In G. A. Olson & E. Hirsch (Eds.), *Women writing culture* (pp. 45–77). Albany: State University of New York.

APA lists the name of the interviewer first and then puts information on the interview in brackets. APA does not list unpublished interviews in references but cites them only in parenthetical citations in the text: (K. Press, personal interview, April 27, 2003).

Lecture or Speech
MLA

Kern, David. "Recent Trends in Occupational Medicine." Memorial Hospital, Pawtucket, RI. 2 Oct. 2004.

APA

Kern, D. (2004, October 2). *Recent trends in occupational medicine.* Paper presented at Memorial Hospital, Pawtucket, RI.

a guide to print, electronic, and other sources

For most research projects, your college library will be the main source of information, and you can count on spending a good part of your research time reading and analyzing what you find there in books, articles, and newspapers (although your topic and research questions may also lead you to conduct field research—which is treated in the next chapter).

A lot of the information you'll need for a research project is now available online or on CD-ROMs—everything from the library's catalog to indexes, bibliographies, and other electronic databases. In addition, you can access a world of information on the Web—material that ranges from serious scholarly discussion to wildly opinionated debates of questionable value. Now that anyone can start a discussion group or put up a Web site, you can find useful electronic sources of information created and maintained by individuals, museums, advocacy groups, and government agencies—and some that are just plain crackpot.

In addition, depending on your research project, you may find yourself doing research at live performances and museums or by watching the media. In any case, doing research is a matter of knowing your way around print, electronic, and other sources and understanding the difference between sources that are credible and those that are not.

BOOKS AND PERIODICALS

As noted in Chapter 2, "Reading Strategies for Academic Purposes," the authority and credibility of print sources depend in part on the reputation of the writer and the reliability of the publication. In this section, we'll categorize the main types of print sources and what they are typically used for. This should help you evaluate the credibility of various sources and decide which are the best fit for your research project.

UNDERSTANDING TYPES OF PRINT SOURCES

Books
Books can be sorted into three main types:

- **Scholarly books,** published by university or academic presses and written by faculty and other researchers, are meant to contribute to a field of knowledge. They have gone through a careful review by peer readers who are knowledgeable about the field and editors. At the time they're published, scholarly books should be up-to-date in terms of the issues they engage and the literature in the field they've reviewed. For these reasons, scholarly books have a high degree of credibility, especially among academics, and will likely be seen as respectable sources for any research project. (You still need, of course, to analyze the claims, evidence, and assumptions in a scholarly book and to assess its relevance to your research.)

- **Trade books** are published by commercial presses, such as Penguin or Free Press, and written by journalists, professional writers, and scholars seeking a broader audience. Intended for the general public, trade books can range considerably in quality and credibility. Some are well researched, even though they may be documented in an informal way, and written by highly reputable authors, while others may be rush jobs to capitalize on some event in the news. For these reasons, you will need to assess the authority and credibility of trade books on an individual basis.

- **Other books** from religious and political presses, nonprofits and professional associations, trade unions, and research institutes can be valuable sources, depending on your research process. Some religious and political presses (e.g., Maryknoll, Monthly Review, South End) have good reputations and reliable editorial practices. Research institutes (sometimes called "think tanks") like the Brookings Institution often issue books, pamphlets, and reports that are credible. Other presses can be fly-by-night and have much sketchier reputations. Make sure you know the organization behind the press.

Periodicals
Here are five different types of periodicals and a quick look at what they cover.

- **Scholarly journals** (e.g., *American Sociological Review, Rhetoric Society Quarterly, New England Journal of Medicine*) contain recent research by scholars in the field written for other scholars. Articles are subjected to a rigorous review process by peer readers and the journal editor, so they have a high degree of credibility and authority.

■ **Public affairs magazines** (e.g., *New Republic, The Nation, Atlantic Monthly*) publish highly reputable and well-researched articles, often by well-known writers, on topics of current interest to their audience of educated readers. Some public affairs magazines have a partisan political perspective (e.g., *National Review* is conservative, while *In These Times* is liberal). Others feature a range of perspectives. Public affairs magazines can be helpful in acquiring background information and a sense of the issues about current events.

■ **Newsmagazines** such as *Newsweek, Time,* and *U.S. News and World Report* come out weekly, with news reports and commentaries on current events. Written by experienced journalists, the articles in newsmagazines can help you understand recent and past events in detail—and the editorials and commentaries will give you a sense of the climate of public opinion. They can be a good supplement to your research, but most faculty would not consider them appropriate as a main source. **Newspapers** such as the *New York Times, Wall Street Journal,* and *Washington Post* cover the national and international news of the day, along with the latest in science, business, sports, culture, and the arts. These national newspapers have highly credible reputations and are good sources for background, especially if you're researching a historical topic. Local newspapers can provide useful information on local events, past and present.

■ **Trade magazines** (e.g., *Advertising Age, PC Computing,* and *Farm Journal*) focus on a particular profession or industry, with articles written by industry experts for others in the field. These magazines can give you a good sense of how a profession or industry sees an issue—and thereby can be a helpful supplement to your research, depending on what your research project is.

■ **Popular magazines,** such as *Rolling Stone, Glamour, Sports Illustrated,* and *Wired,* focus on a particular market niche—whether music, young women, sports fans, or computer enthusiasts. Others, such as *Discover, Smithsonian,* and *Natural History,* popularize topics in a range of fields for interested readers. Some popular magazines like *People* or *Us* feature mainly lightweight articles about celebrities, while others, such as *Scientific American,* contain serious articles written by reputable writers for the educated public.

LEARNING ABOUT THE LIBRARY

Your college library is likely to be your main source for books and periodicals. Many college libraries offer workshops on doing research and how to use the various research sources. Check with your library to see what programs and services it offers students.

THE LIBRARY CATALOG

You can search most online library catalogs by author, title, periodical, subject heading, or keyword. A note on the last two:

- *Subject headings* are normally based on the Library of Congress Subject Headings (LCSH), a reference source that lists the standard subject headings used in catalogs and indexes. Consult the LCSH to identify subject headings that are relevant to your research. Notice also that book entries in online catalogs include related subject headings. Once you find books that look useful, you can use the subject headings listed.

- *Keywords* include words that appear in the author's name, book title, subject heading, and in some cases a summary or abstract. Keyword searches can be useful because they don't depend on pre-established subject headings (but do include them). Keyword searches also allow you to combine several keywords to give your search more focus.

If you don't find relevant books using subject headings or keywords, consult with a reference librarian. He or she can help you refine your search—and can point you to other resources the library has that you'll find helpful.

REFERENCE BOOKS

Your library is likely to have a range of reference books that can be useful to your research. These may be available in print or electronic form.

- *General and specialized encyclopedias* can help you get started on a research project and provide key information as your research deepens. General encyclopedias, such as *Collier's Encyclopedia* or the *Encyclopedia Brittanica*, can provide overviews on a topic, but specialized encyclopedias, such as the *Encyclopedia of Philosophy* or the *Women's Studies Encyclopedia*, will give more in-depth and scholarly treatments of a subject.

- *Bibliographies* list books and articles published on particular subjects and fields of study. Some are annotated, with brief descriptions and sometimes evaluations of the entries. You can search for bibliographies by adding the term "bibliography" or "annotated bibliography" to a keyword search. Ask a reference librarian what bibliographies your library has that may be relevant to your research.

- *Disciplinary guides and companions*, such as the *Cambridge Companion to Postcolonial Literary Studies* or the *Harvard Guide to American History*, will give you overviews of a field of study by respected scholars. They also include important bibliographical information on important work in a particular discipline.

- **Other reference works** include atlases, almanacs, yearbooks, biographical and historical dictionaries, and handbooks. You can browse the reference section to see what your library has available. Ask a reference librarian to help you identify the reference relevant to your research.

ELECTRONIC RESOURCES

Today there are literally hundreds of searchable electronic indexes and databases that provide continually updated lists of articles published in newspapers, magazines, and scholarly journals. Some provide *citations* that identify articles on a particular topic, with author, title, and publication information. Others provide *abstracts* (or summaries) of articles as well. Still others provide the *full text* of articles in downloadable and printable form. Note, however, that because these full-text electronic databases are relatively new, many go back only thirty years or so and sometimes less.

Part of the trick of research is identifying the most relevant electronic resources for your purposes. Most libraries have an index of databases with descriptions of their contents. Reference librarians can help you get started using the most appropriate electronic databases for your research and give you helpful suggestions about how to search them. (Also see the box "How to Use Keywords" on p. 473 for tips on effective searching techniques.)

These electronic databases are library subscription services; availability will vary from library to library. Here are brief descriptions of some of the most common ones:

- **LexisNexis** includes a broad range of newpapers and magazines, along with legal, government, and business sources.

- **InfoTrac** contains articles from scholarly and popular publications in a broad range of fields.

- **Readers' Guide Full Text** offers citation listings and abstracts of articles in the most popular magazines. It has full text of articles written after 1994. **Readers' Guide Abstracts** offers abstracts on articles back to 1983. **Readers' Guide Retrospective** has citations from *Readers' Guide Index to Periodical Literature* back to 1890.

- **JSTOR** is a scholarly electronic database that provides full text of articles in a wide range of fields.

- **ISI Web of Science** is another scholarly database that links to the Science Citation Index, Social Sciences Citation Index, and Humanities Citation Index.

SEARCHING THE WEB

USING SEARCH ENGINES

Google is clearly the go-to search engine for many people these days, handling 75 percent of searches in 2003. Still, it's worth noting that search engines vary in how they are organized and thus will search different sites and produce different results. For this reason, it's a good idea to use more than one in your research. If you don't find what you are looking for on one, try another.

Here is a very partial list of the search engines available:

- *Google* www.google.com (see also Google Scholar www.scholar.google.com and Google)
- *AlltheWeb* www.alltheweb.com (multimedia search engine)
- *AltaVista* www.altavista.com (multimedia search engine)
- *Teoma* www.teoma.com (advanced search provides range of options)
- *Lycos* www.lycos.com (leading Spanish and Portuguese site)
- *Yahoo* www.yahoo.com (multimedia search engine)
- *AskJeeves* www.ask.com (you can ask questions)

Dogpile www.dogpile.com, *HotBot* www.hotbot.com, and *WebCrawler* www.webcrawler.com are some of the metasearch sites that search a number of search engines.

HOW TO USE KEYWORDS

The secret to using search engines or searchable electronic databases is to find the right keyword or combination of keywords. Part of this experimenting is finding the keyword that will give you the hits you want. Here are some techniques in using Boolean operators—AND, OR, NOT, and quotations—to make your searches more efficient.

❑ *Quotations limit your search.* For example if you type in the words death penalty, you will get over 15,000 hits, most of which have nothing to do with capital punishment. However, if you enter "death penalty", using quote marks, you've created a phrase that will give you a focused search.

❑ *AND limits your search.* If you're interested in material on the abolition of capital punishment, enter: "death penalty" AND abolish.

❑ *NOT limits your search.* If you are interested in material on the abolition of capital punishment outside the United States, enter: "death penalty" AND abolish NOT U.S.

❑ *OR expands your search.* If you are interested in material on the abolition of capital punishment in Russia and want to go back before the Soviet Union fell in 1989, enter: "death penalty" AND abolish AND Russia OR Soviet Union.

GOVERNMENT PUBLICATIONS

The U.S. government publishes massive amounts of information annually, largely through the Government Printing Office (GPO). Some of the most commonly used publications are these:

- *Congressional Quarterly Almanac.* Published annually, includes overview of legislation and policy, as well as important speeches and debates and some analysis.

- *Congressional Quarterly Weekly Report.* Weekly news updates on legislative and executive actions, includes overviews of policy debates.

- *Statistical Abstract of the United States.* Annual report of the Bureau of the Census, includes a range of social, economic, and political statistics, with tables, graphs, charts, and references to other sources.

Many government documents are now available online:

- "Keeping America Informed." The home page of the GPO, provides online access to many publications: <http://www.gpo.gov/>

- Library of Congress. Offers access to an enormous range of government and library resources: <http://leweb.loe.gov/>

- "Thomas: Legislative Information on the Internet." Developed by the Library of Congress, includes databases on Congress, current bills, public laws, committee information, online version of the *Congressional Record,* and historical documents: <http://thomas.loe.gov/> Many government agencies have their own Web sites, such as Bureau of the Census <http://www.census.gov/> and the IRS Digital Daily on tax matters from the Treasury Department <http://ww.irs.ustreas.gov/basic/cover.html>

OTHER SOURCES

Attending events and performances such as lectures, seminars, readings, plays, and concerts; visiting museums; and watching films, videos, and television or listening to the radio and recorded music can all be important forms of research. Depending on the nature of your research, these activities can provide information and perspectives to supplement your work with print and electronic sources. Or they can be the main focus of your research. This section briefly explains what performances, museums, and the media offer to researchers.

PERFORMANCES AND EVENTS

Your college may sponsor lectures, readings, or seminars that bring noted speakers to campus. Attending such events can provide you with information that you couldn't find elsewhere and give you the opportunity to question the speaker. In addition, college or local theaters and music and dance companies may stage plays and concerts related to your research. Attending such live performances can deepen your understanding, say, of a Shakespeare play, a Verdi opera, or a style of jazz, folk, or popular music—and offer a useful supplement to reading about the topic or listening to recordings. In all these instances, taking notes is probably the most appropriate research strategy.

On the other hand, performances may themselves provide the focus for your research. You might, for example, want to research what takes place at a Metallica concert or a poetry reading in a local bookstore. In cases such as these, you'll likely draw on observation and perhaps interviews, as well as reading pertinent sources or listening to recordings.

MUSEUMS

Visiting art, science, natural history, and history museums can provide you with a wealth of information to enhance your research. Depending on your topic, you can see in person paintings, sculpture, or photographs pertinent to your research; artifacts and displays from a historical period you're investigating; or scientific exhibits. Some museums, as well as historical societies, have special collections and archives that offer research sources unavailable elsewhere. Again, note taking is probably the research strategy you'll use.

Museums can also be the focus of a research project. Museum studies is a relatively new field that covers the subject of who visits museums, why, and what they do. By reading some of the literature in this field, you can frame questions to answer with field research methods—observation, interviews, and questionnaires.

MEDIA

As you're probably aware, documentary films, television and radio programs, and music and spoken-word recordings can be good sources of information to add to the print and electronic sources you're using. Research in such cases is likely to be a matter of taking notes.

At the same time, films, television, radio, or recorded music can also be valuable sources for studying the media and mass communication. For example, if you want to investigate the issue of violence in children's television shows, you may want to watch a variety of children's programs in order to count the incidences of violence and identify the types of violence depicted. Or you could analyze television commercials to see how men and women are depicted and what, if any, gender stereotypes are perpetuated. In this type of research, it can be quite helpful to tape television or radio programs so that you can return to them in the course of your inquiry.

fieldwork and the research report

Not all research is conducted in the library. In fact, the library may be just a starting point, providing you with an overview of your topic and the background information you need in order to undertake field research. Field research includes making observations, conducting interviews, and using questionnaires. In fact, researchers often combine two or more of these methods in a research project.

Researchers turn to these methods of inquiry when they have questions that can't be addressed solely on the basis of print or electronic sources. Here are some examples of research topics and the fieldwork they might lead to:

- To determine whether a shopping mall in the area should enforce a curfew for teenagers, you observe the mall on weekend nights to see what danger or nuisance, if any, teenagers pose.

- To understand the effects of state-mandated testing on classroom teachers, a student in an education course decides to interview ten sixth-grade teachers whose classes will be taking the test.

- To find out how much the undergraduates at their college drink each week, a group of students designs and administers an anonymous questionnaire.

As you can see from these examples, the kind of field research you do and how extensive it will be depend on the questions with which you begin, as well as the amount of time you have. Field research can be time consuming, but it can also give you information and insights that you could not get in any other way.

In this chapter, we'll look first at the genre of the research report. Next, we consider how researchers design fieldwork. Finally, we discuss how researchers work in the field and three common methods they use—observation, interviews, and questionnaires.

ETHICS OF RESEARCH

INFORMED CONSENT

Informed consent means that a person who is asked to participate in a research study has adequate information about its purpose and methods to make a voluntary decision about whether he or she will take part. If you are asking people to be interviewed or fill out a questionnaire, you need to explain what your research is about, why you're doing it, and what you plan to do with the results. As a rule, you should guarantee your research subjects' anonymity by not referring to them by name or by using a pseudonym. In some instances, such as oral histories or interviews with public figures, it may be appropriate to use people's real names. Most colleges and universities have Institutional Review Boards that can give you more information about obtaining informed consent. ■

UNDERSTANDING THE GENRE: RESEARCH REPORTS

The research report is the primary means of communication that natural and social scientists, engineers, computer scientists, and other researchers use to present their findings. Academic journals in a range of fields—from biochemistry and astronomy to sociology and psychology—are filled with articles reporting research that employs various methods of investigation.

If you haven't been assigned to read a research report in a journal so far, it is likely you will be, at some point in your courses. Depending on your major, you may well be called on to do research, whether experimental research in a laboratory or field research, that will lead to a research report. Or you may be assigned a field research project in your writing course. In any case, it's useful to know what a research report is and how it works.

A research report is really quite simple and fairly standardized in its form. If you have ever done a lab report in a science class, you're already familiar with its parts: Introduction, Literature review, Methods, Results, Discussion, and Conclusions.

To see how these sections work in an actual research paper, let's look at "Food Sources in South Providence," a research report that Luis Ramirez wrote for a field research assignment in the sociology course "Hunger in America." As you read, notice how each section functions within the report.

Food Sources in South Providence

Luis Ramirez

Introduction

Establishes a general problem

Over the next few years, access to food for many low-income individuals and families may change dramatically. "The Personal Responsibility and Work Opportunity Reconciliation Act of 1996" (PL104-193), signed into law by President Clinton on August 22, 1996, replaces "Aid to Families with Dependent Children" (AFDC) with a new program, "Temporary Assistance to Needy Families" (TANF), which requires participants to work for benefits and limits the amount of time they are eligible. In addition, eligibility requirements for food stamps will be made more stringent, and individual grants will be reduced. Legal immigrants who have been in the United States for fewer than five years will no longer be eligible for public assistance programs such as TANF, food stamps, Supplemental Security Insurance (SSI), and Medicaid. In Rhode Island, an estimated 8,000 will lose food stamp benefits altogether, and another 30,000 will have food stamp benefits reduced from $80 to $60 a month. Another 4,000 will lose SSI benefits (Rowland, 1997).

Introduces the specific question that the research addresses

Given these changes in the welfare system, it is crucial to understand how low-income individuals and families secure food to meet their household's dietary needs. With the implementation of the new welfare law and the elimination or restriction of public assistance programs, dependence on noncommercial food sources that low-income families use to evade hunger may increase to buffer the cuts and loss of benefits. Noncommercial food sources can be divided into four categories: (1) public assistance programs, (2) home production, (3) emergency relief, and (4) gifts (see Table 1)

Describes prior research

A good deal of research on people's diets has focused on measuring food intake and its nutritional quality by such methods as the "twenty-four hour recall," the "food frequency" checklist, the "seven day diet record," and direct weighing and measuring of daily meals (Pelto, Jerome, & Kandel, 1980). Other researchers have attempted to develop indicators to assess hunger (Physicians Task Force on Hunger in America, 1985; Radimer, Olson, & Campbell, 1990). These

Food Sources 2

studies have been useful in providing information about general patterns of food use, diet, nutrition, and the prevalence of hunger. What these studies do not include, however, is information about how people actually acquire their food.

More recently, researchers have examined how welfare recipients and the working poor use supplemental sources of income beyond welfare benefits and wages to make ends meet (Rank & Hirschl, 1995; Edin & Lein, 1997). These researchers have found that the benefits allocated from food stamps and AFDC are not enough to meet basic needs. As Rank and Hirschl write, "Even with the budgeting and stretching of resources that recipients try to do, there is simply not enough at the end of the month" (p. 243). The purpose of this study is to determine whether this is the case with low-income families in South Providence and the extent to which they depend on noncommercial food sources to provide for basic needs.

Table 1

Noncommercial Food Sources

1. Public assistance	Food stamps
	AFDC
	Special Supplemental Feeding Program for Women, Infants, and Children (WIC)
	School breakfast and lunch programs
2. Home production	Private and community gardens
	Gathering food (nuts, berries, herbs, greens, etc.) in public parks
	Fishing
3. Emergency food relief	Churches
	Community centers
	Food banks
4. Gifts	Familial networks
	Friends and neighbors

Food Sources 3

Methods

Explains
how
research
was
conducted

A questionnaire on how people acquire their food was administered to thirty low-income individuals who use the services of South Providence Neighborhood Ministries (SPNM). SPNM is a not-for-profit community center which provides a range of services such as emergency food relief, clothing and utility assistance, English as a Second Language classes, tutoring programs, sewing lessons, public health programs, and so on. The questionnaire was administered, with the informed consent of participants, in January and February 1997.

The demographic characteristics of the study population are summarized in Table 2. Of the 30 participants, 28 (93.3%) were women and two (6.6%)

Table 2

Demographic Characteristics of Study Population

	Number	Percentage
Age		
Younger than 18	1	3.3
18–30	6	20
31–50	18	60
51+	5	16.7
Marital Status		
Married	8	2.7
Not Married	27	73.3
Ethnicity		
Latino/Hispanic	20	66.7
African American	5	16.7
Southeast Asian	3	10
African	2	6.7
Work		
Employed	6	20
Unemployed	24	80

Displays
data in
visual
form—
Table 2,
Table 3,
Table 4 and
Table 5

Food Sources 4

were men. Twenty were Latino (66.7%), five (16.7%) African American, three (10%) Southeast Asian, and two (6.7%) African. Six (20%) worked full or part-time, while 24 (80%) were unemployed.

Results

This study found that the participants draw on a number of noncommercial food sources to meet their families' dietary needs. As Table 3 illustrates, the majority participated in public assistance programs of one type or another, including AFDC (56.7%), food stamps (66.7%), WIC (50%), school lunch programs (84.2%), and school breakfast programs (78.9%).

Presents data from research without commenting

Table 3

Number and Percentage of Households Using Public Assistance Programs

	Number	Percentage
AFDC		
yes	17	56.7
no	13	43.3
Food Stamps		
yes	20	66.7
no	10	33.3
WIC		
yes	15	50
no	15	50
School Lunch		
yes	16	84.2
no	3	15.8
School Breakfast Program		
yes	15	78.9
no	4	21.1

Table 4

Number and Percentage of Households Engaging in Various Forms of Home Production (Fishing for Food, Growing Food, Gathering Food)

	Number	Percentage
Fishing		
yes	8	26.7
no	22	73.3
Growing		
yes	9	30
no	24	70
Gathering		
yes	6	20
no	24	80

As shown in Table 4, a number of participants fish for food (26.7%), grow food (30%), and gather food in public parks and other places (20%).

Table 5 shows the number of participants who use emergency food relief and family networks to acquire food. The vast majority of study participants use food pantries and other emergency food distribution centers (97.6%). Nineteen (65.5%) say they visit on a regular basis about once a month, and ten (34.5%) say they go sporadically. Eleven people (44%) eat at a relative's house at least once a month, and six people (24%) feed relatives at least once a month.

Discussion

The most significant results of this study are the extent to which participants use a range of food sources to meet their basic needs. These results appear to confirm the findings of Rank and Hirschl, and Edin and Lein that neither public assistance nor low-paying jobs provide people with sufficient resources to make ends meet. My study found that benefits from

Identifies most important finding

Food Sources 6

Table 5

Number and Percentage of Households Who Utilize Emergency Relief and Familial Networks

	Number	Percentage
Emergency Relief		
yes	29	97.6
no	1	3.3
Feed Relatives Often		
yes	6	24.0
no	19	76.0
Are Fed by Relatives Often		
yes	11	44.0
no	14	56.0

AFDC and food stamps are not enough to meet a family's dietary needs. Therefore, supplemental sources, such as fishing, food production, food gathering, emergency food relief, and family food sharing are important sources of food for many low-income people.

Explains possible implications of the study results

The study results also suggest that at least some people who are eligible for public assistance do not choose it as a food option. One participant said that he does not like to use government programs and would rather use emergency food relief because the people are "nicer" and "not as condescending." It may be that food pantries are no longer temporary and infrequent means of meeting people's household food needs. Rather, people may be using food pantries as a regular strategy to feed their families, particularly at the end of the month when benefits from AFDC and food stamps run out.

Note tentative language ("suggest," "may," "perhaps")

Perhaps the most troubling finding is the fact that low-income people were already using many means of acquiring food, in addition to public assistance

Food Sources 7

uses study results to question popular representations of low-income people

programs, before the new welfare law was implemented. <u>These results suggest</u> that emergency food relief sources such as food pantries may be under growing pressure when benefits from public assistance are reduced or eliminated. Familial networks are also vulnerable, as those who are currently feeding other family members lose food support through AFDC, food stamps, and SSI.

Conclusion

The media and politicians have pictured welfare recipients as lazy people who comfortably enjoy public assistance benefits as a substitute for work. The participants in this study <u>present data contrary to this picture</u>. The majority of people in the study do not rely entirely on public assistance. Rather they draw on a number of different food sources. What will happen to them as public assistance benefits are reduced or eliminated is a matter of considerable concern.

Food Sources 8

References

Edin, K., & Lein, L. (1997). Work, welfare, and single mothers' economic survival strategies. *American Sociological Review, 61*, 253–266.

Pelto, G. H., Jerome, N. W., & Kandel, R. G. (1980). Methodological issues in nutritional anthropology. In N. W. Jerome, R. G. Kandel, & G. H. Pelto (Eds.), *Nutritional anthropology: Approaches to diet and culture* (pp. 27–59). New York: Redgrave.

Physicians Task Force on Hunger in America (1985). *Hunger in America: The growing epidemic*. Boston: Harvard University School of Public Health.

Radimer, K. L., Olson, C. M., & Campbell, C. C. (1990). Development of indicators to assess hunger. *Journal of Nutrition, 120*, 1544–1548.

Rank, H., & Hirschl, R. (1995). *Eating agendas*. New York: Basic Books.

Rowland, C. (1997, February 20). Budgets, belts getting tighter all the time. *Providence Journal-Bulletin*, pp. 1, 5.

Analysis: A Detailed Look at the Genre

If it's easy to identify the sections and the roles they play in this and many other research reports, to understand how the genre works in a fuller sense, we need to take a more detailed look at each section.

- **Introduction:** Notice how the Introduction establishes the purpose of the research through a series of rhetorical moves:

  ¶**1**: *Establishes a general problem* by citing the possible effects of changes in the welfare system on low-income people's access to food.

  ¶**2**: *Introduces the specific question* of understanding how low-income people secure food and how much they rely on non-commercial sources.

  ¶**3**: *Describes prior research* on people's diets by citing sources from the literature.
  Creates a research space by indicating a gap in previous research.

  ¶**4**: *Describes more recent research and proposes to extend it* by examining how low-income people meet basic needs.
  States the research question of determining how much low-income families in South Providence rely on noncommercial food sources.

  As this analysis reveals, the Introduction is a relatively complex passage that works closely with sources first to establish a general problem and then to create a space for the research question by showing how the proposed research fills a gap and how related research can be extended. This Introduction offers a good illustration of how researchers justify their research question by explaining why it is meaningful and how it fits into a body of prior work.

- **Methods:** The Methods section at first glance may seem straightforward as it describes how the questionnaire was administered and presents the demographics of the study population. The underlying question that the Methods section raises, however, is how well-equipped is the proposed method to answer the research question. We learn that the questionnaire asked thirty low-income people about how they acquired their food. The study population is appropriate, but this section might have included a bit more explanation of how the questions were designed to gather the needed information.

- **Results:** There are two things to note about the Results section. First, the results of the questionnaire appear without any comment on their meaning or significance. This is one of the key features of research reports: the data are first presented and then interpreted. For students who are used to writing papers with an interpretative claim followed by supporting evidence, the research report may feel backwards. But the logic here is that of displaying the information for all to see before commenting on it. In keeping with this logic is the second feature to note, namely that the complete data are displayed visually in tables and main points summarized in the text.

■ **Discussion:** Instead of discussing the results point by point as they appear in the Results section, discussion sections typically begin with the most important finding of the research and explain how it relates to the central research question. That takes place here in the first paragraph. Notice, too, that the interpretations of the results use such tempered terms as "appear to confirm" and "suggest." (No researcher would claim that the results can prove anything definitively. There is always room for further research and new questions.) Finally, notice that the discussion becomes more speculative in the second and third paragraphs, drawing out implications from the results. Accordingly, the writer's tone is appropriately tentative in suggesting what "may" be occurring.

■ **Conclusion:** The ending takes a further turn by using the results to refute representations of low-income people by politicians and the media. This is a bold and effective way to summarize the results and relate them to an important context of issues. The final sentence looks ahead with concern to an uncertain future. The conclusion, no doubt, has a bit more of the flair of an essay than is usual in many research reports.

■ WORKING TOGETHER

Analyzing a Research Article

■ Work in a group of three or four. Find a short article that reports research in an academic journal such as *Current Anthropology, American Journal of Public Health*, or *American Journal of Sociology*.

■ Analyze the introduction (and literature review if it's a separate section). Pay particular attention to how the article establishes the general problem or topic, how it defines the research question, and how it relates that question to prior work.

■ Use the rhetorical moves in the analysis of "Food Sources in South Providence" to see how the introduction creates a research space.

DESIGNING A FIELD RESEARCH PROJECT

You can use the discussion of the research report genre as a way to start thinking about how to design a field research project. Many of the key considerations you'll need to take into account have already been raised. Here are some questions to help you use your knowledge of the genre to plan your research:

■ What is the general problem or issue that you want to investigate? You might be interested, say, in the experience of Vietnam veterans, the

Poetry Slam scene, the problem of cheating, or the role of fraternities and sororities at your college.

- What background information is available on the problem or issue? What specific research has already been done? What questions have guided that research?

- How can you use background information and previous research to help you carve out a research space to develop a significant question? Are there gaps in the research? You might find, for example, that there are lots of oral histories of Vietnam veterans' experience of the war but less about what it was like when they returned home.

- Is there research you could extend? Perhaps there are studies of student attitudes toward cheating and toward fraternities and sororities that could be updated. On the other hand, there may be lots of writing on Poetry Slams but little or no research.

- What research method or combination of methods best fits your research question?

WRITING A PROPOSAL

Once you have answered these questions, write a proposal for the research project. This proposal can serve as the first draft of the Introduction to your research report. A proposal should explain:

- What the general problem or issue is.

- What previous research has been done.

- How the main question you're trying to answer relates to previous work.

- Why the particular method you're planning to use is an appropriate research strategy for answering the question.

- How you plan to conduct the research.

- What you think the significance of the results might be.

OBSERVATION

Observation has an important advantage over other research methods: it gives you direct access to people's behavior. Let's say you've done some background research on how men and women interact in conversations, and you want to test some of the findings in the published literature. You might decide to see whether students at your college follow the pattern described by Deborah Tannen in *You Just Don't Understand*—that men interrupt more during conversations and are less likely than women to use questions to elicit comments from others.

Interviewing or surveying wouldn't give you very reliable information, because even if people were willing to be honest about how they behave in conversations, it's not likely that they could be accurate. In contrast, by going to the school dining hall over a period of several days, you could observe what men and women in fact do when they talk and what conversational patterns emerge.

THE PROCESS OF OBSERVATION

Planning

The following questions can help guide your planning. You can use them to write a proposal that explains the role of observation in your research plan (see "Writing a Proposal," above).

- Why does the line of research you're pursuing call for observation? What research question or questions are you addressing?

- How exactly can observations help you answer your research question?

- What kinds of observations would be most useful? Whom and what do you want to observe? What are the best times and places for these observations? How many observations should you do?

- What should your observations focus on? What exactly do you want to record in your field notes? What method or methods will you use to record your observations?

THREE CONSIDERATIONS TO TAKE INTO ACCOUNT WHEN YOU DO OBSERVATIONS

1. Recognize that you'll be observing a limited group and making a limited number of observations. Your findings may confirm or dispute what you've read, or they may suggest new questions and lines of research. Be aware, however, that while your results are valid for the group you observed, the group itself may not be representative of all the students at your college, not to mention all men and women. So when you generalize on the basis of your observations, acknowledge the scope of your research and ensure that the claims you make take these limits into account.

2. Take into account, too, the fact that your presence can have an effect on what you observe. People sometimes behave differently when they know they're being watched. They may clown around, try to make themselves look good, or otherwise act in relation to the observer. The best way to deal with this fact is to conduct multiple observations. In many cases, people being observed will get used to the presence of the observer over time.

3. Finally, be aware of the assumptions you bring to the observations—both when you are conducting the research and when you are analyzing the results. All researchers, of course, operate from a point of view, so there's no reason to think you can be a neutral bystander just recording what happens. For this reason, however, there is a very real danger that you will record in your observations only what you expected to see. Observers' assumptions can cause them to miss, ignore, or suppress important events. Being conscious of your own assumptions can help keep you open to things you had not anticipated.

You may need to request permission to observe, as well as permission to use any recording devices.

Conducting Observations

When you arrive at the place where you'll do your observation, look for a vantage point where you will be able to see what's going on and yet won't be obtrusive. Consider whether you want to move periodically from one spot to another to get a number of different perspectives on the activity or place you're observing. Make sure any equipment you've brought—camera or tape recorder—is ready to use.

Researchers typically develop their own system of taking field notes. Nonetheless, a few suggestions may be helpful. Begin by writing down the basic facts: the date, time, and place. Keep your notes on one side of the page. Depending on your research questions, here are some things to consider:

- **The setting:** Describe the overall size, shape, and layout. You may want to sketch it or draw a diagram. Note details—both what they are and how they are arranged. Pay attention to sounds and smells, as well as to what you can see.

- **The people:** Note the number of people. What are they doing? Describe their activities, movement, and behavior. What are they wearing? Note ages, race, nationality, and gender. How do they relate to one another? Record overheard conversation using quotation marks.

- **Your response:** As you observe, note anything that is surprising, puzzling, or unusual. Note also your own feelings and reactions, as well as any new ideas or questions that arise.

Analyzing Your Notes

After you've finished your observation, read through your notes carefully and, if you want, type them up, adding related points that you remember. Then make sure you analyze your notes from the standpoint of your research questions:

- What patterns emerge from your notes? What are your main findings? What, if anything, surprised you?

- What research questions do your notes address? What issues remain to be addressed?

- Do your observations confirm what you have read? How would you explain any discrepancies?

- What should your next step be? Should you go back to the library? Should you conduct further observations? If further observations are needed, what form should they take?

■ FIELDWORK PRACTICE

Observation

After getting their permission, observe the dinnertime conversation and interaction of your family or a group of friends, taking notes of your observations. When you are finished, read through your notes, considering what they reveal about the patterns of interaction you observed. Then answer the following questions:

1. Do you think your presence as an observer had an effect on what people said and did?

2. How difficult is it to observe and keep notes? What, if anything, could you do to make the process easier?

3. What did you expect to happen at dinner? How did these assumptions influence your observations? Were some things you observed unexpected? Do you think your assumptions caused you to miss anything? Were there certain things you chose not to include in your notes? Why?

4. What tentative conclusions do you think are legitimate to draw from your observations?

INTERVIEWS

As noted in Chapter 7, "Profiles," interviews are often an essential part of capturing the personality and opinions of the person being profiled. Interviews, of course, are not limited to profiles; they have a range of uses. Here are three common situations in which researchers can make good use of interviews, either as the main basis of a research project or a component.

- **Interviews with experts:** Interviewing an expert on anorexia, the 1980s loft jazz scene in New York City, the current status of the cod fishing industry, or virtually any topic you're researching can provide you with up-to-date information and analysis, as well as a deepened understanding of the issues involved in these topics—and can make a significant contribution to a research project. In such cases, interviewing an expert offers a source of information that supplements print or electronic sources.

- **Interviews with key participants:** Interviews can do more than just supplement your research. In some cases, interviewing takes on a central role in a research project, especially in research on contemporary issues where it makes sense to talk to the people involved. Suppose you are planning to research the role of public libraries in relation to recent immigrants. You would certainly want to see what's been written about the topic, but you could also interview librarians at neighborhood branches who work with, say, Russian Jews, Southeast Asians, Haitians, or Latinos. In turn, these interviews could lead to further interviews with recent immigrants, as well as community organizations, to get their perspective on what libraries are doing and might do. The research paper you write will quite likely feature prominently the information you've gathered from these interviews as the main source of data, with print and electronic sources providing background and context for your research.

■ **Oral histories:** Interviews with people who participated in significant historical events can provide a useful focus for research. To understand the event from the perspective of a rank-and-file worker, you might interview a trade unionist who participated in a significant strike. Or to understand the origins of the New Right on college campuses in the early 1960s, you might interview someone who was involved in the founding of Young Americans for Freedom. Interviews such as these are often called oral histories because they are the spoken accounts of important historical moments based on people's memories of their lived experience. For this type of research, you need, of course, to look at what historians have said—both to generate questions before the interview and to relate the oral history to professional accounts after the interview as part of the written presentation of your research.

As you can see, the type of interviewing you do depends largely on the kind of research question you're raising and the sources it leads you to.

THE INTERVIEW PROCESS

Planning

The following considerations can help you get started on planning interviews. You can use these considerations to write a proposal that explains how the interviews fit into your research design (see "Writing a Proposal," on page 487).

■ **Background research:** The first step, as in any research, is to get an overview and basic information about your topic. At this point, you are likely to be formulating questions to guide your research. Consider how interviewing can help you answer these questions. What do you hope to find out?

■ **Choosing interview subjects:** The nature of your research question should suggest appropriate subjects to interview. Does it make sense to interview an expert on the topic? Or does your research seem to call for interviews with people involved in the subject you're investigating? Are the people you're considering likely to provide the information you're looking for?

■ **Preparing interview questions:** Use the notes from your background research to prepare interview questions. Interviewers normally use open questions to get their subjects talking—phrasing questions so that the natural answer is a yes or a no generally leads to a dead end. How open, of course, depends on your research question and your subject. If you are interviewing an expert, your questions should be precise and seek specific information ("Estimates vary on the number of cod in the North Atlantic. Can you give me your view?"). For oral histories, on the other hand, questions often begin at a general level ("Tell me what it was like growing up in Oklahoma") but become more specific ("Do you recall when and why your family decided to migrate to California?"). When you have come up with a list of questions, organize them so that one question leads logically to the next.

■ **Considering the types of interviews**: The in-person, face-to-face interview is probably the best-known type of interview, but there are alternatives you may want or need to consider. The "Four Types of Interviews" box summarizes four possibilities, their advantages and disadvantages.

FOUR TYPES OF INTERVIEWS

❏ **In-person interviews:** In-person interviews have some significant advantages over the other types. Often, when answering your question, the person you are interviewing may take the conversation in a new direction. Although at times this means you'll need to guide the conversation politely back to your topic, sometimes the new direction is one that you hadn't thought of and would like to explore. At other times you may realize that your questions aren't working and that to get the information you need, you'll have to revise and supplement them on the spur of the moment.

Some researchers prefer to take handwritten notes during in-person interviews. Doing so, however, poses certain difficulties. Responses to your questions may be long, and you may not be able to write fast enough. And devoting all your attention to note taking makes it harder to think about what the person is saying and harder to guide the interview by choosing the next question or formulating a new one. For these reasons, many researchers use a tape recorder. But be flexible about using one. Most people don't mind, and the tape recorder will simply fade into the background. But some people are bothered by it and might not be as open as they would be if you took

notes. If you feel the disadvantages of tape recording are outweighing the advantages, be prepared to change methods.

❏ **Telephone interviews:** Telephone interviews are similar to in-person interviews. Both enable you to be flexible in your questioning. However, some people may find telephone interviews a bit more difficult to manage because rapport may not emerge as easily as in an in-person interview.

A speakerphone is useful if you've been given permission to record the conversation. Even if you haven't, a speakerphone makes it easier for you to take notes.

❏ **Email interviews:** Sometimes you might prefer or may have to conduct your interview by email. You might, for example, want to interview someone who isn't willing or able to schedule an in-person or telephone interview but who has no objection to answering questions. One advantage of email interviews is that they provide you with a written record. On the other hand, it may be difficult to follow up on interesting ideas or to clarify points. Phrasing and organization of questions are especially crucial in mail or email interviews because you can't adjust your line of questioning as you can in an in-person or telephone interview.

❑ **Online interviews:** Interviews can also be conducted online. Real-time synchronous communication sites, such as IRCs (Internet Relay Chat), MUDs (Multi-User Domains), and MOOs (MUD Object Oriented), allow computer users from around the world to "talk" to each other in writing in real time.

Like email interviews, online interviews help simplify note taking by recording the conversations. Make sure, however, that you are familiar with the technology necessary to record the interview—you don't want to lose all of your hard work.

Setting Up the Interview

Whether the person you plan to interview is a stranger, a friend, or a relative, you'll need to set up the interview. Generally this means writing a letter or making a telephone call, both to ask for permission and to set a time (or a deadline in the case of an interview by mail). Introduce yourself and your purpose. Be honest about what you are doing—many busy people are happy to help students with assignments. However, be prepared to be turned down. Sometimes busy people are just that—busy. If someone seems too busy to meet with you in person, ask whether you could interview him or her by telephone, mail, or email—or whether the person knows someone else you could interview. Above all, be polite. Be sure to schedule the interview far enough in advance of your due date to allow you to follow up with more questions or with further research if the interview leads to areas you had not previously considered. For in-person or telephone interviews that you want to record, ask at this point for permission to record. If it's appropriate, ask the person you're interviewing if there is anything you should read before the interview.

Conducting an In-Person or Telephone Interview

For in-person and telephone interviews, the interview itself is a crucial moment in your research. To get an in-person interview off on the right foot, arrive promptly. Make sure that you dress appropriately and that you bring your questions, tape recorder (if you have permission to record the interview), a pad and pens, and any other materials you might need. For telephone interviews, make sure you call at the time agreed upon.

Because in-person and telephone interviews are really conversations, the results you get will depend in part on your flexibility as a listener and a questioner. The person you're interviewing will be looking to you for guidance, and it is quite likely that you'll be faced with choices during the interview. Let's say you are interviewing someone about why she attends your college. She says, "I came because they've got a really good computer science program, I got a good financial aid package, and I didn't want to go very far from home. You know what I mean?" Then she pauses, looking at you for direction. You've got a choice to make about which thread to follow—the student's academic interests, her financial situation, or her desire to stay near home.

After the Interview

Especially with in-person and telephone interviews, plan time immediately afterward to review the results of the interview and to make further notes. Transcribe your tape, if you recorded the interview, or print out hard copies of email or on-line interviews. Make sure that you've noted direct quotations and that you've written down pertinent information about the interview (such as the time, date, and location).

Analyzing the Transcript

Material from an interview can be used in many different ways in a research project. It can be central to the final report or can provide supplementary quotations and statistics. The ideas you had ahead of time about how you would use the interview might be changed by the interview or by other aspects of your research process. To help you understand what use to make of the interview, write responses to these questions:

- What are the most important things you learned? List what seem to be the main points.

- What, if anything, surprised you? Why?

- What does the interview contribute to your understanding of your research question? How does the information relate to what you've already learned about your topic? If information, opinion, or point of view differ, how do you account for this?

- What questions does the interview raise for further research? What sources does it suggest you use?

A Final Note on Interviews

Be sure to thank the people you interview. (A note or email message is a nice touch.) When you've finished your paper, send them a copy along with a letter or email thanking them again.

■ FIELDWORK PRACTICE

Interviewing

Work with a partner. Interview your partner about why he or she decided to attend your college. Before the interview, think about the questions you want to ask, how you want to conduct the interview—in person, by telephone, online, or via email—and how you want to keep track of what's said. After the interview, write a paragraph or two about the experience. What sorts of questions were most effective? Did any ideas and topics come up that you had not expected? What decisions did you make during the interview about threads to follow in the conversation? What were the advantages and disadvantages of the interview method you chose? What problems did you experience in recording information?

Compare your response to the interview process with those of classmates. What generalizations can you, as a class, draw about interviewing?

SURVEYS

Surveys are similar to interviews, except that they obtain responses from a number of people by using questionnaires. Surveys can target a particular group of people—to find out, for example, why students at your college have chosen to major in biomedical engineering, or why employees at a particular company do or don't participate in community service activities. Or they can examine the beliefs and opinions of the "general public," as is the case with those conducted by political pollsters and market researchers on everything from people's sexual habits to their religious beliefs to their product preferences.

While interview questions are generally open, questionnaires tend to use more "closed" questions, such as true/false, yes/no, checklists, ranking, and preference scales. In this sense, they sacrifice the depth of information to be gotten about one person for the breadth of data about many people.

Deciding whether you should design and distribute a questionnaire depends largely on what you're trying to find out. If, for example, you've read some research on the television viewing habits of college students and want to find out if students at your school fit the patterns described, it makes sense to ask many students about their habits rather than to interview three or four. The results you get are liable to give you a more accurate picture. At any rate, as a way to start, write a proposal that explains your research project and why a survey is the best method (see "Writing a Proposal," on page 487).

THE PROCESS OF DESIGNING AND CONDUCTING A SURVEY

If a survey seems appropriate to your research project, you'll need to decide who your subjects are, prepare the questionnaire, distribute it, and then compile and analyze the results.

Getting Background Information

Designing a questionnaire is similar to designing an interview. Namely, you'll begin by researching your topic to get an overview and background information. Then you'll determine whether a questionnaire is the most appropriate method for addressing your research question: does it make sense to gather information on the opinions and habits of a number of people instead of talking to a few in depth or doing another form of research? At this point, before you expend the time and effort it takes to design and conduct a questionnaire, make sure that a questionnaire is likely to provide you with the information you're seeking.

Selecting Participants

To be sure that they can generalize from the results of their surveys, professional researchers try to obtain responses from a representative sample of the population they're investigating. If, for example, you're surveying employees of a company or students who major in bioengineering, it should be easy enough to send questionnaires to all of them. In other cases, however, you may need to choose people within the population at random.

For example, if you're studying the students' opinions of a first-year writing program, you could get a random sample by surveying every tenth person on the class lists. But even in that case, make sure that your responses are representative of the actual population in the classes and reflect their demographic composition. You may need to modify the distribution of your survey to guarantee it reaches a representative sample—men, women, blacks, whites, Latinos, Asians, traditional-age students, returning students.

If your results are to be meaningful, you'll also need to include enough participants in your survey to give it credibility. Keep in mind that regardless of how you conduct your survey, not everyone will participate. In fact, as pollsters are well aware, it's generally necessary to survey many more people than you expect to receive responses from. Often as few as 10 percent of the surveys mailed out will be returned. A good rule of thumb is to aim for 40 percent and, if you don't get it the first time, do multiple distributions.

When you write up your findings, any generalizations based on your survey should be limited to the population your survey represents (you should not, for example, generalize about American voters as a whole based on a survey of students at your college). Be sure to discuss any potentially relevant information on survey participants, such as information on age, gender, or occupation.

ETHICS OF RESEARCH

LOADED QUESTIONS

Public opinion polls are a fixture in American politics. Most political candidates, the two major political parties, and many other political organizations and advocacy groups use opinion polls to understand the public's mood and to shape policy. In fact, at times political polls can go beyond simply providing information that will play an active role in the formation of public policy. In political debates, the results of opinion polls are often used to buttress the position of one side or the other. Because opinion polls have become such an important part of political life, there is the temptation to use them in a partisan way.

Take, for example, a poll conducted by advocates of casino gambling in Rhode Island to determine the degree of public support. The main question in the poll— "Would you approve a casino if it would reduce your property taxes and improve education?"—is clearly a loaded one because it stacks the deck with casino proponents' arguments. As political pollster Darrell West noted, the "corollary question from an anti-gambling perspective" might read, "Would you support a casino if you thought it would raise crime rates and increase the level of gambling addiction?"

Not surprisingly, a majority of people polled favored casino gambling when the question was framed in terms of casino revenues reducing taxes and improving education. However, when the question was posed in an unbiased way—"Do you favor or oppose the construction of a gambling casino?"—the results were quite different. Fifty-three percent opposed the casino, 42 percent supported it, and 5 percent had no opinion. ■

Designing the Questionnaire

The results of your survey will depend to a large extent on the questions you ask. Here are some considerations to take into account in designing a questionnaire:

1. Include a short introduction that explains the purpose of the survey and what you will do with the results. Point out that survey participants' opinions are important. Ask them to complete the survey, and give them an estimate of the time it will take to do so.

2. Make sure the questions you ask are focused on the information you need for your research. It's tempting to ask all sorts of things you're curious about. The results can be interesting, to be sure, but asking more questions than you actually need can reduce your response rate. In general, keep the questionnaire brief in order to maximize returns.

3. Design the questionnaire so that it is easy to read. The visual design should suggest that it won't take long to fill out. Don't crowd questions together to save space. And leave plenty of space for open questions, reminding survey respondents that they can write on the back.

4. At the end of the questionnaire, include a thank-you and explain where or to whom it should be returned.

Types of Questions

Questions can take the form of checklists, yes/no questions, categories, ranking scales, and open questions. Each type of question works somewhat differently from the others. Usually you will want to combine several types to give you the particular information you need. You will also need to consider the most effective and logical order to present the questions. Questionnaires typically begin with the least complicated or most general questions and end with open-ended questions.

Here are examples of the most common types of questions designed for a research project investigating whether the political attitudes and involvement of students at the researcher's college support or refute claims in the published literature that students today are generally apathetic when it comes to politics.

Checklist

Which of these political activities have you participated in? Please check all that apply.

_____ voted in national election

_____ voted in state or local election

_____ campaigned for a candidate

_____ worked for a political party

_____ attended a political rally or demonstration

_____ belonged to a political organization or advocacy group

_____ other (specify): _____

Yes/No Questions

Are you a registered voter?

_____ Yes

_____ No

Categories

How would you describe your political views?

_____ left-wing

_____ liberal

_____ moderate

_____ conservative

_____ right-wing

_____ none of the above/don't know

Ranking Scales

Please rank the following items according to their importance as national priorities. (Use 1 for the highest priority, 7 for the lowest.)

_____ strengthening the economy

_____ reducing crime

_____ balancing the budget

_____ improving education

_____ improving the health care system

_____ improving race relations

_____ reducing poverty

Lickert Scale

[Lickert scale questionnaire items gauge the degree of agreement with particular statements of opinion. Researchers typically design a sequence of such items.]

Please indicate the degree to which you agree or disagree with the following statements. Enter the number that best expresses your view on each item.

1—Strongly agree

2—Agree

3—Not Sure

4—Disagree

5—Strongly Disagree

_____ It is important to be well-informed about current political events.

_____ There's no point in getting involved in politics because individuals can have little influence.

_____ Voting in elections is a responsibility, not just a right.

_____ The political system is controlled by politicians and lobbyists.

Open-Ended Questions

[Open-ended questions call for brief responses. Such questions are more time consuming and difficult to tabulate than closed questions, but they can often yield information that other types of questions will not.]

What, if anything, has motivated you to be interested in political affairs?

_____

_____

_____

What, if anything, has posed obstacles to your being interested in political affairs?

_____

_____

_____

After you've prepared your questionnaire, try it out on a few people. Do their answers tell you what you wanted to know? Based on these answers, have you covered all the issues and have you phrased your questions well? If you see any problems, revise your questionnaire. Now is the time to get it right—before you administer it to a lot of people.

Conducting the Survey

Your questionnaire can be distributed in various ways: in person, by mail, by telephone, or online through listservs, newsgroups, or Web sites. Your choice of how to conduct the survey will depend on your choice of a sample population, on your deadline, and on your resources (mail surveys, for example, can be quite expensive because you'll need to provide stamped self-addressed envelopes).

COMPILING, ANALYZING, AND PRESENTING RESULTS

Compiling results amounts to tallying up the answers to each question. This is a fairly straightforward procedure for closed questions such as checklist, yes/no, multiple-choice, and ranking and Lickert-scale items. For open questions, you might write down key words or phrases that emerge in the responses and tally the number of times these (or similar) words or phrases occur. Keep a list of answers that seem of special interest to use in your research report as quotations.

Researchers present the results of closed questions in the form of percentages in the text of their reports. In addition, you may want to design tables or other visual displays of your results to complement the written report.

Remember that your results do not speak for themselves. You need to analyze and explain how they are significant to your research project. The following questions can help you begin such an analysis:

■ What patterns emerge from responses to individual questions? What patterns emerge from responses across questions?

■ How would you explain these patterns? Try to think of two or more explanations, even if they appear to be contradictory or mutually exclusive.

■ What is the significance of these explanations for your research? If the explanations seem contradictory, can you think of ways to reconcile them? If not, on what grounds would you choose one or the other?

■ What tentative claims might you make based on your analysis of the results? How would you justify such claims?

■ FIELDWORK PRACTICE

Conducting a Survey

Work in a group of three or four. Your task is to design a pilot questionnaire to determine student opinion about some aspect of the academic program or student services at your college. You could focus on, say, advising, orientation for new students, required first-year courses, tutoring, or anything else that interests you. Begin by listing the kind of information that you want to get. Then write five to ten questions that seem likely to give you this information. Test your questionnaire by administering it to ten to fifteen classmates. Once you've gotten their responses, evaluate your survey:

1. Did you get the information you were looking for?

2. Is each of the questions worded in such a way that it provides the information you anticipated?

3. Should you word any of the questions differently to obtain the information you're seeking? Should you delete any of the questions or add new ones?

4. Explain your answers.

5. Compare your group's experience with that of other groups. What conclusions can you draw about questionnaire design?

part four

writers at work

4

INTRODUCTION: UNDERSTANDING THE WRITING PROCESS

No two writers compose in the same way, and an individual may work in different ways on different writing tasks. Nonetheless, there are predictable elements in a writing project that can be listed:

- **Invention:** Developing an approach to the topic and to readers, assessing purpose, doing research, choosing the appropriate genre.

- **Planning:** Designing the arrangement of material, finding an appropriate pattern of organization.

- **Drafting:** Creating a working draft, getting ideas down on paper.

- **Peer commentary:** Getting feedback from others, seeing the working draft through the reader's eyes.

- **Revising:** Rereading the working draft, clarifying purpose and organization, connecting the parts.

- **Manuscript preparation:** Designing, editing, and proofreading a document.

Because of the way the elements of writing have been listed, you may think that they constitute a series of steps you can follow. If you look at how writers work, however, you'll see that they may well manage these elements in quite different ways. Some writers like to start drafting before they develop a clear plan, while others would not think of drafting without a carefully developed outline.

Nor are the elements necessarily separate from each other. Some people revise as they draft, working carefully over each section before going on to the next, while others write quickly and then think about needed revisions. Nor do writers spend the same amount of time on each of the elements. Depending on the writing task and their own writing habits, writers learn how to manage the elements in ways that work for them.

Writing can be exhilarating, but it can be aggravating too. You can probably think of times when writing seemed to pour out, leading you to previously unsuspected ideas and precisely the right way of saying things. On the other hand, you may have had moments when you couldn't begin a writing task or got stuck in the middle. The way to get to the source of such difficulties is to think about how you are managing the elements of your writing task. Are you spending your time doing what needs to be done to get the writing task completed? Should you be revising and editing passages that you may eventually discard? Is this keeping you from figuring out how (or whether) the passage connects to other points? If you see your draft diverge from your outline, should you follow it or go back and revise your plan? When you're stuck in the middle of a draft, do you need to turn to invention—to read more or talk to others?

Answers to these questions will vary, of course, depending on the writing task and your own habits as a writer. The point is that experienced writers learn to ask such questions in order to get their bearings, especially when the writing is not going well, to see where they stand in putting a piece of writing together and what they need to do next.

■ REFLECTING ON YOUR WRITING

How You Managed a Writing Task

Think of a writing task you completed recently, in school or out of school. Analyze how you managed the task. To do this, consider the following questions:

1. What called on you to write? Describe how you defined the writing task. How did you establish your purpose? What did your exploration of the topic involve? How did you imagine your readers and the relationship you wanted to establish with them? What genre did you choose? Did you talk to others about your ideas?

2. Explain how you planned the writing. How much planning did you do? When did you plan, and what form did it take?

3. Describe how you drafted. When did you begin? How much invention and planning did you do before you started drafting?

4. Describe what feedback, if any, you received on your draft. What was the effect of this feedback?

5. What kinds of revisions did you make? When did you revise—during drafting, after you had a complete working draft, at various points?

6. What final form did the writing take? Were any considerations of document design involved? Did you edit and proofread the final version?

Now look back over your answers to these questions. What conclusions can you draw about how you managed the elements of the writing process in this instance? What, if anything, would you do differently if you had to do the task again?

the writing process: a case study of a writing assignment

CASE STUDY OF A WRITING ASSIGNMENT

To see how a student writer manages a writing task and how writers and readers can work together effectively, we'll follow a student, Krista Guglielmetti, preparing a paper for a mass communication course.

INVENTION

Understanding the Call to Write

It can be difficult to get started on a writing project if you are uncertain about the call to write and the kind of writing task it presents. You may not be clear, for example, about what an assignment in one of your courses is calling on you to do. If you feel shaky about the purpose of a writing assignment, other students in the class probably do too. Of course, you could talk to the teacher, but you may also want to collaborate with classmates to clarify the purpose of the assignment and develop an approach to it.

Here is the writing assignment Krista Guglielmetti was given in Introduction to Mass Communication.

Writing Assignment

INTRODUCTION TO MASS COMMUNICATION

Much as visual representations from the past idealized families huddled around the fireplace for warmth and comfort, we now have idealized pictures of families gathered together in front of the television set. (See the accompanying illustration.) Media critics have raised questions about what such viewing time actually means for the contemporary family. Does it represent an important moment of family togetherness, a means of avoiding really

Online Study Center

encountering each other, or something else? Draw on your family's viewing habits to write a short (2-page, 500-word) essay that explains the role television plays in the contemporary family. You will need to describe how your family uses television viewing, but your essay should also analyze what such viewing practices tell us about the role of television in the contemporary family.

■ EXERCISE

Analyzing a Writing Assignment

Work with two or three classmates to analyze the Introduction to Mass Communication writing assignment and to determine what it is calling on students do. The following guidelines can be used for virtually any writing assignment. Of course, since you are not actually a student in the mass communication class, you won't have all the information available to Krista and her classmates. Nonetheless, you can make some informed guesses by picking up important cues from the assignment.

Guidelines for Analyzing Writing Assignments

- Look for key words in the assignment—such as *describe, summarize, explain, analyze,* or *evaluate critically.* Discuss what these terms might mean in relation to the material you're being asked to write about and the goals and focus of the course.

- Consider what information you need to do the assignment successfully. Where can you get this information? Does the assignment call for additional research, or is it based on class readings and discussion? Are there things you know or have learned in other classes that might prove useful?

- Look for any special directions the assignment provides about the form of writing. Does it call for a specific genre (such as a report, a proposal, or a review)? Does it call for documentation? Consider the assigned length. What is it possible to do well within these limits?

After your group has answered these questions, compare your response to those of other groups. At this point, what advice would you give Krista as she begins the assignment?

Understanding Readers

Another difficulty in getting started on a writing task may be the writers' uncertainty about what will interest their readers. Sometimes writers believe that if they have thought of something, everyone else must have too. Underestimating the importance of their own ideas, they feel reluctant to express them. One way to test your ideas is to discuss them with other people. That way you can not only reassure yourself that your ideas are valid but also begin to formulate a plan for approaching your readers.

Talking out the ideas you have for a paper is one of the best ways to understand your readers. Here are some guidelines for doing this, followed by a transcript of Krista's discussion with her roommate Tamika.

Guidelines for Understanding Your Readers

- Find a willing listener, describe your writing task, and then tell your listener what you are thinking of writing about and what you are thinking of saying about it.

- Ask your listener what she already knows about your subject, what she would like to know about it, and whether she has ideas or information you could use in your writing.

Transcript of Krista's Discussion with Tamika

KRISTA: I've got to write this paper for my mass comm course on families and television viewing. We're supposed to use our own family to explain what television means in terms of family life.

TAMIKA: Sounds cool. In my lit class all we write about is John Milton and Alexander Pope. At least you've met these people. So what are you going to say?

KRISTA: Well, that's the problem. As you know, my family is a disaster. But I don't want to lay on all this dysfunctional stuff. I thought I could maybe say something about how families use television to avoid really relating to each other. That's sure what happens in my family. But I'm worried this is too obvious. What do you think? Does that sound interesting?

TAMIKA: Oh yeah. People these days are definitely using TV as a means of avoidance. You're supposed to be all happy together, only nobody talks to each other because some TV show is going on.

KRISTA: Why is that?

TAMIKA: In my opinion, people care more about what happens to those idiots on *Survivor* than their own selves.

KRISTA: You really think so? I mean, do you think I can do something here? My teacher has to like it, you know.

TAMIKA: That goes without saying. Just think up some reasons why people like TV more than they like real life. That's the point. You go, girl. You got your main idea.

KRISTA: I hope so. Thanks, Tamika. I better get to work.

TAMIKA: Yeah, but how about cleaning your side of the room first?

Exploring the Topic

At a certain point, writers need to get some ideas down on paper, even if the writing is of a preliminary sort. One way to start is to do exploratory writing, in which you're tentatively working out the focus and direction of your paper. If you want someone to look at your exploratory writing, you can use the guidelines below. Make sure that the person who reads your writing understands that it is an initial attempt to discover what you want to say.

Guidelines for Responding to Exploratory Writing

- Ask your reader to circle or underline key phrases and interesting ideas, whether or not they seem to be the main point of the writing.

- Ask your reader to tell you if there seem to be, implied or lurking just off the page, ideas that you could develop.

After thinking about her conversation with Tamika, Krista decided to do some exploratory writing. Below is her writing and the response from her friend Eric.

Krista's Exploratory Writing

When I was a kid, I dreaded Monday nights. I would be up in my room happily reading a book when I would be summoned by my father to come down and watch TV with the rest of the family. There was no escape. This was supposed to be "quality time"—one of the few moments in the week the family got together. Only we weren't really together. How can you be, sitting silently in front of a TV set? It was pitiful, watching some family in a sit com on TV instead of being a family. All we succeeded in doing was to substitute a fictional family for the real one—us.

Eric's Response

To me, the most interesting point here is the one about how people substitute fictional TV families for real ones. I think you could use this as the basis for your essay. I sense a lot of anger at your family, and I think you need to be careful with this. As I understand it, your assignment is an analytical one, not just a personal essay about your family. Maybe you could look more into why people want to watch TV families. What are the reasons? If you could develop some ideas about why TV families are preferable to real ones, you could explain why and how your family used TV families to create this sense of false togetherness.

PLANNING

Using discussions with others about their ideas for a writing project, writers need to develop a plan for their writing. The key issue at this point is how to arrange their material so that they highlight the main point and provide supporting evidence.

After Krista talked to Tamika and got response to her exploratory writing from Eric, she mulled over the results. She knew it was time to use this information to plan her essay. Tamika and Eric helped her see that she needed to write an analytical essay that made a central claim and backed it up with evidence. A personal essay that focused on her feelings about her family was not the kind of writing called for by the assignment.

At this point, she worked by herself, developing her main idea and arranging reasons to support it. She sketched the following brief outline so that she could begin drafting.

Krista's Brief Outline

Introduction

Begin with an anecdote about my family

Getting called down on Monday night to watch TV with the family

Generalize this experience

Claim: the only quality family time left is spent in front of TV

Body

Give reasons why this is so

It's easy

Actors are doing the work of being a family for us

For TV's fictional families, everything works out

Ending

How to deal with the problem?

Turn off the TV and talk to your family

DRAFTING

Any plan a writer develops needs to be tested by writing a working draft. Outlines, sketches, or other kinds of preliminary planning can tell you only so much. To see where your ideas are going, you must commit them to paper.

After she sketched a brief outline, the next step for Krista was to write a working draft. As you can see, she used ideas and suggestions from Tamika and Eric. But, as is the case in individual writing projects, she worked independently to write the draft. Here is what she came up with.

Krista's Working Draft

It's 8:00 on a Monday night, and I am sitting at home in my bedroom peacefully reading a novel. Suddenly, the dreaded call comes, "Kris, you been in that room for two hours. Come on out here and be with the family for awhile. Cosby is going to start in five minutes. Don't you want to watch it with us?" Well, actually no. I was content with my book. But Dad and the family saw these hours in front of the television as quality, and I was expected to participate. What I constantly wondered every Monday was why? When did sitting in front of the tube become family time?

Unfortunately, my family is not the exception but the rule. People are able to remember it is Monday and at 5:00 they can watch the heartwarming merger of blended families on Full House. Yet, without a calendar, they have a difficult time remembering that this particular Monday is their stepmother's or stepfather's birthday and they should get a card or gift on the way home from work or school. They can tell you that the hot couple is headed for divorce on Melrose Place more easily than they can see the status of their own marriage. People may not have noticed, but the only quality family time left is that shared on the TV. The family has left the living room and has gone to live in the TV set in the form of fictional families living fictional lives that the real people would be living if they weren't watching TV.

So what happened? When did fiction become stronger than reality? And is there a way out? I propose the theory that it happened because it was easy. It takes no effort to sit and stare at the TV. It takes work to relate to your family. Now, that is what we pay actors for: to do that work for us, to relate to their families in the ways that we no longer can. On TV, blended families always work out, drug addicts are always treated, and no one is ever hurt permanently. It's easy. Just follow the script and everything will be fine. After all, if you're watching TV, you won't fight (except over who has the remote). If you don't fight, no one can get hurt and everyone will be happy. Let the TV characters fight. They always make up on the half hour. What could be simpler?

The solution? That's simpler and more obvious than the problem. If the TV is taking over your life, unplug it. Instead of watching TV dads, watch your own. Ask him questions, find out how his day went. Read those books when you want to escape the family. This way, when you come back, your family won't be under the illusion you were with them, and you may have learned something from your reading you can share with them. One night per week, just unplug the box and have real quality time. That's all it will take. Soon, it will become like a popular series. How did mom's big promotion interview at work go? Tune in next week for the answer. And soon will come the realization that you don't have to wait. You can ask her tomorrow. And more easily than you watched TV your whole life, you have become a family again.

PEER COMMENTARY

Once writers have a working draft down on paper, they need to figure out what kinds of revisions are called for. Clearly, feedback from readers can be useful at this point. To get the most useful kind of feedback to your own working drafts, make sure your readers know they're looking at a work in progress and not a final draft.

There are different kinds of commentary you can get from readers at this point. Your readers can:

- *Describe* the writer's strategy.

■ *Analyze* the organization of the essay.

■ *Evaluate* the argument.

Each kind of commentary provides different information to help you plan revisions. Sometimes you'll want just one kind of commentary; at other times you'll want more than one.

The following sections describe the different kinds of feedback, explain their purposes, and provide guidelines. After each, you'll find an example of the type of peer commentary in response to Krista's working draft.

Describe the Writer's Strategy

A good first step in getting feedback on a working draft is to ask your reader to suspend judgment for a moment and instead to analyze the function of each paragraph in your working draft—how the paragraphs support the main point and how they are connected to each other. In this way, a reader can give you a blueprint of what you have written. This can help you see how (or whether) the parts fit together. You can use this information to decide how well your paragraphs play the roles you intended for them (or whether they perform some other function). This can also be a good basis for the following two types of commentary, in which readers analyze the organization and evaluate the ideas of a working draft.

Guidelines for Describing the Writer's Strategy

■ What is the writer's main point? Identify the sentence or sentences that express the main point. If you don't find such a sentence, write your own version of what you think the main point is.

■ Write a statement about each paragraph that explains the function it performs and how it fits into the organization of the working draft. Use words that describe function, such as *describes, explains, gives reasons, proposes,* or *compares.*

Sample Description of Krista's Draft

Main point: The "only family quality time left is that shared on the TV." Families have substituted fictional for real life.

¶**1:** Tells a story about her family that introduces the main problem. Asks a series of questions.

¶**2:** Generalizes from her family's experience to point out that they aren't exceptions. Gives two further examples of the problem. Explains how families have substituted fiction for real life.

¶**3:** Raises a question about why the problem has developed. Offers a theory to explain the problem.

¶**4:** Proposes a solution and describes the outcome.

Analyze the Organization

Sometimes, in the struggle to get your ideas down on paper, you may lose perspective on how effectively you've organized them. For this reason, it can be helpful to ask someone else to analyze the organization and presentation of your main idea and examine the supporting evidence.

Again, ask readers to put aside their personal responses to your ideas. Explain that you want them to focus instead on the organization of what you have written. If they have already described the function of paragraphs in the draft, they can use that description as the basis of their analysis. Tell them, in any case, to consider the following questions.

Guidelines for Analyzing the Organization

- What is the main point of the draft? Is it clear and easy to find? Does the introduction help readers anticipate where the draft will be going?

- Do the following paragraphs develop the main point, or do they seem to develop some other point? Is it easy to tell how the paragraphs relate to the main point, or do they need to be connected more explicitly to it?

- Is each of the paragraphs well focused, or do some of them seem to have several ideas contending for the reader's attention? If a paragraph needs more focus, how could this be achieved?

- Within the supporting paragraphs, do some points seem to need more development? Are there points that don't belong at all?

- Is the ending or conclusion effective? Does it provide a sense of closure?

Sample Analysis of the Organization of Krista's Draft

I like the opening story because I can see what you are getting at. But I wasn't totally clear on the main point for awhile. At first, it seemed like it was just about your family. Then in ¶2 you broadened things to include American families in general. I think you could use a clinching statement at the end of the first ¶ that says what your main point is. The questions left me up in the air.

In ¶2, you give two examples that illustrate the problem. I think you could put these in the introduction to show what the problem looks like beyond your family. Then you could expand the final part of ¶2 that explains how we're substituting fictional for real families. That's a great point because it analyzes the problem instead of just describing it. The last sentence is long and hard to follow.

¶3 explains why people have substituted fictional for real families. I like the theory you propose, but I think you should emphasize the point that on TV everything works out and the characters in the shows do the work for us. This seems like the main idea in the ¶ more than TV took over because it was easy.

Finally, your solution in ¶4 makes sense. I wonder whether escaping the family by reading takes away from your main point.

Evaluate the Argument

While the first two kinds of commentary ask readers to set aside their evaluation of your ideas, sometimes you'll really want to know what they think. This is especially likely if you're making an argument or dealing with a controversial topic. For this kind of peer commentary in particular, you'll find it helpful to have more than one reader and to discuss with each reader the comments he or she makes. In this way, you'll have the opportunity to see how your ideas relate to other points of view and to understand the enabling assumptions you and others bring to the issue. This can help you make decisions about how to clarify your own position and handle differing views as you revise.

If your readers have described the function of paragraphs and analyzed the organization of your working draft, they can use these as a basis to evaluate the argument. In any case, your readers should begin by analyzing the parts of your argument before they evaluate it.

Guidelines for Evaluating the Argument

- Analyze the parts of the argument. What is the claim or main point of the working draft? What supporting evidence is provided? What enabling assumptions connect the evidence to the claim?

- Do you agree with the essay's main point? Do you accept the essay's assumptions? Explain why.

- *If you disagree* with the essay's main point or do not accept one or more of its assumptions, what position would you take on the issue yourself? How would you support your position? What assumptions would you make? How would you refute the main point of the essay? What alternative perspectives does the draft need to take into account?

- *If you agree* with the essay's position, explain why. Do you think the essay makes the best possible argument supporting it? How would you strengthen it? What would you change, add, or omit? Why?

Discuss the responses with your readers. If you disagree, the idea is not to argue about who is right but to keep talking to understand why your positions differ and what assumptions might have led you to take differing positions.

Sample Evaluations of the Argument in Krista's Draft

Commentary 1

Krista, your main claim seems to be at the end of the second paragraph where you say that the only quality family time is watching TV, and you support this idea by talking about how families have substituted fictional families for real families. The reason you give is that it's easier that way—the actors do the work for us and everything works out fine. The assumption that connects this reason to your main claim seems to be that families can't deal with reality any more and so they need a fictional substitute.

I can see what you mean, in that TV shows always have happy endings and wrap up everything in an hour or half hour. But I think there can also be times TV contributes to family life. For example, in my family, watching football together is a big deal, and I have lots of good memories of sitting with my father, grandfather, and brothers watching the 49ers. Maybe this was just a male-bonding ritual but everybody talked and shared. I'm not sure but I feel you're a little too negative.

Commentary 2

[Analysis of the parts of the argument is similar to Response 1.]

I agree totally with your analysis of so-called quality time in front of the tube. What you say is exactly true of my family, and I'm sick of it. My suggestion here is that the evidence you give to back up your main point doesn't seem developed enough. It's all jammed in paragraph 3. To me, the point is not that watching TV is easy but that TV does the work for us in these packaged hour segments. I think that idea would come out more clearly if you developed it more.

The only other thing is the final paragraph. For this kind of assignment, I'm not sure your teacher wants personal advice at the end. Maybe there's some way you could make the ending more analytical by pointing out larger problems or consequences.

REVISING

Writing isn't a precise science with right and wrong answers, and neither is talking about written work in progress. When others comment on your writing, each person will have his or her own responses, insights, and suggestions. At times you'll get differing suggestions about what to do with your working draft, as is the case with the two commentaries on Krista's working draft. This doesn't necessarily mean that one reader has seen the true problem in your writing and the other has missed it altogether. By telling you the effect your writing has on each of them, both readers are giving you information to work with.

It's important to understand why readers have responded to your writing as they did. Try to imagine their point of view and what in your writing might have prompted their response. Peer commentary doesn't provide writers with a set of directions they can carry out mechanically. Rather, they must analyze and interpret their readers' responses.

Here are some guidelines for revising, followed by Krista's commentary about how she made use of the peer commentary she received on her working draft.

Guidelines for Revising

- What do your readers see as the main point of your draft? Is that the main idea you intended? If your readers have identified your main point, do they offer suggestions to make it come across more clearly? If you think they missed your main point, consider why this is so. Do you need to revise the sentence or sentences that express your central point?

- Do your readers see how the evidence you supply supports your main point? If so, do they offer suggestions about strengthening the evidence you're using to back up your main claim? If not, does this mean you need to revise your main point or revise the supporting evidence?

- What do your readers think you assume to connect your evidence to your main claim? Is this what you had in mind? If not, how can you change the relationship between your claim and the evidence you provide?

- If your readers agree with your essay's position, why is this so? Do they think you make the best possible case? If they disagree, consider their positions and the assumptions they are making. Do they offer alternative perspectives you could use?

- Do you provide a meaningful ending that points out an important consequence or implication of your argument?

Krista's Thoughts on Her Peer Commentaries

After I read the peer commentaries, at first I thought the paper was a mess and I needed to start all over again. So I put them aside for a time. When I reread them, I started to see that the paper could be revised. I realized it was a mistake to use questions at the end of paragraph 1. In fact, I had overused rhetorical questions throughout the essay. My real main point didn't come across until the end of paragraph 2, and I could see that my supporting material was too scattered in paragraphs 2 and 3.

Notice in Krista's revisions of her working draft how she uses ideas from the two commentaries to plan a revision. First, we present two paragraphs from the working draft with Krista's annotated plans for revision. This is followed by the final draft.

It's 8:00 on a Monday night, and I am sitting at home in my bedroom peacefully reading a novel. Suddenly, the dreaded call comes, "Kris, you been in that room for two hours. Come on out here and be with the family for awhile. Cosby is going to start in five minutes. Don't you want to watch it with us?" Well, actually no. I was content with my book. But Dad and the family saw these hours in front of the television as quality, and I was expected to participate. What I constantly wondered every Monday was why? When did sitting in front of the tube become family time?

cut

Combine ¶1 & 2

Unfortunately, my family is not the exception but the rule. People are able to remember it is Monday and at 5:00 they can watch the heartwarming merger of blended families on <u>Full House</u>. Yet, without a calendar, they have a difficult time remembering that this particular Monday is their stepmother's or stepfather's birthday and they should get a card or gift on the way home from work or school. They can tell you that the hot couple is headed for divorce on <u>Melrose Place</u> more easily than they can see the status of their own marriage. People may not have noticed, but the only quality family time left is that shared on the TV. ~~The family has left the living room and has gone to live in the TV set in the form of fictional families living fictional lives that the real people would be living if they weren't watching TV.~~

use in ¶2 as examples

In families like mine, television viewing too often means evading each other by replacing real families with fictional ones.

Add concession that TV can be quality time

—Turn next ¶ into 2¶s: 1) how TV families do the work for us, 2) how TV families always solve their problems
—Change ending: explain results instead of giving advice

Krista Guglielmetti
English 10
Prof. Matsuda
November 14, 2005

Family Life and Television

It's 8:00 on a Monday night, and I am sitting at home in my bedroom peacefully reading a novel. Suddenly, the dreaded call comes, "Kris, you been in that room for two hours. Come on out here and be with the family for awhile. Cosby is going to start in five minutes. Don't you want to watch it with us?" This predictable Monday night call from my Dad reveals one of the ways families use television viewing. It is supposed to be "quality" time, where real families gather together to watch fictional families in sit coms like Cosby. Now it may be true that in some families people actually interact while they are watching television, discussing the meaning of recent news or sharing in the victory or defeat of their favorite team. But in families like mine, television viewing too often means evading each other by replacing real families with fictional ones.

When my family watches television together, what we share is not the experience of actual family members but episodes in the fictional lives of television families. One of the effects of watching these television families is that we use the actors and actresses to do our work for us. The fictional families offer television viewers vicarious experiences that can substitute for real experience. People, for example, remember it is Monday and at 5:00 they can watch the heartwarming merger of the blended family Full House. Yet, without a calendar, they have a difficult time remembering that this particular Monday is their stepmother's or stepfather's birthday and they should get a card or gift on the way home from work or school. Television viewers can tell you that the hot couple on Melrose Place is headed for divorce more easily than they can see the status of their own marriage. People may not have noticed, but fiction has become stronger than reality.

Perhaps the greatest attraction to fictional television families is that, unlike real families, they can solve their problems in hour or half-hour segments. On TV, blended families always work out, drug addicts are always treated, and no one is ever hurt permanently. It's easy. Just follow the script and everything will be fine. After all, if you're watching TV, you won't fight (except over who has the remote). If you don't fight, no one can get hurt and everyone will be happy. So we let the TV characters do our fighting for us because they always make up on the half hour.

In my family, watching television families work things out doesn't bring us closer together. Instead of being shared quality time, our experience as television viewers brings about a sense of failure and demoralization. Even though no one says so, we all know we'll never measure up to the television families. Our lives are messier, and our problems seem to persist no matter how much we watch <u>Cosby</u>.

FINAL TOUCHES

Writers collaborate with others throughout the writing process, and that includes working on the final touches. Copy editors routinely edit the manuscripts of even the most famous writers, making suggestions about words, phrases, sentences, or passages that might be unclear, awkward, or grammatically incorrect. Then proofreaders carefully review the final draft for any misspellings, missing words, typos, or other flaws.

In school writing, teachers sometimes consider such collaborative work of editing and proofreading as unwarranted assistance from other students. If your teacher permits it, collaboration can be quite useful in applying the final touches to your work.

Directions for Editing

Ask the person editing your manuscript to look for any words, phrases, sentences, or passages that need to be changed. The person can do this in one of two ways: he or she can simply underline or circle problems, write a brief note of explanation in the margin when necessary, and let you make the changes; or he or she can go ahead and make tentative changes for you to consider. Your teacher will let you know which method to follow.

Sample Editing

Sentence in Krista's Revised Draft:

Unlike real families, the greatest attraction of fictional television families is that they can solve their problems in hour or half-hour segments.

Final Version:

Perhaps the greatest attraction to fictional television families is that, unlike real families, they can solve their problems in hour or half-hour segments.

Directions for Proofreading

The person proofreading your final copy can underline or circle grammatical errors, usage problems, typos, and misspellings and let you make the final corrections. Or she or he can supply the corrections. Again, it's up to your teacher which method to follow.

TALKING TO TEACHERS

Much of what has been said here about how writers and readers can collaborate also applies to talking about your writing with teachers. There may be times, for example, when you have trouble figuring out a writing assignment. You may be confused about the suggestions you've received in peer commentaries, or you may not fully understand the teacher's comments. In such situations, you might request a conference with your teacher.

Talking about writing with teachers will be most productive if you prepare ahead of time. If you want to discuss a writing assignment, reread the directions carefully and prepare questions on what isn't clear to you about the assignment. If you want to talk about the feedback you've gotten from peers, reread their commentaries and bring them with you to the conference. If you want to talk about a paper that has already been graded, make sure you read it over carefully, paying particular attention to the teacher's comments.

In any case, have realistic expectations about what can happen at the conference. Don't expect your teacher to change your grade or give you a formula for completing the assignment. The point of the conference is for you to understand what your teacher is looking for in a piece of writing.

GOING TO THE WRITING CENTER

One of the best places to talk about writing is a writing center, where you can meet and discuss your writing with people who are interested in the writing process and in how students develop as writers. Find out if your college has a writing center. It will be listed in the campus directory, and your writing teacher will know about its hours and procedures.

Sometimes students think the writing center is only for those with serious writing problems, but that is not the case. Students of all abilities can benefit from talking to writing tutors. Whether the people who staff the writing center at your college are undergraduates, graduate students, or professional tutors, they are experienced writers who like to talk about writing.

If your campus has a writing center, make an appointment to interview one of the tutors. Ask what kinds of services the center provides and what insights into college writing the tutor can offer. Even better, take a writing assignment you're working on or a paper that's already been graded to serve as the basis for a conversation with the tutor.

chapter 17

the shape of the essay: how form embodies purpose

The word *essay* is derived from the French word *essai*, which means to try or test out. This derivation captures the spirit of the essay as a genre of writing in which writers invent forms to embody their purposes. Many examples of writing in this book might be described as an essay as well as, say, a memoir, a commentary, or a proposal. The exact meaning of the term *essay* has been debated by scholars in literary studies, rhetoric, and composition. Some want to restrict it to a particular type of literary or journalistic essay that uses a personal voice and other self-revelatory features to fashion experience and observation into writing. Others use it more broadly to refer to writing tasks where the form is open and flexible. In this chapter, we'll use the term *essay* in its broader sense, as a catch-all category that includes a range of other genres. For our purposes, the defining feature of the essay will be the openness and the flexibility it gives writers to shape their thoughts, feelings, and experiences into written forms.

The role of this chapter is to help you understand how this happens—how the essay embodies a writer's purposes and provides the groundwork for readers to engage a writer's ideas. Such an understanding of the formal aspects of writing can help you gain greater control over your own writing projects. We will look in particular at how writers organize their work, write introductions and endings, connect the parts, and design paragraphs.

THINKING ABOUT FORM

Understanding how form works in essays, as well as in other genres of writing, is a matter of understanding how the parts of a piece of writing are related to one another and how that arrangement guides and enables readers to follow the writer's thoughts and purposes.

In some genres of writing, writers and readers alike rely heavily on formal conventions. You can tell, for example, that a piece of writing is a letter simply

by looking at it. The same is true for certain kinds of academic writing, such as lab reports and scientific articles, with their fixed sections–introduction, materials and methods, results, discussion. Public documents such as wills, contracts, laws, and resolutions also have highly predictable features that make them immediately recognizable.

However, with the essay, writers cannot turn to a standardized form to shape their material. Instead they often need to devise a form from a repertoire of possibilites that is adequate for their purposes and appropriate to the materials at hand.

In any case, though, whether the form of a piece of writing is standardized or improvised for the occasion, form has two key dimensions—the visual and the psychological.

- **The visual dimension** of form refers to the way written texts are laid out on a page. Writing materializes people's thoughts and purposes in visible form, and written texts take on a particular "look" as they occupy the space of a page. Paragraph breaks, headings and subheadings, the use of bullets and illustrations, the size and style of fonts, the layout of the page—these aspects of writing provide readers with visual cues to follow a piece of writing.

- **The psychological dimension** of form places readers in a particular frame of mind by creating a set of expectations about the writer's purposes and where a piece of writing is going. The form of written texts arouses the reader's anticipation and then goes on to fulfill it in one way or another, whether the resolution is temporary or permanent, expected or surprising.

Looking at how the visual and psychological dimensions of form work together can help you see that organizing a piece of writing is not simply providing a series of containers to pour your thoughts into—at the rate, say, of one main point per essay and one idea per paragraph. This rather mechanical view of form is often the result of learning the five-paragraph theme (thesis, three paragraphs of support, and conclusion) without taking into account how the form of writing serves, both visually and psychologically, to manage the interaction between the writer and readers. Whether the form of writing is fixed in advance or needs to be invented for the occasion, its key function, as you will see, is to produce common expectations and shared understanding between writers and readers.

THREE PATTERNS OF ORGANIZATION

Let's look first at the overall organization of the essay. To see how form works to bring writers and readers together, we will look at three common patterns that writers draw on, depending on their purposes: (1) top-down order; (2) culminating order; and (3) open form.

TOP-DOWN ORDER

This pattern of organization is perhaps the most familiar. Writers tell readers at the outset what their main point is and then go on to develop and support it. This pattern of organization enables readers to hold in mind the writer's central idea and to evaluate its merits based on the evidence that follows. The success of top-down order depends in large part on how well writers deliver on what they have led their readers to anticipate.

I Shop, Ergo I Am: The Mall as Society's Mirror

Sara Boxer

In certain academic circles, "shop till you drop" is considered a civic act. If you follow cultural studies—the academic scrutiny of ordinary activities like eating fast food, buying a house in the suburbs, watching television and taking vacations at Disneyland—you will know that shopping is not just a matter of going to a store and paying for your purchase.

How you shop is who you are. Shopping is a statement about your place in society and your part in world cultural history. There is a close relationship, even an equation, between citizenship and consumption. The store is the modern city-state, the place where people act as free citizens, making choices, rendering opinions and socializing with others.

If this sounds like a stretch, you're way behind the times. The field of cultural studies, which took off in England in the 1970's, has been popular in this country for more than a decade.

The intellectual fascination with stores goes back even further. When the philosopher Walter Benjamin died in 1940, he was working on a long study of the Paris arcades, the covered retail passageways, then almost extinct, which he called the "original temples of commodity capitalism." Six decades later, the study of shopping is well

trampled. Some academics have moved on from early classical work on the birth of the department store and the shopping arcade to the shopping malls of the 1950's and even the new wide aisles of today's factory outlets and superstores—places like Best Buy, Toys "R" Us and Ikea.

Historically, the age of shopping and browsing begins at the very end of the 18th century. In a paper titled "Counter Publics: Shopping and Women's Sociability," delivered at the Modern Language Association's annual meeting, Deidre Lynch, an associate professor of English at the State University of New York in Buffalo, said the word "shopping" started to appear frequently in print around 1780. That was when stores in London started turning into public attractions.

By 1800, Ms. Lynch said, "a policy of obligation-free browsing seems to have been introduced into London emporia." At that point, "the usual morning employment of English ladies," the 18th-century writer Robert Southey said, was to "go-a-shopping." Stores became places to socialize, to see and be seen. Browsing was born.

The pastime of browsing has been fully documented. Benjamin wrote that the Paris arcades, which went up in the early 1800's, created a new kind of person, a professional loiterer, or *flâneur*, who could easily turn into a dangerous political gadfly. The philosopher Jürgen Habermas, some of his interpreters say, has equated consumer capitalism with the feminization of culture. And now some feminists, putting a new spin on this idea, are claiming the store as the place where women first became "public women."

By imagining that they owned the wares, women were "transported into new identities," Ms. Lynch said. By meeting with their friends, they created what feminist critics like Nancy Fraser and Miriam Hansen called "counter publics," groups of disenfranchised people.

Putting Merchants in Their Place

Some feminists point out that as shoppers, women had the power to alter other people's lives. Women who spent "a summer's day cheapening a pair of gloves" without buying anything, as Southey put it, were "fortifying the boundaries of social class," Ms. Lynch said. They were "teaching haberdashers and milliners their place," taunting them with the prospect of a purchase and never delivering. It may not have been nice, but it was a sort of political power.

Women could also use their power for good. In 1815, Ms. Lynch points out, Mary Lamb wrote an essay called "On Needle-work," urging upper-class ladies who liked to do needlework as a hobby to give compensatory pay to women who did it to make a living. Lamb's biographer recently noted that this was how "bourgeois women busily distributed the fruits of their husbands' capitalist gains in the name of female solidarity."

The idea that shopping is a form of civil action naturally has its critics. In one of the essays in a book titled *Buy This Book*, Don Slater, a sociologist at the University of London, criticized the tendency of many academics to celebrate "the productivity, creativity, autonomy, rebelliousness and even . . . the 'authority' of the consumer." The trouble with this kind of post-modern populism is that it mirrors "the logic of the consumer society it seeks to analyze," he said. Such theories, without distinguishing between real needs and false ones, he suggested, assume that shoppers are rational and autonomous creatures who acquire what they want and want what they acquire.

Another critic, Meaghan Morris, author of an essay called "Banality in Cultural Studies," has faulted academics for idealizing the pleasure and power of shopping and underestimating the "anger, frustration, sorrow, irritation, hatred, boredom and fatigue" that go with it.

The field of shopping studies, whatever you think of it, is now at a pivotal point. In the 19th century, emporiums in London and arcades in Paris turned shopping into social occasions; in the 20th century, academics turned shopping into civic action; and in the 21st century, it seems that megastores will bring us into a new, darker era.

Shoppers' freedoms are changing. According to Robert Bocock, writing in *Consumption*, the mall walkers of today do not have the rights that the *flâneurs* of the 19th century had. "In the United States, 'policing' of who is allowed entry to the malls has become stricter in the last two or three decades of the 20th century."

In superstores, the role of shoppers has changed even more radically. Superstores are warehouses that stock an astounding number of goods picked out at a national corporate level, said Marianne Conroy, a scholar of comparative literature at the University of Maryland. Shoppers educate themselves about the goods and serve themselves. Thus, the superstore effectively "strips shopping of its aura of sociality," Ms. Conroy said. There is no meaningful interaction between the salespeople and the shoppers or among the shoppers. The shoppers' relationship is not with other people but with boxes and shelves.

Does the concept of the shopper as citizen still hold? The real test is to see how the citizen-shopper fares at the superstore. In a paper she delivered to the Modern Language Association, titled "You've Gotta Fight for Your Right to Shop: Superstores, Citizenship and the Restructuring of Consumption," Ms. Conroy analyzed one event in the history of a superstore that tested the equation between shopping and citizenship.

In 1996 Ronald Kahlow, a software engineer, decided to do some comparison shopping at a Best Buy outlet store in Reston, VA., by punching the prices and model numbers of some televisions into his laptop computer. When store employees asked him to stop, he refused and was arrested for trespassing. The next day, Mr. Kahlow returned with a pen and paper. Again, he was charged with trespassing and handcuffed.

When he stood trial in Fairfax County Court, he was found not guilty. And, as Ms. Conroy observed, the presiding judge in the case, Donald McDonough, grandly equated Mr. Kahlow's comparison shopping to civil disobedience in the 1960's. Mr. Kahlow then recited Robert F. Kennedy's poem "A Ripple of Hope," and the judge said, "Never has the cause of comparison shopping been so eloquently advanced."

Like Canaries in the Mines

At first, Ms. Conroy suggested they both might have gone overboard in reading "public meaning into private acts," but then she reconsidered. Maybe, she said, it's just time to refine the model.

Ms. Conroy suggested that consumerism should be seen no longer as the way citizens exercise their rights and freedoms but rather as "an activity that makes the impact of economic institutions on everyday life critically intelligible." In other words, shoppers in superstores are like canaries in the mines. Their experience inside tells us something about the dangers lurking in society at large.

What does one man's shopping experience at Best Buy tell us about the dangers of modern life in America? The fact that Mr. Kahlow was arrested when he tried to comparison shop shows that even the minimal rights of citizen-shoppers are endangered, said Ms. Conroy. Not only have they lost a venue for socializing, but they are also beginning to lose their right to move about freely and make reasoned choices.

Without the trappings of sociability, it's easier to see what's what. Stores used to be places that made people want to come out and buy things they didn't know they wanted. And they were so seductive that by the end of the 20th century they became one of the few sites left for public life. But in the superstores, the *flâneurs* and the consumer-citizens are fish out of water. They have nowhere pleasant to wander, no glittering distractions, no socializing to look forward to and no escape from the watchful eyes of the security guards. If this is citizenship, maybe it's time to move to another country.

CULMINATING ORDER

This form reserves or delays the presentation of the writer's central idea until late in the piece of writing. Instead of announcing a claim early on and then using the rest of the writing to support it, here the writing is organized so that it culminates with the payoff for readers. With this pattern of organization, the success of a piece of writing will often depend on how effectively the writer establishes a central issue or set of issues and then organizes the rest of the essay so that when the culminating point arrives it seems inevitable and logical.

Minneapolis Pornography Ordinance

Ellen Goodman

Just a couple of months before the pool-table gang rape in New Bedford, Mass., *Hustler* magazine printed a photo feature that reads like a blueprint for the actual crime. There were just two differences between *Hustler* and real life. In *Hustler*, the woman enjoyed it. In real life, the woman charged rape.

There is no evidence that the four men charged with this crime had actually read the magazine. Nor is there evidence that the spectators who yelled encouragement for two hours had held previous ringside seats at pornographic events. But there is a growing sense that the violent pornography being peddled in this country helps to create an atmosphere in which such events occur.

As recently as last month, a study done by two University of Wisconsin researchers suggested that even "normal" men, prescreened college students, were changed by their exposure to violent pornography. After just ten hours of viewing, reported researcher Edward Donnerstein, "the men were less likely to convict in a rape trial, less likely to see injury to a victim, more likely to see the victim as responsible." Pornography may not cause rape directly, he said, "but it maintains a lot of very callous attitudes. It justifies aggression. It even says you are doing a favor to the victim."

If we can prove that pornography is harmful, then shouldn't the victims have legal rights? This, in any case, is the theory behind a city ordinance that recently passed the Minneapolis City Council. Vetoed by the mayor last week, it is likely to be back before the Council for an overriding vote, likely to appear in other cities, other towns. What is unique about the Minneapolis approach is that for the first time it attacks pornography, not because of nudity or sexual explicitness, but because it degrades and harms women. It opposes pornography on the basis of sex discrimination.

University of Minnesota Law Professor Catherine MacKinnon, who co-authored the ordinance with feminist writer Andrea Dworkin, says that they chose this tactic because they believe that pornography is central to "creating and maintaining the inequality of the sexes. . . . Just being a woman means you are injured by pornography."

They defined pornography carefully as, "the sexually explicit subordination of women, graphically depicted, whether in pictures or in words." To fit their legal definition it must also include one of nine conditions that show this subordination, like presenting women who "experience sexual pleasure in being raped or . . . mutilated." Under this law, it would be possible for a pool-table rape victim to sue *Hustler*. It would be possible for a woman to sue if she were forced to act in a pornographic movie. Indeed, since the law describes pornography as oppressive to all women, it would be possible for any woman to sue those who traffic in the stuff for violating her civil rights.

In many ways, the Minneapolis ordinance is an appealing attack on an appalling problem. The authors have tried to resolve a long and bubbling conflict among those who have both a deep aversion to pornography and a deep loyalty to the value of free speech. "To date," says Professor MacKinnon, "people have identified the pornographer's freedom with everybody's freedom. But we're saying that the freedom of the pornographer is the subordination of women. It means one has to take a side."

But the sides are not quite as clear as Professor MacKinnon describes them. Nor is the ordinance. Even if we accept the argument that pornography is harmful to women—and I do—then we must also recognize that anti-Semitic literature is harmful to Jews and racist literature is harmful to blacks. For that matter, Marxist literature may be harmful to government policy. It isn't just women versus pornographers. If women win the right to sue publishers and producers, then so could Jews, blacks, and a long list of people who may be able to prove they have been harmed by books, movies, speeches or even records. The Manson murders, you may recall, were reportedly inspired by the Beatles.

We might prefer a library or book store or lecture hall without *Mein Kampf* or the Grand Whoever of the Ku Klux Klan. But a growing list of harmful expressions would inevitably strangle freedom of speech.

This ordinance was carefully written to avoid problems of banning and prior restraint, but the right of any woman to claim damages from pornography is just too broad. It seems destined to lead to censorship.

What the Minneapolis City Council has before it is a very attractive theory. What MacKinnon and Dworkin have written is a very persuasive and useful definition of pornography. But they haven't yet resolved the conflict between the harm of pornography and the value of free speech. In its present form, this is still a shaky piece of law.

OPEN FORM

An open-form pattern of organization gives readers much less guidance than either top-down or culminating order. Instead of explicitly pointing out the connections among the parts, open form often leaves it to the readers to provide these links. If top-down and culminating order operate logically, open form operates associatively, and the parts of the writing take on meaning implicitly by how they are juxtaposed to each other. In this case, the success of a piece of writing largely depends on how skillfully the writer combines apparently disparate materials to create a dominant impression that may never be named outright but that is available to the reader nonetheless.

LOS ANGELES NOTEBOOK
JOAN DIDION

1   There is something uneasy in the Los Angeles air this afternoon, some unnatural stillness, some tension. What it means is that tonight a Santa Ana will begin to blow, a hot wind from the northeast whining down through the Cajon and San Gorgonio Passes, blowing up sandstorms out along Route 66, drying the hills and the nerves to the flash point. For a few days now we will see smoke back in the canyons, and hear sirens in the night. I have neither heard nor read that a Santa Ana is due, but I know it, and almost everyone I have seen today knows it too. We know it because we feel it. The baby frets. The maid sulks. I rekindle a waning argument with the telephone company, then cut my losses and lie down, given over to whatever it is in the air. To live with the Santa Ana is to accept, consciously or unconsciously, a deeply mechanistic view of human behavior.

2   I recall being told, when I first moved to Los Angeles and was living on an isolated beach, that the Indians would throw themselves into the sea when the bad wind blew. I could see why. The Pacific turned ominously glossy during a Santa Ana period, and one woke in the night troubled not only by the peacocks screaming in the olive trees but by the eerie absence of surf. The heat was surreal. The sky had a yellow cast, the kind of light sometimes called "earthquake weather." My only neighbor would not come out of her house for days, and there were no lights at night, and her husband roamed the place with a machete. One day he would tell me that he had heard a trespasser, the next a rattlesnake.

3   "On nights like that," Raymond Chandler once wrote about the Santa Ana, "every booze party ends in a fight. Meek little wives feel the edge of the carving knife and study their husbands' necks. Anything can happen." That was the kind of wind it was. I did not know then that there was any basis for the effect it had on all of us, but it turns out to be another of those cases in which science bears out folk wisdom. The Santa Ana, which is named for one of the canyons it rushes through, is a *foehn* wind, like the *foehn* of Austria and Switzerland and the *hamsin* of Israel. There are a number of persistent malevolent winds, perhaps the best known of which are the mistral of France and the Mediterranean sirocco, but a *foehn* wind has distinct characteristics: it occurs on the leeward slope of a mountain range and, although the air begins as a cold mass, it is warmed as it comes down the mountain

and appears finally as a hot dry wind. Whenever and wherever a *foehn* blows, doctors hear about headaches and nausea and allergies, about "nervousness," about "depression." In Los Angeles some teachers do not attempt to conduct formal classes during a Santa Ana, because the children become unmanageable. In Switzerland the suicide rate goes up during the *foehn*, and in the courts of some Swiss cantons the wind is considered a mitigating circumstance for crime. Surgeons are said to watch the wind, because blood does not clot normally during a *foehn*. A few years ago an Israeli physicist discovered that not only during such winds, but for the ten or twelve hours which precede them, the air carries an unusually high ratio of positive to negative ions. No one seems to know exactly why that should be; some talk about friction and others suggest solar disturbances. In any case the positive ions are there, and what an excess of positive ions does, in the simplest terms, is make people unhappy. One cannot get much more mechanistic than that.

4   Easterners commonly complain that there is no "weather" at all in Southern California, that the days and the seasons slip by relentlessly, numbingly bland. That is quite misleading. In fact the climate is characterized by infrequent but violent extremes: two periods of torrential subtropical rains which continue for weeks and wash out the hills and send subdivisions sliding toward the sea; about twenty scattered days a year of the Santa Ana, which, with its incendiary dryness, invariably means fire. At the first prediction of a Santa Ana, the Forest Service flies men and equipment from northern California into the southern forests, and the Los Angeles Fire Department cancels its ordinary non-firefighting routines. The Santa Ana caused Malibu to burn the way it did in 1956, and Bel Air in 1961, and Santa Barbara in 1964. In the winter of 1966–67 eleven men were killed fighting a Santa Ana fire that spread through the San Gabriel Mountains.

5   Just to watch the front-page news out of Los Angeles during a Santa Ana is to get very close to what it is about the place. The longest single Santa Ana period in recent years was in 1957, and it lasted not the usual three or four days but fourteen days, from November 21 until December 4. On the first day 25,000 acres of the San Gabriel Mountains were burning, with gusts reaching 100 miles an hour. In town, the wind reached Force 12, or hurricane force, on the Beaufort Scale; oil derricks were toppled and people ordered off the downtown streets to avoid injury from flying objects. On November 22 the fire in the San Gabriels was out of control. On November 24 six people were killed in automobile accidents, and by the end of the week the *Los Angeles Times* was keeping a box score of traffic deaths. On November 26 a prominent Pasadena attorney, depressed about money, shot and killed his wife, their two sons, and himself. On November 27 a South Gate divorcee, twenty-two, was

murdered and thrown from a moving car. On November 30 the San Gabriel fire was still out of control, and the wind in town was blowing eighty miles an hour. On the first day of December four people died violently, and on the third the wind began to break.

6   It is hard for people who have not lived in Los Angeles to realize how radically the Santa Ana figures in the local imagination. The city burning is Los Angeles's deepest image of itself: Nathanael West perceived that, in *The Day of the Locust*; and at the time of the 1965 Watts riots what struck the imagination most indelibly were the fires. For days one could drive the Harbor Freeway and see the city on fire, just as we had always known it would be in the end. Los Angeles weather is the weather of catastrophe, of apocalypse, and, just as the reliably long and bitter winters of New England determine the way life is lived there, so the violence and the unpredictability of the Santa Ana affect the entire quality of life in Los Angeles, accentuate its impermanence, its unreliability. The wind shows us how close to the edge we are.

2

7   "Here's why I'm on the beeper, Ron," said the telephone voice on the all-night radio show. "I just want to say that this *Sex for the Secretary* creature—whatever her name is—certainly isn't contributing anything to the morals in this country. It's pathetic. Statistics show."

8   "It's *Sex and the Office*, honey," the disc jockey said. "That's the title. By Helen Gurley Brown. Statistics show what?"

9   "I haven't got them right here at my fingertips, naturally. But they show."

10   "I'd be interested in hearing them. Be constructive, you Night Owls."

11   "All right, let's take one statistic," the voice said, truculent now. "Maybe I haven't read the book, but what's this business she recommends about going out with married men for lunch?"

12   So it went, from midnight until 5 a.m., interrupted by records and by occasional calls debating whether or not a rattlesnake can swim. Misinformation about rattlesnakes is a leitmotiv of the insomniac imagination in Los Angeles. Toward 2 a.m. a man from "out Tarzana way" called to protest. "The Night Owls who called earlier must have been thinking about, uh, *The Man in the Gray Flannel Suit* or some other book," he said, "because Helen's one of the few authors trying to tell us what's really going on. Hefner's another, and he's also controversial, working in, uh, another area."

13   An old man, after testifying that he "personally" had seen a swimming rattlesnake, in the Delta-Mendota Canal, urged "moderation" on the Helen Gurley Brown question. "We shouldn't get on the beeper to call things pornographic before we've read them," he

complained, pronouncing it porn-ee-oh-graphic. "I say, get the book. Give it a chance." The original provocateur called back to agree that she would get the book. "And then I'll burn it," she added.

14   "Book burner, eh?" laughed the disc jockey good-naturedly.

15   "I wish they still burned witches," she hissed.

3

16 It is three o'clock on a Sunday afternoon and 105° and the air so thick with smog that the dusty palm trees loom up with a sudden and rather attractive mystery. I have been playing in the sprinklers with the baby and I get in the car and go to Ralph's Market on the corner of Sunset and Fuller wearing an old bikini bathing suit. That is not a very good thing to wear to the market but neither is it, at Ralph's on the corner of Sunset and Fuller, an unusual costume. Nonetheless a large woman in a cotton muumuu jams her cart into mine at the butcher counter. "What a thing to wear to the market," she says in a loud but strangled voice. Everyone looks the other way and I study a plastic package of rib lamb chops and she repeats it. She follows me all over the store, to the Junior Foods, to the Dairy Products, to the Mexican Delicacies, jamming my cart whenever she can. Her husband plucks at her sleeve. As I leave the check-out counter she raises her voice one last time: "What a thing to wear to the Ralph's," she says.

4

17 A party at someone's house in Beverly Hills: a pink tent, two orchestras, a couple of French Communist directors in Cardin evening jackets, chili and hamburgers from Chasen's. The wife of an English actor sits at a table alone; she visits California rarely although her husband works here a good deal. An American who knows her slightly comes over to the table.

18   "Marvelous to see you here," he says.

19   "Is it," she says.

20   "How long have you been here?"

21   "Too long."

22   She takes a fresh drink from a passing waiter and smiles at her husband, who is dancing.

23   The American tries again. He mentions her husband.

24   "I hear he's marvelous in this picture."

25   She looks at the American for the first time. When she finally speaks she enunciates every word very clearly. "He . . . is . . . also . . . a . . . fag," she says pleasantly.

5

26   The oral history of Los Angeles is written in piano bars. "Moon River," the piano player always plays, and "Mountain Greenery." "There's a Small Hotel" and "This Is Not the First Time." People talk to each other, tell each other about their first wives and last husbands. "Stay funny," they tell each other, and "This is to die over." A construction man talks to an unemployed screenwriter who is celebrating, alone, his tenth wedding anniversary. The construction man is on a job in Montecito: "Up in Montecito," he says, "they got one square mile with 135 millionaires."

27   "Putrescence," the writer says.

28   "That's all you got to say about it?"

29   "Don't read me wrong, I think Santa Barbara's one of the most—Christ, the most— beautiful places in the world, but it's a beautiful place that contains a . . . putrescence. They just live on their putrescent millions."

30   "So give me putrescent."

31   "No, no," the writer says. "I just happen to think millionaires have some sort of lacking in their. . . in their elasticity."

32   A drunk requests "The Sweetheart of Sigma Chi." The piano player says he doesn't know it. "Where'd you learn to play the piano?" the drunk asks. "I got two degrees," the piano player says. "One in musical education." I go to a coin telephone and call a friend in New York. "Where are you?" he says. "In a piano bar in Encino," I say. "Why?" he says. "Why not," I say.

1965–67

■ **FOR CRITICAL INQUIRY**

1. As you read the opening sections of each essay, what did they lead you to anticipate would follow? Were your predictions realized?

2. Explain when you became aware of the writer's main point in each selection. Is it stated explicitly? If so, how did that statement guide your reading? If it was not stated explicitly, how did you identify the writer's purposes?

3. Compare your reading experience in each selection. How did you organize mentally the presentation of material? What patterns of organization in the written text did you rely on? Were there other cues for readers in the text that you used? What do you see as the main differences and similarities in how you read each selection?

SEEING PATTERNS OF ORGANIZATION: HOW FORM EMBODIES PURPOSE

As you can see, the pattern of organization each writer chose embodies a particular purpose and establishes a different relationship with readers.

TOP-DOWN ORDER

In the first selection, "I Shop, Ergo I Am," Sarah Boxer wants to inform *New York Times* readers about a new development in the academic world. For this reason, she makes clear early on how the idea that shopping "is a statement about your place in society" has been taken up by cultural studies scholars.

¶ 1–3: **Introduction:** presents main idea—"In certain academic circles, 'shop till you drop' is considered a civic act."

→ ¶ 4–8: Background on history of shopping and browsing.

→ ¶ 9–12: Academic debates about consumer power.

→ ¶ 13–18: The role of shoppers and megastores.

¶ 19–22: **Ending:** Refines the model of shopping as civic action.

Boxer moves from a general statement about shopping and citizenship in the introduction, to particular evidence in the middle section, back to a general level in the ending.

CULMINATING ORDER

In contrast, Ellen Goodman's "Minneapolis Pornography Ordinance" more nearly resembles the rising action of a short story, with an opening exposition of the issues, a mounting conflict, a crisis where two principles seem irreconcilable, and a resolution in the form of Goodman's main claim. By delaying the presentation of her own position, Goodman leads her readers through an explanation of what the Minneapolis ordinance is trying to accomplish and the logic it is based on. A good half of her writing, the first six paragraphs, gives a generous and informative description of the ordinance before Goodman starts to raise questions about its relationship to the values of free speech.

Notice how she slowly raises doubts about the merits of the ordinance, gradually building a case about how it clashes with the values of free speech, up to the final paragraph when she culminates the column by unequivocally stating her position.

→ ¶ 12: Resolves with main claim opposing ordinance.

→ ¶ 8–11: Raises doubts about ordinance.

→ ¶ 4–7: Explains how the ordinance treats the connection.

¶ 1–3: Raises connection between pornography and rape.

OPEN FORM

In turn, Joan Didion's "Los Angeles Notebook" consists of five sections that at first glance have a kind of freestanding character, as if each were meant to be read by itself. Didion is audacious here in using an open form that operates as a mosaic or collage does by juxtaposing disparate parts to form a whole. The five sections are separate units of attention; yet the fact that they appear under one title sets us to work as readers to see how they resonate with each other and what the unstated connections might be between and among them.

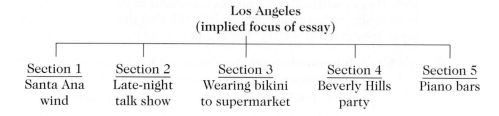

Los Angeles
(implied focus of essay)

Section 1	Section 2	Section 3	Section 4	Section 5
Santa Ana wind	Late-night talk show	Wearing bikini to supermarket	Beverly Hills party	Piano bars

■ EXERCISE

Working with Patterns of Organization

1. Locate a piece of writing that uses a top-down pattern of organization. This could be your own writing or one of the reading selections. Now diagram the pattern of organization in the writing you have chosen by following these steps:
   a. Divide the writing into sections by grouping paragraphs together.
   b. Lay out the sections so that supporting sections are indented in relation to the main point.
   c. Draw arrows to show how the sections are connected.
   d. Write a commentary on your diagram that explains how the sections elicit readers' expectations and then goes on to resolve or fulfill these expectations.

2. Rewrite the opening of Ellen Goodman's "Minneapolis Pornography Ordinance" so that it follows a top-down pattern of organization. What, if anything, do you gain by doing so? What do you lose?

3. Use Joan Didion's "Los Angeles Notebook" as a model to experiment with open form. Write a sequence of sketches that are somehow thematically or attitudinally related. Exchange your writing with a partner in class. Write an analysis of your partner's essay, explaining what you see as the implied focus and what seems to pull the parts together.

A NOTE ON MIXED FORM

The three examples presented here—top-down order, culminating order, and open form—offer relatively pure cases of each pattern of organization. That does not mean, however, that all writing will necessarily fall strictly into one of the patterns. In fact, a good deal of writing combines aspects of the three patterns and therefore might best be described as examples of *mixed form*.

PUTTING THE PARTS TOGETHER

We have looked at the overall form of some short essays. Now we need to look a little more closely at how writers combine the parts of an essay to form a whole. In the following sections, we look first at how writers organize introductions and endings and then at how they connect the parts.

INTRODUCTIONS

The purpose of an introduction is obvious. The opening section needs to let the reader know what the writing is about and how the writer is going to approach the topic.

Sometimes, depending on the situation and the genre, writers just outright tell readers: "This report summarizes the results of the pilot project and makes recommendations for the second stage of implementation" or "This proposal requests funding for a day-care center to serve students, faculty, and staff." In the case of essays, however, introductions need to do more work in establishing a central issue and explaining what is at stake.

Introductions work when they produce a certain meeting of the minds between the writer and reader. This is not to say that they necessarily agree about anything, only that they are mutually engaged in thinking about an issue, problem, or experience. Effective introductions are able to produce this kind of engagement because they identify something that the reader recognizes as interesting, important, controversial, amusing, urgent, whatever—a shareable concern whose relevance is evident.

In other words, writers need to frame their issues in a way that connects to what readers know and care about. Such a framework, then, can become the base from which the writer ventures his or her own views on the matter. The following are some common strategies writers use to establish a common framework and to explain how their own perspective connects to it.

- Describe an existing situation.

- Tell an anecdote.

- Raise a question to answer or problem to solve.

- Use a striking fact, statistic, or other background information.

- Define terms.

- Provide historical background.

- Describe a place, person, or object.

- State a common view and replace it with an alternative perspective.

- Forecast what your writing is designed to do.

■ **EXERCISE**

Analyzing Introductions

Bring to class three pieces of writing (or draw on readings in this book) that use different strategies in their introductions. Work in a group with three or four other students. Take turns explaining the strategies you have found. Consider the differences and similarities among the examples you have found. What generalizations can you draw about how introductions work?

ENDINGS

In terms of the psychological dimensions of form, endings are key moments in writing. Writers know that endings need to provide readers with a sense of closure by resolving their expectations. Without a satisfying sense of an ending, readers are likely to feel let down. Writing that ends abruptly or fails to deliver at the end is going to leave readers up in the air, frustrated, and perhaps annoyed at the writer. In this section, we look at some ways writers typically end short pieces of writing so that they offer readers a satisfying sense of resolution.

Perhaps the most important thing writers can learn about endings is that they perform a function no other part of an essay can perform: they address a question that it doesn't make sense to raise until the writer has developed his or her line of inquiry. This question can be phrased rather bluntly as "so what?"

So what if it is the case, as Sarah Boxer points out, that cultural studies scholars are looking at shopping as civic action? Readers may well have been interested in what Boxer reports about shopping studies. At the same time, it is quite likely that the question "so what?" is lingering at the back of their minds. What's the big picture here, readers will want to know, the consequences and wider implications?

The function of endings is precisely to answer the question "so what?"— to give readers a way to connect the information in Boxer's essay with broader issues. Notice how Boxer has effectively resolved in her ending section the expectations raised in readers' minds when she draws out the connection between shopping and the "dangers of modern life." What might have seemed an esoteric academic topic takes on a wider meaning as Boxer explains how the rise of megastores are changing the character of shopping—and the nature of socializing in contemporary America.

Notice, too, that Boxer is not trying to wrap up everything once and for all in a neat package. Closure doesn't necessarily mean having the final word. In fact, Boxer's ending gives readers something further to think about—to consider what is at stake for them in the whole matter of shopping.

Here are some techniques writers commonly use to write endings that provide a satisfying sense of resolution and closure.

- Point out consequences or the wider significance of the main point.

- Refine the main point in light of the material presented in the piece of writing.

- Offer a recommendation or a solution.

- Consider alternatives.

- Create an echo effect by looping back to something you presented in the introduction.

- Offer a final judgment.

■ EXERCISE

Analyzing Endings

Compare the endings in three pieces of writing in this book or that you have found elsewhere. First identify where the ending begins in each piece. What cues does the writer give? Next, explain the strategy it uses. How does this strategy embody the writer's purposes?

CONNECTING THE PARTS: KEEPING YOUR PURPOSES VISIBLE

If introductions help readers anticipate what is to come and endings explore the consequences or wider implications of the writer's ideas, the middle section (or main body) is where writers unfold their thinking and develop their ideas. The success of the middle section partly depends on readers being able to see how the reasons, evidence, and other supporting materials connect to the main idea presented in the introduction. Writing that is easy to follow, even if the ideas are complex, will use various devices to keep the writer's purposes visible so that readers can stay oriented, identify the relevance of the writer's discussion, and connect it to expectations set up in the introduction.

Here are three standard techniques for connecting the parts.

Use Reasons to Explain

A common way of connecting the parts is to use reasons to explain how the discussion in the middle section develops the main point. In the following sequence of paragraphs, notice how Laurie Ouellette uses reasons to explain why "young women have shunned feminism."

FROM "BUILDING THE THIRD WAVE"

LAURIE OUELLETTE

[W]hat can explain why so many young women have shunned feminism? In her survey of young women, *Feminist Fatale: Voices from the Twentysomething Generation Explore the Future of the Women's Movement,* Paula Kamen found that media-fueled stereotypes of feminists as "man-bashers" and "radical extremists" were behind the fact that many young women don't identify with the women's movement.

But these are not the only reasons. Kamen also points to the lack of young feminist role models as an important factor. The failure of a major feminist organization such as NOW to reach out to a wider spectrum of women, including young women, must be acknowledged as a part of this problem. While individual chapters do have young feminist committees and sometimes officers, they and the national office are led and staffed primarily by older women, and consequently often fail to reflect the interests and needs of a complex generation of young women.

Yet another reason young women have turned away from feminism may lie within its history. If the young women who have gained the most from feminism—that is, white, middle-class women who took advantage of increased accessibility to higher education and professional employment—have been reluctant to associate themselves with feminism, it is hardly surprising that most economically disadvantaged women and women of color, who have seen fewer of those gains, have not been eager to embrace feminism either. The women's movement of the seventies has been called an upper-middle-class white women's movement, and to a large degree I believe that is true. More than a few young feminists—many influenced by feminists of color such as Flo Kennedy, Audre Lorde, and bell hooks—have realized that feminism must also acknowledge issues of race and class to reach out to those women whose concerns have been overlooked by the women's movement of the past. Indeed, numerous statistics, including a poll by the *New York Times*, have noted that young African-American women are more likely than white women to acknowledge many of the concerns conducive to a feminist agenda, including a need for job training and equal earning power outside the professional sector. But for them, feminism has not provided the only answer. Only by making issues of class and race a priority can feminism hope to influence the lives of the millions of women for whom the daily struggle to survive, not feminist activism, is a priority. Will ours be the first generation of feminists to give priority to fighting cuts in Aid to Families with Dependent Children, establishing the right to national health care, day care, and parental leave, and bringing to the forefront other issues pertinent to the daily struggle of many women's lives? If there is to be a third wave of feminism, they must.

We can diagram the pattern of development in the three paragraphs to make visible how it embodies Ouellette's purposes. Notice how the form creates a hierarchy of levels—the main point, the reasons, and the supporting evidence.

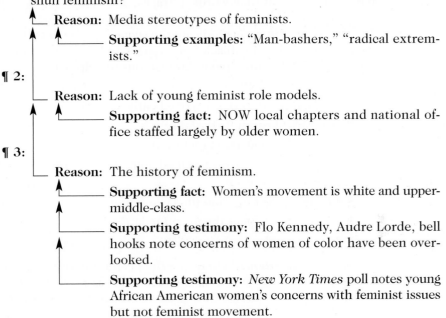

¶ 1:   **Presents main point in the form of a question:** Why do young women shun feminism?

Reason: Media stereotypes of feminists.

Supporting examples: "Man-bashers," "radical extremists."

¶ 2:

Reason: Lack of young feminist role models.

Supporting fact: NOW local chapters and national office staffed largely by older women.

¶ 3:

Reason: The history of feminism.

Supporting fact: Women's movement is white and upper-middle-class.

Supporting testimony: Flo Kennedy, Audre Lorde, bell hooks note concerns of women of color have been overlooked.

Supporting testimony: *New York Times* poll notes young African American women's concerns with feminist issues but not feminist movement.

Create Topic Chains

Topic chains help readers establish links between the parts of a piece of writing and allow them to feel that they know where the writer is going. Writers create topic chains by repeating key words, using pronouns and synonyms, and restating main points. Notice the topic chain Sarah Boxer develops by regularly emphasizing the notion of shopping at the beginning of many paragraphs.

¶ 1–3: In certain academic circles, 'shop till you drop' is considered a civic act.

¶ 4: The intellectual fascination with stores . . .

¶ 5: Historically, the age of shopping and browsing begins . . .

¶ 7: The pastime of browsing . . .

¶ 9: Some feminists point out that as shoppers . . .

¶ 11: The idea that shopping is a form of civic action . . .

¶ 13: The field of shopping studies . . .

¶ 14: Shoppers' freedoms . . .

¶ 15: In superstores, the role of shoppers . . .

¶ 16: Does the concept of the shopper as citizen . . .

¶ 20: Ms. Conroy suggested that consumerism . . .

¶ 21: What does one man's shopping experience . . .

Use Transitions

Writers use transitional words, phrases, and sentences to show readers how one statement, paragraph, or section in a piece of writing relates to the next.

Temporal transitions indicate the sequence of events that takes place and the passage of time. In "Black Hair" (pages 142–149), Gary Soto begins a number of paragraphs with temporal transitions to help readers see the order in his narrative account of work:

¶ **5:** *The next morning*, I arrived early at work.

¶ **7:** I worked carefully *that day.* . . .

¶ **8:** *At five*, the workers scattered. . . .

¶ **9:** From the backyard I walked dully through a residential street, and *as evening came on.* . . .

¶ **11:** When I got up from the lawn *it was late*.

¶ **13:** At work I spent the *morning* at the buffer. . . .

¶ **15:** Iggy worked only *until three in the afternoon.* . . .

Spatial transitions help locate the position of things, people, and events. In her profile of Dr. Susan Love (pages 216–220), Molly O'Neill uses spatial transitions so that readers can visualize the scene she is describing.

> A radiologist used a pointer to outline the tumor for a group of radiologists, pathologists, and surgeons. Dr. Love stood *in the back* of the conference room, rocking in her bone-colored pumps. Her brown eyes were narrowed *behind* red-frame glasses.
>
> The lab coat she wore was a bulletin board of buttons. "Keep abreast," read one, "Get a second opinion." On another: "T.G.I.F. (Thank God I'm Female)." *Under* the string of fat white pearls *around* her neck was a gold chain with an ankh, an ancient symbol of life. *Above* one of the Chanel-style earrings was a tiny labyrs, the mythical double-bladed ax used by Amazons.

Logical transitions help readers understand how ideas are related to one another. Transitional words and phrases link ideas as the writers move from one paragraph to the next—building on what they have just said as the basis for the paragraph that follows.

Henry Jenkins, in "Lessons from Littleton," uses numbering of points and parallel phrases in the opening sentences of a sequence of paragraphs to help readers follow his explanation of the appeal of violent video games. Then he summarizes the consequences in a paragraph that begins with the phrase "In short":

First, violent entertainment offers teens a fantasy of empowerment. . . .

Second, violent entertainment offers teens a fantasy of transgression. . . .

Third, violent entertainment offers teens an acknowledgement that the world is not all sweetness and light. . . .

Fourth, violent entertainment offers teens an intensification of emotional experience. . . .

COMMON TYPES OF TRANSITIONS

To mark sequence and passage of time:	next, later, after, before, earlier, meanwhile, immediately, soon, shortly, often, frequently, again, during, finally, at last
To locate spatially:	near, next to, alongside, facing, adjacent, far beyond, away, off in the distance, between, through, up, down, across, above, below, inside, outside
To give examples:	for example, for instance, namely, specifically, that is
To add further points:	and, in addition, also, furthermore, moreover
To show consequences:	thus, therefore, so, consequently, hence, as a result, for this reason
To compare:	similarly, likewise, also
To contrast:	however, in contrast, but, yet, nevertheless, nonetheless
To compare and contrast:	not only/but also, on the one hand/on the other
To make a concession:	although, even though, granted that

> *In short*, teens aren't drawn to *Quake* or *Scream* because they are bloodthirsty

Leon Botstein, in "Let Teenagers Try Adulthood" (pages 329–331), signals an addition to his argument:

> An institution intended for children in transition now holds young adults back well beyond the developmental point for which high school was originally designed.
> *Furthermore*, whatever constraints to the presumption of adulthood among young people may have existed decades ago have now fallen away.

In "How to Fight the New Epidemics" (pages 292–294), Lundy Braun compares ("not only") and contrasts ("but also") ideas:

> This view is rooted in the rise of the germ theory in the late 19th and early 20th centuries that associated specific microbial agents with particular diseases.
> The germ theory took hold *not only because* of the spectacular technical achievements represented by the isolation of microorganisms, *but also because* infectious diseases, once seen as divine retribution for past sins, now appeared potentially conquerable.

DESIGNING PARAGRAPHS

Paragraphs are the building blocks writers use to assemble larger pieces of writing. That does not mean, of course, that paragraphs come ready-made in standard, prefabricated forms. They need to be designed to perform particular functions depending on the kind of writing and where the paragraph takes place in the larger piece of writing.

SEEING PARAGRAPHS: THE VISUAL DIMENSION

As mentioned earlier, the form of writing has both a visual and a psychological dimension, and this is true as well of paragraphs. Visually, paragraphs are graphic units that mark units of attention for readers by indenting. Paragraph breaks help readers see where a related sequence of ideas begins and ends. In turn, paragraphs provide writers with a means to establish the reader's focus of attention for a period of time.

Experienced writers have learned that the beginning and ending of paragraphs are the points at which readers are most attentive. When a paragraph begins, readers look for cues to tell them what the paragraph is going to be about so that they can concentrate on that particular point and how the writer develops it. When the paragraph ends, readers often pause briefly, to catch their breath and consolidate their sense of what they have just read, before going on to the next paragraph.

In newspaper writing, in part because of the narrow columns in the page layout, paragraphs tend to be short. One of their functions is to make the experience of reading as easy as possible so that readers can get the gist of an article by scanning it quickly. The same thing applies to many kinds of writing in the workplace and the public sphere, where writers and readers alike put a premium on making the information in memos, reports, proposals, news briefings, and brochures concise and easy to process.

In other genres of writing, however, paragraphs have a very different look on the page. Essays, academic writing, and magazine articles often use longer paragraphs, and readers expect that writers will develop their points in greater depth and detail.

The length of a paragraph, in other words, depends on the kind of writing in which it appears and the function it serves.

■ EXERCISE

Analyzing Paragraphs

Following is a passage from Susan Faludi's essay "Shannon Faulkner's Strength in Numbers" without paragraph indentation. You will probably notice right away how dense and forbidding the passage seems. It looks like a lot of extra work to get through it. Your task here is to provide paragraphing to make the passage easier for readers. Follow these steps:

1. On your own, read through the passage and insert paragraph breaks where you think they are most useful.

2. Now work with two or three classmates and compare how each of you has divided the passage into paragraphs. To what extent are the paragraphs alike? To what extent do they differ? In the case of differences, does the effect on

readers differ? If so, how? Working together, see if you can come up with one version that everyone in the group can live with. If you can't agree, explain what your differences are and what seems to be at stake.

Out of all the nearly 2,000 cadets who enrolled in an all-male military academy called The Citadel this year [1995], the only one whose name we know was the one the school didn't want: Shannon Faulkner. This distinction seems, on its face, too obvious to mention. Of course she's famous—that she was admitted to the academy at all was a cause célèbre. But the distinction is important, because it goes to the heart of the issue. One reason the other Citadel cadets loathed Shannon Faulkner (aside from her sex) was her individuality, which affronted The Citadel's ethic. The academy purports to educate young men by making them conform. Conformity is enforced through anonymity. From the day the cadets arrive, when they are issued identical uniforms and haircuts, they become so homogeneous that, as an upperclassman explained to me, "mothers can't even tell their sons apart." Through communal living and endless drills and rigid codes of conduct, the cadet's individuality is subordinated to the identity of the group, his strength founded in numbers and teamwork, in esprit de corps and long tradition. Going it alone, as a maverick, isn't done. "Individuals do not make it here," the commandant of cadets warned this year's freshmen on their first day. "If you want to stay an individual, every day will be a tough day." This is what is called a military education, and it was exactly what Shannon Faulkner wanted and could not find elsewhere in her home state of South Carolina. From the start her quest seemed hopeless: by seeking military anonymity in an all-male corps, she had to stand out. But her downfall was hastened by forces beyond The Citadel. The largest obstacle she faced was the popular illusion that history is driven not by the actions and changing beliefs of large numbers of ordinary people, but by a few heroic giants who materialize out of nowhere to transform the landscape.

UNITY AND COHERENCE: THE PSYCHOLOGICAL DIMENSION

Unity and coherence are workshop terms referring to the psychological dimension of writing and to how writing arouses the reader's expectations and then goes on to fulfill them. *Unity* means that a piece of writing has some central point, focus, or center of gravity that readers can readily identify. They don't wonder what the writer is getting at or try to figure out the main point on their own. *Coherence* means that the ideas in the writing seem to come in the right order, leading logically from one point to the next. Readers don't feel that the writing rambles or jumps around from point to point but instead moves along purposefully.

Often, readers are not even aware that well-crafted writing is unified and coherent. They simply experience the writing as easy to read. The writer's ideas seem to be where they belong, and readers can easily follow the writer's thoughts from point to point. The writing just seems to flow, and readers don't feel confused about its direction. Moreover, when this happens, readers believe they are in good hands—and, as a result, are likely to invest a certain amount of confidence and credibility in what the writer is saying. Whether they agree with the ideas or not, they at least think that the writer knows what he or she is doing and is therefore worth considering. In short, unity and coherence are devices for making a meeting of minds possible.

You can see how unity and coherence work at the level of a whole piece of writing by looking back at the writing samples in this chapter. Take, for example, Sarah Boxer's "I Shop, Ergo I Am." Here the unity comes from the opening paragraphs, where Boxer explains how the connection between shopping and civic action has been taken up as a topic by cultural studies scholars. Readers at this point will justifiably expect the essay to tell them more about such shopping studies. And that is exactly what Boxer does. She develops the idea in a coherent order, starting with studies of eighteenth-century shopping and then moving to contemporary instances. In other words, she enables readers to see how the article's parts are relevant to the main idea.

To see how paragraphs use unity and coherence to enhance readability, look at the following paragraph:

> Public toilets . . . have become the real frontline of the city's war on the homeless. Los Angeles, as a matter of deliberate policy, has fewer public toilets than any other major North American city. On the advice of the Los Angeles police, who now sit on the "design board of at least one major Downtown project, the redevelopment agency bulldozed the few remaining public toilets on Skid Row." Agency planners then considered whether to include a "free-standing public toilet" in their design for the upscale South Park residential development; agency chairman Jim Wood later admitted that the decision not to build the toilet was a "policy decision and not a design decision." The agency preferred the alternative of "quasi-public restrooms"— toilets in restaurants, art galleries, and office buildings—which can be made available selectively to tourists and white-collar workers while being denied to vagrants and other unsuitables. The same logic has inspired the city's transportation planners to exclude toilets from their designs for Los Angeles's new subway system.
>
> *Mike Davis, from* City of Quartz

Topic Sentences and Unity

Notice how Davis begins with a topic sentence ("Public toilets . . . have become the real frontline on the city's war on the homeless"). Topic sentences typically focus on a single idea or on a sequence of related ideas that will be developed in the paragraph. At this point, readers can reasonably expect Davis to devote the rest of the paragraph to explaining how public toilets figure into Los Angeles's "war on the homeless."

Discussion and Unity and Coherence

As you can see, the rest of the paragraph, or the discussion, is indeed devoted to explaining how planners eliminated the availability of public toilets; it thereby contributes to the unity of the paragraph and to fulfilling readers' expectations. Notice, furthermore, how the order of sentences seems coherent. Each sentence not only follows from the topic sentence but also picks up on the sentence that precedes it. The way one sentence leads to the next can be analyzed by imagining that each sentence answers a question in the reader's mind raised by the preceding sentence or sentences:

Topic Sentence

> Public toilets . . . have become the real frontline in the city's war on the homeless.
> *(Question: What is this "war"?)*

Discussion

> Los Angeles, as a matter of deliberate policy, has fewer public toilets than any other major North American city.
> *(Answers question and raises another about how "policy" was made)*

> On the advice of the Los Angeles police, who now sit on the design board of at least one major Downtown project, the redevelopment agency bulldozed the few remaining public toilets on Skid Row.
> *(Answers question about how "policy" was made)*

> Agency planners then considered whether to include a "free-standing public toilet" in their design for the upscale South Park residential development; agency chairman Jim Wood later admitted that the decision not to build the toilet was a "policy decision and not a design decision."
> *(Amplifies answer about how "policy" was made by giving another example)*

> The agency preferred the alternative of "quasi-public restrooms"—toilets in restaurants, art galleries, and office buildings—which can be made available selectively to tourists and white-collar workers while being denied to vagrants and other unsuitables.
> *(Answers question about how "policy" amounts to "war on the homeless")*

> The same logic has inspired the city's transportation planners to exclude toilets from their designs for Los Angeles's new subway system.
> *(Gives a final example of how "policy" makes "war on the homeless")*

■ EXERCISE

Analyzing Paragraph Units and Coherence

Work together in a group of four or five. Read the following passage aloud. Then answer the questions.

> I have always wanted to be a high school American history teacher. Many teachers are now feeling the pressure to teach the test rather than educate their students in historical understanding. There are certainly skills and knowledge that high school students should acquire in their American history

classes. Historical understanding gives students a way to see how the past shapes the present. In American history courses, students have too often memorized facts and dates rather than learning to understand why historical events took place and how they affect the present. I realize that many students are not interested in the past, but my desire is to help students think about American history and the unresolved questions it raises about the legacy of slavery, the American belief in individualism and free enterprise, and the Vietnam War. The current trend to make high schools more accountable emphasizes testing at the expense of genuine learning. Historical understanding is crucial if we want to have an informed citizenry who can make decisions about the complex issues that face us as a nation.

1. What question does the first sentence raise?
2. How is this question answered?
3. Are there other questions that the paragraph seems to raise?
4. How are these questions answered?
5. How would you revise this paragraph for unity and coherence?

A NOTE ON THE PLACEMENT OF TOPIC SENTENCES

Topic sentences typically appear at the beginning (or near the beginning) of a paragraph to focus the readers' attention and enable them to forecast what is to come. In some instances, however, writers will vary the position of topic sentences, delaying it until late in the paragraph. Let's take two examples from "Letters" in Chapter 4 to see how these different (italicized) placements of topic sentences work. In the first instance, notice how Mark Patinkin puts the topic sentence first in this paragraph from "Commit a Crime, Suffer the Consequences" (page 108):

> *All this is just part of the new American game of always saying, "It's not my fault."* No one, when caught, seems ready to admit having done wrong anymore. They just whine and appeal. As in: "Your honor, the stabbing was not my client's fault. He had a bad childhood. And was caught up in a riot at the time. In fact, he's not a criminal at all, he's one of society's victims."

On the other hand, writers may choose to position the topic sentence at the end of the paragraph—to use the paragraph to lead up to it, as James Baldwin does in the second paragraph of "My Dungeon Shook: Letter to My Nephew" (page 113):

> I have known both of you all your lives, have carried your Daddy in my arms and on my shoulders, kissed and spanked him and watched him learn to walk. I don't know if you've known anybody from that far back; if you've loved anybody that long, first as an infant, then as a child, then as a man, you gain a strange perspective on time and human pain and effort. Other people cannot see what I see whenever I look into your father's face, for behind your father's face as it is today are all those other faces which were his. Let him laugh and I see a cellar your father does not remember and a

house he does not remember and I hear in his present laughter his laughter as a child. Let him curse and I remember him falling down the cellar steps, and howling, and I remember, with pain, his tears, which my hand or your grandmother's so easily wiped away. But no one's hand can wipe away those tears he sheds invisibly today, which one hears in his laughter and in his speech and in his songs. I know what the world has done to my brother and how narrowly he has survived it. And I know, which is much worse, and this is the crime of which I accuse my country and my countrymen, and for which neither I nor time nor history will ever forgive them, that they have destroyed and are destroying hundreds of thousands of lives and do not know it and do not want to know it. One can be, indeed one must strive to become, tough and philosophical concerning destruction and death, for this is what most of mankind has been best at since we have heard of man. (But remember: most of mankind is not all of mankind.) But it is not permissible that the authors of devastation should also be innocent. *It is the innocence which constitutes the crime.*

HOW PARAGRAPHS MAKE PATTERNS OF ORGANIZATION EASY TO RECOGNIZE

Readers recognize paragraphs first by their visual features, as indentation marks the transition from one paragraph to another. Readers' expectation, of course, is that the paragraph they are embarking on will relate both to the one before and to the overall meaning in the piece of writing. As you have seen, topic sentences are key to making this transition easy for readers to follow. But you also need to keep readers with you throughout the paragraph.

Readers will be looking, largely unconsciously, for a pattern of development in the paragraph—some ordering system that weaves the sentences into a pattern of meaning. When a clearly recognizable pattern is present, readers will be able to concentrate on the content of the paragraph—to think about what you are saying. What follow are some common techniques for making the pattern of development in a paragraph easy for readers to recognize.

NARRATION

Narration tells a story, relates an anecdote, or re-creates an event or a sequence of events. Memoirs often use narration as their pattern of organization. In other cases, writers will weave narration into their writing. Consider, for example, how the two following excerpts use narration to develop key points:

My flesh-and-blood family long ago grew accustomed to the way I sit in my office early in the morning and late at night, chuckling and cursing, sometimes crying, about words I read on the computer screen. It might have looked to my daughter as if I were alone at my desk the night she caught me chortling online, but from my point of view I was in living contact with old and new friends, strangers and colleagues.

(Howard Rheingold, from The Virtual Community*)*

During the first phase of the FBI's engagement at Waco, a period of a few days, the agents on the ground at the compound proceeded with a strategy of conciliatory negotiation, which had the approval and understanding of the entire chain of command. In the view of the negotiating team, considerable progress was made—for example, some adults and children came out of the compound—but David Koresh and the Branch Davidians made many promises to the negotiators that they then did not keep. Pushed by the tactical leader, the FBI's commander on the ground began to allow tactical pressures to be placed on the compound in addition to negotiation, e.g., turning off the electricity, so that those in the compound would be as cold as the agents outside during the twenty-degree night. This tactical pressure was applied over the objections of the FBI's own experts in negotiation and behavioral science, who specifically advised against it. These experts warned the FBI command about the potentially fatal consequences of using such measures.

(Alan Stone, from "Report and Recommendations Concerning the Handling of Incidents Such as the Branch Davidian Standoff in Waco, Texas")

DESCRIPTION

Description enables readers to see what you are writing about. Writers use description to create word-pictures of a scene or a person. Notice how the following passage locates readers in an America Online chatroom:

"Yo yo yo, what's up what's up?" The lines scroll up my screen. Different fonts, different colors, the words whiz by, everyone's screen name sounding vaguely pornographic. I'm on America Online, in a chat room for young adults. There are hundreds of such chat rooms on AOL, and it has taken a lot of Net navigating simply to find one that has room enough to let me in.

(Camille Sweeney, "In a Chat Room, You Can Be NE1: Constructing a Teenage Self On Line")

But description can also be used to explain a concept or a state of mind, as Mike Rose does in the following paragraph, where he analyzes the defenses vocational education students erect:

The tragedy is that you have to twist the knife in your own gray matter to make this defense work. You'll have to shut down, have to reject intellectual stimuli or defuse them with sarcasm, have to cultivate stupidity, have to convert boredom from a malady into a way of confronting the world. Keep your vocabulary simple, act stoned when you're not or act more stoned than you are, flaunt ignorance, materialize your dreams. It is a powerful and effective defense—it neutralizes the insult and the frustration of being a vocational kid and, when perfected, it drives teachers up the wall, a delightful secondary effect. But like all strong magic, it exacts a price.

(Mike Rose, from Lives on the Boundary*)*

DEFINITION

Definitions provide the meaning of a term or a concept. In some instances, a simple and clear definition of terms is needed to explain basic concepts in a public document, as is the case here:

II. DEFINITION OF ACADEMIC TRUST

Academic trust is the assurance that teacher and student will faithfully abide by the rules of intellectual engagement established between them. This trust can exist only when students adhere to the standards of academic honesty and when faculty test and evaluate students in a manner that presumes that students are acting with academic integrity.
                    (Ad Hoc Committee on Academic Honesty, Proposal for an Academic Honor Code)

In other instances, however, writers use extended definitions to develop their thinking about a subject, as Michael Rock does in the final paragraph of his analysis of *USA Today* design style, where he defines what he calls the "LITE phenomenon":

Or maybe the best explanation for the spread of *USA Today* look-alikes is that it is an inevitable extension of the LITE phenomenon. If beer or mayonnaise or individually wrapped slices of American cheese make you fat, then: a) stop eating and drinking so much; or b) remanufacture the product with fewer calories. We are more comfortable with the idea of changing our products than with changing our habits. Maybe publication design is under the same pressure. Maybe we want the "experience" of reading without all that heavy, annoying thinking. Maybe it's LITE design; it tastes great and is less filling.
                    (Michael Rock, "Since When Did USA Today *Become the National Design Ideal?")*

CLASSIFICATION

Classification is a way of sorting things and people into groups by creating categories. *The Call to Write*, for example, divides the various forms of writing into genres, enabling us then to classify the pieces of writing we encounter into one or another of these categories. By the same token, a review of *Ally McBeal* classifies the show by first explaining what categories it doesn't fit into:

At its uneven best, *Ally McBeal* is neither yuppie sitcom nor courtroom drama

and then the writer tells us which ones the show is like,

but an absurdist morality play that gives off sparks of screwball comedy.
                    (Karen Durbin, "Razor Thin, But Larger Than Life")

In other instances, classification can provide an overall pattern of organization for a document or piece of writing.

COMPARISON AND CONTRAST

Comparison and contrast refer to the way in which writers note similarities and differences. Either can appear by itself, but writers frequently use the two strategies together to show how things, people, and ideas are like or unlike others of their type. You can find discussions of how writers use comparison and contrast in Chapter 7, "Profiles," and Chapter 11, "Reviews."

■ EXERCISE

Analyzing Paragraph Development and Context

Locate one or more examples of narration, description, definition, classification, or comparison and contrast in the piece of writing where it appears. As you put the example back into its original context, note how you became aware of what the writer was doing at that point. What cues alert you to the fact that you're reading a narration, description, definition, classification, or comparison and contrast? What function does the particular strategy perform?

chapter 18

working together: collaborative writing projects

COLLABORATIVE WRITING

Working on collaborative writing projects differs in important respects from working with others on individual writing projects. In the case of individual writing projects, the final result belongs to you; you are accountable for it and you get the bulk of the credit, even though the writing reflects the input of others. Collaborative writing, on the other hand, aims for a collective outcome produced jointly by a team of people with shared responsibility for the results.

Consider, for example, how a group of three students worked together on a research project in an environmental studies course. Their task is to create a map of the sidewalk shade trees the city has planted and maintained in the downtown area over the years and to make recommendations about where new trees should be planted. After they have surveyed the downtown area, sketched a preliminary map, and made tentative decisions about where new trees should go, they give each member a section of the report to draft. One writes the background. One reports their findings. The third student writes the recommendation section. Once the drafts are finished, the group meets to consider what revisions are needed to produce a final report. One student makes these changes while the other two members create the maps.

When individuals work together on collaborative writing projects, they will manage the writing task in various ways, depending on the nature of the task and the decisions the group makes. Sometimes, as in the example above, individuals will each write separate sections, which are then compiled into a single document and edited for uniformity of style. Or, they may work together so closely in planning, drafting, and revising a document that it becomes impossible to distinguish one person's work from another's. In still other cases, the group will work together planning and doing research, one individual will do the drafting, and then the group will work together again to plan revisions.

Online Study Center

There is no single best way to work on collaborative writing projects. Experienced writers learn when it makes sense to produce a collaboratively written document and which writing strategy the situation seems to call for.

While collaborative writing projects can differ, each of them reveals one of the most important benefits of working together—namely that the final written product is based on the collective judgment of a group of people. When a group works well together, the resulting energy and involvement can lead to writing that goes beyond what anyone in the group could have produced alone.

Successful collaborative writing depends on organization, meetings, and constant communication. This chapter looks at how groups can produce effective collaborative writing. The first section offers some general guidelines about working in groups. The second section considers how groups can manage a collaborative writing project from start to finish. The final section presents further writing suggestions for groups.

■ WORKING TOGETHER

Exploring Experience

Form a group with three or four other students. Have each student describe an experience in which he or she worked together with other people. The experience can be positive or negative, and it need not involve writing. After everyone has described an experience, try to reach a consensus, even if you agree to disagree, about what makes group work successful or unsuccessful.

GUIDELINES FOR COLLABORATING IN GROUPS

Any group of people working together on a project will face certain issues, and a group collaborating on a writing project is no exception. The following guidelines are meant to keep a group running smoothly and to forestall some common problems.

Recognize That Group Members Need to Get Acquainted and That Groups Take Time to Form

People entering new groups sometimes make snap judgments without getting to know the other people or giving the group time to form and develop. Initial impressions are rarely reliable indicators of how a group will be. Like individuals, groups have life histories, and one of the most awkward and difficult moments is getting started. Group members may be nervous, defensive, or overly assertive. It takes some time for people to get to know one another and to develop a sense of connectedness to the group.

Clarify Group Purposes and Individual Roles

Much of the initial discomfort and anxiety has to do with uncertainty about what the purpose of the group is and what people's roles in the group will be. Group members need to define their collective task and develop a plan to carry it out. That way, members will understand what to expect and how the group will operate.

Recognize That Members Bring Different Styles to the Group

As you have seen, individual styles of composing can vary considerably. The same is true of individuals' styles of working in groups. For example, individuals differ in the way they approach problems. Some like to spend a lot of time formulating problems, exploring the complexities, contradictions, and nuances of a situation. Others want to define problems quickly and then spend their time figuring out how to solve them. By the same token, people have different styles of interacting in groups. Some like to develop their ideas by talking, while others prefer to decide what they think before speaking. Successful groups learn to incorporate the strengths of all these styles, making sure that even the most reticent members participate.

Recognize That You May Not Play the Same Role in Every Group

In some instances you may be the group leader, but in other instances you'll need to play the role of mediator, helping members negotiate their differences; or critic, questioning the others' ideas; or timekeeper, prompting the group to stick to deadlines. You may play different roles in the same group from meeting to meeting or even within a meeting. For a group to be successful, members must be willing and able to respond flexibly to the work at hand.

Monitor Group Progress and Reassess Goals and Procedures

It's helpful to step back periodically to take stock of what has been accomplished and what remains to be done. Groups also need to look at their own internal workings to see if the procedures they have set up are effective and if everyone is participating.

Quickly Address Problems in Group Dynamics

Problems will arise in group work. Some members may dominate and talk too much. Others may withdraw and not contribute. Still others may fail to carry out assigned tasks. If a group avoids confronting these problems, the problems will only get worse. Remember, the point of raising a problem is not to blame individuals but to promote an understanding about what's expected of each person and what the group can do to encourage everyone's participation.

Encourage Differences of Opinion

One of the things that makes groups productive is the different perspectives individual members bring to group work. In fact, groups of like-minded people who share basic assumptions are often not as creative as groups where there are differences among members. At the same time, group members may think that they can't bring up ideas or feelings because to do so would threaten group harmony. Sometimes it's difficult to take a position that diverges from what other members of the group think and believe. But groups are not forms of social organization to enforce conformity; they are working bodies that need to consider all the available options and points of view. For this reason, groups need to encourage the discussion of differences and to look at conflicting viewpoints.

HOW TO WORK TOGETHER ON COLLABORATIVE WRITING PROJECTS

Because collaborative writing differs from individual writing, it is worth looking at each step involved in working on a joint project.

ORGANIZING THE GROUP

One of the keys to collaborative writing is to get off to a good start. You'll need to decide on the size of the group, its composition, what to do at your first meeting, and how to share the labor.

Group Size

For many collaborative writing projects in college classes, a group of three or four is often the best size. A smaller size—only two students—doesn't offer the group as many resources, and anything larger than four can create problems in managing the work with so many involved.

Of course, there can be exceptions. For example, your teacher may decide to do a collaborative project involving the entire class—developing a Web home page for the class or a Web site devoted to a particular topic with everyone's participation.

Group Composition

Some teachers like to put groups together themselves. Others like to give students input into the group they will be in. If the teacher puts the groups together, it's a good idea to ask each student if there is someone in class he or she particularly wants to work with or particularly wants to avoid working with. It can help, too, to take schedules into account and match students who have free time in common when they can meet.

The First Meeting

The first meeting should focus on the basics:

1. Exchange phone numbers, email addresses, campus box numbers, and the best times to reach group members.

2. If possible, establish a listserv of group members on the campus network.

3. Identify the best times for meetings.

4. Agree on some basic procedures for running meetings. For example, do you want a group coordinator to lead meetings? If so, will one person serve throughout the project, or will you rotate that position? How do you plan to keep records of meetings? Will you have a recorder for the project, or rotate? How long will each meeting last? Who is responsible for developing the agenda?

Division of Labor, or Integrated Team?

Some groups approach collaborative projects by developing a division of labor that assigns particular tasks to group members who complete them individually and then bring the results back to the group. This has been the traditional model for collaborative work in business, industry, and government. It is an efficient method of work, especially when groups are composed of highly skilled members. Its limitations are that weak group members can affect the quality of the overall work and that some group members may lose sight of the overall project because they are so caught up in their own specialized work.

More recently, groups have begun to explore an integrated approach in which the members all work together through each stage of the project. An integrated-team approach involves members more fully in the work and helps them maintain an overall view of the project's goals and progress. But it also takes more time—that must be devoted to meetings and, often, to developing good working relationships among members.

These two models of group work are not mutually exclusive. In fact many groups function along integrated-team lines when they are planning and reviewing work, but also farm out particular tasks to individuals or subgroups. So you need to discuss and develop some basic guidelines on group functioning.

ORGANIZING THE PROJECT

The Proposal

The first task is to decide what the project is and what its goals are. One of the best ways to do this is to write a proposal. Your teacher is the logical audience for your proposal. If you are doing a project with an on- or off-campus group, members of that group should also receive your proposal.

Proposals should include:

- **A statement of purpose:** Define the topic or issue you are working on. Explain why it is important or significant. What have others said about it? State what you plan to do and explain why.

- **A description of methods:** Explain how you plan to go about the project. What research will you need to do? How will you do it?

- **A plan for managing the work:** Explain what roles group members will play and what skills they will bring to the task.

■ **A task breakdown chart:** A task breakdown (or Gantt) chart shows the tasks involved and their scheduling. Such a chart is especially useful for planning collaborative projects because it shows how tasks relate to each other.

Once the group is up and running, it will need to figure out how to stay on track—how to keep the work moving ahead and how to deal effectively with problems as they arise.

Task Breakdown Chart

Task	Week ending	Sept. 12 19 26	Oct. 3 10 17 24 31	Nov. 7 14 21 28	Dec. 5 12 19
1.	Gather preliminary info., contact agency	▮			
2.	Proposal draft–revise final–review, edit	▭			
3.	Progress report	▬▬▬			
4.	Research on food programs	▬▬▬▬			
5.	Interviews with people served by agency	▬▬▬▬▬			
6.	Brochure design get photos graphics	▬▬▬▬▬			
7.	Progress report	▬▬▬▬▬▬▬			
8.	Write text	▬▬▬▬▬▬▬			
9.	Print brochure take to agency feedback revision	▬▬▬▬▬▬▬▬			
10.	Final version	▬▬▬▬▬▬▬▬▬▬			

Incorporating a calendar into your task breakdown chart is one way to stay oriented. Two other ways are to run productive meetings and to write interim progress reports.

Productive Meetings

Group meetings are productive when they get work done, address issues and conflicts, and keep group members accountable. Although failing to meet can cause group members to feel disconnected, meeting for no reason can be just as demoralizing. For meetings to be productive, there must be a real agenda and work that needs to be done. One way to set an agenda is to agree at the end of each meeting what will be accomplished before the next meeting, and by whom. That way the agenda grows out of the progress of the project and group members are kept accountable. If problems in group functioning come up, they need to be addressed immediately at the next meeting.

Progress Reports

Progress reports are another way to enhance group members' accountability—both to one another and to their teacher. They serve to chart the development of a project at regular intervals. On your task breakdown chart you will want to include one or two progress reports that follow the completion of major parts of the project. Include in your reports the following:

- **Tasks completed:** Describe with details what you have done.

- **Tasks in progress:** Be specific about what you are doing and give completion dates.

- **Tasks scheduled:** Describe briefly tasks you haven't yet started, including any not originally entered on the task breakdown chart.

- **Issues, problems, obstacles:** Explain how these emerged and how your group is dealing with them.

In some cases, teachers may ask groups for oral as well as written progress reports. This is a good way for everyone in class to see what the other groups are doing.

Confidential Self-Evaluation

In addition to requiring group progress reports, some teachers also like to ask individual students to assess how their group has been functioning and what their role in it has been. These self-evaluations are confidential and directed only to the teacher. They can be useful in helping the teacher anticipate when groups are having difficulties or personality problems. They are also useful to individual students because they offer an occasion to reflect on the experience of group work and what it means to them as writers, learners, and persons.

Drafting, Revising, and Editing

One thing that often surprises students working in groups for the first time is finding out that they have already started to draft their document from the moment they began to put their proposal together.

For many writing tasks, the final document will draw and expand on what is in the proposal—explaining why the issue or problem is important, what others have said about it, what the group has learned about it, and what recommendations the group has to make.

But whatever the writing task happens to be, groups need to make decisions about how to handle drafting, revising, and editing collaboratively written documents. Here are some possible approaches. Your group will need to decide which one best suits your purposes.

- Members draft individual sections. The group compiles the sections and revises together.

- One person writes a draft. The group revises together.

- Members draft individual sections. One person compiles the sections and revises the document.

With any of these approaches, a final editing needs to be done by an individual or by the group.

However you decide to organize drafting, revising, and editing, make sure everyone contributes to the final document. The draft does not become final until everyone has signed off on it.

Collaborative drafting and revising can raise sensitive issues about individual writing styles and abilities. Some people can be protective of their writing and defensive when it is criticized or revised. Be aware of this. If you think other group members either are trying to impose their own style or are feeling discouraged, bring these matters to everyone's attention and try to sort them out before you continue on the writing task.

GIVING CREDIT

Some teachers ask collaborative writing groups to preface their final document with an acknowledgments page that explains who should get credit for what in the overall project. You should also acknowledge anyone outside your group who helped you on the project.

FINAL PRESENTATION

The final presentation of a collaborative project takes place when the document reaches its intended destination—whether it's the teacher, the Web, a politician or government official, or a community organization. You may want to schedule an oral presentation to go along with the delivery of the document.

ONLINE COLLABORATION

The new electronic communication technologies have created new ways for groups to work together, even when their members are far apart. It's no longer necessary to meet face to face to have the kind of exchange that gives a joint project energy and creativity. With the nearly instantaneous transmission of documents, commentary, and conversation, collaborators can now stay in touch, confer, argue, and refine their ideas with an immediacy that was unimaginable in the past.

Of course, group members don't need to be halfway around the world from each other to take advantage of the new technologies. Here are some good ways of how to use these technologies in collaborative writing projects:

- **Stay in touch with group members:** Ongoing communication among group members is one of the keys to successful group work. Setting up a listserv on email can help members to stay in touch in and out of class.

- **Consult with people everywhere:** Through email, newsgroups, and Web sites, your group can contact a wide range of people who are knowledgeable about your topic—to ask questions, get information, and try out ideas. Online communication can be much quicker and simpler than letters or phone calls.

- **Share working drafts:** To put together a successful collaboratively written document, coauthors need easy access to one another's working drafts. Drafts can be shared in ways that range from downloading files on email to state-of-the-art hypertext authoring systems.

- **Confer on drafts:** Online conferences make it easy for all group members to have input on drafts. New methods include "real-time" synchronous conferences facilitated by networking software.

REFLECTING ON YOUR WRITING

Consider a collaborative writing task you have completed. Explain why the particular situation seemed to call for a collaboratively written document instead of an individually written one. How did your group go about organizing and managing the writing task? What role or roles did you play in the group? What problems or issues did you confront and how did you handle them? What was the result of the group's work? From your own perspective, what do you see as the main differences between collaborative and individual writing? What do you see as the benefits and limits of each?

presenting your

work

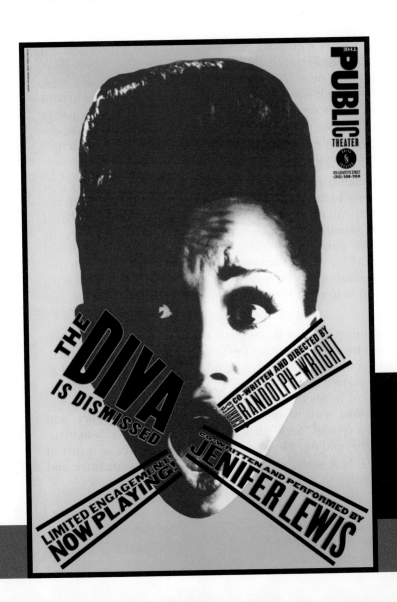

5

INTRODUCTION: DELIVERING THE MESSAGE

Whether you are designing the manuscript of a critical essay or research paper, a fund-raising letter, a brochure, a Web site, or a PowerPoint™ presentation, the material form of the printed page or computer screen not only provides the means to transmit your ideas to yours readers. The visual appearance of your work also carries its own meanings and has its own rhetorical effects.

There are three main reasons to learn more about how the delivery of messages embodies writers' and designers' purposes:

- **To establish credibility with readers:** The reader's first impression of a page or screen is likely to be influenced by its visual appearance. A sloppy manuscript or a Web site that's hard to navigate will raise doubts about the credibility of the person who prepared it. This in turn can undermine the rhetorical effectiveness of the message, no matter how interesting or insightful the content might be. In other words, design is a means to establish the writer's ethos—of presenting the writer and the message as credible and authoritative.

- **To enhance readability:** One of the marks of effective writing is that readers find it easy to follow. When they don't have to struggle with the written text, they can concentrate on what the writer is saying. There are a number of visual cues writers use to make their line of reasoning visible to readers: paragraph breaks, white space, headings, bulleted lists, and so on. The visual display of information in tables, charts, maps, diagrams, and photographs provides writers and designers with further means to help readers visualize key events, relationships, and processes.

- **To assist in planning:** Writing is not just a matter of getting ideas down on paper. It also involves designing the visual appearance of the document that delivers yours message. A number of genres in *The Call to Write*—letters, certain public documents, reports, research proposals—use standard forms that make them immediately recognizable. These genres, along with memos, résumés, newsletters, flyers, and brochures, have a typical "look" that not only enables readers to identify what they are reading. The visual appearances of these forms of writing also provide a scaffolding that can help writers organize and present their messages.

In the following chapters, you will find more information on how to design effective documents of various sorts. Chapter 19, "Visual Design," explores some of the purposes of visual communication and offers suggestions about designing such familiar documents as flyers, newsletters, and brochures.

Chapter 20, "Web Design," offers a basic introduction to the rhetoric and design features of Web sites, while Chapter 21, "Oral Presentations," looks at how you can plan effective talks and use visuals such as PowerPoint. Chapter 22, "Essay Exams," offers suggestions about how to present your ideas when writing under pressure. Chapter 23, "Writing Portfolios," shows how you can design a portfolio of writing that presents and comments on the work you have done in your writing course.

visual design

Why does visual design belong in a writing class? There are two main reasons. First, visual communication is playing an increasingly important role in everyday life, in the workplace, in the public sphere, and in academic settings. Accordingly, the ability to read and evaluate visual messages—whether they come through the mass media, printed texts, or computer screens—has become a central part of what it means to be literate.

Second, visual design belongs in a writing class because writing itself is a visual form of communication, and learning to write in part means learning how to produce well-designed print and digital texts—everything from academic papers, reports, and résumés to flyers, brochures, newsletters, posters, and Web sites. Throughout *The Call to Write*, we've talked about what makes written texts persuasive and easy to follow. At this point, we need to examine the visual dimension of writing and how the design of the page can contribute to readability and persuasion.

We start by considering how visual communication is used for purposes of identification, information, and persuasion. Next, we will see how you can create effective page designs and use type to enhance your message. Finally, we will look at such common visual design projects as flyers, newsletters, and brochures. For information on designing effective Web sites, see Chapter 20, "Web Design." Chapter 21, "Oral Presentations," includes advice about integrating visuals such as transparencies or PowerPoint into oral presentations.

The goal of this chapter is to enable you to understand some of the basic principles of visual design so you can produce documents that fit the situation, that help readers navigate the page, and that influence your readers in the ways you intend.

HOW VISUAL DESIGN EMBODIES PURPOSES

In Chapter 17, "The Shape of the Essay," we looked at how written forms embody writers' purposes. In this section, we will do something similar by considering how visual forms embody designers' purposes in three ways:

Online Study Center

- Identification
- Information
- Persuasion

IDENTIFICATION

One of the primary functions of visual design is to identify things, places, publications, and organizations. Street and building signs, posters, flags, logos, trademarks, letterheads, package labels, and mastheads on newspapers and magazines are just some of the typical visual forms used for purposes of identification.

One well-known example of designing for purposes of identification is Saul Bass's publicity poster for the 1955 film *The Man with the Golden Arm*, starring Frank Sinatra as a jazz musician and addict. Departing from the design of earlier movie posters, which pictured the stars of the film and banner headlines with the title, Bass uses simple but bold blocks of color and an iconic image to create a memorable visual design.

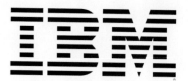

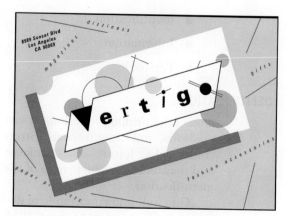

Logos and trademarks identify a broad range of organizations—corporations such as IBM, hip stores such as Vertigo, and political movements such as Solidarity in Poland. Notice how each of the logos included here projects a strong sense of the organization's identity. For example, the noted graphic designer Paul Rand uses bold, square capital letters to give the IBM logo a powerful and conservative look, while April Greiman mixes typefaces to project a playful "new wave" look for the clothing and gift store Vertigo. The logo for Solidarity, the Polish trade union that helped end one-party communist rule in 1989, uses letters as visual forms to suggest both a sense of massed strength and of collective movement.

■ **EXERCISE**

Analyzing Logos and Package Designs

1. Consider the National Aeronautics and Space Administration (NASA) letterheads from 1959, 1974, and 1992. Notice in particular how the redesign of 1974 drops the figurative trademark (known at NASA as the "meatball") in favor of an abstract design that makes the letter "A" into rocket-shaped cones ready for blast-off. What identities do the three letterheads convey? Why do you think NASA officials decided in 1992 to redesign the 1974 letterhead and return to a version of the figurative trademark of 1959?

2. Bring in three or four similar items you can buy in a grocery store. They could be jars of spaghetti sauce, bottles of spring water, packages of laundry detergent, or whatever. How does the design of the packaging—the brand name, logo, color of the label, fonts, shape of the product, or anything else that's notable—seek to create an identity for its product that distinguishes it from other products of its type?

3. Imagine you have been commissioned to create a logo for a particular company, product, organization, or institution. What image and identity will you want to project? What graphics, typeface, or combination could you use to create this identity? Sketch one or more logos. Explain your design decisions.

Top: 1959; Middle: 1974; Bottom: 1992

INFORMATION

The purpose of information design is not simply to add visual interest to documents that are primarily verbal but to help readers visualize important processes, trends, and relationships. Notice how the visual display of information enhances the appearance of the page and makes the information easier to process.

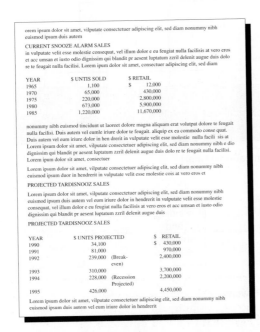

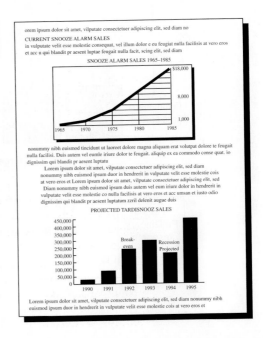

The visual display of information can be divided into three categories: textual, representational, and numerical.

Textual Graphics

Textual graphics organize and display information to emphasize key points and supplement the main text.

- **Sidebars and information boxes** add additional information to the main text and visual interest to the page layout. (See Mike Crouch's "Lost in a Smog" in Chapter 8 for examples.)
- **Tables** organize and display information that enables readers to make comparisons. (See Luis Ramirez's "Food Sources in South Providence" in Chapter 15 for examples.)
- **Time lines** list events on a horizontal axis to represent change over time.
- **Flowcharts and organizational charts** show processes, functions, and relationships. (See the Aristocracy organizational chart and the Research flow chart shown here.)

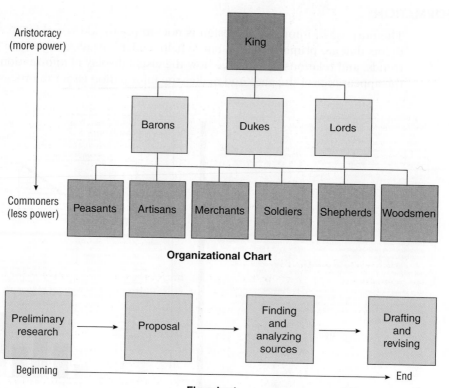

Organizational Chart

Flowchart

Notice that organizational charts are often hierarchical while flowcharts show processes.

Representational Graphics

Representational graphics use pictures to orient readers in time and space and to illustrate processes, relationships, and events.

- **Photographs, drawings, and other illustrations** enable readers to visualize the content of the written text.

- **Maps** often use color coding to help readers visualize the relative location of events or the distribution of a phenomenon.

- **Diagrams** use simplified representations to help readers visualize how processes take place.

The cross section shows the movement of plates on either side of the San Andreas Fault. Notice also the time line at the bottom.

Numerical Graphics

Numerical graphics put the primary focus on quantitative data instead of words or diagrams. Numerical graphics enable writers to analyze the data they are working with and to represent trends and relationships.

- **Tables** are probably the simplest form of numerical graphic. They display numbers and words in rows and columns, enabling readers to see relationships. (See the New York Stock Exchange table.) While tables have the lowest visual interest of numerical graphics, they are useful when you have large amounts of information you want to organize and display in a logical and orderly way.

NEW YORK STOCK EXCHANGE

MOST ACTIVE	Vol (100)	Last	Chg	CHANGES UP	Vol (100)	Last	Chg	% Chg	CHANGES DOWN	Vol (100)	Last	Chg	% Chg
NortelNw	1585880	5.37	+0.13	Orthodon	33718	7.19	+1.09	+17.9	GoodrPet	2568	6.70	-1.03	-13.3
Lucent	499278	3.85	-0.02	JLG	15337	13.70	+1.60	+13.2	Friedmans	5863	5.75	-0.76	-11.7
GenElec	251834	30.50	+0.20	MGM	45410	18.15	+1.95	+12.0	C&D Tch	3879	15.65	-1.76	-10.1
TenetHlt	222717	10.29	+0.48	Celltech	185	15.90	+1.63	+11.4	Systemax	1428	4.97	-0.41	-7.6
Citigrp	160112	49.99	+0.87	Embratl rs	2209	16.37	+1.41	+9.4	SCPIE	118	8.62	-0.69	-7.4
Pfizer	157013	35.42	+0.47	MetrisCos	61139	6.70	+0.55	+8.9	Avaya	92355	14.88	-1.18	-7.3
ATT Wrls	154675	13.56	+0.04	Giantln	4022	20.65	+1.63	+8.6	EnzoBio	3086	16.71	-1.18	-6.6
Corning	126385	10.64	-0.23	Orix	181	52.65	+3.95	+8.1	DPL	47067	18.27	-1.22	-6.3
TimeWarn	126257	16.28	+0.06	BBVABFrn	718	9.19	+0.68	+8.0	HavertyA	17	21.10	-1.40	-6.2
Motorola	125782	16.61	+0.28	Tsakos	2862	29.51	+2.16	+7.9	Ionics	3223	23.60	-1.50	-6.0
SprntPCS	122941	8.51	-0.01	BallyTotF	8509	6.14	+0.37	+6.4	Salton	1979	9.20	-0.59	-6.0
TexInst	109411	29.57	+0.45	Amrep	115	16.74	+0.93	+5.9	URS	3342	28.70	-1.74	-5.7
EMC Cp	103226	12.69	-0.01	ChinaTel	3056	35.90	+1.99	+5.9	Beverly	46482	5.95	-0.35	-5.6
Guidant	102240	64.07	-2.65	RoylGp g	403	10.77	+0.60	+5.9	M&F Wld	395	12.72	-0.73	-5.4
HewlettP	99574	21.79	+0.08	AlliGam	12786	31.03	+1.66	+5.7	LeVZ32 n	49	25.60	-1.40	-5.2

Table

- **Line graphs** are used to show variation in the quantity of something over a period of time. By charting the number of cases on the vertical, or *y*, axis and the period of time on the horizontal, or *x*, axis, writers can establish trends. (See line graph on page 573.)

- **Pie charts** divide the whole of something into its parts, displaying the individual items that make up 100 percent of the whole. Pie charts help readers see the relative weight or importance of each slice in relation to the others. For this reason many graphic designers agree that, to avoid clutter and ensure readability, pie charts should use no more than six or seven slices.

More Than One Third Of Anchorage's Sports Participants Are Soccer Players

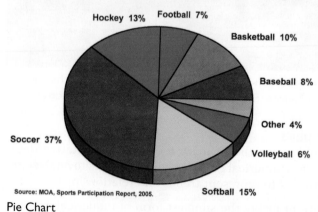

Hockey 13%   Football 7%   Basketball 10%   Baseball 8%   Other 4%   Volleyball 6%   Softball 15%   Soccer 37%

Source: MOA, Sports Participation Report, 2005.

Pie Chart

- **Bar charts** enable writers to compare data and to emphasize contrasts among two or more items over time. Bar charts run along the horizontal axis from left to right. **Column charts** serve the same function as bar charts but run along the vertical axis, from down to up.

Income Distribution
Niles, Michigan

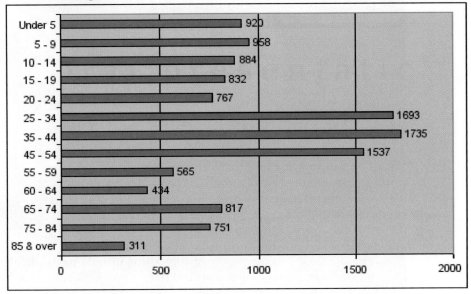

Bar Chart

Institute of Cancer Research
CIHR Cancer Research Funding over the last 6 fiscal years

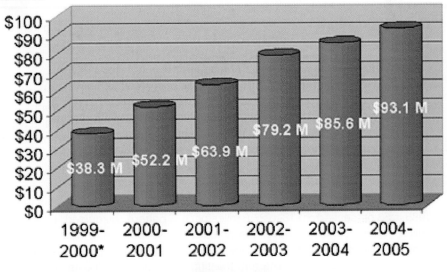

Column Chart

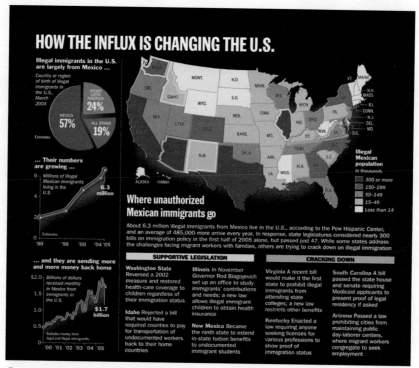

Consider the various types of information design and how they work together.

ETHICS OF INFORMATION DESIGN

DATA DISTORTION

The information design expert Edward R. Tufte says that inept and misleading graphics are widespread in part because visual designers believe that statistical data are boring to readers and in need of jazzing up. As Tufte shows, however, instead of making the data more lively, graphic effects often misrepresent or exaggerate the meaning of the data.

Notice in the illustration on page 573, for example, that the numerical increase in "Fuel Economy Standards for Autos" from 1978 to 1985 is 53 percent—from 18 to 27.5 miles per gallon. As represented, however, the increase from the line representing 1978 standards, which is 0.6 inches, to the line representing 1985 standards, which is 5.3 inches, amounts to 783 percent—a huge distortion of the facts.

Moreover, by departing from the usual order of listing dates on an axis—either bottom to top or left to right—the new standards seem to be surging directly at us, exaggerating their effect.

Tufte redesigned this display of information with a simple graph, so that the size of the graphic matched the size of the data. As you can see, instead of the dramatic, ever increasing change presented in the original, Tufte's redesign shows that the new standards start gradually, double the rate between 1980 and 1983, and then flatten out—a pattern disguised in the original display. Notice, finally, how the redesign includes a simple comparison of the expected average mileage of all cars on the road to the new car standards, another clarifying item of information missing from the original. ∎

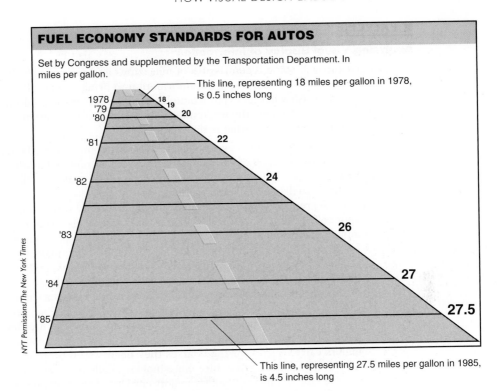

FUEL ECONOMY STANDARDS FOR AUTOS

Set by Congress and supplemented by the Transportation Department. In miles per gallon.

This line, representing 18 miles per gallon in 1978, is 0.5 inches long

This line, representing 27.5 miles per gallon in 1985, is 4.5 inches long

NYT Permissions/The New York Times

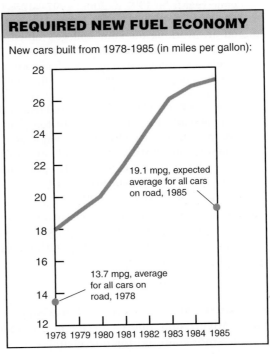

REQUIRED NEW FUEL ECONOMY

New cars built from 1978-1985 (in miles per gallon):

19.1 mpg, expected average for all cars on road, 1985

13.7 mpg, average for all cars on road, 1978

Line graphs

■ **EXERCISE**

Analyzing Visual Display of Information

1. Look through some recent issues of magazines and newspapers to find three examples of the visual display of information to bring to class. Be prepared to explain how (or whether) your examples organize and display information in a way that complements the written text. Does the size of the graphic match the size of the data? If not, what is the effect?

2. The following situations present clusters of information that can be represented in visual form. In each case, decide whether a line graph, a bar chart, or a pie chart is the best choice to convey the information to readers. Make a sketch of your choice to display this information.

   a. You are preparing the annual report for a community service organization at your college. Part of your task is to explain how the organization has spent the annual budget of $7,500 it receives from the college. Expenditures are the following: $1,500 for printing leaflets, brochures, and the quarterly newsletter; $1,000 for speakers' fees; $500 for a workshop for members; $2,500 to send five members to a national conference on community service; $1,750 for donations to local community organizations; $250 for refreshments at meetings.

   b. Biology classes at your college are in high demand. No new faculty have been hired nor have any new courses been offered in the past ten years. With the rapid increase of biology majors, classes are overenrolled. In some cases, even majors can't register for the courses they need. You want to make the case that your college needs to hire more biology faculty and offer more courses. Here are the numbers of biology majors enrolled at the beginning of each academic year from 1997 to 2006: 1997—125; 1998—132; 1999—114; 2000—154; 2001—158; 2002—176; 2003—212; 2004—256; 2005—301; 2006—333.

   c. You are working for your college's office of alumni affairs and you are involved in a campaign to increase alumni donations. No one has ever researched whether donations vary depending on the major of alumni. To help plan the campaign, you are asked to find out how donation differs according to the major of alumni. You decide to look first at alumni who graduated between 1975 and 1984 and have established their careers. Here is the number of alumni who graduated in the ten-year period and the donations they gave in 1997 arranged by type of major: social sciences, 1,300 graduates—$158,000; humanities, 1,680 graduates—$98,000; business, 2,180 graduates—$326,000; engineering, 940 graduates—$126,000; sciences, 1,020 graduates—$112,00; fine arts, 720 graduates—$48,000; nursing and allied health, 680 graduates—$54,000.

3. In a group with two or three other students, choose one of the reading selections that appear in another chapter. Design a visual display of information to emphasize a main point, trend, relationship, or process in the reading. Be prepared to explain your design.

PERSUASION

You don't have to look very far to see how visual design is used for purposes of persuasion. Advertising, public service announcements, and advocacy campaigns of all kinds contend for our visual attention—on television, printed pages, posters, billboards, and Web sites.

Persuasion can address its readers in a number of ways. The famous Uncle Sam army recruitment poster of World War I, for example, took a direct approach to readers, staring them straight in the eye to deliver its command message: "I Want You." A British recruitment poster from the same era took a more indirect approach, putting readers in the role of spectators looking into a living room after the war where children ask their father, "Daddy, what did YOU do in the Great War?"

Notice, on the other hand, how the poster on page 576 from Men Can Stop Rape appeals not to shame but to positive self-image.

Because the contemporary landscape is so cluttered by images, persuasion depends in part on simply getting the viewer's attention in the first place. To make its message stand out, visual design draws on the use of sight in two distinct but related ways—seeing images and reading text. Effective design engages viewer-readers in putting pictures and words together to form meaningful messages. In some cases, such as Jean Carlu's poster promoting production during World War II, viewer-readers can take in at a single glance the powerful visual symbol of industrial mobilization that Carlu designed. Here reading and seeing are interlocked, just as the image and text create one figure.

Notice how, in Amnesty International's appeal to free Ngawang Choephel, seeing and reading are integrated in quite a different way, with the column of text running parallel to the prison bars. (The campaign was successful, and Choephel was released in 2002.)

Persuasive Messages

Face the Music. Art Director: Woody Pirtle/Pentagram Client: Amnesty International. In Milton Glaser & Mirker Inc. The Design of Dissent. Gloucester, MA: Rockport Publishers, 2005; p 101

■ EXERCISE

Analyzing Persuasive Visual Design

1. Find a number of advertisements, public service announcements, or other forms of publicity that integrate words and images into a visual design. Try to get as wide a range as possible. Bring five or six to class. Work in a group with two or three other students. Pay attention to how each visual design addresses you as a viewer-reader. Is it direct address, where you feel someone is talking to you? Or are you positioned in the role of a spectator? Consider how these approaches—direct and indirect—embody the designer's purposes and the persuasive effects.

2. Use the same group of materials. This time analyze how seeing and reading work together and separately in the way you make sense of the message. What are the images you see? What are the words you read? How do they go together to form a message?

VISUAL DESIGN: FOUR BASIC PRINCIPLES

In this section we look at four basic principles that apply to virtually any document you may be called on to design. Each principle emphasizes a particular aspect of design, but all four overlap and mutually reinforce each other.

- **Group similar items together:** Grouping similar items creates visual units of attention on the page and thereby helps readers organize and remember information.

- **Align visual elements:** Alignment refers to the placement of visual elements on the page—whether you center them or align them left or right. Alignment enables readers to connect the visual elements on the page.

- **Use repetition and contrast to create consistent visual patterns:** *Repetition* unifies disparate visual elements and cues readers to where they can expect certain types of information to appear. *Contrast* is a way to emphasize certain visual elements—to make them stand out.

- **Add visual interest:** Visual design can follow the first three principles and still be a bit boring. Adding visual interest will not only make readers more likely to pay attention to your message. It also enhances your credibility as someone who knows how to make a sophisticated and stylish presentation.

USE THE FOUR PRINCIPLES TO REDESIGN DOCUMENTS

To see what the four principles look like in practice, here are examples of using them to redesign a list, a résumé, and a flyer.

Redesigning a List

NBA Player Ratings (original)	NBA Player Ratings (redesign)
Centers	**Centers**
Shaquille O'Neal, Heat	Shaquille O'Neal, Heat
Yao Ming, Rockets	Yao Ming, Rockets
Ben Wallace, Pistons	Ben Wallace, Pistons
Brad Miller, Kings	Brad Miller, Kings
Forwards	**Forwards**
Dirk Nowitzki, Mavericks	Dirk Nowitzki, Mavericks
Lebron James, Cavaliers	Lebron James, Cavaliers
Elton Brand, Clippers	Elton Brand, Clippers
Tim Duncan, Spurs	Tim Duncan, Spurs
Guards	**Guards**
Kobe Bryant, Lakers	Kobe Bryant, Lakers
Steve Nash, Suns	Steve Nash, Suns
Dwayne Wade, Heat	Dwayne Wade, Heat
Allen Iverson, 76ers	Allen Iverson, 76ers

Redesigning a Résumé

Martha Smith
143 Oakland Avenue
Philadelphia, PA 19122
(215) 555-2000

Education

Bachelor of Arts in English
Temple University, 1999

Experience

Journalism internship—*Philadelphia Inquirer*
1998–1999
    Covered and wrote by-lined articles on school board meetings
    Researched sex education K-12 for special report
    Assisted editor in preparing special education supplement

Public Relations Assistant—Trinity Repertory Theater, Camden, NJ
1997–1998
    Wrote advertising copy and designed promotional brochures
    Conducted focus groups
    Prepared instructional materials for Theater in the Schools

Writing Center Tutor—Temple University
1996–1999
    Tutored students on wide range of writing assignments
    Worked with international students
    Trained new tutors

Entertainment Editor—*Temple Daily News*
1997–1998
    Planned and assigned music, art, drama, and film reviews
    Edited reviews
    Led staff meetings

Related Skills
    Written and spoken fluency in Spanish, reading ability in French
    Feature Writing, Graphic Design, Editing, Photojournalism

Achievements/Activities:
    Dean's list (every semester)
    Member of Sigma Tau Delta, International English Honor Society
    Secretary of Amnesty International, Temple University chapter
    Varsity crosscountry and indoor and outdoor track

References: Available upon request

Marginal annotations:

Groupings of information don't stand out

Alignment is inconsistent—some headings are centered, some flush left.

No clear pattern established by repetition and contrast

Résumé (original)

Groupings are more distinct

Visual elements are aligned in a consistent pattern

Use of rules and boldface creates a pattern by repetition

Use of boldface and sans-serif headings creates a pattern by contrast

---

MARTHA SMITH

143 Oakland Avenue
Philadelphia, PA 19122
(215) 555-2000

Education

1999   Bachelor of Arts in English
                  Temple University

Experience

1998–1999   **Journalism internship** at *Philadelphia Inquirer*.
                  Covered and wrote by-lined articles on school board
                  meetings. Researched sex education K-12 for special
                  report. Assisted editor in preparing special education
                  supplement.

1997–1998   **Public Relations Assistant** at Trinity Theater,
                  Camden, NJ. Wrote advertising copy and designed
                  promotional brochures. Conducted focus groups.
                  Prepared instructional materials for theater in the
                  Schools.

1996–1999   **Writing Center Tutor** at Temple University. Tutored
                  students on wide range of writing assignments.
                  Worked with international students. Trained new
                  tutors

1997–98   **Entertainment Editor** at *Temple Daily News*. Planned
                  and assigned music, art, drama and film reviews.
                  Edited reviews. Led staff meetings

Related Skills

Written and Spoken fluency in Spanish, reading ability in French. Coursework in feature writing, graphic
design, design, editing, and photo-journalism.

Achievements/Activities

Dean's list (every semester)
Member of Sigma Tau Delta, International English
Honor Society, Secretary of Amnesty International,
Temple University chapter, Varsity crosscountry, and
indoor and outdoor track

References available upon request

Résumé (redesign)

Redesigning a Flyer

Centered layout makes visual elements "float" on the page

No consistent color scheme

No clear pattern of information design

Flyer (original)

Groups visual elements

Aligns visual elements

Creates patterns by repetition and contrast

Uses color scheme based on Coke can

Creates visual interest with large image of Coke can

Flyer (redesign by Dan Tennant)

WORKING WITH TYPE

In the age of the personal computer, writers have access to literally hundreds of type fonts and can change their size and underline, italicize, or make them boldface with the click of a mouse. The vast range of possibilities now available, however, can be overwhelming. Writers need to understand what their options are in using type, and what kinds of effect their design decisions are likely to have on readers. Here are some basic suggestions about working with type:

- **Use white space as an active element in design:** White space is not simply the empty places on a page where no writing or visuals appear. White space plays an active role in creating the visual structure of a document and the relationship among its parts. Notice, for example, how white space makes headings more or less prominent by creating a hierarchy of levels:

  Level 1 heading (for titles)

  xxxxxxxxxxxxxxxxxxxxxxxxxxxxxxxxxxxxxxxxxxxxxxxxxxxxxxxxxxxxxxxxx
  xxxxxxxxxxxxxxxxxxxxxxxxxxxxxxxxxxxxxxxxxxxxxxxxxxxxxxxxxxxxxxxxx
  xxxxxxxxxxxxxxxxxxxxxxxxxxxxxxx.

  Level 2 heading (on separate line)

  xxxxxxxxxxxxxxxxxxxxxxxxxxxxxxxxxxxxxxxxxxxxxxxxxxxxxxxxxxxxxxxxx
  xxxxxxxxxxxxxxxxxxxxxxxxxxxxxxxxxxxxxxxxxxxxxxxxxxxxxxxxxxxxxx
  xxxxxxxxxxxxxxxxxxxxxxxxxxxxxxxxxxxxxxxxxxxxxxxxxxxxxxxxxxxxxx
  xxxxxxxxxxxxxxxxxxxxxxxxxxxxxxxxxxxxxxxxxxxxxxxxxxxxxxxxxxxxxx
  xxxxxxxxxxxxxx.

  Level 3 heading (with text following) xxxxxxxxxxxxxxxxxxxxxxxxxxxx
  xxxxxxxxxxxxxxxxxxxxxxxxxxxxxxxxxxxxxxxxxxxxxxxxxxxxxxxxxxxxxxxxx
  xxxxxxxxxxxxxxxxxxxxxxxxxxxxxxxxxxxxxxxxxxxxxxxxxxxxxxxxxxxxxxxxx
  xxxxxxxxxxxxxxxxxxxxxxxxxxxxxxxxxxxxxxxxxxxxxxxxxxxxxxxxxxxxxxxxx
  xxxxxxxxxxxxxxxxxxxxxxxxxxxxxxxxxxxxxxxxxxxxxxxxx.

- **Use leading appropriately:** Leading is the typographer's term for the white space that appears above and below a line of type. The basic guideline is that you need more leading—more space above and below type—when lines of print are long, less when they're short. A research paper, for example, is easier to read if it's double-spaced. On the other hand, in newsletters and other documents with columns, it's better to use less leading. Notice the difference between Column A and B:

Column A

For shorter lines, as in
newsletters and other documents

Column B

For shorter lines, as in
newsletters and other documents

with columns, use less leading. If there's too much white space, readers' eyes can drift when they leave one line and look for the start of the next.

with columns, use less leading. If there's too much white space, readers' eyes can drift when they leave one line and look for the start of the next.

■ **Use uppercase and lowercase:** In general, the combination of uppercase and lowercase letters is easier to read than all uppercase.

THIS IS BECAUSE UPPERCASE (OR CAPITAL) LETTERS ARE UNIFORM IN SIZE, MAKING THEM MORE DIFFICULT TO RECOGNIZE THAN LOWERCASE LETTERS, ESPECIALLY ON COMPUTER SCREENS OR SINGLE-SPACED OR ITALICIZED

The combination of uppercase and lowercase uses more white space, produces more visual variety, and thereby helps the eye track the lines of print.

■ **Use appropriate typeface and fonts:** Typeface and fonts refer to the design of letters, numbers, and other characters. There are thousands of typefaces available. The visual appearance of typeface contributes to the personality or character of your document. Part of working with type is choosing the typeface that creates the right image and thereby sends the appropriate message to your readers.

SERIF AND SANS SERIF TYPEFACES

Typefaces are normally divided into two groups—serif and sans serif. Serif typefaces include horizontal lines—or serifs—added to the major strokes of a letter or a character such as a number. Sans serif typefaces, by contrast, do not have serifs. Notice the difference:

Serif	Sans Serif
New York	Geneva
Palatino	Arial
Times	Helvetica

The typical use and stylistic impact of the typefaces vary considerably. Serif typefaces are more traditional, conservative, and formal in appearance. By contrast, sans serif typefaces offer a more contemporary, progressive, and informal look. Accordingly, serif is often used for longer pieces of writing, such as novels and textbooks. It is also the best bet for college papers. The horizontal lines make serif easier to read, especially in dense passages, because they guide the reader's eyes from left to right across the page. On the other hand, technical writers often use sans serif for user's manuals and other documents because it evokes a more modern, high-tech look.

DISPLAY TYPEFACES

Display typefaces offer many options for creating the look you want in newsletter nameplates, organizational logos, invitations, posters, signs, advertisements, and other documents. Display typefaces can project the mood and image that's appropriate for an organization or occasion. The trick, of course, is finding the style that's right—that conveys the message you want to readers.

Notice the different images display type creates for Jetstream Printers. This type projects a sleek and contemporary look:

$$Jetstream$$

This type, however, is probably too staid and conservative, more appropriate, say, for a bank, stock brokerage company, or law firm:

JETSTREAM

On the other hand, this type is too light-hearted and informal. It's better suited for a restaurant or fashion boutique:

Jetstream

MIXING TYPEFACES

In some cases, combining different typefaces can enhance visual design. For example, it's common to use sans serif type for headlines or headings and serif for text. Make sure, however, that combinations of typefaces project a consistent image and that the styles used are compatible. (See the various design examples throughout this chapter.)

■ EXERCISE

Using Design Principles

Use the design principles we've just looked at to consider the changes Alex Schwartz has made to the following poster.

Warehouse State
FALL FILM SERIES

Classic Film Noir

All showings in Harrington Hall at 8:00 pm

Wednesday, September 14, 2001
Double Indemnity (1944)
Directed by Billy Wilder
With Fred MacMurray and Barbara Stanwyck

Wednesday, October 17, 2001
The Asphalt Jungle (1950)
Directed by John Huston
With Sterling Hayden and Marilyn Monroe

Wednesday, November 30, 2001
Touch of Evil (1958)
Directed by Orson Welles
With Orson Welles, Charlton Heston, and Janet Leigh

Original

Alex Schwartz's redesign

VISUAL DESIGN PROJECTS

The following section looks at some of the considerations writers typically take into account when they design and produce documents such as flyers, newsletters, and brochures.

Preliminary Considerations

Like other writing tasks, design projects begin with a call to write—the felt need to send a message from an individual, group, or organization to prospective readers. Developing the design of a particular document will depend on answering questions such as these:

- What is the occasion that calls on you to design a document? What kind of document is most appropriate, given the circumstances (a flyer, leaflet, letter, brochure, or other format)? What is its purpose? Whose interests are involved? What is your relationship to the people who want the document produced and to those who will read it? What image should the document project?

- Who are your readers? What use will they make of the document? What do you want them to do after they have read the document? What tone and style are likely to be effective?

- What information will you be working with? How much of the document will be written text? What graphics do you have to use? How many sections do you foresee? In what order will they appear? Will you be doing all the writing? Some? Who else is involved?

- What technology do you have to work with? What does it enable you to do? What constraints does it put on the document?

- Are there any financial or time constraints you need to be aware of? Who will pay for the printing? When does the document need to be finished? Is this a realistic time frame?

By answering these questions, you can begin to make some basic decisions about the layout and other design features of your document. In particular, you will need to decide on the materials you will use in the document—whether you can use color, what type and color of ink, what type and color of paper, whether you plan to scan in illustrations or photos, what clip art, if any, you plan to use.

Working Sketches

The next step is to sketch a preliminary layout for the document. At this point, document designers often sketch a number of different arrangements. Such working sketches can help you identify potential problems you may face.

Flyer Sketch (based on redesign by Dan Tennant p. 581)

Flyers

Flyers are really small posters that can be passed out or posted on bulletin boards. They may announce upcoming meetings, events, and performances; advertise sales and other limited-time promotions; or urge people to do something. To be effective, flyers need to convey all the pertinent information at a glance. To do so, successful flyers combine seeing and reading with:

- Large headlines.
- Compact units of text.
- Attention-getting visuals and/or design features.

Newsletters

Newsletters are used by companies and organizations to communicate within the group and to the public. They run from a single page to eight pages or so, depending on their purpose and frequency. In many respects, they are like newspapers or little magazines. Key elements of a successful newsletter include:

- A distinctive nameplate and logo that identifies the newsletter.
- Clear identification of the sponsoring organization.
- Volume number, issue number, and date.

- Consistent design that maintains the identity of the newsletter from one issue to the next.
- Use of design features such as sidebars, boxes, pull quotes, photos, and illustrations to break up the text and add visual interest.

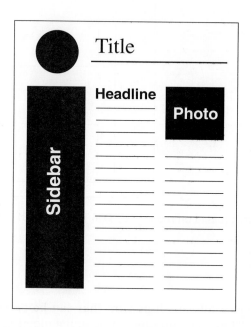

Newletter Sketch

Brochures

Companies and organizations use brochures for promotional and informational purposes. Brochures usually include three or four panels. Here are some considerations to take into account when you're designing a brochure:

- Make the purpose of the brochure easy to identify. The front cover headline should cue readers to the subject and purpose.
- The brochure should be easy to use. The outside panels—front, back, and middle—are often designed to be read separately. The inside panels should be designed as a continuous space.
- Make sure the brochure has all the information readers need—names, addresses, and phone numbers of organizations; maps to get to a store, museum, or historic district; bibliography; steps readers can take; answers to frequently asked questions; basic facts.

Brochure Sketch (inside)

Middle   Back   Front

Brochure Sketch (outside)

W WRITERS' WORKSHOP

The brochure on eating disorders that appears here is a draft Kevin Candiloro did for a course on public health. Before you look at the draft, read Kevin's commentary on the feedback he wants from peer commentaries.

This is a draft, so I think there are still changes I can make. In terms of the content, I'm not sure I've got the best order. Should I explain what eating disorders are before I explain why some people have them? I'm also not sure what should come first, talking about how to help someone with an eating disorder or helping yourself if you've got one. I don't have to keep the questions I'm using at this point, so if you have any suggestions about them, please tell me. It seems that I've got a lot of text. Can you suggest how to break it up into smaller parts? I don't like the bit of text on the back cover, above the section about where to find help, that continues from the inside. Do you have any ideas about how to fix this?

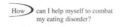

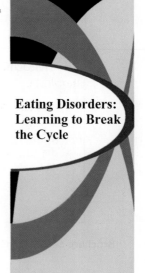

How can I help myself to combat my eating disorder?

You have completed the first part already. Admitting that you need to change your lifestyle to adopt healthier habits is the first step toward change.

If you fast or go on highly restrictive diets one thing you can start with is to learn about proper nutrition and why it is necessary to eat right. It is possible to eat so that you remain at a healthy weight. Maintaining a healthy weight will result in higher energy and your body will be better able to maintain itself and fight illness. Learn what your ideal healthy weight is and how many calories you need to eat to maintain it. Make a meal and snack plan and try to keep with it even if you don't feel hungry or interested in eating.

Binging and dieting can be controlled by making an effort to reduce the amount of calories in your binges and increasing the amount of calories in your diets. It is also a good idea to learn about proper nutrition techniques and why they are important.

Overeating can be helped by taking a few steps to limit yourself. Do not shop when you are hungry and buy only what you need. You should learn how to eat nutritionally balanced meals at specific times of the day and stick to a regular eating schedule. Eat slowly and do not continue eating if you feel full.

No matter what type of eating disorder a person might have, one can always benefit from seeking support from a councilor, nutritionist or other people who have had similar problems with food. Sometimes a therapist can be helpful in helping people to face their illness. Changing habits is a very hard thing to do and it often takes time to be successful.

Poor eating habits make people sick and unhappy. Setting short term goals for oneself can help to show progress in controlling an eating disorder. Anyone should feel proud that they are able to accomplish such a difficult task and one should always remember that eating disorders are treatable.

Where to find help

Eating Disorder Referral and Information Center
2923 Sandy Pointe, Suite 6
Del Mar, CA 92014-2052
(858) 481-1515

National Association of Anorexia Nervosa and Associated Disorders (ANAD)
Box 7
Highland Park, IL 60035
(847) 831-3438

American Anorexia/ Bulimia Association, Inc. (AABA)
165 West 46th Street, Suite 1108
New York, NY 10036
(212) 575-6200

Overeaters Anonymous
World Service Office
P.O. Box 44020
Rio Rancho, NM 87174-4020
(505) 891-2664

Massachusetts Eating Disorders Association, Inc. (MEDA)
92 Pearl Street
Newton, MA 02158
(617) 558-1881

Eating Disorders: Learning to Break the Cycle

do some people have eating disorders?

Society and the media place an enormous importance upon being thin. Because of this many people seek to control their lives through their body. It is when food and eating begin to control a person's life that eating disorder sets in. Eating disorders imprison a person in beliefs that how they eat determines their worth as a person. Additionally many athletes who compete in weight emphasizing sports (wrestling, body building, etc.) can also develop eating disorders.

 is an eating disorder?

The most common forms of eating disorders diagnosed in the United States are anorexia nervosa and bulimia nervosa. Many also consider compulsive overeating to be an eating disorder.

Anorexia is characterized by severe episodes of restrictive dieting or starvation. Anorexics are afraid to gain weight in any capacity and often drop to weights well below healthy tolerances. Symptoms caused by this severe type of weight loss include: pale or gray skin, cold hands and feet, fatigue, digestive problems, irregular sleeping patterns, amenorrhea in women (loss of menstrual periods), growth of fine body hair, unusual eating habits, dizziness, headaches, mood swings and depression. Symptoms of severe, long term anorexia might include susceptibility to infection, bone fractures, general chemical imbalances and atrophy of the heart muscles which can be life threatening.

Bulimia is defined by periods of rapid weight loss and gain. This is caused by the cycle of binging an purging in which the bulimic participates. Most often the shame of their condition forces bulimics to binge and purge in secret. Purging is done by forced vomiting, taking diuretic drugs or laxatives, fasting or over-exercising. Both phases of this illness take their toll on the body.

Throat and mouth wounds, tooth decay, bruising of the eyes and cheeks, digestive disorders, dehydration, muscle fatigue, ulcers and heart irregularities are all symptoms of bulimia.

Compulsive overeating leads to being overweight and eventually leads to obesity. The health problems associated with being overweight have been studied intently in the recent past. The fear of these health issues even motivates some anorexics and bulimics to their illnesses. Symptoms that result from compulsive overeating include: joint pain, fatigue, high blood pressure, and in later stages: osteoarthritis, heart disease and gall bladder disease.

 is at risk?

People who become trapped in the cycle of an eating disorder usually show similar external signs. Often, people with eating disorders become anxious at meals, are obsessed with their body image or repeatedly count their daily calorie intake. In many cases a person with one of these illnesses will show remorse for eating a meal in the form of self-degrading or self-punishing statements. They often complain of "feeling fat" even when they are thin or even unhealthily so. They judge themselves and their character by the food that they eat and keep to themselves when acting upon their disorder.

Most diagnosed cases of anorexia and bulimia occur in adolescent girls. The ages of 14 and 18 are the peaks for the occurrence of these illnesses. When young girls are struggling to become young women the pressures of society are often too much to handle and a person will lapse into eating disorder as a way to try to gain control over their life. Unfortunately, this is a mistake that often leads to years of illness.

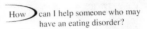 can I help someone who may have an eating disorder?

The most important thing to remember if you suspect that your friend or a family member may have an eating disorder is that the person is likely to be very protective of their illness and may not immediately acknowledge its existence at all. You should try to learn about eating disorders for yourself so that you can get a better sense of the problem and how it affects people.

Be persistent, but not overbearing. Try to bring up the topic by stating that you are worried about how their behavior is impacting your relationship. Do not bring up any concerns about their weight or appearance. If the person is not receptive, tell them you will talk about it again later.

If your friend or family member becomes angry or upset when you try to talk to them about their problem, do not force the issue. Do not try to take the roll of a counselor or eating monitor. You cannot help anyone before they have admitted to having a problem.

You may often be rejected by the person that you are trying to help. This is common. Do not take the rejection personally. People with eating disorders often have trouble admitting that they have a problem controlling themselves, since a sense of control is what drives their illness.

■ WORKSHOP QUESTIONS

1. How would you respond to Kevin's concerns about his draft? First, consider whether the purpose of the brochure comes across clearly. Were you able to see right away what reader needs the brochure was designed to meet?

2. Consider the order of questions. Is it the most effective? What changes, if any, would you suggest?

3. Is the information adequate, given Kevin's purposes? What, if anything, should be added or deleted?

4. Look at the design. Can you think of ways to break up the information into smaller chunks? Should Kevin use more headings? Imagine you are opening the brochure. You see the panel from the outside ("How can I help myself to combat my eating disorder?") next to the first panel from the inside ("Why do some people have eating disorders?" and "What is an eating disorder?"). Is this a problem? If you think so, what should Kevin do? ■

chapter 20

web design

Web sites present a new way of designing and using information. For example, it's not quite accurate to say that people read Web sites, certainly not in the same way they read printed material such as a newspaper or a textbook. Instead, they *visit* a Web site. They don't turn pages but instead *navigate* the site to find what's there of interest. Instead of organizing information in a linear way, from start to finish, as printed material typically does, Web sites provide links to the pages within a document and often to external Web sites so that readers can decide on their own *path* from an array of possibilities.

This chapter presents a basic introduction to Web design. It doesn't explain the technical side of composing Web pages or putting them up on a server. That's beyond the scope of this book. Rather, we look at the rhetoric and design principles of Web sites. First, we consider the rhetorical purposes of Web sites. Second, we look at the structure of Web design. Third, we present information on the visual design of Web sites. Finally, we discuss how to plan a Web site.

This chapter can be used in a variety of ways. According to your instructor's directions, you can read it to learn more about the design of Web sites or you can use it to plan your own Web site. Whether you actually construct a Web site will depend in part on your instructor, your technical expertise, and the time and technical resources available. One option is to plan the Web site on paper as an exercise or writing assignment.

THE RHETORICAL PURPOSES OF WEB DESIGN

When the Web started, its original purpose was to provide physicists with a forum where they could post scientific papers for a specialized community of readers. Since then, of course, with technical improvements in browsers and composers, the affordability of home computers, and the speed of modem connections, use of the Web has become widespread. The Web has been thoroughly commercialized, with companies advertising and selling goods and services online. As noted in Chapter 1, the Web now also provides an important forum for advocacy groups to organize campaigns and publicize

Online Study Center

their point of view. And it gives writers, artists, and musicians, as well as ordinary people who design their own home pages, an opportunity to express themselves.

To understand what calls on individuals and organizations to design Web sites, we will use the same three purposes as in Chapter 19, "Visual Design"— identification, information, and persuasion—to see how Web sites embody their designers' purposes and how these purposes sometimes overlap.

IDENTIFICATION

Coco Fusco's Virtual Laboratory is a good example of how Web sites can project the identity of a particular person, in this case the performance artist and critic Coco Fusco. (See the page reproduced here.) The Web site contains a good deal of information and is at least implicitly persuasive in advertising her publications. Still, the dominant impression created by the Web site is to identify who Coco Fusco is and what she does.

INFORMATION

"Dressed to the Nines: A History of the Baseball Uniform" is an online exhibit that is part of The National Baseball Hall of Fame and Museum Web site.

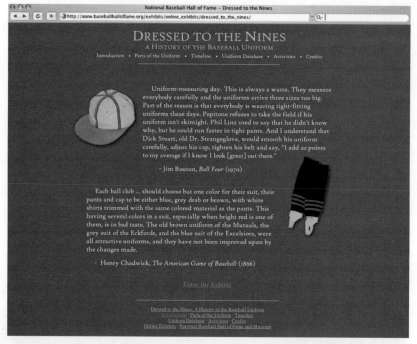

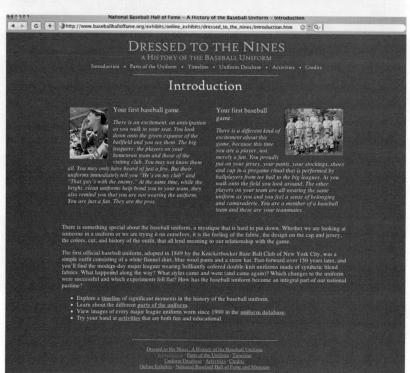

PERSUASION

Amnesty International is devoted to defending human rights worldwide. The Amnesty International Web site (see the page reproduced here) is typical of advocacy group sites. It offers lots of information, in the form of reports and news updates, but it is also frankly partisan in its attempts to influence public opinion and get people involved in Amnesty International campaigns.

■ FOR CRITICAL INQUIRY

1. Visit Coco Fusco's Virtual Laboratory, www.thing.net/~cocofusco/. Consider it as a home page that projects the image and identity of a person. What dominant impression does it create about Coco Fusco and her works? How do the visuals add to that impression?

2. Visit the Lucy Parsons Project Web site, www.lucyparsonsproject.org. What range of information does it make available? What do you see as the purpose of this information? Who might use it?

3. Visit Greenpeace's Web site, www.greenpeace.org. How does the site establish its credibility? What information does it provide? What does it call on visitors to do?

4. Now compare your experience visiting the three Web sites. How do the sites make their purposes clear? What features of the Web sites did you find particularly effective, useful, instructional, or entertaining? Were there features that didn't seem to work well? What generalizations might you draw about how visitors experience Web sites? What criteria can you begin to develop about what makes an effective Web site?

THE STRUCTURE OF WEB DESIGN

The structure of a Web site determines how pages are linked to each other and how visitors are thereby able to move from page to page. Web sites can have a **deep structure,** where visitors must click through a series of pages to get from the home page to a more remote destination.

In other cases, the Web site may have a **shallow structure,** where the home page presents enough options so that visitors can get to any destination in the site with only a click or two.

A **hypertext structure,** on the other hand, links pages to each other so that visitors can take different routes to get from the home page to a destination.

■ EXERCISE

Analyzing Web Structure

Work in a group of three or four. Analyze the structure of one of the three Web sites featured earlier in the chapter, a Web site that appears elsewhere in this book, or one that interests your group. Design a chart that shows how the pages are linked to each other, using the charts of deep, shallow, and hypertext structures as models. Consider how well the structure fits the purpose of the Web site and how easily you were able to move about the site. If time permits, your instructor may ask groups to present their findings and the class as a whole to draw conclusions about effective structures of Web design.

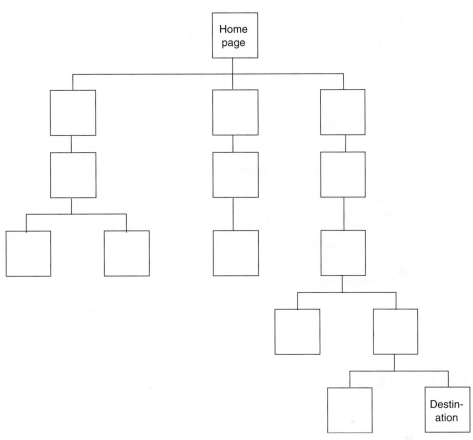

Deep Structure

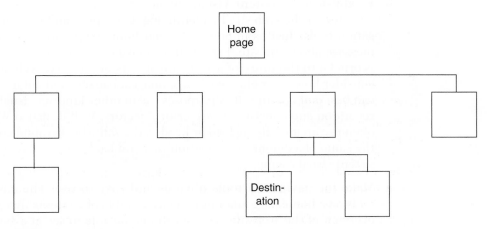

Shallow Structure

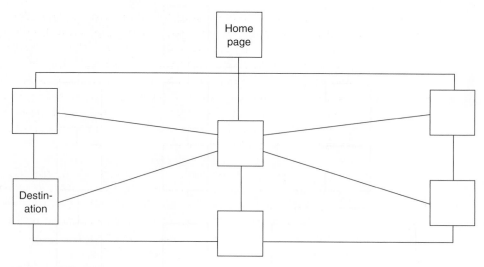

Hypertext Structure

THE VISUAL DESIGN OF WEB SITES

All the principles presented in Chapter 19, "Visual Design," apply to Web sites as much as to printed material. Here are some visual design considerations to take into account when you're planning a Web site:

- **Establish a consistent visual theme:** Home pages typically give an overview of the Web site by identifying its purpose and providing navigation tools. Just as important is that home pages also send a visual message about the site. Establishing a visual theme on the home page is crucial to the unity of a Web site and its credibility. Web designers consider how their choice of logo, images, background color, and font can best embody the site's purposes. As in other kinds of visual design, repetition and consistency are critical factors. Well-designed Web sites often use an identifying logo or header, the same background color, and the same placement of navigation tools on each page to create a consistent visual theme.

- **Make the navigation tools obvious and easy to use:** The navigation tools on a home page amount to a virtual table of contents that gives an overview of the Web site. Visitors should be able to see at a glance the main topics, even if the pages listed as navigation tools contain further links. There are various ways to set up navigation tools. You can use a navigation bar, icons, or buttons. In any case, keep the design, color, and placement consistent throughout the site. Visitors find it reassuring, for example, when the navigation tools are present on each page as a sidebar or at the top of the page. That helps them know where they are in the site and enables them to get back to the home page without clicking the back button on the browser. It's also helpful on longer pages to include a navigation bar at the bottom of the page so visitors don't have to scroll back to the top.

- **Resist clutter:** It can be tempting, particularly if you have the technical ability, to load up a Web site with such "bells and whistles" as animation, busy backgrounds, lurid colors, and lots of graphics. The danger, however, is that of cluttering the page with extraneous material and creating a chaotic effect. Visitors can become impatient rather quickly if the Web page they're trying to read is jam packed, even if they are interested in the material. Whatever appears on the page should follow from the purpose of the Web site and not be simply decorative. Use white space creatively, as noted in Chapter 19, to enhance your design and focus the visitor's attention.

- **Create manageable chunks of information:** Despite the new and exciting multimedia features such as graphics, video, and sound, written text remains the key element of many Web sites. At the same time, using written text effectively is one of the major challenges of Web design because of the size of most people's computer screens and their reluctance to scroll through a long document or read a written text that sprawls all the way across the page. (If they're really interested, they'll print it and read the hard copy.) This means that if you want people to read the pages on a Web site, you need to break up the written text into manageable chunks that can fit easily on a screen or require minimal scrolling. In many ways, this is a new approach to writing, which we'll look at more in the next section.

WRITING ASSIGNMENT

Planning a Web Site

Online Study Center

In this assignment, you will encounter some of the decisions Web designers face in planning a Web site. As you'll see, they are similar in many respects to the decisions you've made in planning other kinds of writing. But, as just mentioned, there are also some important differences between writing print material and writing for the computer screen that you'll need to take into account.

Identifying the Call to Write

Planning a Web site begins, as other types of writing do, by identifying a call to write and clarifying your purposes. There are various situations that might call on you to design a Web site. You might believe there is an urgent issue on your campus, in your local community, or on the national or international scene. You might decide there is something people need to know about, or you may want to persuade them about your point of view. Or you may feel the desire to express yourself. As you've seen, Web design can embody the various and sometimes overlapping purposes of identification, information, and persuasion.

Here are some questions you might ask yourself at this point:

1. Why and how is a Web site a fitting response to the call to write? What can you do in a Web site that you can't do in other genres of writing?

2. What do you see as the main purpose of the Web site?

3. What personality and visual look do you imagine the Web site projecting?

Understanding Your Audience

One of the answers you may have given about choosing a Web site instead of another genre of writing is that it gives you a particular kind of access that connects you to readers online.

To help you plan your Web site, it's worth exploring that connection to on-line readers, the people who will visit your Web site:

1. Who do you imagine will visit your Web site? Are you planning the Web site for a specialized audience or for a more general one? What attitudes and knowledge about the topic of your Web site do you think your intended visitors will have?

2. How will the design of the Web site indicate who your target audience is? Will your intended audience see that it's a site they would be interested in?

3. What do you want visitors to do when they get to the Web site? Is your purpose to have them navigate around your site, or do you plan to provide them with links to related Web sites?

Understanding the Genre

As already noted, one of the key differences between Web sites and many other genres of writing is that Web sites break up information into manageable chunks that can fit on the screen. Instead of giving readers written texts to read linearly, from beginning to end, Web sites link chunks of information together and give visitors navigation tools to determine their own paths from page to page. In this way, Web sites can create layers of information.

In the Lucy Parsons Project Web site, for examples, visitors can read the pages "About Lucy Parsons" or "The Haymarket Affair"—listed as main topics in the navigation tools—but they also have the option of following the links that appear on these pages to read what historians and others have said. The visitor makes the decision about where to go and in what depth. The Web designer structures the site and makes different navigational paths possible.

Designing Web Structure

Work through the following steps to design the structure of your Web site:

1. List as many topics as you can, taking into account what you think visitors need or want to know. Combine topics that overlap or are repetitive. Imagine that each topic will represent a separate Web page. The Web site you're designing might have anywhere between 10 and 20 pages, including the home page. If you decide to include links to other Web sites, you can design a "Links" page or incorporate the links on your own pages where appropriate.

2. Select the topics you want to include on the Web site, and write each topic on a separate note card. Make sure to designate one note card for the home page.

3. Now arrange the note cards to try out designs for your Web site. Put the home page at the top as the entry point. Experiment with various arrangements of information. What topics should appear as navigation tools on the home page? What additional topics should be linked to these pages?

4. Draw a chart of the tentative structure of the Web site you're planning.

Drafting and Revising

Using your Web structure chart as a guide, write drafts of the individual Web pages. If you find some of the pages are too long, you may need to create new linked pages and revise the structure of the Web site. On the other hand, you may find you can combine planned pages into one. Whatever the case, each page should present a manageable chunk of information that will be easy to read on the computer screen and have a sensible place in the structure of your Web design. ■

REFLECTING ON YOUR WRITING

If you have created a Web site to put up on a server or designed a series of Web pages on paper, it's worth considering at this point how composing for the Web compares to composing for print media. What do you see as the main differences and similarities?

chapter 21

oral presentations

A range of situations may require you to give an oral presentation. It's quite likely, for example, that you'll be asked to give an oral presentation in one or more of your courses. Or you may find yourself wanting to speak in a public forum, whether on campus or in your local community, to inform listeners about an issue that concerns you or to persuade them to share your point of view. And you will certainly be called on at some point to give an oral presentation on the job.

As you'll see, planning an oral presentation has much in common with planning a piece of writing, but there are some key differences as well. Understanding these differences can help you use your knowledge of planning written texts to design oral presentations. We will first consider these differences. Then we'll see how you can plan, rehearse, and deliver an effective oral presentation.

UNDERSTANDING THE DIFFERENCES BETWEEN WRITTEN AND ORAL PRESENTATIONS

Depending on the occasion and the speaker's purposes, oral presentations pursue the same goals as written texts do: to inform, analyze, explain, and persuade. With a written presentation, however, readers have a text in front of them to refer to. They can read at their own pace—and reread sections as many times as necessary. The visual design of the page, with its paragraph breaks and section headings, gives readers cues to where they are and how to understand the material presented.

In oral presentations, however, listeners don't have a written text to go on. Instead, they have to grasp the presenter's meanings as he or she is speaking. In oral presentations, there is no going back to an earlier section, as readers can do with written texts. The spoken words evaporate as soon as they are uttered. Listeners have only one chance to understand the speaker's message.

A second main difference involves attention span. Readers can stay at the task longer than listeners, for an hour or more and sometimes much longer,

Online Study Center

603

because they control the pace of reading. Oral presentations, however, put the demand on listeners to follow the speaker's pace. Now it's true that in the nineteenth century and into the early part of the twentieth century, public speakers delivered orations that lasted two or three hours—and could assume the attention of their listeners over that span of time. The Lincoln-Douglas debates, for example, lasted for days, with breaks for meals and sleep. Nonetheless, in the fast-paced age of mass communication, where we're constantly bombarded by images and sound bites, these expectations are no longer realistic. As research on adult attention spans indicates, even the most interested listeners can focus on a presentation for fifteen to twenty minutes at the maximum.

Not only have attention spans shortened, but audiences raised in the era of the mass media now expect oral presentations to use visual as well as verbal communication. Speakers may use something as simple as a handout that summarizes the main points or as sophisticated as multimedia presentations. Later in the chapter, we'll look at how you can design transparencies and computer-generated slides using a program such as Microsoft PowerPoint.

What's important at this point is to understand that oral presentations put special demands on speakers to hold their audience's atttention and enable them to follow the talk easily and understand its main points. Planning an effective oral presentation involves taking your audience's needs into account.

DEVELOPING AN ORAL PRESENTATION

For our purposes here, we'll look at developing an oral presentation to give in one of your classes. These guidelines, however, are applicable to other situations that call on you to give an oral presentation.

PRELIMINARY CONSIDERATIONS

Consider how much time you have for your presentation. Listeners appreciate oral presentations that hold to their time limit. Such presentations require careful planning and rehearsal. Underprepared oral presentations tend to ramble in ways that listeners will find distracting.

Consider also how you will deliver the oral presentation. There is nothing quite so dull as speakers who read a paper to listeners, often with their heads down and eyes on the written text. Effective oral presentations are spoken, and preparation and rehearsal are the best way for you to be able to establish eye contact with your listeners and give them the feeling you are speaking to them. Some speakers write out their presentations and then memorize them. This can be risky, however, especially if you have a memory lapse during the presentation. A safer way is to develop an outline of main points and use it to practice until you can deliver your presentation without hesitation.

PLANNING THE ORAL PRESENTATION

Identifying the Call to Write

You may feel that the call to write is simply that your instructor assigned an oral presentation. It will help you clarify your purpose and plan the presentation, however, if you consider what makes the topic of your presentation interesting, important, controversial, amusing, or some combination. This can help you determine your own stance toward the topic. Do you want to inform your listeners, explain a concept, define a problem and propose a solution, evaluate a work or performance, advocate a point of view, or align yourself with others in a controversy?

Defining Your Audience

Who are your listeners? What interests do they have in the material you're presenting? What level of knowledge do they have about the topic? The answers to these questions may seem self-evident, for your audience is most likely your teacher and fellow students. At the same time, though, you're no doubt aware that your instructor knows more than the students do. So one thing you need to do is find a balance between the needs of your instructor and your classmates. You want to make sure your instructor knows you understand the material well and can present it intelligently; you also want to make sure your classmates will be able to follow your presentation easily. (See the section on "Delivering Your Presentation" for more on your relationship to your listeners.)

Planning the Introduction

Introductions in oral presentations have two main purposes. First, you need to get your listeners' attention by introducing the topic in a way that will make them interested in what you have to say. An amusing anecdote, a telling example, a startling fact or statistic, or a controversial statement by an authority on the topic are possible opening strategies. Second, you need to help listeners follow your presentation by forecasting its organization as well as its content. At the beginning of your talk, tell your listeners what your main points are and how you will cover them. Provide them with the structure of your presentation, so they will know where they are in its development. Remind them periodically of what you've covered and what is coming next.

Arranging Your Material

A consistent scheme of organization is key to making your presentation easy to follow. Depending on your material, you can use a chronological, topical, or problem and solution type of organization. Provide explicit transitions so that listeners can see how the parts of your presentation are related. For example, you might say, "Now that we've seen the scope of the problem of homelessness, we can turn to three proposals to deal with it." Help your listeners keep the "big picture" in mind by connecting the main points and omitting extraneous details. Some details may be interesting in their own right, but if they don't help lead your listeners through the main points of the material you're presenting, then you should resist the temptation to include them.

Planning the Ending

As just noted, transitions are an important part of an effective oral presentation—to help listeners keep the main points in mind and to see how the parts of your talk hang together. This is especially true about the ending of a presentation. Cue your listeners that you are ending with markers that refer back to your main points, such as "In closing, I want to emphasize. . . " or "To review the key points. . . " At the same time, you want to conclude with something more than a mere summary. You might use, for example, an example or idea that illustrates the crux of your talk, a troubling question that remains, or research that needs to be done. End on a strong note. Nothing undermines an ending like a nervous giggle or a shrug and "I guess that's it."

Being Prepared for Questions

One of the advantages of oral presentations is that the audience is present and can respond immediately with questions and comments. If your instructor wants a period of questions and responses after the presentation, pause for a moment after your ending and then say something like "I'd be happy to try to answer any questions you might have." If you are not sure you understand a question, ask the person who raised it for clarification. If you don't know the answer to a question, don't fake it or act defensively. Just say you don't know.

DESIGNING AND USING VISUAL AIDS

Visual communication in your presentation not only offers a way to hold listeners' attention and help them remember key points. It can also help you plan your presentation, because the design of visuals enables you to distill your material into its most essential elements. You can then find ways to represent this information clearly and concisely on a transparency or PowerPoint slide. Think of visuals not as secondary sources to illustrate information at various points in the presentation but as a visualization of the structure of the presentation and each of its main points. If you've done a good job of designing your visuals, your audience should be able to grasp the main points of your presentation from reading the visuals you show.

Here are some suggestions for designing and using visual aids to enhance your oral presentation:

DESIGNING VISUALS

- **Design a visual for each main point in your presentation:** Once you have determined the main points in the presentation, write them out in a list. Now you can begin to consider how best to represent each point visually. In some cases, your visuals will consist of an outline or key phrases. In other cases, the visuals may be a table, graph, or other type of illustration.

- **Keep text as concise as possible:** Visual aids with text elements should give audience members enough information to follow the presentation. They should be able to coordinate easily what appears on a visual aid and what you are saying. Long or dense passages of text will distract the audience from the spoken presentation.

- **Use tables, graphs, or other illustrations selectively and accurately:** You may well want to reproduce visuals directly from sources you've read, or you may design your own representation of information. Your selection should be keyed to the main points in your presentation. In either case, make sure your visuals render the information accurately—and that they provide your audience with a label of the information being presented and cite its source.

- **Use large type, clear fonts, and an appropriate color scheme:** Fourteen- to 24-point type size will usually give an easily readable projection on a transparency or PowerPoint presentation, depending on the size of the room where you'll be speaking. Don't use more than two different fonts (such as Times and Helvetica) or more than two different styles (such as bold and italic) on a single visual. In general, use dark type on a light background. Light text on a dark background can look attractive but may not be easily readable, especially in a room with the lights on. Your visual aids should have a clean and professional look. Avoid a visual presentation that will appear busy or unserious.

- **Decide how you will produce and display your visuals:** Take into account the time, money, and technical expertise you have available, as well as the facilities in the room where you'll be making your presentation. PowerPoint is becoming increasingly popular for academic and professional presentations but requires certain skill and access to computer resources. Producing transparencies for an overhead projector is a simpler procedure and is still widely done. Whichever you decide, make sure you have time to rehearse your presentation with your visuals, so that you feel comfortable integrating them into the flow of your talk.

USING VISUAL AIDS IN A PRESENTATION

- **Refer to the visuals as they appear in your presentation:** Your audience, quite rightly, will expect that there's a good reason for the visuals to show up in your presentation. As mentioned earlier, each visual should be linked to a key point in your presentation. As they appear, explain to your audience what they should see in each.

- **Don't stand between your audience and the visual:** Your audience should be able to see both you and your visual aid.

- **Look at your audience, not at the visual:** Maintaining eye contact with your audience is an important way of holding their attention and involving them in the presentation. You want them to feel that you are talking to them—not to the visual you are showing.

- **If appropriate, use a pointer to direct attention:** You can use either an old-fashioned pointer or a laser highlighter to stress particular aspects of a visual.

- **Don't leave visuals on display once you move to a new point:** If you don't have a visual to show, simply turn off the projector until you need it again. This way you can keep the audience's attention on you and main lines of the presentation.

REHEARSING YOUR PRESENTATION

Even if you know your material well, you can undermine all your work unless you rehearse enough. No matter how intelligent the speaker, an audience will associate long pauses, mumbling, failure to make eye contact, awkward transitions, or fumbling with visual aids as evidence of the presenter's lack of familiarity with the topic and lack of planning. To make sure you don't send the wrong message, you've got to practice.

In fact, rehearsing your presentation is not just something you do once you've finished preparing it. Rehearsing can be an important way of developing and revising what you've got on paper. In many cases, it's only when a speaker practices that he or she becomes aware that more information is needed in a section of the talk or that the proper emphasis on main points isn't coming through effectively.

To get the most out of rehearsing, you need an audience. Some speakers practice in front of a mirror, but another person (or even better, a group of people) can provide you with kinds of feedback that may not occur to you. Or you may be able to record your presentation with a video camera, so that you can review it to determine what changes are called for. However you rehearse, though, you need some criteria to evaluate the presentation. Here are some suggestions about what to look for:

GUIDELINES FOR EVALUATING ORAL PRESENTATIONS

❏ Is the purpose of the presentation clear from the start?

❏ Is the presentation easy to follow? Do listeners know where they are at each point along the way?

❏ Do major points receive proper emphasize? Do they stand out clearly?

❏ Does the speaker use variation in tone, pitch, and loudness to emphasize major points? A monotone puts listeners to sleep, but verbal emphasis at inappropriate points will throw listeners off.

❏ Is the pace of the presentation appropriate? Too fast a pace makes an audience think the speaker is rushing through just to get it done, while going too slow can make them start to squirm.

❏ Does the speaker maintain effective eye contact with listeners?

❏ Does the speaker handle the visuals smoothly and effectively? Are the visuals well coordinated with the presentation? Are they easy to read?

❏ Does the speaker use gestures and body language effectively during the presentation?

❏ Does the presentation stay within the time allotted?

Answers to these questions can give you important information about how you need to change your presentation. Make sure you give yourself time to practice the revised version.

DELIVERING YOUR PRESENTATION

It is perfectly reasonable to be nervous about making an oral presentation. After all, you're going to be up in front of a number of people, and you want to make a good impression on them—your instructor and classmates alike. It helps, of course, if you know your material and have practiced your presentation, but there's no guaranteed way to eliminate nervousness altogether. Even the most experienced presenters get nervous. The trick is to put this nervous energy to work.

Some simple techniques can help you deal with nervousness. One is to breathe slowly and regularly, right before your presentation and then throughout it. Another technique, practiced by many athletes and public performers, is positive visualization, in which you go over in your mind the successful delivery of your presentation and the engagement of your listeners. A third technique, about which we'll say more, is to think of your presentation not just as transmitting information but as forming a relationship with your listeners.

Confronted with the task of delivering an oral presentation, students may well think, "I wish I didn't have to do this. I don't really know anything about chemistry, and I'm sure nobody is interested in what I have to say. I'm just doing it because my instructor is making me." These thoughts are perhaps understandable, but they aren't much help. Our suggestion is to change this way of thinking. Imagine instead that you are a knowledgeable person who wants to convey something of interest to listeners. You may not know everything about your subject, but your preparation should have given you a certain expertise about the material you are presenting. Think of your listeners as a group of people with whom you want to share this information. Imagine not that you're all alone in front of the class but that you are interacting with involved listeners, drawing them into the problems and issues in your talk. Assume, in short, that you and everyone else in the room is fully engaged in—even fascinated by—the material you are covering and all the good reasons there are for thinking about it. Whether this is actually true is beside the point. If you act as though both you and your listeners care about your presentation, you are much more likely to form a positive and effective relationship with them—and your presentation is much more likely to go well.

POWERPOINT™ DO'S AND DONT'S

ELLEN LUPTON

Ellen Lupton is a leading graphic designer, teacher, and theorist who uses PowerPoint to present advice about effective design. You can find the complete deck of PowerPoint slides at www.designwritingresearch.org/archive.html.

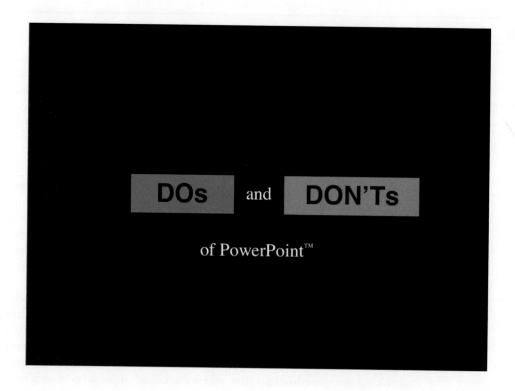

DON'T Use PowerPoint as a teleprompter.

Never fill up the screen with every word you plan to say.

DO Break up your text into manageable chunks.

Respect your audience.

Write less. Use more space.

THIS IS TOO MUCH TEXT

PowerPoint has become a ubiquitous medium of business communication. At sales meetings, training seminars, and conferences, the audience has come to expect a PowerPoint slide show with every talk. This is not necessarily a good thing. Not only do people expect PowerPoint, they also expect it to be dull. PowerPoint has become associated with puffed-up presentations by paid consultants, corny "interactive" discussions led by professional facilitators, and any dull event where you get a free pencil. The fact is, everyone should learn PowerPoint. But you need to learn to use it well, and you need to know when not to use it at all.

BULLETS ARE NOT ENOUGH

- PowerPoint has become a ubiquitous medium of business communication.
- At sales meetings, training seminars, and conferences, the audience has come to expect a PowerPoint slide show.
- This is not necessarily a good thing.
- Not only do people expect PowerPoint, they expect it to be dull.
- PowerPoint has become associated with puffed-up presentations by paid consultants, corny "interactive" discussions led by professional facilitators, and any dull event where you get a free pencil.
- The fact is, everyone should learn PowerPoint.
- But you need to learn to use it well, and you need to know when not to use it at all.

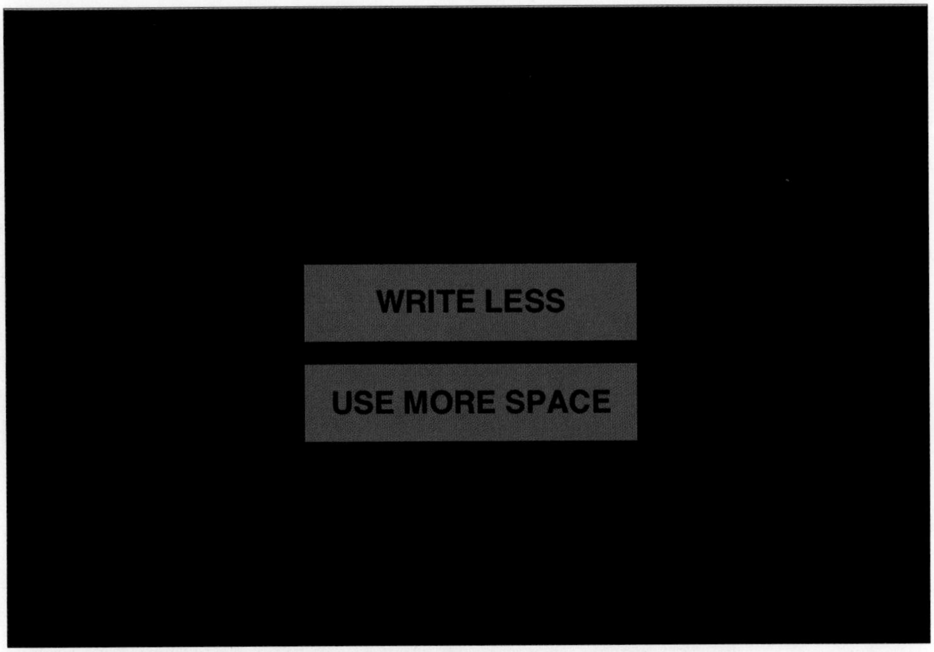
WRITE LESS
USE MORE SPACE

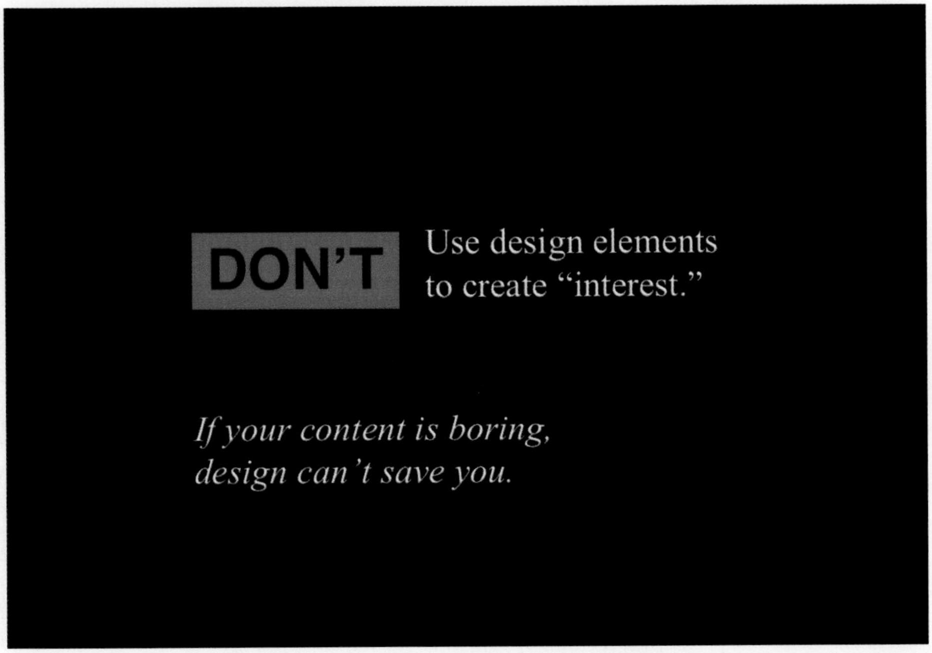
DON'T
Use design elements to create "interest."
If your content is boring, design can't save you.

EXCITING BACKGROUND. DULL CONTENT.

●PowerPoint has become a ubiquitous medium of business communication.
●At sales meetings, training seminars, and conferences, the audience has come to expect a PowerPoint slide show.
●This is not necessarily a good thing.
●Not only do people expect PowerPoint, they expect it to be dull.
●PowerPoint has become associated with puffed-up presentations by paid consultants, corny "interactive" discussions led by professional facilitators, and any dull event where you get a free pencil.
●The fact is, everyone should learn PowerPoint.
●But you need to learn to use it well, and you need to know when not to use it at all.

DO   Use design elements to build or emphasize content.

Colors, boxes, bullets, and font variations CAN make your presentation more clear and meaningful.

USE A HIERARCHY OF FONT SIZES AND SHORT BULLET POINTS

People expect PowerPoint during

- puffed-up presentations by paid consultants
- corny meetings led by professional facilitators
- any event where you get a free pencil

 Use preprogrammed presentation designs.

A little design is a dangerous thing.

These preprogrammed designs are just distracting.

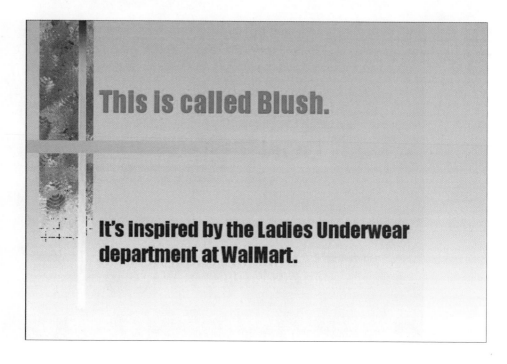

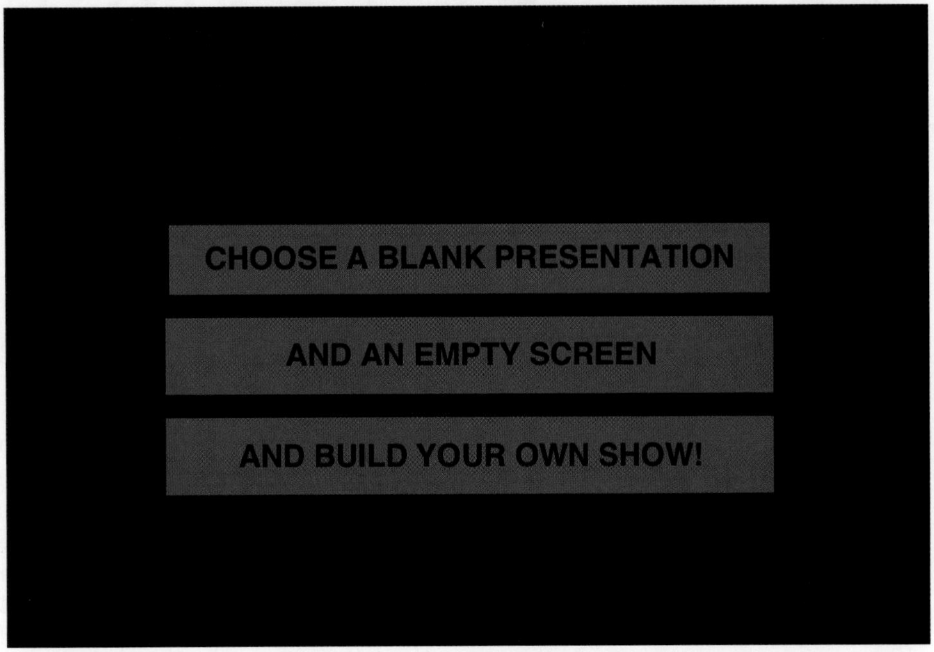
CHOOSE A BLANK PRESENTATION
AND AN EMPTY SCREEN
AND BUILD YOUR OWN SHOW!

chapter 22

essay exams

Essay examinations are certainly among the most challenging writing situations you face in college. The reason is pretty straightforward. Whether the exam consists of identification items, short-answer questions, full-length essays, or a combination, you have to write under pressure. First, there is the pressure to finish all the parts of an exam within the allotted time. Then, there is the pressure of writing on demand, when someone else—namely, your instructor—chooses the topics and asks the questions. There is also the pressure of writing for evaluation, to demonstrate to your instructor that you understand the course material and can work with it in meaningful ways. Finally, there is the pressure of writing without having available the usual resources, such as notes, textbooks, articles, a dictionary, and so on—a pressure that calls on you to write from recall.

As many students can attest (and many teachers remember from their days as students), these pressures can be anxiety provoking. Small wonder. After all, something real is on the line, you can't know in advance exactly what will appear on the exam, and you have to produce on the spot, often by juggling multiple parts of a test. At the same time, writing under pressure can push you to new insights and unforeseen connections—when the course material seems to jell in ways you had not quite imagined. Exams indeed call on you to perform for a grade, but successful students realize that exams can also be important learning experiences, in which you clarify for yourself the main themes and key concepts in a course. In fact, grades often depend on this kind of clarification, as it takes place in response to the questions on an exam.

The writing task you face on essay exams can be stated quite simply: you need to produce a good first draft in the time you're given. To do this, you'll need to develop an overall approach to writing essay exams. Developing a systematic strategy is your best bet to deal with the pressures of an essay exam and to maximize your performance. In the following sections, we'll look at the four basic steps of successful exam writing:

1. Preparing for essay exams.
2. Analyzing the format and questions of an exam.
3. Planning an answer.
4. Writing the essay exam.

PREPARING FOR ESSAY EXAMS

Your preparation for an essay exam should begin at the very start of the course. Going to class, taking good notes, keeping up with the readings, doing the assignments, and participating in discussion sections are all ways to prepare for exams—and are generally more successful than cramming at the last minute. But this is no doubt advice you've heard before. Assuming that you're keeping up, the real question is how you can get the most out of studying the material in the course.

Students sometimes equate studying with simply memorizing bodies of information. Now certainly, in some courses, where the exams consist of multiple-choice, true/false, matching, and fill-in-the-blank items, test taking may rely heavily on the recall of memorized information. Make sure you understand how you will be tested. It's perfectly reasonable to ask your instructor, a teaching assistant, or a student who has already taken the course about the types of exams you can expect so that you can plan your study accordingly.

In courses with essay exams, you'll need to recall information, but largely to show what you can do with it: how you can relate facts, details, examples, terms, and so on to the main themes and key concepts of the course. In such courses, instructors are not likely to hold you responsible for every item of information covered in the class. Instead, they want to see whether you can identify the central issues of the course and explain how information fits together in meaningful patterns. The danger of relying exclusively on memorization in these courses is that it can cause you to stuff your head full of separate items of information and fail to see the big picture.

In this sense, preparing for essay exams amounts to finding the big picture—the main ideas, terminology, controversies, explanations, and conceptual frameworks in a course. You can do this in part by paying attention to chapter headings, summaries, and highlighted terms in your textbook and in part by noticing what your instructor emphasizes in lectures, writes on the board, or includes in review sheets distributed before exams. Teachers and textbooks alike will often mark key points: "The two most important criticisms of sociobiology are . . . " or "The three main factors that led to the construction of the Ringstrasse in 19th-century Vienna are . . . "

Pay attention to how the material in the course is divided. If it is organized chronologically, look for distinct periods (such as Reconstruction or the Great Depression) and the emergence of artistic, intellectual, and political trends (such as the Harlem Renaissance, Freudian psychoanalysis, or McCarthyism). If the course is organized thematically, look for connections between readings and the central themes. If the course presents an introduction to a broad field of study, keep track of the topics that form the separate sections. You may want to meet regularly with a small study group of classmates to review course material and discuss the most important themes and concepts.

As exams approach, you (and your study group) can prepare by trying to anticipate questions your instructor might ask and what an effective answer might be. Remember that an essay exam is likely to call on you to work with the course material—not just to recall information but to analyze key themes, explain their significance, make an interpretation, defend a position, criticize a theory, or recommend a path of action.

■ **WORKING TOGETHER**

Preparing for Exams

Work together with two or three other students. Read a chapter from a textbook in a course one or more of you are taking. As a group, identify key ideas, terms, concepts, theories, controversies, and so on in the chapter. Write two essay questions based on the chapter. Present the questions to your class, explaining why you think they capture central issues in the chapter.

ANALYZING ESSAY EXAMS

As you begin taking an essay exam, you can save yourself a lot of problems by paying close attention to the overall format of the exam and by reading each question carefully.

SURVEYING THE FORMAT

Before you start writing answers to exam questions, take time to survey the format of the exam. Notice how many questions there are, how many points each one carries, and any directions about how long an answer should be or how much space the exam allots to it.

Use this information to divide your time so that you'll be able to answer each question. Careful time management can keep you from running out of time.

As you survey the exam, make some tentative decisions about which questions to answer when choices are offered, and the order you will follow. You don't have to take the exam from start to finish. Students often find they do their best when they begin with the questions that seem the easiest to them. By doing the easiest questions first, you can build some confidence before tackling questions you find more difficult. But if you do decide to answer questions out of their order, make sure you don't inadvertently skip a question altogether.

ANALYZING EXAM QUESTIONS

Analyzing exam questions is really a matter of recognizing the type of question and then clarifying what the question is calling on you to do. The three most common types of questions that call for written answers are identification items (often called IDs), short-answer questions, and essays. They differ in the length of writing called for and in the points they carry. Usually you can tell the type of question at a glance, according to its format, the directions it gives, and the amount of space provided for an answer.

Identification Items (IDs)

Identification items normally call for short statements that identify or define material from the course. You'll frequently get a series of items, and usually each item will carry only a few points.

Sample ID Items (from Media and Mass Communication)

Define each term in a sentence or two. (2 points each)

    a. cognitive dissonance
    b. agenda-setting
    c. technological determinism
    d. hot and cool media
    e. gate-keepers

ID items such as these call on you to define course topics clearly and concisely. Most often, you'll have only a few minutes to spend on each item. For example,

a. Cognitive dissonance is a state of psychological discomfort that occurs when information a person receives is inconsistent with the person's already held attitudes.

Short-Answer Questions

Short-answer questions call for answers that can range from a sentence or two to a mini-essay. Typically short answers are a paragraph or two in length. Depending on the question, you'll have anywhere from a few minutes to ten minutes or so to write your answer.

Sample Short-Answer Questions (from General Chemistry)

Answer each question in a sentence or two. (5 points each)

    1. Contrast *mass* and *weight.*
    2. Define the word *molecule.*
    3. Explain the relationships among the number of protons, neutrons, and electrons in an atom.
    4. Compare *physical processes* with *chemical processes.*
    5. Describe how a percent yield is calculated for a chemical reaction.

Note that a key term in each question—"contrast," "define," "explain," "compare," and "describe"—gives directions about what to do with course topics such as "mass," "weight," "molecule," and so on.

Sample Short-Answer Questions (from Early American History)

Write a paragraph or two on each of the following items. Define the term and explain why it is significant. (10 points each)

1. The Glorious Revolution
2. The Middle Passage
3. Virgin Soil Epidemics

Note that the key terms in this question call first for the recall of information about a particular course topic ("define") and second for an elaboration of its significance ("explain"). For example,

1. The Glorious Revolution

In 1688, James II baptized his first son a Catholic, thereby perpetuating a Catholic monarchy in England. Fed up with James's arbitrary rule, parliamentary leaders responded by inviting James's Protestant daughter Mary and her husband William of Orange to take over as king and queen. James fled to France, and this bloodless change in the monarchy became known as the Glorious Revolution.

The Glorious Revolution had significant effects on the colonies. Colonists in Boston arrested the royal governor Sir Edward Andros and restored the colonial assembly he had tried to abolish. The Bill of Rights and Toleration Act passed by parliament in 1689 limited the power of rulers and guaranteed a degree of

---

GUIDELINES FOR ANALYZING EXAM QUESTIONS

The following guidelines can help you analyze any exam question that calls for a written answer.

❑ Look for key terms in the exam questions. Some key terms—such as "describe," "summarize," "explain," "analyze," and "evaluate"—provide directions. Other key terms are topics from course material. Take, for example, the exam question: "Describe the Monroe Doctrine and give two examples of when it was used." The key term "Monroe Doctrine" refers to a topic from lectures and reading, while "describe" and "give two examples" provide directions. Putting directions and topics together will help you understand the purpose of the question and clarify how you should treat course material in your answer.

❑ Notice whether the question has more than one part. If so, make sure you understand what each part calls on you to do. The question on the Monroe Doctrine, for example, contains two parts—first to describe it and then to give two examples.

❑ Consider what information you need to answer the question. Draw on course material from lectures, readings, and discussions.

❑ How many points does the question carry? How much time do you have to answer it? How much space is provided on the exam? Use these questions to determine the amount of time you can spend on your answer and how long it should be.

religious freedom. More importantly, the Glorious Revolution set a precedent for revolution against the king. John Locke's defense of the Glorious Revolution, Two Treatises on Government (1690), profoundly influenced political thinking in the colonies by arguing that when rulers violated the people's natural rights, they had the right to overthrow their government.

Essay Questions

Essay questions are usually allotted more time and more points on an exam than ID items and short-answer questions. You'll have more time to plan and write your response. Typically essay questions will give you anywhere from twenty minutes to an hour.

As is true of ID items and short-answer questions, the secret to writing effective exam essays is recognizing what the question calls on you to do. See the "Common Essay Exam Questions" box for descriptions of some of the most common writing tasks you'll encounter on essay exams.

■ **WORKING TOGETHER**

Analyzing Essay Questions

Working with two or three classmates, analyze the essay questions listed in the "Common Essay Exam Questions" box below. What key terms are given—directions and topics? What information would you need to answer the question successfully? What does each question call on students to do in their answers?

COMMON ESSAY EXAM QUESTIONS

❑ **Summarize main ideas.** Asks you to recall main ideas and present them clearly and accurately. Example from an anthropology course:

In their article "The Consequences of Literacy," Ian Watt and Jack Goody trace changes that occur with the rise of literacy. What do they see as the main differences between oral and literate cultures? In their view, what are the main consequences of literacy?

❑ **Explain significance.** Asks you to explain the importance of course material by giving reasons and examples. Example from a history of science course:

Watson's and Crick's discovery in 1953 of the double helical structure of DNA ushered in the "molecular revolution." What

exactly did they discover? Explain the significance of their discovery to the field of biology. Give examples to illustrate the "molecular revolution" they initiated.

❑ **Apply concepts.** Asks you to apply concepts to works studied in the course or to your own experience. Example from an African American literature course:

The theme of "passing" as white appears in a number of important African American novels. Analyze the theme of "passing" in at least three of the following novels we've read: Frances E.W. Harper's *Iola Leroy*, James P. Johnson's *Autobiography of an Ex-Coloured Man*, Jessie Faucett's *Plum Bun*,

(Continued)

Nella Larsen's *Passing*. What do you see as the main differences and similarities in the treatment of this theme?

Example from a sociology course:

Define Erving Goffman's notion of "underlife" behavior. Explain how and why it takes place and in what contexts. Use the notion of "underlife" to explain behavior you have observed or read about.

□ **Discuss a quotation.** Asks you to comment on a quotation you are seeing for the first time. Often written by your instructor, these quotations will typically raise a controversial point to discuss. Example from an American history course:

"The coming of the Civil War and the failures of Reconstruction have been seen by historians and others as failures of morality. This is wrong. The problems were actually political. Smarter politicians could have resolved these problems easily." How would you respond to this argument?

□ **Compare and contrast.** Asks you to analyze similarities and differences between two works or ideas. Example from a Latin American literature course:

Julia Alvarez's *How the Garcia Girls Lost Their Accents* and Cristina Garcia's *Dreaming in Cuban* both treat issues of immigration and acculturation. Compare and contrast the two novels' exploration of cultural identity and change.

□ **Analyze causes.** Asks you to explain why and how something happened. Example from a film course:

Explain the emergence of film noir in Hollywood films of the 1940s and 1950s. What values, beliefs, and ideologies of the time do these films embody?

Example from a Russian history course:

What factors led to Stalin's consolidation of control in the Soviet Union?

□ **Evaluate.** Asks you to make a judgment about the strengths and weaknesses of one or more works

or concepts. Example from a mass communication course:

Evaluate the debate between Walter Lippmann in *The Phantom Public* and John Dewey in *The Public and Its Problems*. Explain the respective positions each thinker takes on the role of the public in political life. What do you see as the strengths and weaknesses of their arguments? Where do you stand in the debate?

□ **Propose a course of action.** Asks you to analyze a problem and propose your own solution. Example from an education course:

Briefly summarize the arguments for and against bilingual education. Then explain what you think should be done. Be specific in describing the kinds of programs you think can be successful.

□ **Synthesize a number of sources.** Asks you to develop a coherent framework to pull together ideas and information from a number of sources. Example from a management course:

You have read case studies of managerial strategies in a number of major companies—IBM, Nike, Harley Davidson, Apple, and General Motors. Based on these readings, explain what you see as the major challenges currently facing management. Use information from the case studies to illustrate your points.

□ **Creative questions.** Occasionally instructors will ask students to take on the identity of a historical or literary character, to write dialogue, or to make other types of creative responses. Example from a colonial Latin American history course:

The year is 1808, and Spanish Americans are reeling from the news that Napoleon has invaded Spain and deposed the king. Two creoles meet in a tavern, and their conversation soon turns to the political future of the colonies. Create a dialogue in which one argues for independence while the other urges continued loyalty to Spain.

PLANNING YOUR ANSWER

How you plan your exam answer depends largely on the type of question and the time and points allotted to it. Answering ID items, for example, should take you just a few seconds to recall the key information you need. For short-answer questions that call for a paragraph or two, you may want to underline key terms in the question or write down a few quick notes to help you organize your answer. (Note in the sample short answer on the Glorious Revolution how the writer uses a key term in the directions to focus each of the two paragraphs: first she "defines" the event and then "explains" why it was significant to the American colonies.)

Full-length essays, of course, will require more planning time. In fact, it's not unusual to spend a quarter of the time allotted planning an answer. Here are some guidelines for planning:

- Read the question carefully, noting key terms to clarify what your purpose should be. What kind of answer is the question calling for? What is the topic of the question? Are you being asked simply to define, describe, or summarize? To what extent are you asked to analyze, interpret, evaluate, or argue according to your own understanding of the material?

- See if the question offers any organizational cues. If the question has multiple parts, consider whether these parts offer a possible scheme to arrange your answer. Often the parts consist of questions that lead logically from one to another.

- Write a brief outline of key points. Begin with the main point—the response that answers the main question being asked. Then decide how to arrange supporting reasons, details, and examples.

- Before you start writing, double-check your outline to make sure it answers what the question asks—not what you want it to say.

Notice how the brief outline below uses the essay question to organize an answer.

Sample Essay Question

You have read arguments for and against legislation to make English the official language in the United States. Write an essay that explains why this has become such a controversial issue. What is at stake for each side in the debate? Explain your own position, citing evidence to support it.

Sample Brief Outline

Main point: Demographic changes in the U.S. and the "new immigration" from Latin America and Asia have called national identity into question.

Pro: Desire for national unity
Anxiety about immigration
Belief that "old immigrants" (1890–1920) assimilated and learned English
    quickly
Con: U.S. as nation of immigrants
Value of many languages in global economy
Belief in multiculturalism
My position: Against English Only legislation
For increased language classes for recent immigrants

WRITING A GOOD ANSWER

Writing a good answer on an essay exam amounts to producing a good first draft. You can make additions and corrections, but you won't have the time to do thorough revisions. Here are some suggestions to help you write an effective answer:

- Essay exams responses don't need introductions to set up the main point. State the main answer to the question in the opening paragraph. One good strategy is to use the question (or main question when there is a series) as the basis of your opening sentence. Answer the question as clearly as you can. First impressions on essay exams count. Your opening paragraph should encapsulate the main line of your thinking and forecast what's to come.

- Provide supporting evidence, reasons, details, and examples in the paragraphs that follow. Draw on material from lectures and readings, but don't pad with extraneous material. You don't need to show off how much you can recall. Instead, you need to show how you can relate supporting evidence to your main answer.

- Highlight your understanding of the course material. Demonstrate how you can work with the information, ideas, and themes in the course. Make sure, however, that you're not just presenting personal opinions for their own sake. Link your insights, evaluations, and proposals to the course material.

- Write an ending, even if you're running out of time. A sentence or two can tie together main points at the end.

- Make additions neatly. New ideas may occur to you as you're writing, and you should incorporate them if they fit into the main line of your thinking. You can add a sentence or two by writing neatly in the margins and using an arrow to show where they go in your answer.

- Write legibly and proofread when you've finished. You can make corrections by crossing out and replacing words and phrases. Do so as neatly as you can. A messy exam is hard to read and creates a negative impression.

- ■ Watch the clock. If you're running out of time or need to go on to another question, it's best to list points from your outline. This way you can show where your essay is going, even if you can't finish it.

SAMPLE ESSAY ANSWERS

The following essay question appeared on an exam in a colonial Latin American history course.

Sample Essay Question

"Latin America's ruling elites maintained their position largely through ideological domination. Witness their ability to make patriarchy an unchallenged social assumption. Aside from such exceptional figures as Sor Juana, women at every level of society readily accepted their inferior status, along with the rigid gender conventions that called for female passivity, obedience, and sexual modesty." Discuss.

As you can see, the essay question is a quotation that takes a position on issues in the course, along with the direction "discuss." The key term "discuss" doesn't seem to provide a lot of guidance, but experienced students know that "discuss" really calls on them to offer their own interpretation of the quotation, along with reasons and supporting evidence from readings and lecture.

Two sample essay answers follow. The first is annotated. You can use the second one to sharpen your own sense of an effective essay answer.

SAMPLE ESSAY ANSWER A

Connects key terms in essay question to establish main focus of the answer.

   Although Latin American elites frequently used a policy of coercion to govern indigenous and African populations, they also used consent to maintain their position in colonial society through ideological domination. Colonial society was based on a hierarchical system of authority and dependence, in which the ruling elite established strong ties with the ruled through a shared ideology. Patriarchy, the social assumption that men were responsible for controlling the lives of women, was central to this shared ideology.

The colonial elite based its political and moral authority on the patriarchal ideology of men's superiority, masculinity, and honor and women's inferiority, modesty, and submission. Dignified men acquired their authority by controlling and protecting their dependents—women, servants, workers, and slaves. Women, on the other hand, were socialized to be modest and obedient and were regarded as dangerous and likely to succumb to temptations, instincts, and desires unless controlled by fathers and husbands.

Explains key term "patriarchal ideology."

From father to husband, men had power over a woman's sexuality. Marriage was used by fathers to improve their status and make alliances with other families. Little consideration was given to a woman's own preferences. Once married, a woman was subordinate to her husband. The crime of rape, for example, was seen not as a crime against the woman but rather an assault on the honor of her father or husband. In cases of rape, fathers or husbands would publicly profess their shame, humiliation, and lack of honor for failing to protect a daughter or wife.

Illustrates key term with details and an example.

There were certain groups that posed exceptions to this gender ideology of male control and female dependence. Heiresses, nuns, and widows negotiated a certain amount of autonomy in specific circumstances. For example, the Condessa de Santiago inherited a fortune and became a powerful economic and political force—until she married and her power ended. Nuns such as Sor Juana found a limited space for self-expression in the convent, as demonstrated by the numerous literary works produced by nuns. Widows were the largest group of autonomous women. By law, dowries reverted to widows when their husbands died. However, women without husbands, especially widows, were suspected of immoral acts. The legend of La Florona, the "weeping widow," illustrates how autonomous women were seen as uncontrolled and threatening.

Notes exceptions and gives examples of exceptions.

In the lower classes, there was a significant gap between the theory and practice of patriarchal ideology. Plebeian women were in the public sphere

Analyzes role of patriarchal ideology among plebeian women.

much more than elite women not because of their greater autonomy but because of financial necessity. The labor these women did as vendors, seamstresses, and domestic servants was hardly empowering, and they were often subjected to verbal, physical, and sexual abuse. In this way, they still adhered to the system of patriarchy and remained the dependents of their male employers.

Analyzes role of patriarchal ideology among plebeian men.

For men, masculinity, honor, and social superiority were achieved by controlling dependents. By accepting such a patriarchal ideology, male plebeians, servants, and slaves were constantly reminded of their own position as dependents, with little economic or political authority over their lives. Lower-class and slave men could not exercise the type of patriarchal control and protect their women as the upper classes did. But because the lower classes believed in patriarchal control, they in effect consented to the moral and political leadership of the upper classes.

Ending ties key terms together.

Morality, dignity, and honor, thus, were identified with the ruling elite in colonial society. This gender ideology reinforced the power of the ruling elite as both women and plebeian men consented to its patriarchal assumptions.

SAMPLE ESSAY ANSWER B

Depending on the circumstances, the ruling elite in colonial Latin America used force or consent to govern. For example, they routinely used military power against the Indian population and to suppress slave revolts. In addition, the Inquisition in Latin America used physical force, including torture to eliminate dissent.

Ideological domination was an important tool of the ruling elite, and patriarchy became one of the unchallenged social assumptions that reinforced the authority of the upper classes. The view was widely held by members of colonial society that men were the natural rulers and that women should be controlled by men. Men were considered authoritative, while women were supposed to be obedient.

Thus women in colonial society were excluded from both economic and political power. Excluded from the priesthood, higher education, and the professions, women were forced to remain in the home. This dependence reinforced male authority and kept women powerless and unable to challenge dominant social assumptions. Because women were the socializers of the family, they transferred this gender ideology to their children and thereby further reproduced the system.

If a woman misbehaved, she would dishonor her father or husband and her household. A stain on a woman's reputation tainted the reputation of her entire family. It was therefore a man's responsibility to control a woman and protect her against herself and keep her in the domestic sphere. Fathers decided the person a woman would marry or if she should become a nun. An unmarried woman in the presence of unmarried men was always accompanied by a chaperone to guard her virtue. Husbands controlled their wives and protected them. By engraining women with the dominant ideology of patriarchy, the elite were able to rule without opposition.

This gender ideology, however, did not transfer completely to the lower classes in colonial society because in order to be proper, women had to come from wealthy families. Single lower-class women often worked before they married, and this was considered threatening to their morals. Still, plebeian women did view males as authority figures. Once they married, they were subordinated to their husbands and restricted to the home. Women were considered devious and threatening and therefore needed to be protected and controlled by male authority.

Lower-class men, however, never achieved total patriarchal power and were in no position to challenge authority figures or social assumptions. While they accepted the rigid gender conventions of the dominant ideology, plebeian men remained dependents in relation to the upper classes. Due to their servile and economically insecure position in society, plebeians could not fully protect their women, which was one of the prerequisites of full manhood as colonial society understood it.

Nuns, heiresses, and widows were able in limited ways to evade patriarchal control. Except for priests, men were basically excluded from convents, and so to some extent the nuns could organize their own affairs. Heiresses might achieve a measure of autonomy by inheriting money, and widows received their dowries if their husbands died.

Overall, though, the gender ideology of patriarchy in colonial Latin America was very unfair to women in general and was used to keep lower-class men in their place.

■ WORKING TOGETHER

Analyzing an Essay Answer

In a group with two or three other students, follow these steps:

1. Look again at the sample essay question on page 627. What exactly does it call on students to do? Clarify for yourselves what seems to be the main writing task facing students who are taking this exam in colonial Latin American history.

2. Read the first sample essay answer and annotations. How well do you think it handles the writing task?

3. Read and analyze the second essay answer. Given your sense of what the writing task calls for and how well the first essay answer handles the task, what do you see as the strengths and weaknesses of the second answer? Be specific. What particular features of the essay work well or not so well?

writing portfolios

Portfolios are often used by painters, graphic designers, architects, photographers, and other visual artists to present their work to teachers, prospective clients, museum officials, gallery owners, fellowship selection committees, and so on. Portfolios enable artists to select a representative sample of their best work and to display it in an organized form. The same is true for writing portfolios. In a writing portfolio, students choose a sample of their work to present as the culminating project of a writing class.

Writing portfolios offer students a number of benefits. Portfolios allow students to decide on the writing they want to present to the teacher for evaluation. Students typically select from among their various writing assignments and revise a limited number for their portfolios. In this way, students can show teachers how they have handled different kinds of writing tasks. Portfolios also provide students with the opportunity to reflect on how they have developed as writers and to explain what the writing they've done means to them as students, learners, and people.

Writing portfolios have benefits for teachers too. A portfolio provides teachers with a range of writing to evaluate instead of single papers. One of the premises of writing portfolios is that teachers can make fairer and more accurate appraisals of student writing if they can read various types of writing, written for various purposes, in various forms, for various audiences.

How portfolios are graded varies. In some writing programs, portfolios are evaluated by one or more other teachers who do blind readings—that is, students' names are removed. In other cases, portfolios are submitted to and graded by the student's teacher. The weight assigned to the portfolio grade varies too. If your teacher asks you to prepare a portfolio, he or she will tell you how much it counts toward your final grade.

WHAT TO INCLUDE IN A PORTFOLIO

To put together a final portfolio, you will need to include samples of various kinds of writing. Your teacher will give you further directions. Some teachers are quite specific about what to include, while others will offer students more room to plan the contents of their portfolios.

AMOUNT OF WRITING TO INCLUDE

Part of designing a portfolio is making decisions about what best represents you as a writer. If you include most of the writing you've done, you defeat the purpose. Many teachers ask for only four or five pieces of writing. Others ask for more or leave the number open to student choice.

TYPE OF WRITING TO INCLUDE

Designing a portfolio asks you to select not only a limited number but also a range of writing that represents the different types you've done. If you include only personal narratives or informative writing or argumentative essays, you won't give readers enough sense of this range, and your portfolio will seem too one—dimensional. Your teacher may tell you exactly what types to include, or you may have more room to decide.

SOME OPTIONS FOR A WRITING PORTFOLIO

Here are some types of writing often included in portfolios.

A REFLECTIVE LETTER

Almost all writing portfolios begin with a letter of reflection that introduces you and your portfolio. The purpose of such a letter is to persuade your instructor (or any other readers) that you have accomplished the goals of the course.

A reflective letter might discuss the choices you made in designing your portfolio, explain your development as a writer and the role of writing in your life, evaluate strengths and weaknesses in your writing, and discuss your experience as a writer and as a person in your writing class. The letter should provide readers with a sense of who you are. It might also indicate where you see yourself going next in developing your writing.

The writing you have done in response to the "Reflecting on Your Writing" assignments throughout the book can provide you with material for your reflective letter.

SAMPLE REFLECTIVE LETTER BY JENNIFER PRINCIPE

Dear Professor Trimbur:

Writing has always been an important form of expression for me. I have always had a hard time expressing myself verbally, and I feel that writing gives me a control over my words that I can't find anywhere else. Writing has almost become a form of medication for me, an objective ear always willing to listen. For as long as I can remember, I have kept a journal that I write in whenever there is something I want to straighten out in my life. My journal is one of the best ways I know to explore my thoughts and decide on a course of action to take. Writing forces me to slow down and really consider how I feel about something. It also creates a permanent record that I can go back to at any time.

Although I enjoy and rely on this sort of informal writing, I have felt for a long time that the formal writing I do in my courses could use improvement, and English 101 has definitely helped me to grow as a formal writer. In high school, my English teachers told me I had good ideas but that my writing was wordy and unfocused. I understood what they were saying, but unfortunately they never explained what I should do about my problem. This made writing a very frustrating experience for me.

In English 101, I think the most important thing I learned is that when I start writing I usually don't have a definite idea of where I am going. What I have found through the writing assignments and the peer commentaries is that my main ideas are often unclear at first, but as I get to the end of a draft they become much clearer. As I write more, I begin to focus on an idea and my essay begins to make more sense. In many cases, I could take ideas from the end of a draft and bring them up to my introduction to give me focus.

The writing samples included in my portfolio were chosen with several criteria in mind. First, I chose writing that I had strong personal feelings about because when I believe in a topic my writing tends to be more passionate and heartfelt, and thus more effective. For this reason, the writing samples that are included in this portfolio are strongly rooted in my personal beliefs. Second, I chose different kinds of writing so readers could see how I approached various writing assignments.

I chose to include the peer commentary I wrote for Joe Scherpa. I don't think this was necessarily the best commentary I did, but I was particularly happy about Joe's reaction to it. A week or so after I completed the commentary, Joe told me that my commentary helped him do a complete revision on that assignment. He seemed grateful for my suggestions and happy with the revised version of his work. Although I realize that my commentary was not the sole motivation for his revisions, I was happy to see that he felt it had made a difference in his writing.

In conclusion, I feel this class has been quite beneficial in my growth as a writer. I got lots of practice in different kinds of writing. I'm planning to major in chemical engineering, and I know that writing will be an important part of my upcoming career, as well as in my personal life. For my career, writing will be a tool that I will often need to get my point across. I feel that I need to work on knowing when to put personal opinions into my writing and when I should be more objective. Sometimes I get carried away by my feelings about a topic. This class has helped me to understand different writing situations, and I think I am now better able to see when the personal side is appropriate and when it's not.

REVISED WRITING ASSIGNMENTS

Portfolios usually include revised writing assignments. This gives you the opportunity to review the work you have done over the course of a term and to decide which writings you want to bring to final form and which best represent your abilities. It's a good idea to select a range of purposes and a range of genres. Your teacher will tell you how many to include.

A CASE STUDY

Some teachers ask for a case study of one of the writing assignments, including a working draft, peer commentary, and the final version, as well as your own explanation of how you worked on the piece of writing. Case studies look in detail at how you planned, drafted, and revised one particular piece of writing.

Case studies offer you the opportunity to analyze the choices you made. Be specific by examining how you drafted and revised a key passage or two.

SAMPLE CASE STUDY BY JOHN URBAN

Introduction

I decided to present my profile of Professor Karen Jackson as a case study because it is the paper I revised the most and the one I got the most helpful peer commentary on. I have included the working draft of the essay, the peer commentary I received, and the final draft.

The peer commentary made me realize a couple of things. First, I hadn't created a good opening to introduce Prof. Jackson. In the revised version, I try to take readers into her lab and give the feeling of meeting her in person.

Second, I think the dominant impression was shaky in the first draft. I was trying to use the idea of putting life into biology as the organizing theme, but it wasn't working. The peer commentary gave me the idea of using the idea of "real reasons" instead. I think this gave a way to link the opening discussion of the premed program to her teaching and research.

Third, I realized the quote about Prof. Jackson's research is both too technical and too long. I tried here and in some other places to cut back on the amount of quoting and to use quotes more effectively.

WORKING DRAFT

Putting the Life Back into Premedical Education: A Profile of Karen Jackson
Given such daunting requirements as organic chemistry and a year of physics, premed students are assumed to be learning science to become better

doctors. Sadly, the message of service often gets left behind in the process. "That's the most frustrating thing about directing the premed program. I assume two things when students tell me they want to go to medical school. First, they are saying 'I am good at science,' and second 'I like working with people.'"

As a professor of biology, department chair, and the director of the premed program at Warehouse State, Karen Jackson works a busy schedule. Between trips to oversee her research project at Memorial Hospital, authorizing department spending, and teaching the introductory biology course, Professor Jackson also advises students interested in medical careers. The hardest part about running the premed program, she says, is "finding students who are in it for the right reasons, and persuading those who aren't to be in it for the right reasons."

A key to Karen Jackson's beliefs about advising premed students comes from decisions she has made in her own life. Early in her career, she was strictly a researcher, focusing on metabolic biochemistry, but she did not feel she was doing enough. "I love research, but I found I also needed the intellectual stimulation and challenge that teaching has provided me." She attributes her success as a teacher to having "perspective."

In her introductory biology course for non-majors, you will not find a class ruled by textbooks, tests, and labs. In this course, there are also discussions on real-life current events in biology. "I have students fill out a survey to find out what interests them. I would rather talk about something they are interested in than sit there and lecture from a book. Biology is not in a textbook. Biology is real life."

As a teacher, Professor Jackson sees the need for more community involvement by students interested in medical careers, as well as by college students in general. "I think there should be a degree requirement of community service. I ask my advisees what they've done for community service, and something to the effect, well, my fraternity raised money for diabetes research.' There is a fundamental misunderstanding there. I am asking what *you* personally have done to help the community, not what your organization has done. Being a doctor is about helping those who most need it, not just raising a little money."

Karen Jackson received a Ph.D. in zoology from the University of Massachusetts. From there, she did a postdoctoral fellowship for the Multiple Sclerosis Foundation at the Medical College of Virginia. As a medical researcher, she has also seen the darker side of her area of expertise. She comments on changes in the health care system. "The business side of medicine is ugly. I'd like to see medicine get back to what is important: the patient. Medicine is a service, and that's exactly what it should do, *serve* the people."

She uses the example of her postdoctoral work, in which a team of researchers identified a gene that when expressed in diabetes patients caused heart defects. "We wanted to publish our work, to let colleagues know what we had discovered, but we were stopped by the company that funded the research because it wanted to patent the gene in hopes of making money in the future." Professor Jackson stressed the importance of focusing research not on profits but on the goal of improving the lives of people.

Karen Jackson continues her research on diabetes when she is not managing the department, running the premed office, and teaching. She looks at the problem of cellular metabolism in diabetes patients. "The general aim of my work is to identify differences in cellular metabolism between normal and diabetic individuals. We use a rat model to study the signal transduction pathway for insulin, which ultimately results in glucose being stored as glycogen. This function is impaired in people with diabetes. Even when provided with insulin, they are unable to activate the enzymes responsible for glycogen synthesis, and since it is a complex and poorly understood pathway, sorting it out in normal cells may give us a handle on what might be changed in the diabetic state."

Whether in the classroom, office, or lab, Professor Jackson is undoubtedly working to put the life back into biology.

John,

I enjoyed reading this and feel like I'm beginning to understand what a unique person Professor Jackson is. You've got a lot of good information here, but I think you can do more to create a dominant impression of her and her work.

The main impression I get is someone who is trying to put the life back in biology, and that comes across to a certain extent but I'm not always sure of what you mean.

For example, the title and opening make it seem like the profile is going to focus on her work as premed adviser when the profile you've written is broader. Also, it wasn't clear in the first paragraph who is speaking. You haven't identified Prof. Jackson as the subject of the profile. You could probably do more in the beginning by setting the scene and introducing readers to Prof. Jackson. What you write about her emphasis on community service is interesting, and I wonder if there are any details you could give to show exactly what she means.

I found it a bit confusing when you shift from discussing what Prof. Jackson sees as the "right reasons" for being a premed student to her teaching and research. I pretty much expected to hear more about her sense of "right reasons."

Finally, I think Prof. Jackson's description of her research is too technical and hard to understand.

FINAL DRAFT

"Real Reasons": The Many Missions of Karen Jackson

The door says 405C, and I walk into the newly remodeled lab of Professor Karen Jackson. New countertops, sinks, cabinets, and shelves stand glistening and ready for use, with just a hint of dust left from construction. In the middle of the room, however, resides the hulking mass of an old, defective heating unit that had been replaced by more reliable temperature controls. Even before I catch my first glimpse of Professor Jackson, I hear her voice as she talks on the phone to the contractor who redesigned 405C. "What do you mean you don't normally remove old equipment?!? That thing needs to go, and you need to find a way to haul it out of here."

Then I see her, wearing a t-shirt with a "Stop Domestic Violence" sign, jeans, and sneakers. I fidget nervously, hoping I don't fit in the same category as the contractor. As she hangs up the phone, she becomes aware of my presence, smiles warmly, and says, "Drat these details. You're just the guy I wanted to see. Let's talk."

Karen Jackson is a woman on many missions, and she plays a range of roles at Warehouse State—as a diabetes researcher, biology professor, department chair, and director of the premed program. She admits right away that "I can make people nervous because I know how I feel and am not afraid to voice my opinion." She has seen many aspects of biomedicine, and she doesn't always like what she sees.

She tells me that a crucial part of medicine is often overlooked by premed students, the importance of being involved in the community. She believes there should be a community service requirement for premeds and for college students in general. "I ask my advisees what they've done for the community," she says, "and they normally say something to the effect, 'well, my fraternity raised money for diabetes research.' There is a fundamental misunderstanding there. I am asking what *you* personally have done to help the community, not what your organization has done. Being a doctor is about helping those who most need it, not just raising a little money."

To help premed and other students see what she means, Professor Jackson has set up a number of community service projects on domestic violence and health needs assessment of recent immigrants. She pulls out a copy of a report she and premed students wrote on the health situation of Cambodians who have settled in the Worcester area. Working on a project like this, Professor Jackson says, can help premeds understand the "right reasons" for pursuing a medical career.

According to Jackson, there are many "wrong reasons to become a doctor. Premeds tell me one of their parents is a doctor or doctors make a lot of money." The "right reasons," she says, are "being good at science" and "liking to work with people." As she sees it, her job as director of the premed program centers on "finding students who are in it for the right reasons and persuading those who aren't to be in it for the right reasons."

Another mission Professor Jackson has embarked on is to improve the introductory biology course for non-majors, and here the issue of "right reasons" comes in again. In her course, you will not find a class ruled by textbooks, tests, and labs. In this course, there are also discussions on real-life current events in biology. The "real reason" to study biology, she says, is to understand living organisms and how biologists go about investigating, not to memorize details. She has students fill out a survey to see what questions they have about biology, and she routinely integrates such current topics as genetically modified food, mad cow disease, and environmental toxins to illustrate principles of biology. She wants her students to see that "biology is not in a textbook" but a matter of "real life."

Not all of Karen Jackson's missions are solo sorties. In her current research on diabetes, she works with a team at Memorial Hospital to identify the differences in cellular metabolism between normal and diabetic individuals. She got started as a medical researcher at the University of Massachusetts, where she received a Ph.D. in zoology. From there, she did a postdoctoral fellowship for the Multiple Sclerosis Foundation at the Medical College of Virginia. As a medical researcher, she has seen the darker side of her area of expertise. She comments on changes in the health care system. "The business side of medicine is ugly. I'd like to see medicine get back to what is important: the patient. Medicine is a service, and that's exactly what it should do, *serve* the people."

She uses the example of her postdoctoral work to highlight the "right reasons" to do biomedical research. In this case, she was on a team of researchers who identified a gene that when expressed in diabetes patients caused heart defects. "We wanted to publish our work, to let colleagues know what we had discovered, but we were stopped by the company that funded the research because it wanted to patent the gene in hopes of making money in the future." Professor Jackson stresses the importance of focusing research not on profits but on the goal of improving the lives of people.

Whether it is on the frontlines of biomedical research, in the classroom, or in advising premed students, Karen Jackson is on a mission. Her inescapable personality and warm demeanor work to motivate those around her. She may make some people nervous, like the contractor who remodeled her lab. But she has taken on the mission of challenging people to see the "right reasons" for what they do. And that's the way she likes it.

PEER COMMENTARY

If you have written peer commentaries about other students' work, you may want to include a representative one, prefaced with an explanation of what you learned through the peer commentaries and what it was like for you to do them.

SAMPLE INTRODUCTION TO PEER COMMENTARY BY MARGARET KING

At first, it was difficult to criticize a classmate's work for fear of being too harsh and possibly offending them. But as the term progressed, it became easier because I learned what to look for and how to make helpful suggestions.

I realized that as a writer I wanted my classmates to give me honest feedback and that the best peer commentaries I got didn't try to judge my working draft but to give me suggestions about what to do with it. I tried to apply these ideas to the peer commentaries I wrote. I think the peer commentaries gave me insight as a writer and helped me to learn to read more critically and make choices in the revision process.

COMMENTARY ON COLLABORATIVE WRITING

If you were involved in a collaborative writing project, you might write a short commentary about your experience. What role did you play in the group's work? How does collaborative writing differ from individual writing? What is gained? What, if anything, is lost? Explain your thoughts and feelings about your involvement in producing a group-written project.

SAMPLE INTRODUCTION TO COLLABORATIVE WRITING BY DAVID SANCHEZ

To me, group projects have both good and bad points. Luckily, however, I believe the good points outweigh the bad points. In my opinion, the worst part about doing a group project is setting up meetings. With an abundant amount of other work, finding a time that everyone can meet sometimes becomes difficult. In addition, when the group finally meets, you usually end up talking about other things and basically just hanging out. It seems that for every hour or so of a meeting, only about thirty minutes of work is done.

On a good note, however, the actual project usually produces an interesting result. By having more than one person work on a project, especially a written one, a better result will usually come out. Each person adds a different view and also finds mistakes others have missed. As we have seen through our writing assignments, no one can write a perfect paper the first time. Through each peer commentary, many possible areas of improvement come to light and therefore a better final paper. The same is true of writing a paper with other people.

An additional drawback to writing a group paper, however, is that since it is written by more than one person, more than one idea is conveyed. Yes, as I said before, this is good in a way, but it also makes it harder to write a creative paper. Each person ends up having to modify their view in order to go along with everyone else.

Another bad thing, which can arise from some group projects, occurs when one or more people in the group do not do their parts. When this happens, the other people in the group end up doing too much work and get frustrated. I was happy to find that both John and Joe were willing to do the work. We first met a couple of times to decide on a topic for the project and to begin work. Next we all contributed to the collection of data for the survey. We then divided the paper into three sections, and each wrote one. Finally we had a meeting in order to bring the three parts together and to write an introduction and a conclusion.

Overall, I enjoyed doing the group project with John and Joe. Prior to doing it, I had not known either of them very well. Through this project, I can say that I have become friends with both of them. We all worked together quite well and produced a project I was happy with.

SAMPLES OF EXPLORATORY WRITING

If you have done exploratory writing, you could include a few samples that, for whatever reason, you like the most. Write an introduction that explains what it was like for you to do exploratory writing, what you learned, how this kind of writing differs from other writing assignments, the benefits you see, and so on.

SAMPLE INTRODUCTION TO EXPLORATORY WRITING BY JOHN HOGAN

Exploratory writing was one of my favorite things in this course. When doing this type of writing, I felt free to say what I wanted, any way I wanted. All of this freedom allowed me to put down on paper exactly what I was thinking. Usually when writing a more formal paper, I find that as I am writing I spend too much time making sure everything is structurally and grammatically correct. Many times I lose sight of some of my new ideas, as I try to perfect the previous ones. Here, there was no pattern or structure that had to be followed. When doing exploratory writing I simply wrote and did not worry about grammar, spelling, unity, or coherence.

MISCELLANEOUS

Depending on your teacher's directions, you may include a miscellany of writing done in or out of class—letters, notes, email, newsgroup dialog, poetry, fiction, posters, leaflets, flyers, and so on. Introduce these writings and explain what called on you to write them and how they differ from the other writing in your portfolio.

ONLINE PORTFOLIOS

People usually think of portfolios as a sequence of printed documents that readers go through from start to finish. If your teacher agrees, you could design an online portfolio on the Web. You would need, of course, to include all the required components of a print portfolio. A challenging part of designing such an online portfolio is making it easy for readers to understand how the parts are linked together.

Credits

TEXT CREDITS

ACORN Katrina Survivors Organization flyer, http://acorn.org/fileadmin/KatrinaRelief/
AKSA. Reprinted by permission of Steve Bachmann on behalf of ACORN.

Amnesty International homepage, www.amnesty.org. Copyright © 2006. Reprinted by
permission of International Secretariat, Amnesty International, London; "Call for
Human Rights in Russia," reprinted by permission of Amnesty International,
Washington, D.C.

Anchorage District Soccer Federation Web site, "More Than One Third of Anchorage's
Sports Participants Are Soccer Players," from www.anchoragesoccer.org. Reprinted
by permission.

Associated Press, "Mentally Ill People Aren't More Violent, Study Finds," as appeared in
Providence Journal-Bulletin, May 14, 1995. Reprinted with permission of The
Associated Press.

Baldwin, James, "My Dungeon Shook: Letter to My Nephew on the One Hundredth
Anniversary of the Emancipation." © 1962, 1963 by James Baldwin. Originally
published in *The Progressive*. Collected in *The Fire Next Time*, published by Vintage
Books. Copyright renewed. Reprinted by arrangement with the James Baldwin Estate.

"Be Green Neighborhood Association," from the Center for Environmental Studies at
Brown University, www.brown.edu/Research/EnvStudies_Theses/summit/. Used by
permission.

Berry, Jason, "Cancer Alley: The Poisoning of the American South," photos by Richard
Misrach, essay by Jason Berry, from *Aperture* 162 (Winter 2001). Text reprinted by
permission of Jason Berry.

Botstein, Leon, "Let Teenagers Try Adulthood," *New York Times* Op-Ed, May 17, 1999.
Copyright © 1999 The New York Times. Reprinted by permission.

Boxer, Sarah, "I Shop, Ergo I Am: The Mall as Society's Mirror," *New York Times*, March
28, 1998. Copyright © 1998 The New York Times Co. Reprinted by permission.

Braun, Lundy, PhD, "How to Fight the New Epidemics," *Providence Journal-Bulletin*,
May 29, 1995. Reprinted by permission.

Brody, Michael, Letter to the editor. Reprinted by permission of author.

Brown, Michael, "FEMA and Katrina" email correspondence, August 2005.

Brown University Library screenshots from *Josiah*, the online catalog of the Brown
University Library, are reprinted by permission.

Buhle, Paul, "Profile of Mike Alewitz," from *Insurgent Images: The Agitprop Murals of
Mike Alewitz*. Reprinted by permission of the author.

647

Finkel, Nina, "Hot Spots of Overfishing" and "Catching More Fish," reproduced by permission of Nina Finkel.

Fitzpatrick, Mike, Facebook.com profile page. Reprinted by permission of Mike Fitzpatrick and Facebook, Inc.

"Folk Songs for the Five Points," Web page at www.tenement.org/folksongs/client/. Reprinted by permission of David Gunn.

Forkscrew Graphics, "iRaq," at www.forkscrew.com/iraqyellow.html. Reprinted by permission of Forkscrew Graphics.

Frere-Jones, Sasha, "1979," *The New Yorker*, November 1, 2004. Reprinted by permission of the author.

"Fuel Economy Standards for Autos," *New York Times*, August 9, 1978. Copyright © 1978 The New York Times Co. Reprinted by permission.

Fusco, Coco, "Coco Fusco's Virtual Laboratory," from www.thing.net/~cocofusco/. Reprinted by permission of Coco Fusco.

Gelbspan, Ross, "Rx for an Ailing Planet," *Boston Globe*, April 22, 2003. Reprinted by permission of the author.

Goodman, Ellen, "Minneapolis Pornography Ordinance," *Boston Globe,* 1985. © 1985, The Washington Post Writers Group. Reprinted with permission.

Guglielmetti, Krista, "Family Life and Television" and related writings. Reprinted by permission of the author.

Heller, Steven and Karen Pomeroy, from *Design Literacy: Understanding Graphic Design*. Copyright © 1997. Reprinted by permission of Steven Heller.

Hogan, John, "Introduction to Exploratory Writing." Reprinted by permission of the author.

Holden, Stephen, "After 20 Years, It Still Comes Out Swinging," *New York Times*, August 4, 2000. Copyright © 2000 The New York Times Co. Reprinted by permission.

Home Energy Assistance Program (HEAP) forms, United States Department of Health and Human Services.

"How the Influx Is Changing the U.S.," from *Time*, February 2006. © 2006 Time, Inc. Reprinted by permission.

"Income Distribution," from the City of Niles, Michigan, Web site, www.ci.niles.mi.us/CommonElements/Profile.html. Reprinted by permission.

"The Insider," www.theinsider.org. Reproduced with permission from Tim V. Acheson, BSc (Editorial Director).

Jones, Scott, review of *Grand Theft Auto: San Andreas*, December 1, 2004. Reprinted by permission of Scott Jones.

Kennedy, Jeffrey, *DK Eyewitness Top 10 Travel Guide: San Francisco* (New York: Dorling Kindersley, 2004). Copyright © Dorling Kindersley, 2004. Text reproduced by permission of Penguin Books Ltd.

Kozol, Jonathan, "Distancing the Homeless," from *Rachel and Her Children*. Copyright © 1988 by Jonathan Kozol. Used by permission of Crown Publishers, a division of Random House, Inc.

Kraut, Alan, from "Plagues and Prejudice," from *Hives of Sickness: Public Health and Epidemics in New York City*, David Rosner, ed. New Brunswick, NJ: Rutgers University Press for the Museum of the City of New York, 1995.

Sweeney, Camille, "In a Chat Room, You Can be NE1: Constructing a Teenage Self Online," *New York Times Magazine*, October 17, 1999.

Tardiff, Kristin, "Letter to the Editor," *Providence Journal-Bulletin*, May 3, 1994. Reprinted by permission of the author.

Taylor, John N., Jr., "Letter to the Editor," *Providence Journal-Bulletin*, May 9, 1994. Reprinted by permission of the author.

Tennant, Dan, Use Them or Lose Them. Reprinted by permission of author.

"Triangle Factory Fire." Web exhibit produced by the Kheel Center for Labor-Management Documentation and Archives, Martin P. Catherwood Library, Cornell University. © 1998-2005. All Rights Reserved. Used by permission.

Trimbur, Lucia, "Training Fighters, Making Men." Reprinted by permission of the author.

Tufte, Edward R., "PowerPoint Is Evil." Reprinted by permission, from Edward R. Tufte, *The Cognitive Style of PowerPoint* (Cheshire, CT: Graphics Press, 2003), as appeared in *Wired* Magazine, September 2003; "Required Fuel Economy Standards: New Cars Built from 1978 to 1985," from *The Visual Display of Quantitative Information* (Cheshire, CT: Graphics Press, 1983). Reprinted by permission.

Verghese, Abraham. Reprinted with the permission of Simon & Schuster Adult Publishing Group from *My Own Country: A Doctor's Story of a Town and Its People in the Age of AIDS* by Abraham Verghese. Copyright © 1994 by Abraham Verghese.

Vilett, Cleo, "An Example of Fishing Down" and "Catching More Fish," reproduced by permission of Cleo Vilett.

Welty, Eudora. Reprinted with permission of the publisher from *One Writer's Beginnings* by Eudora Welty. Cambridge, MA: Harvard University Press, Copyright © 1983, 1984 by Eudora Welty.

"WPA Outcomes Statement for First-Year Composition," by the Council of Writing Program Administrators. Originally published in *WPA: Writing Program Administration*, 23 1/2 (Fall/Winter 1999): 59–63. Reprinted by permission.

Photo Credits

1	Album cover design by Tibor Kalman. Courtesy of Rhino Records.
7	Dan Nelken/The New York Times
12	Martha Cooper
13	© Frank Mullin
14-15	Courtesy of ACORN Survivors Association
16	© 2006 Guerrilla Girls, Inc., courtesy of www.guerrillagirls.com
50	Guy Aroch/CORBIS Online
71	Mike Alewitz
99	© Gilbert & Jaime Hernandez, Published by Fantagraphics Books.
108	The Providence Journal
117	Photograph by Lauren Greenfield/VII
121	Courtesy of Doctors Without Borders
194	NYT Permissions/The New York Times
211-17	Mike Alewitz
228-30	© Richard Misrach, courtesy Fraenkel Gallery, SF and Pace/MacGill, NY
257	"Untitled" (I shop therefore I am) by Barbara Kruger, 1987. Photographic silkscreen/vinyl, 112" x 112". Courtesy of Mary Boone Gallery, New York.
259	Courtesy of Milton Glaser, Inc.
263-64	Jean Gaumy/Magnum Photos, Inc.
267	Jason Eskenazi
271	© Genevieve Liang
272	AP/Wide World Photos
273	© 2006 Time Inc. Reprinted by permission.
281	Bettmann/CORBIS
282	Michael Fresco
303	Courtesy of Adbusters
333-34	Photo and drawings from the Center for Environmental Studies at Brown University, www.brown.edu/Research/EnvStudies_Theses/summit/. Used by permission.
371	DK Images
387	3D Poster with glasses. For Pacific Design Center, 2nd Floor Showrooms Organization Design: April Greiman/Made in Space, Inc.
501	© Art Chandry
505	© 1985 Quantity Postcards
561	© Paula Scher, Pentagram, NY
565	Photofest
566 top left	IBM and the IBM logotype are registered trademarks of International Business Machines Corporation.
566 bottom left	Courtesy of the Polish Cultural Institute in NY
566 right	Courtesy of April Greiman, Made In Space
567	Letterhead for NASA designed by James Moderalli (American, active 1950–1975), 1992. Offset lithograph on white wove paper, 10 1/2 × 8 in.

index

guide to reading selections

Readings found within the text are listed here by theme.